Accession no.
36137108

LAW AND JUSTICE ON THE SMALL SCREEN

Law and Justice on the Small Screen is a wide-ranging collection of essays about law in and on television. In light of the book's innovative taxonomy of the field and its international reach, it will make a novel contribution to the scholarly literature about law and popular culture. Television shows from France, Canada, the United Kingdom, Germany, Spain and the United States are discussed. The essays are organised into three sections: (1) methodological questions regarding the analysis of law and popular culture on television; (2) a focus on genre studies within television programming (including a subsection on reality television), and (3) content analysis of individual television shows with attention to big-picture jurisprudential questions of law's efficacy and the promise of justice. The book's content is organised to make it appropriate for undergraduate and graduate classes in the following areas: media studies, law and culture, socio-legal studies, comparative law, jurisprudence, the law of lawyering, alternative dispute resolution and criminal law. Individual chapters have been contributed by, among others: Taunya Banks, Paul Bergman, Lief Carter, Christine Corcos, Rebecca Johnson, Stefan Machura, Nancy Marder, Michael McCann, Kimberlianne Podlas and Susan Ross, with an Introduction by Peter Robson and Jessica Silbey.

Law and Justice on
The Small Screen

Edited by

Peter Robson
and
Jessica Silbey

LIS - LIBRARY

Date	Fund
09/05/14	lw-Che

Order No.

2500152

University of Chester

WITHDRAWN

·HART·
PUBLISHING

OXFORD AND PORTLAND, OREGON
2012

Published in the United Kingdom by Hart Publishing Ltd
16C Worcester Place, Oxford, OX1 2JW
Telephone: +44 (0)1865 517530
Fax: +44 (0)1865 510710
E-mail: mail@hartpub.co.uk
Website: http://www.hartpub.co.uk

Published in North America (US and Canada) by
Hart Publishing
c/o International Specialized Book Services
920 NE 58th Avenue, Suite 300
Portland, OR 97213-3786
USA
Tel: +1 503 287 3093 or toll-free: (1) 800 944 6190
Fax: +1 503 280 8832
E-mail: orders@isbs.com
Website: http://www.isbs.com

© The editors and contributors severally, 2012

The editors and contributors have asserted their right under the Copyright,
Designs and Patents Act 1988, to be identified as the author of this work.

All rights reserved. No part of this publication may be reproduced, stored in a retrieval
system, or transmitted, in any form or by any means, without the prior permission of Hart
Publishing, or as expressly permitted by law or under the terms agreed with the appropriate
reprographic rights organisation. Enquiries concerning reproduction which may not be
covered by the above should be addressed to Hart Publishing Ltd at the address above.

British Library Cataloguing in Publication Data
Data Available

ISBN: 978-1-84946-269-3

Typeset by Compuscript Ltd, Shannon
Printed and bound in Great Britain by
TJ International Ltd, Padstow, Cornwall

MIX
Paper from
responsible sources
FSC® C013056

Acknowledgements

This book is a labour of friendship, born of a mutual conviction that law, and its goal of justice, has much to learn from popular culture. We have been friends through the interdisciplinary law and film circles for many years. However, it was not until 2009 that we decided to work together to produce a collection of essays on law and TV to offset the focus on law and film. We decided to not just approach those whom we knew were interested and working in this area, but to spread the net wider to involve those who had not published in this area before. We are glad we did. As Stella Bruzzi reminded us in her December 2011 review of *Film and the Law: The Cinema of Justice* (Greenfield, Osborn and Robson) published in the journal *Law and Humanities*, TV forms a significant part of the teaching in courses on popular culture. It has, however, hitherto been underrepresented in the published law and culture scholarship. We seek to redress this imbalance. Attention needs to be paid to the 'small screen', which is, we believe, exceptionally powerful in shaping expectations and desires about law and justice. We thank the contributing authors who patiently took each step with us, from the call for papers to final submission. Thank you all for sticking to the deadlines we imposed. Your work brings the value to this book. Thanks also go to the anonymous reviewers who helped us select and guide the final versions found in this collection. We could not have finished this book without the exemplary copy-editing help from three superb Suffolk University Law Students: Daniel Morton-Bentley, Patrick McDonough and Christopher Siteman. All three will be first rate lawyers in light of their persistent efforts and acute attention to language. Thank you Dan, Patrick and Chris. Finally, we would like to thank our friends at Hart Publishing. We are grateful for your patience and support.

Peter Robson, Glasgow, Scotland
Jessica Silbey, Boston, United States
November 2011

Contents

Acknowledgments v
Contributors ix

Introduction..1
Peter Robson and Jessica Silbey

Part I: Method/Context **13**

1. Measuring Humanity: Rights in the 24th Century............................15
   Lief H Carter and Michael McCann

2. Television, Pleasure and the Empire of Force: Interrogating
   Law and Affect in *Deadwood*..33
   Rebecca Johnson

3. Making 'Bad Apples' on *The Bridge*: A Production Study
   of the Making of a Police Drama 63
   Anita Lam

4. Testing Television: Studying and Understanding the Impact of
   Television's Depictions of Law and Justice.......................................87
   Kimberlianne Podlas

5. Let's See How Far We've Come: The Role of Empirical Methodology
   in Exploring Television Audiences...111
   Cassandra Sharp

Part II: Genre Studies **133**
A. The Evolved Law TV Genres

6. Dark Justice: Women Legal Actors on Basic Cable.........................135
   Taunya Lovell Banks

7. A Third Rapist? Television Portrayals of Rape Evidence Rules 153
   Paul Bergman

8. Prosecutors and Psychics on the Air: Does a 'Psychic Detective Effect'
   Exist?...173
   Christine A Corcos

9. Lawyers in Terrorism Thrillers 193
   Tung Yin

B. Reality Law TV 209

10. *Til Debt Do Us Part*: Reality TV and the Financial Literacy
   Regulatory Project..211
   Freya Kodar

11. Judging Reality Television Judges 229
   Nancy S Marder

12. Television Judges in Germany...251
   Stefan Machura

13. Judge Judy: Constructions of 'Justice with an Attitude'................271
   Marilyn Terzic

14. Reality TV and the Entrapment of Predators 289
   Mark Tunick

Part III: Specific Shows **309**

15. Bordering on Identity: How English Canadian Television
   Differentiates American and Canadian Styles of Justice................311
   Ummni Khan

16. Television Divorce in Post-Franco Spain: *Anillos de oro (Wedding Rings)* 347
   Anja Louis

17. 'McNutty' on the Small Screen: Improvised Legality and
   the Irish-American Cop in HBO's *The Wire* 361
   Sara Ramshaw

18. Torture and Contempt of the Law in '24': Selling America
   New 'Patriotic' Values..381
   Ryan J Thomas and Susan Dente Ross

19. Decoding the Dark Passenger: The Serial Killer as a Force for Justice.
   Adapting Jeff Lindsay's *Dexter* for the Small Screen 403
   Angus Nurse

20. Canada: ADR and *The Associates* 425
   Jennifer L Schulz

21. Stranger Danger?: Sadistic Serial Killers on the Small Screen 441
   Annette Houlihan

Index...455

Contributors

Taunya Lovell Banks is the Jacob A France Professor of Equality Jurisprudence at the University of Maryland School of Law where she writes about race, gender, class and law in popular culture. She is a contributing co-editor of *Screening Justice—The Cinema of Law: Films of Law, Order, and Social Justice* (Fred B Rothman & Co, 2006). Her articles have appeared in numerous law journals including *Harvard Civil Rights—Civil Liberties Law Review*, *U.C.L.A. Law Review*, *New York University Review of Law & Social Change* and *Michigan Law Review*. Professor Banks is a former member of the Association of American Law Schools' Executive Committee, and a two-term Trustee of the Law School Admissions Council. She also served on the Editorial Boards of the *Journal of Legal Education* and the *Law & Society Review*.

Paul Bergman is Professor of Law Emeritus at UCLA. His publications relating to law and popular culture include the book (with Michael Asimow) *Reel Justice: The Courtroom Goes to the Movies* (Andrews McMeel Publishing, 2006) and articles such as 'Emergency! Send a TV Show to Rescue Paramedic Services' in the *University of Baltimore Law Review* (2007) (selected as one of the top entertainment-related essays of 2007) and 'The Movie Lawyers' Guide to Redemptive Law Practice', in *Lawyers' Ethics and the Pursuit of Social Justice* edited by Susan D Carle (NYU Press, 2005). Paul has also written four books for Nolo Press, explaining civil and criminal law and processes to non-lawyers. Paul has also co-authored books on client-centred counselling, trial advocacy, deposition strategies, evidence rules and inferential reasoning.

Lief H Carter taught at the University of Georgia from 1973 to 1995. Before going to Georgia he received college and law degrees from Harvard, served in the Peace Corps in Bolivia, and earned his PhD at the University of California, Berkeley. He served as Colorado College's McHugh Distinguished Professor from 1995 to 2004. Professor Carter has published major texts in constitutional law, legal reasoning, and administrative law. He was the first faculty member at the University of Georgia to receive the top award for teaching in two different years, and he won the 2010 national award for teaching and mentoring in law and politics from the American Political Science Association. Lief has served as visiting professor at Brown University and the University of Washington. In 2001 he was a scholar in residence at the Rockefeller Foundation's Bellagio Center in Italy. He has an avid amateur interest in classical music.

Christine A Corcos is Associate Professor of Law, Louisiana State University Law Center and Associate Professor of Women's and Gender Studies, Louisiana State University A&M, Baton Rouge, Louisiana. She received a BA with High Honour from the Honors College, Michigan State University, and holds an MA from Michigan State and the JD from Case Western Reserve. She is a member of Phi Beta Kappa and Phi Kappa Phi. She has published numerous law review articles in the area of media law, human rights, European legal history, and law and popular culture. Her most recent publications are *Law and Magic: A Collection of Essays* (Carolina

Academic Press, 2010), which includes her own chapter 'Ghostwriters': Spiritualists, Copyright Infringement, and the Right of Publicity', and 'Magic Images in Law' in *Explorations on Courtroom Discourse* (Ashgate, 2011). She is a member of the editorial board of the *International Journal for the Semiotics of Law*. She runs the Media Law Prof Blog (http://lawprofessors.typepad.com/media_law_prof_blog/), the Law and Magic Blog (http://lpcprof.typepad.com/law_and_magic_blog/), and the Law and Humanities Blog (http://lawlit.blogspot.com/), the official blog of the Law and Humanities Institute, for which she is the Secretary and a member of the Board of Governors.

Dr Annette Houlihan is an adjunct research fellow in the Socio-Legal Research Centre in the Griffith Law School. Annette's research interests include various areas of law and criminology within the broad theme of intimacy and criminality. Her interest in sadistic serial killers stems from her research on HIV prosecutions. This research examines criminal responses to HIV risk in Australian and other common law jurisdictions. This body of research includes analysis of sadomasochism-related prosecutions, especially within the context of perceived HIV risks. Her work has examined prosecutions of risky HIV bodies, as well as socio-cultural issues around HIV, moral panics and sexual Otherness. Her other area of interest is violence and the law with particular emphasis on socio-legal processes which perpetuate myths about 'stranger danger', while silencing the corporeality of violence within intimate/familial relationships. Her work includes analysis of case law and legislation in these areas, along with cultural and media analyses of mixed and conflicting images of crime within sociality (eg film, television, news media).

Rebecca Johnson is a Professor of Law at the University of Victoria, British Columbia, Canada. After laying her educational roots in Music, Law and Management (BMus, LLB, MBA), she was a law clerk to Madame Justice Claire L'Heureux-Dube at the Supreme Court of Canada. She received her LLM and SJD from the University of Michgan. She has taught courses in the areas of constitutional law, criminal law, legal theory, legal method, business associations, and law and film. A law and society scholar, she frequently finds herself drawn to the practices of power operating at the intersection of law and culture. Recent projects focus on: the relationships between reason, passion and the law in judicial dissent; sexuality as a flashpoint in conflicts around religious diversity; and the linkages of capitalism and informal colonialism in the economic imaginary. She is one of the co-editors of *Storied Communities: Narratives of Contact and Arrival in Constituting Political Community* (UBC Press, 2011).

Ummni Khan is an Assistant Professor at Carleton University, Department of Law. Her research focuses on the overlapping ways that sexuality, gender and the racialised body are constructed, policed and put into discourse in law and culture. She has published articles on the socio-legal construction of sexual deviancy, transgendered subjects, and media and pop cultural representations of law. She is currently completing a book that comparatively analyses the construction of sadomasochism in law, psychiatry, film and feminism.

Freya Kodar is an Assistant Professor at the Faculty of Law, University of Victoria, British Columbia, Canada. Her research, writing and teaching focuses on the regulation of debt and credit, pension law and policy and tort law.

Anita Lam is an Assistant Professor of Criminology at York University. She recently completed her doctoral work at the University of Toronto, where her dissertation research examined the television production of Canadian crime dramas through the lens of actor-network theory. Her previous work has appeared in *Cinéaction*, and the *Canadian Journal of Criminology and Criminal Justice*.

Anja Louis is an Associate Lecturer at Sheffield Hallam University and Honourary Research Fellow at the University of Sheffield. She specialises in the interdisciplinary field of law and culture in the Hispanic world. Her book *Women and the Law: Carmen de Burgos, an Early Feminist* (Tamesis Books, 2005) analyses the representation of law in the work of the Spanish feminist Carmen de Burgos (1867–1932). Dr Louis' research interests lay in the field of Hispanic Cultural Studies, in particular the interface of law and culture, gender studies, and popular culture. Her current research project examines the representation of lawyers in Spanish film and television. Recent publications include 'Whatever Next: Women's Rights in Sáenz de Heredia's *Los derechos de la mujer*' *(Bulletin of Spanish Studies)*.

Stefan Machura has worked at Bangor University, North Wales since 2006. In 1995, he started teaching classes on law and film at the Ruhr-Universität Bochum (Germany) and conducted empirical research on the interplay of direct experiences with law and media influences. Furthermore, he is interested in the lessons lay people and legal personnel take from interacting with another. As part of this, he has surveyed lay judges in Germany and Russia, as well as experiences of students, defendants and citizens generally with lawyers, courts and the police in Germany and the UK. His latest empirical study addresses multi-agency cooperation in safeguarding children. His book publications include: *Procedural Justice* (with Klaus F Röhl) (Ashgate, 1997); *Law and Film* (with Peter Robson) (Blackwell, 2001); *Fairneß und Legitimität* (Nomos Verlagsgesellschaft, 2001) (on lay assessors at German criminal courts); *Ehrenamtliche Richter in Südrussland* (with Dmitrij Donskow and Olga Litvinova) (Lit 2003) (on Russian people's judges); *Politik und Verwaltung* (Verlag für Sozialwissenschaften 2005) (on the interplay of politicians and administration in Germany); *Ehrenamtliche Verwaltungsrichter* (Lit 2006) (on lay assessors at German administrative courts); *Understanding Law in Society* (with Knut Papendorf, and Kristian Andenæs) (Lit 2011).

Nancy S Marder is Professor of Law and Director of the Jury Center at Chicago-Kent College of Law. She is a graduate of Yale College, where she majored in English and Afro-American Studies, and holds an MPhil from Cambridge University, where she was a Mellon Fellow. She received her JD from Yale Law School, where she was an Articles Editor of the *Yale Law Journal*. Professor Marder has clerked at every level of the United States federal court system, including a two-year clerkship with Justice John Paul Stevens at the US Supreme Court (1990–92). Professor Marder has written numerous articles, essays, and book chapters on juries, judges, and courts. Her articles on juries have appeared in law reviews such as *Northwestern University Law Review, Texas Law Review,* and *Southern California Law Review*. She has also contributed book chapters on law and literature and law and television. Professor Marder also writes on law and film, and organised a law review symposium on the *50ᵗʰ Anniversary of '12 Angry Men'*. Professor Marder has presented her work at many conferences and symposia in the United States and abroad and regularly teaches law school courses on Legislation, Juries, and Law & Literature.

Michael McCann is Gordon Hirabayashi Professor for the Advancement of Citizenship at the University of Washington. He served as founding Director of the Law, Societies, and Justice programme for over a decade and was formerly a chair of the Political Science Department. He is the author of *Rights at Work: Pay Equity Reform and the Politics of Legal Mobilization* (Chicago, 1994) and (with William Haltom) *Distorting the Law: Politics, Media, and the Litigation Crisis* (Chicago, 2004). McCann is also editor and lead author for *Law and Social Movements* (Dartmouth/Ashgate, 2006); and co-editor, with David Engel, of *Fault Lines: Tort Law as Cultural Practice* (Stanford, 2009). He is currently co-authoring two books on law and struggles for egalitarian change, as well as serving a two-year term (2011–13) as President of the Law and Society Association.

Dr Angus Nurse is Visiting Lecturer in Criminal Investigation at Birmingham City University where he teaches and researches criminology and criminal justice. He was Research Fellow at the University of Lincoln's Law School from January 2008 until October 2011, researching civil justice systems, criminal justice and human rights, and teaching in constitutional law and human rights on the University's LLB and LLB with Criminology degrees. Prior to this, Angus was an Investigator for the Commission for Local Administration for England (the Local Government Ombudsman) from February 2000 to January 2008. He is a graduate of the University of Leicester with a Master's degree in Criminal Justice Studies, has a PhD in criminality and criminal justice policy from Birmingham City University, and a BA (Hons) in Humanities with Literature from the Open University. Angus has research interests in criminality, critical criminal justice, anti-social behaviour and green criminology. He is particularly interested in the nature of criminality and the reasons why people commit crimes; the enforcement of wildlife and environmental law; and representations of crime and criminal justice in the media, cinema, and television. Angus has also researched and published on the links between violence towards animals and human violence.

Kimberlianne Podlas is an Associate Professor at the University of North Carolina at Greensboro who teaches primarily Media Law, Television Appreciation, Intellectual Property and Production Law. Her research attempts to build both an empirical and theoretical foundation for understanding the relationship between law and pop culture, specifically television (eg, *CSI*, *Judge Judy*, *South Park*). Her research also considers emerging legal issues pertaining to entertainment media. Not only has she seen attorneys on TV, but she is one—prior to joining academia, she practised criminal and appellate law in New York.

Dr Sara Ramshaw is a Lecturer in Law at Queen's University Belfast. She obtained both her LLB and LLM from the University of British Columbia in Vancouver, Canada. She clerked at the Ontario Court of Justice (General Division) in 1998–99 and was called to the Bar of the Law Society of Upper Canada in 2000. She then worked as a Research Lawyer at the Superior Court of Justice, Family Court in Ontario before commencing postgraduate studies at Birkbeck School of Law, University of London, England. Her doctoral thesis, completed in 2007, examined the legal regulation of jazz musicians in New York City (1940–67) through the lens of post-structural theory informed by feminism, race theory and musicology.

During the 2008–09 academic year, Sara was a Post-doctoral Fellow with the Social Science and Humanities Research Council of Canada (SSHRC) Major Collaborative Research Initiative (MCRI) Project, 'Improvisation, Community and Social Practice' (ICASP) in partnership with Centre de recherche en éthique de l'Université de Montréal (CRÉUM), Montréal, Québec, Canada. For more information on this research project, see www.improvcommunity.ca. In September 2009, Sara joined the ICASP project as a Research Associate and a member of the Research Website Editorial Board.

Peter Robson has an LLB from St Andrews University and a PhD from Strathclyde University. He is solicitor and sits as a judge in the Appeals Services dealing with disability issues. His principal professional work is in Housing Law on which he has published extensively. He has been Professor of Social Welfare Law at the University of Strathclyde since 1992. In the past decade he has extended his early focus, writing on legal theory and sociology of law from the work of judges into coverage of how popular culture affects the practice of law. In addition, he has developed undergraduate and postgraduate courses on Law, Film and Popular Culture which he has taught in Universities in Scotland, Portugal, Spain and Argentina. He has written widely on law and film in journals and edited collections including co-editing *Law and Film* (with Stefan Machura) in 2001. His most recent work (with Steve Greenfield and Guy Osborn), *Film and the Law: The Cinema of Justice*, was published in 2010 and updates the influential 1st edition. He has authored essays on British lawyers on TV and is completing a book on TV lawyers. He has recently started to examine law and the theatre.

Susan Dente Ross is Professor of English at Washington State University, a writer of creative nonfiction, and director of Paxim, a peace research consortium. An expert in media representation and media law, she is published widely in edited volumes as well as communication, media, and law journals.

Dr Jennifer L Schulz is an Associate Professor, the Associate Dean of Research and Graduate Studies at the Faculty of Law, University of Manitoba, and the Executive Director of the Manitoba Legal Research Institute. She has studied law at the Universities of Cambridge, Toronto, and Harvard and has taught law at both the JD and LLM levels at Osgoode Hall, Windsor, and the University of Toronto. Dr Schulz was the first Canadian invited research fellow at the Program on Negotiation at Harvard Law School, she is a nationally recognised mediation scholar, a SSHRC recipient, and has won a teaching award. She presents across North America on mediation, mediator liability, and mediators in popular culture, is the author of many refereed articles and chapters on those topics, and is a practising mediator.

Cassandra Sharp is Senior Lecturer in the Faculty of Law at the University of Wollongong. She has a combined Bachelor of Arts (English Literature)/Bachelor of Laws (Hons) and a PhD from the University of Wollongong. Cassandra's primary research interest lies within the broad field of law and popular culture. In particular, her PhD explored the transformation process of first year law, and the use of popular stories by students in constructing identity. Of further interest is the way in which understandings of ethics are challenged or maintained through popular stories of law. In addition to teaching the core subjects of Foundations of Law, Contracts and Honours Research, Cassandra found much enjoyment from developing and teaching the inaugural Law and Popular Culture elective in the Faculty of Law in 2010. Cassandra's ongoing projects include exploring public ideas of justice; media reporting of sentencing; and the superhero phenomenon.

Jessica Silbey is a Professor of Law at Suffolk University Law School in Boston. She received her BA from Stanford University and her JD and PhD (Comparative Literature) from the University of Michigan. Professor Silbey's scholarship primarily engages in a cultural analysis of law. She writes within the interdiscipline of law and film, exploring how film is used as a legal tool and how it becomes an object of legal analysis in light of its history as a cultural object and art form. Questions she addresses in her research are: How does automated surveillance film become testimony in a court of law? How do cultural perceptions about film affect its evaluation by jurors, advocates and judges? How might legal actors and lay citizens mobilise the audiovisual technology of our twenty-first century to further the promises of our justice system? Professor Silbey is also currently working on a book to be published by Stanford University Press about intellectual property law, investigating common and conflicting narratives within legal institutions and private organisations that explain intellectual property protection in the United States. She is especially interested in the connections between cultural narratives of creation, discovery, incentive and labour and their legal counterparts in cases, statutes and litigation. Professor Silbey teaches courses in intellectual property and constitutional law.

Marilyn Terzic is an international award-winning, interdisciplinary scholar. She has authored numerous articles examining the dynamic interplay between the theories of perception, cognition, and composition as it relates to the design of and viewers' responses to persuasive communications. She also maintains an interest in media policy and law.

Ryan J Thomas is a doctoral candidate and instructor in the Edward R Murrow College of Communication at Washington State University. His research interests include media roles and responsibilities, media representations of social class, and media representations of organised labour. His research has been published in *Journalism Practice*, *New Media and Society*, and *Journalism Studies*.

Mark Tunick is Professor of Political Science and Associate Dean at the Wilkes Honors College, Florida Atlantic University, where he teaches political theory and constitutional law. He is author of several books and articles on political and legal theory, including *Hegel's Political Philosophy*, *Punishment: Theory and Practice*, and *Practices and Principles: Approaches to Ethical and Legal Judgment*. He has also written articles on topics including privacy, property, and the political theories of Hegel, Kant, and JS Mill, and is currently working on a book about privacy and free speech. He received BS degrees in Political Science and Management from Massachusetts Institute of Technology and his PhD in Political Science from the University of California, Berkeley.

Tung Yin is Professor of Law at Lewis & Clark Law School, where he teaches courses in criminal procedure, national security law, terrorism and the law, and federal criminal law. His academic research has focused primarily on the domestic legal issues arising out of the United States' prosecutorial and military responses to the 11 September 2001 terrorist attacks. Although he recognises the sheer implausibility of *24*, he confesses to having been an avid fan of the show during its run on Fox.

Introduction

PETER ROBSON AND JESSICA SILBEY

Scholarship on law and television has developed slowly over the past 30 years. It began alongside the study of film and law, but its trajectory and import differ in significant ways. This Introduction provides both an overview of the earlier work on law and television and context to the current collection of essays.

There are several putative beginnings to law and television scholarship, all dating to the 1980s. The early work of both Stewart Macaulay[1] and Lawrence Friedman[2] featured the role of television in the development of popular legal culture. Their influential essays form the starting point for the study of popular culture in shaping the public's conception of the law. Around the same time, studies of Perry Mason complemented those describing the popularity of the pioneering legal drama *LA Law*.[3] Others explored television's role in conceptualising law in the modern era.[4] Steven Stark's 1987 article, 'Perry Mason meets Sonny Crockett: The History of Lawyers and the Police as Television Heroes', is emblematic and examines the substantial amount of 'law and order' oriented programming on American television in its first 30 years as a mass medium of entertainment.[5] By 1990, a mere three years later, one finds the majority of scholarship on law in popular culture focused on television. However, by the beginning of the new century the emphasis switched to film, with only modest contributions in the late 1990s to the study of law and justice on the small screen.[6]

---

[1] Stewart Macaulay, 'Images of Law in Everyday Life: The Lessons of School, Entertainment and Spectator Sports' (1987) 21 *L&SR* 185.

[2] Lawrence Friedman, 'Law, Lawyers and Popular Culture' (1989) 98 *YLJ* 1579.

[3] See Stephen Gillers, 'Taking LA Law More Seriously' (1989) 98 *YLJ* 1607. See also: Robert Rosen, 'Ethical Soap: LA Law and the Privileging of Character' (1989) 43 *UMLR* 1220; Charles Rosenberg, 'An LA Lawyer Replies' (1989) 98 *YLJ* 1625.

[4] See David Leonard, 'From Perry Mason to Kurt Waldheim: The Pursuit of Justice in Contemporary Film and Television' (1988) 12 *LSF* 377. See also Anita Sokolsky, 'The Case of the Juridical Junkie: Perry Mason and the Dilemma of Confession' (1990) 2 *YJL&H* 189.

[5] Steven Stark, 'Perry Mason Meets Sonny Crockett: The History of Lawyers and the Police as Television Heroes' (1987) 42 *UMLR* 229.

[6] See Rorie Sherman, 'Small Screen Takes Shine to Lawyers' (1991) 13 *TNLJ* 9. See also: Robert Jarvis and Paul Joseph, *Prime Time Law* (Durham, Carolina Academic Press, 1998); Chris Jackson, 'Film and TV Drama Com-mentary' (2000) 24 *LSF* 321; Joan Marek, 'The Practice and Ally McBeal: A New Image for Women Lawyers on Television' (1999) 22 *JAC* 77; Joseph, 'Saying Goodbye to Ally McBeal' (2003) 25 *UALR* 459.

In the twenty-first century comparative law and television scholarship grew, with studies of law and justice on television in Canada,[7] France,[8] Australia[9] and the United Kingdom.[10]

Television was not always its own object of study in the interdisciplinary field of law and popular culture. Media departments and cultural studies programmes today, however, study television as a unique medium with its own representational systems, production mechanisms and distribution channels. The beginnings of the law and culture field did not treat television differently from film and literature.

I. Overview of Law and Television Studies

The earnest study of law and popular culture began in the mid-1980s with its mixed focus on literature, film and television. Out of the law and literature movement the interdisciplinary field of 'law in culture' studies rose, which soon evolved into a study of law and popular culture, including both film and television. Over the last 20 years, there has been an explosion in the number of books, edited collections and individual essays devoted to law and popular culture. The vast majority of these have centred on film. Since 1996, more than 16 monographs have been written in the field of law and film, and over a dozen edited collections or special journal editions have been published. (See the references at the end of this Introduction.) Conspicuously absent from the larger body of this more recent scholarship, however, is a focus on television.

While scholarship on law and film has flourished, there has been relatively little published on lawyer and legal processes on the small screen. Even in light of the major developments in Spain, where cultural images of law have been examined in extensive detail under the heading 'cine y derecho',[11] that work has neglected the broader 'cultura popular y derecho' and television representations do not feature prominently. The same is true for French and German scholarship. This dearth of scholarship devoted to television in the law and popular culture field is ironic. Television reaches the vast majority of the population. It is more democratic in its processes and distribution mechanism than film. It provides news, dramas, documentaries and comedies seven days a week, 24 hours a day. Cinema, the pre-eminent source of mass entertainment since the early 1920s, is on the decline. Visiting the cinema is now a luxury and is reserved for a relatively small population of Western audiences. The rise of television as the dominant source of entertainment and information, in light of the world's growing focus on the rule of law and international relations, demands consideration in the law and culture scholarship. Robust studies of law and television will complement

---

[7] See Mary Jane Miller, 'Mirrors in the Robing Room: Reflection of Lawyers and Law in Canadian Television Drama' (1995) 10 *CJL&S* 55.

[8] See Barbara Villez, *Séries Télé: Visions de la Justice* (Paris, Presses Universitaires de France, 2005).

[9] See Jason Bainbridge, 'Rafferty's Rules: Australian Legal Dramas and the Representation of Law' (2006) *MIA* 136.

[10] See Peter Robson, 'Lawyers and the Legal System on TV: The British Experience' (2007) 2 *IJLC* 333.

[11] See Robson, 'Law, Hollywood and the European Experience' (2009) *LP&S:SF* 117.

law school courses on law and literature, law and film, and law and popular culture more broadly.

Most television scholarship about law focuses on the police and prison system and not on legal processes or lawyering.[12] This is likely because the adjudication phase of law, with its lawyers and courts, does not feature in the vast majority of police or prison television dramas. The separateness of the trial process from detention and imprisonment is a consistent feature of a considerable body of programmes in Britain and the United States. One result of this separateness is that lawyer shows rank as a mere sub-genre in the field of legal television studies and criticism. The present volume seeks to begin filling that gap with several chapters focusing exclusively on the adversarial process and/or the 'lawyer-as-character' on television.

There may be legitimate institutional and material reasons for both the dearth of scholarship on legal television programming and for a growing future in the area. As discussed elsewhere in greater detail,[13] practical problems exist in assembling the material. Given this, scholars have frequently worked on individual shows that were accessible on video.[14] As far as the British and American series are concerned, easy access to material up to the present day has been limited. Only two of the pre-2000 British fiction-based law-oriented shows appeared in video/DVD format until very recently.[15] Unfortunately, tapes of the vast majority of the programmes from 1958 to the present day have been destroyed or are only available at considerable cost. The same appears to be the case in the United States. At the time of writing, programmes such as *The Defenders*, *LA Law* or *Petrocelli* appear to be unavailable. Although these are not insuperable obstacles,[16] they reinforce the unarticulated hierarchy in cultural products in which television comes after literature and film.[17]

Television programming has become more available in the DVD era and more recently shown series are now easier to access. Availability is, however, patchy. Despite these hurdles, there has been a slow and partial recognition of the significance of television in this area.[18] Now, with the expansion of digital channels, the rise in sales of DVD players and 'home cinema' devices, there are fruitful possibilities for more widespread viewing and research. Whether or not scholars of the law and legal system

---

[12] See Nicole Rafter, *Shots in the Mirror* (Oxford, Oxford University Press, 2006).

[13] Robson, 'Lawyers and the Legal System on TV' (n 10); Robson, 'Developments in Law and Culture: The Case of the TV Lawyers' (2007) in *Representations of Justice* (Brussels, Lang Publishing, 2007) 75.

[14] Robson, 'Law and Film Studies: Autonomy and Theory' in *Law and Popular Culture* (Oxford, Oxford University Press, 2005) 21.

[15] These are *Rumpole* and *Kavanagh QC*. By contrast, four of the many other shows have gone to DVD, eg, *Judge John Deed*, *Outlaws*, *New Street Law* and *Kingdom*. The pioneering series *Law and Order* (1978) (no relation to the American series) is also now available.

[16] Robson, 'Lawyers and the Legal System on TV' (n 10).

[17] There is also the question of volume. The sheer quantity of material even in the most modest series is huge, and for some a barrier to research. Typically, even a modest run of a series involves a dozen one-hour episodes. The attraction of looking at a single two-hour film as opposed to at least 12 and possibly 40 hours of television programming may be irresistible. Yet anyone wishing to undertake a serious study of any series is required to undertake a longitudinal study of the series. Many chapters in this volume accomplish this Herculean task.

[18] See Elayne Rapping, *Law and Justice As Seen on TV* (New York, New York University Press, 2003). See also: Villez, *Séries Télé: Visions de la Justice* (n 8); Robson, 'Lawyers and the Legal System on TV' (n 10); Robson, 'Developments in Law and Culture' (n 13); Michael Asimow, *Lawyers in Your Living Room!: Law on Television* (Washington DC, American Bar Association, 2009).

will turn seriously to television is by no means certain. (Certainly, in media and communication departments, the study of television has been a mainstay since the 1970s.)[19] The most extensive recent publication in the field, for instance, is deliberately non-scholarly and general in its appeal.[20] Coverage is also focused primarily on the United States.[21] In contrast, the present volume spans a consideration of shows aired in North America and Europe, and it aims for a comparative view of law and justice on television.

II. Contrasting Theoretical Approaches to Lawyers in Popular Culture

The scholarly approach in law and film studies varies, and this diversity informs the structure of the current volume. There is the 'law-in-film' approach, which is primarily concerned with the ways in which law and legal processes are represented in film.[22] The 'law-in-film' approach considers film as a jurisprudential text by asking how law should or should not regulate and order our worlds by critiquing the way it does so in film.[23] Whether the filmic legal practice is accurate interests a range of writers from Bergman and Asimow[24] to James Elkins.[25] Others are concerned with the relationship between the law and its operative social context, tracing the changes in emphasis as regards both the lawyers depicted in the film and the kinds of socio-political framework operating within and beyond the film.[26] Hence, the emergence of women as protagonists in courtroom dramas has been of interest to a considerable body of scholars, especially for the light these changes in cultural representations may shed on changing sexual politics in the late twentieth and early twenty-first century.[27]

There is also a 'film-as-law' approach, which asks how films about law constitute a legal culture beyond film. This approach pays special attention to film's unique qualities as a medium and asks how its peculiar ways of world-making shape our expectations of law and justice in our world at large.[28] Writings in the 'film-as-law'

---

[19] See (describing the evolution of the field of television studies) Robert Allen and Annette Hill (eds), *The Television Studies Reader* (London, Routledge, 2004) 3–6.

[20] Asimow, *The Lawyer in Your Living Room* (n 18).

[21] Ibid.

[22] See Anthony Chase, *Movies on Trial: The Legal System on the Silver Screen* (New York, New Press, 2002) (describing films about law as a vehicle to explore popular beliefs about law and politics). See also (for essays discussing film stories about law) John Denvir (ed), *Legal Reelism: Film as Legal Texts* (Chicago, University of Illinois Press, 1996).

[23] See (for reading 'law films' as feminist critiques of power struggles in law to imagine a more inclusive and compassionate legal order) Orit Kamir, *Framed: Women in Law and Film* (Durham, Duke University Press, 2006).

[24] Paul Bergman and Michael Asimow, *Reel Justice: The Courtroom Goes to the Movies* (Kansas, Andrews & McMeel, 1996).

[25] James Elkins, 'Reading/Teaching Lawyer Films' (2004) 28 *VLR* 813.

[26] Steve Greenfield, Guy Osborn and Peter Robson, *Film and the Law* (New York, Cavendish, 2001).

[27] Cynthia Lucia, *Framing Female Lawyers: Women on Trial in Film* (Austin, University of Texas Press, 2005).

[28] See Jessica Silbey, 'Patterns of Courtroom Justice' (2001) 28 *JL&S* 97. See also (showing how the genre of 'the female lawyer film' both emboldens and undermines women's authority in law and society)

vein often explore the rhetorical power of film to affect popular legal consciousness.[29] They also tend to look closely at film's capacity to persuade us of a particular view of the world, to convince us that certain people are good or bad or guilty or innocent by positioning the audience as the judge or jury.[30] As Ruth Buchanan and Rebecca Johnson, in their 'film-as-law' scholarship, saliently explain:

> [V]iewers are actively positioned by film to identify with certain points of view; to see some groups of people as trustworthy, dangerous, disgusting, laughable; to experience some kinds of violence as normal; to see some lives as lightly expendable.[31]

Thus, by this latter approach, film and law are compared as epistemological systems, formidable social practices that, when combined, are exceptionally effective in defining what we think we know, what we believe we should expect, and what we dare hope for in a society that promises ordered liberty.[32]

Moving from the big screen to the small screen should be an inevitable step for legal scholars working within either of the above-mentioned approaches. Betting that the sheer ubiquity and influence of television ought to attract those interested in the impact of popular culture on legal (or other socio-political) systems, we embarked on collecting the essays for this volume.

III. Noteworthy Television and Law Books of the Past

Several books about law on the small screen deserve mention before setting out the structure of the present book. *Prime Time Law*[33] was an early examination of television lawyers and legal procedure. A main interest of this collection by Robert Jarvis and Paul Joseph is its spotlight on television lawyers. It consists of 17 essays written by a combination of academic lawyers, historians and specialists in the media. Eleven essays focus on individual shows that span four decades of television: *Perry Mason*, both versions of *The Defender* (both from the 1960s), *Paper Chase* and *Rumpole of the Bailey* (from the 1970s), *Matlock*, *LA Law* and *Hill Street Blues* (from the 1980s), and *NYPD Blue*, *Murder One*, *Picket Fences* and *Law and Order* (from the 1990s).[34]

Lucia, *Framing Female Lawyers*. See also Rebecca Johnson, 'Leaving Normal: Constructing the Family at the Movies in Law' in Lori Beaman (ed), *New Perspectives on Deviance: The Construction of Deviance in Everyday Life* (Scarborough, Prentice-Hall, 2000) 163.

[29] Silbey, 'Patterns of Courtroom Justice' (n 28).

[30] Silbey, 'Criminal Performances: Film, Autobiography and Confession' (2007) 37 *NMLR* 189; Silbey, 'Filmmaking in the Precinct House and the Genre of Documentary Film' (2005) 29 *CJL&A* 107; Silbey, '*Judges as Film Critics: New Approaches to Filmic Evidence*' (2004) 37 *UMJLR* 493. See also Jennifer Mnookin, 'Reproducing a Trial: Evidence and Its Assessment in Paradise Lost' in Austin Sarat, et al (eds), *Law on the Screen* (Palo Alto, Stanford University Press, 2005).

[31] See Ruth Buchanan and Rebecca Johnson, 'Strange Encounters: Exploring Law and Film in the Affective Register' (2008) 46 *LP&S* 33.

[32] See (for comparison of film and law as knowledge systems) Silbey, 'A History of Representations of Justice: Coincident Preoccupations of Law and Film' in *Representations of Justice* (n 13).

[33] Jarvis and Joseph, *Prime Time Law* (n 6).

[34] In *Hill Street Blues*, *NYPD Blue* and *Murder One* lawyers make only limited appearances. These would be more accurately described as 'police shows' rather than 'lawyer shows'.

The subjects of the essays varied from the social themes (love triangles and work life) to the pursuit of justice through lawyering and detective work. The contribution of the individual essays to the field of 'law and television' studies was initially limited to considerations of the changes over time in the content of certain programmes or, in some cases, across programmes and genres.

Elayne Rapping's *Law and Justice: As Seen on TV* is a sustained argument on the representation of legal process on television and its interrelationship with social justice more broadly.[35] Therein, she examines the wide-ranging and diverse law-related programmes from the 1940s to the present, touching especially on the advent of televised trials in the United States. She also focuses on *Law and Order* specifically, as well as some of the more notorious trials of the past three decades (including that of OJ Simpson and the Menendez brothers). Rapping argues that the public consumption of law in the forms it has taken on television (mostly crime shows, whether fictional or not) implicates the political growth of the conservative right in the United States. Hers is a trenchant and vigorous critique of the social construction of the legal imagination through popular culture.

Barbara Villez's *Television and the Legal System* is principally a survey of television shows in the United States spanning the decades since the 1960s.[36] She categorises the decades in terms of their programming content, describing the individual case-focused dramas of the 1960s and 1970s as depicting lawyers who are 'guardian angels of the law'.[37] The shows of the 1980s, such as *LA Law*, focused more on the lawyer's professional office life and the relationships between lawyers and paralegals.[38] What Villez calls the final 'third generation of television lawyer[s]' centres on the personal and professional lives of female lawyers, as originally exemplified by shows such as *Ally McBeal* and *Judging Amy*,[39] a short list to which one might now also add *Damages* and perhaps *Fairly Legal*. Villez's contribution to the literature is significant, but it does not describe a universal phenomenon and is limited to the United States.[40]

These seminal works aside, recent empirical work on popular attitudes towards law and lawyers based on television and other media suggest that interest in popular culture and law is growing.[41] In this research, however, an emphasis on film remains and television still plays a mere tangential role.[42] The current volume about law on

---

[35] Rapping, *Law and Justice As Seen on TV* (n 18).
[36] First published in French under the name *Séries Télé: Visions de la Justice* (n 8).
[37] Ibid 37.
[38] Ibid 48.
[39] Ibid 54.
[40] Robson, 'Lawyers and the Legal System on TV' (n 10) 340.
[41] See Kimberlianne Podlas, 'The CSI Effect—Myth and Reality' (paper delivered at Annual Meeting of the Law and Society Association, Baltimore, July 2006). See also Robson, 'Lawyers and the Legal System on TV' (n 10) and 'Developments in Law and Popular Culture' (n 13).
[42] However, there are two exceptions: (1) a transnational study conducted in Argentina, Australia, England, Germany, Scotland and the United States where we looked at the sources of students' perspectives on various aspects of justice, M Asimov, S Greenfield, J Guillermo, S Machura, G Osborn, P Robson, C Sharp and R Sockloski, 'Perceptions of lawyers: a transnational study of student views on the image of law and lawyers' (2005) 12 *International Journal of the Legal Profession* 407, and (2) a similar empirical study inquiring of first year law students as to their knowledge of the cinema of justice, television lawyers and role models in film, television and literature, V Salzmann and P Dunwoody, 'Do Portrayals of Lawyers Influence How People Think About the Legal Profession' (2005) 58 *Southern Methodist University Law Review* 411.

the small screen aims to fuel both the interpretative and empirical work on television programming and its various relationships to our national justice systems.

IV. Theoretical Perspectives on Television and Law Studies

In this book we sought to take stock of the diversity of approaches to the study of law and television, and to craft a preliminary taxonomy that enriches analysis in the field. The structure of this volume is not the only way to account for the field of 'law and television' studies, but in light of the field's history and its major contributors thus far, we thought it sensible to build on the founding texts and to derive some broader categories in which to delve more deeply.

Building on some of the earlier empirical and historical work on television production and media reception, Part I of this book investigates the method and context of doing law and television scholarship. All five authors included in Part I approach the question of 'doing law and television scholarship' from slightly different angles, but each is uniquely interested in the 'how' of television rather than the 'what' of its programming. These essays make some of the most unique contributions to the field, and it is for this reason that we have put them at the beginning of the book.

Part II builds on the formidable scholarship of the past that investigates television genres as a mechanism for understanding the programme's meaning and impact. The first section of Part II contains four essays that bring the field into the twenty-first century, evolving understandings of past law and television genres for a contemporary audience. Taunya Banks' piece investigates race and gender in cable television shows about law. Hers is an inquiry into the transformation of the primary television format, from network broadcasts to cable-based programming, and the complex and crucial categories of identity (vis-à-vis race and gender) as they are there represented in fictional stories about law. Paul Bergman explores what he calls 'rape-centred' law and justice television shows to analyse whether the period of law reform directed at prosecuting rape cases more effectively (the 1980s and 1990s) was reflected in or reinforced by the popular media representations of criminal rape cases. Christine Corcos identifies a new American genre of television show about law: psychic detective dramas, whether they be fictional or reality-based. Her chapter explores these shows in detail, offering theories on the reasons behind their popularity and their relationship to the rise in scientific evidence's role in establishing legal-truth claims, and in offering the added dimension of scientific authentication to the legitimacy of legal verdicts. Tung Yin explores yet another new American law and justice television genre: the terrorism thriller. His chapter focuses generally on the content of these newly popular shows since 11 September 2001, and also more specifically on the characterisation of lawyers within the stories. Yin compares the (mostly negative) characterisation of criminal defence lawyers in these shows with real life examples of lawyers involved in real-time counterterrorism operations as a way to critique and challenge the portrayal of lawyers in this new genre of television programming.

The second section of Part II focuses exclusively on one genre of law and television programming: 'reality TV'. Although 'reality TV' as it relates to law has been around in the United States at least since trials were first televised in the early 1980s, the explosion throughout the world of court television and reality police shows in the late 1990s and the 2000s implies more than a trend, it is an obsession. These chapters exemplify the diversity in 'reality TV' programming today. In her chapter, Nancy Marder analyses six 'courtroom reality' shows during a week of programming in the Chicago metropolitan area. Marder conducts a qualitative and quantitative content analysis of these shows to draw conclusions about the character and role of television judges as they relate to our understanding of actual judging and courtroom practice. Marilyn Terzick also writes about 'courtroom TV', but focuses solely on the wildly popular *Judge Judy* in the United States. Terzik's approach contrasts with Marder's in that she investigates the process of 'message design' in the television aesthetic, that is, the 'manipulation and planning of signs and symbols that can be produced for the purpose of modifying the cognitive or affective behavior of viewers'. Indeed this chapter, combined with Marder's, forms a vibrant and contrasting pair of essays on reality court television.

Freya Kodar uses empirical and historical methods to analyse the reality television show *Til Debt Do Us Part*, which airs primarily in Canada and is about debt management. Kodar's analysis situates this new reality television show within the context of 'reality' law shows as well as game shows, the latter of which clearly have a much longer pedigree than courtroom television shows do. Despite the obvious differences in the content and context of this type of show from the two previous examples, Kodar's analysis parallels many of the others in the book by exploring, at its conclusion, the role of television (especially 'reality' television) in constituting popular notions of responsibility and legal and social fairness, as well as the role of the State in promoting national welfare.

Mark Tunick analyses a new genre of reality television that combines twenty-first century surveillance and communication techniques to target criminal predators. Tunick's analysis of the four years of *To Catch a Predator* contains in-depth content analysis of the programming, as well as a critical examination of the role of surveillance tactics—including those involving television—in the criminal justice system. This chapter is both an examination of a particularly horrifying feature of our criminal justice landscape, as well as a trenchant analysis of the complicity of television and television viewing in exacerbating the social ills the programme claims to be exposing.

Stefan Machura brings the discussion to Germany, where he analyses the lengthy history of 'courtroom television' in that country from the 1960s to the present. Machura is particularly interested in the changing trends of that programming as it relates to the commercial pressure on television broadcast companies to increase their audiences. Indeed, he notes a trend in the programming that is also reflected in the other chapters in this section: the legal conflicts have grown exaggerated over time but the image of the judge as revered legal hero who brings peace and order has not. Ultimately, however, whether or not we can call this patterning 'reality-reflective' or 'reality broadcasting' is the focal question underlying the analytical framework of all the contributions included in this section.

Part III returns to the roots of law and television scholarship. The essays in this last section focus on individual shows in order to examine contemporary themes of law and justice. The innovation of this last section is threefold. First, these chapters are the most international of the volume, focusing on programmes from Canada (Ummni Khan, Jennifer Schultz), Spain (Anja Louis), Australia (Jennifer Schultz), Britain (Jennifer Schultz) and the United States (Annette Houlihan). Second, these chapters focus on the particularly contemporary manifestations of legal programmes: national identity in a world with increasingly blurry national boundaries, alternative dispute resolution, terrorism and law (Ryan Thomas and Susan Ross), vigilante justice in societies with decreasing levels of social welfare (Sara Ramshaw), and the relationship between surveillance powers and law enforcement (Angus Nurse). Third, as compared to the other sections of the book, a larger number of the authors in Part III are new to the field of 'law and popular culture' studies, some of them engaging in 'law and television' scholarship for the first time.

So, in short, to those who have recently joined the conversation, welcome—we are proud to have your work in this volume. To the others who have returned to contribute to scholarship about law and popular culture, we thank you for joining us in this particular volume on law and justice on the small screen.

References

Allen, R and Hill, A (eds), *The Television Studies Reader* (London, Routledge, 2004).

Asimow, M (ed), *The Lawyer in Your Living Room: TV Lawyers* (Washington, American Bar Association, 2009).

Bergman, P (2005) 'Emergency! Send a TV Show to Rescue Paramedic Services!' in M Freeman (ed), *Law and Popular Culture* (Oxford, OUP, 2005) 130.

—— and Asimow, M, *Reel Justice—The Courtroom Goes to the Movies* (Kansas, Andrews and McMeel, 1996).

Berlins, M, 'Whatever Happened to Trials on TV?' *Guardian*, 2 February 2009, 14.

Black, D, *Law in Film: Resonance and Representation* (Urbana and Chicago, University of Illinois Press, 1999).

Bounds, D, *Perry Mason, the Authorship and Reproduction of a Popular Hero* (Westport, Ct, Greenwood Press, 1995).

Bourdieu, P, *On Television and Journalism* (London, Pluto Press, 1998).

Brown, S, *Crime and Law in Media Culture* (Buckingham, Open University Press, 2003).

Chase, A, *Movies on Trial: The Legal System on the Silver Screen* (New York, The New Press, 2002).

Denvir, J, 'Law, Lawyers, Film and Television' (2000) 24 *Legal Studies Forum* 343.

—— (ed), *Legal Reelism: Movies as Legal Texts* (Urbana and Chicago, University of Illinois Press, 1996).

Doherty, M, *Heroes and Villains: Moral Panic and the Anti-Comic Book Campaign of the 1950s* (M.Phil Thesis, Queen's University, Belfast, 2000).

Elkins, J, 'Reading/Teaching Lawyer Films' (2004) 28 *Vermont Law Review* 813.

Epstein, M, 'For and Against the People: Television's Prosecutor Image and the Cultural Power of the Legal Profession' (2003) 34 *U Tol L Rev* 817.

—— 'From *Willy* to *Perry Mason*: The Hegemony of the Lawyer Statesman in 1950s Television' (2003) 53 *Syracuse Law Review* 1201.

—— 'Judging Judy, Mablean and Mills: How Courtroom Programs Use law to Parade Private Lives to Mass Audiences' (2001) 8 *UCLA Ent L Rev* 129.

—— 'The Evolving Lawyer Image on Television' (1994) 27 *Television Quarterly* 18.

—— (1998) 'Young Lawyers' in R Jarvis and P Joseph (eds), *Prime Time Law: Fictional Television as Legal Narrative* (Durham, MC, Carolina University Press) 249–64.

Freeman, M (ed), *Law and Popular Culture* (Oxford, OUP, 2005).

Friedman, L, 'Law, Lawyers and Popular Culture' (1989) 98 *Yale Law Journal* 1579.

Gillers, S, 'Taking L.A. Law More Seriously' (1989) 98 *Yale Law Journal* 1607.

Greenfield, S, Osborn, G and Robson, P, *Film and the Law* (London, Cavendish, 2010).

—— 'Judge John Deed: British TV Lawyers in the 21st Century' in ibid 205–16.

—— 'Matlock—America's Greatest Lawyer—A Transatlantic Perspective' in M Asimow, *The Lawyer in your Living Room: TV Lawyers* (Washington, American Bar Assocation, 2009) 101–16.

Guéry, C, *Justices à l'écran* (Paris, Institut des Hautes Etudes sur la Justice, 2007).

Gunn, D (ed), *The Lawyer and Popular Culture: Proceedings of a Conference* (Littleton, Fred B Rothman, 1993).

Harris, T, *Courtroom's Finest Hour in American Cinema* (NJ & London, The Scarecrow Press, Inc. Metuchen, 1987).

Herman, D, 'Juliet and Juliet Would be More My Cup of Tea' in Freeman, *Law and Popular Culture*, 2005, 470.

Jackson, C, 'Film & TV Drama Commentary' (2000) *24 Legal Studies Forum* 321.

Jarvis, R, 'Legal Tales from Gilligan's Island' (1998) *39 Santa Clara Law Review* 185.

—— 'Situation Comedies' *in R Jarvis and P Joseph (eds), Prime Time Law: Fictional Television as Legal Narrative* (Durham, NC, Carolina Academic Press, 1998).

Joseph, P, 'Saying Goodbye to *Ally McBeal*' (2003) *25 University of Arkansas at Little Rock Law Review* 459.

—— 'Science Fiction' in R Jarvis and P Joseph (eds), *Prime Time Law: Fictional Television as Legal Narrative* (Durham, NC, Carolina Academic Press, 1998).

Kamir, O, *Framed: Women in Law and Film* (Durham, North Carolina, Duke University Press, Durham, 2006).

—— 'X- Raying Adam's Rib: Multiple Readings of a (Feminist?) Law-Film' (2000) 22 *Studies in Law, Politics and Society* 103.

Kennedy, E, 'The Gorgeous Lesbian in L.A. Law: The Present Absence?' in D Hamer and B Budge (eds), *The Good, the Bad and the Gorgeous: Popular Culture's Romance with the Lesbian* (London, Pandora, 1994).

Kuzina, M, 'Military Justice in American Film and Television Drama: Starting Points for Ideological Criticism' in Freeman, *Law and Popular Culture*, 2005, 160.

Lenz, T, *Changing Images of Law in Film and Television Crime Stories* (New York, Peter Lang, 2003).

Leonard, D, 'From Perry Mason to Kurt Waldheim: The Pursuit of Justice in Contemporary Film and Television' (1988) *12 Legal Studies Forum* 377 or 379.

Levi, R, *The Celluloid Courtroom: A History of Legal Cinema* (Westport CT, Praeger, 2005).

Linera, MAP and Rivaya, B (eds), *Una introducción cinematográfica al derecho* (Valencia, Tirant lo Blanch, 2006) [A Cinematic Introduction to Law].

Lucia, C, *Framing Female Lawyers: Women on Trial in Film* (Austin, University of Texas Press, 2005).

Macaulay, S, 'Images of Law in Everyday Life: The Lessons of School, Entertainment and Spectator Sports' (1987) *21 Law and Society Rev* 185.

Machura, S and Robson, P (eds), *Law and Film* (Oxford, Blackwell, 2001).

Marder, N, 'Television in the Courtroom' (Paper presented to the Sociology of Law Meeting, Milan, July 2008).

Marek, J, '"The Practice" and "Ally McBeal": A New Image for Women Lawyers on Television (1999) *22 Journal of American Culture Spring* 77.

Millbank, J, 'It's About *This*: Lesbians, Prison, Desire' in Freeman, *Law and Popular Culture,* 2005, 449.

Moran, L, 'Cause Lawyering "English Style"' in A Sarat and S Scheingold (eds), *The Cultural Lives of Cause Lawyers* (Cambridge, CUP, 2008) 297–330.

—— Sandon, E, Loizidou, E and Christie, I (eds), *Law's Moving Image* (London, Glasshouse Press, 2004).

Nieto, FS and Fernandez, FJ, (2004) *Imágenes y Justicia: el derecho a través del cine* [Images and Justice; Law through Cinema] (Madrid, La Ley, 2004).

Peltz, R, 'On a Wagon Train to Afghanistan: Limitations on *Star Trek*'s Prime Directive' (2003) *25 University of Arkansas at Little Rock Law Review* 635.

Podlas, K, 'The CSI Effect—Myth and Reality' (paper delivered at the Annual Meeting of the Law and Society Association, Baltimore, July 2006).

Puaux, F (ed), 'La justice à l'écran' (2002) 105 *CinémaAction.*

Rafter, N, *Shots in the Mirror* (Oxford, OUP, 2000 (1st edn); 2006 (2nd edn)).

Rapping, E, *Law and Justice As Seen on TV* (New York, New York University Press, 2003).

Reichman, A, 'The Production of Law (and Cinema): Preliminary Comments on an Emerging Discourse' (2008) 17 *Southern California Interdisciplinary Law Journal* 457–507.

Robson, P, 'Lawyers and the Legal System on TV: The British Experience' (2007) *International Journal of Law in Context* 2.4, 333–62.

—— 'Developments in Law and Popular Culture: The Case of the TV Lawyer' in A Masson and K O'Connor (eds), *Representations of Justice* (Bruxelles, Peter Lang, 2007) 75–93.

—— 'Law and Film Studies: Autonomy and Theory in Freeman, *Law and Popular Culture,* 2005, 21–46.

—— 'Law, Hollywood and the European Experience in A Sarat (ed), *Studies in Law, Politics and Society Symposium on Film* (Dartmouth, Dartmouth, 2009) 117–46.

Rosen, R, 'Ethical Soap: *L.A. Law* and the Privileging of Character' (1989) *43 University of Miami Law Review* 1229.

Rosenberg, C, 'An L.A. Lawyer Replies' (1989) *98 Yale Law Journal* 1625.

Sarat, A (ed), *Studies in Law, Politics and Society*, 2009.

—— Douglas, L and Umphrey, M (eds), *Law on the Screen* (Stanford, Stanford University Press, 2005).

Schwabach, A, 'Harry Potter and the Unforgivable Curses: Norm-formation, Inconsistency, and the Rule of Law in the Wizarding World' (2006) *11 Roger Williams University Law Review* 309.

Sherman, R, 'Small Screen Takes Shine to Lawyers' (1991) *13 The National Law Journal* 9.

—— *When Law Goes Pop: The Vanishing Line Between Law and Popular Culture* (Chicago, University of Chicago Press, 2000).

Sokolsky, A, 'The Case of the Juridical Junkie: Perry Mason and the Dilemma of Confession' (1990) *2 Yale Journal of Law & the Humanities* 189.

Stark, S, 'Perry Mason Meets Sonny Crockett: The History of Lawyers and the Police as Television Heroes' (1987) *42 University of Miami Law Review* 229.

Strickland, R, Foster, T and Banks, T (eds), *Screening Justice—The Cinema of Law: Significant Films of Law, Order and Justice* (NY, Hein, Buffalo, 2006).

Tetzlaff, T, 'Why Law Needs Pop: Global Law and Global Music?' in Freeman, *Law and Popular Culture*, 2005 316.

Villez, B, 'Séries Télé: visions de la justice' (Paris, Presses Universitaires de France, 2005).

—— *Television and the Legal System* (London, Routledge, 2010).

Part I: Method/Context

1

Measuring Humanity: Rights in the 24th Century

LIEF H CARTER AND MICHAEL MCCANN*

[W]orks of art are the most intimate and energetic means of aiding individuals to share in the arts of living. Civilization is uncivil because human beings are divided into non-communicating sects, races, nations, classes and cliques.

—John Dewey, *Art as Experience* (1934)

The ultimate measure of a man is not where he stands in moments of comfort and convenience, but where he stands at times of challenge and controversy.

—Martin Luther King, *Strength to Love* (1963)

I. Introduction

The ninth episode of the second season of *Star Trek: The Next Generation*, entitled 'The Measure of a Man', tackles a familiar, profound, and recurring question in politics, philosophy, and literature—who and what qualifies as 'human' or, if not human, nevertheless qualifies for the legal rights and protections granted to humans by communities and tribes?[1] In politics this question has surfaced for centuries in often xenophobic debates about race and alien status, among others. More recently, the question has been raised in debates about foetal status, gay and lesbian rights, and rights for animals. Much of the world does not yet accord equal legal status to women in meaningful ways. The US Supreme Court's extension, in January of 2010, of the right of unlimited political participation to corporations on the ground that they are,

* Lief Carter thanks his Colorado College colleagues Jonathan Lee, David Mason, and Emily Chan and psychology student Daniel Lenzen. Michael McCann thanks Lief Carter and Marilyn Vickers for inviting me to view, discuss, and eventually collaborate in writing about this extraordinary television episode.
[1] Screenplay by Melinda Snodgrass, original air date directed by Robert Scheerer, 13 February 1989, draft version at www.twiztv.com/scripts.nextgeneration/season2/tng-209.txt, transcript of final aired episode at www.chakoteya.net/NextGen/135.htm DVD Paramount Pictures, 2002. Ms Snodgrass took the title of this episode from Dr Martin Luther King's epigraph quoted above. (Email to Lief Carter, 9 February 2010.) See 'What is Man?' in Martin Luther King, Jr, *The Measure of a Man* (Philadelphia, Fortress Press, 1959).

for legal purposes, like people, also invokes the question.[2] A philosophical version of the question crystallises in the existentialism of Sartre. 'Pinocchio' poses the question for children. Shakespeare's Caliban, the 'monster' offspring of a sorceress in *The Tempest*, Mary Shelley's Frankenstein, King Kong in film, and dramas about witchcraft, eg Arthur Miller's *The Crucible*, pose the question for adults.[3]

The *Star Trek* episode's treatment of this perennial question, namely what counts as a 'life form' worthy of equal legal and moral status with humans, is recurrent in science fiction literature and film.[4] The twenty-fourth century, at least as conceived by Gene Roddenberry, the creator of the original *Star Trek* series and adviser to its reprise in 'the next generation', operates on the principle of 'sentience'. Non-human races such as Klingons and Romulans have the same legal status as those of the human race because they are sentient. But what counts as sentience? More specifically, are androids—sophisticated computer robots designed and constructed by humans so as to resemble humans and to accomplish tasks that humans cannot or will not reliably do— sentient 'life forms', or are they machines and hence property, as both slaves and women have been? And is the abstract issue of sentience sufficient to resolve this dispute?

'The Measure of a Man' applies these questions to the case of Lieutenant Commander Data, a 'one-off' sophisticated android designed by a scientist who died without leaving plans for replicating this uniquely valuable entity. Data, like Spock in the original *Star Trek* series, has superhuman strength and analytical powers, powers enhanced in Data's case by programming that prevents emotion from clouding his decision-making skills under any circumstances.[5] He has repeatedly proved his value as a crew member of the star ship *Enterprise*, captained by Jean-Luc Picard.

Headquarters has sent a robotics expert, Commander Bruce Maddox, to requisition Data from the *Enterprise*, transfer 'it' (Maddox's term) or 'him' (the crew's term) to headquarters, and disassemble Data so as to learn how to replicate him so that other star ships can benefit from his unique abilities. Commander Maddox insists that the chances that Data will not be reassembled successfully after complete analysis of his engineering and electronic circuitry are 'negligible', but Maddox cannot deny that Data may experience some degree of amnesia after his reconstruction, or that such amnesia might be permanent. Data and Picard both refuse to honour the transfer order, but a JAG officer newly arrived on board, Phillipa Luvois (with whom Picard

---

[2] *Citizens United v Federal Election Commission*, 130 S Ct 876 (2010).

[3] Other academic treatments of this episode include R George Wright, 'The Pale Cast of Thought: On the Legal Status of Sophisticated Androids' (2001) 25 *Legal Studies Forum* 297, a neo-Kantian analysis of the nature of 'personhood' that, unfortunately, relies on the original draft script that was not filmed or aired. Jeffrey Nesteruk, 'A New Narrative for Corporate Law' (1999) 23 *Legal Studies Forum* 281. Susan Lentz and Robert Chaires, 'What Color Is an Android: Some Reflections on Race and Intelligence in Star Trek' in Robert Chaires and Bradley Chilton (eds), *Star Trek Visions of Law and Justice* (Dallas, TX, Adios Press, 2003) 219–33.

[4] Steven Spielberg's film *AI: Artificial Intelligence* (Warner Bros. Pictures, 2001) deals explicitly with the complexities of human love for a lifelike robot, and of the robot's capacity to love a human. Stanley Kubrick had begun the project, presumably with the goal of extending the human-like qualities of the computer HAL in Kubrick's *2001 A Space Odyssey* (MGM, 1968), but died without realising the project, which Spielberg completed in Kubrick's honour.

[5] It hardly spoils the plot for this chapter's readers to use the personal pronoun rather than the impersonal pronoun to describe Data, if for no other reason than that readers will intuit that this television episode will not kill off a valuable member of its permanent cast.

has had a romantic and antagonistic professional relationship in the past), checks various fleet regulations about computer equipment and personnel transfers and concludes that, regardless of Data's ultimate status, he cannot refuse the order transferring him back to headquarters.

At this point, Data, who is wholly opposed to this disassembly procedure, resigns his commission in the fleet to avoid it. His decision to resign thus forces the immediate question. If he is a sophisticated computer, he is fleet property. He has no more right to resign than the *Enterprise*'s main frame computer does. The fact that he resembles a human is not legally relevant, since he could just as well be 'a box on wheels'. Indeed, Maddox argues that Data's sympathisers are duped into treating him as rights-bearing only because his outer appearance resembles a human rather than a machine. Luvios conducts further research and finds that 'the Acts of Cumberland, passed in the early 21st century' dictate that Data is a machine. She summarily rules that Data has no right to resign, saying, 'He is a toaster'. Picard, on Data's behalf, then demands a formal hearing. Lacking any staff, by regulation Data's defence falls to the Captain, Picard, and First Officer William Riker must represent Maddox. Riker initially refuses to oppose Data: 'Data's my comrade. We have served together. I not only respect him, I consider him my friend'. However, Luvois insists that without someone to represent Starfleet's position, she will reinstate her order prohibiting the resignation and order the transfer. Thus the stage is set whereby an adversarial legal proceeding focuses and resolves the tensions of plot and character created by the larger dramatic setting.

Our analysis begins with a brief rumination about the study of television entertainment as a constitutive component of legal culture. While cultural texts can be analysed in many different ways, our approach primarily analyses the substantive content of the episode for important insights about the politics of contested legal rights and claims to justice. Our approach is especially conducive to the types of engagement that teachers might undertake in a college classroom. The remainder of the chapter develops some reflections on a variety of themes related to legal processes and constructs of 'human rights' that are provocatively addressed in the episode.

II. Commercial Television and Popular Representations of Legal Practice

We ground this analysis of classic cult TV entertainment in the recognition that images of law, legal processes, and legal practices saturate contemporary popular culture. Mass-mediated narratives and images are arguably among the most pervasive and powerful social forces expressing, shaping, and transforming law and social life.[6] Indeed, a great deal, and perhaps most, of what most people know about legal institutions, discourse, and process derives from mass media news sources and

---

[6] Austin Sarat, Lawrence Douglas, and Martha Merrill Umphrey (eds) *Law on the Screen* (Stanford, CA, Stanford University Press, 2005); Austin Sarat and Thomas R Kearns (eds) *Law in the Domain of Culture* (Ann Arbor, University of Michigan Press, 1998).

entertainment-like TV, films, novels, cartoons, and other such visual sources. As Ewick and Silbey put it,

> The law seems to have a prominent cultural presence ..., occupying a good part of our nation's popular media, providing grist for both news and entertainment.... Thus the law is experienced as both strange and familiar; an episodic event and a constant feature of our lives; deadly serious and a source of humor and entertainment; irrelevant to our daily lives and centrally implicated in the way those lives are organized and lived.[7]

Or, in Richard Sherwin's words, 'Where else can one go but the screen.... It is where people look these days for reality ...'[8]

It is not surprising that the socio-legal study of law in/and of popular culture, including television, has grown rapidly in recent decades into a serious scholarly enterprise. 'Turning our attention to the recurring images and scenarios that millions of people see daily projected on TV and silver screens across the nation, is no idle diversion', notes Sherwin.[9] Prominent law and society scholars such as Stewart Macauley and Lawrence Friedman were among the first to encourage expanding socio-legal study to include legal images, narratives, and representations in popular culture, blurring the boundary between official and unofficial law.[10] While these authors recognised that analysing such cultural texts can be intrinsically valuable, they also urged attention to the unrealistic or distorting character of such depictions.

Other socio-legal studies have investigated how popular constructions of legal issues are actually complicit in developments of official legal norms or practices, often in ways that arguably undercut social justice. For example, in the 1970s, Stuart Hall and his colleagues showed how media representations contributed to the construction of mugging as a prevalent practice and fed the demand for more vigorous policing and punitive policies.[11] Moreover, popular constructions of law in mass media can influence actual practices. Popular culture can shape the public's expectations regarding police, lawyers, judges, and jurors. Haltom and McCann, for example, have shown how news coverage and popular entertainment contributed to the perception of a litigation crisis in the US that both nurtured demands for legal reform and altered the relationships and practices of civil disputants, including at trials.[12] Other scholars have similarly focused on the production of legality in mass media, how media legality shapes legal practice, and especially how legal narratives on screen are received and made sensible.

Our focus in this chapter is motivated by a different agenda, however. We make no claims about how *The Measure of a Man*, or the Star Trek series generally, has

---

[7] Patricia Ewick and Susan S Silbey, *The Common Place of Law: Stories from Everyday Life* (University of Chicago Press, 1998) 16.

[8] Sherwin, cited in Austin Sarat, Lawrence Douglas, and Martha Umphrey, 'On Film and Law: Broadening the Focus' in Sarat, Douglas, and Umphrey (n 6) 1.

[9] Ibid.

[10] Stewart Macauley, 'Images of Law in Everyday Life: The Lessons of School, Entertainment, and Spectator Sports' (1987) *Law & Society Review* 21, 185; Lawrence Friedman, 'Law, Lawyers, and Popular Culture' (1989) *Yale Law Journal* 98, 1580.

[11] Stuart Hall, et al, *Policing the Crisis: Mugging, the State, and Law and Order* (New York, Halmes and Meir, 1978).

[12] William Haltom and Michal McCann, *Distorting the Law: Politics, Media, and the Litigation Crisis* (Chicago, University of Chicago Press, 2004).

shaped actual legal practice or understanding, even for the subculture of devoted 'trekkies' (or 'Trekkers').[13] Nor are we interested in identifying how this entertaining fable distorts or misrepresents formal legal processes. Our goal instead is to interrogate *The Measure of a Man* as a provocative text from which we can learn interesting lessons about law, how it works, and how it shapes social interaction and disputing. For our purposes, the difference between low and high art matter little; both provide indeterminate yet rich texts for constructing meaningful reflections about law's practices and possibilities. As such, our approach fits what Douglas Goodman has called a 'semiotic' interpretation rather than either a 'transmission' or 'institutional' study of the television show.[14]

We are especially interested in two interrelated topics intrinsic to the TV narrative construction of law. One is the homology between legal form (especially the form of an adversarial courtroom trial) and narrative form. *The Measure of a Man* is but one of many TV shows that begins with an interpersonal dispute or alleged wrongdoing and culminates in a trial. Episodes of the various versions of *Law and Order* routinely climax in a courtroom confrontation. The popularity of shows such as *Judge Judy* presumably rest on the same capacity to simplify and clarify. Many analysts have recognised not just the extreme fascination with entertainment that focuses on legal trials, but the parallels between the narrative form of film dramas and trial structure. As Carol Cover put it, 'trials are already movie-like to begin with and movies are already trial-like to begin with'.[15] In his closing statement on Data's behalf, Captain Picard says, 'Your Honor, the courtroom is a crucible. In it we burn away irrelevancies until we are left with a pure product....' And such is the logic of the entire episode, which begins by exploring a conflict over a fundamental question of rights and justice in various trial-like exchanges that precede the formal trial proceeding.[16]

One interesting feature of the episode is that it works to extend the life of the twentieth century US model of 'adversarial legalism' into the distant future. The episode takes place in a completely unfamiliar and unknowable setting, the future in the twenty-fourth century. Data, the robotic machine with human-like qualities, is purely imagined; there is no equivalent in the scientific or industrial world. In the case of *Star Trek* particularly, its creator, Gene Roddenberry, conceived of a series that imagined a social world that expressed ideals of a post-racist, post-sexist, post-religious (and implicitly post-capitalist) and peaceful earth governed by a unitary government, conditions that did not exist in Roddenberry's lifetime and do not exist today. Indeed, the series' familiar infinitive-splitting tag line expressly declares its goal: 'to boldly go where no man has gone before'. One could argue that this represents a noble quest for

---

[13] On trekkies and Trekkers, see the Wikipedia entry for 'Trekkie', available at http://en.wikipedia.org/wiki/Trekkie.

[14] Douglas J Goodman, 'Approaches to Law and Popular Culture' (2006) *Law & Social Inquiry* 31, 757–84.

[15] Carole J Clover, 'Law and the Order of Popular Culture' in Austin Sarat and Thomas Hearns (eds), *Law in the Domains of Culture* (Ann Arbor, University of Michigan Press, 1998) 97–120. See also Jessica Silbey, 'Patterns of Courtroom Justice' in Stefan Machura and Peter Robson (eds), *Law and Film* (Oxford, Blackwell, 2001).

[16] It is also relevant that the curious US phenomenon of quiz shows and 'reality television' series, from *Jeopardy* to *Survivor* to *American Idol,* are perennially popular because they, too, are competitive games— another form of adversarial contest with rules, procedures, and enforced if often disconcerted closure.

a universalised, non-relativistic conception of human law and justice, a timely quest in an age of globalising law and 'universal human rights'. But, from another angle, the drama's central conceit represents a bold act of normalising and naturalising a current, time-bound, and contingent but familiar reality as a timeless expression of legal form, process, and substance.

It is important, however, to underline that 'The Measure of a Man' is not just about a trial. Just as law 'is more than litigation, legal movies are more than courtroom drama'.[17] Indeed, in less than 60 minutes the episode displays legally infused practices and legal themes in a variety of modes across multiple contexts. The drama opens with a friendly poker game, which shows us how Data's inherently mechanistic view of rule determination is trumped by superior players who strategically 'bluff' and tactically exploit the indeterminacy of rules. We see other figures shift in and out of distinctively legal discourses as they meditate on past intimate relations, relationships to Data, the work culture on the Enterprise, and the like. Indeed, law is 'all over' this episode, and it takes different modalities with each setting as it is mixed with and confronts other discursive or normative frameworks. In this regard, while the drama of the dispute ends up with a clean and ostensibly satisfying ending, the inquiry into law is anything but simple, neat, and complete.

This shifting in law's modalities among different contexts enriches the central development of themes relevant to the question of Data's status as a rights-bearing individual. Data's 'humanity' and debated rights-bearing status shift from informal contexts that underline personal connection to increasingly formalised, rationalistic, impersonal, and even antiseptic modes in the trial. The abstract, even ungrounded character of formal legal contestation is eventually disrupted by the key central scene with Guinan,[18] who shifts the terms of discussion from ritualistic deference to corporate prerogatives of property ownership to the legacy of slavery, once again expanding the legal frame by analogy with a social history widely accepted as profoundly unjust and inconsistent with basic legal rights.

Our analysis will give some attention to how law plays out in these different contexts, but our primary goal is to inquire into jurisprudential content, to how the episode offers complex ways of understanding law in practice, its limitations, and its possibilities for advancing justice. As such, we treat 'The Measure of a Man' as a text and aim to provide a reading of it that address how law works, constructs legal subjects, and shapes social practice. In this way, the entertaining episode provides something of a mirror for reflecting and, specifically, reflecting on the varied manifestations of legal practice in different settings. But the episode's imagining of a distant future and novel legal dispute also disrupts and challenges our expectations and invites us to think critically, even subversively, about the promises and limits of legal processes and their

---

[17] Anthony Chase, *Movies on Trial: The Legal System on the Silver Screen* (New York, The New Press, 2002) xii.

[18] Guinan is a survivor of a people whose homeworld had been invaded and who escaped into diaspora. Played by African American actress Whoopi Goldberg and often dressed in traditional African clothing, Guinan clearly symbolises the experiential knowledge of a colonised and racially subjugated population. She appears on numerous episodes as a wise figure whom Picard trusts. See the *Wikipedia* entry for 'Guinan', available at http://en.wikipedia.org/wiki/Guinan_(Star_Trek_character)#Guinan.

capacity for generating justice. The episode may aspire to be 'timeless', but it is also timely in many regards.

III. Law and Justice in the 24th Century

A. The Episode as Teaching Material

Films and videos can and do make the subject matter of college courses relevant and vivid for students. *12 Angry* Men, a direct response to McCarthyism, dramatises major differences between critical thinking and mob rule. *The Thin Blue Line* (a dramatised version of actual events) describes the corruption of a legal system and the conviction of an innocent man in order to punish 'someone' for the murder of 'one of our own'. *Breaker Morant* (also based on historical events) dramatises how perceived political necessities at times corrupt due process. Here, in the Boer War, Lord Kitchener ordered the conviction and execution of legally innocent soldiers accused of assassinating a German missionary in order to strip the Germans of an excuse to enter the war on the Boer side and thus threaten British access to mineral wealth in southern Africa. How useful might a teacher of an undergraduate introductory course in American legal process find 'The Measure of a Man'?

'The Measure of a Man' seems enthralled with the basic elements of the adversary system and shows, as does *12 Angry Men*, the virtues of conversation, adversarial debate, and the exchange of multiple viewpoints over summary judgment in decision making. The episode, however, is more nuanced and penetrating than the typical crime show trial that reveals the lies and deceits of a wrongdoer. This episode, by contrast, describes the more common cases where well grounded, defensible values conflict, where 'people of good conscience', as Luvois observes, find themselves deadlocked in a seemingly zero-sum game. Each side presents persuasive arguments; arguments which, particularly for teaching purposes, square neatly with the elements of legal reasoning, ie arguments made cogent because they integrate and harmonise relevant rules, acknowledged facts, and widespread values.[19]

On Maddox's side, military rules authorise superiors to put military personnel 'in harm's way', to risk death for the greater good of the societies and institutions they represent, and members of the military accept these risks. (Picard admits privately that 'I've had to send people on far more dangerous missions'.) During the hearing, Riker shows that Data is a machine by detaching one of his arms and presenting it, its wiring clearly visible, to the Court. Riker then flips a switch on the back of Data's neck, shuts off Data's power supply, and Data slumps motionless in the witness chair. 'Pinocchio is broken. Its strings have been cut', he says. The parties agree that the ship's mainframe computer, which, like Data, is designed and programmed by humans, is a machine, is fleet property, and is regularly retrofitted and updated.

---

[19] Lief Carter and Thomas Burke, *Reason in Law,* 8th edn (New York, Pearson Education, 2008) 10–11.

But Data's case also rests on arguments grounded in established law. Through case law, 'The Federation' has developed the standard of 'sentience' to determine which newly-encountered life forms are 'rights-bearing'. Sentience, as Maddox the protagonist himself agrees, consists of intelligence, self awareness, and consciousness, and Data, on the witness stand, demonstrates each of these capacities during the hearing. For example:

> Picard: Commander Data, what are you doing now?
>
> Data: I am taking part in a legal hearing to determine my rights and status. Am I a person or property?
>
> Picard: And what is at stake?
>
> Data: My right to choose. Perhaps my very life.

Picard then analogises the problem to the evils of slave-based labour. On the stand, Maddox says he would like to construct 'thousands' of Datas 'if necessary' for the benefit of the fleet, but Picard, in his summation, argues that a ruling that Data is property:

> [W]ill reach far beyond this courtroom and this one android. It could significantly redefine the boundaries of personal liberty and freedom, expanding them for some, savagely curtailing them for others. Are you prepared to condemn him and all who come after him to servitude and slavery? Your Honor, Starfleet was founded to seek out new life. Well, there it sits. Waiting.

Luvois justifies her ruling that Data has the right to resign his commission in Sartrean language:

> This case has dealt with metaphysics, with questions best left to saints and philosophers. I'm neither competent nor qualified to answer those. I've got to make a ruling, to try to speak to the future. Is Data a machine? Yes. Is he the property of Starfleet? No. We have all been dancing around the basic issue. Does Data have a soul? I don't know that he has. I don't know that I have. But I have got to give him the freedom to explore that question himself. It is the ruling of this court that Lieutenant Commander Data has the freedom to choose.

'The Measure of a Man' thus portrays a legal proceeding where the result meets standards of impartiality and persuasive reasoning struggling to make sense amidst conflicting, indeterminate rules. Luvois bases her decision on the legal elements presented to her 'on the record'. As do the jurors in *12 Angry Men*, she changes her mind. She deliberately avoids any essentialist determination of what Data 'really' is or what 'property' and 'sentient life forms' really are. Data has demonstrated sentience and the capacity to choose according to the criteria Maddox himself has accepted.

While the episode vastly simplifies the complexities and tedium of actual litigation, it offers vivid representations of law in action. For example, neither rules nor precedents decide the case, and certainly general principles of fairness and justice do not.[20] Nor does 'rights talk', for all its documented capacity to mobilise people to support

---

[20]   *Cf* Robert Burns: 'It is not just, as Kant reminds us, that there are no rules for the correct application of rules (in this case empirical generalizations); it's that there are no rules at all.' *A Theory of the Trial* (Princeton, Princeton University Press, 1999) 170.

and participate in political action, do any heavy lifting at the point of decision, as in this exchange leading up to the demand for a full hearing:

Maddox: Data must not be permitted to resign.

Picard: Data is a Starfleet officer. He still has certain rights.

Maddox: Rights! Rights! I'm sick to death of hearing about rights! What about my right not to have my life work subverted by blind ignorance?

The opening scene of the episode makes the same point. It shows Data, having learned the rules of poker, playing his first actual round of poker, a game of five-card stud, with his crewmates. Data finds the game extremely simple because all one need do is calculate the odds based on one's down card and the other cards showing. This is something that Data instantly does. Data faces Riker, who bets aggressively on a possible flush showing. Data, possessing three queens, folds. But Riker was only bluffing, an act of deception that Data struggles to master. That 'the rules of the game' do not determine the game describes the episode's legal proceedings that follow. The case could go either way, and it goes via Luvois' discretionary judgment. That judgment reflects the rhetoric, familiar in 1989, of the abortion debate between the value of choice and the value of foetal life in the first trimester of pregnancy, although here 'choice' and 'life' align. The realistic point, then, is that law is never just about 'law', it is always about 'something else', and often that something else is up for grabs.

The episode also realistically describes how law, to reach closure, must socially construct realities and create simplistic fictions. The binary quality of a legal decision—Data may or not legally resign from Starfleet and avoid disassembly—requires vastly simplifying the issues in the case. Nothing like a utilitarian calculation shapes the decision. Data's proven ability to solve dilemmas that save the ship and the lives aboard it make a strong case for replicating him. But his defence counters with a very different utilitarian calculation—legally deciding that Data and many more to be made like him are machines that lack rights will lead to the social disruptions which were seen during the enslavement of African-American people and the racism that followed abolition. Luvois must 'make a ruling that speaks to the future', but because law demands a binary decision under severe time constraints, she does not and cannot evaluate the potential costs (that Data will not be successfully reconstructed and lost to his own crew in the process) against the benefits to other ships if the project succeeds against the costs of replicating the horrors of slavery. The adversarial proceeding forecloses any ability to engineer a compromise.

The episode realistically portrays law's 'thinness' in other ways. Luvois never responds to the argument that Data's status as a sentient being is irrelevant because all military personnel accept the risk of dying for the larger sake of their mission. She never addresses the heart of Picard's argument that a decision against Data could set a precedent permitting the replication of slavery. She never returns to 'The Acts of Cumberland'. She never addresses the intractable problem of pinning down the nature of 'consciousness'.[21] Indeed, her justification is, logically, entirely circular.

---

[21] See, eg Steven Pinker, 'The Mystery of Consciousness' (*Time.com*, 19 Jan 2007), available at www.time.com/time/magazine/article/0,9171,1580394,00.html. Pinker argues that, with specific reference to the case of Lt Commander Data, the nature of consciousness is probably unknowable.

It assumes its conclusion that Data is a rights-bearing entity. Her justification's very circularity reminds us that adversarial legal proceedings function primarily to resolve conflicts, not determine 'the correct', or 'the just', decision. As Morse Peckham wrote of art, law resolves the conflict by *selecting and imposing* one of many possible definitions of concepts like 'sentience', and this imposition of 'order, meaning, and value' must happen in order to reach closure and move on. This 'illusion' is 'essential to maintaining life'.

The clever, appealing TV fantasy provides an accessible yet provocative opportunity for critical reflection about law, rights, and justice. Other dramatic treatments of law equally well describe law functioning badly. In either case, these fictionalising dramas succeed because they replicate law's own fictions. The legal hearing confirms Robert Burns' analysis of trials when they function well: '[T]he theatrical nature of the trial proceeding serves to communicate nonverbal information, redirect aggression, encourage impartiality, and induce creativity in judgment.'[22] But nothing guarantees that they will work well. In the episode's last scene, First Officer Riker, unsure that Data can remain his friend, apologetically tells Data, 'I came that close to winning', as indeed he did. However, to limit the analysis of this episode to its accurate description of official law as a 'thin', fictionalising activity would miss the thicker issues that the episode (and not the law within it) raises. The drama is about the problematic relationship of law to conceptions of rights and justice; our remaining reflections are devoted to this theme.

B. Justice, Solidarity, and Loyalty

> What we are interpreting is ourselves, and the past and present social worlds that make us what we are....[23]

Imagine the following two philosophical models that apply to the central problem posed by this episode, that is, the problem of how to determine what beings are and are not 'rights-bearing'. The first model, labeled for simplification purposes as the Kantian/Rawlsian model, identifies two components of justice. The first component entails recognising common essences in the nature of 'humanness', and the second, extending from the first, notes that one such essence is the human capacity for reason and rationality. Recognising a common 'humanity', in this model, leads people to pay costs and incur risks to protect others from cruelty. Behind the Rawlsian veil of ignorance, humans in this model have the capacity to generate reasoned ways of optimising the spread of social benefits as equally as possible to all members of the human community.

The alternative model—which one could label the postmodern 'anti-essentialist' model—pits such thinkers as Richard Rorty and Michael Walzer against Kant and

---

[22] Burns, *A Theory of the Trial* (n 20) 137. Screenplay author Melinda Snodgrass earned a law degree at the New Mexico School of Law, specialising in constitutional law, jurisprudence, and legal history. She practiced law for three years before turning to science fiction writing as her career. Website of Melinda Snodgrass, 'About', available at www.melindasnodgrass.com/about.html.

[23] Ronald Beiner, *Political Judgment* (University of Chicago Press, 1984).

Rawls. This position rejects the premises of the first as philosophically and empirically unsupportable. Yes, people socially construct essences, but these essences quickly collapse in the face of counter examples and mutually incompatible starting premises.[24] The mental dichotomy or opposition between 'reason' and 'feeling' presumed by the first model has no empirical basis, either in personal experiences or in the findings of cognitive psychologists and neuroscientists. In the second model, humans extend protection to whatever 'others' their own communities come to define as 'one of us'. This is an organic process and it is highly contingent, that is dependent on cultural 'givens' combined with changing situational conditions. Thus, as Rorty noted, the Danes and Italians who sometimes took extraordinary measures to hide their Jewish neighbours from the Nazis did not do so from a superior sense of justice or a sense of common humanity. Rather, they lived in a social world that defined these Jewish neighbours as 'one of us', as 'fellow members of the same union or profession, or a fellow bocce player, or a fellow parent of small children', and not as 'Jews' in the first place.[25] The Belgians who turned their backs on their Jewish neighbours did not act inhumanly or cruelly; they just lived in a different, but equally contingent world that did not socially construct a neighbour simply by virtue of humanness or proximity, as 'one of us' unionists or bocce players or parents.[26]

Does the legal drama described in 'The Measure of a Man' seem more consistent with one model or the other? It is of course possible for a Kantian to say that Data was granted 'the freedom to choose' because he sufficiently demonstrated the qualities of human rationality, or 'sentience', as defined in his case. Yet he is at the same time admittedly a machine whose engineering may differ only in its superficial human-like appearance from that of an intelligent main-frame computer—or any 'box on wheels'—of the twenty-fourth century. Thus the episode makes a far stronger case for the contingent, anti-essentialist, and indeterminate model, a model that embraces the possibility of including animals, trees, and planets as 'others' whom those in power may come to spend costs and incur risks to protect.[27] Following Bernard Williams, Rorty describes how rooting obligations to others in rational morality inevitably entails the creation of qualitative distinctions between deserving ('rational') and undeserving ('irrational') humans, and that those distinctions reinforce in turn those feelings of moral purity that trigger, not reduce, human brutality.[28]

'Reason' plays a constructive role in 'The Measure of a Man', but not in any deductive or rationalist sense. Instead, the argumentative acts of adversaries, which include

[24] For a definition of essentialism and a summary of some of the reasons why answers to questions are contingent, context-dependent, and never objectively and universally 'correct', see Lief Carter, 'Law and Politics as Play' (2008) 83 *Chicago-Kent Law Review* 1333, 1340–42. In his recent book *The Idea of Justice* (Cambridge, Harvard University Press, 2009), Amartya Sen categorically rejects the feasibility and utility of grand abstract theories of justice.

[25] See Richard Rorty, *Contingency, Irony, and Solidarity* (Cambridge and New York, Cambridge University Press, 1989) 190–91.

[26] Ibid 191.

[27] *Cf* ibid 192: 'There is natural cut in the spectrum of similarities and differences which spans the difference between you and a dog, or you and one of Asimov's robots—a cut which marks the end of the rational beings and the beginning of the nonrational ones, the end of moral obligation and the beginning of benevolence'.

[28] See generally Barrington Moore, *Moral Purity and Persecution in History* (Princeton, Princeton University Press, 2000) and discussion in Carter, 'Law and Politics as Play' (n 24) 1356–58.

not only Picard/Data against Maddox but also Picard and Luvois, who bait each other and spat, based on past mutual affronts, throughout the episode, create an interactive setting in which people develop bonds of connectedness and solidarity in such a way that the 'other' becomes 'one of us'.[29] The episode, in other words, describes one contingent set of circumstances in which a group expands its sense of who/what is 'one of us'. The episode thus reminds us of John Dewey's epigraphic quote at the beginning of this chapter, and of the point that Dewey made in many contexts that there is more than an etymological connection between the words 'common', 'community', and 'communication'. Arguably, the extension of recognition of Data's rights occurs *because* the process does not maintain the distinction between reason and feeling in Western philosophy from Plato to Kant but, instead, describes bonding that comes as acts of reasoned argumentation interweave with feelings, in this case feelings generated by Data's confession, while on the witness stand, of affection for his comrades and for a woman, now absent, with whom he was once 'intimate'.[30]

Rorty proposed that reasoned argument can build bonds of solidarity (which Rorty called, borrowing from Wilfred Sellers, 'we intentions') when argument generates 'overlapping consensus', but the episode suggests, both in the poker game and in the trial, that competition itself can generate such bonds. Towards the end of the hearing, Maddox vehemently maintains that he is correct and Data is a machine. Yet once Luvois announces her decision, Maddox the loser cancels the transfer order so that Data need not resign. He says simply, using the gendered pronoun for the first time, 'He's remarkable'.[31] 'The Measure of a Man' thus confirms the anti-essentialist model of justice in which justice equates with expanding loyalties and pragmatic rationality.[32] The episode does describe a fascinating and hyper-fictionalised instance of courtroom law at work, but this is not where the episode touches on the profound. Rather, it is the episode's substituting for a familiar, classical, but increasingly untenable understanding of justice, a newer postmodern sense of how justice happens—this is where the television episode arguably rises to an authentically profound level.

---

[29] George Orwell's *1984* describes a system of social control that succeeds because it prevents the formation of groups at all levels in which such bonding and solidarity can develop. See Rorty, *Contingency, Irony, and Solidarity* (n 25) 169–88.

[30] Skeptics may doubt the frequency with which interpersonal bonding between and among strangers comes about through the process of arguing differences through a combination of reasons and feelings. However, a remarkable 'law on the small screen' episode of *Frontline* captures this dynamic in a film of an actual jury deliberation. The 12 jurors' initial divisions and disagreements was transformed, by discussion, into uncoerced 'overlapping consensus'. As the anti-essentialist model would predict, when the final holdout for conviction said he would change his vote so as to avoid a mistrial but said, keeping back some tears, 'I will never feel good about it', the remaining jurors, sensing his obvious pain, insisted on continuing to talk about it until the holdout found a way to change his vote and stay true to his feelings and his conscience. 'Inside the Jury Room' (New York and other Cities: *Frontline*, Public Broadcasting System, FRON-410T (1992).

[31] In spite of the history of antagonisms between Picard and Luvois, never fully explicated in this episode, their relationship survives and appears to strengthen as their disagreements during the episode progress. When they first meet, in the episode's second scene, they joke about their past love-hate relationship. She says 'It brings a sense of order and stability to my universe to know that you're still a pompous ass. And a damn sexy man.' After the hearing ends, they arrange a dinner date.

[32] See Rorty, 'Justice as Larger Loyalty' in Stepanaints Bontekoe (ed), *Justice and Democracy: Cross-Cultural Perspectives* (Oahu, University of Hawaii Press, 1997) 9–22.

The argument in this section may well defeat itself, for it implies that academic writing by its very nature cannot recreate the experience of viewing the episode's artfulness. Acknowledging that limitation, however, we provide two further snapshots of how the episode embodies the postmodern and contingent model of justice as solidarity and larger loyalty.

First, in section III A above, we noted the thinness of Acting Judge Luvois's decision. She eschews 'philosophy and metaphysics'. She makes no essentialist attempt to determine whether Data has a soul, nor does she respond to Picard's argument against recreating slavery, or evaluate whether the criteria for sentience provides a 'correct' definition of sentience, or determine what is or is not truly a machine. The episode does, however, repeatedly dramatise the dynamics of solidarity. The agonistic poker game at the beginning of the episode only confirms that Data the android is, in the community of his shipmates, already 'one of us'. Riker at first refuses to represent Maddox's side in the hearing because 'I consider [Data] my friend'. Perhaps most telling—and her expression communicates it on screen in ways which her words do not—Acting Judge Luvois prefaces her judgment, quoted above, with 'It sits there looking at me, and I don't know what it is'. But of course she does know that 'it' deserves her protection because they have already 'personally' engaged.

Second, Maddox attempts to persuade Data that the probabilities of successfully reassembling Data are very high. Data, accepting at least for the sake of argument that his physical reassembly will succeed, responds by rejecting, as the episode itself does, the classical dichotomy between reason and feeling. Data analogises to the surprising lesson he learned in the poker game at the beginning of the episode, namely that mechanical logic—the basis on which Maddox is confident that he can reassemble Data—does not fully capture reality or experience:

Maddox: …Your memories and knowledge will remain intact.

Data: Reduced to the mere facts of the events, the substance, the flavor of the moment, could be lost. Take games of chance.

Maddox: Games of chance?

Data: Yes, I had read and absorbed every treatise and textbook on the subject, and felt myself ready and prepared for the experience. Yet, when I finally played poker, I discovered that the reality bore little resemblance to the rules.

Maddox: And the point being?

Data: That while I believe it is possible to download the information contained in the positronic brain, I do not think you have acquired the expertise necessary to preserve the essence of those experiences. There is an ineffable quality to memory which I do not believe can survive your procedure.

Data, the supremely rational entity, thus argues that the very process of thinking rationally will require developing corresponding flavours and feelings—emotions—in order to fully understand and analyse reality; it is these very flavours and feelings that either expand or contract the spheres of solidarity, loyalty, and justice.

The episode confirms the anti-essentialist sense of how justice does and does not operate in human affairs, but it also raises and suggests answers to a range of empirical questions. To take one example—what are the specific psychodynamic processes that generate an expanded definition of 'who is one of us', and hence justice? The episode's answer centres on visualisation. We and the characters see Data's physical similarity to humans. The fact that his same skills and talents might just as well be built into 'a box on wheels' is irrelevant. We and they see his pain in losing his relationship with a former lover. We and they see his fondness for his crewmates expressed through the medals and gifts that he packs to take with him believing that, whether or not he wins or loses in the hearing, he will have to leave his friends.

This facet of the drama finds support in many research quarters, including Frans de Waal's extensive work with primates. De Waal suggests that facial expressions are critical to the development of empathy, as they are to other emotions:

> With impoverished facial expression comes impoverished empathic understanding, and a bland interaction devoid of the bodily echoing that humans constantly engage in. As French philosopher Maurice Merleau-Ponty put it, 'I live in the facial expression of the other, as I feel him living in mine'.[33]

De Waal proceeds to describe the pioneering work of the Russian primatologist Nadia Kohts with the chimpanzee Yoni, who read and responded to Kohts' facial expressions with 'extreme concern and compassion'.[34]

The persistent referencing to the theme of 'empathy' provides an interesting pathway to reflections on a more contemporary legal drama—the confirmation hearing of Supreme Court Justice Sonia Sotomayor. The most controversial part of her record was Sotomayor's claim that 'a wise Latina woman, with the richness of her experiences, would more often than not reach a better conclusion than a white male who hasn't lived that life'. This claim set off a surprising and animated public debate about the role of experience and appropriateness of 'empathy' in legal decision making. Was the nominee violating legal conventions or, as we have suggested, expressing the logic of practice in clear ways that violated only formalised decorum, the rituals and myths that sustain the processes to which she eventually deferred?[35] Is it surprising that Judge Luvois's impersonal, even cold, adjudicatory style resists both connecting Data's situation to the experiential history of denying rights to women and displaying the virtues of empathy toward marginalised others? The episode provides a rich source of parallels about the rituals of legal practice and dynamics of legal contestation and judicial performance.

---

[33] Frans de Waal, *The Age of Empathy* (New York, Harmony Books, 2009) 83.

[34] Ibid 84–88. Recent but controversial research into the function of 'mirror neurons' in the development of empathy in both animals and humans is of course consistent with the visualisation hypothesis. In this particular case it might be argued that Judge Luvois rules for Data by mirroring his unbroken display—which is of course in his character's 'nature'—of trust and civility throughout the proceedings.

[35] See Rachel Sanders, 'Justice at Trial: Dramatic Ironies of the Postracial State' *Journal of Law, Culture, and Humanities*, published online first on May 25, 2011, http://lch.sagepub.com/content/early/recent. Print version forthcoming 2012.

IV. From Legal Philosophy to Social History and Back: Guinan's Slavery Analogy

Justice Sotomayor's controversial claim and disavowal about being 'a wise Latina' capable of empathy connects with yet another powerful and potentially subversive element of 'The Measure of a Man'—that of law's historical complicity in racial subordination. We have noted that the philosophical debate over the essential elements of human-ness that qualify for rights, and over sentience in particular, is the central focus of most of the episode, both leading up to and especially during the trial. The turning point in the drama, however, comes in a very short scene in Act Five, during a recess in the trial, when Guinan offers an entirely new angle to the frustrated and seemingly resigned Picard. 'I've lost, and I'm not even sure I mind', confesses Picard. 'Data is a machine. But there is something bothering me. Something I'm missing.' In the dimly lit Ten Forward lounge, Guinan, performed by African American actress Whoopi Goldberg, dramatically shifts the discussion from questions of personal history between Picard and Maddox to the social history of racial domination. 'Unfortunately the past always resonates in the present, and decisions made today reach into the future', the script has her philosophising. If Riker wins the case and Maddox is permitted to disassemble Data, she surmises, thousands of droids will be constructed to do the bidding of their owners.

> Guinan: Consider that in the history of many worlds there always have been disposable creatures. They do the dirty work. They do the work that no one else wants to do, because it's too difficult or too hazardous. And an army of Datas, all disposable? You don't have to think about their welfare; you don't have to think about how they feel. Whole generations of disposable people.
>
> Picard: You're talking about slavery…
>
> Guinan: I think that's a little harsh.
>
> Picard: I don't think that's a little harsh. I think that's the truth. But that's a truth that we have obscured behind a … comfortable, easy euphemism. 'Property.' But that's not the issue at all, is it?

Picard uses this new legal and ethical angle to win the case in the final minutes of the show. The synthesis of his earlier frame about Data's sentience, now as a 'self conscious' creature, with the new politically charged argument about slavery, is awkward but effective. Picard defiantly puts forward the following argument:

> A single Data is a curiosity, a wonder, but a thousand Datas, doesn't that become a new race? And aren't we going to be judged as a species about how we treat these creations? If they're expendable, disposable, aren't we? What is Data?

Nothing in the episode suggests that this argument convinces Luvois, but it clearly transforms the substantive trajectory and intensifies the drama of the episode. The invocation of a consensus about the evils of slavery works, specifically, in reconstructing a sense about the relevant community of who 'we' are and our fundamental constitutional values.

It is tempting and productive to connect this episode to an obvious historical parallel (which the episode's script writer credits)[36]—Martin Luther King's essay 'What is Man?' in his little read tome, *The Measure of a Man*.[37] King's meditation likewise proceeds through a litany of reflections on the essential qualities that define humanity, before concluding with a more political point about democratic governance and the lessons of history. King quickly shifts from recognition that we are all equal as sinners before God to the Founding Declaration of Independence's stipulation that 'all men are created equal and endowed with their inalienable rights'. King then charges America with trampling over 'sixteen million of [its] brothers'. King continues: 'You have deprived them of the basic good of life. You have treated them as if they were things rather than persons.' He ends with a prayer that America returns to its first principles. The *Star Trek* episode diverges dramatically, however, in that its indulgence in metaphysics bypasses serious engagement with Christianity or God at all, which is at the heart of King's solemn meditation. However its conclusion is close to King's: 'This case has dealt with metaphysics, with questions best left to saints and philosophers. I am neither competent, nor qualified, to answer those', confesses Luvois as she renders her judgment in defiance of abstract argument.

We find the most interesting and provocative point of theoretical engagement not King, however, but the important critical race theorist Patricia Williams. Her very powerful essay collection, *The Alchemy of Race and Rights*,[38] offers a profound set of narrative accounts that ponder the legacy of rights in the US from the era of slavery until the present post-civil rights period. We invite readers of this chapter to view the Star Trek episode and read Williams, especially her essay 'The Pain of Word Bondage' (chapter eight). Williams' narrative accounts are complex, subtle, provocative, and not easily reduced to simple points, but one enduring theme is the tension between the American proprietarian tradition of rights grounded in domination of things and people treated as things, on the one hand, and a more inclusive, egalitarian, transformative if submerged rights tradition, on the other. Like King, Williams offers a deeply tragic but hopeful reflection that can add gravity to the brief intervention of Guinan on the TV show. As Williams defines it, rights are at once elusive, ephemeral, and potentially transformative when joined to political struggle. The key is not to just mimic existing rights traditions but to transform and recreate their very meaning with every struggle, small or large:

> The task ... is not to discard rights but to see through or past them so that they reflect a larger definition of privacy or property: so that privacy is turned from exclusion based on self-regard into regard for another's fragile, mysterious autonomy; and so that property regains its ancient connotation of being a reflection of the universal self.[39]

In many ways, this is exactly the transformation in the debate over rights that develops in 'The Measure of a Man'.

---

[36] See n 1.

[37] See King, 'What is Man?' in *The Measure of a Man* (n 1).

[38] Patricia J Williams, *The Alchemy of Race and Rights: Diary of a Law Professor* (Cambridge, Harvard University Press, 1991).

[39] Ibid 164.

Williams' book is filled with painful, tragic incidents that connect an enduring legacy of racial subordination from the past to the present and the future. It is often dark and disturbing, but it is also at various points wistful and optimistic. Williams' plea is to 'expand private property rights into a conception of civil rights, the right to expect civility from others'. In our reading, Williams beckons us to accord respect, the respect that rights confer, on all persons and things on which our lives are interdependent. We must 'give' rights away, she implores:

> Unlock them from reification by giving them to slaves. Give them to trees. Give them to cows. Give them to history. Give them to rivers and rocks. Give to all of society's objects and untouchables the rights of privacy, integrity, and self-assertion; give them distance and respect.[40]

And thus give rights to Data, and to all other androids, the television episode seems to add in hearty agreement. But would Williams agree? We expect so. In any case, the television drama is a powerful invitation to reflect on the continuing relevance of the historical role of legal rights in both supporting and challenging the social hierarchy that Williams interrogates.[41]

V. Some Implications

Some applications to contemporary events in the early twenty-first century may follow from and further confirm this episode's jurisprudential framework. Why, after the most destructive earthquakes ever recorded in the Western hemisphere, did the massive amounts of contributions from utter strangers, people of different races and nationalities and languages, pour in to aid agencies to relieve the pain and suffering of Haitians in Port au Prince? Why did President GW Bush's apparent indifference to the televised suffering in New Orleans after Hurricane Katrina so damage his political status? It is plausible that the small screen medium of television, just as it did after the Indonesian tsunami and the earthquake in the remote hills of northern Pakistan, made viewers see the victims as 'one of us' because, just as Data resembles a human and not 'a box on wheels', their faces and their pain and suffering seem more like our own?

On 5 November 2008, Thomas Friedman was moved to write in *The New York Times* that the previous evening, with the election of Barack Obama, 'the Civil War ended'. Here, too, television presumably expanded the sense that Obama, in spite of his mixed-race background and his suspiciously Islamic middle name and his transnational upbringing—all of which are familiar sources of xenophobic rejection—was instead 'one of us' because he looked and talked and expressed feelings as we do. Viewers of early 2010's blockbuster movie *Avatar* (a movie whose success is built on state-of-the-art three dimensional visual effects) frequently reported that they

---

[40] Ibid 165.

[41] For another more recent, profound, and even darker meditation on the linkages between the legacy of slavery and law's continuing rituals of making and unmaking of persons as in/eligible for full rights status, see Colin Dayan, *The Law is A White Dog* (Princeton, Princeton University Press, 2011).

abandoned their loyalty to the human characters in the film and instead developed their primary loyalties to the Pandorans, a race that the film's human characters try to exploit.[42]

Television may, by allowing us to visualise 'them' as 'us', reduce opposition to the extension of rights to gays and lesbians. It is not so clear that the US Supreme Court's extension of First Amendment free speech rights to corporations in *Citizens United v Federal Election Commission* has such a strong psychological basis. As Justice Stevens wrote in dissent: 'Corporations have no consciences, no beliefs, no feelings, no thoughts, no desires ... they are not themselves members of "We the People" by whom and for whom our constitution was established.'[43] And of course the very dynamic noted in the episode may equally well explain political phenomena that many find dysfunctional. The ability of interpersonal interaction to generate bonds of trust may explain the extraordinary effectiveness of face-to-face lobbying in the hammering out of legislative details, details that seem so frequently to include 'pork' for small interests rather than serve the collective good. The bonds of solidarity built among those united in opposition to the expansion of gay and lesbian rights and other forms of expanding the definition of who is 'one of us' may, because of these same psychodynamics, be very strong.

Viewers of 'The Measure of a Man' can find a powerful resource for reflecting on all these issues. And if this is so, it confronts academic writers with a disturbing corollary—academic analyses of social justice (including that of the authors of this chapter) may never significantly steer people in the direction of larger solidarities, loyalties, and therefore justice. This is due to the abstract character of academic writing and because all such writing lacks the visual and tactile elements that connect reason and feeling. The more visual and public media of theatre, film and television, for all their capacity to reinforce xenophobia, hatred, and cultural shallowness, can also contribute to the work of promoting social justice. The text is rich, indeterminate, provocative, and redolent with images and words that speak to the fragile relationship between law, justice, and humanity.

---

[42] The very fact that the extension of rights to non-humans depends in part on situational and contingent variables means that under different contingencies those rights will be contracted or withdrawn. Thus Rorty wrote, in 'Justice as Larger Loyalty' (n 32) 9–10, that 'Most of us today are at least half-convinced that the vegetarians have a point, and that animals do have some sort of rights.' But a sense of loyalty to an animal species will contract to the degree that preventing cruelty to animals in turn threatens our narrower and more primary loyalties. Suppose that the cows, or the kangaroos, turn out to be carriers of a newly mutated virus, which, though harmless to them, is invariably fatal to humans. I suspect that we would then shrug off accusations of 'speciesism' and participate in the necessary massacre. Rorty, 'Justice as Larger Loyalty' (n 32) 9–10.

[43] *Citizens United v Federal Election Commission* 130 S Ct 876, 972 (2010) (Stevens, J, dissenting).

2

Television, Pleasure and the Empire of Force: Interrogating Law and Affect in *Deadwood**

REBECCA JOHNSON

> ... derided as simple, dismissed as inferior to film, famously characterized as a vast wasteland, television nonetheless exerts an undeniable, apparently inescapable power in our culture.[1]

I love television. I really do. I rarely say that so boldly. I have spent many years teaching a seminar in legal theory using film as the primary text, and when asked, I will truthfully respond that, 'I love film'. Yet if pressed, my confession would be that my deep affections are not tied to the big screen, but to the small one. Many of the powerful affect-laden memories of my childhood circulate around television. The sounds and music of television are deeply imprinted in my psyche. In less than four notes, I can be pulled back in time and space, and situate myself in front of an episode of *Sesame Street*, *Bugs Bunny/Roadrunner*, *Gilligan's Island*, *Bonanza*, or *The Twilight Zone*. It is not just a question of the particular programmes watched (or the ones forbidden, the ones which became objects of desire), but also of the times and places where I watched—at home or a friend's house. Friendships were built around TV programmes shared, and I continue to feel a deep affection not only for the friends with whom I watched, but also with the TV characters we came to know so intimately. Because TV was both a matter of weekly programming, and of Friday night movies,

* I am deeply grateful to Jessica Silbey and Peter Robson for first encouraging and then enabling me to return to *Deadwood*, which I had first talked about in R Johnson, 'Living *Deadwood*: Imagination, Affect, and the Persistence of the Past' (2009) *Suffolk University Law Review* 62(4): 809–22. I have benefited from their insights and suggestions. I have also been the beneficiary of supportive provocations from colleagues and fellow TV addicts at the University of Victoria and elsewhere, and particularly John Borrows, Ruth Buchanan, Gillian Calder, Stacy Chappel, Arta Johnson, Orit Kamir, Freya Kodar, Maxine Matilpi, Jim Tully, and Jeremy Webber. Many thanks.
[1] Kristin Thompson, *Storytelling in Film and Television* (Boston, Harvard University Press, 2003) back cover.

my experiences of television have always been driven by questions of adaptation, transformation and the echoes across genres.[2] It is impossible to disaggregate even my love of film from my affection for the small screen, for even my lingering love affair with movies took shape not in the darkened space of the local cinema, but at home in front of the TV screen, snuggled on the sofa beside parents, siblings and friends. However I look at it, I find the end-point is the same: I love television.

In this chapter, I want to take those complicated emotions and resonances as a point of entry for a discussion of the place of affection—or rather, of 'affect'—in the study of law on the small screen. Attention to affect can help us understand more about the politics of pleasure, and the relationship of television to what Simone Weil calls 'the empire of force'.[3] In identifying and understanding television's affect-based tools of persuasion, we are in a better position to explore how those tools, un-interrogated, may work to rationalise and sustain the underlying ways of thinking, talking and imagining law that make the empire of force possible.

To particularise this discussion of affect and law in television, I want to spend some time in the imaginative world of the HBO series, *Deadwood*. The series is set in the 1870s, in the shadow of the Black Hills of what is now South Dakota. The territory was to be protected through a treaty with the Lakota,[4] but the hills held the lure of gold, and so an outlaw town sprang up to support the prospectors and settlers who illegally flooded into the area despite the treaty. The illegal settler camp of Deadwood is captured as a place supposedly beyond law, outside of law. The series is filmed in a mode of gritty realism, in the palette of dirt, blood, sweat, and mud. The dialogue balances on the thinnest edge between the exquisitely poetic and the discomfitingly profane (rather like Shakespeare meets *The Sopranos*). Each episode is loaded with explicit scenes of physical, racial, gendered and semiotic violence.

I love *Deadwood*, and want to keep that affection squarely centred while thinking about what there is to learn from (and with) the series. For even as I love *Deadwood*, I find myself unsettled by that very affection. A great deal of my research and affective energies are currently invested in projects that have de-colonisation at their centre. In response, I find myself wondering how I take so much pleasure in a television series which explicitly traffics in colonial/racial/gendered violence and oppression. It is a puzzle. Thus, in what follows, I ask myself what might be learned by exploring the

---

[2] Ibid ch 1. One might note, when one is talking about television, that it is not uncommon for discussions to blur the various ways of thinking about television: as the physical object on which we view things (where, if the sales people at Futureshop are to be believed, size may well matter to the viewing experience); as programmes produced specifically for television (though there may be differences between shows designed with attention to advertising breaks, and those designed for markets like HBO, where shows can run without advertising); as the totality of programming made available for home viewers (which includes programming made-for-TV, as well as movies released theatrically and shown in reruns on TV with commercials inserted into the flow). Discussion of TV can certainly take up subjects such as objects, products, production, technology, advertising, reception and more. Here, I agree with Thompson that the study of television is undoubtedly enriched by attention to each of these sites of TV's power. In the context of this discussion, my focus is largely on storytelling in television, and its relation to culturally proliferated 'structures of feeling'. More on this will follow below.

[3] The term 'empire of force' comes from Weil's essay on the *Iliad*. See Simone Weil, 'The Iliad or the Poem of Force' in G Panichas (ed), *The Simone Weil Reader* (New York, David McKay Company, 1977).

[4] Fort Laramie Treaty of 1868, 15 Stat 635 (1868).

ways *Deadwood* offers its critique of the colonial past, while simultaneously inviting the viewer to feel so affectively bound to the violence of that very past.

I. Preliminary Comments on Theory

I begin with a few comments on the tools one might use for exploring law on the small screen. In this exploration of *Deadwood*, I draw on two different traditions of scholarship: first, postcolonial scholarship on imperialism, and second, scholarship on law and film. Through the first of these, I share concerns raised by postcolonial scholars about persistent inequities of power and wealth in the world we currently inhabit. While it has been many years since the former Great Empires participated in the processes of formal decolonisation,[5] postcolonial scholars have long noted that this formal divesting of colonial power has seemingly left the patterns of economic and political power that marked the period of high empire untouched.[6] In light of this consideration, the question is this: given what we know, how is it that these patterns of colonial inequality persist?

In *Imperialism and Civic Freedom*,[7] Jim Tully discusses various strategies of colonial rule including 'replication imperialism' (the implantation of European settler colonies in the Americas, Australia and New Zealand), 'indirect colonial rule' (where small colonial administrations or trading companies rule along/over local legal systems, as in India) and 'free trade imperialism' (where imperial power permits self-rule within a zone in which resources, markets and labour are kept fully open to the outside).[8] This last form, most commonly referred to as 'informal and interactive' imperialism, is paradoxical: it involves a complex form of rule (informal and indirect); but this form of rule is simultaneously rendered invisible, as the imperial powers treat the former colonies as equal sovereigns.[9]

Through his exploration of how this modern form of imperialism has been woven into contemporary understandings and practices of modern constitutional democracy, Tully points to the importance of discursive formations.[10] That is, he points to the ways in which language works to suggest that this state of affairs is natural and inevitable; that it is the culmination of anonymous world historical processes of which there is 'no one…in control', and that, in short, 'life is just like this'. These formulations suggest that there is nothing to do but 'get on board' (so to speak), and such language of inevitability, Tully reminds us, is itself a neo-imperialistic achievement,

---

[5] See generally (for a discussion of the various paths of colonialisation and decolonisation) Robert Young, *Postcolonialism: An Historical Introduction* (Oxford, Blackwell Publishers, 2001).

[6] See also Amy Bartholomew (ed), *Empire's Law: The American Imperial Project and the 'War to Remake the World'* (London, Pluto Press, 2006). See also Jodi Dean and Paul Passavant (eds), *Empire's New Clothes: Reading Hardt and Negri* (New York, Routledge, 2004).

[7] James Tully, *Public Philosophy in a New Key: Imperialism and Civic Freedom* (Cambridge, Cambridge University Press, 2008) vol 2.

[8] Ibid 211–12. See also Claire Cutler, *Private Power and Global Authority: Transnational Merchant Law in the Global Political Economy* (Cambridge, Cambridge University Press, 2003).

[9] Ibid 196.

[10] Ibid 208.

playing its part in the maintenance of relations of force. In this, Tully's approach echoes that of Simone Weil. In speaking of 'the empire of force', Weil was concerned not only with brute force of the kind that might be applied by police or soldiers, but also with the ways that such relations of force were sustained by certain ways of thinking, talking and imagining the world.[11]

Edward Said, similarly interested in the persistence of imperial patterns of rule, suggested it was crucial to consider not only politics and economics, but also the cultural realm. In *Culture and Imperialism,* Said turned to the nineteenth century novel to explore the ways in which British novels, in telling stories about the past, participated in creating particular 'structures of feeling' that supported, elaborated and consolidated the practice of empire.[12] Literature, he argued, and particularly stories about our past, may tell us less about that past than they do about cultural attitudes in the present. Cultural attitudes, he argued, play a crucial role in any society's social and legal structuring, sometimes predisposing a society for domination of another, or preparing it to relinquish that domination. Said does not stand alone in taking such a view of the power of stories, though his articulation certainly asks us to consider the persuasive power of contemporary stories about imperial forms of order. Said's argument about affect and colonialism was sketched out against the context of the nineteenth century novel. Yet one can profitably take his argument about structures of feeling, and explore it in the context of television, one of the twenty-first century's most powerful locations for storytelling.

Given this matrix of interpretation, I ask what might be revealed about empire if *Deadwood* is taken as the point of entry. To explore this question, one can draw on and adapt the methodological tools of a second body of scholarship, that of 'law and film'. Over the past 10 years, I have been teaching a seminar in legal theory using film as the primary text. In that context, discussion of the filmic texts has occurred on three axes.[13] The first axis focuses on the narrative structure of the text. That is, one can focus on 'the story' and its structure. Here, all the tools of law, literature and narrative analysis can be brought to bear, asking about the story, the characters, the implied narrator, the point of view, the setting, the genre and its expectations, the implied trouble, and more.[14] Second, we explore questions of 'reader response'/spectatorship.

---

[11] Weil (n 3). See also (for similar argument about the need to resist forces of inhumanity built into habits of speech and thought, and to practice languages that affirm humanity and sustain the life of the imagination) James Boyd White, *Living Speech: Resisting the Empire of Force* (Princeton, Princeton University Press, 2006). See also White, 'Law, Economics, and Torture' in H Jefferson Powell and White (eds), *Law and Democracy in the Empire of Force* (Ann Arbor, University of Michigan Press, 2008) 265–84.

[12] The term 'structures of feeling' comes from Raymond Williams in *Marxism and Literature* (Oxford, Oxford University Press, 1977) 131–32. Williams argued the material structures of our world condition our culture-phenomenon and used the notion of 'structures of feeling' to try to capture the 'meaning-giving' side of culture. Said drew on Williams' use of the term, arguing that stories of the past can tell us much about cultural attitudes of the present. See Edward Said, *Culture and Imperialism* (New York, Vintage Books, 1994) 14.

[13] See (for a discussion of the ways in which people in law use film) Rebecca Johnson and Ruth Buchanan, 'Getting *The Insider*'s Story Out: What Popular Film Can Tell Us About Legal Method's Dirty Secrets' (2001) 20 *WYAJ* 87.

[14] There is a wealth of literature here. In classes where students first encounter narrative and storytelling theory, they often find Bruner's series of lectures on stories provides a helpful map of categories and concepts. See Jerome Bruner, *Making Stories: Law, Literature, Life* (Cambridge, Harvard University Press, 2002).

This involves questions about the constitution of audience,[15] questions that can be approached with different levels of empirical rigor.[16] In class, there are protracted discussions between the students about their experience of watching, discussion that generally helps to make the ways that meaning is inevitably constructed in the spaces between a text and its many readers visible, and the ways stories are understood as running with or against the grain.[17] The final axis is one that focuses attention on the 'cinematic' medium in which these stories are told. On this axis, questions of 'affect' stand front-and-centre, as the place of 'brute perception' in the constitution of our visions of justice, and the affective resonance of those visions, is considered. Put another way, we come to 'know' not only through what we read (through the narrative structure of the story), but also through what we see, hear, smell, and feel. Or, as Augusto Boal might put it, 'the whole body thinks'.[18]

Seeing a film is not just an exercise in imagining alternatives; it is an unfolding experience in time, an event shaded with embodied dimensions that are particular. The body experiences an affect-laden auditory, visual and tactile encounter. As such, that experience is another way to understand how film and TV not only represent the world, but participate in the making of that world.[19] Thus, on the third axis of discussion, there is room for an exploration of the cinematic nature of film as medium. The technical details (lighting, filters, camera angles, sound) can provide useful vocabulary for discussing particular moments, but the concern is not simply with the details of film production. The cinematic text, like any other text, enters into a relationship with the spectator. Part of the pleasure lies in a closer study of that relationship, an exploration of the ways that spectators can make sense of these affect-laden encounters of cinematic tactility, these invitations to understand and experience our encounters in certain ways.

My sense is that, in law, we are generally much more comfortable with the first and second than with this third axis. Part of the challenge is that discussions of affect slide

---

[15] See (for classic law and literature scholarship exploring the ways that communities of readers are constituted through practices of reading) White, *When Words Lose Their Meaning: Constitutions and Reconstitutions of Language, Character and Community* (Chicago, University of Chicago Press, 1985).

[16] See David Morley, *The Nationwide Audience: Structure and Decoding* (London, British Film Institute, 1980). One can take approaches that look more specifically at who is or is not watching what, or interview them on how they have understood things differently.

[17] Ranciere's work is very helpful in disrupting assumptions that a given work 'has' meaning completely independent of practices of interpretation and use. There are approaches that look exclusively at texts, and those that study texts 'taken up' (ie, the life of the text in the world beyond the screen). See Jacques Rancière, *The Emancipated Spectator* (London, Verso, 2009). See also (on resistant practices of reading against the grain and the work of the reader in constituting the story) Ross Chambers, *Story and Situation: Narrative Seduction and the Power of Fiction* (Minneapolis, University of Minnesota Press, 1984), and Jacqueline Bobo, *Black Women as Cultural Readers* (New York, Columbia University Press, 1995).

[18] Augusto Boal, *The Aesthetics of the Oppressed* (New York, Routledge, 2006). See also (for rich discussion of the place of the body in law) G Calder, 'Embodied Law: Theatre of the Oppressed in the Law School Classroom' (2009) 1 *MOJLaw&T* 1.

[19] See (for a fuller elaboration of this argument) R Buchanan and R Johnson, 'Strange Encounters: Exploring Law and Film in the Affective Register' (2009) 46 *SLP&S* 33. The influence of D'Amasio's work on neurocognitive behaviour is increasingly present in political and legal theory. See, eg William Connolly, *Neuropolitics: Thinking, Culture, Speed* (Minneapolis, University of Minnesota Press, 2002), and ch 7, 'Relinquishing Control: Autonomy, the Bodymind, and the Psyche' in Jennifer Nedelsky, *Law's Relations: A Relational Theory of Self, Autonomy, and Law* (Oxford, Oxford University Press, 2011) ch 7. See also (for a popularised account of these issues) Malcolm Gladwell, *Blink: The Power of Thinking without Thinking* (Boston, Little, Brown, 2005).

easily into discussions of feeling and emotion, and law has long attempted to police the boundary between reason and emotion.[20] It is useful here to distinguish questions of 'emotion' from those of 'affect'. While affects may well obviously generate emotions in viewers, the preliminary registration of sensation in the body in the scale of affect and intensity, movement and change, is worthy of exploration. As Alison Young articulates it, in the act of viewing, one has an experience of cinematic tactility; one's body registers sensations relating to what one is seeing without undergoing or having undergone what is depicted.[21] The challenge is to return to the encounter with a cinematographic approach. That is,

> [i]nterrogating both the image's cinematographic dimensions (a dimension that includes not only its content and context, but also its formal choreography through cinematography, lighting, camera angle, music, and editing) and its affective engagement with the spectator (which means addressing the pleasures and anxieties generated by our relation to the image as image).[22]

It is important to note that those studying television may find themselves drawing more or less heavily on film theory in their consideration of the visual structures of particular television programmes. For even if both film and TV involve the deployment of sight and sound, they do not always do so in the same way. Some TV programmes have drawn very heavily on the traditions of cinema (for example, *Deadwood,* or the *Miami Vice* series of the 1990s), and others have steered in different directions: the visual conventions for news broadcasts, reality TV, daytime soaps, comedy programmes, and crime series may differ significantly. Still, while TV programmes are not always cinematic 'in the same way' as traditional film, attention to the cinematic side of television can nonetheless be helpful in exploring the ways that TV's stories participate in the production and maintenance of structures of feeling, in both the story world and the world beyond the living room doors. Thus, these theoretical approaches in their aggregate seemingly ask us to consider the ways in which TV, like film, works through the harnessing of 'image, sound, affect, memory, plot episode, character, story, and event'.[23]

The challenge is to explore the place of *affect*—of how we come to *feel*—in the filmic and televisual texts that bring us to judge our own world in a particular fashion. Given this, it is incumbent upon us to extrapolate what might be understood about the persistence of colonial patterns of order by exploring the structures of feeling that operate in the cultural stories of our own time. Drawing on the resources above, I want to return to my love of *Deadwood,* and the structures of feeling it generates in me. On the one hand, the series contains a sophisticated and incisive description and critique of settler colonialism. On the other hand, it makes that past seem inevitable and unavoidable. Embedded in its narrative there seems a vision of law itself as powerless against the implacably forward driving forces of economy. The series makes the erasure of indigenous peoples visible, and yet leaves me feeling not only that the erasure was inevitable, but also that I am, in complicated ways, somehow complicitous in that erasure.

---

[20] See S Bandes (ed), *The Passions of Law* (New York, New York University Press, 2001). See also (for fuller exploration of this dynamic in the context of judicial reasoning) MC Belleau and R Johnson, 'Faces of Judicial Anger: Answering the Call' in M Jézéquel and N Kasirer (eds), *Les Sept Péchés Capitaux et le Droit Privé* (Montréal, Éd Thémis, 2007) 13–56.
[21] Alison Young, *The Scene of Violence: Cinema, Crime, Affect* (New York, Routledge, 2010) 8–9.
[22] Ibid 23.
[23] Ibid 7.

In what follows, drawing on the theoretical resources sketched out above, I want to delve into the series to explore three ways in which *Deadwood* invites the viewer to be pulled in this affective direction. It is a direction which suggests that economic forces are beyond the power of law and justice to stop, and which further suggests that colonial appropriation of lands and resources (even the genocidal erasure of first peoples) is inevitable, even if morally wrong. Further, it affectively positions its viewers on the side of colonial appropriation. There are three places to explore how these structures of feeling are embedded and performed in the series. First, I consider *Deadwood*'s place in the Western genre, and how its narrative arc implicates law, economy and 'Indian' lands. Second, focusing on the place of 'seriality' in the television series, I will explore how the episodic nature of the show positions viewers to both see and not see the violence performed against indigenous peoples. Third, I will turn to the more cinematographic aspects of the series to see how one particular scene of violence is structured to again allow viewers to participate in erasures that position the violence as, if not justified, at least understood.

Let us then turn to *Deadwood*.

II. 'No Law at all in Deadwood?': *Deadwood*, the Western and the Drivers below the Surface

Deadwood draws on and disrupts the genre of the American Western. Created with a contemporary audience in mind, it positions itself in a dialogue with the sedimentary traces of the (typically) North-American frontier myth.[24] The 'moral truth' of this line of stories of the Wild West, Slotkin would assert, was the principle that 'violence and savage war were the necessary instruments of American progress'.[25] Yet, writer David Milch, in reimagining this myth, takes us somewhat away from any explicit focus on cattle drives and 'Indian' wars.[26] We see very few cowboys, and even fewer

---

[24] See (on the centrality of the frontier myth) Frederick Jackson Turner, *The Significance of the Frontier in American History* (Indianapolis, Bobbs-Merrill, 1893). There are arguably some interesting differences in Canadian appropriations and elaborations of this myth, captured in, for example, RCMP films with M Pickford. See Ed Morgan, 'The Mild, Mild West: Living By a Code in Canadian Law and Film' (2006) 2 *JLC&H* 115–35.

[25] Richard Slotkin, *Gunfighter Nation: The Myth of the Frontier in Twentieth-Century America* (New York, Atheneum, 1992) 77.

[26] In reading drafts of this paper, some have suggested that the word 'Indian' should be removed, or at least placed in quotation marks. I find myself pulled in two directions on this issue, and thought it worthwhile to articulate the reasons why. First, there are many pressing questions about naming practices, and their relationship to histories of exclusion and dispossession. As Linda Tuhiwai Smith reminds us, 'they came, they saw, they named, they claimed'. See LT Smith, *Decolonizing Methodologies: Research and Indigenous Peoples* (London, Zed Books, 1999) 80. There is a worry that, in using the word 'Indian' in the present, one is sustaining an ongoing practice of injury and erasure. In some contexts, one can argue that it is better to shift to contemporary labels like 'native', Native American', 'First Nations' or 'Indigenous Peoples'. And yet, those are not the words used in *Deadwood*, and so the shift to what are seen by some as more politically acceptable terms could serve to take attention away from the ways that the older (racialising) terms are central to the story that *Deadwood* tells and the way it tells it. Further, while a term like 'Native American' may have a less negative history, it similarly hides the specificity of particular tribes/ nations (ie Lakota, Anishnabe, Sioux, Cree) behind a single label. Of course, what we see in the world of *Deadwood* is precisely this effacing of the specificity of the particular people onto whose territory the

Native Americans. Attention is not on what grows on the land (be it cattle or crops), but on the extraction of resources that lie below, and on the ways gold is pulled into the larger economy through a service economy providing goods, food, drink, gambling and prostitution. Viewers are positioned to re-inhabit the camp of Deadwood in this time of change, to consider how it might have been that order was built from chaos, that law flowed into the space of lawlessness. The town is populated by a range of compelling characters, some of whom are fictional, others historic (Calamity Jane, Wild Bill Hickok, and George Hurst). The story, David Milch asserts, is less about the people than about the camp itself. It is, he says, 'about something larger, about drivers below the surface, moving the characters and the action forward'.[27]

In this context I find *Deadwood*, and Milch's comments about it, important locators in thinking about our cultural imaginings, and how they effectively participate in build-ing structures of feeling that support, elaborate and consolidate practices of empire. What I am particularly interested in are the ways by which the series invites us to imag-ine the relationship between law and economy, between first nations and settlers. For *Deadwood* is the performance of an imaginative return to one particular moment in the American colonial experience. Though 'the government' is ostensibly absent in the outlaw camp of Deadwood, we see the implantation of American/European settlers in territory that is not 'theirs'. Many of the settlers are immigrants: Seth is from Canada, Al from England and Sol from Austria. Yet, they bring with them common ideas about law and economy, ideas that are the product of 'western' ideals. They lay their own ver-sion of 'law' on top of the law of the indigenous peoples on whose territory they stand, and wait them out, wait for them to be bargained with through unequal (and broken) treaties, or put on reservations, or for them to be gradually exterminated.[28]

Indeed, Deadwood is a town illegally built in Lakota territory, the town's very exist-ence evidencing a 'western' rape of the land, a rape that constitutes the town's very existence. Without the moment of illegal foundations, there would be no town. The series thus echoes one of the primary themes of the Western, that of the violent and illegal founding of the society.[29] Taking Milch at his word, it is the life of this illegally

---

colonists illegally came. While it would be historically more accurate to use the term Lakota, in the diegetic world of *Deadwood*, the Lakota are not named or recognised as a particular nation, but only as generic 'Indians'. It is against this backdrop that the placing of quotes around the word 'Indian' might be seen as an effort to disrupt the way the word functions. While sympathetic to that view, I am also conscious that the impulse to soften the harshness of the term may be part of a desire to soften (or deny) the harshness of the past, or indeed to make it less real. I hope the readers will see in the various word choices used an echo of concern with the implications of our practices naming, both in the past and in the present.

[27] *Deadwood* (season one bonus features).

[28] This is a case of what Tully would identify as 'replication imperialism'. See Tully (n 7) 211. There is an argument to be made that this can also be seen as inflected by 'informal or free trade imperialism'. Here, the imperial power permits self-rule to induce the people to open their resources, labour and markets to free trade. This might be a better explanation of the logic that eventually brings the town of Deadwood back under the control of the sovereign US (as we move to season three, and annexation to the Dakotas. Of course, by this time, the indigenous peoples are completely out of the frame of the series, and the imagina-tion of the viewers).

[29] This question of founding violence is taken up in Peter Fitzpatrick, *The Mythology of Modern Law* (New York, Routledge, 1992). See also (the classic work on the place of violence in the sacrifice of the scapegoat) René Girard, *Violence and the Sacred* (Baltimore, Johns Hopkins University Press, 1977). See also (for more on this moment of founding violence in the context of the Western genre in the film *Unforgiven*) Buchanan and Johnson (n 19).

founded community that is the object of our attention. This is a tale of community building, of nation building, and provides a structure of feeling that allows us to erase that initial act of colonial violence, to accept the inevitable logic of the myth of progress and economic development.[30]

This series is designed for 'sophisticated modern viewers'. It does not seek to conceal this moment of originary violence, but is up front with the colonising, racialising and gendering themes of its time. Milch makes no attempt to hide the flaws of the characters. Instead, we are able to return to that past with the more politically correct eyes of the present, to live in it in a way that allows us the pleasures of vicarious identification, indulged in at a suitable distance. *Deadwood*, like the nineteenth century novels of which Said speaks, adopts a realistic format: the streets of Deadwood are full of mud, shit, piss, and vomit. Throats are cut, and blood is spilled; the language is coarse but coupled with a sense of the poetic that invites one to hold the coarseness in a new esteem. Further, as already noted, the show skates the line between fact and fiction. The series plays at the margins of an explicitly re-imagined vision of how things might have been, giving the series both the 'authenticating' power of 'the real', but also the power to utilise truth-telling valences that can sometimes be better delivered through fiction.[31] Yet, it also produces a structure of feeling that justifies and legitimates certain views of progress, colonisation and imperialism.

Taking all this into account, it seems essential that we ask how the story, through its truths and its pleasures, in its narrative and affective modes, participates in creating this 'structure of feeling'. This is particularly so given that this structure of feeling directly addresses the place of settler/indigenous relations in North America. Of course, the genre of the Western is not comprehensible without its imagined native inhabitants.[32] It requires a back-story about the relationship between indigenous and settler orders. The story situates itself as beginning in a place of 'non-law' subject to particular sets of relations between the settlers and the land on which they settle.

The first episode begins by making the colonial character of the past explicit, opening not in the Black Hills, but in Montana, focusing on a brief interchange between Sheriff Seth Bullock and his prisoner, Clell Watson:

Clell: No law at all in Deadwood? Is that true?

Seth: Bein' on Indian land.

Clell: So then you won't be a marshal?

Seth: Takin' goods there to open a hardware business. Me and my partner.

Clell: If I'd a got there, I'd a been prospectin'. Jesus Christ Almighty. No law at all. Gold you can scoop from the streams with your bare hands.

---

[30] See (for an exploration of the ways that American's interpretations of themselves and their past has often been the result of a paradoxical blending of a powerful imperial desire with an equally powerful anticolonial temperment) John Carlos Rowe, *Literary Culture and U.S. Imperialism: From the Revolution to World War II* (Oxford, Oxford University Press, 2000).

[31] David Dow, 'Fictional Documentaries and Truthful Fictions: The Death Penalty in Recent American Film' (2000) 17 *Constitutional Commentary* 511–53.

[32] Armando Prats, *Invisible Natives: Myth and Identity in the American Western* (New York, Cornell University Press, 2002).

Here, the colonial ground is laid. There is no law in Deadwood—because Deadwood is on native land. In such a place there is 'no law', but what that means within this narrative is not so readily obvious. For Clell, the notion of a place with no law is the stuff of fantasy: in the absence of law, all a man need do is reach out and scoop wealth from the land. Seth, who will be one of our moral compasses in the series, is introduced to us as a man about to remove his badge and become a settler in 'Indian Territory'. He is but a step removed from the direct exploitation of the land. His dream is to be part of the service economy, providing goods to others. He is leaving law for business. Still, justice there will be in the new community he is preparing to join, although that justice will be tethered to an economic rather than a judicial order. We do get some sense of what 'law' means in this context as Seth performs his last job as Sheriff, hanging Clell himself rather than letting the job be done by the lynch mob at the door. There is an unavoidable contradiction at work in his supposed commitment to the law at the very moment he is preparing to remove his badge to pursue his fortune on illegally occupied land where he knows he has no legal authority. However, in asserting the absence of 'law' on 'Indian' land, the show invites us to forget the fact of colonial encounter that structures the town as existing in a legal void, rather than existing in a space of active illegality.

Within the next few minutes of the episode, we also see that the description of Deadwood as a place with 'no law at all' requires elaboration. In quick succession, we see a number of transactions that bear all the hallmarks of a legal order: Seth and Sol enter into a rental agreement for land; Trixie authorises Jewel (in an agency arrangement) to sell jewellery to purchase a gun; Brom negotiates the sale of a claim with spit and a handshake ('Done, witnessed'). No law in Deadwood? It appears this is not quite the case. Law rules in Deadwood, but it is not juridical law. It is the law of power, economy and the market. Deadwood may be an illegal camp on native land, but the people of Deadwood clearly function in the shadow of a binding economic order in which their settlers' societal understandings of exchange, property and contract continue to operate. That is, there are at least two ways of focusing on the presence of 'law' in the world of Deadwood. One could attend to law in the juridical sense of the word, exploring the constitutional structures and capacities of law. This would be the law of jurisdiction, of legislators, police, judges and bureaucrats. This is the law of morality, sheriffs, courtrooms, rules, regulations and procedural fairness. However, one can equally focus on law in a more 'natural law' way: a pre-constitutional world of private ordering and contract, of markets and agreements, and reciprocity. This is the law of Locke and Hobbes, a legal order rooted in nature, or natural law, the law of a sort of 'pre-founding' moment.[33]

It is into this space of (natural) market law that we as viewers are flung. While we, like Seth, arrive in the town ahead of the juridical order that will follow, we do not arrive in a space outside of law. There may be no sheriff, but there is law, and it is enforced. Al Swerengen, the owner of the Gem Saloon, decides whether or not space on the street will be rented. He decides whether violators of (his) law will receive mercy

---

[33] In both cases, these legal orders are constituted not only through written texts, but also through mythic tales of origin. See (for exploration of narrative foundations and supports to origin stories of law and legal ordering) Jessica M Silbey, 'The Mythical Beginnings of Intellectual Property' (2008) *GMLR* 15, 319–79.

or a trip to Mr Wu's pig farm. It is Al, the man of business, who is effectively 'the law'. Far from there being 'no law in Deadwood', questions of law run everywhere, directly impacting our two central characters (each of whom functions as a foil to the other). Seth, formerly a man of law, is now a man of business. Al Swerengen, formally a man of business, is informally a man of law. We have, as Tully might note, a performance of replication imperialism, a system where the great powers govern through freedom— the freedom of the settlers who carry with them very particular understandings of law and economy as they displace the local populations.[34] Certainly, in Al and in Seth, we see the ways these two legal orders (moral and economic, if you will) interact with, and indeed sustain, each other. Thus, here represented we find two primary strands in our mytho-constitutional social ordering.

Because of the ways these legal orders are shown in relation to each other, the series suggests that economic development and 'progress' are inevitable, even if they have been constructed on acts of colonial appropriation.[35] Merrick, the editor of the town's newspaper, articulates it in the following way:

> Paradoxes, the massacre at Little Big Horn signalled the Indians' death throes, Mr. Utter. History has overtaken the treaty which gave them this land. Well, the gold we found has over- taken it. I believe within a year, Congress will rescind the Fort Laramie Treaty, Deadwood and these hills will be annexed to the Dakota Territory, and we, who have pursued our des- tiny outside law or statute, will be restored to the bosom of the nation. And, that's what I believe.

Merrick acknowledges the fact of the violent illegality of the colonial settlement, but frames it in the language of 'paradox'. In his language, Merrick shows no linguistic disrespect to the Native Americans. He acknowledges the violence done to them, but situates it in the flow of a paradoxical history that eventually legitimates those vio- lent actions, that sees them as inevitable to the founding of a new state. Here, we see the weight of Tully's arguments about the languages supporting colonialism. History overtakes them all; the fact of the gold overtakes the treaty, and makes the passing of an indigenous way of life inevitable.

Merrick discusses the colonial violence done to the Native Americans in language capable of reproduction in the mainstream press. Beyond him, the series sees other characters describing the original inhabitants in explicitly racist ways, projecting the savagery of settler appropriation of the land onto a mythic 'red man', speak- ing of them as savage, lawless and heathen. This semiotic violence is enacted not only in obviously racist characters, but also in characters that viewers will become strongly attached to over the seasons.[36] Of course, the series also shows us clearly

---

[34] See Tully (n 7) 211–12.

[35] In this respect, *Deadwood* follows in the tradition of Westerns like *The Man Who Shot Liberty Valance*. *Deadwood* makes 'the myth' visible, but leaves us feeling that we are better off going forward with a myth to paper over the reality of the violence that, at some level, we know. See (for more on this) Cheyney Ryan, 'Print the Legend: Violence and Recognition in *The Man Who Shot Liberty Valance*' in J Denvir (ed), *Legal Reelism: Movies as Legal Texts* (Urbana, University of Illinois Press, 1996) 23.

[36] Even Ellesworth, for example, in episode one of season one, speaking of his desire to succeed by the labour of his own hands, describes the 'Indians' as savage: 'I may have fucked my life up flatter than ham- mered shit, but I stand here before you today beholden to no human cocksucker. And workin' a payin' fuckin' old claim. And not the US government sayin' I'm tresspassin' or the savage fuckin' red man himself or any of these limber dick cocksuckers passin' themselves off as prospectors had better try and stop me'.

that the savagery of the indigenous peoples is at least as much 'constructed' as 'real'. In episode one, though Al is perfectly aware that it was road agents rather than 'Indians' who were responsible for the brutal murder and scalping of a settler family, he participates in the collective attribution of the act to 'them heathens, bloodthirsty savages'. Indeed, Al, worried that people will spend the evening hunting down those responsible (rather than spending their gold on drink and women), gives a rousing speech in which he offers a bounty of $50 for 'the decapitated head of as many of these godless heathen cocksuckers anyone can bring in. Tomorrow. With no upper limit!'

Deadwood not only describes the erasure of indigenous peoples, it also performs it. For, although the town of Deadwood is on native land, the viewer only gets a glimpse of two 'Indians' during the entirety of the series' three seasons, both of whom end up dead. In neither case are we given a fully fleshed out character that carries a name or a history, in neither case are we given the chance to hear the character speak words in ways that would enable us to identify with the character. Nor are we given the conditions for cross-cultural empathy.[37] I explore these deaths, each of which is linked to one of the show's two main characters: Al, and Seth. In the first context, the focus will be on 'seriality', in the second context, on 'cinematic technique'.

III. Seriality: Getting in Al's ('Indian') Head Space

It seems trite to observe that *Deadwood* is a serial drama. Yet, for those who take television seriously, it is useful to draw its seriality to the foreground. Stedman argues that it is in the broadcast serial that 'the crafts of playwright and novelist come together with some distinction'.[38] In short, television serial dramas offer something that regular cinema does not. It enables the production of a story with a dense and layered narrative arc, indeed, a narrative arc closer to that of a novel (the initial publication of many of Dickens' novels in a serial mode here comes to mind). A series can offer multiple narrative arcs, some resolving within particular episodes, some over several episodes, others over one season, some continuing through to the end of a series.[39] The series offers time for the more robust delineation of character, and for exploring the minutiae of life since it does not have to press forward the dramatic action at the same speed that film must.

Certainly, because of this slower reiterative return, viewers also have the opportunity to live deeply with one of the pleasures of serial television: getting to know the characters, and watching them grow and change. TV in this respect is much more like

---

[37] See (for a discussion of ways readers can be denied the conditions to practice cross-racial empathy) Katie Rose Guest Pryal, 'Walking in Another's Skin: Failure of Empathy in to Kill a Mockingbird' in MJ Meyer (ed), *Harper Lee's To Kill A Mockingbird: New Essays* (UK, The Scarecrow Press, Inc, 2010) ch 12.

[38] RW Stedman, *The Serials: Suspense and Drama by Installment*, 2nd edn (Oklahoma, University of Oklahoma Press, 1977) 273.

[39] See also Thompson (n 1).

'life'. Audiences develop much stronger relationships with the characters. As Stedman puts it:

> With each episode watched, the viewer invests more deeply in the undertaking. The continuing characters, expanded by the illusion of reality that accompanies the extended action, become as real as neighbours. More real, perhaps because the viewer knows every secret... this detailed knowledge adds nuance to each piece of action.[40]

In response to this, we must ask how the seriality of *Deadwood* works to support a structure of feeling that sustains colonial orderings. For at least a partial answer to the question, let us return to Al and his relationship to the natives on whose land he operates the Gem Saloon.

In episode one, we hear Al offer a bounty of $50 per 'Indian' head. This foreshadowing becomes real at the end of episode four: there we are shown a Mexican riding through the town on horseback, waving a severed head.[41] The man whose head we are presented with in the episode's closing has no name and no history, but his death and decapitation were called for in Al's earlier offer. This visual image of the severed head, presented immediately after the scene in which an unsuspecting Wild Bill Hickok is shot in the back of the head by Jack McCall, seems to link these two deaths: the unheroic passing of the old at the hands of a new order, motivated not by honour, but by a mix of cowardice and greed.

At this point in the series, Al's complicity in the death of the native is unavoidable. For the benefit of viewers who might have missed the link, episode five makes the connection explicit: it opens with Seth passing a man on the street selling 'tufts...[of hair from the head of] a recently decapitated Indian'.[42] Later in the episode, Al calls his bar hand Johnny in to deal with the head:

Al: Come here (Holds out the Indian head wrapped in burlap—Johnny takes it) Get this outta here.

Johnny: Get rid of it?

Al: Did you hear me announce the other night that I'd pay a $50 bounty for every fuckin' Indian head?

Johnny: I was right next to ya, Al.

Al: That's the first head. Some chili chomper's out there somewhere spendin' my 50. You get rid of that head, you'd better know of another place with a position open for an idiot.

Johnny: Alright. Got a couple places I can keep it, I guess.

Al: Yeah, 'til after the trial.

Johnny: Well, what do ya do with it then? Put it somewhere in the bar? It's a nice conversation piece. I mean if it's handled the right way.

---

[40] Stedman (n 38) 490.

[41] *Deadwood*, season one, 'Here was a Man': the script states that it is a Mexican who brings in the head, displacing the violence called for onto a racialised character.

[42] The point is also emphasised in a conversation between Cy and Al. Cy says, 'didn't some Mexican bring the head in for bounty?' Al responds, saying, 'If it's important to ya, I'll look it up in my yesterday's diary'.

LIBRARY, UNIVERSITY OF CHESTER

This is the last we see of the head for a while, but our episodic encounter with the characters of *Deadwood* continues, and works to create an increasing attachment on the part of the viewers to the characters. This attachment happens not simply through time spent, but also through active work done by viewers to make sense of the characters and events.

In his work on Dickens, Sean O'Sullivan points out that there are three important terms in seriality: the new, the old, and the gap between. These three terms give serial fiction much of its compelling power. As he puts it:

> [T]he serial, by its nature, exists at the crossroads of the old and the new. Unlike the stand-alone novel, or a feature film, which present itself to us in toto, the serial offers constantly the promise of the new…the serial also draws us into the past, as old characters appear and disappear, as old green covers pile up by our nightstand, or old episodes of a program burrow into our memory, creating a history commensurate with our lifespan, unlike the merely posited past and present of a text we can consume in a few hours or day. Every reading, or every watching, requires a reconnection of old and new, an iteration of past and present.[43]

Viewers work at connecting the new in subsequent episodes, with the old in those which have past. Sullivan emphasises a third term in seriality: it is not simply 'the old' and 'the new', but 'the gap' between them. It is in the gap that viewers spend much of their time, wondering how to link together the old and the new. It is in the gap, 'swaying between the ignorance of the new and the knowledge of the old, [that] we are most active, most enmeshed in the narrative'.[44]

The 'Indian head' takes us through the old, the new and the gap between. The head, handed by Al to Johnny, acts as a reminder of the illegitimate violence done to the natives on whose territory this illegal town has been built. The head is gone, but not fully forgotten. Before the head returns, the episodic nature of the series relentlessly draws the viewer closer to Al Swerengen. As the series unfolds, we see Al actively working to establish an informal government to deal with the plague running through the camp. We are increasingly drawn toward him, seeing him suffer (both from the loss of Trixie's affections, and in a series of episodes featuring his bout with kidney stones), and seeing him do the hard work that others are not sufficiently brave enough to do (like mercifully suffocating the reverend who is dying of a brain tumour). We are drawn to Al not only through what we see him do, but also by what we hear him say. In many ways Al is an unappealing character, violent, and murderous. Yet, he is a man of words, and it is through his tongue we hear articulated the 'drivers below the surface', the tensions and paradoxes moving within the narrative. He is from elsewhere, but has made himself in Deadwood. At his centre is a will to stabilise, to democratise, to tolerate, to do what is ugly but necessary in the interests of stability. He is also honest (when not lying) and loyal (to those who deserve it). The series shows Al as the dark underbelly of the inevitable. It is Al who can do what is ugly but necessary, who

[43] Sean O'Sullivan, 'Old, New, Borrowed, Blue' in D Lavery (ed), *Reading Deadwood: A Western to Swear By* (London, IB Tauris, 2006) 115, 117.

[44] Ibid 123. This gap is the interpellative space of literature and film, the gap into which subjects are hailed. See also Louis Althusser, 'Ideology and Ideological State Apparatuses' in Ben Brewster (trans) *Lenin and Philosophy and Other Essays* (New York, Monthly Review Press, 1972) 121–76.

knows when the innocent must be sacrificed in the interest of saving others. He is, in short, at the heart of America.

The semiotic value of the 'Indian head' is next evoked in episode nine ('No Other Sons or Daughters'), where Johnny, getting a promotion at work, says 'Al, I have hoped for this conversation ever since you give me that Indian head to hide'. Its mention might be expected to remind us of the violence of the native's death, but it is brought back to our attention immediately after the episode in which Al's competitor, Cy, enacted a moment of violence against two young would-be thieves, violence sufficiently upsetting to displace Al as our 'bad guy'. So, even as we are reminded of the head, our sense of the violence involved in its former owner's murder has already paled against the backdrop of our increasing attachment to Al, and our discomfort over the more recently witnessed violence. Although we are invited to remember Al's incitement to genocide, it does not seem as laden with malice, and our response to the head is partially drained of its once potent emotional effect.

Certainly, by the mid-point of season one, our orientations as viewers change with respect to Al's character. What is significant is the way that this happens: through powerful monologues involving moments of profound exposure, where he speaks of truth, suffering and the past. We hear the pain of the abandoned child, of love lost, of sorrow and sickness. In these moments of truthful disclosure, we draw close to Al in understanding and affiliation. While he is certainly a rough character, he is also the one whose psyche and internal world we most deeply penetrate. What is striking is that these moments of proximity occur in two (upsetting) contexts.

The first site for one of Al's intimate monologues occurs when he is in the midst of having a prostitute perform fellatio on him; she does so as he discourses on his contemporary travails. His recitation of his thoughts is only interrupted when he stops to correct her on issues of technique, or to barrage her with insults, which foregrounds troubling gaps between what we see and what we hear. Further, to the extent that much of the monologue draws us closer to Al, we are also made to grapple with our response to his immediate behaviour. At the same moment that we are invited to peer deeper into Al's 'soul', we are made witnesses to his sexual exploitation of the prostitute. This technique, blending the base and sublime, has a hypnotic effect. Sexual violence is played out before us at the same moment we experience the pleasures of drawing closer to the man out of whose mouth the show's particular set of 'the drivers below' are articulated.

The second site that compels examination of Al's monologues involves the 'Indian head'. Remember, in keeping with the power of the serial form, the viewer must wait before the old returns to be re-woven with the new. In season two, episode 19, the audience is treated to a monologue in which Al, addressing a brown paper wrapped box tied with twine, articulates his strategy in an ongoing struggle for power and control in Deadwood. Here, viewers must make sense for themselves of Al's seemingly bizarre attachment to the box, a box he refers to as 'Chief'.[45]

---

[45] *(Al is in his room, staring at a shot glass, leaning against his bed facing his office.)* 'A man, as it happens a rival of mine, learning the secret of a great man's lieutenant, would make that lieutenant his slave. My rival knows that expanding the circle of the informed, dilutin' his power, will confound his intention, so he takes precaution to be sole sharer of his secret'. *(chuckles)* 'Then the world being the world...' *(drinks)* 'along comes a half-assed knight-errant, Utter, Hickok's ex-partner, to put all my rival's plans at risk. I'd seek audience with Utter, verify my thinking. He earns his bread shipping packages. And as the dimwit

On the fan sites this episode generated dialogue, as viewers tried to make sense of this package, of Al's expressed attachment to it, and of his addressing it as 'Chief'. What, viewers asked, was in the box? With fair speed, people began suggesting a connection to the 'Indian head' from the first season.[46] This connection was confirmed in episode 20, in an exchange between Al and his right-hand-man, Dan Dority:

Dan: Sometimes I hear you speakin' in here when I know there's nobody in here but you.

Al: You have not yet reached the age, Dan, have you, where you're moved to utterance of thoughts properly kept silent?

Dan: Been known to mutter.

Al: Not the odd mutter. Habitual fuckin' vocalizing of thoughts best kept to yourself. I will confide further. Lately... I talk to this package: the severed rotting head I paid bounty on last year of that murdered fuckin' Indian.

Weaving the new with the old, something interesting happens. The head, appearing at this juncture, does not operate as a reminder of genocide that distances us from Al. Now, it functions to draw us closer to him. The head no longer 'bears witness' to past crimes. The 'Chief' has moved from the role of victim to the role of confidant,[47] a shift made possible by television's seriality.

With each return to the head, we return to the memory of the violence, but it is positioned and repositioned against shifts in our understanding of Al's character. We have seen other dimensions of his self, and we have become affectively attached to him through layered experiences. The reality of his violence is remembered, but its present sense is altered. This early act of violence has become a much smaller part of how we understand him. We have shared in the narration of his history as an abandoned and abused child, know of his pain in relation to Trixie's love for Sol, and have watched his hidden acts of kindness to the crippled Jewel. While he is a pimp, his treatment of women is exemplary compared to the more brutal Tolliver and the murderous Wolcott. With each episode, we see and feel the loyalty that Al commands even from those he seems, on the surface, to treat harshly. We come to appreciate the gap between his surface presentation, and his deeper self. As viewers, we thus come to see the severed head as a ghostly presence marking past violence, but now facilitating Al's efforts to bring health, stability, prosperity and democracy to Deadwood.

The head returns again in season three, a season in which ruthless robber baron George Hurst comes to town, bringing a new vision of big business and capitalist

---

nobility that made him intercede may now make him reticent, you, Chief, will be my prop and ploy. Whilst I seek to draw him out'. *(He walks over to the chair in front of his desk where there is a package on it. He sets his shot glass down on the desk and sits in a neighbouring chair.)* 'I congratulate myself on having kept you around. Why make a show of disposing of you was my fucking thinking'. *(Pours another shot.)* 'It's not like we need the storage space. And if there's a chance in a thousand you people have been praying right' *(looks up)*, 'why get your boss's attention?' *(Drinks.)* 'Anyways, I've no plans of us partin' company'. *(He gets up, takes the package by a rope handle.)* 'As you will note...I have inscribed—' *(opens door)* 'no address'. *(He leaves.)*

[46] On the fan sites (18 October 2005), one can follow the discussions as people try to figure out what was in the box. See www.quartertothree.com.

[47] See (for helpful exploration of the difference between the role of the witness in the context of 'bearing witness of trauma' and the role of the priest/confessor in practices that are confessional) Roger Hallas, *Reframing Bodies: AIDS, Bearing Witness, and the Queer Moving Image* (London, Duke University Press, 2009) 10–17.

empire. With Hurst, we have the heralding of the end of one age, and the beginning of another; the town, now legitimate, seems pressed inexorably toward a future where ordinary people will have even less control over their own destiny, and will be ruled by larger (and more implacable) corporate capitalist forces. One of the prostitutes, Trixie, taking matters into her own hands, makes an unsuccessful attempt on Hurst's life. In episode 36, to save Trixie from retaliation, Al must sacrifice the life of a different prostitute, one innocent of any crime. Working through what needs to be done, Al speaks to the box; it is the 'Chief' who enables Al to articulate his grief at the actions he must take, actions we are positioned, similarly, to understand as both grievous and inevitable.[48]

In this particular monologue, it is not simply that we enter into Al's psyche, as in the other instances of his asides to the head. Here, we listen as he articulates the tensions that we too feel. We agree with him, that he must kill one woman to save another. We are complicit in what he is about to do, acknowledging the injustice and yet providing justifications for the act. Addressing the head, Al's monologue (and indeed his monologues in general) draws up echoes of Hamlet speaking to the skull of Yorick. Unlike Hamlet, however, Al is responsible for the death of the man to whose head he now speaks. His indictment of the 'Chief', his assertion that the head's former owner was responsible for his own demise, links us to the struggles of the third season and to the acts of colonial violence on which the town was built.[49] Season three is certainly about adaptation (and the penalties attendant on those who fail to adapt): the illegal settlement adapted to its status as town, and the informal settler economy of the town is being made to adapt to the implacable forward movement of globalising capital. The adaptation may require a certain kind of loss, and thus grieving, but in Deadwood (as elsewhere) life on both the individual and communal scale is an 'adapt or die' proposition. The monologue works to construct not just the 'Chief', but the entire 'Indian Nation', as responsible for his/its own demise. We see the violence that must be done, but are narratively positioned to understand it as unavoidable, as inevitable. The episodic monologues, with the prostitutes and the head, enable us to enter Al's psyche, but at the cost of being asked to remember (and forget) the violence that is part of the setting. His soliloquies resonate with the discursive formulations of colonial inevitability, enabling us to see selectively. While we know the head is present, we are not required to see it as it is: we are not made to

---

[48] Fetishising the dead is certainly a timeless tradition. Here, we have Al making a talisman of those he has conquered. While this is perhaps emblematic of warrior culture, what we seem to have in Al is not a warrior, but a businessman. Yet maybe this is in part the point. The series traces the beginnings of white collar corporate empires. As J Silbey nicely pointed out to me, the relationship Al has with the head serves as a comment on the ways these totemic fetishes persist into the present, doing so in ways that evacuate the power of the violence they supposedly 'remember'. For surely Al's relationship to the head does serve as a comment on the erasure of violence through business norms enacted by businessmen. The head is idolised (like the crucifix), and it is internalised as an individual totem rather than something through which one might empathise to rebuild community.

[49] Al Swearengen: *[talking to the Indian head in the box]* 'This fuckin' place is gonna be a fuckin' misery. Every fuckin' one of them, every fuckin' time I walk by, "Ooh, how could you? How could you?" With their big fuckin' cow eyes. The entire fuckin' gaggle of 'em is gonna have to bleed and quit before we can even hope for peace. What's the fuckin' alternative? I ain't fuckin' killing her that sat nights with me sick and takin' slaps to her mug that were some less than fuckin' fair. I should have fuckin' learned to use a gun, but I'm too fuckin' entrenched in my ways. And you ain't exactly the one to be levelin' criticisms on the score of being slow to adapt. You fuckin' people are the original slow fuckin' learners!'

confront the violence of the decapitation. Instead, we see the head 'as Al sees it': we see it as an occasion for reflection, an opportunity for entering Al's mind. In sum, this attachment through seriality enables us to see not through our own eyes, but through Al's mind, and as a result we become complicit in his way of seeing.

IV. Cinematic Technique and Visual Violence: Affect and the (in)Visibilisation of Law

Let us then turn to the questions of cinematic technique as we consider the second of the two 'Indians' that appear in Deadwood. Although Al is involved in many moments of violence throughout the series, we do not physically see him being violent to the Native American whose head becomes his close companion. While Al is in part responsible for the death, the actual killing is done by someone else, and is done off screen: we are never shown the murder. Rather, the act is left to our imaginations. Compellingly, although the seriality of the narrative enables the 'Chief' to function as a character, his character can be captured through a box on a desk. This is yet another example of selective seeing afforded by the narrative. This 'Indian' is portrayed as a present absence—before our eyes, but beyond our sight—with the box itself functioning as both the character and a symbol for the native people in general, summed up in the form of an undeliverable package, a makeshift coffin.

Although we are located in tribal lands in the entirety of the three seasons of *Deadwood*, there is only one appearance of a living, speaking native character.[50] In the opening minutes of episode six, a lone 'Indian' appears and attacks Seth. The two men fight, and Seth beats the man to death. The series thus gives us two killings of natives: our 'bad guy' is responsible for the death of one, and our 'good guy' is responsible for the death of the other. That the only living 'Indian' we see is violently killed by Seth, our representative of law and the narrative's supposed moral compass, is a point of significance, as is the fact that the scene is one of the more visually violent in the series.

Violence as portrayed in film and on television, far from involving a homogenised category of aesthetic approaches, can function in very different ways, raising different questions about affect.[51] Here, I do not mean simply that different people react to scenes of violence in different ways, though this is of course true.[52] Rather, I share

---

[50] The 'Indian' is played by JK Linn. There is a note of irony here. I had a very difficult time trying to credit an actor for the role. On IMBD site (the Internet Movie Data Base site, found at www.imdb.com), the list of credits for the 'Plague' episode makes no reference to the character of the 'Indian'. I finally tracked down David Midthunder, credited as the 'Consultant: Native American Sioux', who told me the role had been played by Linn. Linn is credited in the episode cast list, not as the 'Indian', but in the role of 'Milliner'. There seemed to be something strange in the difficulties I had in attempting to simply credit the actor who played the role of an unnamed 'Indian'.

[51] See Henry Giroux, *Fugitive Cultures: Race, Violence, and Youth* (New York, Routledge, 1996) 55–88.

[52] In our own collaborative work, R Buchanan and I have worked with and around this issue. My own tolerance for filmic violence is quite high. Hers is quite low. Thus, we are constantly pressed to discussions around our quite different affective responses to the same scenes of violence. As well, this question is a live one for those who teach criminal law, where bloodiness and violence become a background feature of the

Alison Young's view that the 'scenographic' set up of different kinds of violence can work to establish different moments of desire for the spectator.[53] In terms of the encounter between Seth and the 'Indian', the scene of violence is set up to enable a multi-layered space of judgement, resonating with dissonant affective pulls. Certainly, my own response to the scene went in a number of directions: confusion, fear, anxiety, horror, revulsion, relief, shame. With that in mind, let me briefly walk us through the first three minutes of this episode in order to reveal the structures of feeling which support persisting colonial relations that this scene of violence makes visible.[54]

Viewers of the series would recall that, at the end of episode five, Seth, our hero, was riding out to capture Jack McCall, who had escaped after shooting Wild Bill Hickok in the back of the head. The establishing shot of episode six is that of a desolate hillside, deadwood littering the ground, a rock-lined trail on the right, pine-covered mountains in the distance. The wind is audible, and we hear the long lonely cry of a bird. We cut to a medium shot which positions the viewer behind a twisted tree trunk, its leafless branches obscuring the view of the mountains beyond. A low foreboding wind whistles. We look up through the dead branches of a tree at a man-made structure of some sort, a platform with something attached and blowing in the wind, a shot not held long enough for us to be certain what we see, but long enough for us to become unsettled. There is an ominous creaking sound, as if someone is moving in the branches of the tree beside us.

Fifteen seconds into the segment, we see Seth approaching from a distance on horseback. The clop of hoof-beats competes with the sound of wind, a chipmunk, and the long, hollow call of another bird. The next shot positions us downhill to the left of the rocky trail, behind a bank of trees, watching from a low angle as Seth passes by, the view of him obstructed by trees. We seem as if to be sharing the visual space with an unknown spectator, but there have been no reverse shots to let us see who it is that is doing 'the watching'. The camera angles, scenes and sound combine to create a feeling of foreboding and uncertainty.

The camera moves ahead of Seth again for another long shot of him passing us (this time from the opposite side of the trail), and then moves into a medium close-up. Seth seems suddenly attentive to a sound. His head swings to the side, we hear an arrow whizzing through the air, then see it bury itself in the side of Seth's horse. What follows is an explosion of rapid shots with possibly 20 different framings, some lasting a quarter of a second or less. This rolls the viewer through a series of angles, allowing the viewer to experience the shock and surprise of the attack from multiple positions. The horse rears up on the screen, and the camera positions us immediately below the horse, as if its hooves are about to come down on our heads. The horse falls to the earth, pinning Seth beneath him. We hear Seth's hyper-intensified breathing as audible gasps. The shots swing us wildly from side to side as Seth struggles to see his attacker. Up to this point, as viewers, we have no sense of who the attacker might be or why

---

terrain, rather than anything to be commented on. For a lovely articulation of the challenges this poses for those teaching criminal law, see Martha Duncan, 'Beauty in the Dark of Night: The Pleasures of Form in Criminal Law' (2010) 59 *ELJ* 1203–44.

[53] See Young (n 21) ch 2.

[54] Season one, episode six 'Plague'. The first three minutes of the episode is (at the time of writing) available on youtube at www.youtube.com.

they are attacking. The scene is one of inexplicable and sudden violence, exploding like a force of nature rather than an orchestrated response to anything we have seen happen. The rapid succession of jump-cuts forces the viewer's pupils to dilate and contract rapidly in an effort to find a point of focus on the screen, supporting an embodied and generalised feeling of anxiety and panic.[55]

As Seth struggles to pull himself out from under the dead horse, we hear the sound of galloping, and then see an 'Indian' approach on horseback. He hits Seth on the head with a club of some sort, knocking him back to the ground. The man then dismounts and approaches Seth. He wears an eagle feather in his hair, an elaborate collar at his throat, and a fringed buckskin shirt decorated with beads from which shanks of hair hang. The man crouches close and low, places his foot on Seth's back, and gives him a shove. He brings his own face down close to Seth, saying (in Lakota) 'wasicu sica' ('wasicu' generally translates as 'non-"Indian"', 'Frenchman' or 'white man' and 'sica' is generally translated as 'someone or something that is "no good" or "bad"').[56] He grabs Seth's head, now bleeding from the forehead, tilting it sideways to ensure direct eye contact as he repeats the phrase 'wasicu sica', and then headbutts Seth in the head.

The Lakota then dances back again, repeating his sentence in between the cries of some song, continually approaching, jabbing Seth with his foot, and then backing up again, inviting him to conflict. Seth makes a tentative grab at the Lakota's foot, and is dragged forwards as the man shakes him loose, knocking him back to the ground with his knee, continuing to dance around him, repeating his sentence, the war cry, and saying to Seth, 'hoka hey' (translated often as 'Today is a good day to die', but also alternately given as 'Welcome to the soul', but can also be translated as 'charge', 'get moving' or 'get animated'). While the roughly 40 shots over this 60-second segment position us to see the fight from a number of angles, many of them position us to experience the violence of the encounter from Seth's point of view. In one particular shot, we find ourselves as if on the ground with Seth, and half of the other man's foot fills the foreground of the screen, seeming to come directly towards us. In another shot, a close up of the other man's face, mouth open in a war cry, fills the frame.

Seth finally crawls onto his hands and knees, and rises to his feet, seeming to respond to the Lakota's words 'hoka hey' by saying, 'Ok, Ok'. Seth then rushes forward, catching the man around the midsection, driving him backwards until he pins him with his back against a tree. Over the next 15 seconds, through a series of shots and reverse shots, we see the two men grapple with each other, hands to throats, as they choke each other. Seth then makes a fist and knocks the man in the jaw, throwing him sideways, and both men fall panting to the ground. For four seconds (which seems a long sustained moment after the rapid cuts we have been following), we are positioned away from the two men, bystanders witnessing a beautifully framed long shot, the wind still blowing, the men audibly panting in the shadowy foreground, a triangle of light illuminating the background.

---

[55] See (for detailed discussion of *Minority Report* and the relationship between visual structure and affective responses) Buchanan and Johnson (n 19).

[56] For a non-Lakota speaker such as myself, the phrase sounds phonetically like 'Wa-shee-chu-shee-cha'. Thanks to Carly Bad Heart Bull (JD Candidate 2011, University of Minnesota Law School) and Neil McKay for their help with translation.

The camera then cuts to a close-up of a jagged rock on the forest floor. Seth's hands reach out to grab it, and he drags it towards himself. He raises it high in the air, then brings the rock down in a crushing blow on the Lakota's head. While the man's head is below our field of view in this shot, so that we do not quite 'see' what happens, the violence of the moment is visceral; the downward swing of the rock is amplified by a grunt of exertion from Seth, a gasp from the other man, and the unpleasant sound of something begin smashed. Any relief at not having actually seen the rock make contact with the head is quickly ripped away; Seth repeats the action, smashing the rock on the other man's head an additional 15 times. The violence is further amplified by the grunts of exertion that escape Seth with each blow. Finally, he drops the rock, and falls across the body of the supine Lakota with a big grunt of exhaustion.

While the killing takes up only 14 seconds of screen time, it is comprised of a virtual visual storm. There are 11 shots in the scene depicting the violence between Seth and the Lakota man, each framed with care, taken from different angles and views: from the left, the right, below, above, long shot, medium close-up. One might imagine, from what is written here, that we are being made to linger in a moment of violence through an elongation of the 'real time' experience through a slow motion technique. We do not have that here. Rather, we operate in 'real time', but are drenched with images of the killing shot from different vantage points. The impact of the encounter is extended through a layering of multiple images, which leaves us with a much denser experience of the encounter and resulting recall of the moment of violence. Heavily panting, Seth lifts himself off the body as the handheld camera tracks him from behind. With the camera situated behind Seth, our view of the dead Lakota is initially obscured by the back of Seth`s own head. As he pulls away and to the side, still panting, we see the dead man's bloodied head, a head that has been obliterated by the violence. We get a close-up reverse shot of Seth's face, a face which seems to indicate a desire to turn away from what he is looking at, yet his eyes remain fixed, seeming to pull him back to the corpse over and again. He, like us as viewers, seems simultaneously repulsed and hypnotised by the sight. He then struggles to his feet, takes a few steps away and collapses to the ground.

Less than three minutes into the episode, Seth is left unconscious on the forest floor; he will not return to the storyline until much later in the episode. As viewers, we are left swimming in a whirlpool of confusion and shock produced by three minutes of scenographic techniques designed to swing the viewers through a number of affective states. We have seen our hero riding across unknown territory, seeking to bring a murderer to justice, suddenly attacked for unknown reasons by an unknown character, speaking an unknown language. We are relieved that Seth has survived the encounter, but are also shocked and repulsed by the violence we have been made to experience in such a visceral way. There is also an uncomfortable politics at work: we do not *wish* to have our hero responsible for the death of an 'Indian', especially because we know Native Americans have been wrongly blamed and killed as a response to a number of murders committed by the settlers themselves. Still, as viewers, we have been given an affective experience that supports a narrative of self-defence: we were shown Seth minding his own business, subjected to an unprovoked act of aggression. Indeed, the encounter bursts upon us like a wave, leaving us shaken and confused. While the camera's point of view is not limited to that of Seth or the Lakota, it frequently places us in Seth's position, causing us to visually and aurally share the dislocation and panic Seth experiences. We are at no time positioned to identify with his assailant. Affectively, the flood of images and angles also works to deny us the space or time to consider alternatives. Rather, we are pressed into a space of shock and dislocation in which the ferocity of an unprovoked attack situates us in the middle of a life-or-death struggle.

A viewer might nonetheless experience a nagging doubt about the magnitude of force visited on the Lakota by Seth. Within the common law system, the law of self-defence has always required that the force used be no more than is necessary to defend oneself, and that there must have been a reasonable apprehension of death for one to have a right to counter with deadly force.[57] Seth's use of force is extreme, and indeed the 15 blows he delivers might seem to suggest a metaphor for the savagery exercised by the colonial society against the indigenous peoples. Yet, even if this question lingers in the background, the scene presses us in the direction of *feeling* that Seth's response is justified, in both juridical and natural law realms. For beyond the common-law's articulation of self-defence there exists a more primordial law, one that aptly applies to the seemingly barren terrain the narrative occupies, the law of nature that dictates that one must 'kill or be killed'. So, visually, the scene invites us to feel the violence of Seth's response as justified and indeed necessary.

Finally, I want to circle back to the question that motivated this exploration of *Deadwood*. Here we turn to the question of how TV, with its narrative arcs, seriality, and tools of visual persuasion, affectively invites the viewer to share a structure of feeling that sustains the colonial empire of force even while seeming to critique those very structures. Let us close by exploring how the visually powerful three-minute segment above is woven into the critique that follows in the remainder of episode six.

V. 'No law at all in Deadwood? Is that true?': Interrogating Structures of Feeling and re-Visualising Law

Halfway through episode six, Charlie Utter, (close companion to Wild Bill Hickock) travelling the trail earlier taken by Seth, comes across a dead horse. Dismounting from his horse and pulling out his rifle, he moves cautiously through the area, eyes roving expertly across the scene to cull clues from the traces of the incident left behind. His eyes sweep across the body of the Lakota's horse, alive and still standing by. The camera, taking Charlie's point of view, focuses our attention on the body of the heavily painted and decorated horse, holding us in Charlie's space as he 'reads' the particular markings there. He then moves through the trees, finding first the dead Lakota, and then Seth lying bloodied and still on the forest floor some distance away.

Minutes later, we return to the scene, where Charlie is now tending to the still unconscious Seth. Close-up shot/reverse-shot techniques place us alternately in

---

[57] In the Canadian context, this is captured in §§ 34–36 of the *Criminal Code*.

Charlie's and Seth's positions.[58] Occupying Charlie's field of vision, we wipe the blood from Seth's face as he lies on the forest floor below us. Switching to Seth's perspective, we are flat on our backs looking up at Charlie's looming face, the sun immediately behind, blurring the scene. Held in this space, we (as both Seth and audience) listen to Charlie interpret the signs inscribed on the horse's body:

> Charlie: The three red hands on the pony's flank, was three men killed, hand to hand. The red circle was one killed on horseback. The white lines on the pony's legs was times that he had counted coup. Hmm, with them whether they mean to kill your man after or you're just showin' off you hit 'em with a gun butt or a stick or a club. That's counting coup. That's why he come for you instead of pickin' you off with an arrow, like he did your horse.

> Seth: Charlie.

> Charlie: Ah, there you are. That was one bad hombre you got by, Bullock.[59]

In reading the violent scene, Charlie reminds us that native territory is not devoid of law. Through years spent travelling with Wild Bill and Calamity Jane in the last of the Great Wild West shows, Charlie is able to identify and name some elements of native law.[60] One of these elements is the practice of counting coup, which explains why the Lakota did not simply shoot Seth in the first place. As Charlie describes it, counting coup appears as a way of showing off by hitting an enemy in close contact, before, presumably, finishing him off. Beyond Charlie's brief discourse on the matter, there are richer accounts of the various practices of counting coup, ones that position it as a more deeply elaborated practice of 'doing law'. Counting coup is in part a practice of establishing one's position in the tribal honour system, where honour does not inevitably involve the death of either party.[61] For the Cheyenne, for example, one of the bravest acts was to count coup on (to touch or strike) a living and unhurt (ie, battle-capable) man, and to leave him alive.[62] The practice of counting coup, according to Arthur Jacob, served to change the enemy's energy, letting him know you were not frightened and could have hurt him if you wanted to:

> [T]his act of physically touching your enemy without seriously hurting him can take away or disarm the enemies' anger. It creates an opportunity for the enemy to think about, and consider what he is doing and gives him a chance to remember that all life is sacred.[63]

---

[58] See (for another exploration of the affects produced by the blurring of the boundary between screen and audience through such techniques) Jessica Silbey's discussion of Hitchcock's *The Paradine Case* in *The Subjects of Trial Films* (unpublished dissertation, UMI 1999) 193–212.

[59] http://turtlegirl76.com/deadwood/previously/Ep06.pdf, for the transcript of the episode. Last accessed April 4, 2012.

[60] Charlie's account of course raises all the questions that circulate around the articulation of Indian law by non-Indians, myself included. For the issue here is not simply 'who' has the right to offer authoritative statements about the nature of indigenous law, but is also the question of how people from differing legal traditions understand, live with, and give voice to the traditions of the other.

[61] See (for a lovely autobiographical account of counting coup, articulated in the context of one Chief's journey from childhood to becoming a warrior—a book written for middle school readers) Joseph Medicine Crow and Herman Viola, *Counting Coup: Becoming a Crow Chief of the Reservation and Beyond* (National Geographic Children's Books, 2006).

[62] mr_sedivy.tripod.com.

[63] www.sonic.net.

That is, counting coup is not *only* about gaining personal honour. It is also a practice of teaching and reminding the other about responsibility, obligation and law.

One might object that such a practice is not generally theorised as 'law'. Western legal traditions have often characterised indigenous law as 'moral' rather than 'legal' principles; but such characterisations make the operations of an imperial impulse visible that tends to either idealise or flatten indigenous law and its sources.[64] In indigenous terms, 'law' is not simply a set of obligations or strictures, but captures a range of practices, protocols, ceremonies, stories, relations, obligations and traditions.[65] In reading the markings on the horse, and speaking of the practice of counting coup, Charlie unsettles Seth's earlier articulation of the classic colonial doctrine of terra nullius, the notion that there is 'no law in Deadwood', on account of it being 'on Indian land'. On the contrary, the fact of Charlie's knowledge makes a competing account of North American history visible, one in which newcomers acknowledged and learned about indigenous societies and their laws.[66]

If we accept Charlie's account of counting coup, there is room for a different explanation of what happened between Seth and the Lakota. We can make some sense of the man's decision *not* to shoot Seth, but rather to strike him with a coup stick. We can also make sense of the way that the man approached Seth without weapons, dancing around and poking at him with his foot, but not striking him. The words used by the Lakota also make sense. He had shouted 'hoka hey' at Seth, calling on Seth to engage with him, to participate in this moment of counting coup, but we are not invited to view the encounter in this way until it is already over. Thus, if we as viewers did not understand the Lakota's words or protocols, we must then ask ourselves whether Seth understood them. Herein resides a certain ambiguity. In episode one we are told Seth is a sheriff in Montana, and that he had lived in the Dakota Territory from the age of 17. Dakota and Lakota languages are related, so there is every possibility that Seth understood. Indeed, he responded to the line 'hoka hey', by holding out one hand, saying 'OK, OK', and getting up off his knees. Still, even if Seth understands the practice of counting coup, he does not leave his enemy alive to contemplate the implications. He responds with vicious blows—not with his hand or a stick, but with a stone—blows meant not to teach, but to obliterate.

---

[64] See (for a rich discussion of sources of indigenous law, living indigenous legal traditions, and the challenges of keeping these discussions open across communities) John Borrows, *Canada's Indigenous Constitution* (Toronto, University of Toronto Press, 2010) and Borrows, *Drawing out Law: A Spirit's Guide* (Toronto, University of Toronto Press, 2011). The first of these explores the sources and scope of indigenous legal traditions in the language of Canadian legal and political theory (particularly in ch 2). The second, combining both fictional and non-fictional elements, juxtaposes Canadian legal policy and practice with more broadly defined Anishinabek perceptions of law, as evidenced through different Anishinabek ways of engaging with the world.

[65] These nuances are nicely captured by Maori scholar J Ruru. See Jacinta Rur, 'Layered Narratives in Site-Specific "Wild" Places' in H Lessard, R Johnson and J Webber (eds), *Storied Communities: Narratives of Contact and Arrival in Constituting Political Community* (Vancouver, UBC Press, 2011) 211–26. In the world of literature, this nuance in visible in Leslie Silko's novel, *Ceremony* (New York, Penguin Books, 1977).

[66] See (on these alternative histories of encounter): Jeremy Webber, 'Relations of Force and Relations of Justice: The Emergence of Normative Community between Colonists and Aboriginal Peoples' (1995) *OHLJ* 33, 4, 623–60. See also (for an extended exploration of encounters, and particularly the ways stories of settler/indigenous 'contact' have sat alongside stories of citizen/immigrant 'arrival'): Lessard, Johnson and Webber (n 65). In *Deadwood*, one sees elements of both 'contact' and 'arrival' narratives struggling for dominance.

Of course, even if the practice of counting coup is foregrounded, the scene is visually rendered with enough detail and complexity to make it difficult for the viewer to be confident that the Lakota sought only to count coup and not to take Seth's life. Charlie tells us also that the 'Indian' was dangerous, that he had killed three men in hand-to-hand combat, and one on a horse. Of course, we know that Seth too has killed, and indeed he killed two men in episode one.[67] Then again, he is a former sheriff. His killings have thus been conducted under the imprimatur of law. As a counterpoint, we know nothing about the contexts for the killings of the four men whose deaths have been ceremonially inscribed on the horse: was it in war, against known enemies, in defence of others or self? While the markings on the horse constitute additional traces of native law, we as viewers do not have the resources to make sense of this law.[68] We are left only with Charlie's assessment that the man was one 'bad hombre', coupled with our sense that there was no reason for the attack on Seth.

As he regains consciousness, Seth himself shows little interest in the question of why he was attacked. Still the lawman, he remains focused on finding Jack McCall. First, he grabs a shovel to dig a grave for the dead Lakota. Charlie tries to dissuade him, and in the text that follows, we are given not only details about the protocols for a proper burial in indigenous law, but also information that suddenly links this episode to the ones that have preceded it:

Charlie: You ain't doin' him no favor. I mean his way to heaven's above ground and lookin' west.

Seth: Well, let's do that, then. (Tosses the shovel aside.)

Charlie: Don't you want to take him over the ridge? This fuckin' hole in the ground and put him up there with his headless buddy? I mean, that's what you nearly got killed for? Interfering with his big fuckin' medicine, burying his fuckin' buddy, over the fuckin' ridge!

Charlie's comment helps us make sense of the unexplained manmade structure we saw in the opening seconds of the episode: it was the raised platform of a funeral pyre. The unseen watcher was not simply a random 'Indian' positioned to ambush the unwary traveller, but was rather a warrior interrupted in a burial ceremony for his dead friend. Seth had unwittingly entered or violated a sacred space. Still, even as we begin to understand why Seth was attacked, we remain able to see him as legitimately acting in self-defence. For even as Charlie points in the direction of indigenous law, in describing this law as 'big medicine', he characterises it as a form of primitive or savage law, enabling us to judge that law as wanting, to see something disproportionate in the Lakota's response to an unwitting passerby. Even more powerfully, the news that

---

[67] The episode opens with Seth hanging Clell, and ends with Seth and Wild Bill Hickok simultaneously firing on (and killing) Ned Mason. Seth tells Ned, 'Get down off your horse or face the consequences'. Ned draws, but Seth and Bill are faster, and Ned is killed. We do not know which man is responsible. Bill asks 'Was that you are me, Montana?' and Seth responds with 'My money'd be on you'.

[68] Battle markings on the horses also point us in the direction of indigenous laws dealing with conflict between various nations. Questions of inter-nation conflicts between indigenous communities have their own long tradition of legality. As is the case for Western societies, indigenous peoples have legal histories of conflict, dispute resolution, and treaty. See (for a discussion of indigenous mechanisms and laws around such conflicts) Val Napoleon, 'Living Together: Gitksan Legal Reasoning as a Foundation for Consent' in Webber and MacLeod (eds), *Between Consenting Peoples* (Vancouver, UBC Press, 2010) 45–76. See also Napoleon, *Ayook: Gitksan Legal Order, Law, and Legal Theory*, (PhD thesis, University of Victoria, 2009).

the dead friend is headless draws everything into relief. We remember Al's offer of a bounty for the head of an 'Indian', and realise that the body of the 'Chief' lies on the funeral pyre. This second encounter with a native inhabitant has been tightly linked to our first. This enables us to see Al as ultimately responsible for *both* their deaths, and suggests that we can legitimately absolve Seth of any complicity in the killing.

Yet, that would be too simple. It matters that it is Seth who does the killing, and it matters who he kills. Charlie describes the Lakota to Seth as 'one bad hombre'. David Midthunder, however, the Native American Sioux consultant who worked on the episode, takes us in a different direction, in his description of the character as a Lakota *akicita*.[69] The word '*akicita*' is a complicated term that can be translated in a number of ways, meaning slightly different things in different contexts, but here, the meaning seems clear. Consider James Walker's explanation:

> If I speak of an Oglala in camp and say he is akicita I mean he is an officer appointed by the council of the camp. This kind of an akicita is the highest officer of a camp. Everyone in the camp is subordinate to the akicita. He is like a policeman and a judge and a jailer and an executioner. All must do as he says, and he can punish anyone, he may even destroy all the property of anyone, or strike anyone, and he may kill anyone. But if he does anything that is not according to the laws of the Oglalas the other akicitapi will punish him, and the council may depose him.[70]

That the Lakota is *akicita* is made visible in what we are shown of his outfit, hair, markings and actions. He is not only a warrior, wearing an eagle feather in his hair, he has the definitive black streak painted down his right cheek from his eye to the lower edge of his jaw, marking him as *akicita*.[71] Charlie was perhaps not far off the mark in calling him 'one bad *hombre*': the *akicita* were, after all, sometimes known for brutality in a fight. Yet to focus on the mere brutality of the warrior in battle skips over the central point: they were responsible for protecting their people, and were willing and ready to die to do so. Given that, the *akicita,* burying the body of another warrior decapitated by an outsider for the sake of a $50 bounty, may have been interested in something more than changing the energies of his opponent. We still must ask, however, whether this means Seth was entitled to so brutally defend himself.

This depends on how one understands the legal order of the territory. For although Seth may not have been directly responsible for killing the 'Indian' now laying headless on the funeral platform, it does not follow that he is 'innocent'. Recall the indictment the *akicita* flung at Seth: '*wasicu sica*.' While these words, uttered eye to eye in a close-up shot, seem generally best translated as 'bad white person', if one were to translate '*wasicu sica*' more literally, it means 'he who takes the fat' or 'he who takes the best part'. From the point of view of Lakota law, Seth is guilty by the very fact of his presence on the land, responsible for *all* the settlers' disrespect, appropriation, excess consumption and waste. Seth's presence on the land is neither accidental nor unintentional. For Seth, like the others in the outlaw town, has full knowledge that

---

[69] Email communication. Thanks here to D Midthunder, who worked as the adviser on Lakota practices for *Deadwood*.

[70] James Walker and Raymond DeMallie, 'Interview with Thomas Tyon, July 4, 1987' in *Lakota Society* (Nebraska, University of Nebraska Press, 1992) 28–29.

[71] Ibid 25 ('The akicita painted a black streak down across the right cheek, from the eye to the lower edge of the jaw, as a badge of his office.').

the sacred territory of the Lakota is protected by treaty, and that he is there illegally. While not directly taking gold from the land, in selling goods to other prospectors, he has actively chosen to function as a vehicle through which that gold enters into a new economy of trade and commerce. He is implicated both indirectly and directly in the violation of 'Indian' law, and in the death of Lakota people.

Just as the *akicita* is not 'just any Indian', Seth is not 'just any settler'. He is the symbolic representative of Western law, riding across 'Indian' land to capture an escaped murderer, to force him to stand trial according to settler law. In this encounter, then, we have not just any man against any man, but a policeman against a policeman, one legal order against another. We are witness to an encounter between two representatives of 'the law', both seeking justice for men who have been murdered. But whose law applies in this space? If we understood the two men as soldiers for justice, we could understand the encounter as between two nations at war, and perhaps that is the way the colonial encounter *should* be understood. However, if we step back from the assertion that there is no law on 'Indian' land, we instead confront a history of the Lakota people, and those illegally on their land.

This then requires us to understand Seth not as a 'lawman', but as a man acting outside of law, one fully responsible for the wrongs he commits. If the series has focused our attention on the distinction between juridical law and economic/natural law, it has taken our attention away from a third form of law. Rather than seeing Seth as entitled to defend himself according to the rules of the common law, we are pressed to ask about his responsibility to bend himself to the law of the territory to which he had travelled. In this case, even if his life was threatened, it does not follow that Seth had a right of self-defence. Just as Seth was legally empowered to take Clell's life in episode one, in the Lakota territory of episode six, the *akicita* had the right to take Seth's.

Even as the episode makes these issues visible, it also provides mechanisms for forgetting them, for giving the viewer a path to move past the discomfort of our settler complicity. Seth helps the viewer respond to this moment of crisis by giving the *akicita* the honour of a burial done in accordance with Lakota traditions. By emphasising that the *akicita* was trying to bury his dead friend, the episode encourages us to now understand these five men (Charlie, Seth, the dead Wild Bill Hickock, and the two dead 'Indians') as symbolically linked. The *akicita* becomes, in a sense, a fallen compatriot, another man seeking justice, the victim of fate, of destiny, of an inevitable, albeit tragic conflict of legal systems. Justice is to be done not through subjecting oneself to 'Indian' law, but only by honouring it at the moment of its passing.

As we approach the end of the episode, we follow Charlie and Seth as they carry the dead *akicita* to the funeral platform together. When we first caught view of this platform, we heard the haunting and hollow sounds of nature. Now, the scene is coloured by emotive extra-diegetic music that plays in the background. The camera lingers on the platform, allowing us to see all that had been withheld from us at the beginning. We see a drum, spear and bow leaning against the side, a number of eagle feathers similarly hung and blowing in the wind. We see the body of the headless warrior. We also see the body of this other warrior's dead horse, its head, eyes and flanks painted in ways that show this warrior, as well, to have been a man of great honour. There is a swell of the music as the *akicita* is lifted up onto the platform. Charlie and Seth exchange a long look in which some sort of understanding seems to pass between them. Then they walk out of the frame, leaving us on the shot of the burial platform, stark against the green of the hills beyond. The music stops, we return to the sound of the wind, the two men walk down the hill, mount their horses, and ride off, again in pursuit of Jack McCall. The demands of settler law are drawn back to the foreground. It is both the 'Indians' and their laws, honourably buried, that we leave behind.

VI. Some Concluding Thoughts

Television is an immensely powerful site of cultural and legal storytelling. *Deadwood*, like other cultural products, offers a chance for us to interrogate the pleasures and the perils of our cultural and legal imaginings. For if Deadwood is the central character of the series (as Milch states), it is the character of the nation in the process of being birthed, a story of a national identity rooted in a particular vision of land, consumption and economy. In the series, we are shown an inexorable drive for more, to provide what the people need (or, as Al might say, what you *want* them to need). We watch as the town shifts from outlaw space towards law, democracy and civilisation. Thereby the series invites us to share in a structure of feeling that justifies the harms of colonial appropriation, and which acknowledges past violence, but enables us to experience it as tragic yet inevitable, as necessary for the foundation of our democracy and its economy. *Deadwood*, through its narrative arc, its seriality, its cinematic structure, works to draw us to its characters, encouraging us to see the harms and damages done by them as inevitable. In doing so, it makes it difficult for us to either imagine that there were alternative paths in the past, or that alternatives are available to us in the present.

Deadwood returns us to a moment in a traumatic past, to a place of genocidal practice, painting the violence of that moment in textures that invite us to look again, see further, and consider how it is that we both remember and forget. Yet, as Henry Giroux reminds us, there is a politics of forgetting; a politics that erases how disparate social identities have been produced, legitimated, and marginalised within different relations of power. This is an apt description of the processes at work in stories about the foundation of the nation, with their identification of 'insiders' and 'outsiders', with their justifications of violence and erasure. The question for those interested in exploring law on the small screen is not *whether* TV's stories do this, but is rather *how* they do this, and how we as consumers of the stories can understand the affective pulls, and push back against them. As Giroux puts it in the context of the movies, 'we must be attentive to the processes whereby meanings are produced in these films and how they work to secure particular forms of authority and social relations'.[72] The point, he says, is not to cast off these texts, but is rather to find additional ways to intervene in them, to help them mean more and different things. Or, as Rustom Bharucha puts it, the challenge is 'to think through images rather than respond to them with a hallucinatory delight'.[73]

---

[72] Giroux (n 51) 108.
[73] Rustom Bharucha, 'Around Ayodhya: Aberrations, Enigmas, and Moments of Violence' *Third Text*, No 24:7 (Autumn 1993) 45–58, 51.

TV offers us both pleasures and challenges. *Deadwood* itself offers one of many places where we can ask how our cultural stories work both to let us 'know' and 'not know' about structures of feeling which, uninterrogated, would have us unconsciously sustaining the empire of force. In *Deadwood*, we can interrogate the complicated blend of anti-colonialism and imperialism that continues to work its spell on us. Attending to television's narratives, its seriality and its visual structures, we can find the space to explore how the stories we tell, consume and celebrate, provide us with both order-maintaining and order-transforming possibilities.[74] The challenge is to take the place of pleasure seriously, to ask more about how these pleasures are constructed, and to look closely at the ways we are invited to think and to feel. As Tom King puts it, 'you have to be careful with the stories you tell. And you have to watch out for the stories you are told',[75] for television's stories are a matter of serious pleasure and serious business.

What else is there to say? I love television. I really do.

---

[74] SN Eisenstadt, 'The Order-Maintaining and Order-Transforming Dimensions of Culture' in R Münch and NJ Smelser (eds), *Theory of Culture* (Berkeley, University of California Press, 1992) 64.

[75] Tom King, *The Truth About Stories: A Native Narrative* (CBC Radio One, 2003) 10.

3

Making 'Bad Apples' on *The Bridge*: A Production Study of the Making of a Police Drama

ANITA LAM

I. Introduction

Socio-legal scholars have been interested in studying fictional television representations of crime and law for their ideological content. By the term 'ideology', I mean the fundamental beliefs held by the majority of people in a society about how the world is structured, who is good or bad, and what kinds of actions are deemed right or wrong.[1] For the most part, socio-legal scholars have examined legal ideology through content analyses of television representations, where they have separated conventional analyses from critical ones.[2] Conventional representations emphasise the law as the primary means through which justice can be served, highlighting punishment of 'bad' lawbreakers by 'good' law enforcers. In contrast, more critical representations do not reassure viewers that justice can be achieved, that villains will not triumph, or that there are even happy endings to be had. Methodologically, these analyses of ideological messages treat the television text as a final product, because the key analytical moment occurs at the point of (scholarly) reception.

In this chapter, I would like to shift the methodological focus from reception to production, and in doing so highlight the *process* of production[3] that is otherwise obscured in academic analyses that only view television shows as final products or

---

[1] This is in line with the definition of ideology found in Nicole Rafter, *Shots in the Mirror: Crime Films and Society* (New York, Oxford University Press, 2006) 8.

[2] See, eg Naomi Mezey and Mark C Niles, 'Screening the Law: Ideology and Law in American Popular Culture' *Columbia Journal of Law and the Arts 28* (2004–05); Timothy O Lenz, *Changing Images of Law in Film and Television Crime Stories* (New York, Peter Lang, 2003); Rafter, *Shots in the Mirror* (n 1).

[3] See Amnon Reichman, 'The Production of Law (and Cinema)' (1997) bepress Legal Series, www.law.bepress.com/expresso/eps/1997. My project is different from the one suggested by Reichman, where he envisions scholars using the language of cinematic production to describe the production of law.

completed texts for mass consumption. While the final product suggests a stable frame of representation of law and justice, an empirical examination of the production process reveals that television writers and producers are constantly working against a backdrop of shifting and unstable frames of representation as production moves forward and changes are made to accommodate the demands of various stakeholders. This chapter's innovative focus empirically examines how ideology becomes incorporated into the particular production of a fictional crime television series.[4]

In studying the production process of a crime television show, ideology cannot be easily attributed to a single authorial source. Instead, ideology is embedded in 1) what television writers know about crime and law, and 2) how they turn that knowledge into particular representations in ways that align with the demands of other players in the production process,[5] such as producers, network executives and insurers. In this conceptualisation of ideology, I connect it to ways of knowing, because ideology is partial knowledge that represents particular interests.[6] I also associate these ways of knowing with ways of representing particular to North American television dramas broadcast on major television networks.[7] Because ideology is understood as an epistemological question, I utilise actor-network theory to study the circulation of knowledge and representation during the television production process. It should be noted that actor-network theory is a novel method for studying television production, and I will discuss it in greater detail in the following section.

Although the insights in this chapter hold true for the production of most North American crime dramas,[8] the bulk of this chapter examines the writing process of a particular police drama. As a Canadian-American (CTV/CBS) co-produced, one-hour television drama, *The Bridge* (2010) tells the story of a street cop who rises to become the head of a police union, and endeavours to clean up the corrupt network of police officers and city politicians. In this case study, I specifically examine the ideology of 'the bad apple' as an explanation for police corruption. The 'bad apple' suggests that there is an individual cause for an act of corruption rather than an organisational cause (eg 'the bad barrel'). Although academics have demonstrated that acts of police corruption are the result of systemic factors,[9] the 'bad apple' persists in entertainment fiction.[10] I argue that its persistence in television fiction is the result of what 1) the television writers of *The Bridge* know about crime and policing, and 2) how that knowledge is shaped into a representation through the input of

---

[4] As another example that looks at the production process of an American police programme, albeit a reality TV series, see Aaron Doyle, *Arresting Images: Crime and Policing in Front of the Television Camera* (Toronto, University of Toronto Press, 2003).

[5] By highlighting the collaborative nature of television production, I am not proceeding under an auteurist framework that praises the work of a single genius creator.

[6] See Richard V Ericson et al, *Visualizing Deviance: A Study of News Organizations* (Toronto, University of Toronto Press, 1987) 9.

[7] In other words, these television dramas are formatted to appease mass audiences as opposed to niche audiences.

[8] I use the terms 'crime drama' and 'police dramas' interchangeably in this chapter.

[9] See Monique Nuitjten and Gerhard Anders (eds), *Corruption and the Secret of Law: A Legal Anthropological Approach* (Aldershot, Ashgate, 2007).

[10] Judith Grant, 'Assault under Color of Authority: Police Corruption as Norm in the LAPD Rampart Scandal and in Popular Film' (2003) *Journal of Business Ethics* 42, 125–49.

quasi-legal entities, such as Errors and Omissions insurance and a broadcast network's Standards and Practices.

II. Production Study and Actor-Network Theory

Even in media and cultural studies, television production studies are rare because of issues of access and the time-consuming labour on the part of the researcher. However, there are two main approaches used by media scholars to study the film and television production process: a political economy approach and a historical approach. For my research, I used neither of these approaches. Instead, I utilised actor-network theory, which has been rarely used in media studies. In this section, I will also explain why these two dominant approaches were not appropriate methods for what I wanted to study.

A. The Political Economy Approach

In North America, political economy scholars have traditionally dominated academic studies focused on the media industries. Often written within a Marxist theoretical framework, these analyses tend to assume that media culture is an ideological extension of powerful capitalist forces, serving to socialise audiences into broader economic interests.[11] More importantly, for methodological purposes, the political economy approach emphasises macro structural factors that make film and television possible *in general*, such as the concentration of media ownership, large-scale market forces and regulatory regimes.[12] Because the political economy analysis focuses on the relationship between states, markets and communication institutions, the method provides a macro view—or a bird's eye view—of production. Because of the broad scale of this perspective, this method is not useful for explaining the particular conditions under which a specific television show is produced. While political economy studies of production examine the concentration and circulation of capital, particularly at the state or global level, these studies have very little to say about the circulation of representations and textual meaning.

By 'meaning,' I refer to both 1) the meaning of representations, and 2) the meaning of processes that lead to particular representations. In contrast to humanities scholars, the political economy approach does not attend to the richness of meaning(s) embedded in representations. Instead, the approach tends to reduce the meaning of a representation to an ideological stance that either supports a specific political position or resists it. For example, Edward S Herman and Noam Chomsky's 'propaganda model' of mass media reduces the meaning of news representations to

---

[11] David Hesmondhalgh, 'Bourdieu, the Media and Cultural Production' (2006) *Media, Culture and Society* 28 211–32.

[12] See, eg Graham Murdock and Peter Golding, 'Culture, Communications and Political Economy' in James Curran and Michael Gurevitch (eds), *Mass Media and Society*, 4th edn (London, Arnold, 2005) 60–83.

how they serve the special interests of state and private activity.[13] Because the news industry is oriented towards profit-making and depends on government officials as sources of information, they argue that the industry imbues its representations with anti-communist ideology. As Michael Schudson notes,[14] the 'propaganda model' is a rather blunt instrument for examining a subtle system that includes more heterogeneity and capacity for change than Herman and Chomsky give it credit for. Herman and Chomsky's neglect of heterogeneity and change within the system can be understood as part and parcel of political economy's emphasis on the 'big picture.'

By focusing on the 'big picture' (ie the larger political economy of society), the approach also tends to miss examinations of the day-to-day practices in journalism[15] or television drama production. As a result, a political economy approach does not attend to the everyday practices of media production, and what those processes mean to the media producers themselves. Because the political economy approach does not attend to a text's semiotic meanings or to the meaning of daily production processes, both of which are especially important in the process of television writing, I did not find this approach to be a fitting means for studying the day-to-day production of particular texts.

B. The Historical Approach

An historical approach can also be used to study the production of a particular television series. Here, the researcher relies on access to production texts.[16] Textual analyses might be supplemented by interviews with key production personnel (eg writers, producers, directors, etc) who are asked to think about their television production in retrospect. I did not use an historical approach for several reasons. First, given the current trend to include additional 'behind-the-scenes' footage and 'making-of' documentaries on the DVD releases of recent American law films and television shows,[17] the average layperson already has access to some of the information necessary to infer a production history of the law-related representations from a particular programme. However, a researcher runs into the difficulty of separating the apparent industrial reflexivity[18] of such bonus material from current Hollywood marketing strategies,

---

[13] Edward S Herman and Noam Chomsky, *Manufacturing Consent: The Political Economy of the Mass Media* (New York, Pantheon Books, 1988).

[14] Michael Schudson, 'The Sociology of News Production' (1989) *Media, Culture and Society* 2, 263–82.

[15] Ibid.

[16] First and foremost, the key production text of a contemporary North American television drama is the series bible. The bible is first used as a sales document to sell the series to network executives. As such, it includes the original conception of the series, the world in which the series takes place, and notes on main characters. Some series update their bible regularly to reflect character and plot developments. Other production texts might include various scripts, network notes, director primers, etc.

[17] In contrast, Canadian television shows rarely provide useful information in their DVD extras, generally because the relevant production company lacks the additional funds to make them.

[18] That is, producers, writers, directors and screen performers reflect on the why and how of what they did to create the film or TV show.

because that reflexivity is at least partially manufactured expressly for the purpose of the film or show's DVD marketing.[19]

Second, there is no guarantee that all television series will be released on DVD at a later date. This is especially true in the case of Canadian[20] crime dramas. As a result, the researcher can only gain the 'behind-the-scenes' perspective by being on set during its production, because the series' production cannot be retraced after the fact. Since Canada's film and television industry operates under a freelance system, key production personnel are often thinking about their next job while performing their current job. Consequently, their memories of what happened during the day-to-day production of a past television series, barring any traumatic or shocking events, tend to be relatively poor.

C. Actor-Network Theory

Actor-network theory (ANT) comes from the growing field of Science and Technology Studies, and is most commonly associated with the work of Bruno Latour, Michel Callon and John Law. Unlike the previous methodological approaches, ANT has only very recently been used by some media scholars to study film and television production.[21] In this section, I will explain ANT by way of an example. As a method, ANT is particularly useful for the study of the production of a particular television series for the following reasons.

i. Beginning Ethnographic Research without Any Assumptions

I was interested in examining the circulation of ideology-as-knowledge in the making of crime dramas. ANT has been used in the larger study of knowledge production. For example, it was originally used by Bruno Latour and Steve Woolgar[22] to study the ways in which scientific facts came to be produced in a particular format and

---

[19] See ch 7 of John Caldwell, *Production Culture: Industrial Reflexivity and Critical Practice in Film and Television* (Durham, Duke University Press, 2008). He argues that one of the DVD's chief innovations lies in its ability to directly discuss production discourses (eg behind-the-scenes information, knowledge about production technology, and working methods) with audiences without interference from critical and cultural middlemen (eg the critical or popular press).

[20] Canadian-American co-produced television dramas are understood as Canadian television productions within Canada. This understanding is attached to government financing, because the Government of Canada funds national film and television projects as a means to promote Canadian cultural sovereignty. This is one of the reasons why American broadcasters undertake such co-productions. For them, the payment of a licensing fee to broadcast a co-produced series is much cheaper than having to financially produce an original, American crime drama of their own.

[21] See, eg Nick Couldry, 'Actor Network Theory and Media: Do They Connect and on What Terms?' *Citeseer* (2009), www.citeseerx.ist.psu.edu/viewdoc/summary?doi=10.1.1.63.6232; Oli Mould, 'Lights, Camera, but Where's the Action? Actor-Network Theory and the Production of Robert Connolly's *Three Dollars*' in Vicki Mayer et al (eds), *Production Studies: Cultural Studies of Media Industries* (New York, Routledge, 2009) 203–13; John Thornton Caldwell, *Production Culture: Industrial Reflexivity and Critical Practice in Film and Television* (USA, Duke University Press, 2008).

[22] Bruno Latour and Steve Woolgar, *Laboratory Life: The Social Construction of Scientific Facts* (Los Angeles, Sage Publications, 1979).

disseminated through scientific articles. While ANT has not been used to study the making of television fictions, entertainment television production can be considered a site of knowledge production, although it consciously produces knowledge of a different kind and in a different form than the scientific fact.

Moreover, given the scholarly assumptions about what television producers and writers know or do not know,[23] I found it helpful to proceed as ANT scholars are urged to proceed—that is, by not bringing any of these initial assumptions into doing my ethnographic research.

ii. Studying Television as a Collaboratively-Assembled, Material-Semiotic Text

Television series format ideological content in a way that maximises financial profit for those involved, but also as a means of artistic and cultural expression.[24] The study of television production must incorporate a discussion of both the resulting text's aesthetic and commercial properties. Favoured by humanities scholars, text-centred approaches examine a text's aesthetic properties without considering its commercial implications. In contrast, the political economy approach analyses the commercial imperatives underlying the production of a cultural text without attending to the text's meanings. ANT is a method that allows a researcher to combine semiotic readings of texts with field research, because it tries to explain how material-semiotic actor-networks come together.

ANT combines textual analyses with interview data and ethnography. Ethnographic research on a television series in production helps demonstrate the professional procedures through which television is written and produced. The method also emphasises the collaborative nature of textual production, which might otherwise be obscured in historical approaches that focus only on data from texts and interviews. Such data do not capture interactions between different production personnel, especially because many of these interactions are fleeting (ie unlikely to be remembered or textually memorialised) due to the fast-paced nature of television production. ANT scholars are interested in capturing these interactions because the method stresses how the formation of actor-networks (discussed below) is contingent and unpredictable.

iii. Studying the Actor-Network by Following Actors

Unlike the macro perspective of the political economy approach, the ANT perspective tends to focus on details.[25] More importantly, the scale of this perspective is somewhat customisable to the object under study. ANT scholars study the actor-network, which

---

[23] See David Black, *Law in Film: Resonance and Representation* (Illinois, University of Illinois Press, 1999). He refers to a large body of law and film scholarship as 'forensic criticism', or as it is termed elsewhere 'corrective criticism'. This academic work seeks to 'correct' incorrect representations of law and justice in film and television.

[24] Eileen Meehan, 'Conceptualizing Culture as Commodity: The Problem of Television' in Horace Newcomb (ed), *Television: The Critical View* (New York, Oxford University Press, 1994) 563–72.

[25] As a result, ANT is not useful for making general typologies, but valuable in making richly detailed case studies.

is not a description of 'a thing out there', but an analytic concept under the control of the researcher.[26] The researcher decides which actors to follow, and more importantly, which actors make up an actor-network.

For example, an ANT researcher might consider the taxidermied moose as an actor and actor-network in the making of the television pilot for the Canadian–American co-produced police drama *Due South* (1994–96). Shot in Canada, *Due South* was a buddy cop show, in which a street-smart, cynical Chicago police officer was partnered with a polite, sensitive Canadian Mountie (RCMP officer). Semiotically, the taxidermied moose was used as a prop metonym for the Mountie and for Canada, but it was also a physical object. As such, the stuffed moose needed to be carried to each of the shooting locations in the event that it needed to be represented on screen. However, the cast and crew began to believe that the taxidermied moose was the culprit behind the many mishaps and accidents that occurred during shooting, leading them to call for the moose's burial as a means of removing the curse on production.

After hearing this story, an ANT researcher does not immediately jump to the conclusion that the cast and crew of *Due South* are a superstitious and delusional lot. Instead, she considers the taxidermied moose an actor in the making of the *Due South* pilot. Actors in the ANT sense are heterogeneous and can include things, people, texts, objects, information codes, ideas, and, in this case, a taxidermied moose. Because ANT is very much a method for studying action and practice, the *doing* of things, the distinguishing feature of an actor is that it moves other actors in the actor-network to do things. To study action, the researcher would follow the moose as it physically circulated around various sets, because ANT privileges the study of dynamic movement and the circulation of actors. In following the moose around, the researcher would observe how the moose created an actor-network when it was translated into certain courses of collaborative action. After all, the actor-network describes a series of translations and transformations. In this case, the researcher might be interested in the following translations: how did the cursed moose translate into practical concerns for cast and crew safety? Or, because the moose's presence was associated with accidents that ended in property damage, how did it translate into increases in the production budget?

III. Access

Before I discuss the making of a 'bad apple' as an actor-network in one episode of *The Bridge,* I will briefly outline how a researcher might gain access to study television productions.

Because my research entailed doing ethnographic fieldwork, the range of my sample was constrained by pragmatic concerns associated with gaining access to television shows that were currently in production. These pragmatic concerns can be summed

---

[26] Bruno Latour, *Reassembling the Social: An Introduction to Actor-Network Theory* (Oxford, Oxford Univerity Press, 2007).

up by the idea of 'being in the right place at the right time' in order to capitalise on as many productions (ie research opportunities) as possible.

A. Being in the Right Place at the Right Time: Choosing a Sample

The feasibility of doing this research entails being located in the 'right place'. For me, the 'right place' was Toronto, Canada, which has been labelled 'Hollywood North'. Because of the city's status as a major production centre for film and television, the Toronto Film and Television Office, a bureaucratic entity responsible for issuing filming permits to all productions, runs a publicly accessible, online list of productions currently filming in the city. This list provides the contact information (telephone and fax numbers) for each of these productions. Using this list, I narrowed down all the productions that were law or crime-related, and this in turn became the potential range of my sample. Over the course of contacting each of those productions, my sample was further narrowed down as I learned about three production types: 1) service productions versus original productions, 2) movies-of-the week versus television dramas, and 3) established versus 'untried' television dramas.

First, Toronto handles a substantial amount of American service productions. Americans will use Toronto as a shooting location for their Hollywood productions, in which Toronto is generally disguised as an American city, due to the high costs associated with using an American city with American production personnel. By and large, Hollywood productions are inaccessible to most researchers,[27] and all personnel tend to be governed through confidentiality agreements that keep knowledge of the production process secret. Because of these agreements, I focused my research on original Canadian productions, although I would argue that my general comments also pertain to smaller, non-Hollywood film and television production centres.

The second consideration of production type relates to the pace of production, and entering production as a researcher at the 'right time'. Timing is not something within the researcher's control. However, the researcher can decide to focus either on the television production process of movies-of-the-week or serial dramas. This sample choice will have certain methodological and theoretical implications for the research process itself. Like film, a movie-of-the-week is a relatively contained set of representations in which a researcher can expect closure at the end of production. It has a plot with a known beginning, middle and end, and production involves shooting the plot of the story. If the researcher were to come into the production process at the time of the movie's shooting, he or she would be entering the process at a point when the writing has stabilised, the roles have been cast, and the set designed. In this scenario, it would not be easy for a researcher to observe how meanings of law-related representations are negotiated during the production process, because many of these salient decisions were made prior to the researcher entering the picture.

While television drama has adapted some of the conventions of film production (eg acting, camera work, composition, editing and sound production), it also retains

---

[27] The exception would be if the researcher personally knew the film or television show's producer, director, or head writer.

a storytelling process that is unique to the medium of television. In a 13-episode television drama, producers, writers and directors are constantly shaping the story and the characters with each episode, and the series' ending is not definitively known by all production personnel.[28] The television drama is an open-ended affair, and only creates an ending once cancellation occurs or when producers feel that the series has run its course. For a researcher interested in the dynamic process of meaning-making and the shaping of representations of law and justice, the production of television drama provides an opportunity to observe this process in action. If the researcher considers each episode as a relatively contained story, a single television show can potentially provide up to 13–22 research opportunities,[29] whereas studying the production process of a law film will count as a single research opportunity. Because of the larger output of episodic stories, the researcher can potentially enter the production process as early as the writing stage of an episode. In contrast to the single, solitary film screenwriter, collaborative team-writing is characteristic of television drama writing. This collaborative action provides a valuable opportunity for a researcher to observe writers thinking out loud about how they imagine policing, crime and criminals, and how these elements ought to interact in a scene.

My third consideration of production type was whether to focus on 'successful', ongoing Canadian legal television dramas or 'untried' television productions. By 'untried', I mean television shows that have not been 'tried' by any audience because they have yet to air as part of any network's programming. Because these shows have not been broadcast, they cannot be deemed 'successful' in terms of Nielsen ratings, television critics' reviews or by level of fan attachment. Overall, I found it much easier to gain access to 'untried' shows than to 'successful' ones. With 'success', ongoing television productions gain publicists who act as gatekeepers to the production, tend to enforce confidentiality agreements and typically hold a certain amount of paranoia that one's research might tarnish the production's positive image. Theoretically, the focus on 'untried' productions is also in line with ANT's starting assumption that success is unpredictable.[30]

B. Being in the Know: Gaining Access and Mobilising Cultural Capital

Access depends on the structural organisation of television production, which varies by country. In contrast to systems of television production in which broadcasting

---

[28] While the head writer has a sense of how the series will end, he/she does not necessarily share this knowledge with the show's other writers, directors or producers.

[29] In North America, a regular full season of a commercial network television show contains 22 episodes. However, most North American networks tend to order 13 episodes of a show prior to ordering a full season. If the television show is deemed sufficiently successful, as measured by weekly viewer ratings, then networks will pick up 'the back nine'—ie, the remainder of the episodes that would make a 22 episode season. The difference in the number of research opportunities might also be a reason why production studies themselves have tended to focus on television shows instead of films, and television programmes with high episodic outputs. For talk shows, see Joshua Gamson, *Freaks Talk Back: Tabloid Talk Shows and Sexual Nonconformity* (Chicago, University of Chicago Press, 1998); Laura Grindstaff, *The Money Shot: Trash, Class, and the Making of TV Talk Shows* (Chicago, University of Chicago Press, 2002). For soap operas, see Elana Levine, 'Toward a Paradigm for Media Production Research: Behind-the-Scenes at *General Hospital*' (2001) *Critical Studies in Media Communication* 18, 66–82.

[30] For an empirical study on prime-time American television that supports this assumption, see William T and Denise D Bielby,'"All Hits are Flukes": Institutionalized Decision Making and the Rhetoric of Prime-Time Network Program Development' (1994) *American Journal of Sociology* 99, 1287–1313.

goes hand in hand with in-house production of programming,[31] independent film and television production companies produce Canada's television dramas and sell these products to broadcasters for distribution. Access would be granted or denied by the independent production company responsible for the particular legal television programme rather than through the television broadcaster. Having pinned down where to look for access (ie production company), the researcher needs to determine who at the production company would be sufficiently 'authoritative' to grant full access to observe the production process of the legal programme. In television production studies, the 'producer's gate' grants much of the access.[32] Unlike film—where directors have the most authority—television is a producer's medium in which directors can come and go while executive producers remain a stabilising force throughout a television series' entire run. My research question required that access be granted by the television producer for spaces in which I could observe the work of the writers' room.

In order to access above-the-line personnel such as the writer's room, a researcher breaches the self-bounded, highly stratified spatial world of television drama production[33] by mobilising his or her own personal cultural capital—the symbolic capital that one accumulates through education and social upbringing—that serves to confer distinction upon an individual.[34] This cultural capital acts as 'a foot in the door', but does not guarantee entry to observe the production process. In contrast to the research choice of 'studying down', where the cultural capital of the academic clearly outweighs that of their subjects of study (eg lay persons), my research required that I 'study up'. The individuals who produce television dramas (eg producers, writers, directors, etc) are in high demand, and have at least as much or more cultural capital than the academic criminologist (eg they have university/college degrees, are successful in their own field, are economically solvent, and are more popular).[35] Thus, it is harder to gain access to my particular research subjects without already being 'in the know'.

By 'in the know', I refer to three particular sets of knowledge that act as social and cultural capital. In the first instance, knowledge is encapsulated through *who* one knows: a researcher might already be socially connected to television producers through one's personal and/or professional affiliations. Film and media/communication studies professors, particularly those who moonlight as editors of the film and television industry's trade journals, have the social and cultural capital to network themselves into researching television production studies through their

[31] See John Ellis, 'Television Production' in Robert C Allen and Annette Hill (eds), *The Television Studies Reader* (New York, Routledge, 2004) 275–92.
[32] See Caldwell, *Production Culture* (n 21). Although there has been some interest in media studies to shift the focus of research from producers (above-the-line creative personnel) to below-the-line workers (eg gaffers, grips, camera operators, etc), this shift in focus would not be useful for my research project. Above-the-line personnel are the only individuals tasked with deciding how images of law, crime and policing are created and represented; below-the-line personnel are only tasked with 'following orders' already set by above-the-line decisions.
[33] Ibid.
[34] Pierre Bourdieu, *Distinction: A Social Critique of the Judgement of Taste*, Richard Nice (trans) (Cambridge MA, Harvard University Press, 1984).
[35] They are more popular in the sense that the media are interested in what they have to say, particularly on the dramas that they produce. Their work is more popular than that of any academic because more people are aware of it and potentially impacted by it.

professional affiliations. In contrast, some researchers lacking that social and cultural capital have gained access through a second sense of being 'in the know': extensive knowledge of a particular television show derived through the researcher's personal attachment to that show.[36] This requires the researcher to act less like a disinterested observer, and more like an enthused fan of the television show.

As a scholar without the requisite pre-existing social capital or the capacity to be a fan because of my sample of 'untried' television dramas, I instead utilised the third sense of being 'in the know': the 'expert' knowledge that I have gained through the academic study of criminology, some of which could be of use to producers and writers of crime television dramas. For example, my knowledge of insurance fraud enabled my access to the production process of a pilot for a 2010 Canadian television drama called *Cra$h and Burn*. By providing television writers with stories that will help fuel their imaginations, which in turn shapes the content of their television programme, the researcher potentially becomes part of the television programme's production process, and gains access to creative meetings as a participant observer. During the process of working with these creative personnel on the television pilot, I also gained social and cultural capital in the field of television production, which in Toronto is a relatively small and tightly-knit community. This accumulation of social and cultural capital was useful for multiplying research sites and subjects through snowball sampling, and it allowed me to later gain access into the writers' room of *The Bridge*.

IV. Case Study: Making a 'Bad Apple' on *The Bridge*

Airing in Canada from early March 2010 and shot in Toronto, *The Bridge* is a Canadian (CTV)/American (CBS) co-production premised upon revealing the politics behind a big-city police force. CTV describes the show as follows:

> After the rank and file unanimously vote street cop Frank Leo (*Battlestar Galactica's* Aaron Douglas) into office as union head, he begins his quest to put street cops first and clean up the force from the ground up. But the old boys' network running the police force and the city's self-serving politicians are not about to sit idly by while a former street cop makes up his own rules. Frank walks a thin blue line as he battles wiretaps and a concerted campaign to bring him down, letting nothing stop him from fulfilling his unwavering vow that when cops are in trouble, he will be there.[37]

The first season of the series was critically well reviewed by both Canadian and American television critics. Because the show was not considered a commercial success in the US, pulling in only four to five million viewers for CBS, it was cancelled before the broadcaster could air the fourth episode. On the Canadian front, CTV initially renewed *The Bridge* for a second season. The broadcast network later cancelled the renewal as it underwent a personnel shake-up.

---

[36] See, eg Levine, 'Toward a Paradigm' (n 29).
[37] CTV, *The Bridge*: About the Show. *CTV* (2010), www.shows.ctv.ca/TheBridge/About.aspx.

For the remainder of the chapter, I will examine the various actors—people, texts, facts, and quasi-legal entities—that make up the representation of a 'bad apple' (ie a corrupt police officer) in an episode. Before analysing how *The Bridge* writers know about 'bad apples' and how that knowledge is translated into a fictional television representation, I want to take a moment to explain why these writers are fixated on 'bad apples' rather than 'bad barrels' in the first place.

A. Actor One: CBS Network Executives

The Bridge was initially a purely Canadian television production. The show was premised on revealing the political machinations and systemic corruption at work in a large metropolitan police force. However, once American broadcaster CBS signed on as co-producer, the broadcaster issued some storytelling guidelines. Specifically, network executives suggested that the show needed to generate 'satisfying cop stories' where the main protagonist Frank Leo took an active role in all of the stories being told. The writers of *The Bridge* translated the broadcaster suggestion for 'satisfying cop stories' into stories where Frank actively solved crimes on a weekly basis. The show transformed from its original premise of revealing systemic corruption to the more standardised format of a police procedural, modelled on other shows that aired concurrently on CBS. While the producers and writers initially aspired to make a show in the vein of American cable series *The Wire* (HBO) or *The Shield* (FX), they ended up writing a show along the lines of *CSI* instead. As one of the show's writers notes,

> [Frank]'s in on a lot of investigations, out in the field giving orders to cops, so on and so forth. So there's not much realistic about that. It's funny. What we've done in some respects is the way that the *CSI* guys, the forensics guys dig for fingerprints and so on; but they're out tailing suspects and doing investigations and so on and so forth. We solve crimes. [...] It's an interesting progression we've taken here.[38]

Because ideology manifests itself in a text not only through its content but through its format, the modular format of a police television series facilitates representations of 'bad apples'. The narrative of a modular episode revolves around a new situation—such as a criminal investigation—that concludes at the end of the episode.[39] Because this format requires narrative closure at the end of each episode, writers need to suggest that a criminal investigation into police misconduct can be easily resolved. The ideology of a 'bad apple' is useful when working under this format, because 'bad apples' can simply be punished or removed from a police unit at the end of an episode. In contrast, a story of systemic police corruption cannot be told through a modular narrative because there is no neat solution to the problem that can be presented. Instead, such a story requires a serialised narrative, which can establish the problematic structural aspects of the organisation over several episodes.

However, large North American broadcast networks tend to prefer more modular narratives because they believe the show's mass audience includes a large number

---

[38] Interview with author (2 June 2009).
[39] Pam Douglas, *Writing the Television Drama Series* (Studio City, CA, Michael Wiese Productions, 2005) 8.

of casual viewers. Modular narratives engage casual viewers—those who tune into a show periodically—who would otherwise be unfamiliar with serialised, ongoing narratives. In their preference for modular narrative, the broadcaster sets down a formatting guideline that orients the writers towards adopting a 'bad apple' approach to conceptualising police corruption.

While the showrunner (ie head writer and executive producer) of *The Bridge* preferred more serialised storytelling, he understood that he was creating a product for a broadcaster that preferred modular storytelling. He was willing to make this creative trade-off in exchange for the additional funding provided by the American co-producing broadcaster. The involvement of an American broadcaster ensured that the show had a higher production value (eg roughly $2 million per episode in comparison to $1 million per episode) and a larger potential audience (on average, 10–15 million American viewers in comparison to one million Canadian viewers). In general, viewers are more likely to watch and enjoy television programmes with high production value. The expensive, slick aesthetic associated with higher production values distinguishes television programmes, particularly for Canadian viewers. Canadian television programmes typically employ a low-budget aesthetic of jerky pacing, sparse sets and fuzzy film stock. As a result of this difference in production value, Canadian viewers opt instead to watch high-budget American television dramas as compared to low-budget Canadian television dramas.[40] Thus, producers of contemporary Canadian television dramas often seek additional funding to increase the production value of their series as a means to enhance a programme's (potential) viewership.

As a result of this material-aesthetic exchange, *The Bridge*'s storytelling engine is fuelled by weekly crimes that revolve around police corruption or misconduct. Thus, the writing staff needs to generate 'a bad apple of the week' as content for each episode. In order to understand how the show's writers come up with 'the bad apple of the week', the researcher needs to enter the writers' room and investigate the process of breaking story. Entry into the writers' room is important because it is one of the few spaces where an outside onlooker can observe the collaborative nature of television writing.

B. Entering the Writers' Room to Encounter More Actors

While the writing of an episode is officially credited to one or two writers, the entire writing team comes together to break an episode's story in the writers' room. The writers' room of *The Bridge* is a sparse, utilitarian setting, consisting of an oval-shaped table, whiteboards and chairs. It is located on the second floor of the film studio in which the show was filmed.

When breaking story, the five-person writing team of *The Bridge* gathers in the room to discuss the story, plot and characters of a particular episode out loud. The process of breaking story literally entails breaking an entire modular story down into

---

[40] In the twenty-first century, an episode of a popular American crime drama is watched by roughly six million Canadian viewers. In contrast, a popular Canadian crime drama is watched by roughly two million Canadian viewers.

its component acts and scenes. This regular procedure for writing television dramas, at least in North America, is meant to help writers envision the entire story as they collaboratively assemble it from scratch in piecemeal fashion. From the writing team's discussions, I treat the representation of the 'bad apple' as an actor to follow, and observe how it assembles an actor-network of knowledge sources and translations. I also pay particular attention to how initial ideas about the 'bad apple' are translated into ways that align with the interests of other actors in the actor-network. After all, in ANT, successful translations are considered the result of the alignment of various actors' interests. Translations fail when such alignment does not occur.

The writers' room is theoretically interesting because it is analogous to the (scientific) laboratory discussed by ANT scholar Bruno Latour. For Latour, the laboratory is the physical space of the actor-network:

> The first part (actor) reveals the narrow space in which all the grandiose ingredients of the world begin to be hatched; the second part (network) may explain through which vehicles, traces, trails, types of information, the world is being *brought* inside those places and then having been transformed there, are being pumped back *out* of its narrow walls.[41]

In the case of television production, I consider the writers' room a laboratory that produces television fiction. This conceptualisation implies that representations are experiments which are always in danger of not making it onto the screen. As a laboratory, the writers' room is a space in which ideas are brought in from the outside world to be assembled into a particular format, prior to being released back into the world as a product. Here, I consider the format to be experimental because it is constantly revised as other actors impinge on the production process.

Methodologically, this unprecedented research access into the writers' room allowed me to retrace the knowledge sources used by *The Bridge* writers to create a fictional 'bad apple'. As previously discussed, these knowledge sources cannot be easily retraced through an historical approach. Thus, in entering the writers' room, I examine the specific construction of a 'bad apple' in the episode entitled 'The Unguarded Moment' (episode 12), although the general procedure by which 'bad apples' are constructed is the same for all other episodes. In doing so, I discuss 1) what kind of knowledge inputs writers use to build their 'bad apple of the week' and how they are brought into the writers' room; and 2) what knowledge moves and translations occur to the writers' initial representation of the 'bad apple' as other actors inform the writing process.

C. Local Knowledge of Policing and Police Corruption

For writers of *The Bridge*, local knowledge is an important factor in the storytelling process. These writers know first and foremost about Toronto policing by 1) reading the local newspapers (factual sources), 2) talking to their technical consultant (human embodiment of personal and professional experience and source of anecdotal real-life police stories), and 3) watching locally-made fictional police dramas. In ANT

---

[41] Latour, *Reassembling the Social* (n 26) 179–80.

terms, these knowledge sources are considered heterogeneous actors, which come together to assemble the representation of a single 'bad apple'.

D. Actor Two: Local Newspapers

Initially, the writers had conceived of this particular episode's 'bad apple' as a member of the police drug squad unit. *As one writer explains to his fellow writers,* 'Think of the drug squad in Toronto. It was said that they stole [drug dealers'] drugs and their money.'[42] The writers then consciously modelled this 'bad apple' on members of the Toronto Central Field Command's drug squad unit. Major Toronto newspapers began reporting the various wrongdoings of the drug squad in 2004. Allegations included charging a 'tax' on and assaulting drug dealers, as well as stealing over $400,000 from safety deposit boxes.[43] However, over the course of breaking this particular episode's story in the writers' room, the writers decided that the 'bad apple' would be primarily represented by a sergeant from the Emergency Task Force, the Canadian equivalent to the American SWAT team. The decision to have a bad Emergency Task Force sergeant was inspired by anecdotes told by the show's technical consultant.

E. Actor Three: Technical Consultant

The use of technical consultants in television dramas, particular procedurals, is fairly standard practice in North America.[44] Technical consultants provide an air of authenticity to the stories being told by writers in several ways. First, the consultant provides writers with technical details about professional procedures, including the relevant professional jargon. In a police show, this might include explaining to writers about proper police procedure or showing screen performers how to hold a gun. More importantly, the technical consultant might be the one to provide the story idea in the first place.

For some crime dramas, the technical consultants remain anonymous by choice. Technical consultants often prefer anonymity when they are still working and affiliated with a professional institution. While the consultants can speak off the record and in their own name, they cannot fully dissociate from the obligations of confidentiality and potential conflicts of interest that tend to characterise their employment as a lawyer or a police officer. For example, the other two fictional Canadian-American co-produced police dramas shot in Toronto around the same time as the production of *The Bridge*— specifically *Rookie Blue* (Global/ABC) and *Flashpoint* (CTV/CBS)—used anonymous

---

[42] Author's field notes (2 June 2009).

[43] Dave Seglins, 'CBC News Investigation: The Report that Led to Charges and the Crown's Problems' *CBC News* (28 April 2008) www.cbc.ca/news/background/torontopolice/.

[44] To date, there has been no published paper on police technical consultants used in the making of television drama series. It is not clear how frequently technical consultants are used in crime dramas, although almost every (entertainment) news report about a crime drama on North American television tends to include some mention of a technical consultant. Attempts to determine the number of technical consultants might be hindered by the consultants' anonymity, particularly because some of them choose to remain uncredited for their work.

police consultants. Consultants for these shows remained anonymous because they were still working in some capacity for the Toronto Police Services.

Because of their continued affiliation with a police force, not all police technical consultants are comfortable speaking about police corruption or misconduct. According to one former writer of *Flashpoint*, the show's writing team had never talked about police 'dirtiness' with their technical consultants, nor had their consultants ever mentioned anything dirty about the elite policing unit. Thus, some police shows rarely venture into representing 'bad apples', much less 'bad barrels', in the first place because of their selection of technical consultants. Instead, these shows traffic in conventional legal ideology by representing the police officer as a heroic crime fighter,[45] precisely because of the cooperation extended to the television production by local police services. For example, the Toronto Police Services helped provide the writers of *Flashpoint* with their technical consultants and had allowed them to tour the relevant police training facilities. The necessity of police cooperation in the production process of such series therefore has the effect of suppressing negative or critical representations of the police.[46]

In contrast, *The Bridge* focuses precisely on police corruption and misconduct, both of which are generally categorised as negative representations of the public police. Instead of using anonymous police consultants, *The Bridge*'s technical consultant (BC) helped create the show. BC was a high profile former president of the Toronto police union whose overall police career was steeped in controversy. As a former beat cop in Toronto, BC made a name for himself by allegedly assaulting a homeless man, and by leading a wildcat strike with officers from Toronto's 51st Division.[47] During his tenure as President of the Toronto Police Association (1997–2003), BC infamously launched a telemarketing campaign for the alleged purpose of funding his (personal) attempts at political espionage. Because of his checkered past, BC seems particularly well-suited to act as technical consultant for a series about police politics and corruption.

BC has two sources of knowledge about police misconduct and corruption. First, in his role as former head of the police union, he is aware of complaints of misconduct filed against certain officers during his tenure. Second, despite his current retirement from the Toronto Police Services, he still has colleagues willing to share information with him about the current police force. As such, he is up-to-date on any potential stories of police wrongdoing, including cases currently being investigated by Internal Affairs. BC translates his knowledge into anecdotal stories for the writers about particular cases of police misconduct. The writers then translate those cases into episodic stories on *The Bridge*.

For this particular episode of *The Bridge*, BC brings himself and all that he knows into the writers' room. The writers initially called him in to help them understand

---

[45] From my research on the production of crime docudramas (eg *Forensic Factor*, *Exhibit A*, and *72 Hours*), these docudramas represent all police officers as competent, even in cases where the writers themselves suspect the officers of some wrongdoing. They do so because the entire production relies on police cooperation. Specifically, producers need police officers to be willing interviewees for their show.

[46] For a similar conclusion, see Doyle, *Arresting Images* (n 4). Doyle writes more generally about police cooperation, but not about police consultants specifically.

[47] A wildcat strike led by Frank Leo was dramatised in the first episode of *The Bridge*.

the police procedures associated with handling a crime scene, but goes on to tell the writers an anecdote about a particularly memorable Emergency Task Force (ETF) member:

> [When I ran the police union], there was only seventy-five [ETF officers]. It's a very small unit, but they're fucking crazy these guys! One guy would wear a turtleneck all the time. And he got shit [on it once...] so he had to go to his house, it was me and X. We go to the house, [...] and it's like in the summer, he's got this turtleneck on. The house is really heated 'cause he had three really big boa constrictors running around the house—thirty feet long. You know why he wore the turtleneck? He had 'White Power' [tattooed] across here [gestures to the neck]. He was a complete skinhead, white supremacy. I'd walk in and there are fucking snakes curled up in the corner! We got to get this guy cleared?!⁴⁸

With this anecdotal input from the technical consultant, the writers change tack: the 'bad apple of the week' is no longer a corrupt drug squad officer but a corrupt ETF officer, specifically one who wears turtlenecks to cover white supremacist tattoos on his neck. The writers are so inspired by the technical consultant's anecdote about this specific ETF officer because it aligns with the writers' own interest in distinguishing their show from local rival show *Flashpoint*.

F. Actor Four: Flashpoint

Flashpoint is a Canadian-American co-produced police drama that made its prime time debut in the summer of 2008 on CTV and CBS. It was produced as a result of the Writers Guild of America strike in 2007 and 2008. As no other TV dramas were being written in the US as a result of the strike, American broadcasters strategically teamed up with Canadian broadcasting networks in order to put content on the air. Both broadcasting networks deemed the show's debut a commercial success. Since 2008, *Flashpoint* has also been cited as proof that Canadian-American co-productions are a viable business model for the future of North American television production.⁴⁹ More importantly, *Flashpoint* is the reason that CTV and CBS teamed up again for the production of *The Bridge*.

As the show's premise, *Flashpoint* focuses on how an elite policing squad—modelled on Toronto's ETF—handles highly dangerous situations that cannot be handled by regular public police officers. In showing these officers as particularly competent, *Flashpoint* traffics in the image of the heroic ETF officer. When *The Bridge* writers want to represent an ETF officer as corrupt, they are therefore interested in deliberately contrasting their show with that of the already established and successful *Flashpoint*. As a television show, *Flashpoint* becomes an actor in the production of this particular episode of *The Bridge*. In this case, *The Bridge* writers use *Flashpoint* as a way to justify their contrasting representation of the ETF: they claim that their representation of the ETF, unlike that of *Flashpoint*, shows these officers as they

---

⁴⁸ Author's field notes (2 June 2009). I have fictionalised parts of this anecdote because this particular ETF officer is still working for the Toronto Police Service.

⁴⁹ Andy Fixmer, 'CBS, NBC Buy Canadian TV Programs to Save on Cost (Update 2)' *Bloomberg* (2009), www.bloomberg.com/apps/news?sid=afYDvToAWJks&pid=newsarchive.

actually are in 'real life'. This notion finds support in anecdotes from their technical consultant, who the writers conceive as their direct line to insider police knowledge and the 'reality' of policing.

Because television dramas achieve their own unique identity through demonstrating semiotic differences from other shows within the same genre, the following exchange between the showrunner and writing staff illustrates the desire for such a difference, where making a 'bad apple' is understood as part and parcel of *The Bridge*'s distinction:

Writer 2: [The technical consultant] said all of the ETF guys were all crazy...

Showrunner: ...which is something we can use, since we've never seen that. We've always seen them as the straight-laced, you know, like on that show [*Flashpoint*] you [Writer 3] used to work on.

Writer 3: They're just gentle souls.

Showrunner: Yeah, let's make them hard motherfuckers. Let's stick it to [*Flashpoint*].[50]

G. Fictionalising and Translations

From these inputs to this particular episode's storytelling, television writers deliberately mix the ingredients of fact (eg newspapers and anecdotes from the technical consultant) and fiction (eg fictional police dramas) in the same analogous way as a chemist might mix different chemicals in a test tube in a laboratory. For the chemist, once a chemical reaction happens, she needs to determine the generalisability of her results. Similarly, the writers of *The Bridge* are wrapped up in the process of generalising their particular representation of 'bad apple' from a specific (real-life) individual into a stock character. However, the generalising process that occurs in the writers' room is not the same as the one that occurs in social scientific research for the purpose of demonstrating external validity. The process is not seeking to ensure that the results of a sample can be generalised to the general population through the randomised selection of a representative sample. Instead, writers are interested in generalisations, not for scientific purpose, but to ensure that their episodic story meets the show's Errors and Omissions insurance requirements. Additionally, the generalisations are thought to enhance the show's commercial and aesthetic appeal. Fictionalising is the process through which writers make their generalisations. By studying this process, we can observe how quasi-legal, commercial and creative interests align with one another as the logics of Errors and Omissions insurance, the showrunner, and CBS' Standards and Practices come together.

H. Actor Five: Errors and Omissions Insurance

All television productions in North America need to purchase Errors and Omissions (E&O) insurance as part of their distribution deal on a large broadcast network. E&O

---

[50] Author's field notes (2 June 2009).

insurance protects producers from the risk of future lawsuits arising out of claims about the content of their production. These lawsuits might arise out of claims alleging copyright and trademark infringement, libel or slander of persons, invasion of privacy, or plagiarism. While E&O insurance covers a range of claims, the producers of *The Bridge* are especially concerned about preventing lawsuits arising out of claims of defamation, such as libel or slander. To do so, the show's writers and producers seek to avoid representing any 'real' person. In order to meet these insurance requirements, the writers engage in a fictionalising process that proceeds through two strategic translation moves.

i. First Translation Move: From Specific Individual to Character Type

As a result of E&O concerns, the writers need to translate the specific 'real-life' individual in Toronto that inspired the 'bad ETF apple' into a character type. Writers create the character type by aggregating together various 'real life' corrupt ETF officers that have appeared in multiple North American news items and Officer.com.[51] Information obtained by writers from both of these sources is considered public domain material, and producers do not need to pay additional copyright fees for use of the material. The use of such public domain material prevents any connection to potential lawsuits regarding infringement of intellectual property rights.

As a result of mixing public domain material, this particular episode's 'bad apple' is transformed into the embodiment of an entire policing subculture that facilitates police misconduct. The entire ETF squad consists of crazy adrenaline junkies that act before they think. As a result of these characteristics, the officers are prone to causing conflicts with civilians. While this might suggest that the writers are moving towards a representation of systemic police misconduct (eg an entire policing unit is organised in a way that makes misbehaviour possible), producers cannot afford to show an entire corrupt squad, but rather only a single corrupt officer. The writers therefore make the 'bad apple' the captain of the ETF squad. While he is meant to be a synecdoche for an entire corrupt ETF policing subculture, the absence of a similarly-minded squad effectively reasserts the representation of the 'bad apple'.

ii. Second Translation Move: From Toronto to 'Anywhere'

As 'real life' individuals are associated with 'real-life' locations, the writers also generalise the setting from the specific location of Toronto to the archetypal, large urban city. This generalisation of setting is particular to the entire series, not this particular episode, and is a consequence of the show's use of BC, the high-profile technical consultant who was a former police officer active in the city of Toronto. As the showrunner notes, 'it's if we make this [setting] Toronto, then they immediately think it's [our

---

[51] The website www.officer.com, on which police officers across North America air out their policing concerns, is frequented by *The Bridge* writers.

technical consultant as Frank Leo]. And if it's BC, then we're in this situation'[52] where the production might be sued for misrepresentation by some local Toronto viewer who assumes his or her previous interaction with BC has been represented on *The Bridge*. As a result, the show never explicitly stated where *The Bridge* took place.

I. Actor Six: The Showrunner

The generalisation of character type and setting also align with the showrunner's vision for the show. Because the showrunner is responsible for making all the creative decisions on the production, he (in this case) must ensure that the series' aesthetic appeal aligns with its commercial appeal. *The Bridge*'s aesthetic appeal and commercial imperative converge on the notion of universal storytelling.[53] Aesthetically speaking, the showrunner has a preference for telling universal stories because he subscribes to the Jungian theory that archetypes exist. For a Jungian, archetypes are more easily attached to individual characters (eg the hero, the trickster, the wise man, the maiden, etc) rather than large-scale social organisations. Because of the focus on the individual,[54] a subscription to Jungian theory facilitates the representation of the individual 'bad apple'. More importantly, the showrunner can use archetypes to resonate with our collective unconscious in a way that bypasses socio-demographic differences. For him, the

> 'whole thing is I want to tell universal stories. [...] I'm more of a Jungian than a Freudian in that way. I mean, I'm always looking for those classic elements. [...] So once I find [the archetypes] in a story, I can then use [them] because drama is—we make sense of the world by telling ourselves the stories of our lives. And that's what drama is.[55]

For commercial purposes, the series takes place in an unnamed city, not only because it corresponds better with the archetypal notion of 'mean streets', but because naming the city actually hampers the production's foreign sales.[56] For Canadian television dramas, their export to the US is a very important commercial imperative, as access to the US market is thought to dictate access to and success on the global market.[57] As the co-producing broadcaster, CBS preferred that the series take place 'anywhere' in order to reach as wide an audience as possible. As a result, in accessing the US market, Canadian producers and writers tend to privilege universal storytelling and de-emphasise storytelling that focuses on local particularities. In the case of *The Bridge*, it is clear that access to the US market was contingent upon the enthusiasm of CBS' network executives.

---

[52] Interview with author (20 March 2009).

[53] In a similar vein, producers of the Canadian show *Degrassi: The Next Generation* have sold the series for American distribution on the promise that the show's representations of youth are universal. See Elana Levine, 'National Television, Global market: Canada's *Degrassi: The Next Generation*' (2009) *Media, Culture, and Society* 31, 515–31. Thus, producers' assumptions of universality are important in the circulation and distribution of television productions in an increasingly global market.

[54] After all, the individual is the psychoanalysist's unit of analysis.

[55] Interview with author (20 March 2009).

[56] *The Bridge* has since been sold to South Africa and Australia for broadcast.

[57] See Serra Tinic, *On Location: Canada's Television Industry in a Global Market* (Toronto, University of Toronto Press, 2005).

J. Actor Seven: CBS' Standards and Practices[58]

Although *The Bridge* writers and showrunner were excited about representing an ETF captain as a 'bad apple' for this specific episode, the CBS network executives were less excited. North American broadcasting network executives govern the content on television series they produce through Standards and Practices (S&P). To conduct self-regulation of programming content, American over-the-air broadcasters, such as CBS, created S&P departments as a way to avoid programming interference from the Federal Communications Commission (FCC). In undertaking this self-regulation, network S&P executives ensure that content on all their television dramas could be deemed 'prosocial'.[59] In practice, this self-regulation translates into an unwritten mandate whereby evil cannot be shown to triumph. If there is crime, it must be punished by the law enforcer. Thus, the work of S&P departments explains to a great extent why conventional legal ideology flourishes in crime dramas airing on major American broadcasting networks. The notion of 'prosocial' content has shaped many television images of police officers as generally competent crime fighters. In contrast, police dramas (eg most notably *The Wire* and *The Shield*) that take a more critical view of legal ideology do not air on American over-the-air broadcast networks, but on cable networks. The FCC does not regulate cable networks, and consequently these networks are not obligated to show 'prosocial' content in the name of public interest, nor do they cater to mass audiences. Because these networks gain their revenue through subscription fees rather than through advertising fees, they are more willing to take creative risks that satisfy their niche audiences.

For the most part, S&P departments of broadcast networks ensure that programmes shy away from the use of graphic language and depictions of nudity. When S&P executives regulate representations of law and crime, they also take into account what is acceptable for their particular network brand.[60] In tailoring representations to the network brand, network executives strive to keep their covenant with the audience, by promising the audience that it will not be unpleasantly surprised.[61] In the case of *The Bridge*, its representations of 'bad apples' are regulated in such a way to ensure that CBS sticks to this covenant.

The CBS covenant is built on the broadcaster's programming history. In the US, CBS is currently the broadcasting network known for its popular fictional crime dramas, including *CSI* (and its spin-offs), *NCIS* (and its spin-off) and the aforementioned *Flashpoint*. None of these crime dramas represent the ETF (or SWAT team) officer as corrupt or potentially evil. Instead, in the CBS universe, ETF and SWAT officers are depicted as heroic figures that fight crime and save the day. To show these heroes in an unflattering light, especially on a new 'untried' show, would break CBS'

---

[58] To my knowledge, writers favoured CBS' review of an episode over the review done by the Canadian broadcaster.

[59] Tad Friend, 'You Can't Say That: The Networks Play Word Game' *The New Yorker* (2001). www.uvm.edu/~jhaig/tv/Youcantsaythat.pdf.

[60] Other American broadcasters may embrace more critical representations of the police as part of their network brand, particularly if they want to appear 'edgy'. Television writers tend to consider CBS to be the most conservative of the four major American broadcasters (Author's field notes, 2 June 2009).

[61] Friend, 'You Can't Say That' (n 59).

unwritten covenant with its audience, tarnishing the perspective that the broadcaster has built over the past decade.

Consequently, the representation of the crazy ETF officer in this particular episode of *The Bridge* was 'killed' by CBS network executives in tandem with the show's writers.[62] In the final cut of 'The Unguarded Moment', the writers ultimately represent the ETF officer as the most straight-laced, morally upright officer on the job. In making this revision, this episode is distinctive precisely because it does not contain a representation of a 'bad apple.' Instead, the writers concentrate on telling the story of a police officer who was injured in the line of duty by drug-addicted career criminals. According to CBS' S&P, the punishment of these career criminals by the police is a permissible representation, and would leave the CBS worldview intact.

V. Conclusion

The case study of *The Bridge* demonstrates that writing a television drama is a collaborative enterprise, which is not just limited to the writers credited with writing a particular episode. Instead, there are a number of heterogeneous actors that come into play, including other rival shows, insurers and network executives. Because of the number of actors involved in the making of a 'bad apple', this representation is constantly evolving. Representation is not fixed or stable, but changes as writers gain new sources of knowledge in their piecemeal way. Specific representations of 'bad apples' are generalised through a process of fictionalisation, which is used to simultaneously address quasi-legal, creative and commercial concerns. More importantly, this case study demonstrates that a representation can fail at any time if it does not align or is unsuccessfully translated into the terms and interests of another actor in the actor-network. It is these failures of translation that are often missing in academic analyses of crime television dramas because they are obscured by the method of analysis. For example, a content analysis of the final product, no matter how good, cannot explain why the ETF officer is represented as the quintessential good guy even though the show's writers had wanted to provide audiences with a different image.

Broadly speaking, this is the first socio-legal study to examine the production of a crime television drama, particularly its writing process. This ANT-inspired ethnographic research was made possible through unprecedented access into the writers' room. Such access allowed me to trace the making of a 'bad apple' representation

---

[62] Network executives provide feedback to television writers, and generally approve an episode's content and format prior to shooting and broadcasting. In the case of *The Bridge*, CBS network executives provided this feedback over a telephone call. Although I was given access to story documents (eg scripts and their revisions) and was permitted to observe activity in the writers' room, I was not given access to listen to these telephone conversations. As a result, I do not know how the executives explained the need for ordering particular revisions. Because the writers wanted to keep their relationship with the executives on good terms, they were also not specific about whether the removal of the 'bad apple' was an outright broadcaster demand. They were only willing to say that the broadcaster wanted the more modular format of a stand-alone episode. Because this episode went through so many re-writes, it is quite possible that the writers simply accepted the network's direction in order to avoid another re-write. As the twelfth and penultimate episode written, the absence of a 'bad apple' was also deemed creatively novel by the writers who had become tired of writing about corrupt police officers.

as an actor-network composed of heterogeneous knowledge sources and translation moves. By going into the writers' room and studying the making of crime television shows, instead of just the final products or their political and social effects, I reveal exactly what is and is not part of the creative process of production. Many socio-legal scholars have assumed that writers and producers of crime television shows subscribe to conventional legal ideology,[63] which they then reproduce in making their shows. However, my research suggests that this is not necessarily the case. Creatively, *The Bridge* might have been a different show if it were only up to writers and producers. It would have been more critical of the police and police politics. It would have been a show that relied less on the 'bad apple' theory of police corruption and more on exploring systemic corruption. However, television drama production includes many more actors than just writers or producers. As a result, there are genre, commercial and quasi-legal considerations that are not subject to change by individual television producers and writers.

Therefore, production research is important because it demonstrates that a crime drama's ideological message should not be treated as self-evident from watching the show. Instead, it should be understood as the outcome of a particular assemblage of people, creative ideas, commercial interests, quasi-legal requirements, and broadcasting networks during the show's production.

References

Books and Journals

Bielby, WT and Bielby, DD, '"All Hits are Flukes": Institutionalized Decision Making and the Rhetoric of Prime-Time Network Program Development' (1994) *American Journal of Sociology* 99, 1287–1313.

Black, D, *Law in Film: Resonance and Representation* (Illinois, University of Illinois, 1999).

Bourdieu, P, *Distinction: A Social Critique of the Judgement of Taste*, Richard Nice (trans) (Cambridge, MA, Harvard University Press, 1984).

Byers, M and Johnson, VM, '*CSI* as Neoliberalism: An Introduction' in M Byers and VM Johnson (eds), *The CSI Effect: Television, Crime and Governance* (Lanham, Lexington Books, 2009).

Caldwell, JT, *Production Culture: Industrial Reflexivity and Critical Practice in Film and Television* (Durham, Duke University Press, 2008).

Douglas, P, *Writing the Television Drama Series* (Studio City, Michael Wiese Productions, 2005).

Doyle, A, *Arresting Images: Crime and Policing in Front of the Television Camera* (Toronto, University of Toronto Press, 2003).

Ellis, J, 'Television Production' in R Allen and A Hill (eds), *The Television Studies Reader* (New York, Routledge, 2004).

Ericson, R et al, *Visualizing Deviance: A Study of News Organizations* (Toronto, University of Toronto Press, 1987).

---

[63] See, eg Michele Byers and Val Marie Johnson, '*CSI* as Neoliberalism: An Introduction' in Michele Byers and Val Marie Johnson (eds), *The CSI Effect: Television, Crime and Governance* (Lanham, Lexington Books, 2009); Elayne Rapping, *Law and Justice as Seen on TV* (New York, New York University Press, 2003).

Gamson, J, *Freaks Talk Back: Tabloid Talk Shows and Sexual Nonconformity* (Chicago, University of Chicago Press, 1998).

Grant, J, 'Assault under Color of Authority: Police Corruption as Norm in the LAPD Rampart Scandal and in Popular Film' (2003) *Journal of Business Ethics* 42, 125–49.

Grindstaff, L, *The Money Shot: Trash, Class, and the Making of TV Talk Shows* (Chicago, University of Chicago Press, 2002).

Herman, ES and Chomsky, N, *Manufacturing Consent: The Political Economy of the Mass Media* (New York, Pantheon Books, 1988).

Hesmondhalgh, D, 'Bourdieu, the Media and Cultural Production' (2006) *Media, Culture and Society* 28, 211–32.

Latour, B, *Reassembling the Social: An Introduction to Actor-Network Theory* (New York, Oxford University Press, 2007).

Latour, B and Woolgar, S, *Laboratory Life: The Social Construction of Scientific Facts* (Los Angeles, Sage Publications, 1979).

Lenz, T, Changing Images of Law in Film and Television Crime Stories (New York, Peter Lang, 2003).

Levine, E, 'National Television, Global Market: Canada's *Degrassi: The Next Generation*' (2009) *Media, Culture, and Society* 31, 515–31.

——'Toward a Paradigm for Media Production Research: Behind-the-Scenes at *General Hospital*' (2001) *Critical Studies in Media Communication* 18, 66–82.

Meehan, E, 'Conceptualizing Culture as Commodity: The Problem of Television' in H Newcomb (ed), *Television: The Critical View* (New York, Oxford University Press, 1994).

Mezey, N and Niles, M, 'Screening the Law: Ideology and Law in American Popular Culture' (2004–05) *Columbia Journal of Law and the Arts* 28, 91–185.

Mould, O, 'Lights, Camera, but Where's the Action? Actor-Network Theory and the Production of Robert Connolly's *Three Dollars*' in V Mayer, et al (eds), *Production Studies: Cultural Studies of Media Industries* (New York, Routledge, 2009).

Murdock, G and Golding, P, 'Culture, Communications and Political Economy' in James Curran and Michael Gurevitch (eds), *Mass Media and Society*, 4th edn (London, Arnold, 2005).

Nuitjten, M and Anders, G (eds), *Corruption and the Secret of Law: A Legal Anthropological Approach* (Aldershot, England, 2007).

Rafter, N, *Shots in the Mirror: Crime Films and Society* (New York, Oxford University Press, 2006).

Rapping, E, *Law and Justice as Seen on TV* (New York, New York University Press, 2003).

Schudson, M, 'The Sociology of News Production' (1989) *Media, Culture and Society* 2, 263–82.

Tinic, S, *On Location: Canada's Television Industry in a Global Market* (Toronto, University of Toronto Press, 2005).

Websites

Couldry, N, 'Actor Network Theory and Media: Do They Connect and on What Terms?' *Citeseer* (2009) www.citeseerx.ist.psu.edu/viewdoc/summary?doi=10.1.1.63.6232.

Fixmer, A, 'CBS, NBC Buy Canadian TV Programs to Save on Cost (Update 2)' *Bloomberg* (2009) www.bloomberg.com/apps/news?sid=afYDvToAWJks&pid=newsarchive.

Friend, Tad, 'You Can't Say That: The Networks Play Word Games' *The New Yorker* (19 November 2001) www.uvm.edu/~jhaig/tv/Youcantsaythat.pdf.

Reichman, A, 'The Production of Law (and Cinema)' bepress Legal Series (1997) www.law.bepress.com/expresso/eps/1997.

Seglins, D, 'CBC News Investigation: The Report that Led to Charges and the Crown's Problems' *CBC News* (2008) www.cbc.ca/news/background/torontopolice/.

4

Testing Television: Studying and Understanding the Impact of Television's Depictions of Law and Justice

KIMBERLIANNE PODLAS

I. Introduction

Most legal scholars and practitioners can find something interesting about law and television: they might enjoy legal dramas for their entertainment value; they might be interested in how law-oriented television affects public opinion of the profession; or they simply might like debating the value of television generally. The same cannot be said about empirical findings regarding law on television. Few people would take the newest study with them on holiday to read or relax by perusing a nice regression analysis. And few people would open this book looking for the chapter on quantitative studies and methodologies. They simply do not have the same appeal.

Notwithstanding, once we begin to analyse television's legal programmes and contemplate their impact, we must determine whether our suppositions are correct. Because television is society's most pervasive and accessible medium, almost everyone has personal experience with it. As a result, it is easy to mistake experience for expertise and to substitute opinion for fact. By subjecting our ideas to empirical analysis, however, we move beyond philosophy and theory into relevance and reality. Doing so not only demonstrates the value of the field but also helps to establish a strong foundation on which it can build.

This chapter considers the empirical research regarding the influences of televisual depictions of law, as well as the primary theories on which that research is based. It does not privilege methodology, but provides theory and research findings as a foundation. It then turns to contemporary law television programmes—in particular judge shows, crime procedurals, and lawyer dramas—and synopsises the research on their effects. Although the chapter focuses on the American legal system and scholarship, its general themes and conclusions are broadly applicable.

II. The Importance of Television to Law

Television's power is undeniable—it is one of society's primary conduits of information and agents of socialisation.[1] Indeed, much of what people know comes from television. Sometimes it supplements information from other sources, such as family, school, and work; and at other times it substitutes for direct experience, taking us into worlds with which we would otherwise have no contact.[2] Nonetheless, the stories that television tells and the way it tells them communicate norms and ideologies, focus us on issues, influence how we think about those issues, and cultivate beliefs.

This is particularly true with regard to the law: research reveals that most of what the public knows, or thinks it knows, about law and the legal system comes from television.[3] For example, although few people have had personal experience with courts, trials, or lawyers, millions have seen them on TV. Indeed, law-oriented programmes have long been a staple of television programming, and, even as their formats have changed, remain popular.

Law on television comes in a variety of programmatic formats, such as reality courtroom programmes, legal dramas featuring lawyers and trials, police procedurals, and even news reports. Independently and cumulatively these tell the public about litigation, nurture assumptions about legal procedures, and promote opinions about the justice system.[4] Because these depictions constitute much of what the public knows about law, it is important to analyse whether, and if so how, they affect members of the public, judiciary, and legal profession.

III. Approaches to Studying the Impact of Television

Whereas many chapters in this book use narrative and qualitative methods to analyse how legal television programmes contribute to legal culture, this chapter focuses on empirical means. Experimental research from a variety of disciplines, such as communication studies, media theory, and psychology, provides insight into the ways that television mediates understandings. While these theories conceptualise and measure television's influence in different ways, they are all premised on the belief that under

---

[1] LJ Shrum, 'Effects of Television Portrayals of Crime and Violence on Viewers' Perceptions of Reality: A Psychological Process Perspective' (1998) *Legal Studies Forum* 22, 257–68.

[2] Kimberlianne Podlas, 'Guilty on All Accounts: *Law & Order's* Impact on Public Perceptions of Law and Order' (2008) *Seton Hall Journal of Sports & Entertainment Law* 18, 11–14; Nancy Signorielli, 'Aging on Television: Messages Relating to Gender, Race, and Occupation in Prime Time' (2004) *Journal of Broadcasting & Electronic Media* 48, 279–80.

[3] Kimberlianne Podlas, 'The CSI Effect, Exposing the Media Myth' (2006) *Fordham Intellectual Property Media & Entertainment Law Journal* 16, 443–44.

[4] Kimberlianne Podlas, 'Broadcast Litigiousness: Syndi-Court's Construction of Legal Consciousness' (2005) *Cardozo Arts & Entertainment Law Journal* 23, 465; Timothy E Lin, 'Social Norms and Judicial Decision-Making: Examining the Role of Narratives in Same Sex Adoption Cases' (1999) *Columbia Law Review* 99, 758–59.

certain circumstances television can impact audiences. Consequently, they converge to form a trans-disciplinary approach to televisual depictions of law.

Television seldom affects viewers in a direct, immediate way,[5] but, rather, in a number of subtle, long-term ways.[6] The followings section provides an overview of the primary paradigms for understanding and analysing those impacts. It does not endeavour to be a research methods primer, but to provide a foundation for understanding how, and the circumstances under which, television law programmes may exert some measurable impact. It focuses on cultivation theory, heuristic processing, framing, social learning, and agenda-setting.

A. Cultivation Theory

Most theories explaining the relationship between television programming and viewer beliefs rest on cultivation theory.[7] According to cultivation theory, the heavy, long-term exposure to television's imagery cultivates in viewers' attitudes and perceptions of social reality that are consistent with that imagery. Cultivation is a subtle, cumulative influence, not a direct, immediate one.[8] In other words, cultivation does not hypothesise that a viewer who sees a programme celebrating vigilante justice will mimic that behaviour by running out and shooting criminals. Rather, it supposes that a viewer who constantly sees a representation on television will presume that that representation is common in the real world. For example, if a heavy viewer of television sees a great deal of violence on television, she will presume that society is violent; if she regularly sees television judges yell at litigants, she will assume that judges yell at litigants.

The first cultivation studies considered the connection between heavy television viewing and beliefs about violence and crime. Numerous content analyses of network television had demonstrated (and continue to demonstrate) that the number of violent acts and crimes on TV greatly exceeded that in the real world.[9] Hence, cultivation theory posited that heavy viewers would have exaggerated beliefs about the amount of violence in society. Consistent with this hypothesis, research found that heavy television viewers both overestimated the incidence of serious crime in society

---

[5] Steven Eggermont, 'Television Viewing, Perceived Similarity, and Adolescents' Expectations of a Romantic Partner' (2004) *Journal of Broadcasting & Electronic Media* 47, 244–65.

[6] Michael Morgan and James Shanahan, 'The State of Cultivation' (2010) *Journal of Broadcasting & Electronic Media* 54, 337–55; Melvin L DeFleur and Sandra Ball-Rokeach, *Theories of Mass Communication*, 5th edn (White Plains, NY, Longman, 1989).

[7] George Gerbner et al, 'Growing Up with Television: Cultivation Process in Media Effects: Advances in Theory and Research' in James Shanahan and Michael Morgan (eds), *Television and Its Viewers, Cultivation Theory and Research* (UK, Cambridge University Press, 2009) 43–47; Morgan and Shanahan, 'The State of Cultivation' (n 6) 337–39; Eggermont, 'Television Viewing'(n 5) 248.

[8] Morgan and Shanahan, 'The State of Cultivation' (n 6) 339; Robert Goidel, 'The Impact of Viewing Television on Perceptions of Juvenile Crime' (2006) *Journal of Broadcasting & Electronic Media* 50, 119–39; Hyung-Jin Woo and Joseph R Dominick, 'Acculturation, Cultivation, and Daytime TV Talk Shows' (2003) *Journalism & Mass Communication Quarterly* 80, 109–27; Jonathan Cohen and Gabriel Weimann, 'Cultivation Revisited: Some Genres Have Some Effects On Some Viewers' (2000) *Communications Reports* 13, 99–115.

[9] Chris Segrin and Robin L Nabi, 'Does Television Viewing Cultivate Unrealistic Expectations about Marriage?' (2002) *Journal of Communication* 52, 247–63.

and harboured numerous inaccurate beliefs about crime and law enforcement.[10] Ultimately, these perceptions can mature into attitudes about legal policies. For instance, a viewer who is fearful or believes society is unsafe may be more supportive of punitive sanctions, capital punishment, and handgun ownership.[11]

B. Genre-specific Viewing

Three decades of research supports the cultivation effect (ie that television makes a small but consistent contribution to viewer beliefs), but the way it defines television's content has narrowed somewhat. Cultivation originally looked at overall television viewing, assuming a uniform message across all television genres and a non-selective viewing pattern in the audience.[12] This was reasonable, since television's five or six channels offered a relatively limited menu of viewing options. Accordingly, any frequent viewer of television was bound to be exposed to the same types of depictions. Today's television environment, however, is different; cable, satellite, and the consequent proliferation of channels give viewers an infinite buffet of programme options. Thus, a frequent viewer can watch 40–50 hours of television per week, but limit their diet of programmes and genre. As a result, one heavy viewer of television does not necessarily see the same content as another heavy viewer of television, and, therefore, these viewers may not be exposed to the same messages.[13] Empirical evidence confirms that genre viewing is not only a valid measure but also a more precise one.[14] Consequently, contemporary cultivation theory now considers exposure to specific types of programmes, rather than total viewing time, to better predict viewer beliefs.[15]

C. Heuristic Processing

Related to, and thought by some to explain the cognitive mechanism by which cultivation operates, is the concept of heuristic processing.[16]

When people make judgements, they use cognitive shortcuts and mental rules of thumb, such as relying on the information that is easiest to recall, most recently

---

[10] Morgan and Shanahan, 'The State of Cultivation' (n 6) 339–43.

[11] Lance R Holbert et al, 'Fear, Authority, and Justice: Crime-Related TV Viewing and Endorsements of Capital Punishment' (2004) *Journalism and Mass Communication Quarterly* 81, 343–63.

[12] Morgan and Shanahan, 'The State of Cultivation' (n 6) 339–40, 350.

[13] Ibid 340, 350–51.

[14] James W Potter, 'Cultivation Research: A Conceptual Critique' (1993) *Human Communication Research* 19, 564; James W Potter and IK Chang, 'Television Exposure Measures and the Cultivation Hypotheses' (1990) *Journal of Broadcasting & Electronic Media* 34, 313.

[15] Segrin and Nabi, 'Does Television Viewing Cultivate Unrealistic Expectations About Marriage?' (n 9) 259–61; Potter, 'Cultivation Research' (n 14) 564; Potter and Chang, 'Television Exposure Measures' (n 14) 313.

[16] LJ Shrum and Valerie Darmanin Bischak, 'Mainstreaming, Resonance, and Impersonal Impact' (2001) *Human Communication Research* 27; LJ Shrum, 'Processing Strategy Moderates the Cultivation Effect' (2001) *Human Communication Research* 27, 97; Shrum, 'Effects of Television Portrayals' (n 1) 262–63.

acquired, or seemingly common.[17] These are known as heuristics. Essentially, our mind accumulates sets of scenarios, along with their meanings and outcomes, and distills them into decision-making rules, eg experts can be trusted, children do not lie about sexual abuse, guilty people run from the police. By distilling knowledge into an orderly and predictable set of scenarios, heuristics help people process information quickly and draw inferences about events.[18] The more often one comes into contact with an example, the easier that example is to recall, and the more powerful it becomes as a heuristic device. (Additionally, the easier something is to recall, the more common we will think it is, which self-validates the heuristic.)

Television programmes, be they factual or fictional, provide many vivid examples of behaviour and causation which we integrate cognitively as heuristic devices.[19] Furthermore, the more a viewer watches television, the more that viewer will come into contact with and reference television's examples to make judgements.[20] Television's stories of law and the biases and values expressed therein serve as heuristics about the legal system. They help us understand how trial evidence will unfold and become the standards against which testimony and behaviours (of witnesses, litigants, attorneys, and judges) are compared.[21] In fact, some research shows that where trial stories conflict or are ambiguous, jurors tend to resolve these issues by favouring the account that most closely resembles the known story.[22] Television's narratives are among the most prominent of those stories.

D. Framing

Another way that television can impact viewers is through framing. Just as television's images can cultivate perceptions, the frameworks it uses to present information can impact the way that people understand it.[23] Studies have shown that, when television consistently frames an issue in a particular way, audiences tend to adopt that frame in thinking about the issue.[24] For instance, when television repeatedly portrays lawsuits in terms of greedy plaintiffs advancing frivolous claims, or depicts rape as

---

[17] Sarah Sun Beale, 'The News Media's Influence On Criminal Justice Policy: How Market-Driven News Promotes Punitiveness' (2006) *William and Mary Law Review* 48, 244; LJ Shrum, 'Magnitude Effects of Television Viewing on Social Perceptions Vary as a Function of Data Collection Method' (2004) *Advances in Consumer Research* 31, 511–13; SS Wineburg, 'Historical Problem Solving: A Study of the Cognitive Processes Used in the Evaluation of Documentary and Pictorial Evidence' (1991) *Journal of Educational Psychology* 83, 77.

[18] Richard K Sherwin, 'Symposium: Introduction: Picturing Justice: Images of Law and Lawyers in the Visual Media' (1996) *University of Southern Florida Law Review* 30, 897.

[19] Shrum, 'Effects of Television Portrayals' (n 1) 257.

[20] LJ Shrum, 'Magnitude Effects of Television Viewing' (n 17) 511–13.

[21] Richard K Sherwin, 'Celebrity Lawyers and the Cult of Personality' (2003) *New York Law School Journal of International & Comparative Law* 22, 149–50; Sherwin, 'Symposium: Introduction: Picturing Justice' (n 18) 654.

[22] Neal Feigenson and Christina Spiesel, *Law on Display* (NY, New York University Press, 2010) 148–50.

[23] Kathryn Stanchi, 'Persuasion: An Annotated Bibliography' (2009) *Journal of Association of Legal Writing Directors* 6, 82; Mira Sotirovic, 'How Individuals Explain Social Problems: The Influences of Media Use' (2003) *Journal of Communications* 53, 132.

[24] Stanchi, 'Persuasion' (n 23) 82.

a crime that can be explained by a female victim's behaviour, the public adopts that framework in thinking through the issue.[25] Although the frame does not tell viewers what conclusion to draw, it provides a lens through which to examine a given issue.[26] By guiding the analytical process in this way, the frame then impacts the opinions we form about those issues.

Of course, the frame can obscure issues, privilege certain interests, or be wholly incorrect. Because framing activates some ideas and attitudes more than others, and television facilitates fairly stable stereotypical or ideology-based judgements, it encourages us to look at the world in a certain way. This, in turn, facilitates certain interpretive constructions over others and encourages specific trains of thought that lead to particular conclusions.[27] The tenor of frames presented on television can be enhanced through editing, lighting, colour, camera angles, and positioning in the visual frame. These visuals and juxtapositions can imply relationships between elements and evoke emotional responses.

Television's frames can find their way into the courtroom and even impact legislation. Insofar as television's frame becomes a template for assessing actions and understanding issues, framing converges with the old litigation adage: 'the best story wins'. Indeed, the purpose of an opening statement at trial is to provide the decision-maker with a framework to understand evidence. Frames can also impact the public's acceptance of legal principles and legislation.[28]

IV. Socialisation and Normative Formation

The behaviours portrayed on television, as well as their consequences and characters' responses to them, can play a role in socialisation and the formation of norms. Socialisation is the process by which people learn the values, behaviours, and expectations of our society or group. According to social learning theory, most human behaviour is learned by observing others and modelling their behaviours.[29] The images on TV, whether accurate or distorted, are one of the ways that people see behaviours and glean society's values. In this way, television helps socialise audiences.[30]

One function of socialisation is to prepare people for employment and establish their occupational identity. Long before entering the workforce, individuals develop

---

[25] William Haltom and Michael McCann, *Distorting the Law* (Chicago, University of Chicago, 2004) 20–25; Kimberlianne Podlas, 'Impact of Television on Cross-Examination and Juror "Truth"' (2009) *Widener Law Review* 14, 500–01; Fuyan Shen, 'Chronic Accessibility and Individual Cognitions: Examining the Effects of Message Frames in Political Advertisements' (2004) *Journal of Communication* 54, 123.

[26] Young Mie Kim and John Vishak, 'Just Laugh! You Don't Need To Remember' (2008) *Journal of Communication* 58, 338–42; Jodi Baumgartner, 'The Daily Show Effect: Candidate Evaluations, Efficacy, and American Youth' (2006) *American Politics Research* 34, 341–43.

[27] Kim and Vishak, ibid 357.

[28] Margaret Bull Kovera, 'The Effects of General Pretrial Publicity on Juror Decisions: An Examination of Moderators and Mediating Mechanisms' (2002) *Law & Human Behavior* 26, 62–65.

[29] Albert Bandura, *Social Learning Theory* (NY, Prentice Hall, 1977) 22.

[30] Ibid 64–68.

ideas, which are reinforced and perpetuated through the television medium, about what certain professionals do and what particular types of jobs entail, as well as where they, themselves, fit into the employment world...[31] In fact, television viewing tends to be associated with the belief that professions depicted on television (such as legal practice) are easier, more lucrative, and more glamorous than they truly are.[32] Television's depictions of attorneys might provide viewers with possibilities for future careers, or might provide future attorneys with a model of behaviour/ ethics.

Similarly, television plays a role in the formation and transmission of norms. Norms are societal expectations of how to behave. They tell us what society deems normal or wrong. These, too, play a part in behaviour.[33] Television contributes to normative formation and inculcation by broadcasting an apparent consensus of attitude or behaviour. The more an audience sees a behaviour on television, the more it will believe the behaviour is normal or imbued with the values depicted. Conversely, the less an audience sees a behaviour, or the more it sees a behaviour criticised, the more the audience will believe that the behaviour is abnormal or socially disfavored.[34]

In some instances, television's legal depictions contribute to the formation and transmission of legal norms. By signalling which actions and injuries justify legal intervention, or whether litigation is stigmatised, legal norms influence our attitudes and behaviours toward litigation.[35] For example, if society stigmatises litigation, legitimately aggrieved people may choose not to pursue legal claims. Conversely, when society deems it 'normal', people may opt for it.

V. Agenda Setting

Television can also influence the public more indirectly through 'agenda setting'.[36] Agenda setting does not focus on what the public thinks about an issue, but on the specific issues it thinks about. Due to television's cultural and technological prolif- eration, when it devotes a great deal of attention to an issue, viewers will assess that issue salient. Essentially, by devoting a significant amount of airtime to an issue (as

---

[31] Cynthia A Hoffner et al, 'Socialization to Work in Late Adolescence: The Role of Television and Family' (2008) Journal of Broadcasting & Electronic Media 52, 282.

[32] Michael Pfau, 'Television Viewing and Public Perceptions of Attorneys' (1995) 21 Human Communication Research 21, 307–30.

[33] Dan M Kahan, 'Social Influence, Social Meaning, and Deterrence' (1997) Virginia Law Review 53; Daniel W Shuman, 'The Psychology of Deterrence in Tort Law' (1993) Kansas Law Review 42.

[34] Tom Tyler and John M Darley, 'Is Justice Just Us?' (2000) Hofstra Law Review 28.

[35] Stephen Daniels and Joanne Martin, 'The Impact that it has had between People's Ears: Tort Reform, Mass Culture, and Plaintiffs' Lawyers' (2000) DePaul Law Review 50, 482–85; Tyler and Darley, 'Is Justice Just Us?' (n 34) 719.

[36] Melvin L DeFleur and Sandra Ball-Rokeach, Theories of Mass Communication, 5th edn (White Plains, Longman, 1989).

opposed to any other issue), television designates it as important or puts it on the public agenda.[37]

Indeed, quantitative analyses have found that the amount of airtime devoted to a political or legal issue is the key factor in whether the public believes the issue is important.[38] For example, although violent crime declined during the 1990s,[39] television news coverage of it increased. This implied that crime was a significant concern.[40] Echoing the television coverage, but eschewing reality, the public's concern about crime increased.[41] More recently, lawsuits regarding fast food and trans fats have taken centre stage. Although these legal claims are hardly common, television devoted airtime to them, thereby sparking public debate about the regulation of trans fats and junk food.[42]

Once an issue finds its way onto the public agenda, it may become part of the legislative agenda and make the public receptive to legal intervention. For instance, although there was little statistical evidence of a litigation explosion (as measured by the number of lawsuits filed, plaintiff's verdicts, or damage awards) in the 1990s, news and entertainment television began broadcasting stories about frivolous lawsuits and undeserving plaintiffs playing the 'litigation lottery'.[43] Reality notwithstanding, the issue found its way to the top of the public agenda, and became the foundation for the American tort 'reform' movement. This included legislation setting damage caps and liability limits to protect 'victimised' businesses. (Decision-makers in civil cases may even consciously attempt to 'self-correct' their damage awards, artificially lowering them, to avoid contributing to the perceived litigation explosion.)[44] The agenda can also shape criminal justice policy. Accumulating social science evidence suggests that the disproportionate coverage of violent crime by the media may foster public opinion favouring punitive penal policies, such as lengthier sentences, mandatory minimums, and trying juveniles as adults.[45]

---

[37] Shanto Iyengar and Donald R Kinder, *News that Matters* (Chicago, University of Chicago, 1987); Kovera, 'The Effects of General Pretrial Publicity on Juror Decisions' (n 28) 45–46.

[38] Jennings Bryant and Dolf Zillman (eds), *Media Effects: Advances In Theory And Research* (Mahwah, New Jersey, Erlbaum, 1994) 4–9; Dennis T Lowry et al, 'Setting the Public Fear Agenda: A Longitudinal Analysis of Network TV Crime Reporting, Public Perceptions of Crime, and FBI Crime Statistics' (2003) *Journal of Communication* 53, 61.

[39] Daniel Romer et al, 'Television News and the Cultivation of Fear of Crime' (2003) *Journal of Communication* 53, 88–104.

[40] Lowry et al, 'Setting the Public Fear Agenda' (n 38) 61.

[41] Ibid.

[42] One sought to prohibit Kraft from selling Oreo cookies to children, asserting that their high trans fat content made them hazardous to children's health. Although Kraft insisted the suit was groundless, it announced that it would eliminate trans fat from its cookies. Ross Silverman, 'The Mass Media's Influence on Health Law and Policy: Symposium' (2005) *Health Law & Policy* 5, 175–85, 183.

[43] Michael J Saks, 'Do We Really Know Anything about the Behavior of the Tort Litigation System—and Why Not?' (1998) *University of Pennsylvania Law Review* 140, 1281–85; Marc S Galanter, 'Reading the Landscape of Disputes: What We Know and Don't Know (and Think We Know) about our Allegedly Contentious and Litigious Society' (1983) *UCLA Law Review* 31, 154–55.

[44] Jennifer K Robbennolt and Christina A Studebaker, 'News Media Reporting on Civil Litigation and Its Influence on Civil Justice Decision Making' (2003) *Law & Human Behavior* 27, 11; Valerie P Hans, *Business on Trial* (New Haven, Yale University Press, 2000) 56–58.

[45] Sara Sun Beale, 'The News Media's Influence on Criminal Justice Policy' (2006) *William and Mary Law Review* 48, 397–418, 402; Nancy Signorielli, 'Television's Mean and Dangerous Worlds, in Cultivation Analysis: New Directions' in Nancy Signorielli and Michael Morgan (eds). *Media Effects Research* (Newbury Park, CA, Sage, 1990) 102.

VI. The Impact of Television's Depictions of Law

These theories and research findings should not be mistaken as proof that every legal television program will produce an effect. Rather, they identify a potential. Even when programmes *do* appear to be associated with some impact, this impact will differ according to each programme's specific story, content, and programmatic structure. In other words, because one television law show influences audiences does not mean that every television law show will, let alone in the same way. Accordingly, it is important to understand which depictions have been shown to produce which type of effect and at what level.

The following section synopsises experimental research findings regarding the connection between exposure to legal programmes and behaviours and attitudes. It focuses on contemporary law programmes, as they possess the greatest potential to impact the public, legal profession, and justice system, as well as to induce speculation about such impact. It features reality courtroom or 'judge' shows, crime procedurals (such as *CSI*), and *Law & Order* and similar lawyer programmes. To underscore that television's depictions are not isolated but reinforce one another, this section is organised according to effects (real or imagined), rather than according to the television programmes themselves.

A. Perceptions of Judge Behaviour

Of the law-related television programmes broadcast, daytime reality courtrooms (or judge shows) are associated with one of the more concrete impacts of television. Specifically, results from several studies suggest that these programmes cultivate in viewers' expectations about judicial behaviour.

These half-hour programmes are modelled on either small claims or general civil courts, and involve 'real people' and 'real cases', albeit ones that are packaged into easily digestible narratives with clear winners and losers. The focus of these shows, however, is on their titular judges, for example Judy, Christina, Brown, and Hatchett. Indeed, these programmes intercut litigant narratives with reaction shots of the judge, such as medium close-ups of the judge rolling her eyes or otherwise indicating disgust (research has found that these editing techniques elicit an 'orienting response' that increases viewer attention and memory).[46]

A set of studies surveyed approximately 600 respondents (including jury eligible adults and prospective jurors) regarding their viewing habits and attitudes about judges and litigation. This included two main components: (1) a content analysis that identified and catalogued reality courtroom content, in order to identify its predominant messages; and (2) two survey instruments that probed whether heavy viewers of

---

[46] Annie Lang et al, 'The Effects of Edit on Arousal, Attention, and Memory for Television Images: When an Edit is an Edit Can an Edit be too Much?' (2000) *Journal of Broadcasting & Electronic Media* 44, 94–96, 104.

reality courtrooms were more, less, or equally inclined to hold views of judges and litigation consistent with television's depictions.[47]

The studies found that, consistent with the reality television courtroom portrayal of judges as vocal, active interrogators who make moral pronouncements, heavy viewers of the genre expected real judges to be vocal, active, and opinionated. Non-heavy viewers, however, did not share this opinion.[48] Moreover, it appeared that some viewers so expected this behaviour that they interpreted a judge's silence during a litigant's testimony as a negative assessment of the testimony. (Although an inquisitorial style is the norm in some countries, it is not in the United States where the study was done.)

Because several reality courtroom shows are broadcast daily, throughout the day, and across channels, they constitute a significant portion of television's information about legal process. Hence, it is reasonable that they impact viewers on some level. Viewers have very little personal experience with judges, let alone with a variety of them, so they possess no other model of judicial temperament. Consequently, when viewers conjure an example of a judge, television judges most easily come to mind. The behaviours of television judges thus influence beliefs about the behaviours of real judges.

Similarly, although there have been no experimental studies confirming it, these programmes might impact audience assessments of judge demeanour in terms of their gender, as well as estimates of the gender and ethnicity of the bench. As Lovell Banks notes, the television reality court bench is not simply diverse, it is largely female and black or Latina.[49] Despite this television integration, many daytime viewers might be surprised to learn that women judges, especially women of colour, are the exception in real courts. Additionally, the visibility of these women judges may reinforce or diminish traditional negative stereotypes about women, especially women of colour.

B. Perceptions of Whether Attorneys are Ethical or Moral

Although the public rarely witnesses real attorneys practicing law, it has many opportunities to do so on television. Television is even an important source of information for first-year law students—a study investigating the source of law students' perceptions of attorneys surveyed first-year law students in six different countries. In several instances, students believed television was more helpful in constructing their image of attorneys than were the comments of friends and family in the legal profession.[50] This survey data cannot tell us how or to what extent television contributes to people's images of attorneys, but it underscores its potential for doing so.

---

[47] Kimberlianne Podlas, 'Broadcast Litigiousness: Syndi-Court's Construction of Legal Consciousness' (2005) *Cardozo Arts & Entertainment Law Journal* 23, 487–93; Kimberlianne Podlas, 'The Power of Stories: Intersections of Law, Literature, and Culture: Symposium Addendum: The Tales Television Tells: Understanding the Nomos through Television' (2006) 13 *Texas Wesleyan Law Review* 13, 49–53.

[48] Podlas, 'Broadcast Litigiousness' (n 47) 483–87.

[49] Taunya Lovell Banks, 'Here Comes the Judge! Gender Distortion on TV Reality Court Shows' (2008) *University Of Baltimore Law Forum* 39, 38–56, 38–39.

[50] Michael Asimow et al, 'Perceptions of Lawyers—A Transnational Study of Student Views on the Image of Law and Lawyers' (2005) *International Journal of the Legal Professions* 12, 421–26.

Indeed, studies have found that the way in which television portrays attorneys may influence positive opinions about the behaviour and ethics of real attorneys. One of the first studies of this type compared *LA Law*'s fictional lawyers—who were generally portrayed as attractive, powerful people of good moral character—with viewer perceptions of real lawyers. Mirroring *LA Law*'s depiction, heavy viewers of *LA Law* described lawyers to be powerful people, exhibiting good moral character. Individuals who did not watch a significant amount of *LA Law* did not share these beliefs.[51]

Additionally, Menkel-Meadow reported that law students' attitudes regarding professional ethics take a cue from television lawyers. While not necessarily representative of reality, these programmes depict the ethical dilemmas that lawyers actually face. But unlike law school's abstract discussions of legal reasoning and ethics, television provides a factual and emotional context for such issues. This enables law students to draw on them, which, in turn, contributes to their beliefs about what behaviours are ethically appropriate or normal. Exemplifying this, students' assessments of attorney behaviours generally coincided with the way that television lawyers behaved, and whether television portrayed that behaviour as acceptable or unethical.[52]

Similarly, the moral characteristics with which television imbues attorneys might translate into general public perceptions of whether, and which, attorneys are ethical or moral. Since the 1990s, the morally-driven assistant district attorneys of the 20-year-old *Law & Order* franchise have dominated television. Various content and narrative analyses have concluded that *Law & Order* promotes a crime-control ideology that situates prosecutors atop the moral high ground of legal practice. Week after week, government prosecutors work through difficult ethical situations, and sometimes must bend 'technical' legal rules in order to achieve justice and punish the morally guilty.[53] By contrast, criminal defence attorneys on these shows are often portrayed as morally repugnant; they help the guilty escape punishment,[54] and raise the 'legal technicalities' that prevent the system from achieving justice.[55]

Consistent with *Law & Order*'s narrative and ideology, surveys show that a majority of Americans believe that prosecutors are moral, whereas defence attorneys are

---

[51] Michael Pfau, 'Television Viewing and Public Perceptions of Attorneys' (1995) *Human Communication Research* 21, 307.

[52] Carrie Menkel-Meadow, 'The Sense and Sensibilities of Lawyers: Lawyering in Literature, Narratives, Film and Television, and Ethical Choices Regarding Career and Craft' (1999) *McGeorge Law Review* 31, 1–2; Carrie Menkel-Meadow, 'Telling Stories in School: Using Case Studies and Stories to Teach Legal Ethics' (2000) *Fordham Law Review* 69, 815; Carrie Menkel-Meadow, 'Can They Do That? Legal Ethics in Popular Culture: Of Characters and Acts' (2001) *UCLA Law Review* 48, 1305.

[53] Elayne Rapping, *Law and Justice as Seen on TV* (NY, New York University, 2003) 6–8; Kimberlianne Podlas, 'Guilty on all Accounts: Law & Order's Impact on Public Perceptions of Law and Order' (2008) *Seton Hall Journal of Sports & Entertainment Law* 18, 17–20; Michael M Epstein, '"Separate" but not "Equally Important"' (2004) *Television Quarterly* 34, 7–8; Laura Quinn, 'The Politics of Law & Order' (2002) *Journal of American & Comparative Cultures* 25, 130–32.

[54] David M Spitz, 'Notes and Comments: Heroes or Villains? Moral Struggles vs. Ethical Dilemmas: An Examination of Dramatic Portrayals of Lawyers and the Legal Profession in Popular Culture' (2000) *Nova Law Review* 24, 733–37; Rapping, *Law and Justice as Seen on TV* (n 54) 1–4, 8–10.

[55] Epstein, '"Separate" but not "Equally Important"' (n 54) 7–8; Podlas, 'Guilty on all Accounts' (n 54) 18. Television had not always portrayed defence attorneys in this way; in television's early years, they were celebrated as social watchdogs who were critical of the way the justice system worked. Spitz, 'Heroes or Villains?' (n 55) 737; Podlas, 'Guilty on all Accounts' (n 54) 18–19; Rapping, *Law and Justice as Seen on TV* (n 54) 2–10.

dishonest.[56] In one study, 48 participants assessed the 'morality' of prosecutors, on a scale of 'very immoral—immoral—neutral (neither moral nor immoral)—moral—very moral'. Participants who identified themselvesas pro-prosecution/ anti-defence or pro-defence/ anti-prosecution, evaluated prosecutor morality consistent with those expressed dispositions; hence, pro-prosecution/ anti-defence individuals evaluated prosecutors as 'moral' or 'very moral', whereas pro-defence/ anti-prosecution individuals evaluated prosecutors more negatively (and had a much higher proportion of 'immoral' or 'very immoral' assessments). Once these extremes or biases were eliminated, however, the overwhelming majority of (remaining) respondents awarded prosecutors relatively high morality assessments (believing that prosecutors are very moral), in line with the pro-prosecution/ anti-defence group.

Although *Law & Order* almost certainly reinforced or contributed to these beliefs, it cannot be said that *Law & Order* caused them. Rather, the results likely illustrate pop culture's symbiotic nature wherein television portrayals reflect and shape the public's beliefs. In fact, the popularity of *Law & Order*'s attorneys coincided with an ideological shift within the United States to a 'law and order era'.[57]

C. The 'CSI Effect'

Perhaps the most talked-about impact of a television law programme, or at least the one with the catchiest name, is the 'CSI Effect'. In the last decade, the media and legal community have speculated that criminal procedurals, such as *CSI: Crime Scene Investigation*, cause a 'CSI Effect'. As most commonly articulated, the 'CSI Effect' refers to a change in juror expectations wherein jurors now expect that every case will include forensic evidence proving guilt, and, unless such evidence is presented, they will not convict.[58] Prosecutors complain that this increases their burden of proof and is causing an epidemic of wrongful acquittals.[59] Despite its prominence in the media, however, the 'CSI Effect' appears to be more myth than reality.

This is not the first time that a television programme has been accused of perverting the decision-making of juries, and it will not be the last. Every decade seems to be associated with some programme-specific effect, depending on what programmes are in vogue. For decades, attorneys complained that the way *Perry Mason* always exposed the real culprit or used cross-examination to force the prosecution's star witness to confess, created a 'Perry Mason Syndrome'. Specifically, defence attorneys claimed that jurors no longer came to court requiring the prosecution to prove guilt beyond

---

[56] Data from the international student study noted above reflects relatively low opinions of attorney's honesty, but the study did not separate out views about prosecutors or attorneys working on behalf of the government. Michael Asimov et al, 'Perceptions of Lawyers—A Transnational Study of Student Views on the Image of Law and Lawyers' (2005) *International Journal of the Legal Professions* 12, 421–27.

[57] Rapping, *Law and Justice as Seen on TV* (n 54) 3–10; Quinn, 'The Politics of Law & Order' (n 54) 132.

[58] Tom Tyler, 'Viewing CSI and the Threshold of Guilt: Managing Truth and Justice in Reality and Fiction' (2006) *Yale Law Journal* 115; Kimberlianne Podlas, 'The CSI Effect, Exposing the Media Myth' (2006) *Fordham Intellectual Property Media & Entertainment Law Journal* 16, 433–34.

[59] Podlas, ibid.

a reasonable doubt, but expected the defence to prove the defendant's innocence.[60] In the late 1980s, many people claimed that *LA Law* glamourised the legal profession, and caused more people to apply to law school. In the mid 1990s, daytime talk shows such as *Oprah* and *Phil Donahue* were blamed for leading to an 'Oprahisation' of jurors. It was asserted that those programmes' discussions of 'cycles of abuse' and sympathetic portrayals of abused wrongdoers caused viewers (when jurors) to absolve previously victimised defendants of their criminal acts.[61]

The basic premise that a popular, long-running television show like *CSI* could impact jurors is plausible. After all, laws and ethical rules governing pre-trial publicity rest on the notion that television can bias jurors. If, however, *CSI* has an effect, it does not appear to be one that harms the prosecution: notwithstanding the attention devoted to the 'CSI Effect', no empirical evidence has found any anti-prosecution 'CSI Effect' on guilty verdicts.[62] Rather, research employing psychological, sociological, and media studies approaches have all concluded that, in rendering 'not guilty' verdicts, frequent viewers of *CSI* are no more influenced by *CSI* factors than are the non-frequent viewers.

Podlas attempted to detect a 'CSI Effect' by using a criminal trial scenario where forensic evidence was neither provided nor necessary. She surveyed 306 college students and asked them to reach a verdict of guilty or not guilty, where the expected or 'legally correct' verdict for the case was not guilty. The results showed no significant differences in the decision-making processes or 'not guilty' verdicts of respondents who regularly watched forensic television programmes versus those who did not. Furthermore, they did not indicate any increased expectation of forensic evidence by *CSI* viewers compared to non-*CSI* viewers. A second study sought to replicate these findings and it specifically focused on the factors used in decision-making. In this study, 538 mock jurors deliberated in small groups about two crime scenarios where forensic evidence was neither necessary, nor referenced. Again, there was no indication that *CSI* viewers relied on forensic evidence or acquitted in cases that warranted convictions to a greater degree than their non-*CSI* viewing counterparts.[63]

To test the impact of *CSI* on juror expectations, Shelton surveyed 1027 prospective jurors, and presented them with various criminal case scenarios. Respondents were asked what types of evidence they expected to be presented at trial and what verdict they would render based on whether certain types of evidence was presented by the prosecution and defence. The results indicated only a marginal difference in responses of *CSI* and non-*CSI* viewers. But, more importantly, *those*

---

[60] Fred Graham, 'The Impact of Television on the Jury System: Ancient Myths and Modem Realism' (1991) *American University Law Review* 40, 628.

[61] Richard K Sherwin, *When Law Goes POP: The Vanishing Line Between Law and Popular Culture* (New Haven, Yale University Press, 2000) 30.

[62] Simon Cole and Rachel Dioso-Villa, 'Media, Justice, and the Law: Article: Investigating the "CSI Effect" Effect: Media and Litigation Crisis in Criminal Law' (2009) *Stanford Law Review* 61, 1335–37; Tyler, 'Viewing CSI and the Threshold of Guilt' (n 59); Kimberlianne Podlas, 'The "CSI Effect" and Other Forensic Fiction' (2006/07) *Loyola of Los Angeles Entertainment Law Review* 27, 119–21; Podlas, 'The CSI Effect, Exposing the Media Myth' (n 59); Kimberlianne Podlas, 'The Power of Stories: Intersections of Law, Literature, and Culture: Symposium Addendum: The Tales Television Tells: Understanding the Nomos through Television' (2006) 13 *Texas Wesleyan Law Review* 13.

[63] Cole and Dioso-Villa, 'Media, Justice, and the Law' (n 63) 1354; Podlas, 'The "CSI Effect" and Other Forensic Fiction' (n 63) 119–21; Podlas, 'The CSI Effect, Exposing the Media Myth' (n 59) 453–61.

differences ran counter to an anti-prosecution effect. Although all subjects expressed high expectations for forensic evidence, these across-the-board expectations did not translate into a requirement for a guilty verdict. The authors suggest that these increased expectations were not due to a 'CSI Effect', but to a universal technical effect that reflects society's increased awareness of technological advances.[64]

Not only is there no direct evidence of a 'CSI Effect', but there is little secondary evidence of it. If a 'CSI Effect' existed, it would manifest itself through an increase in acquittals. Thus, Cole and Dioso-Villa conducted linear regression models that compared federal acquittal rates before and after *CSI*'s premier in 2000. They did not find any discernable increase in acquittal rates; in fact, they found a decrease.[65] Consistent with this, Loeffler found no increase in acquittals in New York, Texas, Illinois, and California,[66] and Benoit Dupont found no discernable increase in Canadian acquittals attributable to *CSI*.[67]

i. The Pro-prosecution Effect

Although *CSI* does not seem to cause an anti-prosecution effect, some scholars suggest that it might produce a pro-prosecution effect, lowering the prosecution's burden and *increasing* the jury's tendency to convict.[68]

The general message of *CSI* is that police forensics is legitimate.[69] It portrays forensics as the ultimate crime-fighting weapon and fosters an aura of forensic infallibility.[70] The experts are never wrong and the science is always absolute.[71] This might encourage jurors to overvalue anything labelled 'forensic' and ignore problems in the evidence presented.[72]

Moreover, *CSI* celebrates policework and the validity of their arrests. Cole and Dioso-Villa believe that these positive portrayals of police 'benefit those professions by making the public's perception of them more favorable'.[73] Even researchers who believe that watching crime procedurals makes jurors more careful in analysing evidence think this simply improves the reliability of verdicts or aids the prosecution: '[C]rime scene

---

[64] Donald E Shelton et al, 'A Study of Juror Expectations and Demands Concerning Scientific Evidence: Does the "CSI Effect" Exist?' (2006) *Vanderbilt Journal of Entertainment & Technology Law* 9.

[65] Cole and Dioso-Villa, 'Media, Justice, and the Law' (n 63) 1360–63.

[66] Charles Loeffler, '"CSI" and the Criminal Justice System: Jury Trials' (*New Republic Online*, 7 June 2006).

[67] Benoit Dupont, 'The CSI Effect: Myths and Reality, Address at 29th Annual Conference of the Canadian Identification Association' (24 Nov 2008).

[68] Podlas, 'The CSI Effect, Exposing the Media Myth' (n 59) 461–62; Cole and Dioso-Villa, 'Media, Justice, and the Law' (n 63) 1372–73; Tyler, 'Viewing CSI and the Threshold of Guilt' (n 59) 1065–71; Saby Ghoshray, 'The CSI Effect: The True Effect of Crime Scene Television on the Justice System: Untangling the CSI Effect in Criminal Jurisprudence: Circumstantial Evidence, Reasonable Doubt, and Jury Manipulation' (2007) *New England Law Review* 41, 560–61.

[69] Tyler, 'Viewing CSI and the Threshold of Guilt' (n 59) 1072–73; Podlas, 'The "CSI Effect" and Other Forensic Fiction' (n 63) 120–21.

[70] Tyler, ibid 1072–73; Cole and Dioso-Villa, 'Media, Justice, and the Law' (n 63) 1370–72.

[71] Podlas, 'The Power of Stories' (n 63) 46–64.

[72] Tyler, 'Viewing CSI and the Threshold of Guilt' (n 59) 1055, 1065, 1071; Podlas, 'The CSI Effect, Exposing the Media Myth' (n 59) 463.

[73] Cole and Dioso-Villa, 'Media, Justice, and the Law' (n 63) 1348.

investigation shows have predominated prosecutorial bias, such as ... never failing to catch the criminals', making juries more prone to convict if objective evidence is available.[74] This is furthered by the narrative of *CSI*. As Podlas argues:

> *[V]iewers are not taught that the prosecutor must present forensic evidence for the verdict to be guilty (or that when the prosecutor does not do so, the only correct verdict is not guilty). Instead, they are taught that all of the scientific investigation took place long before trial and led to the defendant's arrest.... [A] juror [may] interpret CSI's dominant narrative (i.e., of perfect forensics identifying the guilty and being the precursor to arrest) to mean that: (1) arrests are based on forensics; (2) forensics proves guilt; and (3) therefore, anyone arrested and on trial has already been proven guilty.*[75]

ii. Reconsidering the 'CSI Effect' Myth

As to the genesis of the myth, some authors opine that prosecutors, like many advocates, overestimate the strength of their cases; the 'CSI Effect' may reflect the disconnection between prosecutors' perceptions of their cases, the probative value of the evidence, and the verdict.[76] Hence, this inference through hindsight is a way to find an external explanation for a verdict they think is incorrect.

Despite the lack of empirical evidence, dearth of academic support, and evidence suggesting that it *helps* the prosecution, the continued vitality of the 'CSI Effect' appears to be an example of media coverage and unstudied opinion converging to become 'fact'. This implicates both agenda-setting and framing effects. Because the media devoted attention to this notion, it led people to believe that a 'CSI Effect' actually existed (hence, agenda-setting), and that this phenomenon harmed the prosecution and caused unjustified acquittals (hence, framing).[77] Essentially, as prosecutors complained of a 'CSI Effect', the media reported it, and as the media reported it, prosecutors complained of it; eventually the public began to believe in this effect.[78] This cautions us not to confuse media coverage and unsubstantiated assertions with logic and empirical evidence.

VII. Factual Legal Knowledge

For the most part, legal-themed television has not been shown to be good at teaching audiences specific legal rules. This is not unique to law-oriented programming, but applies to television, generally. Audiences exhibit very little knowledge gain in the form of concrete facts, except from news, typically political debates and stories

---

[74] Ghoshray, 'The CSI Effect' (n 69) 560–61.
[75] Podlas, 'The "CSI Effect" and Other Forensic Fiction' (n 63) 105–06.
[76] Tyler, 'Viewing CSI and the Threshold of Guilt' (n 59) 1077–78; Cole and Dioso-Villa, 'Media, Justice, and the Law' (n 63) 1371–72.
[77] Cole and Dioso-Villa, ibid 1346–47, 1371–72.
[78] Ibid 1338–43.

about catastrophic national events. Even then, however, knowledge gain is modest or insignificant.[79]

The factual content people learn from television tends to involve rote learning of a uniform, concrete message that is consistent and across programmes, somewhat like learning the refrain of a popular song.[80] The best example is that most Americans know the *Miranda* warnings (*Miranda v Arizona*, 384 US 436 (1966)), but did not learn this in school or as a result of an arrest. Presumably, they heard it repeatedly on television programmes and in films, and eventually remembered it. (Nonetheless, the fact that the audience can repeat these words does not mean that they can apply or explain the rule.)

Beyond remembering phrases and simple rules, it does not appear that viewers learn much legal content from television. One study administered a quiz on the legal principles commonly stated on television, and then compared test scores based on the amount of television that test-takers watched. The study hypothesised that, if people learned legal content from legal television, they would score higher on the test. Heavy viewers, however, scored no better than non-viewers.[81] The study author suggested that viewers might not discern legal content from television, because it is secondary to the plot, or that the emotional aspects of the story (which highlight attitude formation) overshadow the factual content. Even if viewers recognise the rule, it might dissipate from memory or not resonate strongly enough to exert a measurable effect.[82] Alternatively, viewers may not comprehend content or be able to apply it outside of the television context. (Therefore, learning is either rudimentary or difficult to discern through empirical testing.) Indeed, investigations of content learning from other types of television have noted such problems in viewer comprehension and extra-episodic application of content, as well as the difficulty in measuring such effects.[83] Consequently, although television can cultivate beliefs, contribute to perceptions, or provide general 'scripts', it seldom succeeds at 'teaching' concrete legal content.

VIII. Norms and Modelling Behaviours

Programmes featuring trials and courtrooms might not teach factual content, but they may provide viewers with models for how to behave in court or normative guides for whether litigation is socially acceptable. Although this assumption is reasonable in light of research on social learning, no law-specific research has been conducted. There is, however, some related information supporting the idea. For example, in the

---

[79] Douglas M McLeod et al, 'Resurveying the Boundaries of Political Communications Effects' in Jennings Bryant and Dolf Zillman (eds), *Media Effects: Advances In Theory And Research* (Erlbaum,1994) 228–30; Kim and Vishak, 'Just Laugh!' (n 26) 339–41.

[80] Kim and Vishak, ibid 340–41.

[81] Podlas, 'The Power of Stories' (n 63) 50–52.

[82] Ibid 52–53.

[83] Shalom Fisch, 'Vast Wasteland or Vast Opportunity?' in Jennings Bryant and Dolf Zillman (eds), *Media Effects: Advances In Theory And Research* (Erlbaum, 1994) 416–20; Kim and Vishak, 'Just Laugh!' (n 26) 340–42.

French legal system, judges are called Monsieur le president or Madame la presidente. A majority of law-oriented programmes on French television, however, are American imports, such as *Law & Order* and *Damages* where judges are referred to as 'Your Honour'. As a result, French audiences hear the term 'Your Honor' rather than Madame la presidente. Consistent with this, Villez reports that French litigants are now calling judges 'Your Honour'.[84]

Some survey evidence suggests that reality courtroom programmes may acculturate audiences to low-stakes litigation or litigation 'for the principle'. One study asked respondents to rate the likelihood of undertaking certain types of litigation (including contract, personal injury, and property damage cases, and ranging from under $100–over $1,500) and the circumstances under which they would do so without the aid of an attorney. A meta-analysis of responses disclosed that a higher proportion of frequent viewers said that they would engage in litigation and do so pro se.[85] Perhaps with repeated viewing, viewers come to believe that civil court is a viable option for the average person, and therefore are more likely to engage in litigation. It is not possible, however, to determine whether viewing causes these beliefs, these beliefs cause viewing, or some other relationship exists explaining the correlation between these factors.[86]

Additionally, television's portrayal of lawyers might help socialise people into the legal profession, by suggesting the law as a possible career or by creating expectations of what that career involves. A content analysis by Salzmann and Dunwoody analysing 63 hours of television lawyer programmes showed that television presents a distorted picture of what attorneys do. On television, attorneys spent more than half of their time in court or meeting with clients, but less than one per cent conducting research or drafting documents.[87] This is hardly surprising since mundane tasks like legal research and drafting documents do not make for entertaining television. It does not, however, appear that this significantly distorts law students' perceptions of what lawyering involves, at least for first-year students. Survey data showed that first-year students estimated that lawyers spent much less time in court and with clients than depicted on TV, and far more time conducting research and drafting documents.[88]

IX. Juror Decision-Making and Verdicts

On a broader level, the accumulation of law portrayals contained within various programmes can influence the mental models and decision-making of jurors. Studies demonstrate that stories are central to juror decision-making: they help juries make

[84] Barbara Villez, 'French Television Lawyers in "Avocats et Associes"' in Michael Asimow (ed), *Lawyers in Your Living Room! Law on Television* (ABA, 2009) 275–77.

[85] Kimberlianne Podlas, 'Broadcast Litigiousness: Syndi-Court's Construction of Legal Consciousness' (2005) *Cardozo Arts & Entertainment Law Journal* 23, 494.

[86] Ibid 494; Kimberlianne Podlas, 'The Monster in the Television: The Media's Contribution to Consumer Litigation Boogeyman' (2004) *Golden Gate University Law Review* 34, 239–83, 270–72.

[87] Victoria S Salzmann and Philip T Dunwoody, 'Prime-Time Lies: Do Portrayals of Lawyers Influence How People Think About the Legal Profession?' (2005) *Southern Methodist University* 58, 437.

[88] Ibid 447.

sense of evidence, prompt inferences, determine causality, and assign blame.[89] Stories have also been shown to influence the analyses and decision-making of judges.[90] Every day, television supplies countless detailed stories about crimes, motives, and legal liability. Whether these are called scripts, heuristics, or something else, they can influence our assessments, by creating expectations and baselines for truth.

Research has demonstrated that in some instances frames or cognitive scripts can make juries more likely to accept allegations as true or believe that certain people have committed a crime. Content analyses demonstrate that television news over-represents African-Americans and Latinos as lawbreakers and criminals.[91] Gilliam and Iyengar assert that this creates a 'crime script' in which criminals are African-American or Latino. As a result, decision-makers may be more likely to believe that an African-American or Latino defendant has committed a crime.[92] In fact, studies have documented that exposure to television crime news seems to produce this type of effect in white viewers.[93] Experimental and survey results further indicate that expo-sure to television's stock script of the black, male, criminal can increase white viewers' punitive attitudes toward crime, as well as their tendencies to endorse dispositional explanations for criminal behaviour and racist beliefs.[94]

Studies also show that decision-makers assess trial evidence that is consistent with known stories as more believable than trial evidence that varies from the known 'script'.[95] Hence, evidence that fits with the known television narrative can be perceived as more believable. Furthermore, script-based expectations can become so mentally persuasive that when people encounter a scenario that lacks information typically in the script, they will 'fill in' that information.[96] One study showed that white viewers, who saw a newscast featuring a white murder suspect, were increasingly likely over time to misidentify the suspect as black.[97] This might also lead decision-makers to presume facts not in evidence. For example, television programmes such as *CSI* and *Law & Order* establish a script of how and under what circumstances an arrest takes place. In this script, the police officers' conclusions of guilt are usually borne out to be correct and based on valid evidence. On television, if an individual is factually innocent, they

---

[89] Nancy Pennington and Reid Hastie, 'Evidence Evaluation in Complex Decision Making' (1986) *Journal of Personality & Social Psychology* 51; Nancy Pennington and Reid Hastie, 'Explaining the Evidence: Tests of the Story Model for Juror Decision Making' (1992) *Journal of Personality & Social Psychology* 62.

[90] Wineburg, 'Historical Problem Solving' (n 17) 77; Chris Riley, 'The Rite of Rhetoric: Cognitive Framing in Technology Law' (2009) *Nevada Law Journal* 9, 503, 507.

[91] Travis L Dixon and Daniel Linz, 'Overrepresentation and Underrepresentation of African Americans and Latinos as Lawbreakers on Television News' (2000) *Journal of Communication* 50, 131; Franklin D Gilliam et al, 'Crime in Black and White: The Violent, Scary World of Local News' (1996) 1 *Harvard International Journal of Press/Policy* 6, 10–12.

[92] Franklin D Gilliam and Shanto Iyengar, 'Prime Suspects: The Influence of Local Television News on the Viewing Public' (2000) *American Journal of Political Science* 44, 560–62.

[93] Robert M Entman and Kimberly A Gross, 'The Court Of Public Opinion: The Practice and Ethics of Trying Cases in the Media: Article: Race To Judgment: Stereotyping Media And Criminal Defendants (2008) *Law and Contemporary Problems* 71.

[94] Ibid 104–05.

[95] Pennington and Hastie, 'Evidence Evaluation in Complex Decision Making' (n 90).

[96] Gilliam and Iyengar, 'Prime Suspects' (n 93) 561.

[97] Mary Beth Oliver, 'Caucasian Viewers' Memory of Black and White Criminal Suspects in the News' (1999) *Journal of Communication* 49, 46.

have been exculpated; but if they are on trial, it is only because a great deal of forensic investigation has occurred that definitively confirms them as the culprit. A juror who is well acquainted with these shows may, therefore, presume that anyone on trial has been identified through this process and proven guilty with forensic evidence, regardless of whether the prosecution and police witnesses mention the process.[98]

The evaluative slant of television news can influence evaluations of guilt,[99,100] or beliefs about how certain crimes unfold.[101] In an experiment by Bull Kovera, participants watched a television news story on rape that had been edited to present pro-defence and pro-prosecution perspectives. Participants then listed what evidence they would need to convict a defendant of rape. The results indicated that the type of evidence participants listed as indicative of guilt seemed to depend on the slant of the news story they had seen. Those who saw a pro-defence story required more inculpatory evidence to convict, but were less concerned about evidence concerning the complainant's credibility.[102] The bias of a frame can also impact responsiveness to witness testimony, sympathy for, and the positive or negative disposition toward the defendant and, ultimately, the verdict. In fact, individuals exposed to pre-trial publicity regarding a defendant tend to render more punitive judgments.[103] These influences can survive the voir dire, limiting instructions, and may even intensify during deliberations.[104]

X. Limitations of Empirical Study

Although this chapter uses the lexicon of empiricism and analyses studies and their evidence, it cannot say with certainty that legal television programmes do or do not produce the enumerated effects. Researchers cannot isolate all of the sources and messages about law that a person has accumulated over a lifetime, so as to conclude that television, alone, is the cause of any particular attitude. Researchers can never know that, but for watching lawyer programmes, a viewer would have a more positive view of the profession, or that if only the news' slant would have been favourable, a jury's verdict would have been different. Moreover, causes and effects seldom operate in isolation, but, rather, interact with or are mediated by other variables. Indeed, media consumption is an active process, where viewers' existing attitudes and beliefs impact how television imagery is interpreted, integrated, and acted upon.

---

[98] Podlas, 'The "CSI Effect" and Other Forensic Fiction' (n 63) 105–06.

[99] Christina A Studebaker and Steven D Penrod, 'Pretrial Publicity: The Media, the Law, and Common Sense' (1997) *Psychology Public Policy & Law* 3, 428.

[100] Ibid.

[101] Margaret Bull Kovera, 'The Effects of General Pretrial Publicity on Juror Decisions: An Examination of Moderators and Mediating Mechanisms' (2002) *Law & Human Behavior* 26; Kurt A Carlson and JE Russo, 'Biased Interpretation by Mock Jurors' (2001) *Journal of Experimental Psychology Applied* 7, 91.

[102] Ibid.

[103] Studebaker and Penrod, 'Pretrial Publicity' (n 100); Jennifer K Robbennolt and Christina A Studebaker, 'News Media Reporting on Civil Litigation and Its Influence on Civil Justice Decision Making' (2003) *Law & Human Behavior* 27.

[104] Studebaker and Penrod, ibid; Robbennolt and Studebaker, ibid.

Furthermore, because viewers exercise some choice in what they watch and how often, viewer motivation and gratification also play a part in this process.

Additionally, there are limitations inherent in any experimental design. Experiments cannot perfectly replicate real-world situations, obtain identically representative participants, manipulate actual, ongoing cases, or statistically measure attitudes as though they are quantifiable numbers. In fact, an underlying hypothesis might be correct, but is difficult to test or adequately measure. Finally, although the above studies follow a model of scientific inquiry, they generally rest on an interpretive foundation—in other words, they begin by analysing a narrative or coding the frequency of television content. A content analysis, however, might focus on the 'wrong' content or code that content according to the researcher's biases; an investigation of framing might find whatever frame it is looking for; narrative analysis may substitute the scholar's interpretation of content for that of the audience. As a result, these methods are subject to the foibles of the researchers employing them, regardless of whether they employ statistics and graphs. This does not mean that the empirical study of legal television is folly, but that its limits should be recognised and its conclusions should not be over-interpreted. Indeed, the information gleaned from methodically testing our assumptions augments our study and keeps us focused on reality and relevance. This ensures that the field can intelligently inform practical perspectives of legal practice, adjudication, and policy.

XI. Conclusion

Law and television is an evolving field dealing with a continuously evolving medium. Although we now recognise that television plays an important role in the construction of popular legal culture, we do not yet fully understand how, to what extent, and with what consequences. Nonetheless, we have begun to develop a corpus of knowledge along with a corpus of theory that can aid our understandings about and encourage further study into this area.

References

Asimov, M, 'Law and Popular Culture: Bad Lawyers in the Movies' (2000) *Nova Law Review* 24, 552–84.
—— et al, 'Perceptions of Lawyers—A Transnational Study of Student Views on the Image of Law and Lawyers' (2005) *International Journal of the Legal Professions* 12, 407–36.
Bandura, A, *Social Learning Theory* (Prentice Hall, 1977).
Baumgartner, J, 'The Daily Show Effect: Candidate Evaluations, Efficacy, and American Youth' (2006) *American Politics Research* 34, 341–67.
Bryant, J and Zillman, D, (eds) *Media Effects: Advances In Theory And Research.* (Erlbaum, 1994).
Carlson, KA and Russo, JE, 'Biased Interpretation by Mock Jurors' (2001) *Journal of Experimental Psychology Applied* 7, 91–103.
Clifford, RA, 'The Impact of Popular Culture on the Perception of Lawyers' (2002) *Litigation* 1.

Cohen, J and Weimann, G, 'Cultivation Revisited: Some Genres have Some Effects on Some Viewers' (2000) *Communications Reports* 13, 99–115.

Cole, S and Dioso-Villa, R, 'Media, Justice, and the Law: Article: Investigating the "CSI Effect" Effect: Media and Litigation Crisis in Criminal Law' (2009) *Stanford Law Review* 61, 1335–73.

—— 'CSI and Its Effects: Media, Juries, and the Burden of Proof' (2007) *New England Law Review* 41, 435–69.

Daniels, S and Martin, J, 'The Impact that it has had between People's Ears: Tort Reform, Mass Culture, and Plaintiffs' Lawyers' (2000) *DePaul Law Review* 50, 453–96.

DeFleur, ML and Ball-Rokeach, S, *Theories of Mass Communication*, 5th edn (Longman, 1989).

Dixon, TL and Linz, D, 'Overrepresentation and Underrepresentation of African Americans and Latinos as Lawbreakers on Television News' (2000) *Journal of Communication* 50, 131–54.

Dupont, B, 'The CSI Effect: Myths and Reality, Address at 29th Annual Conference of the Canadian Identification Association' (24 Nov 2008).

Eggermont, S, 'Television Viewing, Perceived Similarity, and Adolescents' Expectations of a Romantic Partner' (2004) *Journal of Broadcasting & Electronic Media* 47, 244–65.

Entman, RM and Gross, KA, 'The Court of Public Opinion: The Practice and Ethics of Trying Cases in the Media: Article: Race to Judgment: Stereotyping Media and Criminal Defendants' (2008) *Law and Contemporary Problems* 71, 93–133.

Epstein, MM, '"Separate" but not "Equally Important"' (2004) *Television Quarterly* 34, 4–7.

Feigenson, N and Spiesel, C, *Law on Display* (New York University Press, 2010).

Fisch, S, 'Vast Wasteland or Vast Opportunity?' in Bryant and Zillman (eds), *Media Effects* 397–426.

Galanter, MS, 'Reading the Landscape of Disputes: What We Know and Don't Know (and Think We Know) About Our Allegedly Contentious and Litigious Society' (1983) *UCLA Law Review* 31, 4–71.

Gerbner, G, 'Growing Up with Television: The Cultivation Perspective' in Bryant and Zillman (eds), *Media Effects* 17–41.

—— et al, 'Growing Up with Television: Cultivation Process' in Media Effects: Advances in Theory and Research' in J Shanahan and M Morgan, *Television and Its Viewers, Cultivation Theory and Research* (Cambridge University Press, 1999) 43–47.

Ghoshray, S, 'The CSI Effect: The True Effect of Crime Scene Television on the Justice System: Untangling the CSI Effect in Criminal Jurisprudence: Circumstantial Evidence, Reasonable Doubt, and Jury Manipulation' (2007) *New England Law Review* 41, 533–60.

Gilliam, FD et al, 'Crime in Black and White: The Violent, Scary World of Local News' (1996) 1 *Harvard International Journal of Press/Policy* 6–12.

Gilliam, FD and Iyengar, S, 'Prime Suspects: The Influence of Local Television News on the Viewing Public' (2000) *American Journal of Political Science* 44, 560–73.

Goidel, R, 'The Impact of Viewing Television on Perceptions of Juvenile Crime' (2006) *Journal of Broadcasting & Electronic Media* 50, 119–39.

Graham, F, 'The Impact of Television on the Jury System: Ancient Myths and Modern Realism' (1991) *American University Law Review* 40, 623–28.

Haltom, W and McCann, M, *Distorting the Law* (University of Chicago, 2004).

Hans, VP, *Business on Trial* (Yale, 2000).

Hoffner, CA et al, 'Socialization to Work in Late Adolescence: The Role of Television and Family' (2008) *Journal of Broadcasting & Electronic Media* 52, 282–302.

Holbert, RL et al, 'Environmental Concern, Patterns of Television Viewing, and Pro-Environmental Behaviors: Integrating Models of Media Consumption and Effects." *Journal of Broadcasting & Electronic Media* 47 (2003): 177–96.

—— 'Fear, Authority, and Justice: Crime-Related TV Viewing and Endorsements of Capital Punishment' (2004) *Journalism and Mass Communication Quarterly* 81, 343–63.

—— 'Political Implications of Prime-Time Drama and Sitcom Use: Genres of Representation and Opinions Concerning Women's Right' (2003) *Journal of Communication* 53, 45–57.

Iyengar, S and Kinder, DR, *News that Matters* (University of Chicago, 1987).

Kahan, DM, 'Social Influence, Social Meaning, and Deterrence' (1997) *Virginia Law Review* 53, 349–95.

Kim, Y and Vishak, J, 'Just Laugh! You Don't Need To Remember' (2008) *Journal of Communication* 58, 338–60.

Kovera, MB, 'The Effects of General Pretrial Publicity on Juror Decisions: An Examination of Moderators and Mediating Mechanisms' (2002) *Law & Human Behavior* 26, 43–72.

Lang, A et al, 'The Effects of Edit on Arousal, Attention, and Memory for Television Images: When an Edit is an Edit Can an Edit Be Too Much?' (2000) *Journal of Broadcasting & Electronic Media* 44, 94–109.

Lin, TE, 'Social Norms and Judicial Decision-Making: Examining the Role of Narratives in Same Sex Adoption Cases' (1999) *Columbia Law Review* 99, 739–94.

Loeffler, C, '"CSI" and the Criminal Justice System: Jury Trials' (New Republic Online, 7 June 2006).

Lovell Banks, T, 'Here Comes the Judge! Gender Distortion on TV Reality Court Shows' (2008) *University Of Baltimore Law Forum* 39, 38–56.

Lowry, *DT et al*, 'Setting the Public Fear Agenda: A Longitudinal Analysis of Network TV Crime Reporting, Public Perceptions of Crime, and FBI Crime Statistics' (2003) *Journal of Communication* 53, 61–73.

McLeod, DM, Kosicki, GM and McLeod, JM, 'Resurveying the Boundaries of Political Communications Effects' in Bryant and Zillman (eds), *Media Effects* 215–68.

Menkel-Meadow, C, 'Can They Do That? Legal Ethics in Popular Culture: Of Characters and Acts' (2001) *UCLA Law Review* 48, 1305–37.

—— 'Telling Stories in School: Using Case Studies and Stories to Teach Legal Ethics' (2000) *Fordham Law Review* 69, 787–815.

—— 'The Sense and Sensibilities of Lawyers: Lawyering in Literature, Narratives, Film and Television, and Ethical Choices Regarding Career and Craft' (1999) *McGeorge Law Review* 31, 1–24.

Morgan, M and Shanahan, J, 'The State of Cultivation' (2010) *Journal of Broadcasting & Electronic Media* 54, 337–55.

Oliver, MB, 'Caucasian Viewers' Memory of Black and White Criminal Suspects in the News' (1999) *Journal of Communication* 49, 46–60.

Pennington, N and Hastie, R, 'Evidence Evaluation in Complex Decision Making' (1986) *Journal of Personality & Social Psychology* 51, 242–58.

—— 'Explaining the Evidence: Tests of the Story Model for Juror Decision Making' (1992) *Journal of Personality & Social Psychology* 62, 189–206.

Pfau, M, 'Television Viewing and Public Perceptions of Attorneys' (1995) *Human Communication Research* 21, 307–30.

Podlas, Kimberlianne, 'Broadcast Litigiousness: Syndi-Court's Construction of Legal Consciousness' (2005) *Cardozo Arts & Entertainment Law Journal* 23, 465–505.

—— 'Guilty on all Accounts: Law & Order's Impact on Public Perceptions of Law and Order' (2008) *Seton Hall Journal of Sports & Entertainment Law* 18, 1–48.

—— 'Impact of Television on Cross-Examination and Juror "Truth"' (2009) *Widener Law Review* 14, 479–506.

—— 'Respect My Authority!: South Park's Expression of Legal Ideology and Contribution to Legal Culture' (2009) *Vanderbilt Journal of Entertainment Law* 11, 491–541.

—— 'The "CSI Effect" and Other Forensic Fictions' (2006/07) *Loyola of Los Angeles Entertainment Law Review* 27, 87–125.

—— 'The CSI Effect, Exposing the Media Myth' (2006) *Fordham Intellectual Property Media & Entertainment Law Journal* 16, 429–65.

—— 'The Monster in the Television: The Media's Contribution to Consumer Litigation Boogeyman' (2004) *Golden Gate University Law Review* 34, 239–83.

—— 'The Power of Stories: Intersections of Law, Literature, and Culture: Symposium Addendum: The Tales Television Tells: Understanding the Nomos through Television' (2006) 13 *Texas Wesleyan Law Review* 13, 31–62.

Potter, WJ, 'Cultivation Research: A Conceptual Critique' (1993) *Human Communcation Research* 19, 564–601.

—— and Chang, IK, 'Television Exposure Measures and the Cultivation Hypotheses' (1990) *Journal of Broadcasting & Electronic Media* 34, 313–33.

Quinn, L, 'The Politics of Law & Order' (2002) *Journal of American & Comparative Cultures* 25, 130–33.

Rapping, E, *Law and Justice as Seen on TV* (New York University, 2003).

Riley, C, 'The Rite of Rhetoric: Cognitive Framing in Technology Law' (2009) *Nevada Law Journal* 9, 495–543.

Robbennolt, JK and Studebaker, CA, 'News Media Reporting on Civil Litigation and its Influence on Civil Justice Decision Making' (2003) *Law & Human Behavior* 27, 5–27.

Romer, D et al, 'Television News and the Cultivation of Fear of Crime' (2003) *Journal of Communication* 53, 88–104.

Saks, MJ, 'Do We Really Know Anything about the Behavior of the Tort Litigation System—and Why Not?' (1998) *University of Pennsylvania Law Review* 140, 1147–1292.

Salzmann, VS and Dunwoody, PT, 'Prime-Time Lies: Do Portrayals of Lawyers Influence How People Think about the Legal Profession?' (2005) *Southern Methodist University* 58, 411–62.

Segrin, C and Nabi, RL, 'Does Television Viewing Cultivate Unrealistic Expectations about Marriage?' (2002) *Journal of Communication* 52, 247–63.

Shelton, DE et al, 'A Study of Juror Expectations and Demands Concerning Scientific Evidence: Does the "CSI Effect" Exist?' (2006) *Vanderbilt Journal of Entertainment & Technology Law* 9, 331–68.

Shen, F, 'Chronic Accessibility and Individual Cognitions: Examining the Effects of Message Frames in Political Advertisements' (2004) *Journal of Communication* 54, 123–37.

Sherwin, RK, 'Celebrity Lawyers and the Cult of Personality' (2003) *New York Law School Journal of International & Comparative Law* 22, 147–156.

—— 'Symposium: Introduction: Picturing Justice: Images of Law and Lawyers in the Visual Media' (1996) *University of Southern Florida Law Review* 30, 891–901.

—— *When Law Goes POP: The Vanishing Line between Law and Popular Culture* (Yale, 2000).

Shrum, LJ, 'Effects of Television Portrayals of Crime and Violence on Viewers' Perceptions of Reality: A Psychological Process Perspective' (1998) *Legal Studies Forum* 22, 257–68.

—— 'Magnitude Effects of Television Viewing on Social Perceptions Vary as a Function of Data Collection Method' (2004) *Advances in Consumer Research* 31, 511–13.

—— 'Processing Strategy Moderates the Cultivation Effect' (2001) *Human Communication Research* 27, 94–120.

—— and Darmanin Bischak, V, 'Mainstreaming, Resonance, and Impersonal Impact' (2001) *Human Communication Research* 27, 187–215.

Shuman, DW, 'The Psychology of Deterrence in Tort Law' (1993) *Kansas Law Review* 42, 115–67.

Signorielli, N, 'Aging on Television: Messages Relating to Gender, Race, and Occupation in Prime Time' (2004) *Journal of Broadcasting & Electronic Media* 48, 279–301.

—— 'Television's Mean and Dangerous Worlds, in Cultivation Analysis: New Directions' in N Signorielli and M Morgan (eds), *Media Effects Research* (Sage, 1990) 85–104.

Silverman, R, 'The Mass Media's Influence on Health Law and Policy: Symposium' (2005) *Health Law & Policy* 5, 175–85, 183.

Sotirovic, M, 'How Individuals Explain Social Problems: The Influences of Media Use' (2003) *Journal of Communications* 53, 122–37.

Spitz, DM, 'Notes and Comments: Heroes or Villains? Moral Struggles vs. Ethical Dilemmas: An Examination of Dramatic Portrayals of Lawyers and the Legal Profession in Popular Culture' (2000) *Nova Law Review* 24, 725–50.

Stanchi, K, 'Persuasion: An Annotated Bibliography' (2009) *Journal of Association of Legal Writing Directors* 6, 75–87.

Stark, SD, 'Perry Mason Meets Sonny Crockett: The History of Lawyers and the Police as Television Heroes' (1987) *University of Miami Law Review* 42, 229–50.

Studebaker, CA and Penrod, SD, 'Pretrial Publicity: The Media, the Law, and Common Sense' (1997) *Psychology Public Policy & Law* 3, 428–60.

Sun Beale, S, 'The News Media's Influence on Criminal Justice Policy: How Market-Driven News Promotes Punitiveness' (2006) *William and Mary Law Review* 48, 397–418.

Tsfati, Y, 'Does Audience Skepticism of the Media Matter in Agenda Setting?' (2003) *Journal of Broadcasting & Electronic Media* 47, 157–76.

Tyler, T, 'Viewing CSI and the Threshold of Guilt: Managing Truth and Justice in Reality and Fiction' (2006) *Yale Law Journal* 115, 1050–85.

—— and Darley, JM, 'Is Justice Just Us?' (2000) *Hofstra Law Review* 28, 707–761.

Villez, B, 'French Television Lawyers in "Avocats et Associes"' in M Asimov (ed), *Lawyers in Your Living Room!* (ABA, 2009) 275–77.

Wineburg, SS, 'Historical Problem Solving: A Study of the Cognitive Processes Used in the Evaluation of Documentary and Pictorial Evidence' (1991) *Journal of Educational Psychology* 83, 73–87.

Woo, HW and Dominick, JR, 'Acculturation, Cultivation, and Daytime TV Talk Shows' (2003) *Journalism & Mass Communication Quarterly* 80, 109–27.

5

Let's See How Far We've Come: The Role of Empirical Methodology in Exploring Television Audiences

CASSANDRA SHARP

The relationship between law and popular culture has invited great interest among scholars over the years. It is a field that invites the merging of disciplinary boundaries and allows for plurality in the ways that law can be understood. Viewing the relationship between law and popular culture from the vantage point of the viewer is an expanding research interest. Given the influential effects wrought by focuses upon cultural diversity and plurality, this interdisciplinary field invites the exploration of law as it is conceived and portrayed within visual cultural forms. Increasingly, scholars are looking beyond traditional legal narratives in order to better understand the various ways in which law is understood and perceived by the general public. This has meant that greater attention has been paid to stories of law as told in popular culture, with many scholars researching film and television as one avenue through which to say something meaningful about the way people respond to the law. Over the years these scholars have examined the way in which 'a popular understanding of the law and lawyers is constituted by interpretive references and devices employed in the communicative mediums of television, film and literature'.[1] These examinations have been accomplished, for example, by making serious studies of the ways in which trials are portrayed in film, or by evaluating portrayals of female lawyers on television. Attracting a variety of scholars from film studies, literary theory, cultural studies, sociology and law, the multidisciplinary nature of such an enterprise enriches the research quantum by enabling points of difference to be rigorously debated. Work in this diverse and seemingly amorphous field is largely connected by a desire to explore the meaning and representation of law within a variety of cultural contexts,

---

[1] R Malloy, 'Symposium on the Images of Law(yers) in Popular Culture: Introduction' (Fall, 2003) 53 *SLR* 1161–3.

and as a body of scholarship it describes the site of a complex encounter between contemporary culture and law.

The argument asserted in this chapter is that, in order to fully explore the interconnections between television and audience, legal research must go one step further by examining the ways audiences transform meaning in relation to the text. It is argued that we must seek to explore the *use* of television vis-à-vis the perceptions of the audience (which, of course, comprises both lawyers and non-lawyers) as they comprehend and interpret the world of legal practice. This chapter will show that there is a void in research about the connections between television representations and the meaning-making processes of audiences in response to them, particularly in the area of in-depth empirical and ethnographic research. Unlike the abundant scholarship that has been produced in the area of media effects[2] showing that public opinion is influenced by fictitious popular culture, evaluating public perceptions of the law through this medium has been largely neglected. Those scholars who delve into such research usually use quantitative analysis to focus on the effects and influence of media rather than on qualitatively exploring the ways in which audiences use the images. Research into audience use of popular culture (in particular popular stories) in relation to the law is crucial to an understanding of the motivations, values and expectations of the public. The more we can understand the connections between the two, the better legal education and public policymakers could perhaps take into account the ways 'popular representations of law feed back into legal discourses and shape contemporary understandings of law'.[3]

This chapter therefore serves two important functions in understanding the intersection of law and culture as regards popular understandings by viewers: first, it illuminates the broad landscape within which an empirical study of law and popular culture is based (by looking to the methods of the recent past); and second, it contextualises this type of study within a new movement in legal research (with a view to possible future endeavours). In the first part of this chapter, through an exploration of some relevant studies in this field, it is argued that although legal scholars have had much to say about various aspects of the portrayal of law in television, there has been somewhat of a void in qualitative empirical research concerning the connections between television representations and viewer *interpretations*. As recent years have shown an exponential rise in the body of legal scholarship on law and popular culture, this part explores the historical rise to prominence of legal research into law and television, and examines some contemporary empirical scholarship that focuses on issues of law and justice as represented in popular culture, particularly television. In identifying an empirical void, the second part of the chapter reflects on some newer methodologies that have been adopted from the cultural studies tradition and comments on their usefulness. The last part of the chapter then looks toward the future of developing the potential for this ethnographic research, which may further illuminate

---

[2] This is a very large disciplinary avenue and encompasses various methodological approaches and supportive theories. For a quick foray into this area, see J Bryant and D Zillman (eds), *Media Effects: Advances in Theory and Research* (New Jersey, Lawrence Erlbaum Associates, 2002).

[3] M Thornton, *Romancing the Tomes: Popular Culture, Law and Feminism* (London, Cavendish, 2002) xiii.

contemporary interactions between viewers and issues of law and justice presented on the small screen.

I. The Research Status Quo

Within the law and popular culture field, there is a dichotomy between law as presented in film and law on television. For the most part a pragmatic decision, scholarship is usually devoted to one or the other;[4] however it would seem that less attention is paid to the phenomenon of television lawyers versus depictions of lawyers in cinema.[5] Interestingly, one of the earliest legal research developments within the law and popular culture movement was the investigation of law as presented on television. The concern was primarily with the way the relationship between legal culture and television portrayals manifested within the minds of the public. As the main catalyst for this burgeoning area of law and popular culture studies, the late 1980s series *LA Law* encouraged scholars to embrace explorations into the effects of such a programme on the public's perception of lawyers.[6] Following in the footsteps of *LA Law*, the mid 1990s saw a resurgent injection of legal dramas into prime-time viewing as a direct response to a public appetite for shows depicting the law, lawyers and legal themes. This in turn created a contagious interest among scholars to explore the realm of fictional lawyers on television. Thus, individual programmes such as *The Practice*, *Ally McBeal* and *Law and Order* were critiqued and evaluated for the type of law and lawyers that they present,[7] or to illuminate themes that are variously presented within fictional television narratives, including issues of morality[8] and gender.[9] Existing within a framework 'which perceives that popular culture is an important source of the public's knowledge of legal rules and the justice system',[10] the majority of the work over the last 10–15 years has largely

---

[4] There are, of course, those scholars who bridge the two by providing a general survey of film and television fiction from underneath the law and popular culture umbrella. See, eg A Chase, 'Lawyers and Popular Culture: A Review of Mass Media Portrayals of American Attorneys' (1986) 11 *ABFRJ* 281; A Strachenfeld and C Nicholson, 'Blurred Boundaries: An Analysis of the Close Relationship Between Popular Culture and the Practice of Law' (1996) 30 *USFLR* 903; J Denvir, 'Law, Lawyers, Film and Television' (2000) 24 *LSF* 279.

[5] P Robson, 'Developments in Law and Popular Culture: The Case of the TV Lawyer' in A Masson and K O'Connor (eds), *Representations of Justice* (Brussels, Peter Lang, 2007) 79.

[6] See, eg the work of S Gillers, 'Popular Legal Culture: Taking LA Law More Seriously' (1989) 98 *YLJ* 1607; R Rosen, 'Ethical Soap: LA Law and the Privileging of Character' (1989) 43 *UMLR* 1229; C Rosenberg, 'An LA Lawyer Replies' (1989) 98 *YLJ* 1625.

[7] See, eg J Marek, 'The Practice and Ally McBeal: a New Image for Women Lawyers on Television?' (1999) 1 *Journal of American Culture* 22, 77 and B Kitei, 'The Mass Appeal of the Practice and Ally McBeal: An In-Depth Analysis of the Impact of These Television Shows on the Public's Perception of Attorneys' (1999) 7 *UCLAELR* 169; see generally E Rapping, *Law and Justice as Seen on TV* (New York, NYU Press, 2003).

[8] D Keetley, 'Law and Order' in R Jarvis and P Joseph (eds), *Prime Time Law: Fictional Television as Legal Narrative* (California, California Academic Press, 1998) 33.

[9] C Corcos, 'Women Lawyers' in ibid 219.

[10] S Greenfield, G Osborn and P Robson, *Film and the Law* (London, Cavendish Pub, 2001) 11.

been concerned with individual television programmes in order to illuminate certain social aspects of the law and public perceptions thereof.[11]

Indeed within this scholarship, an orthodoxy setting parameters and methodology has already emerged, which includes, as a dominant feature, a focus on questions of representation.[12] Textual critique and content analysis have become by far the most commonly used methods to research the connections between law and popular culture,[13] and so much of the work within these fields is directed at exploring portrayals of legal players, legal themes and/or textual analysis of legal films.[14] Greenfield, Osborn and Robson have also argued that despite the diverse styles and levels of theoretical abstraction that can be found among film and law scholarship, it is possible to identify two major strands that are principally given attention,[15] and the same could be said for work on television. The first strand is indicative of work which seeks to provide panoramic perspectives on law and its portrayal in this medium, and '[s]ome writers in this category have concerned themselves broadly with the nature of law and justice as seen in film and what the underlying messages or ideologies are'.[16] The second strand involves investigating individual popular cultural texts and using them as a basis for considering persistent legal themes such as criminal justice, gender and the environment. For example, evaluations have been made of portrayals of gender relations,[17] law in the courtroom,[18] and social issues like divorce,[19] capital punishment[20] and images of justice,[21] allowing thematic explorations of law in popular culture

[11] See generally J Elkins, 'Reading/Teaching Lawyer Films' (Summer, 2004) 28 *VTLR* 813; R Malloy, 'Symposium on the Images of Law(yers) in Popular Culture: Introduction' (2001) 53 *SLR* 1161; J Silbey, 'What We Do When We Do Law and Popular Culture: Richard Sherwin, When Law Goes Pop' (2002) 27 *Law and Social Inquiry* 139; L Scottoline, 'Law and Popular Culture: Get Off the Screen' (2000) 24 *Nova LR* 655; J Denvir, 'Law, Lawyers, Film and Television' (2000) 24 *LSF* 279; C Jackson, 'Film and TV Legal Drama Commentary' (2000) 24 *LSF* 321; B Kitei, 'The Mass Appeal of the Practice and Ally McBeal: An In-Depth Analysis of the Impact of These Television Shows on the Public's Perception of Attorneys (1999) 7 *UCLAELR* 169; R Rotunda, 'The Legal Profession and the Public Image of Lawyers' (1998/1999) 23 *TJLP* 51; L Friedman, 'Law, Lawyers and Popular Culture' (Summer, 2004) 28 *VTLR* 813; S Macaulay, 'Popular Legal Culture: An Introduion' (1989) 98 *YLJ* 1545; D Gunn (ed), *The Lawyer and Popular Culture: Proceedings of a Conference* (Colorado, Fred B Rothmann & Co, 1993). Later works such as J Denvir (ed), *Legal Reelism: Movies as Legal Texts* (Illinois, University of Illinois Press, 1996); Greenfield, Osborn and Robson, *Film and the Law* (n 10); and T Lenz' *Changing Images of Law in Film and Television Crime Stories* (New York, Peter Lang, 2003) have all contributed to the wider promotion of law and popular culture as a useful scholarly discipline.

[12] L Moran et al (eds), *Law's Moving Image* (London, Cavendish, 2004).

[13] L Gies, 'Law and the Media: the Future of an Uneasy Relationship' in S Greenfield and G Osborn (eds), *Readings in Law and Popular Culture* (Oxon, Routledge-Cavendish, 2008) 65.

[14] For an example of articles about legal players see S Greenfield, 'Hero or Villian? Cinematic Lawyers and the Delivery of Justice' (2001) 28 *JLS* 25; for examples of legal themes see I Lurvey and S Eiseman, 'Divorce Goes to the Movies' (1996) 30 *USFLR* 1209; for textual analysis of a legal film see R Sherwin, 'Cape Fear: Law's Inversion and Cathartic Justice' (1996) 30 *USFLR* 1023.

[15] Greenfield, Osborn and Robson, *Film and the Law* (n 10) 12.

[16] Ibid.

[17] S Caplow, 'Still in the Dark: Disappointing Images of Women' (1999) 20 *WRL Reporter* 55; C Shapiro, 'Women Lawyers in Celluloid: Why Hollywood Skirts the Truth' (1995) 25 *UTLR* 955.

[18] P Bergman and M Asimow, *Reel Justice: the Courtroom goes to the Movies* (Missouri, Andrew McMeels, 2006); G Uelmen, 'The Trial as a Circus: Inherit the Wind' (1996) 30 *USFLR* 1221.

[19] Lurvey and Eiseman, 'Divorce Goes to the Movies' (n 14) 1209; M Asimow, 'Divorce in the Movies: From the Hays Code to Kramer v Kramer' (2000) 24 *LSF* 221.

[20] R Harding, 'Celluloid Death: Cinematic Depictions of Capital Punishment' (1996) 30 *USFLR* 1167.

[21] R Berets, 'Changing Images of Justice in American Films' (1996) 20 *LSF* 473; Sherwin, 'Cape Fear: Law's Inversion and Cathartic Justice' (n 14) 1023; J Brooks, 'Will Boys just be Boyz'N the Hood? African American Directors Portray a Crumbling Justice System in Urban America' (1997) 22 *OCULR* 1.

to grow in dominance in the field of legal scholarship.[22] Yet, the primary objectives for much of this scholarship have been a focus either on the text itself or the *perceived* impact of various representations on public perception.

More recently there seems to be a growing 'awareness of the value of developing a more sophisticated approach to the cultural products of television'.[23] This is evidenced by Rapping's contribution, *Law and Justice as Seen on TV*,[24] which takes the scholarship beyond an exploration of the significance of the images presented. That is, she outlines the 'shifts in television's dominant ideology about law and justice, crime and punishment, and the way these shifts have coincided with broader trends in legal and political policy and history'.[25] In particular Rapping juxtaposes fictional legal entertainment and non-fictional forms, such as televised trials, and finds that recent television programming across all genres presents a blurry but visible general ideological slant towards social issues and crime and punishment.[26] Using seemingly contrasting programmes, such as the melodramatic *The Practice* and Court TV's *Crime Stories*,[27] Rapping shows there is a widespread tendency within American life 'to define and approach all social issues and problems within the narrow terrain of criminal law'.[28] She concludes that television, whether fictional or non-fictional, is a 'useful handmaiden to those who have an interest in maintaining this broad consensus'.[29] In a similar vein, Lenz's contribution,

---

[22] This second strand of writing has also opened up the possibility of discussing films that are not directly about law. Gangster movies, westerns, comedies and thrillers were among the film texts examined by Denvir and his colleagues in *Legal Reelism: Movies as Legal Texts* (n 11) where notions of justice are explored from a postmodern and feminist perspective. The essays in this collection are by non-specialists in film that use film as a tool to better understand the operation of law in the wider community. This is not to say that the law film itself has been ignored. Indeed, much attention within the scholarship is directed at evaluating the presentation of law and legal themes within obviously legal films, such as courtroom dramas (*A Few Good Men*) and movies about lawyers (*The Firm*). Considerable attention has also been given to circumscribing the legal film genre, with this concern as a major theme within two major contributions to this area: Greenfield, Osborn and Robson's *Film and the Law* (n 10); and S Machura and P Robson's edited collection of essays *Law and Film* (Oxford, Wiley-Blackwell, 2001); see also Elkins, 'Reading/Teaching' (n 11) 869–70 (Appendix A), where he suggests that it is possible to outline the structural features of a lawyer film genre. Although the courtroom drama is the usual suspect for any classification of law films, both these major works seek to show that the genre is not so clearly defined. Of particular note, Greenfield, Osborn and Robson suggest that in order to speak meaningfully about the subject of law or lawyers as portrayed in film, the scholar must adopt a broad approach and consider 'what the role and function of law is within society and how this is translated into film': Greenfield, Osborn and Robson, *Film and the Law* (n 10) 23. Chase too goes beyond the courtroom drama trope to include a wide and possibly unexpected variety of films (for example *Wall Street* and *Fight Club*) within his definition of the legal film genre: 'Just as law is more than litigation, legal movies are more than courtroom drama': A Chase, *Movies on Trial* (New York, The New Press, 2002) xii. They conclude that, more than simply courtroom dramas, the key concept of law films is the enforcement of justice, which enables various sub-categories of the genre to be created: Greenfield, Osborn and Robson, *Film and The Law* (n 10) 24. This analysis could equally be applied to the television medium.

[23] P Robson, 'Developments in Law and Popular Culture: The Case of the TV Lawyer' in A Masson and K O'Connor (eds), *Representations of Justice* (New York, Peter Lang, 2007) 89.

[24] E Rapping, *Law and Justice as Seen on TV* (n 7).

[25] Ibid 13.

[26] Ibid 17.

[27] With the rise of the courtroom as a television arena, Rapping argues that although non-fictional programmes are expected to be taken seriously by engaged thoughtful viewers (unlike fictional series), they come 'complete with editorial narrative commentary from legal "experts" who lead us to the "correct" political conclusions': ibid.

[28] Ibid.

[29] Ibid.

Changing Images of Law in Film and Television Crime Stories,[30] charts the change in criminal justice policies from liberal to conservative through an exploration of images of law and crime stories in popular legal fiction. Although examining both film and television, Lenz argues for a better understanding of the relationship between public opinion and legal policy by exploring shared expectations about justice in legal culture.

While distinctive contributions such as these from Rapping and Lenz may serve to stimulate interdisciplinary and empirical scholarship in this field, they do not focus attention on actual viewer responses. Gies argues that despite the benefits that content analysis or ideological critique offer, such methods do not provide convincing support for their claims about the extent to which popular culture and media actually influences audiences.[31] Audience research on the other hand, with its variety of statistical, qualitative and experiment-based methods, centres not on the content of popular culture, but instead on audiences and how they interpret and use popular images.[32] It is this change in emphasis that puts the focus on exploring, understanding and challenging the role of ascendant discourse within popular views of social and legal issues that is advocated later in the chapter. Certainly, in the media effects and cultural studies tradition there is abundant scholarship that has been produced through the study of television audiences that both accept and challenge the notion that public opinion is influenced by fictitious popular culture,[33] yet equivalent empirical work on audiences of law-related media (until quite recently) has remained largely unchartered territory.[34]

This is not to say that legal scholars are uninterested in audience response.[35] Asimow has argued that viewers constantly form opinions, attitudes and ideas that are based on material extracted from television;[36] and other scholars have argued

---

[30] Lenz, *Changing Images of Law in Film and Television* (n 11).

[31] Gies, 'Law and the Media' (n 13) 65.

[32] Ibid.

[33] For example see L Shrum, 'Crime and Popular Culture: Effects of Television Portrayals of Crime and Violence on Viewers Perceptions of Reality: A Psychological Process Perspective' (1998) 22 *LSF* 257; C Barker, '"Cindy's a Slut": Moral Identities and Moral Responsibility in the "Soap Talk" of British Asian Girls' (1998) 32 *Sociology* 65; I Ang, *Living Room Wars* (London, Routledge, 1996); R Allen (ed), *To Be Continued... Soap Opera Around the World* (Oxfrod, Taylor & Francis, 1995); D Morley, *Television, Audiences and Cultural Studies* (London, Routledge, 1992); R Silverstone, *Television and Everyday Life* (London, Routledge, 1994); T Liebes and E Katz, *The Export of Meaning. Cross-Cultural Readings of Dallas* (New York, Oxford University Press, 1993); I Ang, *Watching Dallas: Soap Opera and the Melodramatic Imagination* (London, Routledge, 1985); C Geraghty, *Women and Soap Opera* (UK, Polity Press, 1991).

[34] Some notable exceptions, for example the works of Podlas, Gies, and Salzmann and Dunwoody, will be discussed in more detail below.

[35] Podlas argues that 'since the advent of television, legal scholars and practitioners alike have contemplated the impact of law-oriented entertainment programming, such as *Perry Mason*, *LA Law*, and *The People's Court*, on the public': K Podlas, 'The CSI Effect, Exposing the Media Myth' (2006) 16 *FIPMELJ* 429, 430.

[36] M Asimow, 'Law and Popular Culture: Bad Lawyers in the Movies' (2000) 24 *Nova LR* 533, 551. For further discussion of audience reception, see S Livingstone, *Making Sense of Television: the Psychology of Audience Interpretation* (London, Routledge, 1998). See also D Spitz, 'Heroes or Villians? Moral Struggles v Ethical Dilemmas: An Examination of Dramatic Portrayals of Lawyers and the Legal Profession in Popular Culture' (2000) 24 *Nova LR* 725, 736 (arguing that all signals and images we experience have an impact on our subconscious and that fictional television has the inevitable effect of informing our psyche).

that television narratives often substitute for direct experience with the legal system.[37] Both Meyer and Sherwin have conducted content analyses to evaluate cinematic influences on real closing arguments in jury trials.[38] In fact there has been intense speculation over the years that information or misinformation gleaned from popular culture has a significant impact on 'law' in the legal realists' sense: 'what judges, jurors, attorneys, legislators, voters and ordinary consumers or producers actually do in their contracting, fact-finding, law-applying, and law-making functions'.[39] And yet, legal research that actually seeks to explore that interaction of law and the everyday world via audiences has been hitherto non-existent. Only in recent times have legal scholars begun to acknowledge that there is great value in empirically exploring the intersection between viewers and their responses to the various forms of popular culture.

Two such examples are separate studies (conducted at a similar time) that attempted to gauge the impact of visual images of law on viewers. The first was a transnational study (of which I was a part) that was primarily concerned with delving behind the cardinal assumptions of impact around the significance of popular cultural images of law.[40] The research was conducted in law schools in Argentina, Australia, England, Germany, Scotland and the United States, and was completed in order to see whether there was any empirical evidence to support these assumptions, as well as to investigate the impact films and television shows might have on the study and subsequent practice of law. First-year viewers from each of the institutions were surveyed in their first law class:

> In particular, the vexed issue of media effects informed the study—to what extent did viewers draw their information and opinions from fictitious stories about law and lawyers in the movies or on television? Would it be possible to show that popular culture had influenced their opinions and would the results vary across the various countries?[41]

The transnational study concluded that news coverage, movies and television are quite helpful to viewers in forming their opinions about lawyers, and that such students also have very strong opinions about lawyer trustworthiness and ethical standards.[42] The

---

[37] Podlas, 'Guilty on All Accounts: *Law & Order's* Impact on Public Perception of Law and Order' (2008) 18 *SHJSEL* 2; Gies argues that 'people lack first-hand experience of law, making them almost entirely dependant on the media for their legal knowledge': Gies, 'Law and the Media' (n 13) 65, 66.

[38] P Meyer, 'Why a Jury Trial is More Like a Film Than a Novel' (2001) 28 *JLS* 133; P Meyer, 'Desperate for Love III: Rethinking Closing Arguments as Stories' (1999) 50 *SCLR* 715; P Meyer, 'Desperate for Love II: Further Reflections on the Interpretation of Legal and Popular Storytelling in Closing Arguments to a Jury in a Complex Criminal Case' (1996) 30 *USFLR* 931; P Meyer, 'Desperate for Love: Cinematic Influences Upon a Defendant's Closing Argument to a Jury' (1994) 18 *VTLR* 721; R Sherwin 'Law and Popular Culture' in A Sarat (ed), *The Blackwell Companion to Law and Society* (Blackwell, 2004) 101. Salzmann and Dunwoody also argue that there is power in referencing popular culture in persuasive courtroom arguments: V Salzmann, 'Honey, You're no June Cleaver: The Power of "Dropping Pop" to Persuade' (2010) 64 *MELR* 241.

[39] Asimow, 'Embodiment of Evil: Law Firms in the Movies' (2001) 48 *UCLALR* 1339, 1341. See also L Friedman, 'Law, Lawyers and Popular Culture' (Summer, 2004) 28 *VTLR* 813; and L Gies, 'Law and the Media' (n 13) 65.

[40] Asimow et al, 'Perceptions of Lawyers—a Transnational Study of Student Views on the Image of Law and Lawyers' (2005) 12 *IJLP* 407.

[41] Ibid 409.

[42] Ibid 407.

study found that a high percentage of law students across all jurisdictions credited popular culture as a significant factor in forming their opinions of lawyers.[43]

Salzmann and Dunwoody conducted the other study and it (in part also using first-year law students) focused upon the accuracy of television portrayals of lawyers' day-to-day activities.[44] Comparing content analysis of television lawyers with a survey of actual lawyers, they confirmed a disparity between reality and television practice. By surveying the first-year law students' perceptions of lawyers and lawyering, they then sought to test the assumption that laypeople were conditioned via popular cultural references.[45] In contrast to the transnational study, Salzmann and Dunwoody's research argued that the claims of popular culture influence might at times be overstated.[46] Although presenting seemingly contradictory results, it could be argued that these two studies had different centres of focus: the work of Salzmann and Dunwoody used viewers to establish the *accuracy* of law images in popular culture,[47] in contrast with the transnational study which was more concerned with viewers' *reflections* of being a lawyer. Nonetheless, as both studies were based on quantitative analysis, it is posited that audience use or interpretation of television images could not have been fully explored in either study. It is for this reason that part II of the chapter seeks to explain the need for more qualitative ethnographic research into the vexed area of audience research.

Another scholar that has been active in testing presumptions about audience responses to law on television is Podlas. Her research includes an empirical investigation of the ideologies and messages cultivated by *Law and Order*;[48] an exploration of the effects of syndicated courtrooms (eg *Judge Judy*) on jurors;[49] and she has shed some light on the myth of the so-called 'CSI Effect' on courtroom behaviours and expectations.[50] In this latter study, Podlas 'sought to uncover any connection between *CSI* viewing and issue-oriented influences on "not-guilty" verdicts'.[51] Using quite detailed survey instruments, respondents were asked to indicate television and *CSI* viewing habits and respond to a criminal law scenario.[52] Interestingly, the results of this quantitative analysis were inconclusive for proving whether there was a 'CSI Effect' at all, and she hints at the need for further empirical investigation to finally settle the matter.[53]

---

[43] 'After news coverage, popular culture was often the most important data source, more even than conversations with friends or even having family members or friends who are lawyers': ibid 427; see also Table 4 at 424.

[44] V Salzmann and P Dunwoody, 'Prime-Time Lies: Do Portrayals of Lawyers Influence How People Think About the Legal Profession?' (2005) 58 *SMULR* 411.

[45] Ibid.

[46] 'Inaccurate portrayals did not seem to impact on laypersons perceptions of lawyering': ibid.

[47] Ibid.

[48] Podlas, 'Guilty on All Accounts' (n 37).

[49] Podlas' research argues that reality courtrooms provide information about the operation of courts that viewers integrate into their beliefs: 'a multi-year study of more than 500 viewers found that daytime television's reality courtrooms seem to impact perceptions about the way that judges behave, as well as the normality of their behaviours.': ibid 1, 12. See also Podlas, 'Please Adjust Your Signal: How Television's Syndi-Courtrooms Bias our Juror Citizenry' (2001) 39 *ABLJ* 1.

[50] Podlas, 'The CSI Effect' (n 35) 429.

[51] Ibid.

[52] Ibid 432.

[53] Ibid 465.

Podlas' empirical work in each instance is heavily reliant on audience research grounded in cultivation theory. This is an oft-favoured media theory that 'posits a relationship between exposure to television content and viewer beliefs, attitudes and behaviours'.[54] Cultivation theorists (originally based in the field of psychology) assess the influence of long-term exposure to television's recurrent stories and images on a consumer's conception of social reality, and argue that heavy television exposure can cultivate different attitudes, values and judgement than it would in viewers with light television exposure. Using cultivation theory, Podlas argues that the link between television watching and behavioural change is subtle and cumulative[55] whereby 'if a viewer repeatedly sees a particular representation on television, she will presume that representation is common in reality. For example … if she repeatedly sees television judges yell[ing] at litigants, she will assume that judges yell at litigants.'[56] In cultivation theory, the relationship between information cultivated and the impact on decision-making is explained via heuristic reasoning.[57] Heuristics are informational snap judgements used for automatic decision-making and causal reasoning, and television's depictions are seen as one source of heuristic knowledge regarding the legal process.[58] Using this theory, Podlas consistently argues that television's 'consistent, repeated portrayal of the behaviour of a legal actor can cultivate in a viewer the beliefs that those behaviours are normal and true to reality.'[59] Cultivation research has been extensively conducted to investigate perceptions in the area of crime and violence, and recent evidence shows that heavy television consumption contributes to an exaggerated belief that crime is rampant.[60] One study for example, examined the relationship between television viewing and public perceptions of the juvenile justice system and crime rates.[61] In this study the researchers found that as viewers watched more crime-related television such as *COPS* and *America's Most Wanted*, 'they were more likely to misperceive realities of juvenile crime and juvenile justice'.[62]

One criticism of cultivation theory however, is that it is too closely connected with the behaviourist approach to media effects where it was assumed that watching television was passive in character 'with the meanings and messages of television unproblematically taken up by audiences'.[63] As such, these types of socio-legal

---

[54] Ibid 447. See also G Gerbner, 'Growing up with Television: the Cultivation Perspective' in Bryant and Zillmann, *Media Effects* (n 2).

[55] Cultivation theory is 'unconcerned with the short term effect (where watching a particular television show directly causes a certain effect), but instead with the long-term impact of stable, repetitive images on perceptions of social reality': Podlas, 'Broadcast Litigiousness: Syndi-Court's Construction of Legal Consciousness' (2005) 23 *CAELJ* 465, 483.

[56] Podlas, 'Guilty on All Accounts' (n 37) 11–12.

[57] Podlas, 'Impact of Television on Cross-Examination and Juror "Truth"' (2008–09) 14 *WLR* 479, 479.

[58] Podlas, 'Guilty on All Accounts' (n 37) 14; see also Shrum, 'Effects of Television Portrayals of Crime and Violence on Viewers Perceptions of Reality' 22 (1998) *LSF* 257.

[59] Podlas, 'Impact of Television on Cross-Examination' (n 57) 495. See also Podlas, 'Guilty on All Accounts' (n 37); and Podlas, 'Please Adjust Your Signal' (n 49) 1.

[60] S Eschholz, 'The Media and the Fear of Crime: A Survey of the Research' (1997) 37 *UFJL&PP*.

[61] R Goidel, C Freeman, and S Procopio, 'The Impact of Television Viewing on Perceptions of Juvenile Crime' (2006) 50 *JBEM* 119.

[62] Ibid.

[63] C Barker, *Cultural Studies: Theory and Practice* (London, Sage Publications, 2000) 269 (cites the example of research that attempted to 'prove' that watching television had certain 'effects' on audiences).

research 'tend ... to ignore the distinction between the content of a media text and audiences' reading of that text',[64] and focus almost exclusively on speculated negative *effects*. Indeed it is this approach that is behind Sherwin's apocalyptic account of the merger between law and popular culture. In *When Law goes Pop*,[65] Sherwin makes it clear that 'the extent to which law today is converging with the popular, and the deleterious effects of this convergence on law's stability and continuing legitimacy in the eyes of the public'.[66] He further argues that the law is succumbing to the various influences of mass media and suggests that the law 'goes pop' when the legitimacy of the law is eroded. It is this flattening of legal meaning, and distortion of legal knowledge that leads Sherwin to view law as in need of rescue from the negative effects of our postmodern culture.[67] His warning that law's legitimacy is being diminished is based on a view similar to behaviourism: that the continual overloading of images in contemporary culture dissolves any distinction between art and reality and that those 'negative effects' involve a 'wholesale repudiation of reason and the efficacy of human will'.[68] While it is entirely appropriate and stimulating for Sherwin to be exploring some difficult questions about the influence of popular culture on our meaningful understanding of law, it is important to note that the postmodernism he eschews (through which he argues that the 'truth' of the law is placed into question) may actually provide positive ways in which to empower individuals towards a questioning and a demystification of the mythic significance of the law. Although Sherwin presents a cautionary tale about law's deligitimation and public disenchantment, this chapter argues that the convergence of popular culture and law can actually be used to provoke in viewers a more critical reflection about the images and narratives they encounter. Indeed, this chapter suggests that a behaviourist approach to socio-legal research, and in particular studies of television, is not necessarily the most effective method for getting to the heart of what audiences really think.

Cultivation theory aside, in combination the work of Podlas does appear to demonstrate strong connections between the visual images on television and popular perception. But her research methodology is based on quantitative content and statistical analysis that can only reveal so much. Interestingly, in her study of *Law & Order*'s impact on public perception, Podlas argues that continuous immersion in the world of *Law & Order* would contribute to the cumulative build-up of presumptions about the legal world and she 'ethnographically' reviews the narrative in order to complement her content analysis.[69] Unfortunately, this is not true ethnography as it does not address the viewer's assumptions, beliefs and values—instead it only really puts Podlas as the researcher in the position of 'viewer'—where she 'systematically

---

This was also described as 'the tap on the knee' approach or the 'hypodermic syringe' approach: Gies, 'Law and the Media' (n 13) 67. See also S Hall, 'Encoding/Decoding' in S Hall, et al (eds), *Culture, Media, Language* (London, Routledge,1981).

[64] Gies, 'Law and the Media' (n 13) 68.

[65] R Sherwin, *When the Law Goes Pop: The Vanishing Line Between Law and Popular Culture* (Illinois, University of Chicago Press, 2000).

[66] Ibid 7.

[67] Ibid.

[68] Ibid 235. See also Gies, 'Law and the Media' (n 13) 65, 68 (where he argues that Sherwin's argument is based on a behaviourist approach).

[69] Podlas, 'Guilty on All Accounts' (n 37) 27.

observes and records concrete legal phenomenon'.[70] Macauley warned that 'armchair self-analysis of our own reaction is not enough'[71] and so it is argued that legal scholars seeking to research television should become increasingly aware of the way in which 'media culture meshes and interacts with other forms of social experience.'[72] As such, the next section explains that qualitative methodologies that encompass true ethnographic methods are better able to focus on the viewer.

II. Filling the Empirical Void—Ethnographic Approaches

In exploring the intersection of law and television studies at the point of analysing viewer understanding, newer research draws heavily on cultural studies theory where the groundwork for much of the work on audience influence has already been laid.[73] As a diverse and eclectic field of inquiry, cultural studies provide varying methods for textual analysis. Although there are several methods for data collection and analysis, each has a particular grounding in qualitative methodology aimed specifically at exploring cultural meaning and understanding.

As 'watching television is a socially and culturally informed activity which is centrally concerned with *meaning*',[74] the limitations of quantitative methods in analysing the phenomenon of watching television are well established, with statistical techniques seen to have a disaggregating effect on the exploration of such a complex activity.[75] Watching television must be seen as 'inevitably enmeshed with a range of other domestic practices and can only be properly understood in this context'.[76] Indeed, Morley argues that a broadly ethnographic perspective will avoid such context isolation and assist in providing a 'thick description' of the complexities of this activity.[77]

With ethnography being an empirical and theoretical inheritance from anthropology, the qualitative concern is focused on details of life while connecting them to wider social processes and existence. As Barker has argued, 'in the context of media oriented cultural studies, ethnography has become a code-word for a range of qualitative methods, including participant observation, in-depth interviews and focus groups'.[78] He remarks that these data collection techniques reflect the 'spirit' of ethnography, which is based on a qualitative understanding of cultural activity in context.[79] This further suggests that the data and analysis produced by qualitative research would be seen as arising from the circumstances of social existence and providing a richness of detail

---

[70] Ibid.
[71] S Macauley, 'Popular Legal Culture: An Introduction' (1989) 98 *YLJ*, 1552.
[72] Gies, 'Law and the Media' (n 13) 10.
[73] Ibid.
[74] Barker, *Cultural Studies* (n 63) 269.
[75] Morley, *Television, Audiences and Cultural Studies* (n 33) 173.
[76] Ibid.
[77] Ibid. 'Thick description' is a reference from C Geertz, *The Interpretation of Cultures: Selected Essays* (New York, Basic Books, 1973).
[78] Barker, *Cultural Studies* (n 63) 28.
[79] Ibid.

that is suited to tolerating the ambiguities, uncertainties and contradictions inevitable within a study of social existence.[80]

Ethnographic methods identify and describe the complexity of social phenomena and break open underlying perceptions and expectations for inspection:

> one cannot understand human actions without understanding the meaning that participants attribute to those actions—their thoughts, feelings, beliefs, values and assumptive worlds; the researcher therefore needs to understand the deeper perspectives captured through face to face interaction.[81]

Ethnographic methods therefore place a particular focus on the participant's frame of reference. As a system of representation, television is one of the key practices by which this frame of reference can exchange and produce meaning. Representations only become meaningful through discourse, and the task of the researcher thus becomes to explore how legal discourse is constituted and challenged by viewers as they talk about television lawyers and perceive the legal world. A qualitative research basis can concentrate on the details of this particular social existence and seek to explore its cultural activity in context. The use of qualitative methods is therefore based on a theoretical framework that is concerned with the way individuals make sense of the legal world they inhabit.[82]

The importance of gaining access to the process of constructing meaning can be illustrated by reference to the aforementioned transnational study.[83] The study was conducted by a number of law schools across six countries and utilised statistical analysis to evaluate student responses to a questionnaire. Thus, the quantitative methods used were able to highlight correlations between student backgrounds and perceptions of law and lawyers, and to examine the role of popular culture within these connections.[84] Although quite informative on one level, these statistical correlations cannot provide a deeper exploration of how students construct meaning about these issues in response to television narratives, nor can they elaborate on how the forming of opinions contributes to identity construction. Indeed, the transnational study itself recognised this limitation on quantitative work and commended any future research that would undertake the task of exploring the nature of popular culture's role in the construction of ideas surrounding law and lawyers.[85]

In taking up this challenge, my own research has utilised ethnographic empirical methods as a way of delving deeper into the issues of both student identity[86] and public ideas of justice.[87] In my law student research, the main goal has been to explore

[80] M Denscombe, *The Good Research Guide for Small-scale Research Projects* (UK, Open University Press, 1998) 221.

[81] C Marshall and G B Rossman, *Designing Qualitative Research* (London, Sage Publishing, 1999) 57.

[82] This ties in with Gies' constructionist approach, referred to in part III, that recognises law as an everyday part of life: Gies, 'Law and the Media' (n 13).

[83] Asimow et al, 'Perceptions of Lawyers' (n 40) 407.

[84] Ibid.

[85] Ibid 429.

[86] See further C Sharp 'The Extreme Makeover Effect of Law School: Students Being Transformed by Stories' (2005) 12 *TWLR* 233–50; Sharp, 'Changing the Channel: What to Do with the Critical Abilities of Law Students as Viewers?' (2004) 13 *GLR* 185–99.

[87] C Sharp, 'Will the 'Real' Justice Please Stand Up? How Australian Public Perception of Justice is Transformed through Stories' (Pilot research undertaken in 2009 funded by a University of Wollongong

the various ways in which students respond to and use television stories to construct identity, attitudes and expectations. As such, the primary method of gaining access to this transformation of meaning was through the use of focus groups, conducted with first-year students. The central methodological aim was to present opportunities for new students to talk informally about television lawyers and to explore from their perspective what it meant to 'be' a lawyer. As a way of gaining insight into the transformed and shared meanings of students, focus group discussions of television lawyers provided a mechanism for students' story articulation and development in a mutually stimulative and spontaneously reactive environment. Of particular concern to me were the ways in which first-year students use popular legal narratives to produce their own stories, not only to articulate and describe their current aspirations and expectations of a career in law, but also to interpret and construct ethical awareness and legal identity.[88]

Such an ethnographic approach facilitated access to students' shared (and contested) understandings and perceptions, and for the exploration of how they structure and give meaning to their lives in relation to their future careers.[89] The choice of using focus groups in this research under the broad banner of ethnography was therefore based firmly on the rationale that a rich exploration into viewer perceptions, understandings and expectations could not be adequately achieved through simply the 'snapshot' approach provided by quantitative surveys or questionnaires. Instead, the complexity of a student's meaning-making process demanded an in-depth approach to the ways in which they draw on legal dramas on television as part of their identity construction.

Indeed, the research demonstrated that students used fictional legal television as a springboard for both referential and critical use.[90] The pilot study revealed that despite an overwhelming sense of participant acknowledgement that the representations of television lawyers are not realistic, students nonetheless used them for projections of what they aspire to and expect from a legal career.[91] In addition, the pilot study demonstrated that at the beginning of their legal education they are

---

Research Committee Small Grant, research on file with author. This particular project deploys focus groups to facilitate conversations about the efficacy of justice within our legal system).

[88] See further C Sharp, '"Represent a Murderer? I'd never do that ..." How Students Use Stories to Link Ethical Development and Identity Construction' in M Robertson et al (eds), *The Ethics Project in Legal Education* (Routledge, 2010); see also C Sharp, 'Scarlet Letter or Chastity Belt? What Legal Dramas of the Twenty-first Century are Telling Law Students about a Career in Law' (2002) 5 *Legal Ethics* 90–102.

[89] 'The analysis of qualitative data allows researchers to discuss in detail the various social contours and processes human beings use to create and maintain their social realities': B Berg, *Qualitative Research Methods for the Social Sciences* (US, Allyn and Bacon, 2001) 7.

[90] Viewers may use the programme referentially as a connection to real life (including their own), utilising it to form expectations and ideas about certain aspects of their lives, or they may use it more critically by showing an 'awareness of the program as separate from reality and concerning themselves with the accuracy of that relationship'. Of course, 'a sophisticated viewer should be seen as a commuter between the referential and the critical': Liebes and Katz, 'On the Critical Abilities of Television Viewers' in Ellen Seiter et al (eds), *Remote Control: Television Audiences and Cultural Power* (1989) 209. Indeed, the data from the primary study revealed that law students constantly commute between the two realms. For example, they make 'critical' statements about the stereotyping of, say, B Donnell on *The Practice* as an assertive male lawyer; and in the next breath speak 'referentially' as if he were real, and personally react to his behaviour as if the show were actually a documentary: see further Sharp, 'Changing the Channel'(n 86) 185–99.

[91] Sharp, 'Scarlet Letter or Chastity Belt?' (n 88) 90–102.

constructing a professional legal identity for themselves that is interested in status and social standing, yet is also committed to notions of altruism.[92] Using the same focus group methods, the primary study also demonstrated the value of ethnographically approaching audience use by exploring student critique of fictional legal television. It was through the interactive discussion within the focus groups that students constantly identified and criticised themes, messages and dramatic function within the narrative in order to critique the portrayal of 'reality' in the various programmes. In relation to this study, I have argued that first-year law students utilise discussions of television lawyers to take part in a type of self-reflection that they might not otherwise have the time or the inspiration to do, and more specifically that legal education should better harness these abilities (by emulating mutually stimulative focus group discussions) in order to encourage students towards self-awareness and identity construction within the larger legal community.[93]

Indeed, notions of identity and the transformation of self have been the dominant concerns in my research with law students. In seeking to engage with the student viewer as a specific cultural entity, I found that empirical methods, such as focus groups, interviews and observations, do have the potential of enabling a full exploration of the types of responses an audience may have to law on television. By discussing their views on the stories of law portrayed on contemporary television, audience members share and transform meaning about the practice of law. It is argued that through such dialogue it is possible to qualitatively explore the ways viewers construct understandings about law. It is further argued that not only do focus groups allow access to this process of transforming and sharing meaning, but they also establish a mechanism for opinion formation. The focus group environment is mutually stimulative and encourages discussion, allowing points of view to be expressed in a spontaneous and reactive process of meaning-making.

A. Researching the Television Audience: The 'Active Audience' Paradigm

The use of focus groups as an ethnographic method is grounded in epistemological assumptions of audience research that recognise the individual's active production and transformation of meaning within their cultural experiences. Television is a polysemic text and the range of meanings it contains can be realised by actual readers as they come to the text.[94] The process of making meaning is largely interpretive, and in terms of audiences we cannot simply isolate a meaning that an audience will produce from watching a programme. Rather we need to explore the meaning that is produced and transformed in the interplay between text and reader. This focus on meaning rather than effects is the basis of the 'active audience' paradigm that squarely shifts the emphasis from the clinic to the living room.[95] Hall's seminal encoding/decoding model heralded a paradigmatic shift away from behaviourism and emphasised the

---

[92] Ibid.
[93] Sharp, 'Changing the Channel' (n 86) 185–99.
[94] Barker, *Cultural Studies* (n 63) 11.
[95] Gies, 'Law and the Media' (n 13) 70.

'possibility of audience resistance in the process of making sense of the media'.[96] So, as 'readers' of legal television shows, viewers create and transform meaning. Barker argues that there is now enough work on television audiences within the cultural studies tradition to conclude that the 'audience is conceived of as active and knowledgeable producers of meaning not products of a structured text' and that 'audiences make application of the meaning to their lives'.[97]

Importantly, rather than being seen as cultural dopes, audiences are now recognised as active producers of meaning from within a cultural context of their own.[98] Watching television is seen as a cultural and social activity and although authors may have a message or theme that they want to communicate, viewers nevertheless decode the meaning for themselves and transform it through the use they make of it in their lives. The legal stories on television provide opportunities to contribute to an individual's expectations and attitudes in relation to lawyers. The various characterisations of lawyers in the show will convey certain messages that are transformed and renegotiated into ideas, attitudes and perceptions by the viewer.

B. What to do with Viewer 'Talk'?

Once ethnographic methodologies have been implemented to access the talk of active viewers, the analysis can be conducted via two methods. The first is philosophically based in hermeneutics and concentrates on the interactive relationship between text and audience,[99] whereby the reader is taken to approach the text with 'certain expectations and anticipations ... [that] are modified in the course of reading to be replaced by new "projections"'.[100] This perspective supports the use of focus groups because it recognises the individual transformative process and allows for the exploration of viewer interpretations of the television stories. It involves an interpretive literary analysis where the discussion or 'talk' becomes the text from which to unpack the understandings of viewers. In this sense, the argument is not so much about *how* the television stories *influence* or *affect* understandings, as it is about the exploration of viewer responses to television lawyers and how this informs their understanding of law in the everyday world. The value of interpreting this talk is not found in

> giving an 'objective' and 'totalising' account of their lives ... Rather its value lies in exploring the resources of language, and the consequences of the specific organisation of discourse, which [viewers] bring to bear.[101]

---

[96] Ibid; S Hall, 'Encoding/Decoding' (n 63).

[97] Barker, *Cultural Studies* (n 63) 269–70. Barker refers to McAnany and La Pastina, 'Telenovela Audiences' (1994) 21 *Communication Research*.

[98] Barker, *Cultural Studies* (n 63) 269. Morley's extensive body of empirical work as evaluated and reconceptualised in D Morley, *Television, Audiences and Cultural Studies* (n 33) which also centres on this notion of the active audience.

[99] See also H Gadamer, *Philosophical Hermeneutics* (New York, Oxford University Press, 1977) and W Iser, *The Act of Reading: A Theory of Aesthetic Response* (Baltimore, Johns Hopkins University Press, 1980).

[100] Barker, *Cultural Studies* (n 63) 271.

[101] Barker and J Andre, 'Did you See? Soaps, Teenage Talks and Gendered Identity' (Nov 1996) 4 *Young* 23.

As such, the transcripts of their text are seen as an interactive and social narrative that transforms events and ideas into story:

> The narrative consists of the cumulative effects of these separate stories as their aggregate meaning comes to light. By organising discrete stories and constructing their 'point', narrative ... represents one collective way of knowing things, one communal way ... [of] grasping the world.[102]

The interpretation of this narrative provided could therefore be conducted using coding strategies aimed at exploring various themes and categories of issues relevant to the transformation of meaning among viewers.[103] As a narrative signifies a broad enterprise that involves both the reception and production of stories,[104] it is a way in which viewers actively experience transformation of meaning. That is, by discussing their responses to popular law stories, viewers can provide insight into the uses they make of the television narratives and concomitantly learn about their own beliefs, values, dreams and fears.[105]

In acknowledging the narrativity of the viewer discussions, a second method could be used to augment the hermeneutic analysis described above. Critical discourse analysis is a tool used 'to demonstrate the place of language in the constitution and regulation of cultures and cultural identities',[106] and acknowledges that the 'talk' of the groups is discursively constructed through language. This technique involves identifying a number of aspects of language that can be systematically identified in the data[107] to identify socially shared understandings and explore the occurrence of discourse as a constitutive part of its local context. In this sense, the talk is understood 'not as representing pre-formed ideas but as formative of them in the context of constructing and maintaining social relationships'.[108] Discourse analysis is therefore used to enrich understandings of how viewers perceive themselves culturally, ethically and socially, and to explore the process of meaning production that is part of their continual negotiation within the legal world. I employed this method in my research of law students in order to delve deeper into the transformative process that first-year students are experiencing. For example, it placed a spotlight on the way various linguistic elements exposed the subtle and nuanced ways in which first-year law students are participating in an ongoing process of ethical development. Using discourse analysis, I argued that students use legal narratives on fictional television as a stimulus for talking through their moral positions and that such talk both explicitly and implicitly illustrates the deep connections between personal ethics and self-identity.[109]

---

[102] J Baron and J Epstein, 'Is Law Narrative?' (Winter, 1997) 45 *BLR* 141, 148.

[103] For an example of particular coding strategies see Liebes and Katz, *The Export of Meaning* (n 33); and Sharp, *Becoming a Lawyer: The Transformation of Student Identity Through Stories* (University of Wollongong, PhD Thesis, 2007).

[104] Baron and Epstein, 'Is Law Narrative?' (n 102) 147.

[105] It is in narrative, which 'suggests a whole world of experience', that we learn these things: Elkins, 'On the Emergence of Narrative Jurisprudence: The Humanistic Perspective Finds a New Path' (1985) 9 *LSF* 123, 135.

[106] Barker and D Galasinski, *Cultural Studies and Discourse Analysis: a Dialogue on Language and Identity* (London, Sage Publishing, 2001) 27.

[107] For example, rhetorical devices and linguistic elements.

[108] Barker and Andre, 'Did you See?' (n 101) 23.

[109] See further C Sharp 'Represent a Murderer?' (n 88).

Each method of data collection and analysis described in this part of the chapter recognises that socio-legal audience research is primarily about exploring social and cultural occurrences as regards meaning-making. This has the potential to inspire further ethnographic engagement with the viewer, and it is this issue that dominates the last section of this chapter.

III. Looking for Inspiration?

Emphasising the importance of exploring how the members of a group or culture understand and attach meaning to things, ethnography is concerned to 'grasp the native's point of view' in relation to how they view the world.[110] From a qualitative perspective the advantages to ethnography are therefore substantial. The method provides access to the ways in which members of a culture perceive their reality and to the ways they attach meanings to their experiences. It aspires to develop and/or test theories, and it can present holistic *descriptions* of the processes that underlie the social realm as it naturally exists.

Yet, in seeking these objectives, it must be recognised that, just as the members of the group construct their social world, the ethnographer's interpretation will also be a *construction*.[111] There is no way that this construction can be neutral or objective in order to describe things as 'they really are'.[112] From within this 'interpretive maze we produce communicative and interpretative achievements [of television and television talk], but not a picture of "reality", for we are engaged in producing that reality'.[113] That is, just as the viewers' discussions are a discursive construction, the description of this talk is also a result of the researcher's discursive interpretation. Thus, an acknowledgment of reflexivity must be inherent within ethnography:

> Ethnographers, like others, interpret social events and are an integral part of the social world they seek to describe. They have no super-human privileged understanding of the social world that is 'objective' and immune to the influence of past experience.[114]

This means that we can view ethnography as producing an acculturated understanding, which requires the researcher to acknowledge the inevitable influence of 'self' on the interpretation process. That is, if the analysis is to be shaped by the researcher's

---

[110] B Malinowski, *Argonauts of the Western Pacific: An Account of Native Enterprise and Adventure in the Archipelagoes of Melanesian New Guinea* (New York, E P Dutton & Co, 1922) 25, quoted in Denscombe, *The Good Research Guide* (n 80) 69.

[111] Drawing on A Giddens' use of the term 'double hermeneutic', Barker describes this process as involving the participants' interpretations and my interpretation of their talk: Barker, Chris, 'Television and the Reflexive Project of the Self: Soaps, Teenage Talk and Hybrid Identities' (1997) 48(4) *British Journal of Sociology* 611; see further Giddens, Modernity and Self-Identity (California, Stanford University Press, 1991); see also Barker and Andre, 'Did you See?' (n 101) 21, 23.

[112] Note that this is the limitation (or some would argue impossibility) of realist epistemology: see further J Clifford and G Marcus (eds), *Writing Culture, The Poetics and Politics of Ethnography* (Berkeley, University of California Press, 1986), which is a critique of the epistemology of ethnography from within ethnography.

[113] Barker and Andre, 'Did you See?' (n 101) 23.

[114] Denscombe, *The Good Research Guide* (n 80) 74.

own cultural competencies, then her assumptions, views and positions need to be made transparent.[115] Although reflexivity in ethnography is often criticised, the active interpretive role of the researcher does not diminish the validity of the project:

> Rather than a presumption that there must be, in theory at least, one correct explanation, it allows for the possibility that different researchers might reach different conclusions, despite using broadly the same methods.[116]

It is a key strength of qualitative methods that holistic explorations focusing on processes and relationships can be interpreted as part of a context rather than describing an abstract concept in isolation.[117] Glaser and Strauss approach the analysis of qualitative data as quite distinct from purely descriptive studies that present such data 'as found', or as a snapshot of a social phenomena. They do not accept the notion that qualitative data can be left to 'speak for themselves'.[118] Thus it is through the methodological explanations behind analytic choices and the constant checking and progressive refinement of the analytic process that enables empirical research to be justified as a voyage of discovery into the broad framework of a viewer's everyday experiences.

Gies argues that recognition of a legal consciousness, 'which firmly situates the law at the heart of everyday life', could provide a very useful connection between audience research and questions about how people use the media in their understanding of the law.[119] Gies calls this a constructionist approach to audience research that, unlike media-centred analysis, acknowledges that people make sense of the world by relying on 'a potentially unlimited range of experiences and narratives, only a limited proportion of which may be located in the media'.[120] This approach is key to understanding that when people engage with the popular culture, they carry with them an enormous amount of ideological baggage, which will have been distilled from a number of broad and eclectic sources.[121] Such an approach aligns snugly with advocates of ethnography. A focus on meaning is an integral role of culture, which

> is not so much a set of *things*—novels and paintings or TV programmes and comics—as a process, a set of *practices*. Primarily, culture is concerned with the production and the exchange of meanings—'the giving and taking of meaning'—between the members of a society or group.[122]

---

[115] For a critique of ethnography along these lines, see generally Clifford and Marcus, *Writing Culture* (n 112). For a discussion and critique of the view that ethnography 'is produced by the collision of two social worlds' see J Radway, 'Ethnography among Elites: Comparing Discourses of Power' (1989) 13 *JCI*. Radway has used ethonography to explore reader responses to and uses of romance novels and book-of-the-month club books: Radway, 'Reading the Romance: Women, Patriarchy, and Popular Literature' (1985) 14 *Politics and Society*; Radway, 'The Book-of-the-Month Club and the General Reader: On the Uses of "Serious" Fiction' (1988) 14 *Critical Inquiry*.

[116] Denscombe, *The Good Research Guide* (n 80) 221.

[117] Ibid.

[118] Ibid 215, referring to Glaser and Strauss, *The Discovery of Grounded Theory* (Chicago, Aldine Publishing Co, 1967).

[119] Gies, 'Law and the Media' (n 13) 74.

[120] Ibid 72.

[121] Ibid; Asimow et al, 'Perceptions of Lawyers' (n 40) 407.

[122] S Hall (ed), *Representation: Cultural Representations and Signifying Practices* (London, Sage Publishing, 1997) 2.

To view culture in this way—as that which we carry around inside us in order to interpret the world in a meaningful way[123]—is to acknowledge that the practice of viewing television is interpretive in nature. The study of audiences then becomes more about the interpretive community within which viewing occurs, and less about the specific media text: 'it is the socio-cultural background of people, and not the media products they consume, which is seen as a more reliable predictor of how individuals construct social meaning'.[124]

Barker has remarked that ethnography should become 'less an expedition in search of 'the facts' and more a conversation between participants in a research process'.[125] In this way, ethnographic methodologies enable researchers to access the rich and complex processes that comprise an individual's lived experience as expressed through that conversation. It has been argued in this chapter, that by exploring the discursive constructions of experience it is possible to make some sense of the ways in which viewers see the legal world and their place within it.

The deployment of ethnographic methods in audience research is a newer avenue for investigation that is only now gaining some momentum. By understanding that viewers will use popular culture, or more specifically television narratives, as one of the many cultural resources through which they will construct meaning, legal researchers could begin to 'provide an antidote for blunt and generalising statements about media influence'.[126] It is argued that recognising law as constitutive of everyday life,[127] and acknowledging that what is important is not what people *know* about the law, but how they *use* it to construct and transform meaning, is the way forward for contemporary explorations of television audience research. Although ethnography may be more time consuming and unfamiliar to some, it has overwhelmingly been my experience that the benefits of gaining a richer exploration into viewers' construction of meaning far outweigh any trepidation, and can supplement and enhance the growing literature in this field.

References

Allen, R (ed), *To Be Continued ... Soap Opera Around the World* (Oxford, Taylor & Francis, 1995).
Ang, I, *Living Room Wars* (London, Routledge, 1996).
—— *Watching Dallas: Soap Opera and the Melodramatic Imagination* (London, Routledge, 1985).
Asimow, M, 'Divorce in the Movies: From the Hays Code to *Kramer v Kramer*' (2000) *Legal Studies Forum* 24.
—— 'Embodiment of Evil: Law Firms in the Movies' (2001) *UCLA Law Review* 48
—— 'Law and Popular Culture: Bad Lawyers in the Movies' (2000) *Nova Law Review* 24.
—— et al, 'Perceptions of Lawyers—A Transnational Study of Student Views on the Image of Law and Lawyers' (2005) *International Journal of the Legal Profession* 12 (3).

---

[123] Ibid 17.
[124] Gies, 'Law and the Media' (n 13) 72.
[125] Barker, *Cultural Studies* 29.
[126] Gies, 'Law and the Media' (n 13) 72.
[127] '[T]he ethnographic tradition of law in everyday life, which clearly adopts a constitutive approach, regards law and something that is deeply embedded in people's consciousness. Consciousness, not knowledge seems to be the crucial issue': ibid 75.

Barker, C, '"Cindy's a Slut": Moral Identities and Moral Responsibility in the "Soap Talk" of British Asian girls' (1998) *Sociology* 32, 1.

—— *Cultural Studies: Theory and Practice* (London, Sage Publications, 2000).

—— and Andre, J, 'Did you See? Soaps, Teenage Talks and Gendered Identity' (1996) *Young* 4:4.

—— and Galasinski, D, *Cultural Studies and Discourse Analysis: a Dialogue on Language and Identity* (London, Sage Publishing, 2001).

Baron, JB and Epstein, J, 'Is Law Narrative?' (Winter, 1997) *Buffalo Law Review* 45.

Berets, R, 'Changing Images of Justice in American Films' (1996) *Legal Studies Forum* 20.

Berg, B, *Qualitative Research Methods for the Social Sciences* (US, Allyn and Bacon, 2001).

Bergman, P and Asimow, M, *Reel Justice: The Courtroom Goes to the Movies*, 2nd edn (Missouri, Andrew McMeels, 2006).

Brooks, JP, 'Will Boys Just be Boyz'N the Hood? African American Directors Portray a Crumbling Justice System in Urban America' (1997) *Oklahoma City University Law Review* 22.

Bryant and Zillman (eds), *Media Effects: Advances in Theory and Research* (New Jersey, Lawrence Erlbaum Associates, 2002).

Caplow, S. 'Still in the Dark: Disappointing Images of Women' (1999) *Women's Rights Law Reporter* 20, 2/3.

Chase, A, 'Lawyers and Popular Culture: A Review of Mass Media Portrayals of American Attorneys' (1986) *American Bar Foundation Research Journal* 11(2).

—— *Movies on Trial* (New York, The New Press, 2002).

Clifford, J and Marcus, G (eds), *Writing Culture, The Poetics and Politics of Ethnography* (Berkeley, University of California Press, 1986).

Corcos, CA, 'Women Lawyers' in RM Jarvis and PR Joseph (eds), *Prime Time Law: Fictional Television as Legal Narrative* (California, California Academic Press, 1998) 19.

Denscombe, M, *The Good Research Guide for Small-scale Research Projects* (UK, Open University Press, 1998).

Denvir, J, 'Law, Lawyers, Film and Television' (2000) *Legal Studies Forum* 24.

—— (ed), *Legal Reelism: Movies as Legal Texts* (Illinois, University of Illinois Press, 1996).

Elkins, JR, 'On the Emergence of Narrative Jurisprudence: The Humanistic Perspective Finds a New Path' (1985) *Legal Studies Forum* 9(2).

—— 'Reading/Teaching Lawyer Films' (Summer, 2004) *Vermont Law Review* 28.

Eschholz, S, 'The Media and the Fear of Crime: A Survey of the Research' (1997) 9 *U FLA JL & PUB POL'Y* 37.

Friedman, LM, 'Law, Lawyers and Popular Culture' (Summer, 2004) *Vermont Law Review* 28, 813.

Gadamer, H, *Philosophical Hermeneutics* (New York, Oxford University Press, 1977).

Geertz, C, *The Interpretation of Cultures: Selected Essays* (New York, Basic Books, 1973).

Geraghty, *Women and Soap Opera* (UK, Polity Press, 1991).

Gerbner, G, 'Growing up with Television: the Cultivation Perspective' in Bryant and Zillman (eds) *Media Effects*, 2002.

Giddens, Anthony. *Modernity and Self-Identity* (California, Stanford University Press, 1991).

Gies, L, 'Law and the Media: the Future of an Uneasy Relationship' in S Greenfield and G Osborn (eds), *Readings in Law and Popular Culture* (Oxon, Routledge-Cavendish, 2008) 65.

Gillers, S, 'Popular Legal Culture: Taking L.A. Law More Seriously' (1989) *Yale Law Journal* 98.

Goidel, RK, Freeman, CM and Procopio, ST, 'The Impact of Television Viewing on Perceptions of Juvenile Crime' (2006) *Journal of Broadcasting & Electronic Media* 50(1).

Greenfield, S, 'Hero or Villian? Cinematic Lawyers and the Delivery of Justice' (2001) *Journal of Law and Society* 28, 1.

Greenfield, S, Osborn, G and Robson, P, *Film and the Law* (London, Cavendish Pub, 2001).

Gunn, DL (ed), *The Lawyer and Popular Culture: Proceedings of a Conference* (Colorado, Fred B Rothmann & Co, 1993).

Hall, S (ed), *Representation: Cultural Representations and Signifying Practices* (London, Sage Publishing, 1997).

—— 'Encoding/Decoding' in S Hall, et al (eds), Culture, Media, Language (London, Routledge, 1981).

Harding, RM, 'Celluloid Death: Cinematic Depictions of Capital Punishment' (1996) *University of San Francisco Law Review* 30.

Iser, W, *The Act of Reading: A Theory of Aesthetic Response* (Baltimore, Johns Hopkins University Press, 1980).

Jackson, C, 'Film and TV Legal Drama Commentary' (2000) *Legal Studies Forum* 24.

Keetley, D, 'Law and Order' in R Jarvis and P Joseph (eds), *Prime Time Law: Fictional Television as Legal Narrative* (California, California Academic Press, 1998).

Kitei, B, 'The Mass Appeal of the Practice and Ally McBeal: An In-Depth Analysis of the Impact of These Television Shows on the Public's Perception of Attorneys' (1999) *UCLA Entertainment Law Review* 7.

Lenz, TO, *Changing Images of Law in Film and Television Crime Stories* (New York, Peter Lang, 2003).

Liebes, T and Katz, E, *The Export of Meaning. Cross-Cultural Readings of Dallas* (New York, Oxford University Press, 1993).

Livingstone, S, *Making Sense of Television: the Psychology of Audience Interpretation* (London, Routledge, 1998).

Lurvey I and Eiseman, S, 'Divorce Goes to the Movies' (1996) *University of San Francisco Law Review* 30.

Macaulay, S, 'Popular Legal Culture: An Introduction' (1989) *Yale Law Journal* 98.

Machura, S and Robson, P, *Law and Film* (London, Cavendish, 2001).

Malinowski, B, *Argonauts of the Western Pacific: An Account of Native Enterprise and Adventure in the Archipelagoes of Melanesian New Guinea* (New York, E P Dutton & Co, 1922).

Malloy, RP, 'Symposium on the Images of Law(yers) in Popular Culture: Introduction' (Fall, 2003) *Syracuse Law Review* 53.

Marek, J, 'The Practice and Ally McBeal: A New Image for Women Lawyers on Television?' (1991) *Journal of American Culture* 22, 1.

Marshall, C and Rossman, GB, *Designing Qualitative Research*, 3rd edn (London, Sage Publishing, 1999).

Meyer, PN, 'Desperate for Love: Cinematic Influences upon a Defendant's Closing Argument to a Jury' (1994) *Vermont Law Review* 18.

—— 'Desperate for Love II: Further Reflections on the Interpretation of Legal and Popular Storytelling in Closing Arguments to a Jury in a Complex Criminal Case' (1996) *USFL Rev* 30.

—— 'Desperate for Love III: Rethinking Closing Arguments as Stories' (1999) *SC Law Review* 50.

—— 'Why a Jury Trial is More Like a Film than a Novel' (2001) *Journal of Law and Society* 28.

Moran, LJ et al (eds), *Law's Moving Image* (London, Cavendish, 2004).

Morley, D, *Television, Audiences and Cultural Studies* (London, Routledge, 1992).

Podlas, K, 'Broadcast Litigiousness: Syndi-Court's Construction of Legal Consciousness' (2005) *Cardozo Arts and Entertainment Law Journal* 23.

—— 'Guilty on All Accounts: "Law & Order's" Impact on Public Perception of Law and Order' (2008) *Secton Hall Journal of Sports and Entertainment Law* 1.

—— 'Impact of Television on Cross-Examination and Juror "Truth"' (2008–09) *Widener Law Review* 14.

—— 'The CSI Effect, Exposing the Media Myth' (2006) *Fordham Intellectual Property, Media and Entertainment Law Journal* 429.

Radway, J, 'Ethnography among Elites: Comparing Discourses of Power' (1989) *Journal of Communications Inquiry* 13(3).

—— 'Reading the Romance: Women, Patriarchy, and Popular Literature' (1985) *Politics and Society* 14(1).

—— 'The Book-of-the-Month Club and the General Reader: On the Uses of "Serious" Fiction' (1988) *Critical Inquiry* 14 (3).

Rapping, E, *Law and Justice as Seen on TV* (New York, NYU Press, 2003).

Robson, P, 'Developments in Law and Popular Culture: The Case of the TV Lawyer' in A Masson and K O'Connor (eds), *Representations of Justice* (New York, Peter Lang, 2007).

Rosen, RE, 'Ethical Soap: LA Law and the Privileging of Character' (1989) *University of Miami Law Review* 43.

Rosenberg, CB, 'An LA Lawyer Replies' (1989) *Yale Law Journal* 98.

Rotunda, RD, 'The Legal Profession and the Public Image of Lawyers' (1998–99) *The Journal of the Legal Profession* 23.

Salzmann, VS, 'Honey, You're no June Cleaver: The Power of "Dropping Pop" to Persuade' (2010) ME L Review 64, 241.

Scottoline, L, 'Law and Popular Culture: Get Off the Screen' (2000) *Nova Law Review* 24.

Shapiro, C, 'Women Lawyers in Celluloid: Why Hollywood Skirts the Truth' (1995) *University of Toledo Law Review* 25.

Sharp, C, *Becoming a Lawyer: The Transformation of Student Identity through Stories* (University of Wollongong, PhD Thesis, 2007).

—— 'Changing the Channel: What to Do with the Critical Abilities of Law Students as Viewers?' (2004) *Griffith Law Review* 13 (2), 185–99.

—— '"Represent a Murderer? I'd never do that ..." How Students use Stories to Link Ethical Development and Identity Construction' *The Ethics Project in Education* (Routledge, 2010).

—— 'Scarlet Letter or Chastity Belt? What Legal Dramas of the Twenty-first Century are Telling Law Students About a Career in Law' (2002) *Legal Ethics* 5 (1), 90–102.

—— 'The Extreme Makeover Effect of Law School: Students Being Transformed by Stories' (2005) *Texas Wesleyan Law Review* 12(1), 233–50.

Sherwin, R, 'Cape Fear: Law's Inversion and Cathartic Justice' (1996) *University of San Francisco Law Review* 30

—— *When the Law goes Pop: The Vanishing Line Between Law and Popular Culture* (Illinois, University of Chicago Press, 2000).

—— 'Law and Popular Culture' in A Sarat (ed), The Blackwell Companion to Law and Society (Blackwell, 2004) 101.

Shrum, LJ, 'Crime and Popular Culture: Effects of Television Portrayals of Crime and Violence on Viewers Perceptions of Reality: A Psychological Process Perspective' (1998) *The Legal Studies Forum* 22.

—— 'Effects of Television Portrayals of Crime and Violence on Viewers Perceptions of Reality' (1998) *Legal Studies Forum* 22.

Silbey, JM, 'What We Do When We Do Law and Popular Culture: Richard Sherwin, When Law Goes Pop' (2002) *Law and Social Inquiry* 27.

Silverstone, R, *Television and Everyday Life* (London, Routledge, 1994).

Spitz, DM, 'Heroes or Villians? Moral Struggles v Ethical Dilemmas: An Examination of Dramatic Portrayals of Lawyers and the Legal Profession in Popular Culture' (2000) *Nova Law Review* 24.

Strachenfeld, AJ and Nicholson, CM, 'Blurred Boundaries: An Analysis of the Close Relationship between Popular Culture and the Practice of Law' (1996) *University of San Francisco Law Review* 30.

Thornton, M, Romancing the Tomes: Popular Culture, Law and Feminism (London, Cavendish, 2002).

Uelmen, GF, 'The Trial as a Circus: Inherit the Wind' (1996) *University of San Francisco Law Review* 30.

Part II: Genre Studies

A. The Evolved Law TV Genres

6

Dark Justice: Women Legal Actors on Basic Cable

TAUNYA LOVELL BANKS

I. Introduction

Mid way through the first decade of the twenty-first century, two basic cable networks in the United States, FX and TNT, premiered law-related shows featuring tough, ambitious, ruthless and deeply flawed female leads. TNT's highly rated show, *The Closer*, which premiered in the summer of 2005, revolves around Deputy Chief Brenda Leigh Johnson, a former Georgia police detective who leads a special high-profile homicide division in Los Angeles.[1] In 2007 TNT began airing *Saving Grace*, a popular show featuring Grace Hanadarko as a heavy smoking, hard drinking and promiscuous Oklahoma City detective.[2] The show ran for three seasons.[3] The same year FX premiered *Damages*, a lawyer-focused show featuring the brilliant but amoral Patty Hewes, the head of a New York City law firm specialising in civil matters. In their professional lives these three tough women act like men. They fight for good causes while breaking or bending the rules in traditionally male domains. Like the strong cowboy heroes in American Westerns, these women are less successful with their personal relationships, preferring their heroic tasks over domesticity.

What is distinctive about the women on TNT and FX is that these networks have not simply replaced male characters with females. Rather, the character flaws and

---

[1] Since its premiere in 2005, *The Closer* has earned numerous ad-supported cable viewership records, ranking as the number one series of all time and scoring the number one series telecast of all time. For its fifth season, the show averaged 7.7 million viewers. 'TNT's *The Closer*, Ad Supported Cable's #1 Series of All Time, Return for Sixth Season Monday, July 12' *TVbytheNumbers* (9 June 2009), available at www.tvbythenumbers.com.

[2] For its first season in 2007, *Saving Grace* was ad-supported cable's top new series of the year. Last summer, the show averaged more than 3.7 million viewers and ranked as ad-supported cable's number one show in its time period among viewers, households and adults in the 25–54 age group. BWW News Desk, 'TNT's *Saving Grace* Starring Holly Hunter to Wrap March 29' *TalkTVworld* (1 March 2010), available at www.tv.broadwayworld.com.

[3] According to one report, the series ended in 2010 because TNT disagreed with the show's producer, Fox TV Studios, about how many episodes to produce: N Andreeva, '*Saving Grace* Will Wrap Next Summer' *The Hollywood Reporter,* 13 Aug 2009, available at www.hollywoodreporter.com.

behaviours displayed by Brenda, Grace and Patty are judged through a gendered lens. In other words, it is impossible to separate their gender from their characters. They do not simply morph into women playing men's roles. Although they appear to be anti-heroes in the traditional sense because of their 'fallibility and ... fundamentally flawed human nature(s)',[4] their flaws do not mimic those of their male counterparts.

Similarly, while the lead characters on *The Closer*, *Saving Grace* and *Damages* believe in gender equality and their actions often reflect strands of feminist philosophy, they are not feminists in the conventional sense of the term. Further, these shows may not owe their existence to pressure from interests groups like the Screen Actors Guild (SAG) or women's advocacy organisations for gender diversity in casting. Rather, market considerations influenced the creation of Patty, Grace and Brenda. In other words, and perhaps it is almost too obvious to mention, economic considerations and branding choices play an important role in the creation and marketing of legalistic television shows. Thus, this particular network focus seems to define and distinguish TNT and FX's legal-drama actresses from their mainstream commercial channel counterparts.

FX historically catered to men, but all references to male viewers stopped once the channel started its 'no box' campaign.[5] Today FX brands itself as a basic cable version of premier cable's HBO, a network that targets a more intellectual and affluent adult audience (between the ages of 18–34) than conventional commercial television.[6] Critics characterise FX's programmes as 'darkly unconventional'.[7] This desire to appeal to a larger and broader audience may also determine how female leads in traditional male roles deviate from conventional ideas about how women should behave. In contrast, TNT wants to, and does, appeal to a broader viewing audience.[8] Thus, TNT's female characters, while somewhat edgier, seem more conventional than the 'darkly unconventional' characters on FX.

---

[4] J Fitch, III, 'Archetypes on the American Screen: Heroes and Anti-Heroes' (2004) *Journal of Religion and Popular Culture* 2, available at www.usask.ca.

[5] According to one media watcher, FX intended to push boundaries and challenge present notions of heroes, fatherhood, the medical profession and the law. In effect, FX is trying to engrain its image in the psyche of the American people, while simultaneously taking artistic risks and expanding its audience base: S Elliot, 'Box? We Don't Need No Box' *New York Times: Media Decoder* (11 Dec 2007), available at www.mediadecoder.blogs.nytimes.com; 'It's Always Sunny on Our Channel, FX Tells Advertisers' *New York Times: Media Decoder* (7 Apr 2010), available at www.mediadecoder.blogs.nytimes.com.

[6] 'FX expanded its total viewership by 10% in 2009, making it No. 9 across all basic cable networks. Among advertiser-beloved 18 to 49-year-olds, FX grew its audience more than any other top 10 basic cable network. Rather than populate his schedule with a wide swatch of programs for all audiences, the FX chief has remained narrowly focused on reaching more mature audiences with darker themes and adult language': L Rose, 'At FX, There is Still No Box' (18 Jan, 2010) *Forbes: The Biz Blog* (18 Jan 2010), available at www.blogs.forbes.com.

[7] J Hibberd, 'FX Launches Major Branding Campaign', *Television Week* (17 Dec 2007), available at www.tvweek.com.

[8] TNT has a viewing audience that is twice the size of FX's audience.

Primetime	Average viewers	Adults 18–49-year-olds
USA	3,202,000	1,087,000
TNT	2,511,000	1,327,000
FX	1,060,000	564,000

B Gorman, 'USA Leads Cable Primetime Viewership: TNT Skies over Adults 18-49 Ratings' *TV by the Numbers* (18 May 2010), available at www.tvbythenumbers.com.

Historically the mass media tended to depict women in one of three ways, as mothers,[9] as sex objects subordinate to the desires of men,[10] or as vigilant feminists.[11] But television images of women have evolved over the past 20 years, reflecting changing contemporary standards about gender roles. Arguably, Grace, Brenda and Patty represent departures from even the newer, but nonetheless stereotypical, images portrayed by legal-drama actresses. First, they clearly are the leads of their shows, still somewhat unusual for females in television who, if they are lucky, usually share the lead billing with a male co-star.[12] Second, the actresses portraying these characters (Holly Hunter as Grace, Kyra Sedgwick as Brenda, Glenn Close as Patty) are acclaimed film stars over the age of 40. To find three older women lead characters on television crime or legal dramas is unusual even in the twenty-first century. According to the Screen Actors Guild, in 2001 there were 'nearly twice as many roles for performers younger than 40. Women over 40 [got] ... just 11 percent of the television and film parts'.[13] Thus the characters of Grace, Brenda and Patty at first glance represent an evolution of women's power and authority on the small screen—they are now playing primary heroic roles.

Media and legal scholars argue that mass media not only reflects and reinforces contemporary society norms,[14] but often also 'extends certain collectively-perceived norms about the world and lays out areas of cultural argumentation'.[15] Thus television series that stereotype women can be particularly damaging to the cause of substantive equality for women. Unlike big screen images, television images have a greater and long-lasting impact because characters evolve over a longer span of time, whether over several episodes or seasons of a show. There is anecdotal evidence that supports this cultural truth, consider, for example, the influence on hairstyles and dress-styles that shows like *Friends* had in the 1990s and the advent of cellular phones in the wake of shows like *Star Trek*. Television's influence is overwhelmingly obvious. Thus, critiques of media programming are important exercises in monitoring gender inequality in the United States.

This chapter examines the character portrayals of Patty Hewes, Grace Hanadarko and Brenda Leigh Johnson. It asks whether they represent a significant departure from the way American television traditionally depicts women lawyers and law enforcement officers, and whether their presence signals a change in America's psyche about women and their workplace roles in twenty-first century society. Finally, this chapter ends by asking whether the success of these shows will influence mainstream

---

[9] E Seiter, 'Feminism and Ideology: The Terms of Women's Stereotypes' (1986) 22 *Feminist Review* 67.

[10] T Higgins and D Tolman, 'Cultural Media[ation], and Desire in the Lives of Adolescent Girls' in M Fineman and M McCluskey (eds), *Feminism, Media and Law* (New York, Oxford University Press, 1997) 178.

[11] D Young, 'Introduction to Portrayals of Feminism' in ibid 7.

[12] R Owen, 'TV welcomes Over-40 Actresses as Never before to Play Series Leads' *Pittsburgh Post-Gazette: TV & Radio* (12 Aug 2007), available at www.post-gazette.com; L Brounstein, 'On Prime Time, Women Lead the Charge', *The Huffington Post* (18 Mar 2010), available at www.huffingtonpost.com.

[13] D Chmielewski, 'Actors, Lawmakers, AARP Tackle Ageism in Hollywood' *San Jose Mercury News* (2 Aug 2002).

[14] See, eg D Hess and G Grant, 'Prime-Time Television and Gender-Role Behavior' (1983) 10 *Teaching Sociology* 371; D Glass, 'Portia in Primetime: Women Lawyers, Television, and LA Law' (1990) *YJL&F* 371, 411.

[15] Glass, 'Portia in Primetime' (n 14) 411.

commercial television networks that cater to larger and broader audiences; and if so, whether the greater exposure of these seemingly evolutionary female images is a good or bad thing for gender equality in the United States.

II. Television Heroes and Anti-Heroes: One Feminist Perspective

'Hero' is an overtly masculine term. For more than half a century the male hero has been a staple of American television. A few masculinities scholars speculate that the pervasiveness of the mythic male (usually white) hero in American popular culture— films, books, music and television—stems from men's need to compensate for their insecurities about the meaning of heterosexual masculinity, especially in the post World War II era.[16] This explanation, the need for a stable model of heterosexual masculinity, explains why traditionally men have been the only characters capable of *real* heroism, even following the rise of the American feminist movement in the late 1960s and early 1970s. This reasoning might also explain why 'heroine', the female counterpart, has no separate meaning. It is 'a definition completely derivative of the masculine type'.[17] Even the adjective 'heroic', a seemingly gender-neutral term, is also inherently masculine.[18] Thus, heroines or women heroes are generally defined in the context of male behaviours, with little opportunity for self-definition.

But it is possible that, after more than 40 years of fast-paced cultural evolution, American women may also be experiencing similar anxieties about the meanings of heterosexual femininity. No matter what the strand of feminist legal theory, the discourse continues to be framed in a way that treats men either 'as oppressors, or as "other"'.[19] The failure of any significant cross-fertilisation between masculinities studies and feminist theory provides few opportunities to ponder the ways in which 'inequalities are complex and interlocking'.[20] Thus at the beginning of the twenty-first century legal scholars like Christine Coros discuss heroism solely in terms of men and women, paying no attention to how male identity is constructed or why men considered powerful by feminists might feel powerless.[21] Corcos argues that film and television disproportionately tend to portray male heroes and anti-heroes, as opposed to heroines or female anti-heroes, as attractive protagonists. 'Fawning females' surround male heroes, however flawed; whereas, women 'making the same choices are likely to be perceived as "not understanding" the sacrifices that the

---

[16] D Holt and C Thompson, 'Man-of-Action Heroes: The Pursuit of Heroic Masculinity in Everyday Consumption' (2004) *JCR* 425; B Traister, 'Academic Viagra: The Rise of American Masculinity Studies' (2000) *American Quarterly* 274.

[17] R Sparks, 'Masculinity and Heroism in the Hollywood "Blockbuster": the Culture Industry and Contemporary Images of Crime and Law Enforcement' (1996) 36 *TBJC* 348.

[18] Ibid.

[19] N Dowd, N Levit and A McGinley, 'Feminist Legal Theory Meets Masculinities Theory' in F Cooper and A McGinley (eds), *Masculinities and Law: A Multidimensional Approach* (New York, NYU Press, 2011) ssrn.com.

[20] Ibid 8.

[21] Ibid 5.

profession—"the game"—entails'.[22] She concludes that heroism is a decidedly male trait not because women necessarily behave differently than men, but because viewers see similar actions by women and men differently.

Often for the male characters on legal dramas, 'heroism may equate with moral integrity, political power and legal prowess, as well as traditional physical action'.[23] Thus these male figures on legal dramas, the ones who follow their own path or adhere to their own beliefs, are seen as heroic. In contrast, when female characters engage in the same sets of behaviours, they 'are repeatedly reminded that they will lose their colleagues' affection, not just their allegiance'.[24] Keeping in mind the cultural influence televisions wields, one finds here a steady diet of television programmes that discourage women from acting and thinking independently while simultaneously encouraging them to adhere to stereotypical gender roles.

Corcos acknowledges that a few films 'attempt to present a woman attorney as heroic without forcing her into the male model allowing her to reconcile her profession and her ethics'.[25] Tellingly, she cites no female television legal heroes. Clearly, Corcos is correct when she writes that women still have 'difficulty ... being viewed as ... significant player[s in crime and legal television dramas], let alone ... hero[es]... [because they] lack the opportunity to exert the power that accompanies the mastery of the law'.[26] Putting it simply, television show storylines continue to provide men with 'more opportunities to emerge as heroes'.[27] Thus, the presence of three women legal heroes on two basic cable networks is noteworthy and warrants closer scrutiny.

III. Women Law Enforcers: Brenda Leigh Johnson and Grace Hanadarko

Perhaps the most celebrated form of late twentieth century American heroism is what some scholars call the man-of-action hero. This hero 'embod[ies] the rugged individualism of the rebel while maintaining their allegiance to collective interests'.[28] In many ways the conventional law enforcement officer typifies the man-of-action

---

[22] CA Corcos, 'We Don't Want Advantages The Woman Lawyer Hero and Her Quest for Power in Popular Culture' (2003) 53 *Syracuse Law Review* 1225, 1229 (discussing women lawyers).

[23] Ibid 1228.

[24] Ibid 1229.

[25] Corcos acknowledges that a few lawyer films, notably *Legally Blonde*, *Adam's Rib* and *The Accused*, 'attempt to present a woman attorney as heroic without forcing her into the male model allowing her to reconcile her profession and her ethics': ibid 1232. Yet a closer examination of Corcos' examples reveals that each 'heroic' woman film lawyer prevails against injustice in ways that reinforce rather than refute sexual stereotypes. Two films involved 'women's issues'. In *Adam's Rib* Amanda Bonner wins her case, emasculating her husband/opponent in the process. See, L Grosshans, 'Accurate or Appalling: Representations of Women Lawyers in Popular Culture' 4 (2006) *CPLP&EJ* 457, 461–62. In *The Accused* the subject is rape. In the third film, *Legally Blonde*, Elle Woods prevails at trial because of her knowledge about hair perms, not legal principles or tactics. Thus these rare legal women heroes arise only in specific settings where their sex-specific empathy or expertise is required to secure justice.

[26] Corcos, *Advantages* (n 22) 1228.

[27] Ibid.

[28] Holt and Thompson, 'Man-of-Action Heroes' (n 16) 428.

hero. Heroism is one of the central values, if not the central value, in the culture of law enforcement. Today, American television crime dramas tend to portray the man-of-action hero as a rebel, a magnetic figure who 'threaten[s] the status quo and challenge[s] societal institutions'.[29]

Both Grace and Brenda, each law enforcement officers, have characteristics consistent with the man-of-action hero model. Brenda's character, however, seems the least evolved from the old gender-stereotypical images. She is brittle, frilly and demurely southern. Viewers quickly learn that she is gifted and outstanding at her job—closing murder cases, and in that sense an exception to the old stereotypes that question women's competencies in relation to traditionally male jobs. But rather than act like a man doing a man's job, Brenda embraces her feminine attributes, often playing the Southern belle to her advantage.

Yet Brenda is not a girly or girlie feminist, a third wave concept that rejects the notion that gender equality is inconsistent with women embracing their femininity.[30] Instead the character uses her femininity as a source of power, because acting like a man undercuts her authority by privileging masculinity as the only source of power. Further, Brenda is not a feminist, or even a strong proponent of women's equality, a point made clear when she resists having her name submitted as the 'woman' candidate for Police Chief by another female officer intent on promoting gender diversity within the police leadership.

Instead, Brenda is a fairly conventional deputy police chief. Her gender is the only thing that separates her from her male counterparts. She continually corrects people and harps about following procedure. This obsession with rules ultimately leads her co-workers and opponents to characterise her as a 'bitch'. Bitch is a derogatory term used to describe an aggressive, bitter and domineering woman.[31] In this sense Brenda's character is a benign version of the vigilant feminist stereotype, only she acts as though she lives in a post-feminist world. Although some twenty-first century feminists now use the word 'bitch' to describe women who have broken free of society's constraints on women,[32] Brenda's character does not fit their definition. Those feminists who claim to have redeemed and redefined 'bitch' define that word as indicating a woman who defies societal expectations and puts her needs in front of others.[33]

---

[29] Ibid.

[30] '[W]hat Girlies radiate is the luxury of self-expression that most Second Wavers didn't feel they could or should indulge in': S Mann and D Huffman, 'The Decentering of Second Wave Feminism and the Rise of the Third Wave' (2005) 69 *Science & Society* 56 (citing J Baumgardner and A Richards, *ManifestA: Young Women, Feminism and the Future* (New York, Farrar, Straus and Giroux, 2000) 161; I Karras, 'The Third Wave's Final Girl: Buffy the Vampire Slayer' (2002) 1 *ThirdSpace*, available at www.thirdspace.ca (Buffy the Vampire Slayer is the 'prototypical girly feminist'); N Adams, A Schmitke and A Franklin, 'Tomboys, Dykes, and Girly Girls: Interrogating the Subjectivities of Adolescent Female Athletes' (2005) 33 *WSQ* 17, 24 (acting feminine is seen as an affirmation of female heterosexuality).

[31] Joreen, 'The Bitch Manifesto' (1969) JoFreeman.com; Y Tamayo, 'Rhymes with Rich: Power, Law, and the Bitch' (14 Feb 2009) *Social Science Research Network*, www.papers.ssrn.com.

[32] V Renegar and S Sowards, 'Contradiction as Agency: Self-Determination, Transcendence, and Counter-Imagination in Third Wave Feminism' (2009) 24 *Hypatia* 1, 7, www.works.bepress.com: 'Some third wave feminist-oriented magazines take negatively connotative identity labels and problematize them by using them as terms of empowerment, such as the magazine *Bitch*. The creators and editors of this magazine use *bitch* to represent the feminist who is outspoken and assertive'.

[33] A male commentator writes about the pejorative use of the term: 'Bitch is a word we use culturally to describe any woman who is strong, angry, uncompromising and, often, uninterested in pleasing men.

For these feminists, mainly third-wavers, the word bitch implies power and control.[34] Bitch redeemed becomes the female equivalent of the male anti-hero, and that term's traditional attribute—defying societal expectations. As in the case of the male anti-hero, the rebellious character of the redeemed bitch has some qualities that cause viewers to identify with her internal struggles. Applying this definition, the character of Brenda fails to measure up. Brenda possesses many negative qualities associated with the typical anti-hero. She is selfish, judgemental, obsessive, insecure, bossy, and lacks empathy. But, unlike most anti-heroes, Brenda is also preoccupied with rules and proper procedure, which perhaps comes from her rule-bound southern upbringing. Brenda's character is a fairly stereotypical portrayal of professional women in a job formerly the exclusive domain of men.

In contrast, Detective Grace Hanadarko, who prefers fast cars, and jeans and boots over dresses or skirts, seems like a typical male anti-hero—a rebel with a flawed character willing to challenge an often unjust legal system.[35] Her heavy drinking and sexual promiscuity suggest the kind of deep character flaws usually attributed to men who perform heroic tasks often using 'methods, manners, or intentions that may not be heroic'.[36] She is willing, for example, to use 'tainted' evidence to secure the conviction of a suspected wrongdoer. Although she has the least power among the three female characters being considered, like typical male anti-heroes on shows like *Law and Order*, Grace regularly challenges authority in the name of justice, and prevails.

More interestingly, Grace is forgiven flaws that traditionally stigmatised and undermined women, but not men, who perform heroic tasks. Unlike conventional female protagonists, Grace's sexual promiscuity does not transform her into a slut.[37] Instead, there is something empowering and masculine about the sex on *Saving Grace*. As presented in the show's narrative arc, there is strength in surrendering to one's primal

We use the term for a woman on the street who doesn't respond to men's catcalls or smile when they say, "Cheer up, baby, it can't be that bad". We use it for the woman who has a better job than a man and doesn't apologize for it. We use it for the woman who doesn't back down from a confrontation'. See A Zeisler, 'The B-Word? You Betcha' *Washington Post* (18 Nov 2007), available at www.washingtonpost.com. The publishers of *Bitch Magazine* wrote 'in the magazine's mission statement, "If being an outspoken woman means being a bitch, we'll take that as a compliment, thanks"', ibid. The term is now used to describe certain types of feminist popular culture. M Sharratt writes that 'Bitch Lit is a smart and subversive celebration of female anti-heroes—women who take the law into their own hands, who defy society's expectations, who put their own needs first and don't feel guilty or get exterminated as a result!' in M Chowdhry and M Sharratt (eds), 'Introduction: Interview with the Editors, So What is Bitch Lit' in *Bitch Lit* (Croscus Books, 2006), www.marysharratt.com.

[34] For a discussion of Third Wave Feminism see Renegar Sowards, 'Contradiction as Agency' (n 32) 1.

[35] Holt and Thompson, 'Man-of-Action Heroes' (n 16) 425 (citing M Kimmel, *Manhood in America* (New York, Free Press, 1996)), use the term man-of-action hero. Another commentator claims that some alleged anti-heroes really aren't heroes, but simply 'anti-Establishment' heroes, 'a "primal man"'. Sparks, 'Masculinity and Heroism in the Hollywood "Blockbuster"' (n 17) 354 (citing David Bingham, *Acting Male: Masculinities in the Films of James Stewart, Jack Nicholson, and Clint Eastwood* (New Brunswick, Rutgers University Press, 1994) 186).

[36] 'Anti-hero: Encyclopedia', *All Experts*, www.en.allexperts.com; A heroine is a woman distinguished and venerated for her extraordinary courage, fortitude, or noble qualities: 'Heroine', as defined in L Brown (ed), *The New Shorter Oxford English Dictionary on Historical Principles* (Oxford, Oxford University Press, 1993).

[37] 'Slut' is defined in the Oxford English Dictionary as a dirty, slovenly woman, a loose woman. In the Urban dictionary, 'slut' is defined as having morals of a man. 'Slut, n', *OED*, dictionary.oed.com. A 'slut' is thought of as a person of low character that has multiple sexual encounters with different men because she lacks the ability to say no. 'Slut', *Urban Dictionary*, www.urbandictionary.com.

desires and doing so without regard to social conventions. Those third-wave feminists who criticise the ideological rigidity of a second-wave feminism, that does not 'allow for individuality, complexity, or less than perfect personal histories',[38] would approve.

To gain audience acceptance of her character, Grace's flaws must be feminised. Her drinking and promiscuity are explainable, the result of two traumatic events. She was attacked by a serial killer and allowed to live, and she also keeps the sexual abuse she suffered as a child at the hands of a priest a secret. Perhaps without these explanations for her rebellious behaviour, television audiences might resist embracing her character. Thus gender still colours how she is perceived, and may explain why the show's producers use Grace's story as a vehicle to discuss the topic of faith, and how difficult maintaining one's faith can be in an imperfect world. This religious twist gives the show a decidedly female appeal.

Grace has lost her faith and seems unable to heal from these traumatising life events. Thus Earl, her 'last-chance' angel, appears to her throughout the series, hoping she will turn away from her more self-destructive tendencies and seek God's help. Grace's anti-heroic determination to live in constant conflict rather than face her own flaws and damaged soul appeals to masculine values. Yet her underlying spiritual struggle is reminiscent of the mainstream commercial series *Touched by an Angel* and the family values movement.[39] That television series, which aired on CBS from 1994 to 2003, featured an angel named Monica who was assigned the task of guiding people at a crossroad in their lives by bringing them messages from God. The gently angelic Monica on *Touched by an Angel*, however, is a sharp contrast to Grace's unconventional angel Earl, a scruffy, tobacco-spitting man matching the gritty realism of the show's settings. In this respect *Saving Grace* is a cross-genre programme, part crime and part inspiration drama.

In true heroic style, Grace does not carry herself like a victim. Throughout the series she seems empowered by her desire to become an avenger for others who have been wronged, ultimately giving her life to save her community from evil, both literally and figuratively. The series ended in 2010 with Grace's heroic self-sacrifice, which she chooses to make in order to save her beloved Oklahoma City from another deadly explosion.[40] But before her sacrificial death she is 'reborn', literally emerging from a body of water healed.

In many respects the lead women on *The Closer* and *Saving Grace* are simply variations of the few earlier woman-led crime shows like *Police Woman* (1974–78) and *Cagney and Lacey* (1981–88). Like the earlier shows their contemporary counterparts on TNT reflect that network's desire to attract more female viewers.[41] TNT was successful. In 2008, for example, approximately 65 per cent of *The Closer*'s and

---

[38] C Snyder, 'What is Third-Wave Feminism? New Directions Essay' (2008) 34 *Signs* 175, 176.

[39] One media studies scholar argues that in the 1990s 'more explicit programs that challenged the traditional television image of family life, such as ... *Married with Children* and *Murphy Brown* ... produced a backlash ... One result has been the scheduling of more "family values" programs, such as ... *Touched by an Angel*, and the emergence of new "family friendly" networks'; S Craig, '*From Married ... with Children* to *Touched by an Angel*: Politics, Economics and the Battle Over "Family Values" Television', presented at 2001 Conference of the Popular Culture Association/American Culture Association, 13 April 2011.

[40] In 1995 the federal building in Oklahoma City, OK was bombed by American terrorists killing 168 people and injuring many more. This traumatic event is an important memory in *Saving Grace*.

[41] M Flaherty, 'Femme Influence Helps Shoot Down Police Brutality' *Variety* (17 Nov 2008) 413, 1:18.

Saving Grace's viewers were women.[42] Unlike the shows of the 1970s and 1980s, however, viewer popularity alone is not enough today to sustain them. DVD sales at home and abroad also are important. One reason given for ending *Saving Grace* after only three successful seasons was the show's inability to generate 'stronger international and ancillary revenue'.[43]

More than anything else the female lead characters in *The Closer* and *Saving Grace* reflect cable network marketing decisions. TNT continues to look for the right formula that will attract more women viewers and also generate other revenue. In fall 2010 the network premiered another woman-led crime show, *Rizzoli & Isles*, drawn from characters created by thriller writer Tess Gerritsen.[44] The show pairs a 'tomboy cop' and 'a fashion-late medical examiner' as Boston crime solvers. Although TNT's crime shows with women leads are a deliberate marketing gimmick, the presence of powerful women crimefighters also reflects what is happening in the real world. If TNT's formula is successful in retaining large audiences and producing substantial revenues, other networks will replicate them and these images will continue to evolve and compete with one another.

IV. Patty Hewes: Darkly Unconventional Heroic Lawyer?

Patty Hewes, the brilliant but amoral lawyer on FX's *Damages*,[45] stands apart from the others because she is the ultimate authority—a truly powerful woman. A high-stakes civil litigator who heads her own firm, Patty represents plaintiffs in class action lawsuits against powerful (male) defendants.[46] Like Brenda and Grace, Patty sees herself as a weapon of justice, a lethal opponent as signalled by the skulls in the show's opening credits. Like Grace, Patty acts and dresses like a man professionally, preferring pants over dresses and skirts. However, unlike in the cases of Grace and Brenda, or stereotypical anti-heroes who we like despite ourselves, viewers do not feel inclined to *like* Patty. She seems almost villainous in her eagerness to secure her brand of justice, perhaps a darker version of the vigilant feminist stereotype. But then an anti-hero can be 'someone with some qualities of a villain, up to and including brutality, cynicism and ruthlessness, but with the soul or motivations of a more conventional Hero'.[47]

On the surface Patty seems like a renegade hero, but rather than operate from outside the legal system, she is deeply embedded in one of society's most traditional legal

---

[42] Ibid.

[43] S Levine, 'TNT Cancels "Grace"' *Variety* (14 Aug 2009) 6,16.

[44] K Tucker, 'The Closer/Rizzoli & Isles' *Entertainment Weekly* (23 July 2010) 73–74.

[45] As late as 2002 only 16% of all women in the legal profession were partners in law firms even though 71% of all women lawyers are engaged in private practice; G Wilder and B Weingartner (eds), *Databook on Women in Law School and in the Legal Profession* (LSAC, 2003).

[46] F Moore, 'Financial Scandal Gives "Damages" Dramatic Payoff' *ABC News Entertainment* (5 Feb 2010), available at www.abcnews.go.com.

[47] 'What is an Antihero?' in *The Gallery of Antiheroes*, available at www.flowerstorm.net.

institutions, the big law firm with a civil practice. As the sole partner she controls the firm, making all the rules and eliminating the need to go outside the institution to secure justice. As a legal renegade who also owns a mainstream law firm, Patty is a bundle of contradictions. She is *sui generis*, a powerful woman in search of a label. In this sense she fits FX's branding as darkly unconventional. Still, there is little agreement about the character of Patty Hewes.

One critical commentator describes Patty as 'an ice-eyed trial lawyer and serpentine liar who disdains white-collar violence in favor of open sadism'.[48] But Glenn Close sees her character differently: 'Patty, for all her complications, doesn't like bullies ... [she] is not always manipulative; for the most part, she's on the side of doing good'.[49] Another commentator argues that Patty

> exacerbates the woman as lawyer stereotype by portraying her as 'the most "revered and reviled" civil litigator in the country ... a vicious trial lawyer who is driven to win cases ... [and who] resorts to "bullying and deception—and other possibly bloodier means—to ... win at all costs"'.[50]

Corcos argues that Patty is consistent with older television images of women lawyers who are seen as 'bitchy, arrogant, and unfeminine because they succeed in a male-dominated profession', citing Rosalind Shays (*L.A. Law*) and Ling Woo (*Ally McBeal*), and adding Karen Crowder in the 2007 legal thriller *Michael Clayton*.[51] At first glance her assessment seems well founded. However, closer scrutiny suggests Patty differs significantly from these earlier women lawyers.

From a feminist perspective, Patty is an interesting fusion of 'bitch' and anti-hero. She is aggressive and merciless, with an undeniable need to be in control at all times and an overwhelming distrust of everybody around her, attributes of male aggression, and virtues often found in heroes and anti-heroes. But aggressiveness is typically not considered a virtue in women. Thus Patty's characterisation as a strong woman, able to put aside societal pressures and do what needs to get done, is off-putting to some critics. The inability to classify Patty using conventional labels like hero, anti-hero, bitch or even redeemed bitch, perhaps illustrates the influence of third wave feminists and proponents of post-feminism.

One interesting debate among academics is not only over whether third-wave feminism is sufficiently distinguishable from second-wave feminism, but rather whether the goals of the late twentieth century feminist movement have been achieved.[52] A few

---

[48] M Raymond, 'On Legalistic Behavior, the Advocacy Privilege, and Why People Hate Lawyers' (2007) 55 *BLR* 929, 946 FN3 (citing V Heffernan, 'Me Fierce? It's All Make-Believe' *New York Times*, 22 July 2007 AR1.

[49] D Goldstein, 'FX Aims for HBO's Cachet' *Business Week* (19 Sept 2005), available at www.businessweek.com.

[50] W Hyland, Jr, 'Creative Malpractice: the Cinematic Lawyer' (2008) *TRESL* 231, 267.

[51] C Corcos, '*Damages:* The Truth is Out There' in M Asimow (ed), *Lawyers in Your Living Room: Law on Television* (Chicago, ABA Press, 2009) 265. According to Corcos, the counter older image is a woman lawyer 'easily intimidated, overly feminine, or not quite smart enough, like A Perkins on *LA Law* and Reggie Love in *The Client*' ibid. For my critique of K Crowder, see T Banks, '*Michael Clayton*: Women Lawyers Betrayed—Again' in H Radner and Rebecca Stringer (eds), *Feminism at the Multiplex*, (Routledge 2011).

[52] A Piepmeier, 'Postfeminism vs. the Third Wave', *Electronic Book Review* (17 Mar 2006), available at www.electronicbookreview.com.

commentators wonder whether we live in an increasingly post-gender world. In other words, they wonder whether many young women no longer define themselves based on their gender.[53] This question is especially apt when the character of Patty Hewes is more closely scrutinised. For, how one judges Patty depends on one's perception of 'acceptable' female behaviour. In many ways her character builds on 'the initial success of [FX's] "white, middle-aged, male antihero" image on shows such as "The Shield" and "Rescue Me"',[54] but with a gendered twist. *Damages* appeals to the same audience— 'viewers from the coveted 18-49 demographic'.[55] The middle-aged Patty appeals to this demographic for the same reason as the characters on *The Shield* and *Rescue Me*. She embodies the desires of anxious Americans, male and female, who feel lost and powerless in the face of increasing corporate unaccountability and power. They long to have power and use it to strike back at all forms of injustice for the benefit of the larger society.

Patty seems modelled on real life renegade industrialist heroes, rugged individualists who nonetheless 'maintain[ed] their allegiance to [the] collective interests [of society]'.[56] The kind of hero who 'pay[s] no mind to ... conventions ... struggle[s] tenaciously against seemingly insurmountable forces, and improbably conquer[s] the establishment'.[57] The ratings success of *Damages*, with its the darkly unconventional female anti-hero, suggests that the anxiety attributed to men and the need for heroic figures may be more universal. Her gender seems less important than her ability to attain control and power in the name of justice. In this sense some might argue that Patty Hewes is the embodiment of post-feminism. While early twenty-first century popular culture celebrates feminism, some scholars argue that it does so 'in such a way as to suggest that the politics of feminist struggles are no longer needed'.[58] Arguably, the character of Patty Hewes might be invoked. Her presence on the small screen as a powerful, successful and independently wealthy woman is an indicator that women have arrived.

There are alternate explanations for Patty's character. In the past audiences tended to view women's behaviour through a gendered lens—the gendered glaze—expecting television women lawyers to 'behave in a certain way, face certain problems, and make certain choices'[59] that are different from their male counterparts. Today, just as the meaning of heterosexual masculinity has become destabilised, so has the meaning of heterosexual femininity, as reflected in discussions about third-wave versus second-wave feminism and post-feminism. In sum, Patty's character may be the first depiction of a truly evolutionary woman lawyer on the small screen. If so, the more pressing question is whether her presence is a positive sign for gender equality.

---

[53] See K Steagill, 'Seeking a Post-Gender Society' *The Michigan Daily* (17 Feb 2009), available at www. michigandaily.com; see also ibid.

[54] Hibberd, 'FX Launches' (n 7).

[55] H Lewis, 'Damages's Audience Much Larger than Ratings Would Indicate' *Business Insider* (18 Feb 2009), available at www.businessinsider.com.

[56] Holt and Thompson, 'Man-of-Action Heroes' (n 16) 428.

[57] Ibid.

[58] A McRobbie, 'Young Women and Consumer Culture: An Intervention' (2008) 22 *Cultural Studies* 531, 533.

[59] Corcos, *Advantages* (n 22) 1228.

V. New Images or Reconfigured Stereotypes?

Many critiques of televised female images by second-wave feminists focus on whether they reinforce older, limiting stereotypes about women's roles in formerly male professions.[60] These feminists might be uncomfortable with Grace's sexual promiscuity and masculine behaviours. Similarly, second-wave feminists would be critical that Brenda's overtly girlish character reinforces traditional stereotypes about women authority figures in traditionally male occupations. Christine Corcos' critique of Patty captures the concerns of this group of feminists: 'Patty', she writes, 'is the kind of person from whom the laws are designed to protect us'.[61]

On the other hand, third-wave feminists, many of the women watching these shows, might respond differently to these characters. Arguably, Brenda, Grace and Patty are reflections of third-wave feminism's diverse approaches to gender equality. In varying degrees all three characters engage in confrontational behaviour with authority figures. As Shugart, Waggoner and Hallstein write, 'Vigorous assertion of one's individuality ... is highly prized by third wavers, such that an "in-your-face," confrontational attitude can be described as a hallmark of the third wave'.[62] Third-wave feminists are also noted for 'embracing contradiction so that apparently inconsistent political viewpoints coexist'.[63] Thus these feminists might embrace, with little difficulty, the three distinct and contradictory images portrayed by the leading women on *The Closer*, *Saving Grace* and *Damages*.

Brenda, Grace and Patty represent new images of women, leading women who exercise power without excuse or hesitation. Yet they are not simply women who have been substituted for men. Rather, their images seem to disrupt the television crime and legal drama genres. Women viewers might analyse the significance of these images differently, based on generational, geographical and even ideological differences. Furthermore, even second-wave and third-wave feminists may disagree over whether Brenda, Grace and Patty advance the cause of women's equality, essentially demonstrating that there may be no single truth about these television characters.

Post-feminists might celebrate the appearance of these complex and contradictory female characters as signalling proof that gender is no longer a bar on the job. Brenda and Patty are in charge and Grace's immediate superior is a black woman. Any limitations these women experience on the job seem attributable to things other than their gender. As political scientist Carisa Showden argues:

> Post- and third-wave feminists seem to believe that because certain actions are open to both liberating and discriminatory readings, the liberating meaning (because it is the one they prefer) is dominant, or at least sufficient, to counterbalance the negative weight of the images

---

[60] See Glass, 'Portia in Primetime' (n 14); S Goldberg, 'Bar Girls? Images of Women Lawyers on TV Slowly Improving' (1988) 76 *ABA Journal* 41; J Mayne, 'Law and Primetime Feminism' (1988) 10 *Discourse* 30.

[61] Corcos, *Damages* (n 22) 272.

[62] H Shugart, C Waggoner, and D Hallstein, 'Mediating Third-Wave Feminism: Appropriation as Postmodern Media Practice' (2001) 18 *Critical Studies in Media Communication* 194, 195.

[63] Ibid 195.

they project. These new feminisms thus disaggregate cultural representations of women's bodies and choices from the political messages they have been tied to and the material effects that have resulted. This does not mean that one cannot engage in 'sexy dressing' and be a feminist, but it does mean that a lack of attention to context and power is not the same as the resistant disruption of heteronormative feminine gender.[64]

On the other hand, legal feminists like Nancy Dowd might respond that Brenda, Grace and Patty reflect the type of tensions and anxieties present in masculinities studies about gender roles in a rapidly changing world. After almost half a century of the gender equality movement in the United States, twenty-first century women are anxious about their role in their society and world. A more cynical argument is that the characters of Patty, Brenda and Grace represent how 'feminism is currently being appropriated and integrated into those aspects of neoliberal discourse (political and popular) that are explicitly directed to young women'.[65]

Finally, it may also be significant that a woman, Nancy Miller, was directly involved in the development of both TNT's *Saving Grace* and *The Closer*. Miller is the creator of *Saving Grace* and was a co-executive producer for *The Closer* during its first season.[66] In contrast, the creators and writers for FX's *Damages* are all male.[67] The implications are self-evident, and while it may be tempting to attribute one particular factor over others to the creation of these female crime and legal drama leads, they are the result of a complex and nebulous set of influences. The interplay of feminism, market considerations, branding choices, and women in positions of power within the television industry may all contribute to this influx of female characters that challenge the acceptable image of women on television.

VI. Conclusion

In the end the presence of Patty, Grace and Brenda on basic cable may say little about the image of lead actresses in legal dramas on television. TNT and FX may be using these powerful female characters as branding devices to attract a certain viewer demographic, thereby enhancing the economic fortunes of these networks. While early twenty-first century popular culture seems to celebrate women's equality, it does so 'in such a way as to suggest that the politics of feminist struggles are no longer needed'.[68] In response to this particularised appropriation of feminist ideology, some feminists genuinely fear that the commodification of feminism may ultimately harm women's equality. Arguably this may be what is happening with the programmes on TNT and FX that feature these seemingly unconventional women.

---

[64] Carisa R Showden, What's Political about the New Feminism? (2009) *Frontiers: A Journal of Women's Studies* 177–178.
[65] A McRobbie, 'A Response to Susie Orbach: On Generation and Femininity' (2008) *Studies in Gender and Sexuality* 239, 240.
[66] 'Nancy Miller' *IMDb*, available at www.imdb.com.
[67] 'Full Cast and Crew for *Damages*' *IMDb*, available at www.imdb.com.
[68] A McRobbie, 'Young Women and Consumer Culture: An Intervention' (2008) 22 *Cultural Studies* 531, 533.

On the other hand, basic cable has more freedom to experiment with programmes and characters than conventional commercial television, and this may explain why Patty, Grace and Brenda have appeared via this venue. Even so, Brenda and Grace are not radical departures from other portrayals of police officers on television. It is not merely their gender, but also the manner in which it is deployed on these shows, that distinguishes these characters from their earlier male counterparts. And further, in the end it may not matter how the more evolutionary character of Patty Hewes is portrayed on television because the American public 'is ambivalent about its lawyers'.[69] A 2002 survey commissioned by the American Bar Association, Section of Litigation, found 'little difference in confidence in lawyers between consumers who watch law related television programs (eg, *The Practice*, *Law and Order*, *Court TV*, *Judge Judy*, and *Ally McBeal*) and consumers who do not watch such programs'.[70] Patty's gender might be irrelevant because public ideas about lawyers do 'not just come from the media, personal experiences bear it out'.[71]

Television lawyers like Patty may simply reflect public attitudes about lawyers as unethical, driven to win at all costs and 'driven by profit and self-interest, rather than client interest':[72]

> High-profile legal cases capture our attention because they often tap into preexisting beliefs about lawyers and justice ... Respondents believe that the media perpetuates these negative perceptions of lawyers by focusing on the highly controversial cases that feed into the public belief system and by ignoring facts and stories that do not.[73]

Nevertheless, advocates for women's equality in the United States should remain watchful. For, as more evolutionary female leads begin to populate the small screen, empirical studies will be needed to gauge their impact on the women and men who watch them.

---

[69] L Shapiro & Assoc LLC, 'Public Perceptions of Lawyers: Consumer Research Findings' (2002) 13 *ABAJ* (April 2002), available at www.abanet.org 4; the public has less confidence in lawyers than it has in judges, physicians and the executive branch. Lawyers rank just below Congress and just above the media. Respondents felt that attorneys were knowledgeable and hard-working, but mercenary. Seventy-four per cent of respondents believed that 'lawyers are more interested in winning than in seeing that justice is served'. Sixty-nine per cent felt that 'lawyers are more interested in making money than in serving their clients'. Seventy-three per cent thought that 'lawyers spend too much time finding technicalities to get criminals released'; however, only a simple majority of 51% felt that 'we would be better off with fewer lawyers'. In addition to this unseemly behaviour, respondents don't believe that bad lawyers are held accountable for their actions. Only 26% said that 'the legal profession does a good job of disciplining lawyers ... [f]ifty-five per cent of respondents who may have needed a lawyer in the preceding year did not plan to hire one'. Note that this study took place in 2002. Given the recent economic downturn, that number might be even lower today.
[70] Ibid. (The study was based on a national survey of 450 households, 10 focus groups in five US markets, and a national survey of 300 households.)
[71] Ibid 9.
[72] Ibid 7.
[73] Ibid 12.

References

Books and Journals

Adams, N, Schmitke, A and Franklin, A, 'Tomboys, Dykes, and Girly Girls: Interrogating the Subjectivities of Adolescent Female Athletes' (2005) 17 *Women's Studies Quarterly* 33.

Banks, TL, '*Michael Clayton*: Women Lawyers Betrayed—Again' in H Radner and R Stringer (eds), *Feminism at the Movies: Understanding Gender and Contemporary Popular Cinema* (Routledge, 2011).

Baumgardner, J and Richards, A, *Manifesta: Young Women, Feminism and the Future* (New York, Farrar, Straus and Giroux, 2000).

Bingham, D, *Acting Male: Masculinities in the Films of James Stewart, Jack Nicholson, and Clint Eastwood* (New Brunswick, Rutgers University Press, 1994).

Brown, L (ed), 'Heroine' in *The New Shorter Oxford English Dictionary on Historical Principles* (Oxford, Oxford University Press, 1993) vol 1.

Chowdhry, M and Sharratt, M, 'Introduction: Interview with the Editors, So what is Bitch Lit' in M Chowdhry and M Sharratt (eds), *Bitch Lit* (Croscus Books, 2006).

Corcos, CA, 'We Don't Want Advantages the Woman Lawyer Hero and Her Quest for Power in Popular Culture' (2003) 53 *Syracuse Law Review* 1225.

—— '*Damages:* The Truth is Out There' in M Asimov (ed), *Lawyers in Your Living Room: Law on Television* (American Bar Association, 2009).

Dowd, NE, Levit, N and McGinley, AC, 'Feminist Legal Theory Meets Masculinities Theory' in FR Cooper and AC McGinley (eds), *Masculinities and Law: A Multidimensional Approach* (New York, New York University Press, forthcoming August 2012).

Fitch, J, III, 'Archetypes on the American Screen: Heroes and Anti-Heroes' (2004) 7 *Journal of Religion and Popular Culture* 1.

Flaherty, M, 'Femme Influence Helps Shoot down Police Brutality' (2008) 413 *Variety* 15, 1.

Glass, DM, 'Portia in Primetime: Women Lawyers, Television, and L.A. Law' (1990) 2 *Yale Journal of Law and Feminism* 371.

Goldberg, S, '*Bar Girls? Images of Women Lawyers on TV Slowly Improving*' (1990) 76 *ABA Journal* 41.

Grosshans, L, 'Accurate or Appalling: Representations of Women Lawyers in Popular Culture' (2006) 4 *Cardozo Public Law, Policy, and Ethics Journal* 457.

Hess, DJ and Grant, GW, '*Prime-Time Television and Gender-Role Behavior*' (1983) 10 *Teaching Sociology* 371.

Higgins, T and Tolman, DL, 'Cultural Media[ation], and Desire in the Lives of Adolescent Girls', in MA Fineman and MT McCluskey (eds), *Feminism, Media and Law* (Oxford, Oxford University Press, 1997) 177.

Holt, DB and Thompson, CJ, 'Man-of-Action Heroes: The Pursuit of Heroic Masculinity in Everyday Consumption' (2004) 31 *Journal of Consumer Research* 425.

Hyland Jr, WG, 'Creative Malpractice: The Cinematic Lawyer' (2008) 9 *Texas Review of Entertainment & Sports Law* 231.

Karras, I, 'The Third Wave's Final Girl: Buffy the Vampire Slayer' (2002) 1 *ThirdSpace* 2.

Levine, S, 'TNT's "Grace" Period Ends' (2009) 304 *Daily Variety* 6.

Mann, SA and Huffman, DJ, 'The Decentering of Second Wave Feminism and the Rise of the Third Wave' (2005) 69 *Science & Society* 56.

Mayne, J, 'Law and Primetime Feminism' (1998) 10 *Discourse* 30.

McRobbie, A, 'A Response to Susie Orbach: On Generation and Femininity' (2008) 9 *Studies in Gender and Sexuality* 239.

—— 'Young Women and Consumer Culture: An Intervention' (2008) 22 *Cultural Studies* 531.

Raymond, M, '*On Legalistic Behavior, the Advocacy Privilege, and Why People Hate Lawyers*' (2007) 55 *Buffalo Law Review* 929.

Renegar, VR and Sowards, SK, *Contradiction as Agency: Self-Determination, Transcendence, and Counter-Imagination in Third Wave Feminism* (2009) 24 *Hypatia* 1.

Seiter, E, *Feminism and Ideology: The Terms of Women's Stereotypes* (1986) 22 *Feminist Review* 57.

Showden, CR, '*What's Political about the New Feminism?*' (2009) Frontiers: A 30 *Journal of Women Studies* 166.

Shugart, HA, Waggoner, CE and O'Brien Hallstein, DL, 'Mediating Third-Wave Feminism: Appropriation as Postmodern Media Practice' (2001) 18 *Critical Studies in Media Communication* 194.

Snyder, C, 'What is Third-Wave Feminism? New Directions Essay' (2008) 34 *Signs* 175.

Sparks, R, 'Masculinity and Heroism in the Hollywood "Blockbuster": The Culture Industry and Contemporary Images of Crime and Law Enforcement' (1996) *The British Journal of Criminology* 348.

Tucker, K, 'The Closer/Rizzoli & Isles' (2010) 112 *Entertainment Weekly* 73.

Wilder, GZ and Weingartner, B, *Databook on Women in Law School and in the Legal Profession* (Law School Admission Council, 2003).

Young, DE, 'Introduction to Portrayals of Feminism' in MA Fineman and MT McCluskey (eds) *Feminism, Media and Law* (Oxford, Oxford University Press, 1997) 3.

Websites

Andreeva, N, 'Saving Grace Will Wrap Next Summer' *The Hollywood Reporter* (13 Aug 2009, available at www.hollywoodreporter.com/hr/content_display/television/news/ e3i12c12e20214456f333d00ec64aa8c3a1.

Anti-hero: Encyclopedia. All Experts, available at http://en.allexperts.com/e/a/an/anti-hero.htm.

Brounstein, L, 'On Prime Time, Women Lead the Charge' *The Huffington Post* (18 March 2010), available at www.huffingtonpost.com/laura-brounstein/on-prime-time-women-lead_b_504995.html.

BWW News Desk. 'TNT's Saving Grace Starring Holly Hunter to Wrap March 29' *TalkTVworld* (1 March 2010), available at http://tv.broadwayworld.com/article/TNTs_SAVING_GRACE_ Starring_Holly_Hunter_to_Wrap_March_29_20100301.

Elliot, S, *Box?* 'We Don't Need No Box' *New York Times: Media Decoder* (11 December 2007, available at http://mediacoder.blogs.nytimes.com/2007/12/11/box-we-dont-need-no-box/.

'Full Cast and Crew for Damages' *IMDb*, available at www.imdb.com/title/tt0914387/ fullcredits#cast.

Goldstein, D, 'FX Aims for HBO's Cachet' *Business Week* (19 Sept 2005), available at www. businessweek.com/magazine/content/05_38/b3951112.htm.

Gorman, B, 'USA Leads Cable Primetime Viewership: TNT Skies over Adults 18-49 Ratings' *TVbytheNumbers* (18 May 2010), available at http://tvbythenumbers.com/2010/05/18/usa-leads-cable-primetime-viewership-tnt-skies-over-adults-18-49-ratings/51800.

Hibberd, J, 'FX Launches Major Branding Campaign' *Television Week* (17 Dec 2007), available at www.tvweek.com/news/2007/12/fx_launches_major_branding_cam.php.

'It's Always Sunny on Our Channel, FX Tells Advertisers' *New York Times: Media Decoder* (7 April 2010), available at http://mediadecoder.blogs.nytimes.com/2010/04/07/fx-tells-advertisers-its-always-sunny-on-our-channel/#more-31755.

Joreen, 'The Bitch Manifesto' *JoFreeman.com* (1969), available at www.jofreeman.com/joreen/ bitch.htm.

Lewis, H, '"Damages" Audience Much Larger than Ratings Would Indicate' *Business Insider* (18 Feb 2009), available at www.businessinsider.com/damages-audience-much-larger-than-ratings-would-indica.

Moore, FAP, 'Financial Scandal Gives 'Damages' Dramatic Payoff' *ABC News Entertainment* (5 February 2010), available at http://abcnews.go.com/Entertainment/wireStory?id=9755131.

'Nancy Miller' *IMDb*, available at www.imdb.com/name/nm0589043/.

Owen, R, 'TV Welcomes over-40 Actresses as Never Before to Play Series Leads' *Pittsburgh Post-Gazette: TV & Radio* (12 August 2007), available at www.post-gazette.com/pg/07224/808316-237.stm.

Piepmeier, A, 'Postfeminism vs. the Third Wave' *Electronic Book Review* (17 March 2006), available at www.electronicbookreview.com/thread/writingpostfeminism/reconfiguredrip2.

Rose, L, 'At FX, There is Still No Box' *Forbes, The Biz Blog* (18 January 2010), available at http://blogs.forbes.com/bizblog/2010/01/18/at-fx-there-is-still-no-box/.

Slut. Urban Dictionary, available at www.urbandictionary.com/define.php?term=slut.

Slut, n. Oxford English Dictionary, available at http://dictionary.oed.com/cgi/entry/50228191?query_type=word&queryword=slut&first=1&max_to_show=10&sort_type=alpha&result_place=1&search_id=vnV6-jTbqpk-3621&hilite=50228191.

Steagill, K, 'Seeking a Post-Gender Society' *The Michigan Daily* (17 Feb 2009), available at www.michigandaily.com/content/2009-02-18/transcending-gender.

Tamayo, YA, 'Rhymes with Rich: Power, Law, and the Bitch' *Social Science Research Network* (14 February 2009), available at http://papers.ssrn.com/sol3/cf_dev/AbsByAuth.cfm?per_id=329885.

Thompson, J, 'Just a girl—Feminism, Postmodernism and Buffy the Vampire Slayer' *Refractory*, vol 2 (March 2003), available at http://blogs.arts.unimelb.edu.au/refractory/2003/03/18/just-a-girl-feminism-postmodernism-and-buffy-the-vampire-slayer-jim-thompson/.

'TNT's The Closer, Ad Supported Cable's #1 Series of All Time, Return for Sixth Season Monday, July 12' *TVbytheNumbers* (9 June 2009), available at http://tvbythenumbers.com/2010/06/09/tnts-the-closer-ad-supported-cables-1-series-of-all-time-returns-for-sixth-season-monday-july-12/53641.

'What is an Antihero?' *The Gallery of Antiheroes*, available at www.flowerstorm.net/disa/Gallery/anti- explain.html.

Zeisler, A, 'The B-Word? You Betcha' *Washington Post* (18 Nov 2007), available at www.washingtonpost.com/wp-dyn/content/article/2007/11/16/AR2007111601202.html.

Newspapers

Heffernan, V, 'Me Fierce? It's All Make-Believe' *New York Times*, 22 July 2007.

Research

Craig, S, '*From Married … with Children* to *Touched by an Angel*: Politics, Economics and the Battle Over "Family Values" Television', presented at 2001 Conference of the Popular Culture Association/American Culture Association, 13 April 2011, www.cas.unt.edu/~rscraig/pdfs/from%20married.PDF.

Shapiro, LJ & Associates LLC. 'Public Perceptions of Lawyers: Consumer Research Findings' *American Bar Association* (April 2002), available at www.abanet.org/litigation/lawyers/publicperceptions.pdf.

7

A Third Rapist? Television Portrayals of Rape Evidence Rules

PAUL BERGMAN*

I. Introduction

Popular legal culture, including law-related television shows, transmits powerful messages about such topics as the fairness of a justice system, the content of legal rules, the processes by which laws are made and cases decided, and the work and attitudes of lawyers and judges. What you may consider the 'Three R's' captures the primary potential interactions between popular legal culture and widely-shared beliefs about law and justice:

— Popular legal culture may REFLECT beliefs about law, lawyers and the legal system.
— Popular legal culture may REINFORCE beliefs about law, lawyers and the legal system.
— Popular legal culture may lead to REVISED beliefs about law, lawyers and the legal system.

This chapter focuses on the depiction of rape evidence rules in law-related and widely-viewed American television series. To the extent that rape-centred episodes from different series that aired at different times present similar images of rape evidence rules, *cultivation theory* suggests that these episodes have the capacity to reinforce and to produce revisions in popular attitudes about the content of the rule and their interpretation by police officers, lawyers and judges.[1]

* Thank you to the UCLA Law School for supporting my research, and to UCLA law librarians Linda O'Connor and Lynn McClelland and UCLA law students Steven Garff, Christine Green and Jeff Boerneke for their research assistance
[1] Cultivation Theory was developed by George Gerbner and Larry Gross and first presented in an article in the 1976 *Journal of Communication* entitled, 'Living with Television: The Violence Profile'.

The potential impact of television shows on popular beliefs about the content and functioning of rape evidence rules is especially significant. The reason is that those beliefs have tended to discourage sexual assault victims from reporting attacks to the police. This is particularly true in 'acquaintance rape' situations. Acquaintance rape occurs when a potential rape complainant has had a previous relationship with her attacker. Acquaintance rape has long been considered to be the most under-reported serious crime in the United States.[2] A common explanation for the reluctance of many women to report sexual assaults by acquaintances to the police is that 'the rules all too often result[] in the victim's being violated a second time by the criminal justice system'.[3] The criminal justice system's violation of sexual assault victims primarily takes the form of allowing defence lawyers to question rape complainants about their general sexual behaviour, while placing accused rapists' sexual characters off limits for the most part. In the words of Susan Estrich, rape evidence rules 'humiliated the victim and protected the defendant'.[4] These evidence rules apply most strongly to acquaintance rape prosecutions, in which consent is a common defence. Thus, potential acquaintance rape complainants may well choose to remain silent rather than to subject themselves to a criminal justice system that allows one-sided and degrading, hostile and irrelevant questioning about their private sexual history.

This chapter examines the images of rape evidence rules presented to viewers by rape-centred episodes of popular television series filmed before and after a period of time which I refer to in this chapter as the 'Get Tough on Rapists Era'. The era roughly corresponds to the decade 1980–90, and was a period of dramatic change in American rape evidence rules in virtually all states, as well as under federal law.[5] During the Get Tough on Rapists Era, the enactment of rape shield laws placed rape complainants' sexual character largely off limits.[6] At the same time, the enactment of character-of-defendant rules allowed prosecutors much greater leeway to offer evidence of accused rapists' violent sexual characters.[7] To the extent that rape stories in popular law-related television series failed to reflect these changes, these series may have forfeited an important opportunity to educate viewers and encourage potential acquaintance rape complainants to *revise* their pre-existing attitudes and become

---

[2] Dr Dean G Kilpatrick, of the National Violence Against Women Prevention Research Center, Medical University of South Carolina, states that 'Rape is the most underreported crime in America': Dean G Kilpatrick, 'Rape and Sexual Assault', available at www.musc.edu/vawprevention/research/sa.shtm[accessed Feb 2010] 1. Susan Estrich has presented a more nuanced view. According to Estrich, rape complainants are extremely likely to report 'stranger' and violent rapes to the police, but far less likely to report 'simple' sexual assaults such as date rape. See Susan Estrich, *Real Rape* (Harvard University Press, 1987) 10.

[3] Estrich, *Real Rape* (n 2) 42. Similarly, the Rape Shield Laws FAQ on a webpage of the National Center for Victims of Crime states that, 'Rape shield laws were designed, in part, to make it more likely for victims to come forward'. See National Center for Victims of Crime, 'FAQ: Rape Shield Laws', available at www.ncvc.org/ncvc/main.aspx?dbID=DB_FAQ:RapeShieldLaws927 [accessed Jan 2010].

[4] Ibid 52.

[5] For the sake of convenience and clarity, I refer generally to rape charges. However, the new rules enacted during the Get Tough on Rapists Era apply to all sexual assault prosecutions, not just those based on rape.

[6] See, eg Federal Rule of Evidence 412; California Evidence Code s 1101(c)(3).

[7] See, eg Federal Rule of Evidence 413; California Evidence Code s 1108.

more willing to report attackers to the police. More critically, the portrayals of rape evidence rules in these series might well make them a 'third rapist'.[8]

II. Rape Evidence Rules before 'Get Tough on Rapists Era'

Before the advent of the Get Tough on Rapists Era, rape evidence rules in the United States were largely congruent with the widespread attitude that the rules were hostile, degrading and unfair to rape complainants. Rape evidence rules typically allowed rape defendants who claimed that sexual intercourse was consensual to attack rape complainants' sexual character. The supposed relevance was that a woman who had previously engaged in consensual sexual behaviour with other men (including a husband) would be more likely to consent to sexual intercourse with the defendant.[9] On this basis, the rules in most states allowed defence counsel to cross-examine rape complainants about the intimate and private details of their sexual history. For example, defence attorneys in consent cases commonly attacked rape complainants' sexual character by inquiring into such topics as:

— their dating history and patterns;
— the age at which they became sexually active;
— how many boyfriends and/or sexual partners they had had;
— how often they engaged in sexual intercourse;
— whether they used birth control; and
— the way they dress.

One of the factors that pre-1980s rape evidence rules ignored was that women are autonomous human beings whose willingness to engage in sexual activity with one partner is irrelevant to their willingness to do so with a different partner. Stated differently, the pre-1980s rules ignored the fact that a woman's 'consent to sexual intercourse is temporally constrained permission that is specific as to act and non-transferable to other people'.[10]

Prior to the Get Tough on Rapists Era, a corollary set of rape evidence rules largely shielded rape defendants' violent sexual characters from exposure at trial. Apart from in narrow circumstances, prosecutors could not offer evidence that a

---

[8] The limited scope of the project means that any conclusions must at best be tentative. I identified what I considered to be highly-rated and serious law-related television series, and then searched websites devoted to those series for episode descriptions suggesting that rape was a prominent part of a story. Thanks to the collections of the UCLA Film and Television Archive and the Paley Center for Media in Beverly Hills, I was able to view a majority of these episodes. However, I did not watch all of them, both because I would not have had the space to discuss them and because I was unable to locate copies of some of the episodes within the timeframe I had to complete this project.

[9] Prof Michelle Anderson has referred to the basis of this inference as a 'chastity requirement'. See Michelle J Anderson, 'From Chastity Requirement to Sexuality License: Sexual Consent and a New Rape Shield Law' (2002) 70 *Geo Washington L Rev* 51.

[10] Ibid 58.

defendant charged with rape (or other sexual assault crime) had sexually assaulted women other than the rape complainant. This was not a special rule for rape cases, rather it was consistent with the more general rule that when deciding whether a charged defendant committed a crime, judges and jurors are to 'judge the act and not the actor'.[11]

III. Television Shows before 'Get Tough on Rapists Era'

Television episodes featuring rape stories were largely absent from law-related television series made before 1980.[12] However, the few episodes that I was able to identify and watch presented viewers with largely accurate messages about the degrading and unfair content of rape evidence rules as they existed prior to 1980. The congruence

---

[11] Federal Rule of Evidence 404 is typical of the general rule that prosecutors cannot offer character evidence to prove that a defendant committed a charged crime.

[12] For example, in virtually every episode of *Perry Mason*, the granddaddy of all television lawyer series (1957–66, starring Raymond Burr), Perry's clients were charged with murder. For summaries of the 271 episodes of the Perry Mason series, see Perry Mason TV Series Wiki, 'Episode/Pages, Episodes', available at www.perrymasontvseries.com/wiki/index.php/EpisodePages/Episodes [accessed Mar 2011]. In *The Defenders* (starring EG Marshall and Robert Reed), the classic 1960s show depicting a father and son law firm that took on such controversial subjects as teen pregnancy and McCarthy-like black-listing, never broadcast an episode with a rape theme. *The Defenders* episode summaries are available at TV.com, 'The Defenders (1961) Episode Guide', available at www.tv.com/the-defenders/show/225/episode.html?tag=prev_episode [accessed Mar 2011]. Similarly, in the series *Petrocelli* (1974–75, starring Barry Newman), Petrocelli was a zealous and combative criminal defence lawyer. However, according to the episode summaries he never defended a client charged with rape. *Petrocelli* episode summaries are at TV.com, 'Petrocelli on TV.com', available at www.tv.com/petrocelli/show/1862/summary.html [accessed Mar 2011]. Finally, *Judd for the Defense* (1967–69, starring Carl Betz) was another series depicting a tough, hard-boiled lawyer loosely based on well-known lawyers F Lee Bailey and Percy Foreman. Among the 53 episodes of the show, only one (*Between the Dark and the Daylight*) featured Judd representing a client charged with rape. Viewers of that episode heard only of an 'attack', the term 'rape' was not used. In addition, Judd's cross-examination of the alleged rape complainant's sexual history was limited to one rather antiseptic inquiry: 'Have you ever been intimate with anyone else?' *Judd for the Defense* episode summaries are available at TV.com, 'Judd for the Defense on TV.com', available at www.tv.com/judd-for-the-defense/show/6245/episode.html [accessed Mar 2011].

One possible explanation for the apparent dearth of pre-1980 episodes of popular law-related series featuring rape stories is that the lawyers in *Perry Mason*, *The Defenders*, *Petrocelli* and *Judd for the Defense*, and many other main lawyer characters, are defence lawyers rather than prosecutors. The shows' producers might not have wanted their stars confronting sympathetic rape complainants with the details of their sexual history. It is also likely that in an era when virtually all television programming was shown on only three advertiser-supported national networks, the networks were squeamish and fearful of alienating viewers and sponsors by airing programmes with controversial themes such as rape.

By contrast, rape stories may have been somewhat more common in pre-1980s films, at least those made after the demise of the Production Code. In the classic 1959 film *Anatomy of a Murder*, Otto Preminger defied the Production Code (and hastened its demise) by making a film centred on a murder trial in which the issue is whether the killer, Lt Manion (played by Ben Gazzara), was temporarily insane at the time he shot the man who had allegedly raped Manion's wife Laura (played by Lee Remick). In accordance with the then-existing rape evidence rules, Prosecutor Claude Dancer (played by George C Scott) thoroughly and nastily probes Laura's sexual history. *Town Without Pity* (1970, starring Kirk Douglas), also depicts a defence lawyer who defends four soldiers charged with rape by attacking the young rape complainant's sexual mores.

between the rules and their depiction on television should not be surprising. The images of smarmy and snarly defence lawyers hectoring trapped and weeping rape complainants with their sexual history fit perfectly into the *mano a mano* world of cross-examination so often depicted in popular legal culture as a staple of American trials.

Perhaps the best example of an episode of a law-related television series providing a realistic depiction of the rape evidence rules as they existed before the advent of the Get Tough on Rapists Era is the 'Victim in Shadow' episode of the extremely popular television series *Owen Marshall Counselor at Law*.[13] As the series title suggests, Owen Marshall was a compassionate and holistic lawyer, often reviewing strategic alternatives with clients and exploring how clients' legal problems affected other aspects of their lives.[14] In the 'Victim in Shadow' episode, Marshall takes Beth home after a dinner date. It is not a romantic evening; Beth and her husband are personal friends and Marshall sees her occasionally while her husband serves as a military officer in Vietnam. After Marshall leaves and Beth begins to get ready for bed, a man with a stocking pulled over his face and a knife in his hand confronts her. Off screen, this man apparently sexually assaults Beth. The details of the attack are vague, and, as we later find out, the medical examiner could not confirm that a rape occurred and found no indication that Beth had struggled against an attacker.

Beth does not remain silent and she reports the attack to Marshall and the police. The police offers are suspicious of rape victims in general and Beth in particular. When Beth tells one of the investigating officers that she recognised her attacker as Gar Kellerman, a man who works in the same hospital as she does, the officer snidely suggests that 'Since you recognized him, you and he must be close friends'.[15] Although the police officer insists that he's only interested in the truth, the officer also tells Beth that "We get a lot of stuff like this. Many are false alarms. Just a lovers' quarrel, often they cool down right away.' Later at the police station, a supervising officer reinforces this demeaning attitude by telling Marshall that 'You'd be surprised how often the women are to blame. They provoke the guy, then get panicky and try to back out at the last minute'.

Eventually, the District Attorney decides that he does not have sufficient evidence to prosecute Kellerman for sexual assault. Beth's summary of the painful experience for Marshall echoes the 'second rapist' perception of the criminal justice system: 'I almost felt that I was a criminal rather than a victim.'

However, the case does go to trial after Beth sues Kellerman in civil court for assault and battery and intentional infliction of emotional distress.[16] Marshall warns Beth ahead of time that 'It can get pretty rough. Most judges allow detailed

---

[13] The episode first aired in 1972.

[14] Arthur Hill played the role of Owen Marshall, a Santa Barbara lawyer; Lee Majors was his associate. The location enabled the beautiful Spanish-style Santa Barbara courthouse to play a prominent role in the series.

[15] Beth's and Gar's prior relationship makes this an 'acquaintance rape' situation, although the term was probably unknown at the time of the show.

[16] By changing the posture of the case from a criminal rape trial to a civil suit brought by the rape complainant, the producers were able to depict rape evidence law without putting Marshall, the show's hero, in the unsavoury role of badgering a rape complainant about her sexual character.

questioning of one's personal life.' Marshall's prediction proves accurate. Beth's testimony is limited almost entirely to sneering defence attorney Shiller's cross-examination, which unfolds as follows:

Counsel: How long have you been married, Mrs. Whitaker?

Beth: Four years this month.

Counsel: Which means that for the most part of your adult life you've been unmarried. And since you're a very attractive woman you must have had many boyfriends.

Beth: I don't know what you mean by 'many.'

Counsel: Well, let's count them together, shall we?

Marshall: I strongly object, Your Honor. That's irrelevant.

Counsel: Your Honor, I think that Mrs. Whitaker's morals are very much an issue here if I'm to properly defend my client.

Judge: Well I agree with you in theory Mr. Shiller. But I must insist that you conduct your interrogation in a manner that is not personally offensive to the witness or to the jury.

Counsel: Mrs. Whitaker, please describe the circumstances of your first date with a boy.

[Beth looks anxious and confused; Marshall whispers to his associate, 'Here we go.' But viewers don't hear Beth's answer.]

Counsel: … this man Jennings that you worked for in New York, did you ever date him?

Beth: We went out to dinner once or twice.

Counsel: But wasn't he married?

Beth: He was separated from his wife for over a year; they were getting a divorce. I've already told you that.

Counsel: Nevertheless he was still a married man?

Beth: Legally, yes.

Counsel: Well, did he go through with the divorce?

Beth: No. Eventually he and his wife reconciled.

Counsel (smirking): So he was a married man. …

Marshall: I object to this entire line of questioning. Counsel is deliberately badgering the witness.

Counsel: That's all right Your Honor. I'm finished with my cross examination. (staring intensely at Beth) But I may wish to recall the witness in the defense portion of the case.

The visual aspects of the cross-examination scene are consistent with the verbal bullying. Defence counsel's facial features and demeanour are alternately menacing and challenging, and he often stands tall over the seated Beth while questioning her. Moreover, the judge and Marshall can offer little assistance to her. In total, the show promotes the message that going public with a rape claim will result in a humiliating ordeal in which rape complainants will be forced to answer questions about their private sexual history.[17]

In an episode entitled 'A Girl Named Tham',[18] Owen Marshall represents accused rapist Gavin Chord. Chord is charged with raping his former girlfriend, Lucy Jamison.[19] Although Marshall is convinced that Jamison is lying because she has become pregnant, he treats her respectfully. Nevertheless, the story emphasises the negative consequences awaiting rape complainants who go public. In one scene, Marshall is in a restaurant interviewing Jamison's roommate when Jamison unexpectedly walks over to the table and confronts him. The story continues as follows:

> Marshall: I should mention that any discussion of the case under these circumstances would be unethical.
>
> Jamison: Unethical? You're trying to keep Gavin Chord out of jail and you talk to me about ethics?
>
> Marshall: Miss Jamison, you know very well that everyone is entitled to a defense.
>
> Jamison: Oh that's great! That is great!
>
> Marshall: Please.
>
> Jamison: Please what? Don't raise my voice? Disappear? You don't care about me or my child. You see Mr. Marshall, you're paid to forget about us.
>
> Marshall: You're wrong if you think that.
>
> Jamison: You know what happens to a girl when she tries to get some justice after she's been raped? Do you? First she calls out to her parents only they don't answer because they're dead. You get dropped by everyone close to you and boys, boys have a way of avoiding you when they know that you're pregnant. You know who gets blamed for the whole ugly mess? But that doesn't matter to Gavin. It doesn't matter to anyone I suppose least of all to you, Mr. Marshall.[20]

In a later scene that takes place in Marshall's law office, Marshall is frustrated at Chord's reluctance to cooperate in the defence. He knows that Chord cares for Jamison and so he unsuccessfully tries to use his power to attack Jamison's morality to induce Chord to talk openly with him about what happened:

> Marshall: Gavin, any lawyer can put Lucy Jamison on the stand, in three minutes of calculated questioning make her out to be a provocative, reckless, immoral girl with no more scruples than a prostitute.
>
> Gavin: No! You can't do that.
>
> Marshall: Then give me an alternative.

---

[17] Beth prevails in the trial after Marshall's questioning of Kellerman about Kellerman's acts of cowardice in Vietnam result in Kellerman's hysterical admission that he sexually assaulted Beth and numerous other women. Thus the episode also served as a critique on the negative psychological effects that fighting in Vietnam had on returning soldiers.

[18] First aired 14 March 1973.

[19] This episode also presents an acquaintance rape scenario.

[20] Commenting shortly afterwards to his secretary about Jamison's outburst, Marshall tells her that Jamison 'seemed so young, so fragile'.

After Chord leaves his office without providing information about his relationship with Jamison, Marshall asks his secretary to gather information that Marshall may have to reluctantly use at trial:

> Marshall: Frieda, we mustn't let this chip away at our determination to give him a good defense. I want to know more about Lucy Jamison. These two blank days during that week, the other men in her life, who else did she date. Let's dig way back.

Despite Marshall's concern for Jamison and his reluctance to attack her sexual character, this episode reinforces the indignities awaiting rape complainants who go public. Close friends and even parents shun them, and it's an easy matter for a defence attorney to portray a rape complainant as a 'provocative, reckless, immoral girl with no more scruples than a prostitute'.[21]

The conclusion of the Get Tough on Rapists Era coincided with the beginning of the show *Law and Order*, by leaps and bounds the most successful law-related television series ever created.[22] Each episode of *Law and Order* focused first on the police investigation of a crime, and then on the prosecution of the suspects. Its stories were often 'ripped from the headlines', and the show sought to present the gritty details of the work of police officers and prosecutors in a realistic, yet dramatised manner. Throughout its long history consisting of well over 400 episodes, *Law and Order* aired only two rape-focused episodes; both aired as the Get Tough on Rapists Era was ending.[23] Neither of the rape-focused episodes delves into a rape complainant's sexual character. They do, however, suggest the unfairness of rape evidence rules by delivering the then-largely accurate message that accused rapists' sexual character is off limits to prosecutors.

In a *Law and Order* episode entitled 'Helpless',[24] police psychologist Elizabeth Olivet takes it upon herself to investigate Dr Merritt, an obstetrician/gyneacologist who she suspects of raping and molesting patients. Posing as a patient, Olivet is sedated and then becomes another of Dr Merritt's rape victims. Dr Merritt testifies that Olivet consented to sexual intercourse, and he is found not guilty after the trial judge accuses the prosecutor of trying to entrap the doctor into committing the crime. The police persuade about 50 women who Dr Merritt had previously attacked but who had remained silent to lodge complaints against him. However, because rape evidence rules of that era generally prevented prosecutors from offering evidence that alleged rapists had attacked women other than the rape complainant, the prosecutor does not offer testimony from any of these women as evidence against Dr Merritt in Olivet's case.[25]

---

[21] The episode concludes with Marshall proving that Chord became impotent as a result of his Vietnamese fiancée dying in a bombing attack. Jamison fabricated the rape story because she did not know that Chord was impotent and thought that he had rejected her.

[22] *Law and Order* was cancelled in 2010. It had aired for 20 years, and is tied with the 1950s–1960s Western *Gunsmoke* as the longest running American television drama of all time. However, in 2010 the show morphed into a new series called *Law and Order Los Angeles*, so the long-running concept had not entirely disappeared.

[23] For episode summaries of *Law and Order*, visit TV.com, 'Law & Order on TV.com', available at www.tv.com/law-and-order/show/180/summary.html [accessed Mar 2011].

[24] 'Helpless' was episode six of season three, and it first aired on 4 November 1992.

[25] Television shows are sometimes a vehicle for alerting viewers to the need for legal change. For example, the pilot episode of what became the highly rated 1970s television series *Emergency!* was a plea

'Discord' was the second episode of *Law and Order* to feature a rape story.[26] This episode also suggests that the rape evidence rules before the Get Tough on Rapists Era were slanted in favour of accused rapists. Naive college student Julia Wood accompanies rock star C Square to his hotel room late at night, ostensibly so he can give her tickets to an upcoming concert. Sexual intercourse takes place. Julia claims that she was raped; C Square claims that the sex was consensual. Before arresting C Square, the police find another woman who tells them that C Square had raped her under very similar circumstances.[27] When the investigating officers report this information to their supervisor, the following exchange ensues:

Officer: It [the other attack] shows predisposition.

Supervisor: Which isn't admissible in court.

The case goes to trial, and in accordance with the supervisor's statement the prosecutor never seeks to offer evidence that C Square had raped another woman.

From the perspective of the '3 R's', referred to earlier, these pre-Get Tough on Rapists Era episodes reflected and no doubt reinforced many viewers' beliefs about the unfairness of rape evidence rules, and the ordeal that acquaintance rape complainants in particular were likely to experience if they reported an attack to the police. The widely held attitude that the criminal justice system was a 'second rapist' found support both in the existing rape evidence rules and in the messages embedded in the few episodes of law-related television series of this era that featured rape stories.[28]

IV. Rape Evidence Rules after 'Get Tough on Rapists Era'

By the early 1990s, virtually all US jurisdictions had enacted legislation that changed rape evidence rules in two major ways. *Rape shield* laws prevented rape defendants from exploring a rape complainant's general sexual character.[29] In addition, *character-of-defendant* rules gave prosecutors more leeway to offer evidence of a rape defendant's

---

for the enactment of new rules allowing paramedics to perform functions that previously were the exclusive domain of physicians. For a discussion of this series, see P Bergman, 'Emergency! Send a TV Series to Rescue Paramedic Services' (2007) 36 *University of Baltimore Law Review* 347–69. The article also appears in (2005) 7 *Current Legal Issues (Law and Popular Culture)* 130–47 and in the *Entertainment, Publishing and the Arts Handbook (2008–2009)*.

[26] 'Discord' was episode three of season four, and it first aired on 6 October 1993.

[27] The other woman's name is 'McCartney', but 'there's no connection' to the famous Beatle.

[28] The nationally-televised trial of William Kennedy Smith on a charge of raping Patricia Bowman took place in 1991 in Florida. Prosecutor Moira Lasch sought to bolster her case by offering evidence that Smith had sexually assaulted three other women. At the time of the trial, Florida rape evidence rules generally excluded evidence of a rape defendant's sexual character. Such evidence was only admissible if the circumstances of the charged crime and the other sexual attacks were nearly identical. Under these rules, Judge Lupo correctly excluded evidence of Smith's other alleged assaults. Thus, just like the televisions episodes of that era described above, the Kennedy Smith trial reinforced the popular perception that the criminal justice system was a hostile arena for rape complainants.

[29] See, eg Rule 412 of the Federal Rules of Evidence.

violent sexual character. These new rape evidence rules both responded to the perception that the criminal justice system was hostile to rape complainants and made it more likely that prosecutors would obtain convictions of defendants charged with acquaintance rape.

The policy underlying rape shield laws is that a rape complainant's general sexual character is irrelevant to the issue of whether she consented to engage in sexual intercourse with an accused rapist. The reach of rape shield laws extends to sexual behaviour generally, not merely to sexual intercourse. For example, assume that a defence attorney seeks to cross-examine a rape complainant about provocative dancing or attire, whether she practices birth control, enjoys pornographic films, or works as a prostitute. All of these are forms of sexual behaviour that rape shield laws exclude as the basis of an inference that a complainant consented to sexual intercourse with an accused rapist.[30]

Character-of-defendant laws[31] are an exception to the general rule of evidence in the United States and other common law countries that evidence of a criminal defendant's propensity to commit crimes is not admissible to prove that the defendant committed a charged crime. For example, a prosecutor trying to prove that a defendant robbed a bank cannot typically offer evidence that the defendant has robbed other banks, forged checks, engaged in mortgage fraud, or committed other crimes. However, if a defendant is charged with rape (or other crimes of sexual violence), character-of-defendant laws allow prosecutors to offer evidence of the defendant's other acts of sexual violence. The theory underlying character-of-defendant laws is that the difficulty of proving what took place during a private sexual encounter makes it legitimate to use evidence of an accused rapist's history of sexual violence to prove that the encounter consisted of sexual violence rather than consensual sexual intercourse.[32]

A brief example illustrates how these two types of laws may operate in the same case. Assume that Ron Johnson is charged with raping Rhoda Hudson. Hudson's story is that she met and danced with Johnson in a club and that Johnson offered to give her a ride home. Instead Johnson drove to a secluded spot and forcibly raped her. Johnson's story is that he met and danced with Hudson in the club, that Hudson went willingly into his car, and that before he drove Hudson home they parked in a secluded spot and engaged in consensual sexual intercourse.

Here, rape shield laws prevent Johnson from questioning Hudson about her sexual character, including, for example, how she was dressed and whether she had, on any other occasion, had consensual sex with a man that she had just met in a club. At the

---

[30] Rape shield laws are subject to limited exceptions. A common exception is that they do not exclude evidence of prior sexual conduct involving the complainant and the accused rapist. Rape shield laws exclude evidence of a rape complainant's general sexual character, and exceptions identify narrow circumstances in which sexual history is relevant without regard to a complainant's general sexual character.

[31] See, eg Rule 413 of the Federal Rules of Evidence.

[32] Judges have discretion to exclude this type of propensity evidence if they conclude that it would be unfairly prejudicial. For example, if the 'other sexual assault' took place many years ago, or under very different circumstances compared to the charged crime, a judge is likely to conclude that the other act's evidence is unfairly prejudicial and exclude it.

same time, the prosecutor could offer evidence that Johnson had been sexually violent towards other women.[33]

V. Television Shows after 'Get Tough on Rapists Era'

The television landscape in the United States after the Get Tough on Rapists Era ran its course was very different from the previous one. By the mid-1990s, the three major television networks had been joined not only by other over-the-air networks, but also by a myriad of channels available to cable and satellite subscribers. In the years following the Get Tough on Rapists Era, cable and satellite services created original programmes that were free of many of the content restrictions that the government placed on over-the-air networks. One result was the creation of more shows with adult themes, including shows depicting rape and its legal consequences. This section analyses the images that these shows provided of the rape evidence rules that were enacted during the Get Tough on Rapists Era.

Although one might reasonably have expected the television series to portray the updated version of rape evidence rules in its stories, the changes to rape evidence rules made during the Get Tough on Rape Era are barely visible in episodes of law-related television series that aired after the era ended. Shows generally ignored the changes or presented them as ineffective or even unjust. Perhaps the reason was that producers and writers were unwilling to forgo the emotional impact of an aggressive criminal defence lawyer exploring a rape complainant's sexual history. Whatever the reason, law-related television shows made after the Get Tough on Rape Era provide little reason for rape complainants to believe that rape evidence rules are fair and that the criminal justice system will treat them with dignity and respect.[34]

The 'Noah's Bark' episode of the hugely popular law-related series *L.A. Law* exemplifies the images of rape evidence rules that law-related television shows presented following the changes to these rules that took place during the Get Tough on Rapists Era.[35] In this episode, a rape complainant testifies that she did not consent to have sex with the defendant, and that she tried to fend off his advances by insisting that

---

[33] Under the typical character of defendant law, the judge has discretion to admit evidence of Johnson's other acts of sexual violence even if he was never formally charged with committing them. Indeed, a judge might admit the evidence even if Johnson had been formally charged with attacking the other women, gone to trial and been found not guilty. Double jeopardy would not prevent their admission because Johnson would not be charged and face punishment for committing them.

[34] For example, the phenomenally successful law-related series *Law and Order* has not aired a single rape-focused episode since the end of the Get Tough on Rapists Era. For information on episode summaries, see n 23.

[35] This episode initially aired on 11 January 1990. Although that was before the formal end of the era, rape shield laws were already common throughout the United States. For a reflection on the significance of *L.A. Law*, see Phillip N Meyer, 'Revisiting L.A. Law' in M Asinow (ed), *Lawyers in Your Living Room! Law on Television* (Chicago, American Bar Association Publishing, 2009).

she was in a monogamous relationship.[36] The defence attorney elicits the following testimony during cross- examination:

Defense Counsel (Miss Jenkins): This monogamous relationship was with who?

Prosecutor: Objection.

Defense Counsel: She opened the door, Your Honor.

Judge: I'll allow it. She can answer.

Defense Counsel: Who is this exclusive relationship with, Miss Gauntleave?

Witness: His name is Victor Sifuentes.[37]

Defense Counsel: Miss Gauntleave, is it possible my client thought that you wanted to have sex with him?

Witness: This was not sex Miss Jenkins, this was violence ... and no it is not possible that he thought I wanted ...

Defense Counsel: Miss Gauntleave have you ever had sex with a member of your crew?

Witness: What is this?

Prosecutor: Objection, past sexual history is not admissible.

Defense Counsel: It is when she raises the issue.

Judge: The objection is overruled.

Defense Counsel: What about it Miss Guantleave, have you ever had sex with a member or plural members of your film crew?

Witness: In the past I have had two relationships with men who have been in my crew.

Defense Counsel: When you say relationships, do you mean exclusive, spend the holidays together, celebrate birthdays together and so forth, that sort of thing? Or do you mean extremely short-lived physical encounters?

Witness: They were two short affairs.

Defense Counsel: Do you make room for the possibility Miss Guantleave that my client, knowing your propensity to be sexually promiscuous ...

Prosecutor: I object.

Judge: Get to it Miss Jenkins.

Defense Counsel: Isn't it possible that he thought you wanted it?

Witness: He threw me down on the floor and ripped my clothes off.

Defense Counsel: Move to strike, nonresponsive.

Witness: He pinned my legs back, stuck his thumb into my throat and he raped me.

Judge: Miss Gauntleave ...

---

[36] This was not an acquaintance rape scenario.
[37] Sifuentes was a regular character on the series; he was played by Jimmy Smits.

Witness: There is no way in hell that any person could think that any woman would want done to her what he did to me.

Judge: Miss Gauntleave that's enough.

Defense Counsel: I have nothing further.

[Defense Counsel then calls Victor Sifuentes as a witness to testify that he and the rape complainant have a sexual relationship that started very shortly after they met.]

To the extent that this episode obliquely acknowledged the existence of rape shield laws, it depicts them as useless. The one line of dialogue that refers to the policy of rape shield laws (the prosecutor's objection that 'past sexual history is not admissible') does not even refer to the rape shield law by name. Moreover, the judge immediately overrules the objection and allows the defence attorney to attack the rape complainant's sexual character. The defence attorney suggests that since the complainant has had consensual sexual intercourse with three men (Sifuentes and two film crew members), therefore it is more likely that she consented to have sexual intercourse with the defendant. This is precisely the type of circumstantial evidence reasoning that the rape shield laws were enacted to prevent. The defence attorney's argument that the rape complainant 'opened the door' to the attack on her sexual character by testifying that she was currently in a monogamous relationship is ludicrous. After all, the rape complainant did not testify that she was a virgin at the time of the rape. All she said was that she was presently in a monogamous relationship, and the rape shield laws render the sexual history of that or her other relationships irrelevant to the issue of whether she consented to sexual intercourse with the defendant.

If one message about rape shield laws is that they are ineffective, another is that they are unjust. Instead of a 'shield' protecting rape complainants against unfair attacks, television shows turn these laws into swords that prosecutors use to obtain unjust convictions. For example, consider 'Rape Shield', an episode of the long-running series *The Practice*.[38] Court-appointed defence attorney Jimmy Berluti defends Derrick Hall, who is accused of raping Jessica Palmer. Palmer testifies that Hall jumped into her car and forced her to drive to her home.[39] Once inside the home, Hall raped her. Berluti's examination of Palmer begins as follows:

Berluti: Did you willingly have sex with my client only to claim rape after your dad walked in?

Palmer: No. He forced me.

Berluti: I see. And have you ever claimed somebody raped you before after having …

D.A.: Objection!

Judge: Sustained. Cut it out, counsel.

Berluti: Isn't it true you invited my client back to your house?

---

[38] *The Practice* was created by David E Kelley, who was also the creator of *L. A. Law. The Practice* ran for eight seasons between 1996 and 2003 and was often ranked among the top 10 shows on television. The 'Rape Shield' episode first aired on 9 November 2003, during the show's last season. A script of the episode is available at www.boston-legal.org/script/tp08x07.pdf [assessed Feb 2010].

[39] This episode does not involve an alleged acquaintance rape.

Palmer: No. It is not true. And I did not extend an invitation to be raped.

Berluti: Nothing further.

A chagrined Berluti belatedly discovers a note in the file indicating that Palmer had previously falsely accused two other men of rape. When the trial resumes the next day, Berluti tells the trial judge that he plans to question Palmer further. When the prosecutor objects, the scene shifts to the judge's chambers:

Berluti: Evidence has come to light that Ms. Palmer has made claims of rape before and—

D.A: This is rape shield. You can't get into this. Her sexual past is off limits. Any questions relating to her sexual past are—

Berluti: This goes to her credibility, not her sexual past.

Judge: This woman alleged rape how many times?

Berluti: Two. Both times to her father, who was dubious himself—

D.A.: You can't say this.

Berluti: I can't say it? If she goes around claiming rape—

D.A.: First of all, you can't prove these claims were false. And even if you could, it still falls within rape shield. False rape accusations by the victim are not admissible unless a four-prong test is satisfied. One prong being, the victim is the only prosecution witness. Which here, she isn't. We have an eyewitness to the rape.

Berluti: Her father.

D.A.: It doesn't matter.

Berluti: I'm not looking to impugn a woman's sexual past. This is only being introduced to impeach—

Judge: I understand. But there's no impeachment exception. And even if there were, you have a slew of problems, counsel. First, Mr. Webb states the law correctly.

Berluti: Your Honor—

Judge: Second, victim's testimony has to be confused or inconsistent. Hers wasn't.

Berluti: Let me question her—

Judge: And third, you have to file all questions regarding her sexual past before trial. You didn't.

Berluti: Because I didn't know.

Judge: And whose fault is that? It was in the file. Did you read it?

Berluti: They buried it deep in the file, barely a footnote, they didn't want us to find it.

Judge: But it was there.

Berluti: Your Honor, come on. This woman has perhaps falsely claimed rape before. How can it be possible that the jury doesn't get to hear this?

Judge: You can write your congressman if you don't like the law, counsel. In here, we simply follow it. Any and all evidence of prior rape accusations will not be introduced.

Berluti tries to explain the judge's ruling to his angry client:

Mills: You can't even raise it?

Berluti: No.

Mills: How can this possibly be?

Berluti: There are specific laws—

Mills: Don't I have the right to confront my accuser?

Berluti: Unfortunately, not in rape cases. Look, I know this is unfair. I don't know what to say.

Mills testifies in his own defence, explaining that Palmer was the sexual aggressor and that the sexual intercourse was consensual. Nevertheless he is convicted of rape.

The episode's clear message is that rape shield rules produce unjust outcomes.[40] The rules deny a defendant a chance to exercise one of the most basic American trial rights: the right to confront an accuser. In order to send this negative message the show has to twist rape shield laws out of all recognisable shape. First, it creates a non-existent 'four prong test' that an accused rapist supposedly has to satisfy in order to question a rape complainant about her sexual history. The second, and even more misleading message, is that rape shield laws prevent accused rapists from offering evidence that a rape complainant has on other occasions made false rape claims. In fact judges in almost all jurisdictions have the power to admit such evidence because it is relevant to the complainant's *credibility* (just as Berluti argued). In all types of cases, civil and criminal, Federal Rule of Evidence 608(b) allows parties to question witnesses about specific instances of lying. If Berluti could demonstrate to the judge that Palmer had in the past falsely accused other men of rape, rape shield rules would not prevent him from confronting Palmer with this information.[41]

The 'Doubt' episode of *Law and Order: SVU* arouses doubts not only as to whether a sexual liaison between a graduate student and her professor was consensual or forced, but also as to the effectiveness and fairness of rape shield laws.[42] After the student tells the police that her professor raped her, a test of her underwear suggests the presence of semen from a second individual. When the student nevertheless insists that she had intercourse only with the professor, two prosecutors privately analyse the strength of the rape case:

Prosecutor # 1: Sooner we get the results from the rape kit the better. I can't draft a complaint unless I know what she is hiding and why.

Prosecutor # 2: Maybe she's just embarrassed about having sex with two men in one day.

[40] Even the trial judge seems to recognise that the guilty verdict was unjust. Talking to a morose Berluti after the trial, the judge seeks to console him by telling him that 'The case isn't over… there's still sentencing'.

[41] See, eg *People v Weiss* 133 P.3d 1180 (Colo. 2006). As the *Weiss* Court states, the general rule is that the fact that an alleged rapist was not formally charged with rape is not by itself sufficient to prove that a rape claim was false.

[42] The episode first aired on 23 November 2004.

> Prosecutor # 1: Well, she'd better get over it. Two samples are enough to get her sexual history admitted.

As this conversation concludes, the professor's defence attorney walks in and hands the prosecutors a 'list of [the student's] numerous sexual partners'. One of the prosecutors replies that 'I don't know how you got this but it's irrelevant'. Not so, says the defence attorney, '[The student's] truthfulness or lack of it is a matter of record'.

This portion of the story suggests that rape shield laws are ineffective. The story suggests that having sex with more than one man opens the door to evidence of a rape complainant's sexual character. It also suggests that a history of multiple sex partners is relevant to attack a complainant's credibility. Neither proposition is accurate.

The show concludes with no resolution of the question of whether the sexual liaison was consensual or forced. However, the defence lawyer's closing argument attacks the fairness of rape shield laws:

> The crime of rape used to be hard to prove, even harder to convict. The victim was on trial, not her rapist. Then the laws changed. Woman's identity was protected, her sexual history excluded, and rapists were rightly brought to justice. But now perhaps the pendulum has swung too far. Women who have sex and later regret it are not entitled to call their partners rapists.

The messages embedded in an episode of *The Practice* entitled 'Do Unto Others' suggest to rape complainants that they cannot take comfort in either the rape shield rules nor the character-of-defendant rules.[43] In this story, a Rabbi is charged with raping a young woman. They had carried on a consensual sexual relationship for nearly a year, and the evidence (including the medical evidence) as to whether their ultimate sexual contact was consensual or rape is conflicting. The episode acknowledges the existence of rape shield rules, but suggests that they are porous. Defence attorney Eugene Young asks his colleague Jimmy Berluti to 'chase down some of her old boyfriends'. When Berluti asks one of the boyfriends about his relationship with the complainant, the conversation proceeds as follows:

> Boyfriend: I'm not comfortable with this at all.
>
> Berluti: Neither am I ... but this is his life ... this is a very beloved Rabbi.
>
> Boyfriend: I thought you couldn't do this in rape cases. Dig up old boyfriends, I thought there were laws against putting the victim on trial.
>
> Berluti: We don't plan to do that.

Later, Young talks to the attorney who the complainant has retained to represent her in the civil lawsuit for damages that she has brought against the Rabbi and the temple that employs him:

> Young: There's some evidence that she likes [sex] a little rough.
>
> Attorney: What?

---

[43] This episode first aired on 2 May 1999.

Young: We talked to some old boyfriends.

Attorney: Rape shield, Eugene.

Young: Rape shield goes to putting the victim's character on trial. This goes to a 'how' issue. I think I can get around rape shield …

Following a pre-trial conference with the judge and prosecutor in the criminal case, Young talks to the Rabbi about the effect of the rape shield law:

Young: At the pretrial conference I said that if they introduce any evidence of vaginal bruising that we'd be offering evidence of her sexual preferences. They tried to get it excluded under rape shield. The Judge said he would hear it depending on our offer of proof. Bottom line I don't think the District Attorney will go near the medicals. That's good.

Here, defence attorney Young uses the threat of the complainant's sexual history to discourage the prosecutor from offering evidence of the complainant's post-intercourse physical condition. As a result, although the prosecutor's direct examination of the complainant explores the alleged rape in great detail, he asks no questions about physical injuries.[44] Again, the message concerning rape shield rules is that defence attorneys can easily circumvent them.

When the complainant's testimony concludes, the prosecutor shocks Young and the judge by asking permission to call a surprise witness. Young's furious objection leads to the following in-chambers discussion:

Prosecutor: We want to call Sheila Keenan. Three years ago she was raped by Rabbi Jacob …

Young: Prior bad acts by a defendant in a criminal case, that's not even close to being acceptable.

Prosecutor: I will be offering it to show pattern.

Young: What pattern? Two?

Judge: I don't like it Mr. Bullock (prosecutor). The only thing that would happen from calling that witness is a guaranteed appeal. A conviction would just be overturned. No chance.

The story hides from viewers the character-of-defendant rules that were enacted during the Get Tough on Rapists Era. Young thunders on about general character evidence rules, but neither the prosecutor nor the judge point out the special rules that were enacted during this era that create exceptions to these rules in sexual assault cases.[45]

---

[44] Young's aggressive cross-examination of the complainant elicits her testimony that the rape didn't result in bruising to either her wrists or her inner thighs. In response to the prosecutor's single follow-up question (called 're-direct examination'), the complainant testifies that the rape caused vaginal bruising. Nevertheless, Young offers no evidence of her sexual history.

[45] Similarly, in an episode of *Law & Order: SVU* entitled 'Consent' that first aired in the year 2000, a college student claims that she was raped by two men at a fraternity party. The investigating police officers contact a woman who tells them that Joe, one of the alleged rapists, had raped her some time earlier. No mention is made either before or during the trial that the prosecution might offer the earlier rape incident to prove Joe guilty of the charged rape.

In an episode of *Shark* entitled 'In the Grasp',[46] two college football players are charged with raping Sydney Blair, a student at the same college, during a party.[47] Blair admits that she had been drinking alcohol and that she willingly accompanied the two defendants into an isolated basement room, but insists that they forced her to have sex with them. The story includes elements that bring into play both types of laws enacted during the Get Tough on Rape Era, and manages to ignore them. As to rape shield laws, at one point prosecutor Shark instructs his associate to 'find out every detail of her [Blair's] life from conception onward'. The context falsely implies that Blair's sexual character is important to the case. The trial itself features this bit of cross-examination that should have, but did not draw a rape shield law objection from the prosecutor:

> Q (Defense Attorney): Earlier that night you had sex with Mr. Carpenter, right?

> Blair: Yes.[48]

Character-of-defendant laws fare no better in this episode. The prosecutor's zealous sleuthing leads her to a young woman named Tandy, who attends the same college as Blair and the defendants. Tandy tells the prosecutor that the defendants had raped her two years earlier, in the same basement. She didn't report the attack to the police, fearing that the college might withdraw her scholarship if she accused two football players of rape. The striking similarities between the two attacks make it almost certain that the judge would have admitted Tandy's testimony under the character-of-defendant laws. However, the prosecutor never bothers to call Tandy to testify.

VI. Do TV Shows Constitute a Third Rapist?

In the years since the end of the Get Tough on Rapists Era, acquaintance rape has remained an under-reported crime compared to other crimes of violence.[49] At least one research study (perhaps now outdated) has concluded that the changes in rape

---

[46] The series starred James Woods as a combative defence lawyer-turned-prosecutor. The 'In the Grasp' episode first aired on 19 October 2006.

[47] Blair initially claims that three men raped her, the two defendants and Josh Carpenter, the football team's star quarterback. She soon recants as to Carpenter, admitting that she and Carpenter had been having consensual sex for weeks and that he wasn't one of the rapists. Thus, the story sows doubt about the credibility of rape complainants.

[48] The earlier consensual sex with Carpenter was not relevant to prove that someone other than the defendants was the 'source of the semen or injury': a common exception in rape shield statutes.

[49] According to the December 2007 Bulletin of the US Bureau of Justice Statistics entitled 'Crime Victimization 2008', about 60.5% of all violent robberies and about 62% of aggravated assaults were reported to the police. By comparison, about 41% of rapes and sexual assaults were reported to the police. The report is available at US Department of Justice, 'Bureau of Justice Statistics Bulletin' available at http://bjs.ojp.usdoj.gov/content/pub/pdf/cv08.pdf [accessed Mar 2011] 6. However, some evidence suggests that rape and sexual assault victims are increasingly willing to report attacks to the police. In 1994, the National Crime Victimization Survey, conducted each year by the US Department of Justice, concluded that only 32% of sexual assault cases were reported to the police. The report is available online at www.icpsr.umich.edu/icpsrweb/ICPSR/studies/22927?classification=ICPSR.XVII.E.&paging.startRow=1&geography=United+States&series=National+Crime+Victimization+Survey+(NCVS)+Series.

evidence rules 'have generally had little or no effect on the outcomes of rape cases, or the proportions of rapists who are prosecuted and convicted'.[50] At the end of the day, however, the effectiveness of the changes to rape evidence rules made during the Get Tough on Rapists Era is uncertain. One writer has concluded that 'courts have not only been generally supportive of rape shield legislation, but have even expanded it beyond the scope of the drafters'.[51] By contrast, another author has concluded that rape shield law 'exceptions routinely gut the protection they purport to offer'.[52] This author admits, however, that

> the cases best suited for scholarly review and criticism—written appellate decisions … are not representative of all decisions in the criminal justice process dealing with a rape complainant's prior sexual behavior … and this limitation hinders the ability to assess the way rape shield laws work at trial.[53]

At the end of the day, a number of factors make it difficult to make blanket pronouncements about the effectiveness of rape shield laws in trials. These include the following:

— Rape shield laws apply only at trial. Potential rape complainants may fear disclosure of their sexual history during pre-trial processes.
— Rape shield laws vary among the states.[54] Some state statutes do little more than remind trial judges that evidence of a rape complainant's sexual character is not admissible unless it is relevant. The less directive a statute, the less confidence it can offer potential complainants about the privacy of their sexual history.
— Even the strictest rape shield laws are subject to exceptions. For example, a common exception allows defendants charged with rape to offer evidence of their own previous sexual activity with a rape complainant. Since shield laws apply most commonly in 'acquaintance rape' situations, this exception often allows defendants to offer evidence of at least a portion of a complainant's sexual history.[55]

Thus, it remains an open question as to whether the drumbeat of negative portrayals of rape shield laws in the television shows described above make it fair to consider them a third rapist. After all, if the portrayals provide potential rape complainants with fair warning that lawyers and judges commonly allow end runs around rape shield laws, then condemning the portrayals would be to unfairly condemn the messenger for providing accurate messages.

Nevertheless, television shows surely do a disservice to potential rape complainants and the proponents who fought so long and hard for the enactment of rape shield laws. None of the episodes described in section V present a positive message

---

[50] David P Bryden and Sonja Lengnick, 'Rape in the Criminal Justice System' (1997) 87 *J Crim L and Criminology* 1194, 1199.

[51] R Klein, 'An Analysis of Thirty-Five Years of Rape Reform: A Frustrating Search for Fundamental Fairness' (2008) 41 *Akron L Rev* 981.

[52] Anderson, 'From Chastity Requirement to Sexuality License' (n 9) 55.

[53] Ibid 95.

[54] Prof Anderson identifies four different categories of rape shield laws. See ibid 81.

[55] Prof Anderson argues that this generally-accepted exception to rape shield laws is unwarranted. See ibid 147.

about rape shield laws. Nor do any of these episodes educate viewers about the laws that often allow prosecutors to offer evidence of accused rapists' commission of other acts of sexual violence. Instead, the episodes suggest that clever defence attorneys easily manoeuver around rape shield laws, that these laws have gone too far and are unfair to men, and that accused rapists' propensity for sexual violence is irrelevant. The repetition of these messages suggest to viewers that rules protecting rape complainants may exist on paper but are of little use in the real world. This is especially true given the breadth and strength of the pre-existing attitude that the legal system is a 'second rapist', the post-Get Tough on Rapists Era episodes have probably reinforced rather than led viewers to revise their beliefs that rape evidence rules are degrading and unfair to rape complainants. To the extent that rape complainants' reluctance to report their attackers to the police is due to their beliefs that the formal legal system will treat all rape complainants like them harshly and unfairly, the television portrayals do constitute a third rapist.

8

Prosecutors and Psychics on the Air: Does a 'Psychic Detective Effect' Exist?

CHRISTINE A CORCOS*

I. Introduction

With this chapter I begin an examination of the effect and influence of psychics and psychic detectives on the legal system and popular culture.[1] Scripted shows,[2] such as the popular *Medium*[3] and the recently cancelled *Ghost Whisperer*,[4] enhance

---

* I would like to thank my fellow panelists and attendees at the 13th Association for Law, Culture and the Humanities Meeting, Brown University, 20 March 2010, for their valuable comments on a draft of this chapter. I would also like to thank H Vey LaPlace (LSU Law '2011), Christopher Rhymes (LSU Law '2012), and Danielle Goren (LSU Law '2012) for patient and faithful editing and research assistance. In addition, many, many thanks to my colleague Professor Grace Barry, who read drafts of this chapter and made thoughtful comments both on the form and the substance.

[1] For reasons of space I limit much of my examination in this chapter to the recently cancelled scripted show *Medium,* and to some of the reality shows that have been or are currently airing. I am currently working on a more extensive study of psychic detective shows, in which I examine the extent to which they have an influence on the legal system. Some of the issues I examine include the ways in which jurors reconcile judges' instructions with what they see on 'psychic TV' and what they think they know about the paranormal, and possible tort and contract liability of psychics for their speech and behaviour.

[2] The word 'scripted' refers to shows that have writers who are (normally) members of the Writers' Guild of America. Prior to the writers' strike of 2004, reality show writers had no representation in the WGA. See W Booth, 'Reality Is Only an Illusion, Writers Say' *Washington Post* (10 Aug 2004) C1. After the strike, the Writers' Guild began to represent reality show writers as well as part of the Nonfiction Writers Caucus. See http://wga.org/content/default.aspx?id=1123.

[3] www.cbs.com/primetime/medium/. *Medium* is based on the experiences of psychic medium Allison DuBois of Phoenix, Arizona. See A DuBois, *Don't Kiss Them Goodbye* (New York, Simon & Schuster, 2005). An early review of *Medium* suggested that the show had something new to offer, but even the writer recognised that it was perhaps old wine in old bottles: '"Medium" is not "The Twilight Zone" or even "The X-Files". It is a conventional police drama with an unconventional twist. Yet the most innovative aspect of the show is not its reliance on extrasensory sleuthing, but the selection of an atypical actress to star in a new drama. For network television, that is paranormal.' See Alessandra Stanley, 'When DNA Fails to Crack a Case, Call a Psychic Friend' *NY Times* (3 Jan 2005) www.tv.nytimes.com/2005/01/03/arts/television/03stan.html?ref=patricia_arquette. Throughout this chapter, I differentiate between the real life Ms DuBois and the television character by referring to the television character as 'TV Allison'.

[4] www.cbs.com/primetime/ghost_whisperer/. CBS cancelled the show in May 2010 after five seasons. See '"Ghost Whisperer" Gone for Good', *Toronto Sun* (28 May 2010) www.torontosun.com/entertainment/

the personal accounts of the psychic detectives on whom they are based, adapting interesting characteristics and stories, and creating entertainment for viewers. Psychic detective shows such as the reality shows[5] *Psychic Detectives*,[6] *Psychic Witness*,[7] and the new series *Paranormal Cops*[8] provide an alternative to the popular crime scene investigation (CSI) shows[9] by opening a window into the legal system for America's TV audience. The CSI shows rely on experts and an exciting array of scientific tools,[10] suggesting that scientific evidence can often be so conclusive that the prosecutor in criminal cases can satisfy the 'reasonable doubt' standard without difficulty. Psychic detective shows seem to present investigative television that appeals to those interested in the spiritual and the unknown, offering a contrast to the certain outcomes of CSI shows by posing questions that seem closer to the realities with which many viewers are more likely to be familiar through their newspaper and TV experiences. Sometimes juries or judges acquit defendants even though they seem to be guilty, or convict the defendants even though evidence might seem to exonerate them. Some members of the public think they have paranormal experiences and regularly go to psychics. Many people read newspaper horoscopes, even if only for entertainment, and love the inserts in their Chinese fortune cookies.

tv/2010/05/28/14173186-wenn-story.html. The show was based on the life story and experiences of psychic medium Mary Ann Winkowski. See MA Winkowski, *When Ghosts Speak: Understanding the World of Earthbound Spirits* (New York, Grand Central Publishing, 2007). James Van Praagh, another well known psychic (*Talking to Heaven* (New York, Dutton, 1997)), wrote the Introduction to her book.

[5] While both the industry and critics argue over what exactly constitutes a 'reality show', at a minimum a reality show holds itself out as 'factual' even if it is not. In her discussion of the reality television genre, Annette Hill surveys the varying definitions given to it by the industry, critics and TV viewers. See A Hill, *Reality TV: Audiences and Popular Factual Television* (London and New York, Routledge Publishing, 2005) 41.

[6] Court TV (now TruTV), aired 2004–to date.

[7] On its Investigation Discovery Channel, TLC airs a programme called *Psychic Witness*. Animal Planet aired a programme called *The Pet Psychic* (2002–?), with Sonya Fitzpatrick as the eponymous psychic. One commentator on the show's message board said, 'Ok for entertainment purposes but she is not real'. But another raved about Fitzpatrick's abilities, saying, 'Sonya really does communicate with animals. It's amazing!... I wish she would explain how the animals understand her—is it telepathic or do they really understand when we speak to them?' See www.tv.com/pet-psychic/show/14241/summary.html.

[8] *Paranormal Cops* (A&E, 2009–) www.aetv.com/paranormal-cops/.

[9] See, eg CSI: Crime Scene Investigation at www.cbs.com/primetime/csi/.

[10] See, eg *CSI* (CBS, 2000–). The 'CSI effect literature' is growing rapidly, although some of it suggests that the effect itself may not exist. For an analysis of its effects on the legal system, see, eg R Catalani, 'A CSI Writer on the CSI Effect' (2006) 115 *Yale Law Journal Pocket Part* 76; CM Cooley, 'The CSI Effect: Its Impact and Potential Concerns' (2007) 41 *New England Law Review* 471; S Cole and R Dioso-Villa, 'CSI and Its Effects: Media, Juries, and the Burden of Proof' (2007) 41 *New England Law Review* 435; H DiFonzo and RC Stern, 'Devil In a White Coat: The Temptation of Forensic Evidence In the Age of CSI' (2007) 41 *New England Law Review* 503; JB Johnston, 'Prosecuting Government Fraud Despite the "CSI Effect": Getting the Jury To Follow the Money' (2007) 41 *New England Law Review* 563; TF Lawson, 'Before the Verdict and Beyond the Verdict: The CSI Infection Within Modern Criminal Jury Trials' (2009) 41 *Loyola University Chicago Law Journal* 119; M Mann, 'The "CSI Effect": Better Jurors Through Television and Science?' (2005/2006) 24 *Buffalo Public Interest Law Journal* 211; TW Nolan, 'Depiction of the "CSI Effect" In Popular Culture: Portrait in Domination and Effective Association' (2007) 41 *New England Law Review* 575; K Podlas, 'Impact of Television On Cross-Examination and Juror "Truth"' (2009) 14 *Widener Law Review* 479; SL Stephens, 'The "CSI Effect" On Real Crime Labs' (2007) 41 *New England Law Review* 591; DE Shelton et al, 'A Study of Juror Expectations and Demands Concerning Scientific Evidence: Does the "CSI Effect" Exist?' (2006) 9 *Vanderbilt Journal of Entertainment & Technology Law* 331; AP Thomas, 'The CSI Effect: Fact or Fiction' (2006) 115 *Yale Law Journal Pocket Part* 70; and TR Tyler, 'Is the CSI Effect Good Science?' (2006) 115 *Yale Law Journal Pocket Part* 73.

Further, such shows emphasise what many viewers may consider to be the fallible side of the legal system, playing on existing viewer fears that defence attorneys can overwhelm prosecutors and juries with their 'tricks'. These fears include those that arise out of the impression that constitutional guarantees such as those embedded in the Fifth, Sixth, and Fourteenth Amendments are 'loopholes' or 'technicalities', which seem to exist solely to give the accused far too many rights at the expense of the victim and his or her family. Linked to that fear is the idea that the police may arrest the wrong person or fail to solve crimes altogether. The news media deluges viewers with stories about cold cases.[11] In addition, TV today also features horror stories about criminals 'inexplicably' allowed to go free, who then proceed to commit additional crimes,[12] and exposés about law enforcement which never apprehends killers.[13] Added to this mix is the public's suspicion that innocent persons may spend years in prison[14] or may well be executed.[15] 'Psychic detective' shows may well present a convenient solution to what seems to some to be a tragically confused and horrific dilemma.

Scholars provide relatively little empirical, as opposed to anecdotal, evidence to support the often-reported notion that many people think the courts 'have gone too far' in protecting the rights of the accused as opposed to the rights of the victim. However, one commentator who has studied the issue notes that, although the public seems to have accepted the consequences of specific Supreme Court decisions (citing those of *Miranda v Arizona*[16] and *Gideon v Wainwright*[17]), it still might not have

embrace[d] the philosophical position of the Court on constitutional protections for the accused. When the rights of those accused of crimes are considered in light of competing concerns, such as the desire to prosecute crime and to ensure that those who are guilty are found guilty, the modern public appears still more closely aligned with an ideological position emphasizing crime control.[18]

---

[11] *Cold Case Files* (A&E, 1999–?). Lawyer/journalist Bill Kurtis hosted the series, which received two Emmy nominations (2004 and 2005). Criminologist Dayle Hinman hosted a similar reality series based on her own experiences called *Body of Evidence: From the Case Files of Dayle Hinman* (2002–). Currently running on Fox is the fictional series *Bones* (2005–), the TV version of the novels by Kathy Reichs about forensic anthropologist Temperance Brennan. See www.kathyreichs.com/. See also *Cold Case* (CBS, 2003–10) www.cbs.com/primetime/cold_case/), and the reality series on Fox *America's Most Wanted* www.amw.com/.

[12] A Rozas and M Owens, 'Murder Exposes Flaws in Parole System' *Chicago Tribune* (11 April 2008) www.chicagotribune.com/news/local/chi-domestic-violence-080411,0,3118283.story.

[13] Famous unsolved crimes include that of the disappearance of Judge Joseph Force Crater (discussed in R Tofel, *Vanishing Point* (Chicago, Ivan R Dee, 2004)); Elizabeth Short, the 'Black Dahlia', (1947), which has been dramatised several times, most recently in the film *The Black Dahlia* (Universal Pictures, 2006); the murder of actor Bob Crane, the star of the television series *Hogan's Heroes* in 1978; and the Christmas 1996 killing of JonBenet Ramsay.

[14] See J Carlton, 'DNA Clears Texas Man Who Spent Thirty Years In Prison' *whtr.com* (2011) www.wthr.com/story/13774045/dna-clears-texas-man-who-spent-30-years-in-prison (discussing the exoneration and expected release of 51-year-old man who has spent three decades in prison for a crime he did not commit).

[15] M Smith, 'Texas Resists Family's Effort to Clear Executed Man's Name' *CNN* (9 Nov 2009) www.cnn.com/2009/CRIME/11/07/willingham.texas.execution.probe/.

[16] 384 US 436 (1966).

[17] 372 US 355 (1963).

[18] AE Lerman, 'The Rights of the Accused' in N Persily et al (eds), *Public Opinion and Constitutional Controversy* (New York, Oxford University Press, 2008) 41, 57.

A television show that offers the vision of a psychic detective who presents the police, the district attorney, and the fact-finder with proof from the victim himself has innate attraction. It gives representatives of the legal system absolute certainty of the identity of the perpetrator. Further, it plays into the traditional narrative of 'the loner' or the outsider—the individual who can address the underlying issue, which is to identify the perpetrator and bring him to justice, particularly when the legal system seems incapable of doing so.[19]

In addition, through the convenience of the camera and other familiar technology that the viewer understands (although she may not quite grasp its application in the psychic and paranormal investigation field),[20] both scripted and reality shows allow the viewer to accompany the psychic as he or she receives messages and makes connections to the afterlife. In a scripted show, the viewer can see either through the psychic's eyes, through the victim's, or through the perpetrator's, a convention used in the scripted shows *Medium* and *Ghost Whisperer*. The camera also serves other functions in such shows. For example, it witnesses and validates the (fictional) experiences of the characters. In a reality show, the camera accompanies the psychic detective to act as a check on his or her activities; it stands in the viewer's shoes. It provides the viewer with what seems to be incontrovertible evidence, and thus allows the viewer to make the connection that the camera presents the truth of what occurs or has occurred. For viewers who have grown up with cameras, the video camera carried along in a documentary style show seems to present proof of psychic detective claims.[21] In scripted shows, cameras tend to serve persuasive and narrative, rather than investigative, functions. On reality shows, which mimic the documentary style, the cameras seem to serve the investigative function. In actuality, I would suggest that they reinforce the narrative function laid out by the off-screen (or voiceover) narrator and the behaviour of the psychic detective.

If some viewers believe that psychic detectives might effectively assist one side or the other[22] in discovering 'the truth', they may well also believe that psychic participants in the legal system do not need any particular legal training in order to validate

---

[19] Common examples of the individual addressing the failure of the legal system to identify the perpetrator include the private investigator, as in the Sherlock Holmes stories, which are notably bare of any paranormal explanation, although Sir Arthur Conan Doyle was himself a believer in Spiritualism. See M Polidoro, *Final Séance: The Strange Friendship Between Houdini and Conan Doyle* (Amherst, NY, Prometheus Books, 2001).

[20] See, eg the show *Ghost Hunters* (Syfy Network), www.syfy.com/ghosthunters/, which uses various pieces of equipment including a tape recorder and digital thermometer (described in Steve's Gear Guide), http://www.syfy.com/videos/Ghost%20Hunters/Steve's%20Gear%20Guide.

The theory behind the use of the equipment is that 'spirits are made of energy', (from the EMF Detector clip) and therefore the equipment can detect them.

[21] Interestingly, the development of the camera and Spiritualism came about at roughly the same time. Indeed, early cameras documented 'spirit photographs' and these pictures seemed to prove the existence of ghosts because few people could understand how camera operators could have falsified them. One prosecutor took pains to find experts who could explain to a court exactly how this could be done. See generally L Kaplan, *The Strange Case of William Mumler, Spirit Photographer* (Minneapolis, University of Minnesota Press, 2008) (discussing the case of the Boston photographer tried for fraud and reproducing the closing statement of the prosecutor). Several recent books and one exhibition have documented the attraction of 'spirit photographs'. See C Chéroux, *Photography and the Occult* (New Haven, Yale University Press, 2005).

[22] Normally, psychics and psychic detectives assist the prosecution; in some cases we see psychics and mediums assisting the defence or victims' families who may not have a particular 'side'.

that participation. After all, the reverse is certainly true. The average potential juror needs no particular knowledge of the law in order to participate on a jury. She might interpret the psychic's lack of legal knowledge as an advantage. Not until the juror receives a judge's instructions might she begin to understand why, for example, she is not allowed to discuss the trial with any other party except other members of her jury panel, why the accused is entitled to confront witnesses against him, and what reasoning underlies the 'best evidence' rule. Prior to these judicial instructions, such a juror might wonder why a psychic should not be allowed to participate in the legal system according to her particular talents. Such a juror might therefore be more likely to accept the argument that if psychic detectives can ensure that the quality of justice improves (whatever that means), the legal system should not bar them from participation.

In addition, shows that feature the psychic detective, whose talents and skills arise not primarily study and training, but from some paranormal power, emphasise the psychic's ability to assist the 'unimaginative'; the lawyers, police and judges in charge of our legal system.[23] The psychic detective who can call on supernatural or paranormal powers to uncover 'whodunit' and who seems to have no bias is an attractive hero to the American viewer, who herself might be called on to sit in a jury box. These shows also suggest that outside, although not necessarily untrained, assistance is necessary for simple justice to prevail. Thus, these shows reinforce the impression that 'legal technicalities' prevent valid testimony from being given in court and justice from being served.[24] These psychics are simply delivering simple truths from beyond and redressing a balance that many viewers may believe is tipped in favour of the defendant.[25] Why should the jurors not listen and, together with the psychic, do justice for the victim, if law enforcement, attorneys, and judges will not or cannot?

II. Common Psychic Detective Claims

What then are the claims that psychics make concerning their abilities to solve crimes? One of the most common of these claims is that law enforcement agencies use psychics to assist them in their investigations, although the agencies will not admit it. Those

---

[23] We sometimes hear psychics in fictional shows discuss the need for training, *Medium*—'Pilot' (aired 3 Jan 2005); and in real life discuss the need for study, DuBois, *Don't Kiss Them Goodbye* (n 3) 58–68, but generally speaking, persons who claim no paranormal ability would, I think, assume that such abilities simply 'come' to the psychic or medium without any development. They are not something that one can 'learn', as one 'learns law' or 'learns medicine' or 'learns' the techniques of policing. Indeed, psychics and mediums reinforce this notion themselves when they talk about their abilities as 'gifts' from above or 'gifts from God'. They may 'develop' these gifts but these abilities still sound like something bestowed, whereas a license to practice law is not.

[24] While I cannot thoroughly address the ways in which psychic shows compete with actual legal proceedings in order to achieve justice in such a short chapter, I do sketch out one way in which one show, *Medium*, offers an alternative narrative to the traditional method of seeking justice. See n 69 and accompanying text.

[25] Lerman, 'The Rights of the Accused' (n 18).

viewers who watch such shows as the recently cancelled *Larry King Live*[26] or psychic detective reality shows that dramatise psychic detective/law enforcement partnerships quickly become aware of the claims. When the writers fold such claims into fictional shows such as *Ghost Whisperer* or *Medium*, such assertions seem 'real' to the viewers because they have previously heard them. In addition, an attractive, personable actor (Jennifer Love Hewitt on *Ghost Whisperer*, Patricia Arquette on *Medium*), familiar to the viewer, helps deliver the claims.[27]

Similarly, psychic detectives who appear on popular interview shows such as *Larry King Live*, or on heavily edited reality shows, understandably wish to demonstrate their abilities to 'hit' on information that other sources, such as police officers, can later verify.[28] Sympathetic interviewers can make psychic detectives seem very successful and very effective.[29] Among the claims that a psychic might make include the following: that law enforcement agencies might employ her to assist with a cold case, or with an ongoing case that has no leads, particularly without disclosing that fact,[30] and that she has been of material assistance in solving particular crimes or disappearances, even if law enforcement did not consult her.[31] Those who try to rebut such claims fret that they get rather less publicity than do psychics and their adherents.[32]

---

[26] *Larry King Live* (CNN), www.cnn.com/CNN/Programs/larry.king.live/. For example, psychic Sylvia Browne appeared on the show on 31 August 2000 and 5 Dec 2003; Browne, psychics John Edward and James van Praagh and Rabbi Schmuley Boteach appeared on 6 March 2001 to respond to skeptics Leon Jaroff and Paul Kurtz. See 'Are Psychics For Real?', *CNN*, broadcast on 6 March 2001, www.archives.cnn.com/TRANSCRIPTS/0103/06/lkl.00.html.

[27] Indeed, Hewitt now asserts that she accepts certain paranormal beliefs, including a belief in ghosts. See T Morales, 'Jennifer Love Hewitt's "Ghost"' (CBS) *The Early Show*, broadcast on 21 Sept 2005, www.cbsnews.com/stories/2005/09/21/earlyshow/leisure/celebspot/main870783.shtml (discussing Hewitt's discovery, with the assistance of Mary Ann Winkowski, that her Los Angeles home housed two ghosts). The evidence, according to Hewitt, included 'feeling very lethargic and you have throat problems or really bad headaches, a lot of times that can sometimes mean there is nothing wrong with you physically, but also that you have a ghost…They're drawing on your energy. They draw on your upset, on your stress, on your tired, on your emotional and whatever else is going on with you at the time. Because they pull your energy, you feel like you're sick.' ibid.

[28] Some researchers have studied claims made by certain well-known psychics and psychic detectives, including Sylvia Browne, Nancy Weber, and several others. Their studies suggest that at best, psychic detectives tend to overstate their claims of accuracy. See R Wiseman et al, 'An Experimental Test of Psychic Detection', (1996) 61 *Journal of Society Psychological Research* 34. The Wiseman study was in part a response to a widely read book, A Lyons and M Truzzi, *The Blue Sense: Psychic Detectives and Crime* (New York, Mysterious Press, 1992). Other researchers have studied the success rate of psychic detectives used specifically by police departments. See M Reiser et al 'An Evaluation of the Use of Psychics in the Investigation of Major Crimes' (1989) 7 *Journal Police Sci & Admin* 18.

[29] See *Larry King Live* (CNN) broadcast on 26 January 2007 (featuring Rosemary Altea and James Randi as guests). Transcript available at www.transcripts.cnn.com/TRANSCRIPTS/0701/26/lkl.01.html. Two researchers have investigated Browne's claims in detail. See R Shaffer and A Jadwiszczok, 'Psychic Defective: Sylvia Browne's History of Failure,' (2010) 34 *Skeptical Inquirer* 38.

[30] See M Irwin, 'There's No Good Proof the Real Medium, Allison DuBois, Has Ever Cracked a Case, But Her Fans Don't Care' *Phoenix New Times* (10 June 2008) www.phoenixnewtimes.com/2008-06-12/news/there-s-no-good-proof-the-real-medium-allison-dubois-has-ever-cracked-a-case-but-her-fans-don-t-care/1.

[31] See generally Jane Ayers Sweat and Mark W Durm, 'Psychics: Do Police Departments Really Use Them?' (1993) *Skeptical Inquirer*.

[32] 'We want to believe psychics can communicate with the dead; we want to believe that Reiki healing works medical wonders. So while the occasional James Randi or Carl Sagan can bring the message to a wider audience, skeptics usually get shut out of television and the popular media. They don't make good copy. They don't get ratings.' M Oppenheimer, 'Pulling the Wool Off Your Eyes: Penn and Teller Declare War On Magicians' Bull' (2003) *Hartford Courant* WLNR 15203130. Note also that in many fictional representations of the psychic detective story such as *Medium,* the skeptical and questioning third party

A frequent convention of the 'psychic' or 'psychic detective' film or television series presents the skeptical or cynical third party (often a reporter or a police officer)[33] as one whom the psychic detective must convince that her abilities are real.[34] This convention holds true both in *Medium*, which apart from its 'psychic detective' spin is a traditional crime drama, and *Ghost Whisperer*. Frequently the psychic is a beautiful woman, as played not just by Arquette and Hewitt, but by Valerie Bertinelli in the film *Claire*,[35] or an attractive or popular leading man that producers and networks expect will encourage high ratings.[36] That device also leaves open the possibility of friction with another character, which then may lead to romance during the course of the story. In most cases, the psychic is female, which seems to conform to the historical record, because Spiritualism is a belief system founded by and dominated by women.[37]

serves as a proxy for such a real-life individual. Often, but not always, in such stories, the psychic manages to persuade this individual that her paranormal abilities are valid and useful. If the fictional character remains unpersuaded, the script often identifies him or her as being either overly cynical or otherwise 'flawed', thus closed-minded, and sometimes 'unredeemable'.

[33] In some cases, the psychic who brings evidence to the police unsolicited may find herself accused; see J Klunder, 'Jury Awards $25,184 in "Psychic Vision" Case' *Los Angeles Times* (31 March 1987) (discussing the case of Etta Louise Smith). Ms Smith approached the local police with a 'vision' concerning the location of a missing nurse's body; the police interrogated her for 10 hours and then arrested her in connection with the case. She sued for false arrest and won. Most jurors accepted her explanation of a psychic vision (or at least they did not believe the police had cause to arrest her and the prosecution did not have a case against her); the police believed she learned of the body's location through neighbourhood gossip or other non-paranormal means. ibid.

[34] *Psych* turns this convention on its head for the purposes of satire but obviously aims to debunk the notion of the paranormal, not just through the characters of Shawn and Gus but also through Shawn's father, Henry Spencer, a retired police officer. *Psych* also spoofs fellow anti-psychic detective show *The Mentalist*, which airs on CBS. *The Mentalist* is more serious, but still takes a debunking position through former 'psychic' Patrick Jane's explanations to his colleagues in the CBI (and thus to the audience) of his work. Another show which tries to explain paranormal behaviour is *Lie To Me* (Fox), www.fox.com/lietome/. The popular television show *Monk*, which starred Emmy winner Tony Shaloub, featured a detective who was extremely observant, but specifically noted that he did not believe in the paranormal. As he says to his personal assistant, 'You've gotta be a little skeptical, Sharona. Otherwise you end up believing in everything—UFOs, elves, income tax rebates.' 'Mr. Monk and the Psychic', aired 19 July 2002, on the USA network.

[35] See *Claire* (Hallmark, 2008) www.hallmarkchannel.com/publish/etc/medialib/shared/titles/Claire/q_a/claire_bertinelliqa.Par.0001.File.dat/Claire_BertinelliQA.pdf+valerie+bertinelli+movie+psychic&hl=en&gl=us [accessed 15 September 2009). (Larry Levinson Productions/RHI Entertainment, 2007). French title 'Des Yeux Dans la Nuit' (literally: 'Eyes in the Night'). For a summary of the action in the film, see 'Inside Look at Valerie Bertinelli's Claire' *MovieWeb* (20 July 2007), www.movieweb.com/news/NENTwPRPZWqpSS. The name may be a reference to the title character's ability to see ghosts, but also (for those who are skeptics) a bad pun.

[36] Ted Danson plays James van Praagh in the TV movie *Living with the Dead* (2002) based on van Praagh's book *Talking to Heaven*.

[37] On 30 March 1848, two young Hydesville, New York sisters, Kate and Margaret Fox, founded the Spiritualist movement in the United States when they scared their mother by making sounds with their knuckles and with an apple by bouncing it against the wall of their bedroom. Spiritualists who communicated with the dead used the term 'medium', not 'psychic', but today the terms seem to be interchangeable. On the Fox sisters see B Weisberg, *Talking to the Dead: Kate and Maggie Fox and the Rise of Spiritualism* (San Francisco, HarperBooks, 2004). On the history of the movement, see A Braude, *Radical Spirits: Spiritualism and Women's Rights in Nineteenth-Century America* (Boston, Beacon Press, 1989) and RL Moore, *In Search of White Crows: Spiritualism, Parapsychology, and American Culture* (New York, Oxford University Press, 1977). Moore questions whether the Spiritualist movement is quite so heavily dominated by women. See RL Moore, 'The Spiritualist Medium In America: A Study of Female Professionalism In Victorian America' (1975) 27 *American Quarterly* 200, 203–204.

That the psychic or psychic detective must persuade law enforcement of her abilities may only make her even more sympathetic and convincing to the viewer. Viewers see what the police do not—verification of the psychic's claims.[38] Television makes this presentation an attractive one, emphasising the psychic's status as underdog, loner, and champion of the victim, a common and popular symbol in American folklore. It recalls the image of the individual who stands alone against the government or some great evil, fighting against the odds, to bring about justice.

Psychic detective shows, whether they are reality shows or fictional dramas, present a view of the legal system that suggests it can and should be opened to those who can simply present 'the truth', 'the right outcome' or 'justice', if necessary circumventing constitutional guarantees. These shows also suggest that, in many cases, those guarantees are simply flaws in the legal system, because they prevent justice from prevailing. For some viewers who watch these shows, the legal system seems to provide uncertainty, particularly because of the 'cold cases' the media often highlights.[39] Thus, in order for victims and victims' families to achieve justice, the legal system really needs the assistance of both the victims themselves, calling out from beyond the grave, and those gifted with psychic ability here on earth, even though such ability might be scientifically unproven.[40] Of course, such shows are what we might consider 'law and order'- or 'prosecutor'-driven shows. That is, they emphasise the necessity of finding 'truth' or 'justice', rather than of validating the legal system's procedures. For example,

---

[38] Like *Medium* and *Ghost Whisperer*, the television movie *Claire* presents an attractive woman who reluctantly becomes involved in an unsolved crime. She does not flaunt her abilities. She has a supportive family, but others are suspicious of her abilities, which is why she is reluctant to become involved in the case. Her law enforcement connection (the retired police officer uncle) convinces her to become involved. Her involvement puts her in danger. She finds romance. Her abilities bring the case to a successful conclusion by pointing the police to clues that they can use to bring the killer to justice (although in this case the killer actually commits suicide). The suggestion is clearly that without Claire, this case would have remained unsolved, either because the police are incompetent or because they simply did not have enough evidence to convict the killer (suggesting a flaw in the legal system). Unlike some psychic detectives, Claire gets involved in the case because her uncle, a retired detective, asks for her assistance, a circumstance that we don't normally see, because police officers, retired or not, normally do not seek out the assistance of psychics, whether or not they are related to them. ibid. Another example is the television movie *Visions of Murder* (1993) starring Barbara Eden as a psychologist who begins having psychic visions of a dead patient. She eventually convinces law enforcement that she knows the identity of the killer. Eden made a follow-up film, *Eyes of Terror* (1994). Similarly, Melissa Gilbert stars in *A Vision of Murder: The Story of Donielle* (2000), in which she has visions of the identity of a serial killer and eventually convinces law enforcement that she can help solve the crimes. The story is based on real events; Donielle Patton claimed to be psychic; see L Farr, *The Sunset Murders* (New York, Pocket Books, 1993) and www.trutv.com/library/crime/criminal_mind/psychology/defending_oneself/11.html.

[39] The manner in which psychic detective shows provide alternatives to traditional legal dramas or real legal proceedings is beyond the scope of this particular chapter. However, in my discussion of *Medium*, and in my discussion of some jurors' and parties' responses to the legal regime, I attempt to show that at least some individuals who are aware of paranormal claims are attempting to reconcile them with that legal regime.

[40] The victims' rights movement has moved ahead with some rapidity. In California, for example, the Legislature has passed Marsy's Law, and its supporters now wish to push forward to make it the basis of a constitutional amendment. See www.marsyslawforall.org/. For an explanation of the popularity of the continuing attraction of belief in the afterlife see Michael Shermer, *The Believing Brain* (New York, Henry Holt, 2011) at 141–63. Shermer suggests non-paranormal explanations for the experiences that observers put forward as evidence of the afterlife and notes 'there is no scientific evidence that [the soul] survives [death] or ever will.' The belief in a psychic's ability to communicate with the dead presupooses a belief in the afterlife.

a psychic who could take the stand in a murder trial to testify that she spoke with a dead victim and could swear, under oath, that the victim told her the defendant was guilty of his murder, could assist in circumventing the right to confrontation afforded by the Sixth Amendment to that defendant. For viewers concerned about justice, that right to confrontation may seem like a 'technicality'. However, that 'technicality' is a funda-mental guarantee.[41] How could the defence attorney effectively cross-examine such a psychic witness if the Confrontation Clause and the hearsay rules do not apply?

For those who accept the possibility of psychic visions, disallowing such testimony because of 'legal technicalities' supports their view that judges and lawyers are more interested in form rather than substance, and in resolving legal disputes rather than in achieving justice. In addition, to many viewers, including those who watch a great deal of television and hear a great deal about defendants' rights gone wild,[42] the balance may seem to have tipped in favour of too much justice for the accused and too little for the victim. Whether the psychic presents herself as someone who 'helps people' voluntarily, as in *Ghost Whisperer*;[43] as someone who works (albeit unofficially) for the government,[44] as in *Medium*; or as someone who works sometimes for free and sometimes under contract, as do many of the psychics who appear on talk shows and reality shows, that person may seem to take on the role of the avenger—an individual who can redress the balance.

In addition, some of these shows may give their viewers the impression that 'cold case' investigators can profit from the assistance of psychics, some of whom also advertise their availability as psychic detectives. Thus, families of cold case victims may find comfort in the words or actions of some who offer the possibility of con-tact with the afterlife. While the notion of a link to the afterlife is not new, because Spiritualism as a belief system has been around for more than 150 years,[45] the linking of psychic contact and the legal system *is* something new and merits investigation.

Talk show host Larry King often invited psychic Sylvia Browne on the show to discuss her work.[46] Browne also gave numerous readings on the (now-cancelled) *Montel Williams Show*,[47] including one to the mother and stepfather of Shawn Hornbeck, who had been missing for months, telling them the boy was dead.[48] FBI agents and police later found Shawn alive.[49] To explain her misses, Browne notes that

---

[41] US Constitution, Amendment VI.

[42] See M Blanding, 'The Long Shadow of Willie Horton' *The Boston Globe Magazine* (8 October 2009), www.boston.com/bostonglobe/magazine/articles/2009/10/18/the_long_shadow_of_willie_horton (discuss-ing unintended effects of the pardon granted Willie Horton by the then Governor Michael Dukakis).

[43] In the episode 'The Gravesitter' (aired 11 April 2008), a blogger named Justin repeatedly describes Melinda as someone who 'helps people'.

[44] TV Allison Dubois, in *Medium*.

[45] On the history of Spiritualism, see generally D Blum, *Ghost Hunters: William James and the Search for Scientific Proof of Life After Death* (New York, Penguin Press, 2006); B Goldsmith, *Other Powers: The Age of Suffrage, Spiritualism, and the Scandalous Victoria Woodhull* (New York, Alfred A Knopf, 1998); and RL Moore, *In Search of White Crows: Spiritualism, Parapsychology, and American Culture*, (n 37).

[46] *Larry King Live* (CNN, 31 August 2000) www.quiz.cnn.com/TRANSCRIPTS/0008/31/lkl.00.html; *Larry King Live* (CNN, 5 December 2003) www.transcripts.cnn.com/TRANSCRIPTS/0312/05/lkl.00.html.

[47] *The Montel Williams Show* (Paramount/Out of My Way Productions, 1991–2008).

[48] www.stopsylvia.com/articles/montel_shawnhornbeck.shtml.

[49] B Pinto, 'Found Alive! Two Boys Went Missing, One For Four Years' *ABC News* (12 January 2007) www.abcnews.go.com/US/story?id=2792051).

only God is infallible.[50] Other psychics who appear fairly regularly on television to attempt to solve crimes or assist law enforcement include Carla Baron,[51] Gale St. John,[52] and Jackie Barrett.[53] Such a proliferation of appearances and shows suggests that the topic continues to interest audiences. The Writers' Guild of America West, which provides its members with access to assistance via its website and through events, offers a transcript of an interview with a psychic to help writers working on scripts with paranormal content.[54]

Medium dramatises the work of real life psychic Allison DuBois, who says she has worked with certain law enforcement agencies, even though those agencies deny having worked with her.[55] Similarly, psychic detective 'reality' shows pull in a decent audience share. On these shows, members of law enforcement agencies present psychics with 'cold cases' (that is, long, unsolved crimes) and ask them to provide assistance with possible solutions. Common claims for nearly all these shows are that the psychics involved have no prior information concerning these cases and have never been to the locations involved. Thus, the audience infers that any clues or pronouncements the psychics deliver must be the result of their paranormal powers. The camera follows along with the psychics as they direct the detectives toward clues and attempt to solve the crimes. As these shows are either half an hour or an hour long, their creators edit them heavily because psychics work on these cases for one to two days, producing a great deal of footage. Narrators assure the viewers of the validity of the proceedings.

On TruTv (formerly Court TV), *Psychic Detectives*[56] garnered a respectable following. A similar show, *Sensing Murder*, was quite popular in its native Australia, and an American version runs periodically on the Discovery Channel.[57] Some commentators have criticised psychic detectives, most notably 'debunkers' like James 'the Amazing' Randi, Penn & Teller, Michael Shermer, and other skeptics, as have some criminal profilers who see such work as unhelpful at best and as exploitative of victims' families at worst.[58]

---

[50] J Ronson, 'Is She For Real?' *The Guardian*, 27 October 2007 www.guardian.co.uk/world/2007/oct/27/usa.jonronson.

[51] *Haunting Evidence* (TruTv), www.trutv.com/shows/haunting_evidence/mystery_meet.html. In this particular show, the psychic detectives involved offer clues, but the episodes tend to conclude without any resolution of the case.

[52] *Psychic Detectives* (TruTv, 2005–09) www.jerrypippin.com/Paranormal_Psychic_Detectives.htm.

[53] See n 83.

[54] See D Faye, 'Occult Status' *Writers Guild of America, West,* www.wga.org/content/default.aspx?id=3566 (interview with Mary Kara).

[55] M Irwin, 'There's No Good Proof the Real Medium, Allison DuBois, Has Ever Cracked a Case, But Her Fans Don't Care' *Phoenix New Times* (10 June 2008) www.phoenixnewtimes.com/2008-06-12/news/there-s-no-good-proof-the-real-medium-allison-dubois-has-ever-cracked-a-case-but-her-fans-don-t-care/1.

[56] The network is now called TruTV, and the programme seems to have been dropped. It ran from 2005 through 2009 and featured Phil Jordan; the narrator was Les Marshak. See www.imdb.com/title/tt0460670/.

[57] www.dsc.discovery.com/fansites/upcomingshows/sensingmurder.html.

[58] CV Zandt, 'Shoe Leather, Not Sixth Sense, Breaks Cases Open' *MSNBC*, www.msnbc.msn.com/id/7320305/. Some psychics have taken such criticism to heart. One psychic, Noreen Renier, won a defamation action against a skeptic who criticised her work in the area, www.badpsychics.co.uk/thefraudfiles/modules/news/article.php?storyid=360. However, she subsequently ran into legal problems when she breached the 1992 settlement agreed to by publishing her account of the lawsuit in a 2005 book, *A Mind to Murder* (New York, Berkley Books, 2005). The defendant in the 1992 case filed suit and when she failed to respond, the judge issued a default judgment in favour of the (now) plaintiff. See *Merrell v Renier*

When contacted, many law enforcement agencies respond that they have never used psychics to assist them in investigating cases.[59] A 1993 survey of police departments in the 50 largest cities in the United States indicated that 65 per cent of the departments did not use psychics. The remaining departments sometimes used them, but none of these departments found the information provided by psychics to be useful in solving crimes.[60] However, police and the FBI still take the position that they must investigate all tips, including those coming from psychics, especially when handling high profile crimes.[61]

For viewers who have suffered loss themselves, or who empathise with the families of victims, the 'scripts' on talk shows, reality shows, and dramas quickly become familiar through repetition. The reasons to use psychics to assist in crime-solving seem obvious: to help get killers off the streets, to assist overworked police and prosecutors, and to bring solace to grieving families.

III. Presentation of Psychic Claims on Scripted Psychic Detective Television Series: Medium

CBS describes its popular show *Medium* as

[A] DRAMA INSPIRED BY THE REAL-life story of research medium Allison Dubois, an extraordinary young wife and mother who, since childhood, has struggled to make sense of her dreams and visions of dead people. Emmy Award winner Patricia Arquette stars as Dubois, a strong-willed, devoted young wife and mother of three girls who has gradually come to grips with her extraordinary ability to talk to dead people, see current events and the future through her dreams and read people's thoughts. Dubois works as a consultant to District Attorney Manuel Devalos, using her psychic abilities to solve violent and horrifying crimes that baffle Phoenix police and others within the criminal justice system. Assisting her crime-solving endeavors is Detective Lee Scanlon, her longtime ally in the local police department. Meanwhile, at home, Dubois' husband Joe, an aerospace engineer, is a supportive husband and father who is also busy launching his own scientific engineering company. Their daughters, Ariel, Bridgette and Marie all seem to have inherited their mother's abilities to varying, expanding degrees.[62]

Case No C06-404JLR, Order issued 22 Jan 2007, commentarybysherlock.com/commentarybysherlock/pdf/012507%20Order_on_Partial_Reconsideration.pdf; *Merrell v Renier* (fees order) issued 5 April 2007, www.noreenrenier.com/order.pdf.

[59] C Crawford, 'Yard Hunt For Clues On Sarah' *Sunday Herald Sun* (26 September 2004) www.infoweb.newsbank.com/iw-search/we/InfoWeb?p_action=doc&p_topdoc=1&p_docnum=1&p_sort=YMD_date:D&p_product=AUNB&p_text_direct-0=document_id=(%201055641EA6BE8035%20)&p_docid=1055641EA6BE8035&p_theme=aggregated4&p_queryname=1055641EA6BE8035&f_openurl=yes&p_nbid=L6EB5BTVMTE4MDAxNzU2MC43MDU1NjA6MTo4OnJmLXNcTE5&&p_multi=AHSB) (Australian police response to questions about the use of psychics in a search for a missing young woman); R Tiffin, 'Police Reject Psychic Advice' *Bay of Plenty Times* (1 February 2006) www.bayof-plentytimes.co.nz/local/news/main-story-police-reject-psychic-advice/3670861/ (discussing police rejection of psychic clues concerning location of woman missing 20 years).

[60] See generally Sweat and Durm, *Psychics: Do Police Departments Really Use Them?* (n 29) 148.

[61] Zandt, *Shoe Leather, Not Sixth Sense, Breaks Cases Open* (n 56).

[62] www.cbs.com/primetime/medium/about/. *Medium* ran on NBC from 2005 to 2009. After NBC cancelled it, CBS picked it up and it has run on that network since the fall of 2009. It is also in syndication in a

I classify this show as having the following characteristics:

— It is based on a 'real-life story'.[63]
— The person on whom the show is based has 'struggled to make sense' of her claimed abilities.
— The character in *Medium* works with law enforcement and with a district attorney, reinforcing the notion that actual psychic detectives work with law enforcement and the individual who inspired the series also does so.
— The character in the show has a law enforcement colleague or colleagues who provide support but also skeptical foils.
— The character in the show has supportive relatives and/or friends who believe in and accept her abilities.[64]
— The character in the show has relatives who are also psychic, which suggests that paranormal abilities are not only real, but that they are genetic (thus scientific and provable).
— While many people are initially put off by the central character's psychic ability claims, they eventually become believers because of her obvious abilities, although she can be somewhat assertive. Sometimes she is initially incorrect, but in the end, she always points the way towards 'the right answer'.[65]

Although the show's website does not make it clear, TV Allison Dubois (as opposed to her real-life inspiration) is generally reticent about advertising her abilities to society.[66]

---

number of markets. Five of its seasons are now out on DVD. Because of its availability on two major broadcast networks, *Medium* is familiar to a fair section of the American viewing audience. Its 2009 premiere won its time slot, crushing NBC's *Dateline*. See R Poter, 'TV "Medium-Sized" Numbers Good Enough For CBS Friday' *ZAP 2 News & Buzz* (26 September 2009) www.blog.zap2it.com/frominsidethebox/2009/09/tv-ratings-medium-sized-numbers-good-enough-for-cbs-friday.html. CBS also aired *Ghost Whisperer* in the 8pm time slot preceding *Medium*; it won its time slot. However, the network cancelled *Ghost Whisperer* at the end of the 2009/2010 season.

[63] A DuBois, *Don't Kiss Them Goodbye* (n 3). See also DuBois' website, which clearly links her to the show *Medium*, www.allisondubois.com/ [accessed 17 March 2010] and on which she mentions her 'favorite' episodes www.allisondubois.com/index.php/Table/CBS.com-Videos/. One obvious difference that DuBois does not mention is that TV Allison dreams a great deal; her dreams are often crucial to solving cases. But the real life Allison states, 'Anyone who knows me knows that I rarely dream at all'. A Dubois, *Don't Kiss Them Goodbye* (n 3) 145.

[64] As played by Patricia Arquette, the television Allison Dubois (note the spelling of the last name) is somewhat assertive and often angry, somewhat more feminist than the soft-spoken Jennifer Love Hewitt as Melinda Gordon in *Ghost Whisperer*, even though Allison is a devoted mother. In some episodes the Dubois marriage shows quite a bit of strain, unlike the Gordon/Clancy marriage in *Ghost Whisperer*, in which the couple seems to be able to work out its problems. Melinda Gordon, the main character of *Ghost Whisperer*, the CBS show, also features these characteristics. Similarly, in the psychic detective 'reality shows', in which females seem to predominate, women tend to be quite assertive. The gendered dynamics of the psychic detective, although beyond the scope of this chapter, certainly deserve some attention, because they are historically of interest if one considers the traditions of Spiritualism, a belief system in which women were finally able to assert themselves. See A Braude, *Radical Spirits: Spiritualism and Women's Rights in Nineteenth Century America*, 2nd edn (Bloomington, Indiana University Press, 2001).

[65] See *Medium*, 'In Sickness and Adultery' (broadcast 31 January 2005) (Allison has a vision of Joe in a clinch with a young woman; later Allison and Joe have dinner in a restaurant; the young woman is at another table, begins to choke and Joe performs the Heimlich manoeuver to save her life. These events correspond to Allison's vision although she initially misinterprets them).

[66] In the third season finale, Allison's position at (and role with) the district attorney's office becomes public knowledge and the public becomes aware of her powers. See *Medium*, 'Everything Comes to a Head' (broadcast 16 May 2007).

Real life psychics say they are reluctant to profit from their abilities However, many of them write books and appear on talk shows. At least some also seem to charge varying fees for psychic readings and personal appearances,[67] and otherwise seem to advertise their gifts. [68]

While TV Allison is not always right initially in the interpretations she gives to the police, her visions always guide her to correct conclusions about the guilty party.[69] The fact that she had originally planned to go to law school, that she often mentions that she studied 'criminal law' as an undergraduate, but that she manages to solve or assist in solving so many crimes without a law degree (particularly in the episode 'In Sickness and Adultery') further emphasises the idea that a medium or a psychic detective is as capable, or more capable, than someone trained in the law to bring criminals to justice.[70] Because Allison works for the district attorney's office, because the district attorney believes he needs her in order to assist in obtaining convictions, and because he cannot admit that he employs her, Allison seems to be even more of a heroine.[71] In addition to the moral outrage viewers may already feel at the idea that 'the legal system' may perpetrate what seems to be injustice, they may also recognise that TV Allison represents a real person (even though that viewer understands that the character is somewhat fictionalised). One can then understand that what TV Allison accomplishes each week by channeling her paranormal abilities through the legal system may seem to be for some viewers a more satisfactory outcome than what currently exists outside the television 'medium.'

---

[67] See the website for Sylvia Browne, a prominent psychic and psychic detective who charges $850 for a 'phone reading', www.readings.sylviabrowne.com/. Note that the website indicates that fees are temporarily reduced given the state of the current economy, www.sylviabrowne.com/. The real Allison DuBois made an appearance on the reality show *The Real Housewives of Beverly Hills* during which she responded to a request for a demonstration of a psychic reading. See Claire Lawton, 'Allison DuBois Makes (Drunk) Appearance on Real Housewives of Beverly Hills', *Phoenix New Times Blogs*, (21 Dec 2010) (http://blogs.phoenixnewtimes.com/jackalope/2010/12/allison_dubois_makes_drunk_app.php).

[68] For many years psychics took the position that they would not use their talents to benefit themselves, but this claim, as one might imagine, sounded hollow, particularly because they charged for their services. One such psychic says: 'I've known few psychics, however, who haven't taken their innate abilities and worked and studied for years to hone their spiritual faculties. Many have invested in lengthy schooling and training, and lead a lifestyle as disciplined as an Olympic athlete's in terms of meditation, habits and focus in order to maintain clear access to subtle energies and information. I see little difference between the training and education of a doctor or teacher or artist and that of a psychic or medium.' See www.everythingunderthemoon.net/psychic-readings.htm.

Many psychics will often say, as TV Allison does, that they cannot foresee clearly what will happen to them, thus forestalling criticisms such as 'If you can see the future, why don't you win the lottery for yourself?' In answer to this question, psychic Rosa Derivviere responds, 'Clairvoyants don't win the lottery because the work that clairvoyants do is based on spiritual guidance and insights. The lottery is about financial gain and it's very unlikely that you will find any clairvoyant or psychic predicting lottery numbers because it's not for your greater good.' See www.videojug.com/interview/life-of-a-psychic.

[69] *Medium*, 'Being Mrs. O'Leary's Cow' (broadcast 25 April 2005). Allison initially assures the district attorney that an airline pilot's missing wife is alive and that the pilot is not implicated in her disappearance, then revises her view, leads the police to the woman's body, and to evidence of the man's guilt.

[70] In the last episode of the series, Allison becomes a lawyer. CBS Website Preview at www.cbs.com/primetime/medium/.

[71] The real Allison DuBois has said in an interview that 'In Sickness and Adultery' is one of her favourite episodes because of the 'smack down' TV Allison administers *sotto voce* to the defence attorney in the courtroom scene. 'Interview', *Medium* Season One DVDs.

In the episode 'In Sickness and Adultery',[72] Devalos uses the information TV Allison gives him to obtain a warrant, then asks her to lie on the stand in order to preserve its validity and thus presumably achieve justice. When the defence attorney, suspecting that a psychic, namely Allison, is involved in the case, he subpoenas her and attacks her testimony on the stand. Devalos' request that Allison back him up by lying, that she say that she has 'independent information' that supports his request for the warrant, offends her tremendously. Her husband Joe simply advises her to do what Devalos asks her to do.[73] Once Allison is on the stand, she manages to 'smack down' the defence attorney by revealing to him in a low tone of voice that she knows, for example, that he asked someone else to take the bar exam for him.[74] Rather than pursue the line of questioning on which he has embarked, which is to find out exactly 'who you are, Ms. Dubois, and what you do for the District Attorney's office', he abruptly abandons his line of questioning and stalks back to his seat, leaving the field of battle clear for the district attorney.[75] But the defence attorney has the right and in the zealous representation of his client an obligation to try to quash the warrant. What Allison does is to frighten him off by blackmailing him, thus protecting her supervisor, and ensuring the conviction of the guilty defendant. Viewers might believe that this outcome is morally justified. However, Allison's psychic knowledge does not justify her use of threats. In effect, she and Devalos are guilty of the same act. He uses her knowledge to get a warrant, and she uses her knowledge to circumvent the defendant's right to a fair trial. In addition, while Devalos uses his access to the formal mechanisms of the justice system and his knowledge of law to circumvent the defendant's right to a fair trial, Allison uses her paranormal powers and her access to the legal system to do the same. The episode presents not simply the notion that the prosecutor might be slightly dishonourable and willing to use TV Allison in ways that she had not anticipated, but that Allison is, as the psychic heroine, completely honest. 'In Sickness and Adultery' also reinforces a major and disturbingly familiar complaint about the legal system, combined with a new assertion about those with paranormal gifts; by itself, the system will not bring about justice, and it needs the assistance of the psychic.[76] But TV Allison's behaviour is questionable. She uses what she believes is her knowledge of the defence attorney's private behaviour to fend off his defence of his client, to help to convict someone she believes is guilty of a crime, and to protect the district attorney, using the rationale that 'the end justifies the means'. While that behaviour may seem honourable to some viewers, it is based on information about the defence attorney and his client that TV Allison has arrived at 'psychically'. Because Allison has no objective proof of this behaviour, her own action validates the behaviour of a district attorney who has arguably broken the law. In effect, TV Allison appoints herself judge and jury in the case.

---

[72] *Medium*, 'In Sickness and Adultery' (broadcast 31 January 2005).
[73] Ibid.
[74] Ibid.
[75] Ibid.
[76] Extensive evidence concerning how some individuals may try to integrate what they have seen in psychic detective shows and interpret about the paranormal with what judges instruct them about their duties as jurors is beyond the scope of this chapter. However I give an example of what some British jurors did in *R v Young* [1995] QB 324.

TV Allison's husband Joe is a physicist and one of the more powerful skeptical voices on the show. He continually challenges her to question her belief not that her visions are real, but that she is interpreting them correctly. Joe also urges Allison to question whether everything in life is fore-ordained. He makes this statement most clearly before they marry, as we see in the flashback episode, 'Allison Rolen Got Married'.[77] Allison has a vision of a missing woman, and then a dream of the death of their, as yet, unborn daughter at the hands of a relative Allison meets for the first time at their wedding. She calls the police to give them the information she received through her vision, but they find the information unhelpful. The script makes clear that this encounter is her first as a psychic with law enforcement.

Because of her vision and dream, Allison is deeply disturbed and believes that in order to prevent her child's murder, she must call off the wedding. Being a believer in free will as well as a critical thinker, Joe points out that any number of events could derail this tragedy, but Allison is adamant. What finally frees Allison to marry Joe is not just Joe's mother's statement to Allison that love is not simply an act of faith but also an act of courage, but also Allison's own second call to the police with additional information about the killer she has seen in her visions. While her first call yields only skepticism from law enforcement, her second provides specific information which leads to the discovery of the missing woman's car and to the arrest of the killer, who is also Joe's relative. The second call represents the free will and the courage of which Joe and his mother speak.

The camera in *Medium* allows viewers to see what TV Allison sees, and also believe what she then conveys to police and to others about her visions. Curiously, what viewers and Allison see is quite often more than what Allison actually says. Allison might urge her law enforcement colleagues on with cryptic or abbreviated messages, particularly early in an episode when she has a limited amount of information. Because her information lacks specificity, her colleagues must then wait, or proceed with their own investigation, until she can point them in the right direction, or confirm their independently discovered evidence with her own visions. As viewers, we *do* believe Allison because we see what she sees, but her colleagues have not seen what we have seen. Thus, Allison's role as somewhat victimised and misunderstood psychic continues, but we understand her colleagues' reactions, and their reluctance to make a leap of faith, which we, the viewers, do not have to make.

While Allison's colleagues may believe her, they must always confirm her information with additional evidence. While she may be able to point her colleagues in the right direction, Allison and the audience must wait, frustrated, while her colleagues ask for warrants, get independent verifications of her visions, or otherwise verify that she is correct when she gives them information. *Medium* episodes thus heighten the dramatic tension that audiences often feel during crime dramas; not only are viewers certain that TV Allison may be or is correct about her visions, but they (and she) feel helpless while the police and the district attorney seem handcuffed by 'legal technicalities'—the need, for example, to stay on the 'right side' of ethical rules.[78]

---

[77] Broadcast 12 March 2010.
[78] *Medium*, 'How to Beat a Bad Guy' (broadcast 10 March 2010) (Detective Scanlon's brother may be involved in the death of an undercover police officer).

Unsurprisingly, some viewers (or at least those who leave comments on the message board) believe that some individuals have genuine paranormal powers and that law enforcement should use them to assist in solving crime.[79] However, others note sadly that the legal system does not accept paranormal evidence.[80] Finally, some enjoy the show, but find its premise, well, otherworldly, and see no legal value in it whatsoever.[81]

IV. Consequences

Viewers' continued interest in paranormal shows, including those that combine law and the paranormal such as the series *Drop Dead Diva*,[82] seem to suggest that their primary interest is not the actual workings of the legal system but a concern with ultimate justice. They may instead have a particular, romanticised view of the legal system as one in which specific individuals mediate spectral evidence in order to provide perfect justice in the event that law enforcement and prosecutors cannot otherwise achieve it. Indeed, some members of the public may believe that psychics can and should act as a check on law enforcement by making sure that the 'real killer' in particular cases is caught if it seems that she or he might escape justice. Programmes such as *America's Psychic Challenge*,[83] *Sensing Murder*,[84] and *Psychic Detectives*,[85] and dramas such as *Ghost Whisperer*[86] and *Medium*[87] may serve to express and/or reinforce viewers'

---

[79] "It does not surprise me that fans of Medium would vote 90 to 10 in favor of forensic psychics. We all know that psychic phenomena is real. I knew a couple of them up in MD that were very helpful with cold cases.' (jbdavis53, posted 30 Oct 2009); 'I believe that there are people like Allison, and what could it hurt to have someone that can pick up on things that the police or others may miss in an investigation. There are all kinds of interties in this world, and who are we to say that they don't exist.' (tr2thmpson, posted 17 Jan 2010). (Comments from www.cbs.com/forum/posts/list/0/82872.page#1566177).

[80] 'I think if the psychic is genuine and not simply a con artist they could be very helpful in investigations. Sadly though it's the judicial system that balks at their talents and typically does not allow the use of that information in court.' (loneworf634, posted 4 June 2010). (Comment from www.cbs.com/forum/posts/list/0/82872.page#1566177).

[81] 'NO way, but it does make for fun TV. There is no way that there could ever be any probably [sic] cause, with the use of a "medium", and the case would get thrown out of court. Or, the criminal would be convicted [sic], and then appeal, and walk free. If there is ONE real psychic in the world, there are one million fakes for that one. It's also scary to me the number of people who believe that cops should use these fake psychics in their investigations. Cops have only limited time and energy and finances, and they need to focus on real evidence, not bogus information that wastes their time or brings them to wrong conclusions. That hurts the real victims, and gives more time to the bad guy to get away, or come up with better alibis. Thankfully, police departments do not use pyschics [sic], or tarot card readers, or astrologers.' (spudscouch, posted 22 April 2010). (Comment from www.cbs.com/forum/posts/list/0/82872.page#1566177.

[82] *Drop Dead Diva* (Lifetime Television, 2009–present), www.mylifetime.com/shows/drop-dead-diva. In this series a model is reincarnated in the body of an attorney.

[83] *America's Psychic Challenge* (Lifetime Television 2007). In this programme, 16 self-proclaimed psychics competed for a $250,000 prize by demonstrating their abilities through a series of tests. Each week, one contestant was eliminated until one remained to win the prize. See www.mylifetime.com/shows/americas-psychic-challenge. The ultimate winner was Michelle Whitedove, who prevailed over Jackie Barrett. Barrett later obtained her own reality show, *Medium PI*, which aired on the BIO channel, beginning in 2009. Her co-star was Sean Crowley, a former NYPD officer. On her website, Barrett says she is 'the official psychic consultant to the Federal Government' I am not sure exactly what she means. See www.jackiebarrett.com/5.html.

[84] *Sensing Murder* (Granada Television, 2006).

[85] *Psychic Detectives* (Court TV/TruTv, 2005–).

[86] *Ghost Whisperer* (CBS, 2006–present).

[87] *Medium* (Paramount, 2005–06; CBS Paramount, 2006–09; CBS Television, 2009–).

beliefs that psychics really can deliver such messages from beyond the grave and that, regardless of the rules of evidence and procedure, such information should make its way to the police and then into the trial. If law enforcement cannot provide evidence that passes muster according to the standards of the Rules of Evidence, some viewers may reason that perhaps we should at least consider the possible persuasiveness of spectral evidence. Such viewers may not think it should be necessarily admissible, but they may think the police and judges ought at least to consider it.[88]

I would suggest that such a view of the possible re-admissibility of spectral evidence causes tension in the legal system. This tension has already begun to create conflict, not just for jurors, but for prosecutors and judges. The following are just a few examples of this tension. In the first example, a psychic attempts to explain her special abilities to a judge and two attorneys:

The Court: Yes, ma'am. What number are you, ma'am? ...

Defence Attorney: Number 123, Your Honor ...

The Court: Okay.

Prospective Juror No 123: I am a psychic and a spiritual counselor. I see auras and —

The Court: Well, can you tell me now what's going to happen, so we can all go home?

Prospective Juror No 123: I see auras and I feel energy. I didn't say I was a mind reader. And I don't feel I can be objective to this in a situation like this. This is why I disqualify myself.

The Court: Okay. What do you —

Prospective Juror No 123: I don't know what you're thinking, but your aura is beautiful. It's sparking out all over the place.

The Court: Sparking?

Prospective Juror No 123: It's sparking out into space.

Prosecutor: I concur.

The Court: Well, thank you.

Defence Attorney: What about mine?

Prospective Juror No 123: You don't want to know. It's very dark.

The Court: Okay. Well—but you'll have to wait until the attorneys ask you questions, and then bring it up and then we'll see what happens.

Prospective Juror No 123: Yes. I know you're confused. That's why your energy is going (gesturing), because of what I said. You were calm and cool until I stood up here.

The Court: Well, cosmic matters concern me.[89]

---

[88] Just one poll taken in 2005 indicates that nearly half the population admits to a belief in ghosts, and that over 20% says it has encountered a ghost. S Alfano, 'Poll: Majority Believes in Ghosts' *CBS News* (30 October 2005), www.cbsnews.com/stories/2005/10/29/opinion/polls/main994766.shtml.

[89] *Texas Bar Journal* (February 2004), www.texasbar.com/PrinterTemplate.cfm?Section=texas_bar_journal1&Template=/ContentManagement/ContentDisplay.cfm&ContentID=5822.

In the second example, a prosecutor's decision to consult a psychic muddied the waters of a Pennsylvania murder case:[90]

> A court ruling has confirmed that Erie County President Judge William R. Cunningham consulted with a psychic on the Kirk case in the early 1990s. Cunningham met with the psychic when he was district attorney and when an investigative grand jury, at Cunningham's request, was reviewing evidence from the Kirk case in secret.
>
> The prosecution and defense disagree over the significance of Cunningham's visit with the psychic... Current District Attorney Brad Foulk said Cunningham's venture into the para-normal has no bearing on how Foulk will proceed with the prosecution of James 'Jamie' Fleming. He was Kirk's boyfriend when the 25-year-old X-ray technician was found dead on a Presque Isle State Park beach. Foulk in August 2000 had Fleming, then 39, charged with homicide, 12 years after Kirk's death.
>
> The defense hopes to use Cunningham's reliance on the spiritual dimension as a multidi-mensional tool to help offset the prosecution's case. Tim Lucas, Fleming's lawyer, contends Cunningham's use of the psychic proves the evidence against Fleming is so 'sorry' that Foulk should not be allowed to bring the case to trial.[91]

The case went to trial later that year, and included the former prosecutor's testimony regarding his use of the psychic,[92] over the objections of the prosecutor then trying the case.[93]

In a notorious 1995 English murder trial, *R v Young,* the defendant obtained a retrial on the grounds that, while they were sequestered, some members of his jury consulted an homemade Ouija Board to communicate with the spirit of the deceased in order to obtain additional evidence of his guilt or innocence.[94]

> The summing up finished and the jury, who had retired to consider their verdicts, were unable to complete their deliberations. They were accommodated at a hotel overnight. As eventu-ally was established, four jurors conducted what purported to be a session with a makeshift ouija board for communicating questions to and receiving answers from the deceased which were highly adverse to the appellant and caused distress to three women jurors present at the session. On resumption the next morning, 23 March 1994, in court the jury returned unanimous verdicts of guilty on each count and the appellant was sentenced to concurrent terms of life imprisonment. Consequent on a juror consulting a solicitor and giving him a handwritten statement of what had occurred at the hotel, communication was made with leading counsel for the appellant.[95]

---

[90] L Thompson, 'Ex-D.A.'s Visit to Psychic Fogs Kirk Case' *GoErie.com* (12 January 2003), goerie.com/apps/pbcs.dll/article?AID=/20030112/FRONTPAGE/101120221.

[91] Ibid. The local retired police chief noted he had never used a psychic and did not think they were 'an appropriate tool' for such an investigation. Ibid.

[92] L Thompson, 'Jury to Unravel Kirk Murder' *GoErie.com* (11 July 2003) www.goerie.com/apps/pbcs. dll/article?AID=/20030711/FRONTPAGE/107110339.

[93] L Thompson, 'D.A. Foulk Tries to Block Hearing' *Erie Times-News* (23 March 2003*)* www.truthin-justice.org/eerie.htm. In this article, the 'psychic' is identified as a 'tarot card reader'. The jury convicted Fleming of involuntary manslaughter. See L Thompson, 'Foulk Friend to Victims: Families Say they Saw Justice when DA Pushed Old Cases' *Erie Times-News* (13 August 2009).

[94] *R v Young* [1995] QB 324.

[95] Ibid 4. Would anyone argue that the statement of the deceased should be admissible had it been a *sworn* statement, witnessed by a notary present at the séance? On contacting the spirits of murder victims, see also D Pannick, 'Cases Haunted by the Spectre of Failure' *Times of London,* 24 March 1998 (on a lawsuit over a haunted piece of Derbyshire property). ('I am indebted to my friend Cyril Glasser... for drawing to

The jurors in *R v Young* had received explicit instructions to suspend deliberations once they retired for the night, but obviously some of them thought contacting the dead victim would aid them in discovering the truth. These and other examples too numerous to include here show that lay participants in the legal system can sometimes have difficulties dissociating their inclinations to accept paranormal beliefs or their willingness to investigate the paranormal as a route to the truth from their duties as members of that system.[96]

V. Conclusion

In a society in which many Americans may have an imperfect understanding of the legal system to begin with, the notion that police, lawyers, and judges should give spectral evidence some credibility should not seem so far-fetched. Non-lawyers may not understand the purpose of evidentiary rules, or the reasons for the Confrontation Clause. Combining such uncertainties with questions about the actual purpose of trials suggests that pressure on law enforcement to use psychics, or at least to continue to consider their use, will continue because many Americans continue to show interest in the paranormal. Comments left on television message boards indicate the extent to which viewers consider the possibility that paranormal abilities exist and that psychics can help to solve crimes, such as those left on the board for *Medium,* or the A&E reality show *Paranormal Cops.*[97] One viewer wrote that he or she was excited about this show, thinking that:

> real police investigators' would bring a whole new world of credibility to paranormal investigations… Instead they walk around with a psychic… your credibility goes to zero with a psychic… Someone walking around claiming they can see the ghosts, hold conversations with the ghosts, can even tell the gender and what they are wearing, well that's just not scientific.[98]

Responded another viewer:

> It doesn't bother me. Many investigations into non-paranormal stuff use rumors and sources that cannot be used in a courtroom. I have no problem seeing the psychic as the paranormal equivalent to hearsy (sic). She might have something invaluable to the investigation, but it isn't evidence that can be used to make the case- just give it a direction to look in.[99]

---

my attention a report in this newspaper some years ago of an investigation into a violent death in India. At a seance, the victim's spirit was asked whether she had been murdered or had committed suicide. She answered: "I shan't tell". Asked why, the spirit replied: "Don't you know the matter is sub judice?").

[96] Lay participants are not the only ones with the problem, of course. As the Kirk case points out, lawyers can also have difficulty. See n 91 and accompanying text. The well-known case of *State v Charbonneau* is another example. In that case, the defence lawyer was convinced his niece, a clairvoyant, was in touch with the victim; on appeal the defendant later unsuccessfully claimed ineffective assistance of counsel. See *State v Charbonneau* 774 P. 2d 299, 307, 310 (Idaho 1989).

[97] *Paranormal Cops* (A&E Television), www.aetv.com/paranormal-cops/. The police officers describe themselves as 'paranormal detectives'.

[98] A&E Community Message Board/Paranormal Cops www.community.aetv.com/service/display DiscussionThreads.kickAction?w=279123&as=119137&d=477992&ac=new.

[99] Ibid.

Clearly, the two commenters both understand that psychic evidence obtained under such circumstances would be questionable, and the second points out that it would not be admissible. But the second also noted that it might take police to a helpful clue, thus supporting the notion that psychics have clearly made this point with the viewing audience.[100]

Fictional programmes such as *Medium*[101] and *Ghost Whisperer* and 'reality shows' such as *Psychic Detectives*, make the claim that psychic detectives can assist both law enforcement and victims and survivors to achieve justice. I suggest that these fictional and 'reality' shows create the assumption for some viewers that alternatives to the current legal system might exist, or that the current legal system could be induced to make room for validated paranormal claims. For these viewers, some individuals seem to have paranormal ability and if they can assist law enforcement, judges, prosecutors, and defence attorneys to do justice then such viewers may not immediately see the harm. These viewers, then finding themselves on a jury, might legitimately question why a psychic's assistance with a police investigation should not be admissible, or whether a psychic's testimony ought not to be heard, and if not, why not?

Neither criticism of psychic detective procedure nor a more deep-seated skepticism of paranormal beliefs seems to dampen audience interest, which should not surprise us. Polls taken in 2007 indicated that at least one-third of the American public believes in ghosts.[102] The First Amendment protects a belief in life after death, and in the right to assert that one can communicate with spirits (and to assert that the communication goes both ways).[103] Yet the idea that murder victims can assist in unmasking their own killers by sending back messages from beyond, and that potential members of a jury panel might think that such messages might somehow be admissible in court is disturbing. Its popularity suggests not only that it taps into the understandable and traditional desire in the lay audience for justice but also either a fundamental misunderstanding and/or a general disagreement about the nature of admissible evidence. It deserves further investigation.

---

[100] See n 60 and accompanying text (discussing the use of psychics by law enforcement).

[101] *Medium* (CBS), www.cbs.com/primetime/medium/. *Family Guy* satirises *Medium* in the episode 'Extra Large Medium' (Fox, broadcast 14 February 2010) in which Peter believes he has extrasensory perception.

[102] 'Boo! One in three people believes in ghosts' *MSNBC* (25 October 2007), www.msnbc.msn.com/id/21477704/. Further, early empirical research suggests that television programming of the *Medium* sort enhances such beliefs. GG Sparks and W Miller, 'Investigating the Relationship between Exposure to Television Programs that Depict the Paranormal Phenomena and Beliefs in the Paranormal' (2006) Presentation to the Research Division of the Broadcast Education Association web.archive.org/web/20061001060134/http:/www.beaweb.org/bea2000/papers/spa&mil.pdf.

[103] While early in the history of Spiritualism, its followers had difficulty convincing courts and legislatures that the law protected their beliefs, they eventually began to succeed. See *City of Chicago v Payne* 160 Ill. App. 641 (1911) (overturning the conviction of a Spiritualist under a Chicago vagrancy ordinance); CA Corcos, *The Scrying Game* (work in progress; manuscript on file with author). On the protection of freedom of religion and the idea that the government does not inquire into the 'truth' of religious tenets, see *US v Ballard* 322 US 78 (1944) (also referred to as the 'I Am' case).

9

Lawyers in Terrorism Thrillers

TUNG YIN

Although modern litigation may resemble gladiatorial combat, it is actually a battle of wits, not brawn. Narrative tensions in successful law-based US television dramas such as *Law & Order*, *The Practice*, *Boston Legal*, and *L.A. Law*, among others, have generally derived from confrontations between tenacious lawyers and mendacious witnesses, as well as presentations of theatrical courtroom arguments and counter-arguments. This formula invariably led audiences of these dramas to focus upon, and to experience an anticipation of, the verdict. Despite television lawyers often facing life-and-death issues, they generally only do so in the context of representing a defendant who is facing the death penalty. It is, therefore, unsurprising if terrorism-focused shows—a popular television staple since the terrorist attacks of 11 September 2001—have completely ignored lawyers, concentrating instead on the here and now of counterterrorism work. Federal agent Jack Bauer, the protagonist of the paradigmatic terrorism show *24*, dealt with terrorists by torturing them for information or killing them, not by cross-examining them on the witness stand or prosecuting them.

Strangely, however, lawyers have in fact appeared in some terrorism-related television shows, generally appearing as antagonists or obstacles to the pursuit and interrogations of the wrongdoers. Counterterrorism agents seeking to interrogate captured terrorists about the location of ticking time bombs find themselves facing Constitution-quoting lawyers who demand due process for the detainees. This chapter examines this mostly negative portrayal of lawyers in American television dramas such as *24* and the mini-series *The Grid*,[1] and examines how such shows exploit the similarly negative public view of criminal defence lawyers, particularly in terrorism-related cases. The chapter then looks to real life examples of lawyers involved in real-time counterterrorism operations. In doing so, it seeks to develop suggestions about the ways in which terrorism-related television dramas could diversify their portrayals of lawyers, taking them beyond the obvious role of those who defend the rights of terrorists, without sacrificing the action-oriented suspense that characterises such thrillers.

---

[1] This chapter focuses on American television shows. While there are European terrorism thrillers, most notably BBC's *Spooks* (which aired briefly as *MI-5* in the United States), an analysis of lawyers in non-American shows would necessarily require comparative analysis of the substantive criminal procedure and legal norms of different countries—a task beyond the scope of this chapter.

I. Lawyers in Television Thrillers as Antagonists or Obstacles

The logical starting point for analysis is to define the category of television shows fall-ing within the concept of terrorism thriller. These shows focus on operational efforts to disrupt and defeat terrorism plots through surveillance, investigation, and the ultimate capture of terrorists. Terrorism thrillers since 9/11 have frequently depicted scenarios where government agents engage in seemingly illegal and immoral actions in order to stop an imminent terrorist attack. The tacit and explicit reasoning put forth in favour of this ethically dubious approach to counterterrorism work is based on a utilitarian 'end justifies the means' argument. As advocates for suspects, defence lawyers are a natural character choice in terms of presenting the legal arguments pro-hibiting such lawless activity. Yet, while not usually shown to be conspiring actively with terrorists, the lawyers nevertheless come across as naively idealistic at best—they are routinely shown to be dead wrong. The counterterrorism agents in these shows, seemingly as a matter of practice, often ignore the lawyers' demands only to then, as a result, avert catastrophe. The implication is obvious: had the agents complied, the terrorists would have succeeded in their deadly plots.

For example, near the end of Season Four of *24*, terrorists have already caused Air Force One to crash, recovered the launch codes from the President's 'nuclear football', and hijacked a US nuclear missile. If the terrorists cannot be found and captured in time, they will be able to launch the missile against any US city of their choosing. Federal counterterrorism agents apprehend Joe Prado, an American suspected of collaborating with the terrorists.[2] The agents believe that Prado is their only source of information for discovering the location of the terrorists. Because Prado is a former Marine, however, the agents do not think he will be easy to interrogate.[3] Agents are preparing to ques-tion Prado coercively, with the aid of pain-inflicting drugs, when the supervising agent orders a halt to questioning. A lawyer named David Weiss is present with a court order 'protecting the rights of one Joseph Prado whom you have in custody'. The federal agents do not know (but the viewer does) that Weiss is alerted to Prado's capture only because the lead terrorist placed an anonymous call to Amnesty Global, the human rights organisation that Weiss represents (a thinly-veiled jab at Amnesty International), to report that the government was about to torture an American citizen.

When counterterrorism agent Jack Bauer wonders why Prado is not already being interrogated coercively, the following conversation ensues:

Weiss: Mr. Bauer, my client is cooperating. He's not trying to go anywhere. All he wants is to be treated like any other US citizen.

Bauer: Your client aided and abetted the people who attacked the President of the United States today.

---

[2] *24*, 'Day 8: 12:00 AM to 1:00 AM' (broadcast on 18 April 2005) Fox Broadcasting Company. All sub-sequent events involving the character Prado discussed in this chapter come from the same episode.

[3] The implication is also that the agents lack enough time to engage in traditional rapport-building interrogation. See generally A Davidson, 'Missed Opportunities' *The New Yorker*, 10 July 2006 (noting FBI agent Ali Soufan's successful interrogation of various terrorism suspects, including Salim Hamdan).

Weiss: You don't know that.

Bauer: As a matter of fact, we do.

Weiss: Then charge him.

Bauer: You and I both know that your client isn't clean. He conspired to steal a US nuclear warhead.

Weiss: All my client wants is due process.

Bauer: Mr. Weiss, these people are not going to stop attacking us until millions and millions of Americans are dead. Now I don't want to bypass the Constitution, but these are extraordinary circumstances.

Weiss: The Constitution was born out of extraordinary circumstances, Mr. Bauer. This plays out by the book, not in a back room with a rubber hose.

Bauer: I hope you can live with that.

In our actual world, Weiss's arguments are reasonable and sensible. We would not know if Prado was truly involved with the terrorists or if he had actionable information. Yet in the world of *24*, the viewer knows that Prado is indeed aiding and abetting the terrorists. Bauer, unable to persuade Weiss that exigent circumstances call for extreme methods of interrogating Prado, decides to violate the judicial order: he suggests to his supervisor that Prado be released from federal custody, at which point Bauer will resign from the government and interrogate Prado as a private citizen. Bauer assaults Prado in his car, breaking fingers until learning the location of the lead terrorist. As a result, Bauer eventually corners the lead terrorist and stops the nuclear missile attack.

The Bauer/Weiss conversation is repeated thematically two seasons later in *24*, when a series of suicide bombing attacks by Islamic terrorists inside the United States has led the government to detain numerous men of Arab descent in holding facilities. FBI agents arrive at the regional office of the Islamic-American Alliance, seeking a membership list for further leads. Meeting the agents are the IAA's regional director, Walid al-Rezani, and his lawyer, Sandra Palmer (who also happens to be the sister of the President of the United States). The following conversation takes place:

Al-Rezani: We take pride in being good citizens and we will cooperate with you in order to stop these attacks.

Palmer: May I see your warrant, gentlemen? I'm Mr. al-Rezani's attorney. I also represent this organisation.

Agent Samuels: We know who you are, ma'am, and I'm afraid we don't have a warrant.

Palmer: Then I'm afraid we can't turn over our personnel records. That information is private, and that privacy is protected by law.

Agent Samuels: I understand, ma'am, but in light of what's happening around the country, we don't think it's unreasonable to ask for the cooperation of our citizens.

Palmer: You're looking in the wrong place. There are no terrorists here, so unless you have a warrant, I'm going to have to ask you to leave.[4]

---

[4] *24*, 'Day 6: 7:00 AM—8:00 AM' (broadcast on 14 January 2007) Fox Broadcast Company.

The agents then leave, but al-Rezani and Palmer continue to debate the wisdom of cooperating with the government:

Palmer: This is getting out of hand.

Al-Rezani: Maybe we should give them what they want.

Palmer: You can't be serious.

Al-Rezani: We have nothing to hide.

Palmer: No, but we have something to protect: the privacy of everyone who's ever worked for this organisation.

Al-Rezani: Maybe we have to sacrifice a little privacy. The country is under attack, Sandra. We cannot pretend it isn't.

Twenty minutes later, the FBI agents have returned with a warrant, which Palmer inspects and challenges as invalid. However, she steps aside. As al-Rezani leads the FBI agents to a room with a data technician to retrieve the contents of the database, Palmer hurries to another computer station and deletes the database. Because of her actions, the FBI agents arrest not only Palmer, but also al-Rezani, who is taken to the local detention centre where men of Middle Eastern descent are being held. At the detention facility, Palmer, having been released from custody because she is the President's sister, is able to meet her client, where she continues to focus single-mindedly on his civil liberties:

Palmer: I'm getting you out of here.

Al-Rezani: I'm not going anywhere.

Palmer: Yes you are.

Al-Rezani: Sandra, listen to me. I think some people in this place have a connection to the terrorist attacks.

Palmer: How would you know that?

Al-Rezani: They were speaking Arabic, which I don't understand. But there was one phrase they used several times: 'Hamsa zawa zirada.' Pass that on to the FBI or somebody. It may help.

Palmer: They're being held illegally. Any statements they make may not be in their—

Al-Rezani: Damn it, Sandra, stop being a lawyer for one damned minute! Look, these guys may be planning something that will harm a lot of people.

'Hamsa zawa zirada' turns out to bear possible relevance to the day's events; an Arabic-speaking federal agent translates it to 'five visitors'. When the terrorists detonate a nuclear weapon just north of Los Angeles, federal agents realise that 'hamsa zawa zirada' may well mean that there are still four other tactical nuclear weapons on US soil in the hands of terrorists—a supposition that turns out to be correct. As a result, federal agents wisely continue a frantic hunt for the perpetrators of the initial nuclear attack. Whatever credibility Palmer might have had in seeking her client's rights is undermined by her criminal actions, coupled with her seeming rebuffing of her client's efforts to help the government stop the ongoing terrorist attacks.

24 does not stand alone in showing scenes where defence lawyers righteously invoke the Constitution, thus hindering the efforts of counterterrorism agents. In TNT's mini-series *The Grid*, a joint US-British anti-terrorism task force seeks to stop a former mujahedeen from carrying out a terrorist plot to wreck the economies of Western nations by destabilising the governments of the oil-producing countries in the Middle East. At one point, US agents capture a suspected terrorist, Foukara, following a failed attempt to assassinate FBI agent Max Canary (played by Dylan McDermott). The following scene takes place as the agents question Foukara:[5]

Lawyer: I am here to protect Mr. Foukara's rights.

Canary: Mr. Foukara tried to kill me.

Lawyer: Allegedly. He hasn't been charged, and he's being held illegally.

Canary: We believe he's connected to a terrorist cell that was involved in the Lagos bombings.

Lawyer: Believe what you will. This is still a free country.

When Foukara refuses to answer any questions, Canary suggests that the government could send him back to Lebanon for questioning, which prompts the lawyer to ask to speak to the agents outside his presence:

Lawyer: Don't you dare threaten him with a rendering.

Agent: He has information about planned attacks here that could threaten thousands of American lives.

Lawyer: And that gives you the right to summarily dismiss Mr. Foukara's rights? Hey, why stop there? Deport all the Muslims in America to win your war.

Canary: I might suggest some rights stop at mass murder.

Lawyer: They don't. And until there is an amendment to the Constitution to that effect, I will protect Mr. Foukara's rights. Charge him with attempted murder, try to have him extradited, but he will receive due process.

Canary: You don't know what you're doing.

Lawyer: The problem America's having in the world right now, Agent Canary, is not because of what I'm doing.

As in the scene above, the lawyers in all of these scenes competently espouse the traditional civil libertarian viewpoint that civil rights should not be undercut even in times of crisis.[6] Yet, given that in the world of *24*, for instance, terrorists are planning devastating attacks with nuclear weapons, the viewer cannot help but see Weiss and Palmer as, at best, unrealistic in their resolute adherence to legal standards.

In fact even Palmer's own client, Walid al-Rezani, expresses momentary exasperation at her intransigence and unwillingness to yield a seemingly minimal amount of

---

[5] *The Grid*, 'Hour 3' (broadcast 26 July 2004) TNT Broadcast Company.
[6] This is the central principle underlying the Supreme Court's decision in *Ex Parte Milligan* 71 US 2 (1866), striking down the use of military commissions to prosecute American civilians during wartime where civil courts remain open and functioning.

civil rights in order to help the government. If the scenario in question involves nuclear weapons and risking thousands (or perhaps millions) of lives, it may seem foolish to adhere to the Constitution just for the sake of principle. The consequentialist argument that laws and morality may have to yield, when the stakes are high enough, is laid out effectively by legal philosopher Michael Moore:

> It just is not true that one should allow a nuclear war rather than killing or torturing an innocent person. It is not even true that one should allow the destruction of a sizable city by a terrorist nuclear device rather than kill or torture an innocent person.[7]

This is not to say *24* offers any persuasive justifications for the use of torture, race-based detention, or other tactics beyond (perhaps) the fictionalised world it depicts on television. The quality of information available to the government agents, not to mention the viewer, simply fails to reflect any real life situations that the country has ever faced,[8] and the suspects seem to capitulate to torture quickly and without any deceit.[9] But television thrives on drama, not necessarily verisimilitude.

II. Defence Lawyers on TV Compared to Defence Lawyers in Real Life Terrorist Cases

As has been shown, lawyers on terrorism-related television dramas often appear naïve, overly idealistic, and perhaps even willfully ignorant of the true threat presented by ongoing terrorism. In effect, shows like *24* have exploited and intensified the conflict of feelings that American society often exhibits regarding the role of defence lawyers in the criminal justice system.

On the one hand, criminal trials are a search for the truth; hence, among other things, the prosecutor has a constitutional obligation to disclose material exculpatory evidence to the defendant.[10] The classic image of the defence attorney—someone who successfully represents the wrongfully accused, innocent person, as exemplified in the classic *Perry Mason* series[11]—fits comfortably within this narrative of the trial as a search for truth.

On the other hand, much of criminal procedure relevant to defendants has the appearance, if not actual effect, of inhibiting the search for truth. A prime example is the exclusionary rule, a legal principle that prevents the jury from hearing about relevant evidence of a defendant's guilt by suppressing it if it was obtained in

---

[7] M Moore, *Placing Blame: A General Theory of Criminal Law* (Gloucestershire, Clarendon Press, 1997) 719.

[8] For more on the so-called ticking time bomb scenario, see J Parry, *Understanding Torture: Law, Violence, and Political Identity* (Ann Arbor, University of Michigan Press, 2010) 73.

[9] See T Yin, 'Jack Bauer Syndrome: Hollywood's Depiction of National Security' (2008) 17 *SCILJ* 279, 284–85.

[10] *Brady v Maryland* 373 US 83 (1963).

[11] See F Nevins, 'Perry Mason' in M Asimow (ed), *Lawyers in Your Living Room!: Law on Television,* (ABA Press, 2009) 51, 55: 'In the Mason novels dating from the late 1930s to the late 1950s ... the clients [are] always innocent'.

violation of the Constitution.[12] Another is the Fifth Amendment privilege against self-incrimination, which allows a factually guilty person to withhold inculpatory evidence, a position largely at odds with the behaviour that parents might expect of children, or that teachers might expect of students.[13] The defence lawyer's duty to provide zealous advocacy on behalf of a factually guilty client means that the lawyer may need to subject a truthful witness to aggressive cross-examination so as to undermine that witness's credibility.[14] As James Kunen has noted:

> How can you defend those people?' is a question frequently put to criminal defense attorneys, often in a tone suggesting that it is not so much a question as a demand for an apology, as though a defense attorney needs to justify his work, in a way that a prosecutor doesn't. Because the question presumes that 'those people' accused of crime are guilty, and that people who are guilty of crimes ought not to be defended, it reflects a profound misunderstanding of our criminal justice system and the defense attorney's role in it.[15]

Considering the devastation caused by the 9/11 terrorist attacks, it may not be surprising that the misunderstanding identified by Kunen has emerged in prominent criticisms of lawyers who represented suspected al Qaeda and Taliban detainees at Guantanamo Bay, Cuba. Terrorists are seen as different from and worse than mass murderers, and terrorism on the scale of 9/11 is viewed by many as much more than a mere crime. The Supreme Court has, for example, consistently noted in dicta that various Fourth Amendment restrictions on searches and seizures might well not apply to counterterrorism efforts.[16]

Thus, in 2007, Charles Stimson, the Deputy Assistant Secretary of Defense for Detainee Affairs, publicly identified a number of prominent US law firms that had been providing *pro bono* legal representation to Guantanamo detainees. Stimson's purpose was apparently to embarrass or shame the firms, for he said:

> I think, quite honestly, when corporate C.E.O.'s see that those firms are representing the very terrorists who hit their bottom line back in 2001, those C.E.O.'s are going to make those law firms choose between representing terrorists or representing reputable firms.[17]

In a similar vein, in March 2010, the conservative organisation, Keep America Safe, produced 'Who Are The Al Qaeda 7?',[18] a video that criticized several lawyers in

---

[12] See *Mapp v Ohio* 367 US 643 (1961). Empirical evidence suggests that this concern is overstated, as only 1–2% of people arrested for felony are not convicted due to the inability to use evidence, suppressed as a result of the exclusionary rule. See *United States v Leon* 468 US 897, 907 n6 (1984).

[13] See H Friendly, *The Fifth Amendment Tomorrow: The Case for Constitutional Change* 37 *UCLR* 671, 680 (1968).

[14] See, eg *United States v Wade* 388 US 218, 258 (White J, dissenting): 'If [defense counsel] can confuse a witness, even a truthful one, or mike appear at a disadvantage, unsure or indecisive, that will be his normal course'; see generally A Dershowitz, *Reasonable Doubts: The O.J. Simpson Case and the Criminal Justice System* (New York, Simon & Schuster, 1996) 145: 'A zealous defense attorney has a professional obligation to take every legal and ethically permissible step that will serve the client's best interest—even if the attorney finds the step personally distasteful'.

[15] J Kunen, *How Can You Defend Those People?: The Making of a Criminal Lawyer* (New York, Random House, 1983) xii.

[16] See, eg *Indianapolis v Edmond* 531 US 32, 44 (2000) (striking down a suspicion-less roadblock for drug interdiction purposes, but noting that 'the Fourth Amendment would almost certainly permit an appropriately tailored roadblock set up to thwart an imminent terrorist attack').

[17] N Lewis, 'Official Attacks Top Law Firms Over Detainees' *NY Times*, 13 Jan 2007 A1.

[18] The video is available at www.youtube.com.

the Obama Administration. This video consisted of a clip of the Attorney General saying, 'We're looking for people who share our values', which is then followed by a narrator saying,

> So who did President Obama's Attorney General, Eric Holder, hire? Nine lawyers who advocated for terrorist detainees. Who are these government officials? Eric Holder will only name two. Why the secrecy behind the other seven? Whose values do they share? Tell Eric Holder Americans have the right to know the identity of the al-Qaeda 7.

The two Justice Department lawyers initially identified by Holder were Deputy Solicitor General Neal Katyal, previously a Georgetown law professor who successfully argued *Hamdan v Rumsfeld*[19] before the Supreme Court; and Jennifer Daskal, previously a lawyer with Human Rights Watch. A few days after the Keep America Safe video debuted, the Justice Department released the names of the other seven lawyers. Prior to their appointments within the Justice Department, all seven had been lawyers at major law firms, such as O'Melveny & Myers, WilmerHale, Morrison & Foerster, and Sidley & Austin, and had represented various Guantanamo Bay detainees in *habeas corpus* proceedings.[20]

It is worth noting at the outset that the attacks by Stimson and Keep America Safe were vague, perhaps intentionally so, as to the motivations of the lawyers in question. In asking whose values they share, the Keep America Safe video not so subtly implies that the lawyers actually share the values of their suspected terrorist clients. In other words, it is one thing to depict lawyers as foolish guardians of the Constitution who cling unrealistically to idealistic principles; it is another to accuse them of wishing that their clients succeeded in what they were suspected of seeking to do.[21] In short, *24* and *The Grid* likely reinforce the negative and inaccurate perception of defence lawyers.

Ultimately, the basic nature of the conflict between enforcement of civil rights versus effective law enforcement remains the same, whether in the world of television thrillers or the real world. What is different in the fictionalised television world is the clarity and certainty of the consequence of recognising those civil rights. As Jack Bauer argued to no avail, if he could not interrogate Joe Prado in whatever fashion was necessary to extract actionable information, then thousands if not millions of Americans were going to die from the next terrorist attack. And as subsequent events demonstrated, Bauer was correct in his belief that Prado had useful information and that no other avenue for tracking down the terrorists was available. Thus, in the context of the story arc, had the government complied with the court order that Weiss obtained, the results would have been disastrous: Bauer would have lost the trail of the terrorist, Marwan, who would have successfully hit Los Angeles with a nuclear missile.[22]

---

[19] 548 US 557 (2006).

[20] See 'Justice Dep't on So-called "Al Qaeda Seven": We Will Not Participate in An Attempt to Drag People's Names Through the Mud' *ABC News* (3 Mar 2010), available at blogs.abcnews.com.

[21] To be fair, the 'al Qaeda 7' ad drew criticism from many prominent lawyers, some who had worked in the Bush Administration. See C Savage and B Becker, 'Holder Did Not Disclose Briefs on "Enemy Combatant"' *NY Times*, 12 Mar 2010 A16.

[22] As it was, Marwan managed to launch the missile. Bauer saved Los Angeles because he recovered Marwan's palmtop computer, which enabled a technical analyst to locate the missile so that it could be destroyed by a fighter jet.

Torture can be objected to on a number of grounds: deontology (torture is immoral and wrong no matter what the circumstances);[23] efficacy (torture only gets people to confess falsely); and epistemological (even if torture was justified and effective, how can we know that our suspect has the information we need?). The implication that Bauer was right and Weiss was wrong about the appropriate course of action regarding Joe Prado puts the show squarely on one side of the torture debate on all of those grounds, and Weiss on the other side (very clearly, at least, on the first and third grounds). Epistemologically speaking, what further skews the portrait of Weiss' lawyering is not just the viewer's knowledge of what happens *after* Bauer tortures Prado, but the quality of knowledge available at the moment that Bauer decides that Prado must be subjected to such treatment. Based on electronic and visual surveillance, Bauer concludes that Prado is associating with a known terrorist. Still, Bauer doesn't know this for certain; he can only infer it from what incomplete information he can access. The viewer, on the other hand, is shown that Prado is not only associating with terrorists, but also knows that they are terrorists and that Prado is willingly aiding and abetting them.

The difference in information to Bauer and to the viewer is important, because events subsequent to the government conduct in question can affect ex post analysis. In a case where the issue is whether the police officer had probable cause to suspect the defendant of criminal activity, the fact that the police officer was correct is likely to tilt the playing field in favour of the officer in a marginal case. This is a known cognitive bias that has been discussed in criminal procedure literature.[24] The quality of knowledge available, at the time an agent is called upon to decide whether to torture a suspect, is an area where the world of television breaks with reality. The television viewer can be put in the position of having almost omniscient knowledge by being made privy to happenstances in scenes involving only terrorists or criminals. Thus, viewers are likely to suffer cognitive biases in favour of law enforcement without having to even see positive results derived from questionable government conduct (ie torture).

III. Suggestions for Additional Ways of Depicting Lawyers in Terrorism Thrillers

In real life, lawyers have played a variety of roles in terrorism cases beyond that of the defence attorney; television writers can accordingly draw upon these other roles to broaden the depiction of lawyers in terrorism thrillers. Of course, terrorism thrillers are not legal courtroom dramas, so the suggestions that follow are not aimed at turning the next *24* into *Law & Order: Homeland Security* or *D.C. Law*. Rather, these suggestions seek to incorporate lawyers into the ticking time bomb scenarios that drive the narrative suspense in such terrorism thrillers.

---

[23] See, eg, International Covenant on Civil and Political Rights arts IV and VII (forbidding derogation of prohibition on torture even '[i]n time of public emergency which threatens the life of the nation').

[24] See, eg, W Stuntz, 'Warrants and Fourth Amendment Remedies' (1991) 77 *VALR* 881.

One obvious suggestion would be to stop depicting lawyers at all. This may seem paradoxical, but if the only purpose of law-related dialogue in these sorts of programmes is to identify that tension exists between national security and civil rights, defence lawyer characters are hardly necessary. Terrorism thrillers often depict non-lawyer government officials discussing whether to undertake some extreme, arguably illegal act in order to forestall or defeat the threat posed by terrorists. Without downplaying the significance of these moral/legal debates, lawyers are hardly necessary to present arguments on this level—that laws must be obeyed or they are meaningless; or that horrific circumstances justify otherwise 'bad acts' to avert greater harms. For example, while Bauer and his fellow agents are blocked from interrogating Prado by the court order that the lawyer, Weiss, obtained, the President and his advisers are debating whether to authorise Prado's torture notwithstanding the court order. The President's chief of staff—a non-lawyer—makes the utilitarian argument in favour of torture, while another adviser argues against torture.[25]

If terrorism thrillers are to include lawyers for a sense of verisimilitude, government lawyers could also be integrated into the narrative. In the lawyer-agent interactions described earlier, the narrative conflict typically involves a pressing need for actionable information that agents believe can be obtained only through illegal means, such as torture. Instead of having a defence lawyer such as David Weiss raise the expected civil libertarian argument, a terrorism thriller could instead dramatise the same kind of conflict with an inverted structure: a field agent or agents could be the ones arguing that they lack the legal authority to press a captured suspect, with a government lawyer being the one to raise the 'end justifies the means' argument. Two well-known real-life examples of US Justice Department lawyers, rather than agents, being the ones to take aggressive legal positions in counterterrorism operations seem perfectly apt examples. These lawyers wrote the 'torture memo' that advised giving an extremely narrow definition to the term 'torture', thereby authorising harsh and coercive interrogation methods that fell outside that definition, and also pushed for interrogating terrorism suspects without giving the usual *Miranda* warnings.[26]

A. Aggressive Legal Positions: The Torture Memo

After the 9/11 attacks, when the United States government captured a number of high-level al Qaeda members, including Abu Zubaydah, Khalid Sheikh Mohammed (KSM), and Ramzi bin al-Shibh, lawyers in the Office of Legal Counsel issued opinions that sought to define torture so that federal agents would have guidance as to which interrogation tactics were permitted and which were prohibited. Because the government believed that these detainees might have had actionable information about future plots, as well as the location of other al Qaeda leaders, interrogators wanted as much leeway as possible to extract such intelligence without running afoul

---

[25] 24, 'Day 4: 1:00 AM—2:00 AM' (25 Apr 2005) Fox Broadcast Company.
[26] In *Miranda v Arizona*, 384 US 436 (1966), the Supreme Court held that prior to any interrogation, the police must instruct a suspect in custody that he or she has the right to remain silent, that anything said can and will be used against the suspect in court, that the suspect has the right to an attorney, and that if the suspect is indigent, an attorney would be appointed at no cost.

of the federal ban on torture. Although there was no specific plot in mind, these captured detainees presented something akin to the ticking time bomb scenario in that the government agents believed that the end justified the means in terms of subjecting the captives to severe interrogation, including in the case of KSM, in which there were over 100 instances of water-boarding.

The Office of Legal Counsel memorandum, officially titled 'Standards of Conduct for Interrogation under 18 USC. §§ 2340-2340A' and dated 1 August 2002,[27] has come to be known as the 'torture memo'.[28] It concluded that the statutory phrase 'severe mental pain or suffering' should be interpreted as meaning pain equivalent in intensity to that 'associated with a sufficiently serious physical condition or injury such as death, organ failure, or serious impairment of bodily functions'.[29] This meant that interrogation conduct that caused pain short of that equivalent to organ failure would not be torture (though it might still be coercive). This conclusion was widely criticised when the memorandum was eventually released,[30] and it was subsequently withdrawn.[31]

A terrorism thriller could create a narrative conflict that involves a government agent balking at subjecting a suspected terrorist to harsh interrogation methods, with a government lawyer arguing—perhaps incorrectly—that such interrogation would not be illegal. This story structure would allow dramatic depiction of the essential elements of the ticking time bomb scenario (time pressure, potentially catastrophic terrorist attack, and perceived need to violate the law in order to stop the attack) with the involvement of a lawyer, but a different kind of lawyer than might be ordinarily expected.

B. More Aggressive Legal Positions: Miranda Warnings

Anyone who has watched more than a few episodes of any police procedural drama knows that police officers must read the *Miranda* warnings to an arrested suspect:

> You have the right to remain silent. Anything you say can and will be used against you in a court of law. You have the right to an attorney. If you cannot afford an attorney, the court will appoint one to represent you.

After *Miranda* was decided, law enforcement groups immediately complained that criminal suspects would no longer confess because they would 'lawyer up'. In point of fact, police detectives continue to extract confessions from many suspects even after reading

---

[27] US Dept of Justice, Office of Legal Counsel, Memorandum for Alberto R Gonzales, Counsel to the President, 'Re: Standards of Conduct for Interrogation under 18 USC. §§ 2340-2340A' (1 Aug 2002), available in the law archives at www.gwu.edu.

[28] See, eg, J Martinez, 'Process and Substance in the "War on Terror"' (2008) 108 *CLR* 1013, 1072.

[29] 'Standards of Conduct for Interrogation' memo (n 25) 6.

[30] For a small sampling, see J Moore, 'Practicing What We Preach: Humane Treatment for Detainees in the War on Terror' (2006) 34 *DJIL&P* 33, 49: 'Torture cannot be limited to the degree of suffering associated with organ failure, given that psychic pain or mental suffering is explicitly within the definition.'; David Cole, 'The Idea of Humanity: Human Rights and Immigrants' Rights' (2006) 37 *Colum HRLR* 627, 636: describing the memo as 'a truly astounding opinion... that treated the torture prohibition as if it were a tax code, and as if the main function of the lawyer was not to ensure that the letter and spirit of the law be honored, but to find loopholes in the code'.

[31] See J Goldsmith, *The Terror Presidency: Law and Judgment Inside the Bush Administration* (New York, WW Norton & Co, 2007) 144-55.

those warnings, largely by persuading those suspects that they would fare better by cooperating with the police than by seeking a lawyer.[32] Nevertheless, if the stakes are high enough, society might rightly hesitate about gambling on a police detective's ability to persuade a captured terrorist to reveal the location of, say, a nuclear weapon. If the suspect were to invoke his right to a lawyer, thereby ending the interrogation, police officers might lose their best chance to find and disarm the weapon of mass destruction. The *legal* thing to do might be to '*Mirandise*' the suspect, but the *necessary* thing might be to skip the warnings and start the interrogation immediately.

In fact, there is a 'public safety' exception to *Miranda*, first articulated in *New York v Quarles*,[33] which allows law enforcement agents to skip *Miranda* warnings in certain situations. In *Quarles*, a suspect was arrested with an empty gun holster; the victim earlier told police that her assailant was armed. The arresting officer, without reading *Miranda* warnings, asked the suspect where the missing weapon was located, and the suspect answered. The Supreme Court ruled that both the gun and the defendant's statement were admissible notwithstanding the absence of the *Miranda* warnings, because the cost to society of a suspect's invocation of his right to remain silent was not just 'the possibility of fewer convictions' but also 'further danger to the public'.

The federal government has actually made use of this public safety exception in terrorism cases. On 3 May 2010, federal agents arrested Faisal Shahzad, a Pakistani-American, on terrorism charges based on suspicion that he had left an explosives-laden truck in Times Square, New York City. The agents who took him into custody did not immediately read him his *Miranda* rights; they instead began to interrogate him.[34] Shahzad was not *Mirandised* until after the initial interrogation dispelled concerns that there might be accomplices planning further car bombing attacks.[35]

In a television thriller like *24*, this scenario would offer another opportunity to show lawyers in a role other than defending terrorism suspects. As with the previous suggestion (about aggressive lawyering to narrow the definition of torture), this suggestion would not alter the fundamental parameters of the ticking time bomb scenario. For example, in depicting the suspenseful situation of needing to extract information quickly from a captured terrorism suspect, a television thriller could invert the usual roles of agents and lawyers, with the law enforcement agents fretting about the need to *Mirandise* the suspect, and a prosecutor pushing for use of the public safety exception.

C. Seemingly Overcautious Government Lawyers

Not all government lawyers need to be portrayed as pushing for aggressive counterterrorism efforts. To the extent that a terrorism thriller wants to generate tension by depicting a lawyer as standing in the way of a field agent's efforts to investigate a suspected terrorist plot, a legal obstacle to that investigation can be placed by a government lawyer

---

[32] For an example of the psychological tactics detectives employ, see D Simon, *Homicide: A Year on the Killing Streets* (US, Houghton Mifflin, 1992) 201–05.

[33] *New York v Quarles* 467 US 649 (1984).

[34] M Mazzetti et al, '*Terrorism Suspect, Charged, Admits to Role in Bomb Plot*' *NY Times*, 5 May 2010) A1.

[35] Ibid A1.

as effectively as a defence lawyer. Such government lawyers could even be shown to the viewer to be, in fact, overcautious in the sense that their insistence on adherence to constitutional and statutory rules would be disastrous if followed.

A couple of real-life examples demonstrate the plot potential in having government lawyers as the people interfering with field agents. The first involves a former Justice Department ethics lawyer named Jessalyn Raddack. After the so-called American Taliban, John Walker Lindh, was captured in Afghanistan in late 2001 while fighting for the Taliban, another government lawyer asked whether FBI agents could interrogate Lindh without a lawyer present.[36] Raddack responded that such interrogation would be problematic, but did suggest that agents consider telling Lindh that his father had found a lawyer for him and then seek a waiver of counsel.[37] Instead, an FBI agent went ahead and questioned Lindh after getting him to waive his *Miranda* rights. Upon hearing this, Raddack advised that the results of the interrogation might need to be sealed and used only for intelligence purposes, not for criminal prosecution.

What happened next sounds like something out of a television drama series itself—Raddack, who previously received merit bonuses and strong work evaluations, received an extremely negative work evaluation, prompting her to resign from her position with the Justice Department. She then came to believe that the government had not, as required by law, disclosed her conclusions in response to a defence counsel request for evidence to support its motion to suppress Lindh's statements to the FBI agent in Afghanistan. As a result, she eventually leaked her documents to a *Newsweek* reporter, who wrote a magazine story about the Lindh interrogation. No doubt embarrassed by the disclosure, the government opened an investigation to identify the source of the leak and quickly homed in on Raddack. Although she was working for a private law firm at this point, the Justice Department effectively blocked her from practicing law by complaining to the Maryland and District of Columbia bars (of which she was a member) that she violated client confidences; and she did not resume the practice of law until four years later.[38]

In other words, a Raddack-type storyline offers the same potential for narrative tension driven by a lawyer's interference with an ongoing interrogation as in the David Weiss storyline, but with a government lawyer as the source of the obstacle. Indeed, using a government lawyer as the obstacle creates the possibility of additional subplots where the lawyer tries to blow the whistle on the potentially illegal government actions, which if successful might further derail the counterterrorism efforts.

The second real-life example of seemingly overcautious lawyers is the group of Justice Department lawyers who blocked FBI agents' request for a special foreign intelligence surveillance warrant to search the laptop of Zacarias Moussaoui, a French citizen who had been detained on immigration charges the summer before 9/11. Moussaoui had been taking flying lessons at a flying school in Minnesota when he aroused the suspicion of a flight instructor based on the fact that he wanted to learn to pilot a 747 passenger jet with only a small amount of past flight experience

---

[36] For a summary of Raddack's involvement in the Lindh interrogation, see D McGowan, 'Politics, Office Politics, and Legal Ethics: A Case Study in the Strategy of Judgment' (2007) 20 *GJLE* 1057, 1060–67.

[37] See email from J Raddack to J DePue (7 Dec 2001) reprinted in ibid 1102.

[38] See ibid 1071.

on a small plane.[39] The flight school managers reported Moussaoui to the FBI, which then arrested him on immigration charges because he had overstayed his visa. This incident provides another clear scenario where government lawyers interfere with and hinder counterterrorism efforts.

The FBI office in Minneapolis sought a special FISA warrant to search the contents of Moussaoui's laptop computer. FISA, or the Foreign Intelligence Surveillance Act,[40] is a statute which was enacted in 1978 to regulate the Executive Branch's gathering of foreign intelligence through electronic surveillance and other means. The difference between foreign intelligence gathering and criminal investigation is that, in the latter, the government must demonstrate probable cause to believe that the target of a search warrant has engaged in or is engaging in criminal conduct, whereas a FISA warrant does not require any showing of criminal wrongdoing. Instead, the FISA standard is that there exists probable cause to believe that the target of the surveillance is an agent of a foreign power. Unlike regular search warrants, issued by any federal trial judge with the appropriate jurisdiction, FISA warrants are issued by a special Foreign Intelligence Surveillance Court.[41]

Although the Minneapolis FBI agents were suspicious of Moussaoui, they did not think they could get a regular search warrant. Because Moussaoui was neither an American citizen nor an American legal resident, it was more likely that it would be argued that he was an agent of a foreign power. However, applying longstanding guidelines that dated back to the Clinton Administration, the Justice Department declined to apply for the FISA warrant. Because FISA had been enacted to curb perceived Executive Branch abuses, Executive Branch lawyers had interpreted the Act to erect a 'Wall' to prevent information-sharing between intelligence agents and criminal investigative agents. The concern was that federal law enforcement agents might resort to FISA warrants in gathering evidence when unable to get a traditional surveillance warrant.[42] However, after 9/11, searches of Moussaoui's laptop and other belongings tied him to a key al Qaeda member who played a major role in helping facilitate the 9/11 attacks.[43]

This incident would also work well within the narrative structure of terrorism thrillers. The Minnesota FBI agents did not know what they would find on the laptop, or even whether Moussaoui really was a terrorist. But in a television show, the viewer would already have been shown that the detained person was in fact a terrorist and that his laptop indeed contained actionable intelligence. From the viewer's standpoint, therefore, there could be considerable suspense and tension created over whether the Justice Department lawyer would overcome his or her reluctance to approve the FISA warrant request.

Lawyers have been crucially involved in decisions about the post-arrest treatment of terrorists such as Shahzad, Lindh, and Moussaoui, among others, and not only as defence lawyers. Naturally, some of the real life instances discussed above are anachronisms under current law. The Wall that was so critical to the FBI's failure to seek a

---

[39] See 'Flight Instructor Gets $5 Million for Catching Terror Suspect' *CNN* (25 Jan 2008), available at www.cnn.com.

[40] 50 USC ch 36.

[41] The members of the FISC are, however, federal judges who serve as FISC judges for a fixed term of seven years.

[42] See generally *United States v Truong* 629 F.2d 908 (4th Cir 1980).

[43] See A Zegart, *Spying Blind: The CIA, the FBI, and the Origins of 9/11* (Princeton, Princeton University Press, 2007) 162.

FISA warrant to search Moussaoui's computer and other belongings was repudiated publicly in 2002 by the Foreign Intelligence Surveillance Court of Review,[44] as well as by the USA PATRIOT Act's amendments to FISA.[45] Yet even if the Wall were not the specific basis for a subplot involving lawyers, it could inspire one through a fictional statute that presented the same balancing of interests.[46] This is not to say that terrorism thrillers should never show defence lawyers engaged in zealous representation of their suspected terrorist clients. Although the public may often question the actions of such lawyers, they are in fact fulfilling their constitutionally envisioned role by defending their clients' interests. It is to say, however, that to the extent terrorism thrillers want to use lawyers primarily as plot devices, such shows can broaden the roles played by lawyers without sacrificing narrative drive and tension.

IV. Conclusion

Lawyers are easy targets of ridicule, as Michael Asimow notes about lawyers on television, '[m]ost people would rather find vampires with chainsaws rather than lawyers in their living rooms'.[47] Still, for a medium that thrives on imagination, television has shown remarkably little of it when it comes to how lawyers can be integrated into terrorism-related shows. As evidence, consider that the dialogue from the David Weiss scene in *24* is interchangeable almost word-for-word with the dialogue from the lawyer scene in *The Grid*. As this chapter has demonstrated, however, such shows can retain their action-suspense nature without becoming legal procedurals and yet incorporate lawyers in ways that go beyond defence lawyers who simply argue that torture or coercion can never be justified.

References

Books

Asimow, M (ed), *Lawyers in Your Living Room!: Law on Television* (ABA, 2009).
Dershowitz, AM, *Reasonable Doubts: The O.J. Simpson Case and the Criminal Justice System* (New York, Simon & Schuster, 1996).
Farber, D, *Lincoln's Constitution* (University of Chicago Press, 2003).
Goldsmith, J, *The Terror Presidency: Law and Judgment Inside the Bush Administration* (New York, WW Norton & Co, 2007).

---

[44] *In re: Sealed Case No. 02-001, 02-002*, 310 F.3d 717 (FISC Rev 2002).

[45] The USA PATRIOT Act changed FISA's requirement that the foreign intelligence gathering requirement of electronic surveillance from 'the primary purpose' to 'a significant purpose'. Now, even if a significant or even primary purpose of the electronic surveillance is criminal prosecution, a FISA warrant would not be precluded so long as the government could plausibly maintain that *another* significant purpose was for foreign intelligence gathering.

[46] Indeed, much of what Hollywood had to say about the PATRIOT Act when invoked in terrorism-related shows has been so grossly inaccurate that it could be said to refer to a fictional statute. See Tung Yin, 'A Government's Trustworthiness: Beyond the USA PATRIOT Act' (2004) 8 *Chi PR* 1.

[47] Asimow (ed), *Lawyers in Your Living Room!* (n 11).

Kunen, J, *How Can You Defend These People?: The Making of a Criminal Lawyer* (New York, Random House, 1983).

Moore, M, *Placing Blame: A General Theory of Criminal Law* (Gloucestershire, Clarendon Press, 1997).

Parry, JT, *Understanding Torture: Law, Violence, and Political Identity 73* (Ann Arbor, University of Michigan Press, 2010).

Rehnquist, WH, *All the Laws But One: Civil Liberties in Wartime* (New York, Vintage, 1998).

Rossiter, C, *Constitutional Dictatorship: Crisis Government in the Modern Democracies* (Princeton, Princeton University Press, 1948).

Zegart, AB, *Spying Blind: The CIA, the FBI, and the Origins of 9/11* (Princeton, Princeton University Press, 2007).

National Commission on Terrorist Attacks Upon the United States, *Final Report of the National Commission on Terrorist Attacks Upon the United States* (New York, Barnes & Noble Books, 2004).

B. Television Shows

24 (Fox 2001–10).
The Grid (TNT 2004) (mini-series).
Law & Order (NBC 1990–10).
Perry Mason (CBS 1957–66).
The Practice (ABC 1997–2004).

B. Reality Law TV

10

Til Debt Do Us Part: Reality TV and the Financial Literacy Regulatory Project

FREYA KODAR*

Citizens in Canada and elsewhere presently carry unprecedented levels of debt.[1] While alarm bells about growing levels of consumer debt sounded before the global financial crisis, they have become louder and seemingly more urgent since the crisis began. One response to this crisis has been to target financial literacy levels: if consumers are more financially literate, they will be better able to understand the contracts and other documents they encounter regularly within the marketplace, and they will make better decisions about spending, saving and taking on debt. Much like concerns about consumer debt, this attention to financial literacy is not new,[2] and there have

* Thanks to Lyndsey Delamont, Claire Farmer, Zoë Macmillan and Chris Tait for research assistance, and to Rebecca Johnson and an anonymous reviewer for their comments and insights. This chapter has also benefited from the feedback of those attending the Law and Reality TV Panel at the Association for the Study of Law, Culture and the Humanities, 12th Annual Meeting at Suffolk University Law School in April 2009, the Western Canada Emerging Scholars Workshop at the Faculty of Law, University of Manitoba in May 2009 and a Law Faculty Seminar at the University of Victoria in August 2009.

[1] Recent estimates put Canadians' household debt in 2009 at $41,740 per person if it were averaged amongst all Canadians. This is 2.5 times more than it was in 1989. Of particular concern is the increasing percentage of household debt taken up by 'revolving credit' such as credit cards and personal lines of credit; and the increasing use of credit for non-durable goods and current consumption. Canadian General Accountants Association of Canada, 'Where is the Money Now: The State of Canadian Household Debt as Conditions for Economic Recovery Emerge' (Canadian General Accountants Association of Canada), my.texterity.com/cgaresearchreports/debt2010#pg1, 15–16, 27–38. There is no shortage of statistics on household debt. In Canada for example, see also: Bank of Canada, 'Financial System Review June 2010' (Bank of Canada, 2010) www.bankofcanada.ca/en/fsr/2010/index_0610.html; Statistics Canada, 'Personal debt' Perspectives on Labour and Income (2007) 8:1, 28–34; and R Sauvé, 'The Current State of Canadian Family Finances 2010 Report' (17 February 2011) Vanier Institute of the Family, www.vifamily.ca/node/783.

[2] For example, a 2004 report for the federal government noted that while 'the ability to read complex documents, contracts and instruction is a key skill, … 40 percent of the Canadian population falls below the minimum desirable threshold of literacy'. Office of Consumer Affairs, 'The Consumer Trends Report' (Ottawa, Industry Canada, 2004), www.ic.gc.ca/eic/site/oca-bc.nsf/vwapj/EN_CTR.pdf/$FILE/EN_CTR. pdf. See also T Williams, 'Empowerment of Whom and for What? Financial Literacy Education and the New Regulation of Consumer Financial Services' (2007) *Law & Policy* 29, 228.

been a number of private and public sector initiatives to improve Canadians' financial literacy. In the province of British Columbia for example, high school students must take Planning 10, a course first introduced in 2004, which includes a significant financial literacy skills component.[3] Nationally, the federal government established a Task Force on Financial Literacy in 2009 to assist in the development of a national strategy to improve financial literacy.[4]

Canadians, and more recently Americans, can also turn to a reality TV show, *Til Debt Do Us Part*, to watch couples struggling with their debts. The show follows them as they receive financial 'makeovers' and learn to manage their finances 'responsibly'. This chapter looks at *Til Debt Do Us Part* on a variety of levels. The first section provides an overview of the series, describes the format of a typical episode, and discusses the mechanisms it uses to encourage audience participation and investment in the programme. The second section situates the television series within the reality TV genre, and looks specifically at the ways in which it fits within the reality TV sub-genres of game shows and lifestyle programming, particularly shows that focus on self-improvement and transformation through consumerism and consumption.

The third part of the chapter analyses *Til Debt Do Us Part* both empirically and textually. It looks first at the socio-economic location of participants, who it turns out generally have the means to become debt-free in a relatively short period of time provided they make 'appropriate' choices. Second, following on from the insights of scholars such as Nikolas Rose and John Fiske about the capacity that television has to promote particular ideologies and choices,[5] it looks at the messages about spending, savings, debt and responsibility that thread through the episodes, and reflects on the kinds of expectations and beliefs about financial management and responsibility that are constituted in the programme's audience. I draw on the literature analysing financial literacy programmes as 'regulatory projects',[6] and ask whether the financial literacy education in *Til Debt Do Us Part* can be understood as empowering—providing participants and viewers with tools to assist them as they participate in the market. Or alternatively, whether it is better understood as (1) reinforcing and normalising individual responsibility for managing risk and financial security; and (2) providing

---

[3] British Columbia Ministry of Education Graduation Program, 'Planning 10: Integrated Resource Package 2007' (British Columbia Ministry of Education, 2007), www.bced.gov.bc.ca/irp/course. php?lang=en&subject=Health_and_Career_Education&course=Planning_10&year=2007. A variety of financial literacy educational resources are approved for the course, including resources developed by the province's Securities Commission and by VISA Canada. British Columbia Ministry of Education Graduation Program, 'Learning Resources: Planning 10' (British Columbia Ministry of Education), www. bced.gov.bc.ca/irp_resources/catalogue_of_learning_resources.htm; See also C Weeks, 'Financial Literacy: With the Boom Gone Bust, Canadians are Scrambling to Learn what they were Never Taught: Money 101' *Globe and Mail* (30 March 2009), www.theglobeandmail.com/servlet/story/RTGAM.20090303.

[4] More information about the Task Force and its mandate, and its recently released report, 'Canadians and Their Money: Building a Brighter Financial Future', can be found at www.financialliteracyincanada. com/eng/. For an overview of additional financial literacy initiatives in Canada and internationally, see Task Force on Financial Literacy, 'Leveraging Excellence: Charting a Course of Action to Strengthen Financial Literacy in Canada' (Task Force on Financial Literacy), www.financialliteracyincanada.com/ documents/Consultation_Report.en.pdf: Appendix B.

[5] N Rose, 'Governing "Advanced" Liberal Democracies' in A Berry et al (eds), *Foucault and Political Reason: Liberalism, Neoliberalism and Rationalities of Government* (London, University College London Press, 1996) 57–58; J Fiske, *Television Culture* (London and New York, Routledge, 1987).

[6] Toni Williams characterises it as such a project in Williams, 'Empowerment of Whom and for What?' (n 2) 228.

cultural support for the regulatory shift under neoliberalism that has been characterised by, among other things, a focus on decentralised governance, limited regulation of the market, and responsibilisation—'a form of regulation by which the state holds individuals accountable for aspects of market governance and social security that it used to provide'.[7]

I conclude that despite some of the empowering financial literacy features of *Til Debt Do Us Part*, the programme is best understood as cultural support for the responsibilisation that underpins the neoliberal regulatory project. The fact that the programme rarely places participants' experiences beyond their individual context is of particular significance here. While viewers can find messages about the rule of law and its prescriptive nature in the opening shot of the bus shelter ad with the words 'Layin Down the Law' next to the photograph of the show's host Gail Vaz-Oxlade, and also in her directives/advice about setting and keeping to a budget, it is *Til Debt Do Us Part*'s messages about self-regulation and individual responsibility for managing risk that connect the programme most strongly to 'the law'. Like the reality-based courtroom TV programme *Judge Judy* and other reality TV programming, *Til Debt Do Us Part* provides cultural support for the neoliberal regulatory project and responsibilised citizenship.[8]

I. *Til Debt Do Us Part*

Til Debt Do Us Part completed its eighth season on Canadian television in June 2010,[9] and it has recently become available to audiences in the United States.[10] Each half-hour episode features a couple struggling with their debt load. The show follows the couple as they attempt to meet various challenges designed to improve their financial situation. If successful, they can receive up to $5,000 to put toward their debts. A typical episode opens with a voiceover—narrated by the show's host Gail Vaz-Oxlade—outlining the couple's situation. The voiceover generally includes details about the couple's occupations, income, living situation, any children, and a breakdown of their consumer (non-mortgage) debt and their monthly spending habits. Often, one or both members of the couple speak directly to the camera about how their financial situation makes them feel and affects their relationship. Then, as the camera focuses on a photograph of Gail in an advertisement for the show on a bus

---

[7] Ibid 227.

[8] SA Kohm, 'The People's Law versus Judge Judy Justice: Two Models of Law in American Reality-Based Courtroom TV' (2006) *Law & Society Review* 40, 693–727; L Ouellette, '"Take Responsibility for Yourself": *Judge Judy* and the Neoliberal Citizen' in L Ouelette and S Murray (eds), *Reality TV: Remaking Television Culture* (New York, NYU Press, 2004) 231–50; G Palmer, '"The New You": Class and Transformation in Lifestyle Television' in S Holmes and D Jermyn (eds), *Understanding Reality TV* (London and New York, Routledge, 2004) 185–88.

[9] *Til Debt Do Us Part* is produced in Canada by Winnipeg-based Frantic Films. Episodes can be viewed online at www.slice.ca, the website of the lifestyle television station Slice™.

[10] The programme can be viewed on NBC Universal's Consumer News and Business Channel (CNBC).

shelter, she indicates that she is 'going to help [the couple] go from red to black' and proceeds to walk out of the photograph to make 'house calls'.

Upon arrival at their home, Gail goes through the rooms focusing on the couples' possessions—the quantity, size, newness—often asking them which items are paid for and which are not yet paid off. By the time she meets them on camera, Gail has seen the couple's interview tapes and reviewed their finances for the previous six months. Gail's first step is to set out and compare their monthly expenses with their income to show them how much debt they create each month. Often, they are surprised to discover just how much they are actually over-spending each month. Gail also tells them how much their debt will be in five years if they continue their current spending patterns. This five-year debt forecast ranges across the episodes from $80,000 to $1,600,000, with an average estimated debt of a little over $500,000.[11]

Gail takes all their credit and debit cards, or in some cases destroys them. She puts the couple on a weekly cash budget for all their variable expenses, with the cash divided into jars for food, clothing and gifts, entertainment, transportation, and miscellaneous. The remainder of the episode follows them as they live on this budget for a month, keep track of all their expenses and undertake her challenges. Gail usually has a 'three-point plan' for the couple, with one point specifically targeting an aspect of their relationship with one another. The three challenges are designed to assist them in implementing the plan. The financial challenges range from researching and planning (eg drawing up a financial plan to pay off debts, researching free activities for children, calculating the cost of going back to work before the end of a maternity leave, finding out if debt can be consolidated on their mortgage, or deciding whether to sell the house); to creating extra income (eg finding additional employment), cash (eg selling things such as cars, stocks) or new habits (eg bringing lunch to work, grocery shopping weekly rather than daily, staying out of the shopping centre). The 'relationship rescue challenge' tends to focus on communication and decision-making (eg setting a budget together, the other person making particular financial decisions, a recreational activity that requires cooperation and trust, such as riding a tandem bicycle). As the episode progresses, Gail does follow-up 'house calls' to discuss the couple's progress and give them further challenges. She may also provide more general financial advice to the viewer through voiceover or in a short scene in which she speaks directly to the camera.

In an episode's last segment she gives her 'final verdict' on how the couple have done, and rewards them up to $5,000 based on her assessment of their efforts. She also explains the monthly budget she has developed in more detail, and tells the couple how long it will take to pay their debt off completely if they stick to the budget. Generally, their budget includes contributions towards debt repayment, an emergency fund, and retirement savings, and will allow the household to eliminate their debt, or at least their non-mortgage debt, within three years. Gail advises the couple that once they have paid off their debts, they should add the monthly sum they were putting towards the debt to their retirement savings, and calculates how much they will have saved on

---

[11] It is not clear in every episode whether this projected debt includes only consumer debt, or both consumer and mortgage debt.

retirement if they follow her advice.[12] The episode closes with statements from one or both members of the couple about their experience—what they have learned, how it has affected their relationship, and how they think they will manage their finances in the future. Those watching the show via the internet can also view short 'Where Are They Now' episodes that provide updates about the situation of some of the couples featured on the show.[13]

In its ninth season, and expanding into the United States, *Til Debt Do Us Part* is clearly a popular show.[14] But why do people like it, one might ask? What is it that encourages audience engagement and brings them back? While my analysis here is a textual and empirical one, and any suggestion about how *Til Debt Do Us Part* is consumed or received by viewers is speculative,[15] one can identify devices in the programme's structure that draw in audiences and encourage their participation in each episode's narrative. For example, when Gail or the participants speak directly to the camera, they acknowledge and include the audience in the narrative, drawing them into its meaning-making. The fact that Gail speaks *to* the audience either directly or in voiceover about the participants, and more particularly that she critiques participants' situation and progress (or lack thereof) in meeting her challenges, encourages audiences to do the same. Moreover, it creates a means through which the viewer can empathise with—or pass judgement on—participants. Viewers may also displace their own insecurities and fears about their financial knowledge and management onto participants.[16] Finally, while the participants change each week, the structure of each episode and its host remains the same—viewers can return again and again, building attachment to the programme as time passes. *Til Debt Do Us Part* also incorporates features of two reality TV sub-genres to encourage audience participation and attachment.

II. *Til Debt Do Us Part* as Reality TV

Laurie Ouellette and Susan Murray define reality TV as a genre 'united ... by the fusion of popular entertainment with a self-conscious claim to the discourse of the real'.[17] Similarly, Su Holmes and Deborah Jermyn suggest that it 'is primarily its discursive, visual and technological *claim* to "the real"' that links the variety of

---

[12] Often, participants receive an additional gift such as a fund to start a Registered Education Savings Plan for their kid(s), or a gift connected to the couple's interests such as a holiday tour or gift certificate.

[13] As of July 2010 there were 10 such 'webisodes': www.slice.ca/Slice/Watch/Default.aspx?ID=v.

[14] Season nine, *Til Debt Do Us Part: Home Edition*, is available online at www.slice.ca. The programme's structure is clearly popular with audiences. Frantic Films recently produced *Princess*, also featuring Gail Vaz-Oxlade, which utilises a similar format but follows only one (female) participant, the 'Princess', in each episode. Episodes can be viewed online at www.slice.ca.

[15] For a discussion of the critical need for more research into how reality TV programming is received see, eg B Montemurro, 'Toward a Sociology of Reality Television' (2008) *Sociology Compass* 2/1, 98–99.

[16] Carol Clover writes about this kind of viewer displacement of anxieties and fear in a very different context, slasher films, in 'Her Body, Himself: Gender in the Slasher Film' (1987) *Representations* 20, 187–228.

[17] L Ouellette and S Murray, 'Introduction' in L Ouelette and S Murray (eds), *Reality TV: Remaking Television Culture* (New York, NYU Press, 2004) 2.

programming understood to be reality TV.[18] Other important features of reality TV programming are its focus on entertainment over education and information,[19] and its voyeuristic appeal—its 'capacity to let viewers see for themselves'.[20]

In presenting an edited version of apparently unscripted actions of 'real people' as they work with Gail to change their very real financial situation, *Til Debt Do Us Part* makes a similar claim to 'the real' and to allowing viewers to 'see for themselves'. The programme follows the couple's efforts to improve their financial situation within a narrative structure of challenges and 'relationship rescues', Gail's voiceover commentary and frequent ridicule or chastisement, a verdict and the promise of a cash prize. The verdict and prize are tied to the extent to which the couple can meet Gail's challenges and improve their situation. In doing so, the programme incorporates features of two reality TV sub-genres—game shows and lifestyle programming—without quite fitting into either category.[21]

Til Debt Do Us Part is not the typical blockbuster spectacle game show like *Survivor* or *American Idol* that features the regular elimination of participants, nor is it quite like the programming in the 'gamedoc' sub-genre which follow 'ordinary' people as they compete against one another to avoid elimination and/or win, such as *Survivor*, *Big Brother*, or *The Amazing Race*. But in following ordinary people as they try to meet the challenges Gail sets in the hope of ultimately 'winning' the full $5,000, *Til Debt Do Us Part* does draw on elements of both types of game show.

The programme also has many elements of reality TV lifestyle programming, or what Beth Montemurro refers to as programmes that 'focus on transformation'.[22] Transformation is 'clearly at the heart of lifestyle television',[23] as this category includes gamedocs such as *The Biggest Loser* where participants compete to lose the most weight, and programmes that follow participants' 'transformations' through plastic surgery such as in *The Swan* or makeovers of their wardrobe, home or lifestyle.[24] *Til Debt Do Us Part* more closely mirrors those lifestyle shows such as *Supernanny* that 'highlight families whose "lives are changed" when an outsider enters their home and provides guidance or new rules and new perspectives on child care or spousal relationships'.[25] Gail clearly plays this outsider role in *Til Debt Do Us Part*, providing

---

[18] S Holmes and D Jermyn, 'Introduction' in S Holmes and D Jermyn (eds), *Understanding Reality TV* (London and New York, Routledge, 2004) 5.

[19] Montemurro, 'Sociology of Reality Television' (n 15) 87; Ouellette and Murray, 'Introduction' (n 17) 3.

[20] A Hill, *Reality TV: Audiences and Popular Factual Television* (London and New York, Routledge, 2005) 53–55. See also Montemurro, 'Sociology of Reality Television' (n 15) 87–88.

[21] Montemurro, 'Sociology of Reality Television' (n 15) 87–92; Hill, *Reality TV* (n 20) 49; Ouellette and Murray, 'Introduction' (n 17) 3–4. It is important to note that the lines between categories of reality TV programming are not always clear, and current programmes are often hybrids of formats that preceded them. J Corner, 'Afterword to *Understanding Reality TV*', in S Holmes and D Jermyn (eds), *Understanding Reality TV* (London and New York, Routledge, 2004) 292; S Murray, 'I Think We Need a New Name For It: The Meeting of Documentary and Reality TV' in Ouelette and Murray (eds), *Reality TV: Remaking Television Culture* (n 8) 40–56.

[22] Montemurro, 'Sociology of Reality Television' (n 15) 91.

[23] Palmer, '"The New You"' (n 8) 72; Montemurro, 'Sociology of Reality Television' (n 15) 91–92.

[24] For a helpful overview describing many of the more popular reality makeover programmes, see RM Huff, *Reality Television* (Westport and London, Praeger, 2006) 67–77.

[25] Montemurro, 'Sociology of Reality Television' (n 15) 92.

guidance and new rules and perspectives about managing money, avoiding debt and communication, and generally 'helping' the family with their 'financial makeover'.[26]

By utilising features of both reality TV sub-genres, *Til Debt Do Us Part's* structure encourages audience participation and investment in each episode. The audience follows people in financial crisis as they attempt to follow Gail's strategies for a financial 'makeover'. Viewers become both voyeurs and supporters as they follow participants to the final verdict to see if the participants can perform the seemingly manageable goals Gail sets for them, and win the full $5,000 prize. This creation of suspense and anticipation about the final verdict helps sustain audience involvement and participation.

While *Til Debt Do Us Part* draws on elements of reality TV game shows and lifestyle programming, its premise—that participants and viewers should live within their means and avoid debt—appears to run counter to the consumerism rampant in lifestyle programming. For while these shows are about participants' transformation, lifestyle programmes' focus on change through consumer purchases also creates strong links to the retail economy,[27] and promotes consumerism as the means to self-actualisation.[28] As Lisa Glabatis Perks suggests, this in turn might ultimately encourage viewers to spend beyond their means.[29]

In many ways, *Til Debt Do Us Part* seems instead to be about how to pick up the pieces of the debt that can result from the mix of consumerism and credit. Most episodes begin with Gail surveying all the 'stuff' in participants' homes. She often asks them why they need particular objects, and whether they bought them with cash or credit. In some episodes, Gail will ask the couple to do tasks that highlight how much stuff is not yet paid for or how much they do not 'need'. For example, in one episode the material goods that are not yet paid for are removed from the home,[30] while in another, the couple has to separate the 'wants' from the 'needs' in four rooms and dispose of all the wants.[31] In other episodes, she suggests to participants that their accumulation of consumer goods—and spending beyond their income—is connected to keeping up appearances, going so far as to make some participants 'come clean' about their financial situation to friends, relatives or complete strangers.[32]

Ultimately though, the programme does not present a sustained critique of consumerism and a consumer-driven economy. Instead, desire for material goods and

---

[26] In an interesting reflection on what Gareth Palmer refers to as the 'decline of experts and the rise of "ordinary people"' [Palmer, '"The New You"' (n 8) 72], *Til Debt Do Us Part's* popularity has helped propel Gail into the role of celebrity commentator on questions of money management. For example, when the Bank of Canada raised its overnight interest rate on 20 July 2010, the online news story in the *Globe and Mail*, a national newspaper, included a sidebar link to an online video featuring Gail discussing debt. R Carrick, 'Control Your Debts, Central Bank Tells Canadians' *Globe and Mail*, 20 July 2010, www.theglobeandmail.com/globe-investor/control-your-debts-central-bank-tells-canadians/article1645853/.

[27] Palmer, '"The New You"'(n 8) 72; L Taylor, 'From Ways of Life to Lifestyle: The 'Ordinari-ization of British Gardening Lifestyle Television' (2002) *European Journal of Communication* 17, 485.

[28] Ouellette, '*Judge Judy* and the Neoliberal Citizen' (n 8) 233–235; LG Perks, 'The Nouveau Reach: Ideologies of Class and Consumerism in Reality-Based Television' (2007) *Studies in Language & Capitalism* 2, www.languageandcapitalism.info/wp-content/uploads/2007/05/slc2-4-perks.pdf.

[29] Perks, 'The Nouveau Reach' (n 28) 103, 115.

[30] *Til Debt Do Us Part* episode 53.

[31] Ibid episode 78.

[32] Ibid see eg episodes 1, 15, 50, 55, 58, 61, 78, 84, 87, 96, 104.

the debt that can result are understood as personal to the participants, as is their ability to overcome their debt and manage to live within their means. This focus on the individual as both the cause and the remedy that we see in *Til Debt Do Us Part* is explored more fully in the next section, which looks at the programme as financial literacy education.

III. *Til Debt Do Us Part* and the Financial Literacy 'Regulatory Project'

With each episode structured around the arrival of an 'expert' outsider who advises both the participants and viewers about financial matters, one can also analyse *Til Debt Do Us Part* as a form of financial education.[33] Examining the messages about spending, savings, debt and responsibility that are threaded through the programme is therefore important. In addition, like those in many reality TV programmes, the participants in *Til Debt Do Us Part* are presented as 'ordinary' people, thus attention should also be paid to participants' socio-economic location. In order to analyse these aspects of *Til Debt Do Us Part*, each episode in its first eight seasons was catalogued and a variety of information gathered.[34] Participants' socio-economic location was constructed by tracking information about their gender, race, sexual orientation, marital and family status, and whether they were living with a disability, along with information about their occupation and income. Details about participants' current and projected debt were also collected. The financial education elements of the programme were catalogued by tracking (1) the details of the budget and the three-point 'rehabilitation plan' participants had to follow; (2) participants' efforts to follow the plan; (3) Gail's assessment of these efforts—both her commentary and the decision about whether they would receive the full $5,000 'prize'; and (4) the participants' reflections on their experiences. The project also compiled the more general financial information provided through the programme.[35]

A. Not Quite 'Ordinary' Debtors: Participants' Socio-Economic Location

Given the play on words of one of the traditional marriage vows in the programme's title, along with the shot in the opening sequence of bride and groom figurines on a wedding cake, it is not surprising that the vast majority of *Til Debt Do Us Part*

---

[33] I note that it was students in my debtor and creditor relations course who brought *Til Debt Do Us Part* to my attention during our discussions of financial literacy, consumerism and credit. It was clear from their comments, and those of colleagues and friends who follow the programme, that they understood or received the programme as both entertainment and education.

[34] I am indebted (the pun is unavoidable) to Lyndsey Delamont, Claire Farmer and Zoë Macmillan for their assistance in compiling this data.

[35] One caveat: all of these details were provided in the vast majority of the episodes catalogued, but not in every one. The discussion that follows is based on the information that could be catalogued, and thus the numbers are approximate.

episodes featured legally married heterosexual couples. There were only two same-sex couples, one gay, one lesbian, and both were legally married.[36] The programme does include some heterosexual couples living together, although they were more likely to be engaged than simply living common law.[37] Moreover, at least two of the common law couples cited debt as one of the reasons they were not yet engaged.[38] Only two episodes featured participants who were not in a conjugal relationship: one featured two sisters, and another featured a single mother.[39] While one episode did focus on the financial situation of a single father, his desire to move in with his girlfriend motivated this participant's decision to deal with his debt.[40] Given the show's premise, it is not surprising that *Til Debt Do Us Part* features couples in a conjugal relationship, but the programme's participant selection reinforces both heterosexuality and marriage.

The majority of participants were parenting children on a full-time basis or—in some cases where one spouse had children from a previous relationship—a part-time basis. This inclusion of a number of blended families captures some of the realities of Canadian family life, but it does so within a context that reifies the traditional hetero-sexual nuclear family and ignores the diversity of forms and relationships of depen-dency that characterise family life in Canada.[41] There were only a few exceptions to this, including an episode in which the married couple cared for their grandchild,[42] along with the two episodes previously discussed. The show's projection of the nuclear family as normative also extended to the household budgets participants had to follow, as couples were only financially responsible for themselves and their children. There were few episodes featuring households that included an extended family.[43] The expenses of these family members did not seem to be included in the household budget, although in one case the brother paid rent to the couple[44] and in another, Gail challenged the wife to ask her parents and sister to contribute to the housing expenses—essentially asking them to pay rent.[45] Moreover, the household budgets designed for participants reflected the fundamental assumption about the hetero-sexual nuclear family that underpins welfare state policy-making in relation to the family in liberal states: that household income is shared within the family unit.[46] The budgets for the couples in a conjugal relationship therefore assumed that the couples should—and did—share incomes, expenses and savings (including future retirement

---

[36] In Canada, the federal Civil Marriage Act, SC 2005 legalised same-sex marriage. *Til Debt Do Us Part* did not include same-sex couples until after the legislation was passed.

[37] While it was made abundantly clear that the same-sex couples were legally married, rather than living common law, the marital status of the heterosexual couples was not always disclosed.

[38] *Til Debt Do Us Part* episodes 44 and 99.

[39] Ibid episodes 36 and 85 respectively.

[40] Ibid episode 58.

[41] See, eg Statistics Canada, 'Family Portrait: Continuity and Change in Canadian Families and Households in 2006, 2006 Census', www12.statcan.ca/census-recensement/2006/as-sa/97-553/pdf/97-553-XIE2006001.pdf.

[42] *Til Debt Do Us Part* episode 31.

[43] In a number of these episodes the couple were living with parents rent-free, or paying below market rent. Again, the household budget only included the couple. In one episode Gail did require the couple to take on more of the household chores in order to 'pay rent'. See *Til Debt Do Us Part* episode 80.

[44] Ibid episode 50.

[45] Ibid episode 11.

[46] J Acker, 'Class, Gender, and the Relations of Distribution' (1988) *Signs* 13, 473–97.

savings), while the show created separate budgets for each of the sisters who shared their home.

Just as the representation of family forms did not reflect the diversity of Canadian families, the programme did not reflect the heterogeneity of Canadians.[47] Out of more than 100 episodes examined, there were only five in which both members were racialised, and slightly more than twice that number in which one partner was racialised. None of the participants nor their children had a visible disability, and in only one episode did the participant's children have what one could characterise as a disability: one of the sisters featured in episode 85 had two children diagnosed with Attention Deficit Hyperactivity Disorder. The only other episode in which a person with a disability was included was one in which a participant—a social worker—received remuneration and a housing allowance to foster a teenager with Fetal Alcohol Spectrum Disorder.[48]

The vast majority of participants were employed and lived in two-income households, with most working for an employer rather than being self-employed. Approximately 20 per cent of the households included participants on maternity leave, doing unpaid carework, or going to school full-time.[49] It appeared that only two participants had recently lost their jobs, and both were receiving employment insurance benefits. Although all the participants had accumulated considerable debt and were spending more than they earned, it is important to note that their median household income was approximately $87,000.[50] This is $23,300 more than the national median of $63,700.[51] It is also more than the income the federal Superintendent of Bankruptcy considers sufficient for households in bankruptcy,[52] and well above the housing and shelter allowances provided to people living on income assistance.[53]

The debt-carrying households and debtors that emerge from this analysis of *Til Debt Do Us Part* are the normative nuclear family—heterosexual, married, non-racialised

---

[47] See, eg Statistics Canada, 'Canada's Ethnocultural Mosaic, 2006 Census', www12.statcan.ca/census-recensement/2006/as-sa/97-562/pdf/97-562-XIE2006001.pdf; Statistics Canada, 'Participation and Activity Limitation Survey 2006: Analytical Report', www.statcan.gc.ca/pub/89-628-x/89-628-x2007002-eng.pdf.

[48] *Til Debt Do Us Part* episode 99. Gail refers to the situation, particularly the housing allowance, as a 'windfall' that will assist the couple in considerably reduce their debt.

[49] The majority of this group consisted of participants on maternity leave. Some of the students also held down part-time jobs.

[50] It was not clear if the incomes disclosed were gross or net after taxes and other statutory deductions. The household incomes ranged from $32,400 to $155,000, and the average household income was $85,600.

[51] This is after taxes. Statistics Canada, 'Income in Canada 2008', www.statcan.gc.ca/pub/75-202-x/2008000/hl-fs-eng.htm.

[52] If they are earning income while they are in bankruptcy, bankrupts must give their trustee any 'surplus income'. Surplus income standards are set annually by the Superintendent of Bankruptcy and are based on Statistics Canada's after-tax Low Income Cut Off (LICO) for urban areas with populations of 500,000 or more. The LICO represents the point at which a household will be paying more than the average household for food, clothing and housing. In 2011, a household of two earning $2,398 a month net ($28,776 annually) or less was not considered to have any surplus income. For a household of four, the surplus income threshold increase to $3,579 per month ($42,948 annually). Superintendent of Bankruptcy, Directive No 11R2–2011, *Surplus Income*, Appendix A.

[53] In the province of British Columbia for example, a household of two adults without disabilities would receive $877.22 per month ($10,526.64 annualised). If this couple lived with two children, the assistance would increase to $1,348.06 monthly ($16,176.72 annualised). Ministry of Housing and Social Development, 'BC Employment and Assistance Rate Table', www.eia.gov.bc.ca/mhr/ia.htm.

with children—with dual incomes and living in property they own. Their debt results largely from a combination of what Gail refers to as 'consumeritis' and credit. Participants do not have to rely on credit for their basic shelter and living costs, and only rarely are they accessing credit in the alternative consumer credit market through payday lenders or pawnbrokers, for example.[54] Their household incomes and expenses are such that for the most part, Gail's revised budget permits them to meet their basic needs and more, while paying off their existing debt and building some savings.

The fact that participants on *Til Debt Do Us Part* are not so 'ordinary' is not particularly surprising. It would be much less entertaining to watch people with insufficient income to meet their basic needs try to manage their financial situation since they would be set up to fail. However, as Montemurro points out in her discussion of the need for more research into representations of identity and diversity, 'reality television has the potential to make a different impact on audiences and perceptions of difference than scripted television, given the identification that viewers may experience in viewing "ordinary" people'.[55] Thus participants' 'un-ordinariness' has important implications for the kind of financial information *Til Debt Do Us Part* provides. More importantly, in terms of thinking about the ideologies and choices the show promotes, this 'un-ordinariness' has implications for the expectations and beliefs the programme inculcates in viewers about the normative family and household, and about debt, credit, financial management and responsibility over the life course.

B. Til Debt Do Us Part as Financial Literacy Education

Susan Block-Lieb, Karen Gross and Richard Wiener have observed that 'we teach remarkably little about money and credit in our schools and within our families'.[56] This lack of education means in turn that '[a] great many of us neither read nor understand the small print on our bills, insurance policies, or student and other loan documents'.[57] *Til Debt Do Us Part* features many couples who appear to have arrived at their situation by failing to keep track of expenditures in relation to their income, spending on credit, and ignoring their bills. In doing so, the programme provides a consistent and weekly message to set and follow a budget, write down every expenditure, and create (and follow) a long-term financial plan that includes debt repayment, and saving for emergencies, large purchases, vacations and retirement. The fact that many of the challenges and relationship rescue tasks focus on communication, trust, cooperation and planning also encourages viewers to talk with their partners and others about spending and saving, something they can do without additional training

---

[54] For an overview of this financial sector in Canada see I Ramsay, 'The Alternative Consumer Credit Market and Financial Sector: Regulatory Issues and Approaches' (2001) *Canadian Business Law Journal* 35, 325–401.

[55] Montemurro, 'Sociology of Reality Television' (n 15) 100.

[56] S Block-Lieb et al, 'Lessons from the Trenches: Debtor Education in Theory and Practice' (2001) *Fordham Journal of Corporate and Financial Law* 7, 507.

[57] K Gross, 'Financial Literacy Education: Panacea, Palliative, or Something Worse?' (2005) *Saint Louis University Public Law Review* 24, 307. While she is writing in the American context, studies of Canadians' financial literacy levels suggest similar problems. See, eg Office of Consumer Affairs, 'The Consumer Trends Report' (n 2); Task Force on Financial Literacy, 'Leveraging Excellence' (n 4) 11–12.

or expertise. Indeed, most of the financial management strategies highlighted in the programme, either through the challenges or through Gail's direct advice, are easily modelled on television, and seem to require only individual willpower to implement.

In addition, the show dispenses more general financial advice in most episodes that is—for the most part—informative and helpful, even if not always practicable.[58] Many viewers will have heard variants of the advice before, or found something similar in the small print of their financial documents. For example, with respect to savings and spending, Gail advises viewers to save 10 per cent of all earnings,[59] and spend no more than 35 per cent on housing,[60] 15 per cent on debt repayment and 25 per cent on 'life'.[61] In terms of planning, she advises participants and viewers to have emergency savings equivalent to six months living expenses to deal with unexpected events such as job loss,[62] to buy life and disability insurance at a young age,[63] and to start saving for retirement early.[64] Finally, with respect to credit, Gail admonishes viewers to be careful about entering variable interest loan agreements[65] or carrying a credit card balance while money earns low interest in a bank account,[66] and to remember that there are no interest grace periods for credit purchases if the balance has not been paid.[67]

On one level, it is difficult to fault the advice and reminders about spending, savings, debt, financial management and communication.[68] On closer inspection, however, a number of concerns emerge when considering *Til Debt Do Us Part* as financial literacy education. The first is the question of the extent to which the programme adds to the financial skills toolboxes of both participants and viewers.[69] Block-Lieb, Gross and Wiener articulate a number of tasks that those 'without adequate financial literacy skills' may not be able to do. These tasks include making appropriate short and long-term financial plans; comparing credit offers and lending practices; understanding that taking a mortgage to pay off consumer debt converts unsecured debt into secured debt; and realising how long it will take to pay back a loan or credit charge based on the monthly payment.[70] This list helps illuminate the fact that people need a wide range of financial skills to navigate daily life, a fact also highlighted by the Task Force on Financial Literacy's recent efforts to comprehensively assess Canadians' financial literacy levels. The Task Force commissioned Statistics Canada to do this by

---

[58] The strong emphasis on avoiding any debt is questionable in some of the situations featured on the programme. For example, it may be prudent to go into debt during periods of reduced income if your income is likely to increase in the short or long-term future as when you are on maternity or parental leave, or between employment contracts. It is precisely these patterns of uneven income that access to credit can help smooth out.

[59] *Til Debt Do Us Part* episode 7.

[60] Ibid episode 40.

[61] Ibid episode 67.

[62] Ibid episode 26.

[63] Ibid episode 59.

[64] Ibid.

[65] Ibid.

[66] Ibid episode 14.

[67] Ibid episode 65.

[68] I must confess to paying a lot more attention to my own budgeting while working on this project.

[69] I am using Karen Gross's toolbox metaphor from 'Financial Literacy Education' (n 57) 309.

[70] Block-Lieb et al, 'Lessons from the Trenches' (n 56) 507.

assessing Canadians' financial capabilities in six areas: balancing household budgets, keeping track of finances, selecting appropriate financial products, planning for retirement and other major purchases, understanding financial matters, and keeping informed about those that affect their personal financial position.[71] Assessed against these enumerated tasks and capabilities, *Til Debt Do Us Part* falls short of providing comprehensive financial literacy education because it focuses largely on balancing the household budget and keeping track of finances, the first two areas of financial capability identified by the Task Force.

Even for these areas of financial capability, it is hard to know the extent to which Gail 'help[s] people *understand* money and debt' as suggested in the introduction to every episode.[72] Writing about financial literacy education for consumer bankrupts, Karen Gross notes that the moment of bankruptcy creates a 'teachable moment'.[73] *Til Debt Do Us Part* creates a similar moment for participants at the start of an episode when Gail shows the couple their monthly expenses and earnings, and predicts their debt load in five years. Moreover, many features of the programme mirror those that have been identified as important for meaningful and effective financial literacy education, and are important for both participants and the audience. These features include: voluntary enrollment; programme delivery in a comfortable and accessible setting; tailoring to participants' financial situation; active and participatory learning; and an incentive to keep participants' involved (and the audience watching).[74]

However, *Til Debt Do Us Part* does not clearly deliver some other key elements of effective financial literacy pedagogy, particularly in terms of empowering learners to make better and more informed financial decisions in the future. First, the programme does not appear to include any follow-up to support participants after an episode finishes, nor is much information provided about getting support with managing debt.[75] And while the learning is active and participatory in that they must learn to follow a strict budget, participants are not generally given assistance with the lifestyle changes that are needed or prescribed by Gail in order to live within the budget, although occasionally experts will be brought in to teach participants skills such as cooking,[76] or assist them with de-cluttering and organising.[77]

In addition, participants (and therefore viewers) do not appear to have the rationale for the various allocations in the weekly budget explained to them, nor is the more general financial advice dispensed throughout the programme explained. A common 'challenge' sees couples creating a short or long-term budget together, but there is little advice about what to consider in creating it. The instructions appear to be limited to the following general parameters: do not take on new debt; plan to be debt-free or at least free of consumer debt within three years; and save for emergencies, retirement

---

[71] Task Force on Financial Literacy, 'Leveraging Excellence' (n 4) 11.

[72] Emphasis added.

[73] K Gross, 'Establishing Financial Programs for Consumer Debtors: Complex Issues on the Platter' in J Niemi-Kiesilainen et al (eds), *Consumer Bankruptcy in Global Perspective* (Oxford and Portland, Hart Publishing, 2003) 347–48.

[74] For a discussion of the considerations that should be addressed in designing effective financial literacy education programmes, see, eg ibid 343–60; Block-Lieb et al, 'Lessons from the Trenches' (n 56) 503–24.

[75] The 'Where Are They Now' webisodes discussed earlier do not feature any support to the participants.

[76] *Til Debt Do Us Part* episodes 35 and 84.

[77] Ibid episodes 40 and 78.

and children's post-secondary education costs. This focus on individual or nuclear family responsibility for all contingencies across the life course highlights another feature of *Til Debt Do Us Part*—its reinforcement of the neoliberal regulatory project.

C. The Financial Literacy 'Regulatory Project'

Neoliberalism as a political practice is associated with a withdrawal or retreat of the state from socialising risks—such as illness or poverty—through collective measures, or providing equality of condition through, for example, income redistribution. The state's role is instead focused on providing individual citizens equality of opportunity to participate in the market to ensure their financial and physical security. This shift towards individual provisioning and responsibility takes regulatory form in measures to decentralise governance and limit direct regulation of the market, along with privatising and reducing social services and income redistribution.[78] Despite the language of 'deregulation' that often surrounds discussions of law under neoliberalism, characterising the regulatory changes as 'new regulation' is perhaps more appropriate because 'in many countries there has been significant re-regulation'.[79] An important neoliberal regulatory tool is 'responsibilisation',[80] the process by which the state essentially transfers to individual citizens direct responsibility for many of the services and protections it previously provided. 'Responsibilised' citizens regulate their behaviour and provide for their own well-being over the life course, and the state assists them to do this by 'fostering the institutional, social, and cultural conditions that support "entrepreneurship of the self"'.[81]

In the context of consumer law, 're-regulation' or 'new regulation' takes the form of measures 'to ensure that individuals become responsible consumers'.[82] Regulatory initiatives to facilitate this responsibilisation include the creation of opportunities for citizen involvement in policy development and implementation; enhanced disclosure requirements for financial service providers;[83] and financial literacy education.[84] In the neoliberal regulatory project responsibilised citizen consumers are understood to be simultaneously regulating themselves and financial markets through their

---

[78] See generally J Fudge and B Cossman, 'Introduction' in B Cossman and J Fudge (eds), *Privatization, Law and the Challenge to Feminism* (Toronto, University of Toronto Press, 2002) 3–37; D Harvey, *A Brief History of Neoliberalism* (Oxford, Oxford University Press, 2007) 64–86; H Lessard, 'Charter Gridlock: Equality Formalism and Marriage Fundamentalism' (2006) *Supreme Court Law Review* 33, 297–303.

[79] I Ramsay, 'Consumer Law, Regulatory Capitalism and the "New Learning" in Regulation' (2006) *Sydney Law Review* 28, 11. Ramsay provides a helpful overview of the literature examining regulation under neoliberalism at 11–18. See also Williams, 'Empowerment of Whom and for What?' (n 2) 231.

[80] N Rose, *Powers of Freedom: Reframing Political Thought* (Cambridge, Cambridge University Press, 1999) 158–60, 174, 215; Williams, 'Empowerment of Whom and for What?' (n 2) 232–33.

[81] Williams, 'Empowerment of Whom and for What?' (n 2) 233 (paraphrasing N Rose, *Powers of Freedom* (n 80) 144). See also P O'Malley, 'Risk and Responsibility' in A Barry et al (eds), *Foucault and Political Reason: Liberalism, Neoliberalism and Rationalities of Government* (London, University College London Press, 1996) 189–207; Rose, 'Governing 'Advanced' Liberal Democracies (n 5) 41, 56–60.

[82] Ramsay, 'Consumer Law' (n 79) 11.

[83] See, eg Credit Business Practices (Banks, Authorized Foreign Banks, Trust and Loan Companies, Retail Associations, Canadian Insurance Companies and Foreign Insurance Companies) Regulations, SOR/2009/257 (9 September 2009).

[84] Ramsay, 'Consumer Law' (n 79) 12–13.

consumption choices,[85] although consumers are not completely sovereign in these choices. For example, in countries in the global north where economies are heavily credit-driven, financial literacy initiatives have focused on the 'responsible' use of credit and debt management rather than on trying to curb consumption.[86]

In sum, the financial literacy neoliberal regulatory project is held out 'as a tool for consumer empowerment and a cure for all that ails our consumer credit economy: financial ignorance, unhealthy debt burdens, predatory lending, mortgage foreclosures, joblessness and susceptibility to savvy lenders and scam artists.'[87] At the same time, the assumption that the financially literate individual should and will successfully negotiate their way through consumer financial markets 'absolves a wide range of other entities, public and private, from responsibility.'[88] This assumption further reinforces the neoliberal focus on individual responsibility for physical and financial well-being, and helps undermine arguments for socialising various risks such as illness and poverty. As Williams suggests, 'future generations may find it difficult to comprehend arguments for the pooling of resources to support those perceived to have failed in the "business of life"'.[89]

In his work on governance, Nikolas Rose highlights the significance of the development and expansion of mass media technologies—such as television—that provide indirect means to 'translate the goals of political, social and economic authorities into the choices and commitments of individuals'.[90] John Fiske similarly argues that television 'work(s) ideologically to promote and prefer certain meanings of the world'.[91] *Til Debt Do Us Part* provides a number of messages that help reinforce and normalise the individual responsibility that underpins the neoliberal regulatory project and responsibilised citizenship. As discussed earlier, in the last segment of each episode Gail explains how her budget will permit participants to pay off their debt, create an emergency fund and build retirement savings. The show reinforces this focus on personal responsibility for physical and financial security over the life course with a general message that no social safety net exists to assist participants if they lose their job or home, or they are injured or fall ill. In featuring participants who are able to meet their basic needs and live relatively comfortably on the budget set for them, supported by an income that allows them pay off their debt and save for emergencies and retirement, the programme reinforces this ideal of responsibilisation—that the right personal choices will lead to short and long-term security.

However, the fact that most participants can become debt-free in a short period of time sends an unrealistic message about how easy it is to do this. In almost every

---

[85] Williams, 'Empowerment of Whom and for What?' (n 2) 233, 243.

[86] Ibid 244.

[87] Gross, 'Financial Literacy Education' (n 57) 307.

[88] Ibid. This assumption that if given sufficient information and financial education, consumers will be able to make responsible choices, is not necessarily borne out by studies of consumer choice. Ramsay, 'Consumer Law' (n 79) 13, fn 19; S Stabile, 'The Behavior of Defined Contribution Plan Participants' (2002) *New York University Law Review* 77, 71–105; Williams, 'Empowerment of Whom and for What?' (n 2) 244–47.

[89] Williams, 'Empowerment of Whom and for What?' (n 2) 243.

[90] Rose, 'Governing 'Advanced' Liberal Democracies (n 5) 58.

[91] Fiske, *Television Culture* (n 5) 20. Brenda Cossman also discusses the relationship between legal discourse and popular culture in *Sexual Citizens: The Legal and Cultural Regulation of Sex and Belonging* (Stanford, Stanford University Press, 2007).

episode, participants follow the budget, pick up extra work as soon as Gail tells them to,[92] consolidate their loans, or negotiate better arrangements with creditors.[93] *Til Debt Do Us Part* also appears to suggest that faced with the financial implications of particular choices, the rational one will be easy to make. In a number of episodes, for example, participants successfully give up smoking or gambling after Gail advises them of the significant costs of the habit.[94] In another episode, a couple accepts her advice that they cannot afford in vitro fertilization treatment.[95]

The show buttresses this responsibilisation message with the fairly regular suggestion that people unable to support themselves have only themselves to blame. In a few episodes, Gail suggests in the voiceover that the participants 'grew up poor and never learned how to handle their money'.[96] Her 'life lesson challenges' include having participants access food banks and feed themselves for a week,[97] spend a night in a homeless shelter,[98] or live for a week on their projected weekly government pension income.[99] All of these challenges carry with them the implication that being homeless or receiving income assistance is 'what happens to people who don't plan their lives'.[100]

Finally, in keeping with its message of individual responsibility, *Til Debt Do Us Part* rarely places participants' experiences beyond their individual context. The ease with which participants build up debt and access credit and credit cards is never more than an individual problem. While Gail often takes multiple credit cards away from participants at the start of each episode,[101] and occasionally destroys them,[102] only rarely does she question credit-granting practices.[103] Nor does the programme situate challenges that participants have, such as finding affordable high quality childcare,[104] or supporting themselves in retirement as reflective of larger social and political choices about who should bear responsibility for these costs and risks. To be fair, *Til Debt Do Us Part* is about helping people manage their debt and live within their means within the current political and economic climate. What I want to suggest is that in doing this in a popular reality TV series, the programme reinforces the neoliberal regulatory project by presenting financial and physical security over the life course as individual responsibilities.

In analysing the messages about financial management and financial responsibility that are constituted in *Til Debt Do Us Part*'s audience and identifying it as providing cultural support for the neoliberal regulatory project, it is important to be clear that

---

[92] See, eg *Til Debt Do Us Part* episodes 47, 53, 72.

[93] See, eg ibid episodes 19, 22, 79.

[94] See, eg ibid episodes 2, 6, 21, 48, 83.

[95] Ibid episode 67.

[96] Ibid episodes 6 and 22.

[97] Ibid episodes 28 and 89. Gail does permit them to supplement the food bank box with fresh fruit and vegetables.

[98] Ibid episode 26.

[99] Ibid episode 51.

[100] Gail Vaz-Oxlade, ibid episode 26.

[101] See, eg ibid episode 1.

[102] See, eg ibid episode 51.

[103] See, eg ibid episode 11.

[104] Gail occasionally comments on the high cost of daycare, but usually in the context of explaining why it is a good financial decision for a mother to stay out of the labour force.

this is not a critique of the programme as 'bad TV'. This is not an argument that *Til Debt Do Us Part* itself needs to be critical of the neoliberal project, although one can imagine such a critique in a documentary or documentary series that follows people as they struggle with a variety of financial situations.[105] And yet, one can take up the images and ask about the ideologies and beliefs that are constituted in the audience, and ask how the narratives might 'be contested and engaged so that we do more than respond to them, as Rustom Bharachua puts it, "with a hallucinatory delight"'.[106] Indeed, if I am 'asking' anyone to be critical, I am asking the audience.

IV. Conclusion

Commentators have noted that lifestyle reality TV promotes self-actualisation and transformation through individual effort, initiative, and spending. While *Til Debt Do Us Part* is firmly situated within this reality TV sub-genre, its messages of responsible spending, planning and living within one's means over the life course appears to run counter to the consumerism that permeates much lifestyle reality TV programming. In a credit-driven economy with low financial literacy levels where many citizens carry unmanageable debt loads and continue to add to them, these are important messages.

A closer examination of the programme as financial literacy education however, raises questions about the extent to which the programme helps participants and viewers add to their financial literacy toolboxes in a meaningful way. Analysis of participants' socio-economic location, the budgets they follow and the 'challenges' they must complete, suggests that there is another lesson being taught indirectly and directly in that the programme provides cultural support for the responsibilised citizenship that underpins the neoliberal regulatory project by reinforcing, as normative, individual responsibility for managing risk and financial security over the life course.

---

[105] The National Film Board's 'GDP—Measuring the Human Side of the Canadian Economic Crisis' is an example of such a series. The 'web documentary' was a year-long project to chronicle the stories of Canadians dealing with the recession. The project created 17 stories which followed the experiences of a variety of Canadians. These can be found on the website www.gdp.nfb.ca/stories.

[106] R Johnson, 'Living *Deadwood*: Imagination, Affect, and the Persistence of the Past' (2009) *Suffolk University Law Review* 42, 824 (quoting R Bharacuha, 'Around Ayodhya: Aberrations, Enigmas, and Moments of Violence' (1993) *Third Text* 7, 51).

11

Judging Reality Television Judges

NANCY S MARDER

I. Introduction

Judge Judy, an extraordinarily successful American television show, has inspired a television phenomenon in which viewers can watch judge shows on television from morning until evening every day of the working week. My intent, after providing a snapshot view of these shows based upon an empirical study I conducted, is to examine the positive lessons these shows offer, as well as the negative ones. On balance, I think that the negative lessons outweigh the positive ones, but television viewers disagree, as suggested by their willingness to watch these shows. In fact, *Judge Judy*, with 6.3 million daily viewers, has recently overtaken *Oprah* as the most popular daytime television show.[1]

For the most part, these television judge shows adhere to the format made famous by *Judge Judy*. They focus on a single judge, whose personality sets the tenor of the proceedings, and whose task is to decide a private dispute between two parties. In many of the cases, the parties could have gone to a small claims court, but instead they appear before a television judge. The television judge decides the case in a brief segment during which there is drama and tension as each side struggles to tell its story in the most sympathetic light possible. Often a party will introduce 'evidence', such as a document, a photo, or a video, in the course of making its case. The parties tell their stories in their own words, and the television judge resolves their dispute in language that the parties, the audience members, and the viewers understand.

What do these shows teach television viewers about the judicial system, and what do they teach them about justice? Some of their lessons are positive, insofar as they give viewers practical information about legal concepts or words or some common-sense notion of what constitutes evidence. Some of the shows' lessons are negative, insofar as they depict a court in which decisions can be made quickly and without recourse to precedent by a judge who seems more interested in making the audience laugh than in struggling to arrive at the correct result. There is no difficulty in reaching

---

[1] '"Judge Judy" Topples "Oprah" from Top Daytime Spot' *New York Times*, 24 September 2010, http://abcnews.go.com/Entertainment/wireStory?id=11721182.

judgment in these television court settings; answers are immediately knowable and always clear-cut according to the judge.

Surprisingly, these shows present a television judiciary that is diverse by race and gender. Such diversity cannot be found in the federal judiciary or the judiciaries of many states. The diversity of the television judiciary may well convey to viewers a positive lesson about who can serve as a judge—at least on television. More practically, however, the television judiciary probably owes its diversity to the need of advertisers to reach different demographic groups. The commercials that accompany these programmes typically track some of the demographics of the judge.

What difference does it make that these television judges reach a vast audience and convey to them some basics about law? In my view, these television judges translate the arcane language of the law and make it accessible to the mainstream public.[2] In doing so, television judges allow a broad swath of the population to gain some knowledge of the law, even though in most instances it is very basic, commonsense knowledge, such as 'don't sign a document unless you read it and understand it'.

What difference does it make that these shows enter viewers' homes every day through the small screen? Television allows regular viewers to become familiar with particular judges. These viewers know the judges on a first-name basis, referring to them as 'Judge Alex' and 'Judge Judy', and they can identify their persona. On one level, the judge is seen as human and demystified, in spite of being cloaked in the traditional symbols of the role, such as the robe, the gavel, and the American flag. On another level, however, television judges become just another form of entertainment; they lack the dignity and gravitas that actual judges have. Even though television judges' courtroom sets mimic actual courtrooms, these shows do not create for viewers the sense of respect and awe that one feels upon entering a courtroom. These shows reach millions of people and make justice seem more accessible and available to them and to the parties, and yet, these shows sow confusion. They blur the lines between judging and entertaining so that viewers might think they have watched a case and now think they have some inkling about what takes place in a courtroom, when in fact they have watched entertainment on a stage set that just happens to have some of the trappings of a courtroom.

II. Description of the Project

In order to study the phenomenon of television judge shows, I focused on about a week's worth of shows that were broadcast from 16 December to 23 December 2009 in the Chicago metropolitan area.[3] I included all television judge shows that follow the *Judge Judy* model, in which a judge, wearing a robe and using a set that looks like a courtroom, hears two parties' versions of the dispute and then resolves the dispute. The parties

---

[2] See Malcolm Gladwell, *The Tipping Point: How Little Things Can Make a Big Difference* (Boston, Little, Brown and Company, 2000) 200.

[3] The Audiovisual Department at Chicago-Kent College of Law recorded all the television judge programmes that were aired from 16 December to 23 December 2009 in Chicago. My two research assistants, Amanda Schackart and Stephanie Thommes, and I worked from the recorded shows. I created a coding sheet, which we used for each case that was presented to a television judge during the time period of this study. I have included the coding sheet as an Appendix.

present their case (an actual dispute, though not always involving a legal claim) to the judge but there is also a bailiff and an audience in the courtroom. There were six television judge shows that fit this pattern.[4] I included two other shows, *The People's Court*[5] and *Divorce Court*,[6] which were precursors to *Judge Judy*, and another show, *Street Court*, which adds a slightly different twist in that the dispute is heard by a television judge at the location where the dispute occurred, rather than in a setting that looks like a courtroom.

This snapshot of television judge shows made it clear just how many shows and cases are available to viewers on a daily basis. Amazingly, a devoted viewer (with a DVD player to record shows that aired at the same time) could watch nine different shows and hear a total of 181 cases in this time period. During the relevant time period, the number of cases heard by each judge was as follows:

Show	Number of Cases
Judge Judy	34
Judge Pirro	32
The People's Court	27
Judge Mathis	25
Street Court	19
Judge Joe Brown	14
Judge Alex	12
Divorce Court	10
Judge Hatchett	8
TOTALS: 9 shows	181 cases

Given that these shows attract millions of viewers,[7] different viewers are likely to have different viewing habits. A particularly devoted viewer could watch all of these shows and perhaps feel that he or she had spent the week learning something about the law, or at least something about the ups and downs of peoples' lives. Of course, a viewer could have a favourite television judge and just watch that judge's shows. Of these shows, *Judge Judy* attracts the largest number of viewers;[8] thus, many viewers might limit their viewing just to *Judge Judy*.

---

[4] The six television judge shows included: *Judge Alex, Judge Pirro, Judge Hatchett, Judge Joe Brown, Judge Judy,* and *Judge Mathis.*

[5] *The People's Court* began in 1981 with Judge Joseph Wapner. See Michael Wilson, '"Street Court" Goes Right to Dispute's Heart, or Front Lawn' *New York Times*, 22 November 2009 ('It has been 28 years since Judge Joseph Wapner heard his first case on "The People's Court". Copycats abounded, some successful (Judith Sheindlin of "Judge Judy") and some less so ....'). Judge Wapner was very popular and probably the best-known 'judge' at the time—more well-known than any of the justices of the US Supreme Court. See, eg Taunya Lovell Banks, 'Will the Real Judge Stand-Up: Virtual Integration on TV Reality Court Shows' *Picturing Justice*, 16 January 2003, http://usf.usfca.edu/pj/realjudge_banks.htm. Currently, the presiding judge on *The People's Court* is Marilyn Milian.

[6] *Divorce Court* began in 1957. See Wikipedia, entry for 'Divorce Court' at http://en.wikipedia.org/wiki/Divorce_Court. The presiding judge is currently Judge Lynn Toler.

[7] See, eg Wilson, '"Street Court"' (n 5) ('"Judge Joe Brown" averages 2.9 million viewers nationwide ....').

[8] In 2009, *Judge Judy* averaged 6.3 million daily viewers. See '"Judge Judy" Topples "Oprah"' (n 1).

Although the television judge shows adhere to the same format, within this format they try to distinguish themselves in small ways. For example, the introduction to *Judge Pirro* is that 'she's an advocate, a mentor, a judge, and a justice with conviction'. She is willing to take on tough issues, like domestic abuse, because she has dealt with such issues in past jobs she has held. In the opening to Judge Mathis' show, he is described as someone who had started out as part of a gang, but who changed the course of his life by putting himself through school, and eventually becoming a judge.[9] His underlying message is that if he can change his life in such a dramatic way, so too can his viewers. The judges not only have different work histories, but they also have different approaches on 'the bench'. Judge Hatchett, for example, seems to believe in 'tough love'. She tries to cut to the chase in disputes and does not let the parties make excuses for themselves. In contrast, Judge Alex, who is described at the opening of his show as having been 'a police officer, a trial lawyer, and a criminal court judge', takes a friendlier, more low-keyed approach to his role as television judge compared to some of the other judges.

III. Gender and Race

One of the most striking ways in which television judges distinguish themselves, particularly because television is a visual medium, is in their demographic characteristics. Of the nine television judges included in this study, five are female (56%) and four are male (44%). This is certainly not a gender breakdown that can be found in the federal judiciary (district courts and courts of appeal), where there were 1260 active and senior status judges in 2009, of which 257 of them were female (20%) and 1003 of them were male (80%).[10] Nor can the gender diversity of the television judiciary be found in state court judiciaries. For example, in Illinois there were 954 state court judges in 2009, of which 264 were female (28%) and 690 were male (72%).[11] Other large states, such as New York and California, have state court judiciaries with similar gender breakdowns. In New York, there were 698 judges as of 2009, and 189, or 27 per cent, were female. In California, there were 1631 judges as of 2009, and 477, or 29 per cent, were female.[12]

The television judges are also racially and ethnically diverse. Of the nine television judges, four (44% after rounding) are African-American (two men and two women) and two (22%) are Latino/a (one man and one woman). Even the three (33%) white judges (two women and one man) are ethnically diverse. Although the three white judges, Judge Pirro, Judge Mazzariello, and Judge Judy, are all New Yorkers, the first judge is of Lebanese ancestry, the second is of Italian ancestry, and the third is Jewish.

---

[9] Charles Leroux, 'The Gavels of TV' *Chicago Tribune*, 11 December 2008.

[10] The numbers are for the federal judiciary in 2009 and are available at United States Courts, History of the Federal Judiciary, www.uscourts.gov/JudgesAndJudgeships/BiographicalDirectoryOfJudges.aspx.

[11] Numbers are from 2009 and are available at American Judicature Society, Diversity of the Bench, www.judicialselection.us/judicial_selection/bench_diversity/index.cfm?state=.

[12] See ibid (providing figures available at www.judicialselection.us/judicial_selection/bench_diversity/index.cfm?state=).

The television judiciary is far more racially diverse than the federal judiciary, where just 113 of 1260 judges (active and senior status judges in district courts and courts of appeal), or nine per cent, are African-American, and just 71 of 1260 judges (active and senior status judges in district courts and courts of appeal), or six per cent, are Latino/Latina.[13] Of the 1260 judges in the federal judiciary (active and senior status in district courts and courts of appeal), 1062 judges, or 84 per cent, are white.[14] In contrast, among the nine television judges, just three out of nine, or 33 per cent (after rounding), are white.

One of the more curious features of these television judge shows is the bailiff. Although almost all the television judges have been actual judges at some point in their careers,[15] all the television judges have a bailiff who is usually played by an actor.[16] The bailiff typically adds to the diversity of the 'court'. In all the shows, if the judge is female, then the bailiff will be male. So, too, if the judge is white, then the bailiff will be African-American; if the judge is African-American, then the bailiff will be white (or Latina in one case); and if the judge is Latino/a, then the bailiff will be African-American. For example, 'Judge Mazz', as Judge Michael Mazzariello on *Street Court* is known, is a white, male judge. His bailiff is an African-American woman. Similarly, Judge Pirro is a white woman. Her bailiff is an African-American man. For all nine programmes, the judge is of one race and the bailiff is of another. In seven out of nine programmes, the judge is of one gender and the bailiff is of another, and in the remaining two programmes, the judge and bailiff are of the same gender (male), but they are of different races. The two charts below show the gender and race of the judge and the bailiff:

Judge	Judge's Gender	Bailiff's Gender
Judge Pirro	Female	Male
Judge Hatchett	Female	Male
Judge Judy	Female	Male
Judge Lynn Toler	Female	Male
Judge Marilyn Milian	Female	Male
Judge Mazz	Male	Female
Judge Joe Brown	Male	Female
Judge Alex	Male	Male
Judge Mathis	Male	Male

---

[13] See United States Courts, History of the Federal Judiciary, www.uscourts.gov/JudgesAndJudgeships/BiographicalDirectoryOfJudges.aspx.

[14] Ibid.

[15] The exception is Judge Mazz on *Street Court*, who has never been an actual judge.

[16] The bailiff is played by an actor except in the following cases: the bailiff on *Judge Pirro* is a member of the Chicago Police Department, see 'Chicago Officer Keith Anderson is Judge Pirro's New Bailiff' (Fox Chicago News) www.myfoxchicago.com/dpp/entertainment/keith-anderson-judge-jeanine-pirro-chicago-police-officer-new-bailiff-20100930; the bailiff on *Judge Joe Brown* worked for the Los Angeles County Sheriff's Department for 19 years, see Judge Joe Brown, Bios, www.judgejoebrown.com/bios.php; and the bailiff on *Divorce Court* worked for the San Bernardino, CA County Sheriff's Department for 30 years, see Wikipedia, entry for 'Divorce Court', http://en.wikipedia.org/wiki/Divorce_Court.

Judge	Judge's Race	Bailiff's Race
Judge Pirro	White	African-American
Judge Judy	White	African-American
Judge Mazz	White	African-American
Judge Hatchett	African-American	White
Judge Mathis	African-American	White
Judge Lynn Toler	African-American	White
Judge Joe Brown	African-American	Latina
Judge Alex	Latino	African-American
Judge Marilyn Milian	Latina	African-American

Thus, the picture that is presented to the television viewer is that the television 'court', consisting of the judge and bailiff, are diverse by gender and race. The judge, who is in a robe and usually has a gavel on the bench and is framed by flags in the background, and the bailiff, who wears a uniform and is present to assist the judge, represent the court. Why is it important to viewers that the judge and bailiff, who constitute the court, are diverse by gender and race? One reason might be to draw viewers to the programme from as broad a swath of the population as possible. The producers and advertisers might think that viewers select the television judge programmes they watch based on how closely they identify with the judge or the bailiff (though admittedly, the bailiff plays a de minimis role compared to the judge). Another reason could be that the bailiff serves as a foil to highlight the gender or race of the judge. The bailiff does this by being of a different gender and/or race than the judge. Yet another reason could be that the shows are trying to be as inclusive and as politically correct as possible, though this seems unlikely because there are many television shows that have all-white casts and are anything but politically correct.

What difference does the race and gender of the television judge make given that the show is based largely on the judge? This is a question that academics who study actual courts have considered, particularly with respect to the gender of actual judges.[17] Usually, they have not found any difference in the judgments that male and female judges reach.[18] Occasionally, they have found that gender makes a difference in terms of the style or manner in which the judicial proceeding has been conducted,[19] and only rarely have they found that gender makes a difference in terms of the result reached by the judge.[20] Some judges, such as former US Supreme Court Justice Sandra Day O'Connor, have argued that gender does not make any difference to

[17] See, eg Carrie Menkel-Meadow, 'Portia in a Different Voice: Speculations on a Woman's Lawyering Process' (1985) *Berkeley Women's Law Journal* 1, 39–63.

[18] See, eg Dermot Feenan, 'Women Judges: Gendering Judging, Justifying Diversity' (2008) *Law & Society* 35, 517 ('In general, women judges did not suggest they would decide differently, but their responses also reflect nuances in understanding the role of judicial office that are not shared by male judges.').

[19] Ibid 510–12.

[20] For one of the rare studies in which male and female (immigration) judges reached different results, see Carrie Menkel-Meadow, 'Asylum in a Different Voice? Judging Immigration Claims and Gender' in Jaya Ramji-Nogales, Andrew I Schoenholtz and Philip G Schrag (eds), *Refugee Roulette* (New York, New York University Press, 2009) 202–26.

judging. In Justice O'Connor's view, judges, regardless of their gender, try to reach 'wise' decisions, and it is harmful to suggest otherwise.[21]

In the controlled world of television judges, however, there are several different ways that the race and gender of the judge could play a role. For example, television producers and advertisers are likely to consider the race and gender of the judge and parties in terms of the viewers they want to attract. Producers want to attract the largest number of viewers possible so that advertisers will pay as much money as possible to run commercials during the show. Advertisers are more willing to pay a lot of money for advertising time if they know the show will reach a large audience, and in particular a large audience of people who are likely to buy the product they are advertising.

This study included commercials as a way of assessing who producers and advertisers think the television viewers are likely to be. This study recorded not only all of the television judge shows that aired between 16 December to 23 December 2009 in the Chicago area, but also all the commercials that were broadcast before, during, and after each case. Over the course of the 181 cases considered by the television judges, there were 1840 commercials. On average, each show had 10.2 commercials per case.

In this study, there are three television judge shows in which the judge is white. These three shows are *Judge Judy*, *Judge Pirro*, and *Street Court* (with Judge Mazz). Interestingly, these three shows also had the highest proportion of cases in which both parties were white as compared to cases in which both parties were African-American or where one party was white and the other was African-American.[22] Almost two-thirds of the cases in *Judge Pirro*, almost four-fifths of the cases in *Judge Judy*, and over one-half of the cases in *Street Court* involved both parties who were white.

My hypothesis is that if the judge and parties are white, the television audience is more likely to be middle class, and possibly white. Although I do not know the racial composition of the television audience, the commercials aired on shows that have white judges and the highest proportion of cases in which both parties were white, were geared more toward a middle-class television audience. For example, *Judge Judy*, a white judge with the largest number of viewers of all the television judge shows,[23] and the largest proportion of cases in which both parties were white, also has commercials aimed at a mainstream, middle-class audience. Almost all the commercials (96%) tend to focus on health products, food (including restaurants and specialty food items), other television programmes, beauty items, household furniture, luxury items, insurance, communications services, clothing/shopping, local events, financial services, and charities. A very small percentage of the commercials (2.8%) during *Judge Judy* cases focused on financial problems, injuries, diseases, and attorneys.[24] In contrast, the two television judge shows that have an African-American judge and the largest proportion of cases in which both parties were African-American (*Judge Hatchett* and *Divorce*

---

[21] Sandra Day O'Connor, 'Madison Lecture: Portia's Progress' (1991) *New York University Law Review* 66, 1557–58.

[22] There were a few shows in which one of the parties could have been Latino or of another race or ethnicity, but it was difficult to be sure. For the purposes of this analysis, I discuss only parties who are white or African-American because these were the two races that appeared most often on the television judge shows and were most easily identified.

[23] See '"Judge Judy" Topples "Oprah"' (n 1) (describing *Judge Judy's* viewership).

[24] The remaining 1.2% of commercials during *Judge Judy* advertised products I could not classify as the product type was unclear from the coding.

Court with Judge Lynn Toler) have commercials aimed at less affluent viewers. *Judge Hatchett* and *Divorce Court* have some types of commercials in common with *Judge Judy* (though not necessarily for the same upmarket products), such as commercials for health products, other television programmes, communications services, insurance, and clothing/shopping. These types of commercials constitute about 62 per cent of the commercials shown during *Divorce Court* and 48 per cent shown during *Judge Hatchett*. However, these two programmes also have types of commercials that *Judge Judy* does not have, such as advertisements that focus on financial problems, diseases or illnesses, personal injury attorneys, school/career programmes, and injuries. These commercials, which are directed to a less affluent population, constitute about 37 per cent of the types of commercials shown during *Divorce Court* and 47 per cent of the types of commercials shown during *Judge Hatchett*.[25] In addition, these two shows have commercials for television programmes starring African-Americans (4% of the commercials during *Divorce Court* and 6% of the commercials during *Judge Hatchett*), which *Judge Judy* does not have. In television judge programmes in which the judge is African-American and a large proportion of the cases involve parties who were both African-American, many of the commercials (roughly one-third to one-half) tend to be directed toward a less affluent population. Thus, the race of the judge and the parties makes a difference, but largely to the producers and advertisers who are trying to reach different segments of the viewing public to sell them either upmarket or cheaper product types.

In terms of gender, I found that in all nine of the television judge shows—regardless of whether the judge was male or female—the largest category of cases involved a man as one party and a woman as the other party, rather than two women or two men as parties. Of the 181 cases in this study, 98 cases (54%) involved parties in which one person was female and one was male.[26] Of these 98 cases, the woman won in 53 cases (54%). The man won in 31 cases (32%). In the remainder of the cases, of which there were 13 (13%), nobody won, both parties won in part, or the coder could not determine who won because of a technical problem with the recording.

These figures suggest that women won more of the cases when one party was female and one party was male and that this pattern persisted whether the judge was male or female. In 64 mixed party cases (one man and one woman) before women judges (Pirro, Hatchett, Judy, Toler, and Milian), women won 31 cases (48%) and men won 21 cases (33%) and 19 per cent could not be determined. In 34 mixed party cases before male judges (Alex, Joe, Mathis, and Mazz), women won 23 cases (68%) and men won 10 cases (29%). In the remaining 1 case (3%), there was no winner, or both parties won in part, or there was a technical problem. My explanation for why women won a higher percentage of cases than men, regardless of the gender of the judge, is that television viewers are more likely to be women than men[27] and that the women

---

[25] In *Divorce Court*, 6% of commercials could not be identified from the coding, while 3% could not be identified in *Judge Hatchett*. The percentages for each programme add up to 100% when tenths are included, rather than rounded to the decimal point.

[26] I excluded cases in which there were multiple plaintiffs of different genders or multiple defendants of different genders.

[27] '"Judge Judy" has been the ratings leader among court reality shows with about 10 million viewers daily (75 percent women)' Charles Leroux, 'There's No Justice Like Show Justice: Reality Court Shows Compete in Strange World of Small Gripes' *Chicago Tribune*, 11 December 2008.

who view these shows are more likely to want to see women as the winners in these disputes. However, this remains merely a hypothesis that has yet to be tested.

Although the gender of the judge did not make a difference in terms of which party won—female parties won more often than male parties whether the judge was male or female—there was a limited gender difference in terms of the kinds of cases that male and female judges heard. For the most part, male and female judges heard the same kinds of cases. Of the 181 cases in this study, there were 54 contract disputes (30% of the cases), 46 property damage/property disputes (25%), 26 billing disputes (14%), 26 landlord-tenant disputes (14%), 11 personal relationship/divorce disputes (6%), 11 domestic abuse disputes (6%), four paternity claims (2%), and three disputes with pain and suffering (2%).[28] The judges, regardless of gender, typically heard four kinds of dispute: contract, property damage/property, billing, and landlord-tenant. Three female judges had niches on which they focused, albeit not always exclusively. Judge Toler on *Divorce Court* heard only divorce cases; she had a niche that none of the other judges had. However, two other female judges heard typical cases (contract, property, billing, and landlord-tenant), but also heard domestic abuse cases (Pirro) and paternity disputes (Hatchett). These three women judges had areas of focus that would be of particular interest to women viewers.

IV. The Positive Lessons that Television Judge Shows Teach

One positive lesson that television judge shows teach is that judges can be of any gender, race, and ethnicity. Although such a diverse judiciary currently exists only on television, and does not yet exist in federal or state judiciaries, it opens up the possibility for viewers that judges can be of any gender, race, or ethnicity; there are no limitations. Perhaps if viewers are able to imagine that judges are not limited to being white and male by watching a diverse judiciary on television, then someday our actual judiciaries will be as diverse as our television judiciaries. Of course, there is also the possibility that viewers will mistakenly conclude that federal and state judiciaries are already diverse because the television judiciary is diverse. This could lead to 'virtual integration', in which viewers think 'the world is more integrated than it truly is'.[29] Based on television judge shows, viewers might even 'fear that women and nonwhite men have taken

---

[28] The cases were difficult to categorise because they could often be put into more than one category. For example, a dispute could involve a tenant and a landlord, but the dispute could also be about furniture that was damaged, so it could be categorised as landlord-tenant or property. Also, there were many disputes in which it was unclear whether the parties had entered into a contract; and if there was a contract, it was usually not one that had been put into writing. Finally, many of the disputes were between people who had some relationship to each other (former roommates, ex-girlfriends/boyfriends, family members) and their argument was ostensibly about money, but underlying that dispute was a disagreement about their relationship. The judge spent much of the time hearing about the relationship, and resolved the money dispute quickly and without much explanation.

[29] Leonard Steinhorn and Barbara Diggs-Brown, *By the Color of Our Skin: The Illusion of Integration and the Reality of Race* (New York, Dutton, 1999) 145–46.

over the courts'.[30] Although these are possibilities, it is hard to predict the effects of a diverse television judiciary. It could hasten change by helping viewers to recognise that judges are not limited to white men, or it could hinder change by persuading viewers that actual judiciaries already look like the television judiciary. I am inclined to view a diverse television judiciary as a positive feature of the television judge show.

Another positive feature is that the judges provide some very basic legal lessons to the parties and viewers. In some instances, these lessons involve more common sense than law, but nevertheless, parties and viewers would benefit if they followed this advice. Out of 181 cases, there were 98 cases (54%) in which the television judge provided a legal lesson, even if it was a very basic lesson. For example, one common lesson that television judges convey to the parties and the television audience is the importance of getting an agreement in writing. Judge Pirro gave this piece of advice to the parties in a case in which the plaintiff sued her former employer for $1500 for work that she claimed she did as a casting director for a pornographic movie, but the employer disputed the claim on the ground that the plaintiff did not complete the work she was hired to do.[31] Judge Milian gave the same advice in a case in which the plaintiff worked as a consultant and was promised a commission and finder's fee for booking the defendant's band; however, the defendant said the booking never happened.[32] Judge Milian stressed the need to put these arrangements in writing. Judge Mazz tried to impart a similar lesson in a case involving a tenant (plaintiff) who said that he had to pay rent twice and a landlord (defendant) who said that he was entitled to the extra money because when the plaintiff's roommate moved out he only received half the rent. The plaintiff won and the lesson was 'when in doubt, write it out'.[33]

On another positive note, the television judge shows often teach parties and viewers the meaning of legal terms or concepts, although again, the explanations are quite basic. Of the 181 cases, 27 (15%) involved a legal term or concept and some explanation, no matter how brief. In a case involving ex-roommates, for example, the plaintiff sued the defendant for non-payment of rent and bills, and the defendant, who had signed a lease, moved out because she said the room was in a terrible state. Judge Hatchett ruled for the plaintiff but explained that the plaintiff had a duty to 'mitigate damages'.[34] In another case in which the plaintiff sued her ex-boyfriend for the down payment on two cars and the cost of laser eye surgery, Judge Judy explained to the defendant that if he was not present for a phone conversation it was 'hearsay' and not admissible; she then dismissed the claims because the loans were old and were made during the time that the plaintiff and defendant lived together.[35] In a case before Judge Milian, in which the plaintiff and defendant shared an apartment, the defendant smoked pot, however the plaintiff was in the military and could not share an apartment with someone who smoked pot. Judge Milian explained that the plaintiff

---

[30] Taunya Lovell Banks, 'Judging the Judges–Daytime Television's Integrated Reality Court Bench' in Michael Asimow (ed), *Lawyers in Your Living Room! Law on Television* (Chicago, ABA Publishing, 2009) 309, 317.

[31] Jeanne Johann v JR & Vicki Rodriguez, *Judge Pirro*, 23 Dec 2009.

[32] Emily Irene McEntee v C Zion Dwayne Earle, *People's Court*, 21 Dec 2009.

[33] Jason Gross v James Shepard, *Street Court*, 21 Dec 2009.

[34] Amanda Johnson v Valerie Boudou, *Judge Hatchett*, 17 Dec 2009.

[35] Marcella Sheehan v Roland Gonzales, *Judge Judy*, 22 Dec 2009.

could move out and get her money back because there had been a 'constructive eviction'.[36] In other words, the defendant's pot-smoking had 'made it so that plaintiff could not live there'[37] because to do so would jeopardise her career in the military. In a case in which the plaintiff sued the defendant for the cost of a new roof that she had put on a house that the defendant owned because the plaintiff thought she was 'leasing to own' the house from the defendant, Judge Alex ruled for the plaintiff.[38] Judge Alex explained that otherwise there would be 'unjust enrichment' for the defendant; the defendant would own the house and have the benefit of the new roof that the plaintiff had installed.[39] In all these instances, the television judge used a legal term and offered a brief explanation of the term.

Another positive lesson that parties and viewers can take away from television judge shows is the importance of evidence and the various forms it might take. Out of 181 cases, 161 cases (89%) included some form(s) of evidence. Admittedly, some of the evidence was more for entertainment than for proof. For example, when a plaintiff, a professional wrestler, showed his ACW Heavyweight Champion belt to Judge Mathis, it was more to entertain than to support his claim that the defendant had distracted him during a match and had caused him to lose money by losing the match.[40] Similarly, when Judge Pirro heard the defendant's rap song in one case[41] or watched the defendant's video of his 'freak dog' in another case,[42] these were solely to entertain the audience. However, in many other cases, the television judges encouraged parties to present evidence and instructed them on the importance of having documents to support their claims. For example, in one case before Judge Alex, he complimented the plaintiff on her presentation of evidence. The plaintiff had sued the defendant because he would not let her take her belongings (valued at $1073) from a house they had shared; he said that she had already taken her belongings.[43] However, the plaintiff had photos showing that her belongings were still in the house after the date the defendant said they were gone and photos of newspapers in the house showing the date on which those photos had been taken.[44] Even the defendant agreed that the plaintiff had 'all the evidence against [him]'.[45]

Parties and viewers learn from television judge shows that plaintiffs have to present appropriate evidence to support their claims. As Judge Milian explained in one case, the plaintiff has 'the burden of proof'.[46] Or, as Judge Pirro explained, albeit more colloquially, 'Don't come to court and not give me evidence'.[47] In a case in which the plaintiff sued a business that supposedly fixed the oil leak in his car and provided a warranty for six months or 6000 miles, the plaintiff had to provide paperwork to

---

[36] Kristin Timms v Dara Persinger, *People's Court*, 17 Dec 2009.
[37] Ibid.
[38] Diana Roth v Fred Farias, *Judge Alex*, 17 Dec 2009.
[39] Ibid.
[40] Jeremy Young v William Ruffin, *Judge Mathis*, 17 Dec 2009.
[41] Nina Coleman v Rapper Compton Young Nino Banks, *Judge Pirro*, 17 Dec 2009.
[42] John Strong v Calvin Owensby, *Judge Pirro*, 17 Dec 2009.
[43] Amber Cobb v Oscar Rogers, *Judge Alex*, 17 Dec 2009.
[44] Ibid.
[45] Ibid.
[46] Irving Placida v Eagle Foreign & Domestic Auto Repair, *The People's Court*, 17 Dec 2009.
[47] Anita Brooks v Emanuel Watson, *Judge Pirro*, 21 Dec 2009.

show that the recurring oil leak was within the warranty period and that the plaintiff had not gone over 6000 miles, as the defendant claimed.[48] In the middle of the case, the plaintiff was allowed to ask his mother to take a photo on a mobile phone of the odometer on his car and to fax it to Judge Milian.[49] Judge Milian ruled in favour of the plaintiff because he had not exceeded the mileage or the time period, and he had not reaped the benefit of the warranty from the defendant. In another case, Judge Pirro explained that the plaintiff, who was suing a former tenant for unpaid rent, could not seek damages for property damage without an estimate.[50] Judge Pirro said that she was not a carpenter, and that even a photo taken on a mobile phone of the property damage could not substitute for an estimate.[51]

Evidence typically took the form of documents, photos, or the testimony of a witness; however, it occasionally took more unusual forms. For example, in one case, a plaintiff claimed that the defendant had damaged his truck by throwing beer cans at it when he tried to break up with her.[52] The defendant explained that she had meant to hit the plaintiff, not the truck, with the beer cans.[53] The plaintiff brought in the truck's fender, which was the part that had been damaged, to show the court; Judge Milian awarded damages to the plaintiff.[54]

Another positive lesson that some of the television judge shows teach is the importance of treating women with respect. Judge Pirro offered this lesson, particularly when she heard cases that involved domestic abuse. She made it clear that there should never be violence towards women. In one case, the plaintiff sued her ex-husband for breaking her nose twice and sought $5000 for medical bills and pain and suffering.[55] Judge Pirro awarded the plaintiff $1892 for medical bills, $500 for pain and suffering, $2400 for child support, and an additional $1000.[56] She explained that the damage award was based on equity rather than law because the statute of limitations had already run. She reminded the parties and audience that 'domestic abuse is passed from one generation to the next', that it is 'a serious subject', and that the plaintiff needs to 'stand up for [her]self'.[57]

A related positive lesson is that men and women need to take a man's role as father and husband seriously. As Judge Pirro explained to one woman who had sued her ex-boyfriend for unpaid medical bills for their five-year-old daughter, unless the father is abusive to the child, the mother has an obligation to facilitate the relationship between father and child.[58] Judge Joe Brown heard the case of a woman (plaintiff) who obtained a cash advance to help her ex-boyfriend (defendant) stay out of jail for past child support payments he owed; Judge Joe wondered why the plaintiff was lending the defendant money.[59] Nevertheless, Judge Joe decided in her favour and she recovered the full amount of the loan. Judge Joe told the defendant that it was his

---

[48] Irving Placida v Eagle Foreign & Domestic Auto Repair, *The People's Court*, 17 Dec 2009.
[49] Ibid.
[50] Anita Brooks v Emanuel Watson, *Judge Pirro*, 21 Dec 2009.
[51] Ibid.
[52] Charles Jappen v Regina Nanista, *The People's Court*, 17 Dec 2009.
[53] Ibid.
[54] Ibid.
[55] April Anderson v Roger Peterson, *Judge Pirro*, 17 Dec 2009.
[56] Ibid.
[57] Ibid.
[58] Sarah Rewerts v Michael Haywood, *Judge Pirro*, 22 Dec 2009.
[59] Cooper v Jackson, *Judge Joe Brown*, 18 Dec 2009.

job to support his children. In a case before Judge Toler on *Divorce Court*, a woman sought recompense from her husband for the damage ($750) he had caused when he kicked her car and dented it.[60] She also complained that he was irresponsible with their children and had a gambling addiction. The judge agreed and advised the man not to marry again until he was 'done being a child'.[61]

In spite of the disputes and personal relationships gone awry on these shows, another positive lesson was that occasionally both parties were satisfied with the judge's decision. This was not acknowledged very often, but it did happen occasionally. It is surprising that it happened at all because one would expect only the winner to be happy. Instead, there were some cases in which both parties admitted satisfaction with the judgment when they were interviewed outside the courtroom after the case. For example, in one case before Judge Alex, the plaintiff recovered damages for her belongings that were still in the defendant's house, even though the defendant had denied that they were there.[62] During the interview after the case, the plaintiff said that the proceeding had been 'fair' and that she was satisfied that the judge had 'listened'.[63] Meanwhile, the defendant also thought that the judge's decision had been fair because 'she had all the evidence against me'.[64] Thus, both sides were satisfied with the proceeding and result. It would be unusual to hear plaintiffs and defendants in actual courts say that they were satisfied with the decision, especially the party that had lost. Usually, so much time has gone by and so much money has been spent that neither side is satisfied, particularly the loser, but on television judge shows, where the case is decided quickly and cheaply for the parties,[65] and both sides tell their story directly to the judge, the parties' response is occasionally quite positive.

V. Television Judge Shows' Broad Role

In addition to the positive lessons that the television judge shows provide for parties and viewers, they perform a broader role in our society. The judges on these shows act, to use Malcolm Gladwell's term, as 'translators'; they translate the esoteric language of the law into plain words and straightforward descriptions that everyone can understand.[66] The television judges educate the large viewing public in the ways and words of the law. Although a judge or lawyer would hardly think that these television judges convey the law, viewers might think that the judge shows provide them with a sense of the law and believe that they are acquiring useful knowledge which they cannot obtain any other way.

---

[60] Jess Jacobus v Jeremy Jacobus, *Divorce Court*, 17 Dec 2009.

[61] Ibid. The judge also asked, albeit rhetorically, 'Why do women do this? If he's an idiot before marriage, he'll be irresponsible after'. Ibid.

[62] Amber Cobb v Oscar Rogers, *Judge Alex*, 17 Dec 2009.

[63] Ibid.

[64] Ibid.

[65] Wilson, '"Street Court"' (n 5) ('There are at least eight court shows on the air, ... sometimes paying the parties appearance fees regardless of the outcome, and generally promising to pay the judgment if the plaintiffs prevail.').

[66] Gladwell, *The Tipping Point* (n 2) 200.

Malcolm Gladwell identified 'translators' as people who take esoteric trends and transform them into trends that are embraced by the mainstream. Although Gladwell was trying to explain why some trends take hold, and the role that translators play in that process, his concept of 'translators' is applicable to television judges. As Gladwell explained, 'translators' are people who take what the visionaries—the Innovators and Early Adopters—experiment with and transform it into something that the Early and Late Majority find acceptable.[67] Innovators and Early Adopters are willing to experiment. For example, they are willing to try new gadgets—the earliest version of iPods and iPads—before the glitches have been worked out and the prices have come down. However, most people are not risk takers; instead, they prefer to wait before they try a new gadget. They want to know that the gadget works and that it is here to stay before they invest in it. The 'translators' take what the Innovators and Early Adopters have experimented with and transform it into something that the mainstream is likely to accept. According to Gladwell, translators 'take ideas and information from a highly specialized world and translate them into a language the rest of us can understand'.[68] It is in this particular way that television judges perform as translators.

Television judges take the specialised ideas and language of the law and explain them in ways that viewers will understand. Television judges do this in several different ways. They perform this function when they impart basic commonsense legal requirements, such as the importance of putting an agreement in writing; when they use and explain legal terms, such as the meaning of 'hearsay' or 'credibility'; and when they insist upon evidence, such as documents or witness testimony, so that a plaintiff can prove his or her case.[69]

Interestingly, television judges occasionally 'translate' events that have happened in the law to viewers watching their programme. For example, in one case before Judge Pirro, the plaintiff ran an animal freak show and had a contract with the defendant to purchase the defendant's puppy which had a fifth leg, but then the defendant changed his mind.[70] Judge Pirro used the case to explain not only about breach of contract, but also about Judge Sotomayor's views on the role of the judge as revealed during her Senate confirmation hearings to become a US Supreme Court Justice.[71] Judge Pirro mentioned that Judge Sotomayor had said during her confirmation hearings that she would follow the law and not be swayed by empathy. Judge Pirro explained that she was an animal lover, but she believed, like Judge Sotomayor, that 'the law is the law' and that her decision in the freaky dog case could not be governed by empathy.[72] Thus, Judge Pirro translated Judge Sotomayor's views to the parties and television viewers and explained that judges are guided by law, not empathy.

However, Judge Pirro was not the only translator in this process. In her response to the Senators, Judge Sotomayor retreated from her earlier description, which she had offered to a specialised audience of women law students, that a judge is inevitably

---

[67] Ibid 198.
[68] Ibid 200.
[69] See text accompanying nn 31–54.
[70] John Strong v Calvin Owensby, *Judge Pirro*, 17 Dec 2009.
[71] Ibid.
[72] Ibid.

shaped by her background and life experiences ('a wise Latina judge');[73] instead, Judge Sotomayor followed the lead set by Chief Justice Roberts during his confirmation hearings, in which he had said that a judge is an umpire simply applying the rules.[74] Thus, Judge Sotomayor simplified her description of a judge when she appeared before the Senate, and Judge Pirro took that simplified view and made it available to a much wider audience, many of whom had probably not watched the Senate confirmation hearings (although they were televised). Both Judge Sotomayor and Judge Pirro served as 'translators', albeit for different audiences. Judge Sotomayor offered her translation to Senators and those who watched the hearings on C-SPAN, and Judge Pirro took Judge Sotomayor's translation, spread it more widely and articulated it more colloquially as one of 'Pirro's Principles: Rule on facts, not empathy'.[75]

VI. Causes for Concern

In spite of the positive lessons and the broad 'translation' function of these shows, they nonetheless raise several serious concerns. One concern, which I have raised before,[76] is that television judges do not act like judges. They lack the essential attributes of a judge, which include fairness and impartiality. Judge Judy is the worst offender. She is rude and insulting to the parties and interrupts them constantly. She uses body language, such as rolling her eyes, finger-pointing, and dramatic pauses, to reveal her biases, which most judges try assiduously to avoid. She reaches quick decisions without recourse to law or explanation. She is the antithesis of how a judge should behave on the bench, and yet, she remains the most popular television judge. Her show has dominated the rankings,[77] garnered numerous awards,[78] and made her a highly compensated television star.[79] Her show has served as the model for the other television judge shows.

Although the other television judges are an improvement over Judge Judy in terms of their portrayal of a judge, these judges still play to the audience. They often engage in banter that is inappropriate for a judge. They try to get a laugh from the audience in the courtroom, which is something most actual judges would not do. Although the television judges who came after Judge Judy do a better job of acting like judges and referring to the law, they still try to entertain the audience. In addition to making jokes, they ask about details that have little to do with the dispute but are titillating, and therefore, likely to keep the television viewers' attention.

---

[73] See Sonia Sotomayor, 'A Latina Judge's Voice' (speech, Boalt Hall Law School, Berkeley, CA, 26 October 2001), www.law.berkeley.edu/4982.htm.

[74] Transcript: Day One of the Roberts Hearings (US Senate Judiciary Committee, Washington, DC, 12 September 2005), www.washingtonpost.com/wp-dyn/content/article/2005/09/13/AR2005091300693.html.

[75] Nina Coleman v Rapper Compton Young Nino Banks, *Judge Pirro*, 17 Dec 2009.

[76] See Nancy S Marder, 'Judging Judge Judy' in Michael Asimow (ed), *Lawyers in Your Living Room! Law on Television* (Chicago, ABA Publishing, 2009) 299, 300–02.

[77] *Judge Judy* even surpassed *Oprah* as the most popular daytime show. See '"Judge Judy" Topples "Oprah"' (n 1).

[78] See Marder, 'Judging Judge Judy' (n 76) 299 (listing the awards the show has received).

[79] Judge Judy was paid $45 million in 2010. See Stephen Battaglio, 'Who Are TV's Top Earners?', www.tvguide.com/News/Top-TV-Earners-1021717.aspx.

Perhaps the greatest cause for concern is that these shows offer a blend of entertainment and judging that could leave viewers confused as to how much is real and how much is fake. The judges, with the exception of Judge Mazz, have all served as actual judges before becoming television judges. Even though they are no longer judges, they play the role of judge on television; they have the traditional accoutrements of a judge (robe, gavel, and flags); and they appear on a set that looks like a courtroom (complete with a bench and a bailiff). As television judges, they hear actual disputes that the parties could have brought to a small-claims court,[80] but have chosen to bring before a television judge. The parties might choose to appear before a television judge rather than a small-claims court because judgments are paid by the producers of the show and both parties receive appearance fees and travel and hotel expenses,[81] or it could just be because the parties want their 15 minutes of fame. On most of these shows, the parties have essentially agreed to arbitration.[82] Occasionally, a party will walk out or will be ejected for having been disrespectful, and the television judge will comment that the party has broken its agreement with the show.[83]

Some judges blur the lines further between entertainment and judging by insisting that they provide judgment not entertainment. For example, in one case before Judge Mathis, the plaintiff was a professional wrestler and ACW Heavyweight Champion, who claimed that the defendant distracted him and caused him to lose a match and money. Judge Mathis explained that what he does as a television judge is 'court arbitration' and 'everything we do is real', as opposed to what the wrestler did during staged matches on television.[84] Judge Mathis told the plaintiff, 'What you do is entertainment. I don't want people to think I'm not a real [judge]'.[85] Television judges' insistence that what they do is real is likely to contribute to viewers' confusion.

These television judge shows are real insofar as they resolve the parties' dispute. Yet, there are many ways in which the television court experience bears little resemblance to actual court experience, at least federal and state courts, although maybe the more apt comparison is with small-claims courts. In television courts, unlike in actual courts, the parties speak directly to the judge and no lawyers are present; the case is resolved without recourse to books or law; the judge seems to know everything he or she needs to know in order to decide the case on the spot; and the judge is the dominant force in the courtroom and delivers most of the funny lines. It is not surprising that, according to one empirical study, potential jurors who watch television judge shows tend to believe that judges should ask a lot of questions, hold opinions, and express these opinions in the courtroom.[86] If viewers relied on television judge shows

---

[80] See Wilson, '"Street Court"' (n 5) (explaining how television judge shows 'mine New York's small-claims courts for cases').

[81] Charles Leroux, 'How the System Works' *Chicago Tribune*, 11 December 2008.

[82] Ibid (explaining that some of the shows, like *People's Court* and *Street Court*, essentially provide 'arbitration the parties have agreed to'); Alessandra Stanley, 'Gavel to Gavel (to Gavel to Gavel) Coverage' *New York Times*, 8 July 2007, www.nytimes.com/2007/07/08/arts/television/08stan.html?scp=2&sq=Gavel%20to%20Gavel%20%28to%20Gavel%20to%20Gavel%29%20Coverage&st=cse ('The chosen sign a waiver agreeing that the television arbitration is final and cannot be pursued elsewhere, though in some cases rulings have been overturned.').

[83] See, eg Nancy & Mark Barton v Autumn Stock, *Judge Joe Brown*, 17 Dec 2009.

[84] Jeremy Young v William Ruffin, *Judge Mathis*, 17 Dec 2009.

[85] Ibid.

[86] Kimberlianne Podlas, 'Should We Blame Judge Judy? The Messages TV Courtrooms Send Viewers' (July–Aug 2002) *Judicature* 86, 38, 39.

to learn about actual judges and courts, they would emerge with a very distorted view. They might believe that the judges' proper role is to entertain, to highlight salacious details, and to decide the case without a moment's hesitation.

The image of the judge portrayed on these television judge shows is of a person unconstrained by law or even by the role of the judge. In fact, some of the judges, such as Judge Mathis, offer their own brand of justice; it is a mix of what they think is right and what they say the law requires. The opening to Justice Mathis' show announces that he offers 'justice that makes a difference'. Judge Hatchett also claims to offer 'real life lessons, real drama' and to 'make a difference in everyday lives'. Thus, these television judge shows offer a view of judges and courts in which judges act based on their own sense of what is right. They are not constrained by law or precedent. The starkest example of this tendency is a new television judge show that will be called *Swift Justice with Nancy Grace* rather than *Judge Nancy*.[87] The judge will no longer be constrained by her role as judge, but will simply offer what she personally thinks is the right answer.

The distinguishing feature of *Street Court* is that there is no need for a courtroom or a robed judge. Although Judge Mazz explained that this was done so that viewers would not mistake him for a real judge, it seems more likely that this approach is intended to distinguish his show from other television judge shows. What it has also done is to show that justice has become unmoored from the courtroom. Justice can be decided anywhere now—in the street, at home, and even on television. A case no longer has to be heard by a judge in a courtroom for 'justice' to be done.

This blurring of the line between judging and entertaining can lead to confusion for viewers of television judge shows in several different ways. Viewers, especially those who are unfamiliar with courts and judges, might think that they are watching actual judges at work. In fact, viewers who submitted complaints about Judge Judy to the California Commission on Judicial Performance made that mistake.[88] When viewers of television judge shows are called for jury duty, they might think that the lessons gleaned from these and other shows can be applied in actual courtrooms. A study by the National Center for State Courts found that 61.4 per cent of those polled relied on prime-time television drama as an important source of information about courts, and 40.5 per cent of those polled said they relied on shows like *Judge Judy* to learn about courts.[89] In fact, Ohio recently added a jury instruction requiring judges to remind jurors either before or after *voir dire* and at every recess to put aside any legal information that they acquired from television shows including *Judge Judy* and 'any other fictional show dealing with the legal system' because these shows 'simply cannot depict the reality of an actual trial or investigation'.[90] The judge also instructs them as follows: 'You must put aside anything you think you know about the legal system that you saw on TV'.[91]

---

[87] Rob Owen, 'Tuned In: Nancy Grace Courts New Audience with "Swift Justice"' Post-gazette.com (10 September 2010), www.post-gazette.com/pg/10253/1086378-67.stm ('Move over, "Judge Judy". There's a new snappish adjudicator coming to daytime TV.').

[88] Podlas, 'Should We Blame Judge Judy?' (n 86) 39.

[89] David Ray Papke, 'From Flat to Round: Changing Portrayals of the Judge in American Popular Culture' (2007) *Journal of the Legal Profession* 31, 127, 151 (citing study).

[90] Ohio State Bar Association (OSBA) Jury Instructions, 1.C. Jury Admonition, available at http://goingpaperlessblog.com/social-media-in-the-legal-profession (listed under 'Ohio'). I thank Thaddeus Hoffmeister for bringing this instruction to my attention.

[91] Ibid.

Of course, actual judges, like actual jurors, are not impervious to the influence of television judge shows. San Diego County Superior Court Judge DeAnn Salcido saw nothing wrong with allowing her courtroom proceedings to be filmed as part of her television audition and for engaging in behaviour that is typical of a television judge, but is inappropriate for an actual judge.[92] The Commission on Judicial Performance charged her with 'willful misconduct and conduct prejudicial to the administration of justice for filming an hour-long TV audition for a "Judge Judy" type of program, and making inappropriate remarks at that hearing and others'.[93] The judge's defence of some of her crude remarks to litigants, who were unaware that their cases were being filmed for her TV show audition, shows that the blurring of judging and entertaining affects not just the layperson, but also the judge, and sows confusion not just about what is real on TV but also about what is proper in the courtroom.

VII. Conclusion: Justice on the Small Screen

It used to be the case that parties had to go to an actual courtroom and appear before an actual judge if they wanted a third party to resolve their dispute. Now, parties can appear on television before a judge who is dressed like a judge but who is not a judge and who presides on a set that looks like a courtroom but is not a courtroom. This television judge can resolve their dispute quickly, cheaply, and without any hesitation.

Just as the parties' experience is different when they choose to go on television rather than go to court, so too is the viewers' experience when they watch television judge shows rather than actual trials in a courtroom. A viewer can watch these programmes, along with millions of other viewers, and yet the experience feels very personal and intimate. The same judges enter their homes day after day. These judges seem familiar to the viewers, who know them by their first names—Judge Judy, Judge Alex, and soon just Nancy. The disputes are explained simply and decided quickly and viewers have access to this process day or night.

However, something important has been lost when disputes are resolved on television rather than in the courtroom. What takes place in a courtroom inspires awe and respect among those who are present. The formality of the courtroom, the dignity of the judge, and the fairness of the procedures are all essential elements. They are essential because they help the decision-maker reach the truth. When adjudication moves from the courtroom to the small screen, something is lost in the translation. Although viewers might appreciate that they are on a first-name basis with their judges and that they do not need to leave their home to watch them, something essential has been lost in the move from justice in the courtroom to entertainment posing as justice on the small screen.

---

[92] Kate Moser, 'Judge Defends Filming TV Show Audition in Courtroom' (law.com, 13 October 2010), www.law.com/jsp/article.jsp?id=1202473252076.

[93] Ibid.

Appendix: Coding Sheet

Name of Program: _____   Case Name: _____

Date of Program: _____   Judge's Name: _____

Time of Program: _____   Channel: _____

Judge's Demographics:

Gender (circle one):   Male   Female

Race (circle one):   White   Black   Hispanic   Other

Other: _____

Litigants' Demographics:

Plaintiff:

Gender (circle one):   Male   Female

Race (circle one):   White   Black   Hispanic   Other

Defendant:

Gender (circle one):   Male   Female

Race (circle one):   White   Black   Hispanic   Other

Setting (circle appropriate one(s)):

Courtroom   Flags   Gavel   Robe

Bailiff's Demographics:

Gender (circle one):   Male   Female

Race (circle one):   White   Black   Hispanic   Other

Case Description: _____

_____

_____

_____

Law or Legal Lessons: _____

Winner (circle one):

Plaintiff   Defendant

Verdict (Brief Description): _____

_____

Commercials (list products):

1. _____   8. _____

2. _____   9. _____

3. _____   10. _____

4. _____   11. _____

5. _____   12. _____

6. _____   13. _____

7. _____   14. _____

Gimmick/Approach of Judge (Brief Description): _____

_____

_____

_____

Types of Evidence Used (circle appropriate one(s)):

Photo   Witness Testimony   Document   Other (specify):

Object   Song   Test Result   _____

Coder (Your Name): _____   **Date of Coding:** _____

References

Banks, TL, 'Judging the Judges–Daytime Television's Integrated Reality Court Bench' in M Asimow (ed), *Lawyers in Your Living Room! Law on Television* (Chicago, ABA Publishing, 2009) 309–20.

Foust, CR, 'A Return to Feminine Public Virtue: Judge Judy and the Myth of the Tough Mother' (Fall 2004) *Women's Studies in Communication* 27, 269–93.

Gladwell, M, *The Tipping Point: How Little Things Can Make a Big Difference* (Boston, Little, Brown and Company, 2000).

Kohm, SA, 'The People's Law versus Judge Judy Justice: Two Models of Law in American Reality-Based Courtroom TV' (2006) *Law & Society Review* 40, 693–727.

Marder, NS, 'Judging Judge Judy' in Asimow, *Lawyers in Your Living Room!*, 2009, 299–307.

Ouellette, L, '"Take Responsibility for Yourself" Judge Judy and the Neoliberal Citizen' in S Murray and L Ouellette (eds), *Reality TV: Remaking Television Culture* (New York, New York University Press, 2009) 223–42.

Papke, DR, 'From Flat to Round: Changing Portrayals of the Judge in American Popular Culture' (2007) *Journal of the Legal Profession* 31, 127–51.

Podlas, K, 'Should We Blame Judge Judy? The Messages TV Courtrooms Send Viewers' (July–Aug 2002) *Judicature* 86, 38–43.

Slipock, S, 'Judge Judy and The People's Court: The Phenomenon of the "Real Court" Television Genre' (Unpublished paper, UCLA Law School, 1998).

12

Television Judges in Germany

STEFAN MACHURA*

A lot of what we know about the world comes from electronic media, especially television.[1] Children, teens and adults spend large amounts of time in front of the small screen. Satellite TV and internet downloads have further multiplied the content available. Given this exposure, many of our impressions and ideas about the world are directly shaped by our interactions with such media. Thus, it seems evident that the portrayal of key social institutions, such as the forces of law enforcement and the larger legal system, ought to attract the attention of socio-legal scholars. American authors, with their empirical approach to law, have long argued that people take lessons from these television shows.[2] In Continental European countries there is much less literature on this popular form of media and its relation to the law. In Germany, the 'law in action' perspective is underdeveloped.[3] Further, scholars were even less prepared to relate law to the flicker of TV shows.[4] The sheer fact that judges gave up their careers to become TV celebrities alone was novel. Even more, the unrestrained style and provocative content of TV courtroom shows, by the private broadcasters RTL and Sat1, shocked its more conservative audience members, as well as the legal profession. More than not judges, lawyers and legal scholars expressed being put off

* The author would like to thank Dr Ruth Herz for several interviews about TV court shows as well as other people involved in producing the shows. Dr Herz has also graciously opened her private archive for an analysis. The German science foundation DFG has generously funded research for almost two years. Professor Klaus F Röhl of Bochum University Law School has, as always, been very supportive.

[1] For the 'cultivation theory', see G Gerbner, 'Die Kultivierungsperspektive: Medienwirkungen im Zeitalter von Monopolisierung und Globalisierung' in A Schorr (ed), *Publikums- und Wirkungsforschungen* (Wiesbaden, Westdeutscher Verlag, 2000).

[2] Early examples: A Chase, 'Towards a Legal Theory of Popular Culture' (1986) *WLR* 527–69; L Friedman, 'Transformations in American Legal Culture 1800–1985' (1985) 6 *Zeitschrift für Rechtssoziologie* 191–205; S Macaulay, 'Images of Law in Everyday Life: The Lessons of School, Entertainment and Spectator Sports' (1987) 21 *L&SR* 185–218.

[3] For the chequered history of sociology of law in Germany, see S Machura, 'Rechtssoziologie' in G Kneer and M Schroer (eds), *Handbuch Spezielle Soziologien* (Wiesbaden, VS Verlag für Sozialwissenschaften, 2010); for German criminology, see S Karstedt, 'Standortprobleme: Kriminalsoziologie in Deutschland' (2000) 23 *Soziologische Revue* 141–52.

[4] The first publication in a German law journal was O Castendyk, 'Recht und Rechtskultur. Das Recht im Fernsehen als „Popular Legal Culture"—ein vielversprechender Ansatz aus den USA?' (1992) 25 *Zeitschrift für Rechtspolitik* 63–67.

by the wave of German television judges appearing in the last decade, and critics quickly predicted severe consequences for public trust in the courts.

This article sets out to explain the legal-cultural significance of commercially televised courtroom shows.[5] How did they develop and how did they differ from previous programmes? In particular, the peculiarity of German TV court shows is examined. With their sensational portrayal of criminal cases, they are distinct from American TV judge shows. Also, a comparison with the most successful TV court series of the late 1960s reveals that the world is now shown as a much darker and more dangerous place. In contrast to psycho-therapeutically oriented chat shows (which comprised the programming aired during the same broadcast hours by other channels), TV courtroom series generally offer an authority figure that puts things right in the end, rather than audience attraction relying merely on the voyeuristic value of witnessing raw emotional outbursts. Yet, in their desperate competition for larger audiences, the channels broadcasting these shows have begun resorting to displaying graphic conflicts in the TV courtroom. It almost need not be said that such scenes would hardly be allowed in real courts, where the procedural investigatory mode prevails.

So, do 'unreal' depictions of courtroom situations alienate audiences from their own national legal systems? Answering this question, which worried a number of lawyer-critics, requires a review of the existing empirical research. Only by delving into such research can these potential trends and cultural effects be adequately perceived—such that, in the end, the allure and influence of TV court shows in relation to regular viewers' attitude and perceptions of the law will have been clarified.

I. From the Royal Court to the People's Court and Beyond

In the late 1960s, the German courtroom-centred series *Königlich-Bayerisches Amtsgericht* (*The Royal Bavarian Magistrates' Court*) appeared on TV. Set in a nineteenth century context, a voiceover narrator with a heavy regional accent set the tone at the beginning of every episode: these were 'lovely times, when his Lordship the Prince-regent still governed Bavaria because the King was melancholic ... [as] life goes on, acquittal or penitentiary and, anyhow, his Honour Magistrate Judge August Stierhammer never sent anyone to the scaffold'.[6] Accompanying the recitation were lavish images of beer gardens; couples in Bavarian folk costumes danced to the tunes

---

[5] Methodological and media-theoretical aspects are discussed in Machura, 'Media Influence on the Perception of the Legal System' in K Papendorf, Machura and K Andenæs (eds), *Understanding Law in Society* (Zurich/Berlin, Lit, 2011). In short, the approach combines elements of 'cultivation' theory, as well as user-centred perspectives and tries to place media influences into their political and economic background, controlling for other forms of experience. TV judge shows are also discussed in S Ulbrich, 'Gerichtsshows als mediales Format und ihre Bedeutung für das Recht' in Machura and Ulbrich (eds), *Recht—Gesellschaft—Kommunikation. Festschrift für Klaus F Röhl* (Baden-Baden, Nomos, 2003), and S Brauer, 'Gerichtsshows als Hybridgenre: Dramaturgie, Inszenierung und Rezeptionsmuster' in K Döveling, L Mikos and J Nieland (eds): *Im Namen des Fernsehvolkes. Neue Formate für Orientierung und Bewertung* (Konstanz, UVK, 2007).

[6] www.br-online.de [accessed 11 May 2010], author's translation.

of a brass band; participants in the trial sipped from their *Weißbier* mugs. The cases tried were often trivial. They usually involved out-moded nineteenth century 'honour', morality and law. The character-types embodied by the various parties were well-known to the audience through traditional folk-theatre: the bigoted elderly lady, the petty thief, the naïve day-labourer, the young couple, the benevolent authority figure, the avaricious farmer and so on. The characters often attacked and insulted each other in open court in humorous ways, which were never overly offensive. The characters were also routinely portrayed by Bavarian actors and actresses, men and women who exploited the comedic value of their given dialect, and with whom the audience would have already been familiar. Eventually, and inevitably, the monocle-wearing Magistrate would overcome his astonishment, ask the right questions and finally issue a lenient yet reasonable verdict. The *Königlich Bayerisches Amtsgericht* was intended as pure entertainment and provided no legal educational value at all. The setting in a historic court alone prevented any misunderstanding that viewers could learn about current law. The absurd fairytale past the show presented assured viewers that these characters and their conflicts were not real, or at least not relevant, as the goings on depicted were entirely unrelated to the viewers' lives and historical context. The series, exported to numerous countries, ran well into the 1970s. Yet, the next entertainment-oriented courtroom-centred series to prove successful on German TV did not occur until much later, in 1999, with the adoption of the format from US courtroom TV shows[7] and the advent of *Richterin (Judge) Barbara Salesch*, a show which emerged as the German equivalent of *Judge Judy.*

Richterin Barbara Salesch proved the most successful of a number of German TV judges. In May 2011, the 2000th broadcast was celebrated. Salesch retired by the end of the same year, but sequels of her show continue to appear regularly on the small screen. Barbara Salesch had already been declared 'quota-queen' of the private Sat1 channel by the leading German TV guide.[8] Yet, just as *Judge Judy* had a more benign predecessor in Judge Wapner of *The People's Court*, Salesch's series followed a show aired by the German public broadcaster ZDF. *Streit um Drei (Dispute at 3pm)* started a few months before Salesch's show aired in 1999, and it followed the lines of *The People's Court*.[9] Both *The People's Court* and *Streit um Drei* basically functioned to assure the public of the validity of traditional values. The shows tacitly stated that, by the very nature of the content of the broadcasts, the laws of the land were being upheld by competent agents of authority. The elderly and experienced Guido Neumann and Joseph A Wapner were near mirrors of one another. Both were known to be actual retired judges and both decided cases with an eye to common sense. Helle Porsdam wrote that Wapner gave an audience suffering from the stresses inherent in radical social change, and afraid of deviant behaviours, the feeling that their norms

---

[7] There were, however, for a number of years, shows like *Ehen vor Gericht* (Marriages at Court) or *Verkehrsgericht* (Traffic Court), which aimed to educate citizens about the law. Although they were not without entertaining moments arising out of various conflicts of interest, the style of these shows was very much in a semi-documentarian vein. They combined enacted scenes, interviews with legal experts and appearances of lawyers and judges. However, in contrast to the later TV shows, there were no stars.

[8] With a quota of 26% *HÖRZU* (17 Aug, 2001) 7.

[9] See H Porsdam, *Legally Speaking. Contemporary American Culture and the Law* (Amherst, UMass Press, 1999) 89–106.

were still valid.[10] This analysis is equally applicable in regards to the German shows. According to Emile Durkheim, the punishment of offenders not only fights lawlessness (anomie), and redraws the lines of the law, but it also strengthens the notions of solidarity within a society.[11] As each mature-minded individual understands, every member of society (whether they consciously realise it or not) has an interest in the administration of justice.[12] In this way, therefore, it becomes evident that law-related media products tap into a basic and very powerful social concern.

In the early afternoon slot that it occupied, *Streit um Drei* (and Richter Neumann) formed a welcomed contrast to the diet of sensationalised pseudo psycho-therapeutic talk shows offered by other broadcasters. On these other talk shows, parties to conflicts expressed their views frankly, sometimes lashing out, but they also performed what amounted to a washing of their dirty laundry in public. This unrestrained self-exposure on the part of the guests, in fact, provided nearly all of the cathartic entertainment value the shows provided, and these exchanges, moderated by the TV hosts themselves, often achieved no real resolution. As a result, critical audience members expressed dismay about the license being given for seemingly anyone to insult others on screen and/or discuss the most private matters in the most shameless way. By contrast, following its educational mission as a public broadcaster, ZDF designed *Streit um Drei* so that it did not only entertain but also taught its audience about the law of the land. Judge Neumann did not only routinely and explicitly explain his verdict. In the wake of Neumann's verdict, there was also a 'legal expert from ZDF' on hand during each episode to be interviewed on the case. In the end, the interviewer never failed to point out that it was generally always better to find a peaceful solution than to file a lawsuit. While the cases that formed the basis for the show came from newspaper reports and/or from rulings reported in law journals, and given that the parts of the various parties were played by professional actors, and that the 'parties' were only involved in small claims disputes, the proceedings never turned vulgar. Of course, characters were, at times, colourful, but a rather calm and polite atmosphere was maintained in the courtroom.

Eventually, *Richterin Barbara Salesch* changed the world of German TV courts. At first, the series had been scheduled in the early evening and did not attract enough viewers. Consequently, it faced the threat of cancellation, so the crew changed the concept radically. Initially, Salesch acted as a mediator, working on small claims cases brought forward by real parties, but in the new edition, she became a judge deciding fictional criminal cases. Actors and actresses played the parts of victim and defendant, as well as other roles, and they often portrayed outlandish characters. If the role was not too difficult, lay actors were employed to preserve an atmosphere of authenticity. The idea for this new concept may have come, in part, from the one roaring success the show had in its initial evening format. In one episode, a lady with a strong Saxonian accent (generally viewed by the rest of the nation as provincial) demanded that her neighbour take away a common snowberry bush which threatened her mesh wire fence. Soon after this episode was broadcast, a TV entertainer and Germany's leading

---

[10]   Ibid.

[11]   E Durkheim, *Regeln der soziologischen Methode* (Neuwied, Luchterhand, 1976) 181.

[12]   A Pepitone, 'Social Psychological Perspectives on Crime and Punishment' (1975) 31 *JSI* 198–99.

country band produced a hit record with clips of the unfortunate woman pronouncing 'Maschendrahtzaun' and 'Knallerbsenstrauch' in Salesch's court. Thus, there was already a certain level of interest generated by the time *Richterin Barbara Salesch* was reformatted and rescheduled to appear earlier in the afternoon. In no time at all the show inherited a significant viewership, in large part made up of the emotional-conflict-loving audiences of those aforementioned talk shows. Simply put, the series proved superior to the talk shows the programme competed against in at least one crucial aspect: Barbara Salesch, as Guido Neumann did before her, rendered a ficti- tious legal verdict over fictitious cases. The definitiveness of each episode's conclusion relieved the audience from having to grapple with uneasy feelings. Nothing was left unresolved, in terms of the value conflicts embodied in the various parties' characters, but also in terms of the cases. In the end, Salesch's show resolved the conflicts through the lens of reason and the law, as opposed to having the loudest and most extreme personality dominating the show, and given this striking juxtaposition (by mere virtue of the broadcast schedule) one can perhaps see clearly the very foundational ethos of the law.

Soon, however, the aggressive behaviour from these pseudo psychotherapeutic talk shows spilled over into the content of the courtroom shows. This cocktail of criminal cases, coupled with lay actresses and actors having their hour in the limelight, with real lawyers and theatrically aggressive behaviour in the courtroom, set in motion a downward spiral. A race to the bottom ensued which saw new court shows flourishing as they distanced themselves further and further from the Neumann model, and which further saw censorship bodies threatening to take action, representatives of judges and lawyers protesting,[13] and the public broadcaster ZDF's withdrawal from the market.

II. The Bootstraps of Entrepreneurial Competition

The morphing format of courtroom TV might easily have been predicted by economic analysts using a forecast model that emphasises the differences between public and private enterprises.[14] In the post-war period, television in West Germany[15] was based on the British Broadcasting Corporation (BBC) model. Licence fees formed a solid economic basis for public TV. In addition, special statutes provided a degree of broadcaster independence from the state that was upheld in various court decisions.

---

[13] Eg, the interview with the President of the Judge Association: N Festenberg and D Hipp, 'TV-Justiz— "Das ist emotionales Theater", Interview mit Geert Mackenroth' (2002) 42 *Der Spiegel* 188–89. For criti- cism see also, eg: S Schnorr, 'Justiz, Medien, Medienrecht' (paper presented at the Tagung der Deutschen Richterakademie, Wustrau, Germany, 2–8 November 2003); M Amann, 'Gerichtsshows im Fernsehen— Folgenreich für echte Richter', www.faz.net.

[14] T Thiemeyer, 'State-Owned Enterprises' in E Grochla et al (eds), *Handbook of German Business Management* (Stuttgart, Poeschel, 1990).

[15] For an overview on the politics and regulation of German media: D Grimm, 'Medien' in W Heun et al (eds), *Evangelisches Staatslexikon* (Stuttgart, Kohlhammer, 2006); G Vowe, 'Massenmedien' in U Andersen and W Woyke (eds), *Handwörterbuch des Politischen Systems der Bundesrepublik Deutschland* (Opladen, VS Verlag für Sozialwissenschaften, 2009).

The public broadcasters were run as non-profit enterprises and they maintained autonomy when it came to programme content. Statutes also demanded that public TV be responsible for political education and generally informing the public. When a new generation of journalists, politicised in the 1960s by the student movement, began occupying jobs in the 1970s, radio and television became cultural battlegrounds. In the 1980s, under the pretext of counter-balancing public programmes leaning to the left, the conservative government of Chancellor Helmut Kohl fostered the addition of private for-profit competition. Radio Television Luxemburg (RTL), together with its main private rival Sat1, won over the younger and more working class audiences. To the dismay of Kohl's conservative followers,[16] the push for private television backfired. Rather than competing directly with public stations, private stations exploited the gaps left by public programming. In short, they began to offer programming with loosened strictures. In the early 1980s, however, thousands of viewers protested when Kommissar Schimanski of the *Tatort* series cursed on a public channel, but by the end of the decade private TV regularly offered much more controversial programme content. An all-out war raged among broadcasters, private and public, pitting RTL and Sat1, each with about a quarter of the German TV market, against the public broadcasters, which together held about 40 per cent.[17] Against this backdrop, the drama of German courtroom TV unfolded.

The public broadcaster ZDF's pioneering judge show, *Streit um Drei*, bordered the area between legal advice shows[18] and civic education. In essence, German private TV companies have no such commitments. They run their shows as profit centres, which have to attract large audiences and big advertisement money. The private channels were destined to fall prey to the temptations of an outstanding entrepreneur feeding them with TV judge shows.

Ironically, the creator of *Richterin Barbara Salesch*, Gisela Marx, started her career as a leftist journalist. Marx owned her own production firm 'filmpool' selling shows to broadcasters. One day, Marx visited the US and saw *Judge Judy*. She returned to Germany with the idea of creating a spin-off. *Richterin Barbara Salesch* is Marx's version of the American series. Even the age and hair colour of the two TV judges are the same.[19] After *Salesch* became a success in the early afternoon with the new concept of a criminal court, Marx was able to sell the same idea again to RTL, Sat1's rival among Germany's private broadcasters. This time the setting for the concept was in a juvenile court, so the show was called *Das Jugendgericht (The Juvenile Court)*. To add insult to injury, the new show directly competed with *Richterin Barbara Salesch*, as it was aired in an early afternoon time-slot. Juveniles not only formed a major part of the TV audience at this time of the day; they are also the preferred target-group of the advertising industry. *Das Jugendgericht*, with its sympathetic judge Dr Ruth Herz, tapped into this market, and the show dealt with cases that were primarily of

---

[16] Note the similarity with the history of US court TV: it was initially favoured by conservative judges who were then deeply disappointed by the actual content: R Sherwin, *When the Law Goes Pop: The Vanishing Line between Law and Popular Culture* (Chicago, University of Chicago Press, 2000) 162–63.

[17] Vowe, 'Massenmedien' (n 15) 421.

[18] These are defined as programmes 'in which real-world lawyers provide information on various legal problems': Machura and Ulbrich. 'Globalizing the Hollywood Courtroom Drama' (2001) 28 *JL&S* 119.

[19] The website www.sat1.de provides photos and other information.

interest to a youthful audience.[20] Ruth Herz and Barbara Salesch received a lot of attention in the press, which further alerted audiences to the show.[21] Sat1 did not wait long to launch its counter-attack and signed a deal with another TV producer, Constantin Entertainment, for a show seemingly geared to a young female audience. Thus, in *Richter* (*Judge*) *Alexander Hold*, the judge took centre stage, a younger, good looking and well-behaved man.[22] RTL took up the challenge and varied the concept yet another time. This courtroom TV show, produced by filmpool again, was called *Das Strafgericht* (*The Criminal Court*) and therefore dealt with adult criminal court cases. As could be expected, Judge Ulrich Wetzel of *Das Strafgericht* was (in the early days, at least) in a bit of a darker mood than his colleagues.[23] In their heydays, five TV judge shows competed on RTL and Sat1 within three hours. A labour court and a family court also convened on TV screens. In addition, Judge Hold had his occasional murder case at primetime slots in the evening.

Amid this fierce competition for viewers, the courtroom shows of RTL and Sat1 resorted to encouraging ever more outrageous and aggressive behaviour by the parties in court. Surprise developments occurred during cross-examinations and in exchanges between 'parties' and 'witnesses'.[24] Provocatively dressed actresses and actors played shrill characters. Cases often had strange sexual ingredients and the contentious parties could sometimes hardly be kept from brawling before the judge. Insults of the worst kind were common. In response to this, the youth protection agency of conservative Bavaria threatened to intervene. The shows, which had been initially welcomed by the press, increasingly attracted public criticism. Representatives of judges and lawyers grew even more alarmed and outwardly condemned the shows. So, to remain free of state interference, the private broadcasters and filmpool emphasised that their shows educated youths about the legal system. They referred to the many schools visiting their studios. TV judges gave interviews stating that being able to educate the public had led them to leave the real courts and enter the world of television. RTL even produced an expansive box set with DVDs and a booklet, purportedly for teachers to be used for legal education. Eventually, however, the ZDF decided to withdraw its much tamer show, *Streit um Drei*, and ultimately the private channels curbed their shows' worst excesses.

In the end, however, viewership began to decline. The effects of the 'Zapping-Kultur'[25] were evident. Employing market research technology, desperate editors tracked the audience share of their stories. Viewer behaviour was measured by the minute to understand when they switched channels. These techniques are, however, not without their perils. Even if most of the audience viewed the shows in disgust, the analysts

---

[20] The figure of Dr Herz and the audience response to her is described in more detail: Machura, 'German Judge Shows: Migrating from the Courtroom to the TV Studio' in M Asimow (ed), *Lawyers in Your Living Room! Law on Television* (Chicago, ABA Press, 2009).

[21] Ibid 323.

[22] Current material can be found at www.sat1.de.

[23] See www.rtl-now.rtl.de.

[24] J Scheerer, 'Die Gerichtsshow als kommunikative Gattung. Eine konversationsanalytische Untersuchung am Beispiel der Sendungen „Richter Alexander Hold", „Richterin Barbara Salesch" und „Das Strafgericht"' (MA dissertation, Potsdam University, 2007) 33–34.

[25] See R Jellen, '"Semiotische und emotionale Kampfzone", Interview mit dem Kulturwissenschaftler Daniel Hermsdorf über gegenwärtige Tendenzen der Fernsehkultur' *Telepolis* (20 Feb 2011) www.heise.de [accessed 20 February 2011].

counted these viewings as a 'success'. RTL got into trouble when Dr Herz left *Das Jugendgericht* and her successors failed to fill her boots. TV courtroom shows had by then acquired a negative image. Although the shows still had audiences, the market no longer supported five and more shows. In the end, only *Richterin Barbara Salesch* and *Richter Alexander Hold* on Sat1 and *Das Strafgericht* on RTL survived.

III. Attractions of Education and Entertainment

TV judges always provide an explanation for their verdicts and tell the audience how the law applies to the given case. This is typically carried off in the minute, or so, before the end of the episode. Barbara Salesch, Ruth Herz and Alexander Hold have each frequently highlighted the assertion that they really try to teach the public about law. In addition, Ruth Herz made an effort to influence the public in favour of a rehabilitation approach to juvenile justice.

This fulfills the viewing desires of at least that part of the audience expressly interested in learning about law and the courts. In telephone interviews in the Bochum area of western Germany,[26] some respondents clearly stated that they watch to learn. Others found TV court shows lightweight and sometimes ridiculous given the aggressive behaviour of the parties. However, it is highly possible that those who do not have direct court experience might be influenced by brief encounters with media of this sort. In her study with Munich students, Barbara Thym classified one fifth of the respondents as 'orientation seekers', who were more drawn to stereotypical views of court proceedings involving heavy disputes and surprise developments. Orientation seekers were more likely to think that witnesses often turn out to be the guilty parties at the hearing, and that the truth comes to light only at trial.[27] An American study on the 'CSI effect' suggests that the more frequently viewers watch a programme, the more they tend to think it is accurate.[28] From the Bochum telephone interviews it seems that the die-hard fans of courtroom shows are prepared to disregard the more appalling aspects of the broadcasts and instead relish those parts of the shows they see as authentic: mainly the application of the law by the superior authority of the judge.

In most German courts, and nearly all criminal courts, cameras are not allowed access during the hearing. One of the attractions of court shows is that viewers can watch real judges at work, or so they might think. Following their US predecessors, German TV judges are retired judges or judges on leave. They certainly carry over their typical behaviour from the bench to the TV studio. The roles of public prosecutors and defence attorneys are also played by 'real' lawyers who have or had their own independent practices

---

[26] Machura, 'Ansehensverlust der Justiz? Licht und Schatten des Gerichtsshowkonsums' in K Döveling, L Mikos and J Nieland (eds), *Im Namen des Fernsehvolkes. Neue Formate für Orientierung und Bewertung* (Konstanz, UVK, 2007).

[27] B Thym, 'Kultivierung durch Gerichtsshows. Eine Studie unter Berücksichtigung von wahrgenommener Realitätsnähe, Nutzungsmotiven und persönlichen Erfahrungen' (MA diss, Ludwig-Maximilians-University Munich, 2003) 113–15.

[28] D Shelton, Y Kim and G Barak, 'A Study of Juror Expectations and Demands Concerning Scientific Evidence: Does the "CSI Effect" Exist?' (2006) 2 *VJE&TL* 346.

(some even became minor TV celebrities with their own series). One can only imagine, however, that their behaviour in real courtrooms would have been much different from their often unrestrained appearances in front of Barbara Salesch and her colleagues. Yet, by contrast, when the shows depict a mixed court, the lay assessors never say a word,[29] again reinforcing the centrality of the presiding judge.

While Durkheim and others stated that the reaction to crime is of interest to all members of a society, a view widely accepted among social scientists, there is now also a growing awareness of the cultural value placed on the fairness of the proceedings, of the process by which decisions are reached. Therefore, procedural fairness is one of the aspects used as a measuring stick in regards to legal authorities. German TV judges conform to universal values of fair treatment. They give parties sufficient opportunity to state their case, treat the people before their courts benevolently, are unbiased and respect everyone's status as citizens with equal rights.[30] Only at first glance does this seem to contradict the public's urge to make rule-breakers pay for their transgressions. Simultaneously, individuals are also suspicious of abuses of power by the authority.[31] This applies to sentencing, as well. The convicted innocent, or the repentant sinner harshly punished, are staple stories from popular legal culture. This wariness about justness also applies to the procedure. German TV judges count as sound examples of procedural fairness. Generally displaying equanimity, they rarely get impatient or display signs of prejudice. Parties and witnesses are given ample opportunity to express their views and emotions[32] and are treated with the utmost respect by the television judges. A study of German lay judges (called *Schöffen*) elicited that concern for fairness even extends to the treatment of defendants.[33] Just as Hollywood productions often place the audience in the jury box, the position of the camera in a TV judge show invites viewers to think like a judge. This is certainly one of the attractions of the format; one show invited viewers to its webpage with the phrase: be an 'online-*Schöffe*'.

In a content analysis, *Jana Scheerer* identified that the shows not only tell the story of a criminal case, but they also have a second, moral story.[34] The TV judge addresses the moral issues that are beyond the reach of law through side commentaries. While there may be a criminal charges case to be resolved, at the same time the episode may deal with a betrayal of trust among some of the participants.

[29] Scheerer, 'Die Gerichtsshow als kommunikative Gattung' (n 24) 30–31.
[30] For criteria for fairness see T Tyler and E Lind, 'A Relational Model of Authority in Groups' in M Zanna (ed), *Advances in Experimental Social Psychology* (New York, Academic Press, 1992) vol 25, 115–91.
[31] Lind, 'Procedural Justice, Disputing, and Reactions to Legal Authorities' *American Bar Foundation Working Paper Series, No 9403* (Chicago, American Bar Foundation, 1994).
[32] Scheerer makes this her main argument: TV judges allow the people involved to express their feelings freely and this would amount to a 'therapeutic effect'; Scheerer, 'Die Gerichtsshow als kommunikative Gattung' (n 24) 33–34. Scheerer goes on to say that the 'therapeutic effect' would contribute to what N Luhmann termed 'legitimation by procedure'. Parties are involved in a role play and have the chance to express themselves until the authority decides in the end; N Luhmann, *A Sociological Theory of Law* (London, Routledge Press, 1985) 203.
[33] Machura, *Fairneß und Legitimität* (Baden-Baden, Nomos, 2001). For a description of the work of *Schöffen* see also Machura, 'Interaction between Lay Assessors and Professional Judges in German Mixed Courts' (2001) 72 *IRPL* 451–79.
[34] Scheerer, 'Die Gerichtsshow als kommunikative Gattung' (n 24) 44–45.

Another attraction is that these shows offer opportunities to learn about those that appear prone to victimisation or come from backgrounds suspected of consistently producing perpetrators. Courtroom shows regularly satisfy such demands when they portray shrill and outlandish people. Often, the characters involved are from the margins of society, sometimes even from the remote stratum of the super-rich. Indeed, if the audience is attracted to the shows by its interest in their society's laws and mores being upheld, it is only logical that the shows should focus on individuals who are commonly suspected of deviating from the rules. The outcome is such that, audiences seemingly take away at least two kinds of lesson from watching these shows: one relates to the behaviour of parties at court, the other to the character of judges and lawyers and the trustworthiness of courts in general.

IV. Learning about Aggressive Behaviour in Court

German courtroom TV shows broadcast on private channels quickly gained a reputation for depicting shameless and aggressive behaviour by the 'parties' in court. TV lawyers often zealously advocate their views and cross-examine parties in a ruthless manner. At the extremities of the episodes, the TV judge is sometimes hardly able to restrain the opposing parties. Insults by defendants, witnesses and from the audience in the courtroom are common. The courtroom thus appears a dangerous place, a place of malignant uncertainty, where people often suffer due to the unfettered aggression of the other trial participants; surprise witnesses and last minute evidence are presented by the parties; on cross-examination witnesses burst into tears and are regularly exposed as culprits plotting against an innocent defendant. All this would rarely happen in real German courtrooms where the atmosphere is sometimes tense but more commonly sedate. Criminal courts follow an investigative mode of procedure. The judge has read the dossier and often formed a preliminary opinion that is put to the test in the public hearing.[35] After all, any criminal case that makes the trial phase has been investigated by the police, further verified by the public prosecutor and then finally vetted by the judge. Parties to a trial have generally, by the time oral arguments are presented, already been told the likely outcome of the proceeding by their lawyers. With this in mind, there are likely to be few surprises.

At the oral hearing, the investigative procedure effectively avoids any dramatisation. Unlike the US or English trial, there is not much of a duel between the representatives of the two parties. Instead, the idea is that the judge and all parties work together to establish the truth.[36] The judge investigates the case based on their knowledge of the dossier. Often, prosecutors and defenders do not ask additional questions. Public prosecutors have to equally weigh evidence both for and against the defendant's case. Lawyers are assigned the function of an 'organ of justice' and, in the German system,

---

[35] R Lautmann, 'Teilnehmende Beobachtungen in der Strafjustiz' in J Friedrichs (ed), *Teilnehmende Beobachtung abweichenden Verhaltens* (Stuttgart, Enke, 1973) 111; C Rennig and Machura, 'Die Zusammenarbeit zwischen Schöffen und Berufsrichtern' in H Lieber and U Sens (eds), *Ehrenamtliche Richter—Demokratie oder Dekoration am Richtertisch?* (Wiesbaden, Kommunal-und Schulverlag, 1999) 69.

[36] Machura, 'German Criminal Procedure in Practice' (2007) 11 *Cuadernos Unimetanos*, Special Issue: 'Derecho y Democracia' (2007).

it pays for prosecutors and lawyers not to force their case but rather to unreservedly collaborate in the search for 'truth'. While German court cases generally run their course without much high emotion and with few surprises, and the professionals involved take care not to offend participants, there are always exceptions. If the accounts of lawyers and judges can be taken as accurate, TV courtroom shows have encouraged some live audience members to shout from their seats. Some witnesses and defendants become unruly. Occasionally, lawyers have stated that their clients wanted them to put on a show and were dissatisfied if they did not actively interfere in the judge's questioning of witnesses. In the absence of systematic studies, it is hard to tell whether or not such observations refer to isolated events. Perhaps it is all too human to remember the odd cases when asked to comment on a social phenomenon. Yet, if it is any indication of at least some frequency in regards to outlandish court-room behaviour, sometimes judges have been cited in the press as warning parties: 'We are not in a court show'.

The personal archive of Judge Ruth Herz contained a letter that had been sent with a small artificial flower:

> Dear Mrs Dr Herz! ... I am looking forward to the next episode of *Das Jugendgericht*! I really like watching your series and I try not to miss any episode. I find your series very exciting, too, because there is something new in every second (eg brawl, shouting etc). Then I sometimes feel frightened.

In one study, Barbara Thym found out that students perceived court trials as dramatic situations. They expected that the proceedings would involve insults and abuses between the various parties. Students thought that witnesses were often revealed as the real culprits, and trials were often seen as emotional, turbulent and entertaining.[37] In a telephone study with respondents from the Bochum area, it was found that the frequent viewing of TV courtroom shows was significantly correlated to individuals holding such views on trials in court.[38] Yet, these stereotypes may not exclusively come from watching these sorts of shows. In classic Hollywood courtroom dramas like *To Kill a Mockingbird*, and in numerous American TV lawyer series like *Perry Mason* or, more recently, *The Good Wife*, lawyers cross-examine lying witnesses until they suffer emotional breaks and engage in arguments with the public prosecutor and/ or judge. German film and TV makers have long detected the dramatic qualities of the adversarial trial—the eternal fight between 'Good' and 'Evil'—and have utilised a fair number of its tactics in their depictions of German courts. The yellow press and private channel TV news also concentrate on sensational cases. These often involve celebrity defendants or famous lawyers deliberately seeking publicity through scandal. Accordingly, in a study among high school and technical college students, the hold-ing of misguided trial stereotypes has been found to be significantly related to being informed by novels and movies, and also by TV and radio reports on courts and law-yers, but not to the consumption of TV judge shows.[39] The image of the dangerous trial is therefore seemingly pervasive in popular legal culture, but it depends on the audience and its habits where they pick it up.

---

[37] Thym, 'Kultivierung durch Gerichtsshows' (n 27) 121.
[38] Machura, 'Ansehensverlust der Justiz?' (n 26) 95.
[39] Machura and A Kammertöns, 'Detered From Going to Court? A Survey at German Schools on Media Influences' (2010) 8 *E&SLJ*.

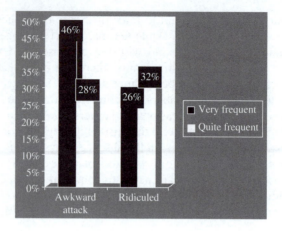

Figure 1: Perceived treatment by the opposing party and its lawyer when in court, telephone survey, Bochum area, 2005, N = 1.015.
Source: Machura, 'Ansehensverlust der Justiz?' 93.

Consequently, if this is how people perceive court hearings, they should be expected to be, and are, often afraid of being a party to a trial. Large majorities of the respondents in the Bochum area study assumed they would be ridiculed in court or would have to suffer awkward attacks (see Figure 1). In the study involving high school and technical college students, 80 and 70 per cent, respectively, feared awkward attacks and ridicule from their opponents in court.[40] While this can partially be attributed to judge shows, as more frequent viewers were more likely to fear ridicule if in court, it seems a significant facet of the popular understandings of legal proceedings in general.

V. Effect on Trust in Courts and Lawyers

Research suggests that audiences take lessons from TV courtroom shows. The public debate, as well as legal practitioner concerns, focused on the effect of the trust placed in the courts and in lawyers. It seems almost too obvious to state, but trust in the legal system is important. Citizens need to have a minimum level of trust in the system or they will not be able to adequately defend their interests with the help of lawyers and the courts. Victims and witnesses have to feel confident enough to voice their testimony in court. Lawyers very much dread that, during their preparations, clients and witnesses have not spoken to them openly about the case. Consequently, scholars have turned to studying media effects on trust and related issues. In an international comparison of first-year law students, respondents at the Ruhr-Universität Bochum consumed TV judge shows less often and indicated watching lawyer movies more often. Combined, these measures correlated with student beliefs that lawyers have

---

[40] Ibid.

high prestige.[41] Three other studies addressed broader groups of students, not just law students. Students in Munich learned from TV judge shows that judges should render a moral judgement and that they should not only follow the law objectively.[42] This would indicate quite a departure from the perspective of the legalistic culture of German courts. Students at the Ruhr-Universität Bochum showed a positive correlation between TV courtroom show consumption and the belief in the high prestige of German courts. Frequent viewers of courtroom shows were also more likely to believe that citizens are treated fairly in German courts.[43] Another study among younger students at technical colleges and high schools did not detect any significant positive or negative effect of TV courtroom shows in relation to their trust in courts, judges and lawyers. In fact, there were few heavy viewers of courtroom shows in the sample. It was also found that general media influence reinforced a climate of trust in the courts and a favourable image of legal professions among the respondents.[44] If anything, these results indicate that the shows are more likely to have a positive rather than negative effect on how much trust young people place in courts and lawyers. After all, they are the primary target audience. Yet, the prototypical viewers are best described as women over 50 years of age having had only a basic education.[45] One, then, wonders what the effect might be on the broader public, as Table 1 and Figure 2 demonstrate.

Table 1: Public Opinion on Courts, Judges and Lawyers (in %)

	Very	Quite	Less	Not at all
1. Judgments of courts just	16	40	37	5
2. Judges trustworthy and ethical	36	45	15	4
3. High prestige of courts	43	36	18	4
4. Citizens treated fairly at court	31	50	15	2
5. Judgments of courts can be corrected	33	40	20	4
6. Lawyers trustworthy and ethical	22	44	27	5
7. High prestige of lawyers	30	38	27	4

Telephone survey April–June 2005 in the area of Bochum, Germany, n = 1.015.
Source 'Media Influence on the Perception of the Legal System' in Knut Papendorf, Stefan Machura and Kristian Andenæs (eds), *Understanding Law in Society* (Zurich/Berlin, Lit 2011) 247.

[41] M Asimow, S Greenfield, G Jorge, Machura, G Osborn, P Robson, C Sharp and R Sockloskie, 'Perceptions of Lawyers—A Transnational Study of Student Views on the Image of Law and Lawyers' (2005) 15 *IJLP* 426–428.
[42] Thym, 'Kultivierung durch Gerichtsshows' (n 27) 121.
[43] Machura, 'Fernsehgerichtsshows: Spektakel des Rechts' (2006) 15 *Paragrana* 185.
[44] Machura and A Kammertöns, 'Recht im Schulunterricht, Medieneinflüsse und die Attraktivität von Rechtsberufen' (2009) 30 *Zeitschrift für Rechtssoziologie* 235–59; Machura and Kammertöns, 'Detered From Going to Court?' (n 39).
[45] F Fleschner, U Martin and V Gustedt, 'Oper des Ordinären' (2006) 32 *Focus*, citing data of the Gesellschaft für Konsumforschung. The advertising industry is less interested in this group as they allegedly have stable patterns of consumption, while youthful customers can still be influenced.

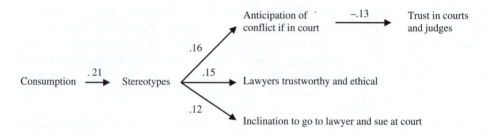

Figure 2: Effects of the consumption of TV judge shows, Bochum area study.

Entries are Pearson correlations, p <.001, 927 < n < 958.
Telephone survey April-June 2005 in the area of Bochum, Germany, n = 1.015.
Source: Machura, 'Ansehensverlust der Justiz?' 95.

In addition, a broader survey was undertaken in the Bochum area involving 1015 residents above 14 years of age.[46] This survey revealed high levels of trust in the courts, judges and lawyers (Table 1). When asked to ascertain the fairness of judges, or to weigh the ethicality and trustworthiness of lawyers and judges, overwhelming majorities answered positively. The degree of trust only wavered when it came to the perceived justice of judgments. It was obvious from the comments in the telephone interviews that this deviation in the degree of trust was directly related to crimes in which no form of civilised punishment could match the suffering of the victims. Other opinion surveys elicited similar results in that Germans tend to trust their courts and their legal personnel.[47]

According to the Bochum study, TV courtroom shows 'cultivate' stereotypes that trials involve aggression, contingence and emotion (see Figure 2).[48] While these stereotypes encouraged viewers to mobilise the law in cases of conflict, it was found that they were far more likely to go to a lawyer or to court when they suffered a specific damage.[49] Those who shared the various prevailing stereotypes about the legal system also expected to be ridiculed by the opposing party, and that they would have to endure awkward attacks if they were party to a trial.[50] The stereotypes also encouraged viewers

---

[46] Machura, 'Ansehensverlust der Justiz?' (n 26) 83–101. Data was sampled from April to June 2005.

[47] For on overview of recent survey results, see Machura, 'Media Influence on the Perception of the Legal System' (n 5). Trust in lawyers is discussed in Machura and Asimow, 'Das Ansehen von Anwälten bei Jurastudenten: Einflüsse von familiärem Hintergrund, persönlichen Erfahrungen, Anwaltsfilmen und TV-Anwaltsserien' (2004) 25 *Zeitschrift für Rechtssoziologie* 4–8.

[48] In Thym's survey students did not learn about crime from TV judge shows. Thym, 'Kultivierung durch Gerichtsshows' (n 27). In a much broader study, Pfeiffer, Windzio and Kleimann found that heavy viewers of television, especially of typical programmes on private channels, among them judge shows, overestimated the increase in crime. This perception then favoured harsh attitudes towards sentencing; C Pfeiffer, M Windzio and M Kleimann, 'Media, Evil and Society: Media Use and its Impacts on Crime Perception, Sentencing Attitudes and Crime Policy in Germany' in J Freilich and R Guerette (eds), *Migration, Culture Conflict, Crime and Terrorism* (Aldershot, Ashgate, 2006) 114–19, 122. The result would coincide with the argument above that TV judge shows tend to portray the world as riddled with dangerous conflict.

[49] Combines answers to items 'go to lawyer when 500 Euro damage by a stranger', 'go to court when 500 Euro damage by a stranger' and 'go to lawyer when 500 Euro damage by an acquaintance' (Cronbach's alpha = .751, n = 989).

[50] See Figure 1 for percentages.

to believe in a positive lawyer character, namely one that depicts lawyers as trustworthy and ethical. This duality is hardly surprising. Arguably, when faced with the dangers of a court trial, people want a guardian angel at their side.

Table 2: Bochum Study, Trust in German Courts, Linear Regression

	B	Std. Error	Beta	Significance
(Constant)	11.098	.966		.000
Self-assessed sources of information:				
— Lawyers among friends and family	.064	.087	.027	.463
— Personal experience with lawyers	−.256	.106	−.110	.016
— Personal experience at court	−.031	.108	−.013	.777
— School education	.361	.112	.115	.001
— Discussions with friends about courts and lawyers	−.132	.100	−.049	.187
— TV and radio reports on courts and lawyers	−.110	.113	−.038	.330
— Novels, telecasts and films on courts and lawyers	.099	.108	.036	.358
Other factors:				
Frequency of watching TV judge shows	.030	.033	.034	.370
Number of law-related films watched from list	−.032	.036	−.033	.377
Age	−.013	.007	−.077	057
Gender = female	.214	.186	.039	.252
Level of school education	−.171	.086	−.080	.047
German family background	−.527	.392	−.047	.179

$N = 841$, $R^2 = .038$, $p = .002$.

Trust in courts measured by items 1 to 5 in Table 1.

School education: 1 = no exam, 2 = basic qualification (_Volksschule_ and similar), 3 = medium qualification (_Mittlere Reife_ and equivalent), 4 = qualification for university of applied sciences (_Fachhochschulreife_ and equivalent), 5 = general qualification for university (_Abitur_ and equivalent)

Telephone survey April-June 2005, in the area of Bochum, Germany, n = 1.015 (Source: 'Media Influence on the Perception of the Legal System' in Knut Papendorf, Stefan Machura and Kristian Andenæs (eds), _Understanding Law in Society_ (Zurich/Berlin, Lit 2011) 261.

Respondents also placed less trust in courts and judges when they assumed having to suffer as a party in court (see Figure 2). Therefore, the effects of courtroom shows on the German audience might not be exclusively positive vis-a-vis the legal institution and its key personnel in the long run. Yet, for the time being the high level of trust in courts typical for the German legal-political culture is not compromised too much by media effects. When a range of direct and indirect experiences were included in multivariate analyses, trust in the courts was significantly related to personal experience of lawyers, and to school education, measured by perceived effect and by formal education attained. Various other measures for media impact were not related to trust, among them the frequency of watching TV courtroom shows (Table 2). The model constant is positive, very substantial and significant. It indicates a general trend to give positive evaluations of the courts which are only nuanced by the factors investigated. This suggests a high degree of consensus that courts can be trusted.

VI. Conclusion

Contrasted against the 1960s *Königlich-Bayerisches Amtsgericht*, today's shows reveal differences and similarities between themselves and their predecessors. The nature of the conflicts involved with current courtroom TV cases is much more serious than in the *Amtsgericht* days, where the crimes considered hardly shook the foundations of society. In current shows, there is more at stake. They depict a constant battle against the most heinous characters and their crimes. The cases sometimes allude to questions that are essentially political because they are also a consideration and reiteration of the basic values of the society; they assert a value system to be defended and a perspective on the various directions in which their creators and participants believe their society should take. A marked difference between the *Amtsgericht* era and now is also highlighted by the varying degrees of dangerousness exemplified by the viewers' fellow citizens. Today's villains often seem hopelessly anti-social. Also, lawyers currently play a much more prominent role in these courtroom shows, further amplifying the conflict between victims and perpetrators, and empirical analysis shows that these portrayals do not fail to impress audiences.

What is still similar between the *Amtsgericht* era and now is that the role of the omnipotent and trustworthy judge who redraws the boundaries of acceptable behaviour is still vitally present. The monocle-wearing Judge August Stierhammer and his successors display the virtues of fairness and common sense, and attempt to set things right to the best of their ability. Cases usually find a solution at the end of every episode. The application of justice is honestly attempted and this aim often seems to be achieved. These judges are in the business of reinforcing the boundaries of not only the law but of decent and morally acceptable behaviour. So in the end, are things set right for all involved in a TV case, including the viewer in front of the screen? Are the participants reassured that they can peacefully live in their shared society together? In the old Bavarian court, every episode closes with a lavishly nostalgic picture of communal harmony restored. Here is yet another contrast: the ending of TV courtroom shows is abrupt; the judge barely has time to announce and to explain the verdict before the credits start to roll. The shows are seemingly in perpetual haste. Moreover, the aggressive behaviours of the various parties in court tend to feed the nagging suspicions and fears of the citizenty. Thus, viewers are put in the position of yearning to see justice done but must run the risk of enduring repeated displays of wicked rage, and so they appear to be caught in a vicious circle.

All in all it seems highly likely that the TV courtroom show is here to stay and that, with little variation, it will be a constant in the popular culture diet. For, even if the majority does not take them too seriously, the shows have their devoted followers, and, as the letter in Judge Herz's archive that was sent with the artificial flower concludes, 'I pledge that I will stay loyal to the *Jugendgericht*'.

References

Books, Journals and Papers

Asimow, M et al, 'Perceptions of Lawyers—A Transnational Study of Student Views on the Image of Law and Lawyers' 9 (2005) *International Journal on the Legal Profession* 15, 407–36.

Brauer, S, 'Gerichtsshows als Hybridgenre: Dramaturgie, Inszenierung und Rezeptionsmuster' in K Döveling, L Mikos and J Nieland (eds), *Im Namen des Fernsehvolkes. Neue Formate für Orientierung und Bewertung* (Konstanz, UVK, 2007) 33–82.

Castendyk, O, 'Recht und Rechtskultur. Das Recht im Fernsehen als "Popular Legal Culture"— ein vielversprechender Ansatz aus den USA?' (1992) *Zeitschrift für Rechtspolitik* 25, 63–67.

Chase, A, 'Towards a Legal Theory of Popular Culture' (1986) *Wisconsin Law Review* 527–69.

Durkheim, E, *Regeln der soziologischen Methode,* edited by René König (Neuwied, Luchterhand, 1976).

Festenberg, N and Hipp, D, 'TV-Justiz—'Das ist emotionales Theater', Interview mit Geert Mackenroth' (2002) *Der Spiegel*, 188–89.

Friedman, LM, 'Transformations in American Legal Culture 1800–1985' (1985) *Zeitschrift für Rechtssoziologie* 6, 191–205.

Gerbner, G, 'Die Kultivierungsperspektive: Medienwirkungen im Zeitalter von Monopolisierung und Globalisierung' in A Schorr (ed), *Publikums- und Wirkungsforschungen* (Wiesbaden, Westdeutscher Verlag, 2000) 101–21.

Grimm, D, 'Medien' in Werner Heun et al (eds), *Evangelisches Staatslexikon* (Stuttgart, Kohlhammer, 2006) 1498–1506.

HÖRZU (August 17, 2001) 7.

Karstedt, S, 'Standortprobleme: Kriminalsoziologie in Deutschland' (2000) *Soziologische Revue* 23, 141–52.

Lautmann, R, 'Teilnehmende Beobachtungen in der Strafjustiz' in Jürgen Friedrichs (ed), *Teilnehmende Beobachtung abweichenden Verhaltens* (Stuttgart, Enke, 1973) 109–19.

Lind, EA, 'Procedural Justice, Disputing, and Reactions to Legal Authorities' *American Bar Foundation Working Paper Series*, No 9403 (Chicago, American Bar Foundation, 1994).

Luhmann, N, *A Sociological Theory of Law* (London, Routledge, 1985).

Macaulay, S, 'Images of Law in Everyday Life: The Lessons of School, Entertainment and Spectator Sports' (1987) *Law and Society Review* 21, 185–218.

Machura, S, *Fairneß und Legitimität* (Baden-Baden, Nomos, 2001).

—— 'Interaction between Lay Assessors and Professional Judges in German Mixed Courts' (2001) *International Review of Penal Law* 72:1/2, 451–79.

—— 'Fernsehgerichtsshows: Spektakel des Rechts' (2006) *Paragrana* 15, 174–88.

——' Ansehensverlust der Justiz? Licht und Schatten des Gerichtsshowkonsums' in K Döveling, L Mikos and J-U Nieland (eds), *Im Namen des Fernsehvolkes. Neue Formate für Orientierung und Bewertung* (Konstanz, UVK, 2007) 83–101.

—— 'German Criminal Procedure in Practice' (2007) *Cuadernos Unimetanos* 11, special issue 'Derecho y Democracia', 157–166.

—— 'German Judge Shows: Migrating from the Courtroom to the TV Studio' in M Asimow (ed), *Lawyers in Your Living Room! Law on Television* (Chicago, American Bar Association Press, 2009) 321–32.

—— 'Rechtssoziologie' in G Kneer and M Schroer (ed), *Handbuch Spezielle Soziologien* (Wiesbaden, VS Verlag für Sozialwissenschaften, 2010) 379–92.

—— 'Media Influence on the Perception of the Legal System' in K Papendorf, S Machura and K Andenæs (eds), *Understanding Law in Society* (Zurich/Berlin, Lit, 2011) 239–83.

—— and Asimow, M, 'Das Ansehen von Anwälten bei Jurastudenten: Einflüsse von familiärem Hintergrund, persönlichen Erfahrungen, Anwaltsfilmen und TV-Anwaltsserien' (2004) *Zeitschrift für Rechtssoziologie* 25, 3–33.

—— and Kammertöns, A, 'Recht im Schulunterricht, Medieneinflüsse und die Attraktivität von Rechtsberufen' (2009) *Zeitschrift für Rechtssoziologie* 30, 235–59.

—— and —— 'Deterred From Going to Court? A Survey at German Schools on Media Influences' (2010) *Entertainment and Sports Law Journal* 8, 2.

—— and Ulbrich, S, 'Globalizing the Hollywood Courtroom Drama' (2001) *Journal of Law and Society* 28, 117–32.

Pepitone, A, 'Social Psychological Perspectives on Crime and Punishment' (1975) *Journal of Social Issues* 31, 197–216.

Pfeiffer, C, Windzio, M and Matthias, K, 'Media, Evil and Society: Media Use and its Impacts on Crime Perception, Sentencing Attitudes and Crime Policy in Germany' in J Freilich and RT Guerette (eds), *Migration, Culture Conflict, Crime and Terrorism* (Aldershot, Ashgate, 2006) 109–32.

Porsdam, H, *Legally Speaking. Contemporary American Culture and the Law* (Amherst, University of Massachusetts Press, 1999).

Rennig, C and Machura, S, 'Die Zusammenarbeit zwischen Schöffen und Berufsrichtern' in H Lieber and U Sens (eds), *Ehrenamtliche Richter—Demokratie oder Dekoration am Richtertisch?* (Wiesbaden, Kommunal- und Schulverlag, 1999) 65–70.

Scheerer, J, 'Die Gerichtsshow als kommunikative Gattung. Eine konversationsanalytische Untersuchung am Beispiel der Sendungen "Richter Alexander Hold", "Richterin Barbara Salesch" und "Das Strafgericht"' (MA dissertation, Potsdam University, 2007).

Schnorr, S, 'Justiz, Medien, Medienrecht' (Paper presented at the Tagung der Deutschen Richterakademie, Wustrau, Germany, 2–8 November 2003).

Shelton, DE, Kim, YS and Barak, G, 'A Study of Juror Expectations and Demands Concerning Scientific Evidence: Does the "CSI Effect" Exist?' (2006) *Vanderbilt Journal of Entertainment and Technology Law* 9, 331–68.

Sherwin, RK, *When the Law Goes Pop. The Vanishing Line between Law and Popular Culture* (Chicago, University of Chicago Press, 2000).

Thiemeyer, T, 'State-Owned Enterprises' in E Grochla et al (eds), *Handbook of German Business Management* (Stuttgart, Poeschel, 1990) vol 2, 2259–68.

Thym, B, 'Kultivierung durch Gerichtsshows. Eine Studie unter Berücksichtigung von wahrgenommener Realitätsnähe, Nutzungsmotiven und persönlichen Erfahrungen' (MA dissertation, Ludwig-Maximilians-University Munich, 2003).

Tyler, TR and Lind, EA, 'A Relational Model of Authority in Groups' in M Zanna (ed), *Advances in Experimental Social Psychology* (New York, Academic, 1992) vol 25, 115–91.

Ulbrich, S, 'Gerichtsshows als mediales Format und ihre Bedeutung für das Recht' in S Machura and S Ulbrich (eds), *Recht—Gesellschaft—Kommunikation. Festschrift für Klaus F. Röhl* (Baden-Baden, Nomos, 2003) 161–74.

Vowe, G, 'Massenmedien' in U Andersen and W Woyke (eds), *Handwörterbuch des politischen Systems der Bundesrepublik Deutschland* (Opladen, VS Verlag für Sozialwissenschaften, 2009) 418–29.

TV Series and Films

Das Jugendgericht. TV-series, Germany: RTL, 2001–07.

Das Strafgericht. TV-series, Germany: RTL, 2002–08.

Ehen vor Gericht. TV-series, Germany: ZDF, 1970–84, 1989–2000.

Judge Judy. TV-series, USA: Worldvision Enterprises, CBS, since 1996.

Königlich-Bayerisches Amtsgericht. TV-series, Germany: ZDF, 1968–72.

Perry Mason, TV-series, USA: CBS, 1957–66.

Richter Alexander Hold. TV-series, Germany: Sat1, since 2001.

Richterin Barbara Salesch. TV-series, Germany: Sat1, 1999-2011.

Streit um Drei. TV-series, Germany: ZDF, 1999–2003.

Tatort. TV-series, Germany: WDR, 1981–91.

The Good Wife. TV-series, USA: CBS, since 2009.

The People's Court. TV-series, USA: Warner Brothers, 1981–93.

To Kill A Mockingbird. Movie, USA: Universal International Pictures, 1962.

Verkehrsgericht, TV-series, Germany: ZDF, 1983–2001.

Websites

Amann, M, 'Gerichtsshows im Fernsehen – Folgenreich für echte Richter' FAZ.NET, www.faz.net/s/Rub867BF88948594D80AD8AB4E72C5626ED/Doc~EB22F3180C31C40E4BBB174EE90A305E8~ATpl~Ecommon~Scontent.html?rss_googlefeed_gesellschaft.

Fleschner, F, Martin, U and Gustedt, V, 'Oper des Ordinären' *Focus* (2006), www.focus.de/kultur/medien/fernsehen-oper-des-ordinaeren_aid_218079.html.

Jellen, R, '"Semiotische und emotionale Kampfzone," Interview mit dem Kulturwissenschaftler Daniel Hermsdorf über gegenwärtige Tendenzen der Fernsehkultur' *Telepolis* (20 February 2011), www.heise.de/tp/r4/artikel/33/33947/1.html.

13

Judge Judy: Constructions of 'Justice with an Attitude'

MARILYN TERZIC

> If you're going to try to make a fool of the justice system by not following the rules, by flaunting its orders, by not abiding by the laws of the place where you live, there is a consequence. I am your consequence.[1]

Judge Judith Sheindlin is the queen of court, just as Oprah Winfrey is the queen of talk. The byplay between Sheindlin and the small-claims combatants who come before her every day is the equivalent of a reality-type soap opera. After all, Americans have indulged themselves in such dramatic programming for over half a century and, in turn, have legitimised and condoned the most aberrant and repulsive behaviours.[2] As a result, television judges confront soap-opera-like disputes in their courtrooms 'And [they] resolve them and say, no, we know you may have seen this [on television], but it is not right.'[3] The success of syndi-court shows is therefore predicated on the audience's desire to see a resolution to a conflict. 'They want to watch someone who has done wrong confronted and see justice prevail ... all in [half] an hour.'[4] Nevertheless, what draws viewers to the show? How do Sheindlin's rulings differ from those issued by other arbitrators? And why, for the last 15 years, has *Judge Judy* dominated the court show genre? The answer is as follows:

> She can see what other judges can't see. She can hear what other judges can't hear. And she can render a decision faster than other judges even think. Still think Judy is like other judges? Think again. America's ultimate truth machine, *Judge Judy*.[5]

---

[1] Judith Sheindlin, interview by Stephen J Abramson, Academy of Television Arts & Sciences Foundation, 2009.

[2] M McFarland, 'Blazing Gavels—No-Nonsense Judges Serve Up Fast, Furious Justice For TV Court Potatoes' *The Seattle Times* (30 Nov 1998), available at www.community.seattletimes.nwsource.com/archive/?date=19981130&slug=278637.

[3] Ibid.

[4] Warner Bros, 'The People's Court: Judge Milian', available at www.peoplescourt.warnerbros.com/about/judge.html.

[5] *Judge Judy* (CBS Distribution, 2010), available at www.cbstvd.com/shows.aspx?showID=14.

Be that as it may, this promotional clip gives rise to a question of considerable importance: What exactly are viewers seeing and hearing? Specifically, how do the audio and visual elements presented in *Judge Judy* shape viewers' perceptions of the litigants and thus influence them to resolve their disputes in Sheindlin's court? To address these questions, this chapter examines the reality television court show by means of a message design approach. Message design, in this context, refers to 'the manipulation and planning of signs and symbols that can be produced for the purpose of modifying the cognitive or affective behavior of viewers'.[6] To that end, the chapter describes and explains the strategies used in the construction of 'justice with an attitude'. However, to inform our understanding of viewers' appreciation of reality television programmes, and thus the implementation of these tactics, we now turn to empiricist theories of media aesthetics.

I. Understanding Television: Mind over Matter

As we all know, the brain processes information in two quite different and parallel ways. The left hemisphere processes information analytically, corresponding to verbal stimuli, whereas the right hemisphere processes information in a holistic way, corresponding to nonverbal stimuli.[7,8,9] Building on the notion of hemispheric lateralisation, research has shown that heavy viewers of television programmes that require lower levels of concentration (eg sitcoms and reality television series)[10] tend toward passive learning, choosing to store information procedurally on the basis of images to which they have been repeatedly exposed.[11] Conversely, television programmes that demand a higher level of concentration (eg documentaries) require viewers to play a more active role in interpreting the content. Hence, viewers of content heavy programmes store information declaratively through intentionally discovered facts.[12] Both memory systems are used in the recognition of television images, 'The extent to which television viewers use one more than the other [depends] on the amount of time spent watching television and the types of television programs they choose to watch'.[13]

---

[6] M Fleming and WH Levie, *Instructional Message Design: Principles from the Behavioral and Cognitive Sciences,* 2nd edn (Englewood Cliffs, NJ, Educational Technology Publications, 1993) iii.

[7] MS Gazzaniga et al, *Cognitive Neuroscience: The Biology of the Mind,* 2nd edn (New York, Norton, 2002).

[8] PJ Holcomb et al, 'Dual Coding, Context Availability, and Concreteness Effects in Sentence Comprehension: An Electrophysiological Investigation' (1999) *Journal of Experimental Psychology: Learning, Memory, and Cognition* 25, 721–42.

[9] J Kounios and PJ Holcomb, 'Concreteness Effects in Semantic Processing: ERP Evidence Supporting Dual Coding Theory' (1994) *Journal of Experimental Psychology: Learning, Memory, and Cognition* 20, 804–23.

[10] Seeing that they are subgenres of reality television, syndi-court shows are also regarded as lighter forms of television programming.

[11] N Metallinos, *Television Aesthetics: Perceptual, Cognitive, and Compositional Bases* (Mahwah NJ, Erlbaum, 1996).

[12] Ibid.

[13] Ibid 102.

To this effect, the author examined the extent to which heavy viewing of reality television programmes affected an individual's comprehension and recall of events presented in a documentary.[14,15] After watching a 10-minute documentary, the author gave subjects an intervening task and attitudinal survey, followed by two tests measuring their recall of the programme's narrative and visual components. The results indicated that the subjects' television viewing habits affected the ways in which they perceived and processed audiovisual information. Heavy viewers of reality television programmes paid greater attention to the visual aspect of the documentary, whereas subjects whose television viewing habits were comprised primarily of documentaries showed more interest in its aural counterpart.[16] The significant differences between the two may be indicative of the more active role undertaken by documentary viewers in interpreting the newly acquired information.

The findings further revealed that the programme's pace and density of its subject matter may have overwhelmed the reality television group, which, in turn, influenced the encoding and storage of semantic memories. Consequently, the effortful processing of visual information could have required most of the subjects' cognitive resources and may not have permitted any additional information to be processed. Thus, the memories of these television viewers were at a lower level, analogous to the stimulus complexity of the programmes the viewers watched. Reality television programmes do not concern themselves with superfluous details. Instead, each episode carefully feeds viewers bits and pieces of information that they need to know (or then again, what the producers want them to know) to make coherent sense of the installment and to maintain their viewership. Thus, viewers of such programmes are not preoccupied with details, only the necessary facts. The same applies to the visual component of reality television programmes. Given that viewers have a tendency to look at the middle of the screen first, directors intentionally centre the majority of their shots. Although directors often do this at the expense of proper framing, the tactic ensures that the attention of viewers will be selectively drawn to the middle of the screen and the surrounding objects or events remain unnoticed. Hence, the directors will have succeeded in designing aural and visual stimuli that require lower levels of information processing.

Finally, subjects in the documentary group tended to store information as conceptual wholes, whereas their counterparts seemed to focus on one aspect (visual stimuli) at the expense of another (detailed verbal content). The added mental effort invested in the visual channel, by the reality television group, may have been due to the graphic complexity of the documentary. A reality television series is presented within a familiar setting that has either been established in previous episodes or by a long shot preceding the scene in question. Likewise, the repeated visual and animated sequences contained in the stimulus materials provided subjects with a form of reinforcement, emphasising

---

[14] M Terzic, 'Reality TV: Altering the Terrain of Factual Programming and Learning' (2008) (paper presented at the Annual Meeting of the International Visual Literacy Association, Blacksburg, VA, 16–19 October 2008).

[15] Additional research with heavy viewers of sitcoms has reaffirmed these findings. After all, reality television programmes have borrowed many conventions from this genre (eg use of an objective point of view and teasers, limited stimulus complexity, pace, and timing).

[16] Each group viewed at least nine hours of reality television and documentary programming per week, respectively.

the desired concepts to be retained, and as such 'their understanding and appreciation of television images and sounds are prejudiced by previously stored information'.[17]

II. Engaging the Viewer: Low Involvement Medium, High Involvement Tactics

As we have seen, there are individual differences in the ways in which people process televised information. Heavy viewers of reality television programmes found concrete and readily visualised information easier to comprehend and recall than semantically and acoustically complex details. They also responded to the documentary in a passive and reactive manner, storing information procedurally through repetition and conditioning. Thus, to effectively draw, engage, as well as entertain their audiences, reality television programmes should be designed to reflect the information-processing styles of their viewers. To that end, the following message design strategies were observed in *Judge Judy*.

Television can have an impact on both the formation and organisation of viewers' concepts.[18] As a result, 'the more [the viewer] can be engaged to actually think about the message (including imagined or actual rehearsal of the recommended behavior), the more likely he or she is to experience appropriate changes in knowledge, attitudes, and behavior.'[19]

Ausubel believes that 'New ideas and information are learned and retained most efficiently when inclusive and specifically relevant ideas are already available in cognitive structure to serve a subsuming role or to furnish ideational anchorage.'[20] Thus, to assist the viewer in organising and interpreting the 'facts', *Judge Judy* presents an overview of the case at the beginning of each scene. Likewise, the show uses teasers to emphasise and draw attention to the pertinent details of the proceedings. Teasers present the viewer with context, not content, and with conceptual frameworks, but not specific details. In fact, these 15- to 30-second promotional tools have been proven effective in aiding viewer comprehension, whether they precede the show, are seen throughout the week, or are seen during the episode itself.[21,22] Teasers also engage the viewer by providing him or her with the necessary organisational structures to guide the assimilation of the new content.

Interestingly, a sequence of desaturated shots often comprises these cold opens. This not only draws the viewer's attention to the contrasting visual materials, but also

---

[17] Metallinos, *Television Aesthetics* (n 11) 101.

[18] DR Anderson and PA Collins, *The Impact on Children's Education: Television's Influence on Cognitive Development* (Washington, DC, Department of Education, 1988).

[19] Institute for Media, Policy, and Civil Society, *Plan the Work: A Handbook for Strategic Communications Planning for Not-for-Profit Organizations* (Vancouver, BC, Author, 2006) 111.

[20] DP Ausubel et al, *Educational Psychology: A Cognitive View*, 2nd edn (New York, Holt, Rinehart and Winston, 1978) 190.

[21] H Chang, 'The Effect of News Teasers in Processing TV News' (1998) *Journal of Broadcasting and Electronic Media* 42, 327–39.

[22] JD Schleuder et al, 'Priming Effects of Television News Bumpers and Teasers on Attention and Memory' (1993) *Journal of Broadcasting and Electronic Media* 39, 437–52.

prompts him or her to take a more active role in interpreting the content, as Zettl suggests:

> Color on recognizable images (people and objects) emphasizes their appearance; thus, [the viewer's] attention is directed toward the outer, rather than inner, reality of an event. But when [the scene is rendered] more low-definition through the desaturation of color ... the event becomes more transparent. It also makes the [viewer] apply psychological closure, that is, fill in the missing elements of the low-definition images. In this way [the viewer] will inevitably get more involved in the event than if [he or she] was looking at high-definition color images.[23]

To demonstrate, let us consider the following clip:

Boyfriend:	She was having an inappropriate sexual relationship with another man.
Announcer:	His jealous rage.
Ex-Girlfriend:	He started acting very angrily and got violent.
Announcer:	Turned into a brutal attack.
Ex-Girlfriend:	*He was strangling me with both of his hands on top of me. When I woke up, I was in the hospital.*
Boyfriend:	*I did not touch her.*
Sheindlin:	*You are a pretty repulsive guy.*
Announcer:	And now his fate is sealed.
Sheindlin:	*You pled guilty.*
Boyfriend:	*In order to avoid a trial.*
Sheindlin:	*Guilty means your guilty.*
Announcer:	Judge Judy.[24] (Italics were added to indicate the times at which the audio track was accompanied by black-and-white images.)

The teaser clearly serves as a preamble to a domestic violence case and further sets the precedent that the case warrants a guilty verdict. However, the alleged strangulation and infidelity have no bearing on the dispute over the return of personal belongings and unpaid rent. Thus, whereas this public denigration may be considered as a form of retribution for the defendant's actions, the sensationalist focus on the conflict at hand undeniably feeds the insatiable appetites of its viewers.

By contrast, mathemagenic strategies aim

> to control the transformation of media symbols ... into learning behaviors ... to provide for 'the effective management of learning processes.' [They seek] to orient [viewers to reality courtroom television programs,] show them what is relevant and important, and then engage them in activities that will ensure the proper encoding of the materials into memory.[25]

[23] H Zettl, *Sight Sound Motion: Applied Media Aesthetics*, 5th edn (Boston, Wadsworth, 2007) 77.
[24] *Judge Judy* (Big Ticket Productions, CBS Distribution, 20 May 2010).
[25] DH Jonassen, 'Learning Strategies: A New Educational Technology' (1985) *Innovations in Education and Teaching International* 22, 30.

Epistemic curiosity is 'a drive reducible by knowledge rehearsal. It is elicited in an individual when a question arises that demands an answer [and is sated] when an acceptable answer is realized.'[26] Hence, the viewer will be motivated to rehearse the responses to Sheindlin's inquiries because of the rewarding effects of reducing conflict.[27] For the most part, these questions appear to be central to gathering and interpreting new evidence. Nevertheless, they are carefully and intentionally integrated throughout the proceedings to call the viewer's attention to specific elements of the case.

These queries also contribute to the game-show-like qualities of the programme. The preliminary set of questions stems from the complaints and defence responses, and thus provides the viewer with the requisite facts from which a logical judgment can be derived. Thereafter, the focus of Sheindlin's interrogation shifts to more personal matters, which, in turn, adds an emotional component to the case and effectively encourages the viewer to exercise his or her subjective judgment in evaluating its outcome. If the viewer correctly guesses the verdict, he or she will gain a renewed sense of confidence in his or her reasoning skills. Otherwise, the viewer will continue to watch the reality-based series in the hope of sharpening his or her legal wit and benefiting from the practical value of such knowledge. Either way, the show presents the exchanges between the judge and the litigants in such a manner that dissuades the viewer from validating, questioning, or evaluating the facts. Hence, viewers of syndi-court programmes not only tend toward passive learning, but previously acquired knowledge influences their understanding of the 'law'.

On the other hand, pauses are psycholinguistic.[28] They provide the viewer with an opportunity to rehearse the newly acquired information and consequently facilitate cognitive learning. Pauses also recapture the minds of those viewers who have strayed and cause those who have been listening to pay closer attention to the information that follows. For this reason, the viewer can observe brief moments of silence after statements that reaffirm Sheindlin's decisions and beliefs.

III. Learning by Design: Visual Practices of Court Television Shows

We live in a highly 'visual culture in which print and graphics, television and tele-communications, video and movies, and computer displays of various size convey information of such intensity that it diminishes the dominance of speech and print

---

[26] LR Mittman and G Terrell, 'An Experimental Study of Curiosity in Children' (1964) *Child Development* 35, 851.

[27] DF Berlyne, 'Curiosity and Learning' (1978) *Motivation and Emotion* 2, 97–175.

[28] VP Richmond and JC McCroskey, *Nonverbal Behavior in Interpersonal Relations*, 4th edn (Boston, Allyn & Bacon, 2000).

media'.[29] Not surprisingly, most individuals are visual learners.[30] However, as far as studio productions are concerned, *Judge Judy* is far from a visual programme per se. Despite Sheindlin's efforts to present the most rudimentary elements of a case, the information density of such programmes requires that all visual elements, in terms of both the set (ie the clothing of the litigants and members of the gallery, and the design of the props) and camera movements, be kept to a minimum. In turn, the absence of visually complex stimuli lessens the cognitive load on viewers and enables the producers to maintain the desired (and unadorned) graphic continuity of the programme.

The plaintiff occasionally employs charts, photographs, and videos to affirm his or her assertions. However, when bank statements, receipts, or copies of correspondence are brought into evidence, the producers highlight select transactions and passages in yellow to draw attention to—and thus reinforce—the significance of the information. Nonetheless, one could argue that *Judge Judy* employs a highly visual approach to learning in terms of the show's reliance on facial expressions. Sheindlin's signs of boredom, disbelief, curiosity, or attentiveness serve as cues as to the appropriateness of the litigants' behaviour or response. Thus, through repetition and conditioning, viewers will shape their perceptions of the judicial system and judges accordingly.

IV. Communicator Credibility: Source Factors in Persuasion

Credibility is more than a mere 'attitude toward a source of communication held at a given time by a receiver'.[31] Rather, this psychological characteristic is a fundamental element of communication. Perloff believes

> It is part of the two-way interaction between communicator and message recipient—a dynamic entity that emerges from the transaction between source and audience member. This means that communicators are not guaranteed credibility by virtue of who they are, their title, or academic pedigree. ... [Instead,] there is something democratic about credibility. Communicators [not only] have to enter the rough-and-tumble realm of persuasion ... [but they must also] earn the audience's respect and win its credibility.[32]

Thus, for a source to be deemed credible, he or she must exhibit at least one of six traits: competence, trustworthiness, goodwill, power, idealism, and similarity.

Competence requires 'more than simply being knowledgeable. It involves a perception that others have of people concerning their degree of knowledge on topics, abilities to command such knowledge, and abilities to communicate this knowledge

[29] JW Marcum, 'Beyond Visual Culture: The Challenge of Visual Ecology' (2002) *Portal: Libraries and the Academy* 2, 189.

[30] M Snell, 'Innovator: Judy Kranzler' DLC (1999), available at www.dlc.org/ndol_ci.cfm?contentid=1234&kaid=110&subid=181.

[31] JC McCroskey, *An Introduction to Rhetorical Communication*, 8th edn (Boston, Allyn & Bacon, 2001) 83.

[32] RM Perloff, *The Dynamics of Persuasion: Communication and Attitudes in the 21st Century*, 4th edn (New York, Routledge, 2010) 166–67.

clearly'.[33] Sheindlin's persona as the feisty femme with an indomitable personality, sharp tongue, and no-nonsense approach to television justice has fuelled the success of *Judge Judy* and, as a result, has increased her perceived level of competence. Even so, Sheindlin continues to remind viewers of the ways in which her countless life and extensive courtroom experiences influence her decision-making.

Sheindlin's high visibility in the media, as well as her representation on television as being real, allow her to be rated highly in terms of trustworthiness. By the same token, the two-sided analogies that capture the essence of a case reflect her genuineness and sincerity. In the matter of *Jordan v Johnson*, the plaintiff sued a limousine company for not providing her with the vehicle she requested. Despite her dissatisfaction, she accepted the terms of service and expected to be reimbursed in full, as the stretch Hummer was not able to accommodate all of her guests. However, as Sheindlin explained, the plaintiff's actions were comparable to those of a restaurant patron who consumes an entire meal and refuses to pay for it:

> Ms. Jordan, this is your problem, madam. I want you to think about going to a restaurant and you order dinner, and the meal comes and you taste it, but you are really not crazy about it, and you send it back and say, 'There is something wrong with this meal, but I am more than happy to pay for my drink, but I am not paying for this meal.' A-OK. But, if you go to the restaurant and you take a bite of the burger and say, 'You know, I am really not crazy about this, but I am going to finish it anyway, and then I am not going to pay for it,' that you cannot do. So, if he did not deliver, Ms. Jordan, what you wanted, you had a perfect right not to use it, and if you felt as if he breached your contract, by not providing you with the size limousine you wanted, you could have sued him for your deposit back, you could have done that ... You ate the hamburger, Ms. Jordan. You ate the burger![34]

Thus, detailing the existence and reasons for the strengths and weaknesses of the litigant's case can help to reinforce trust between the viewer and the arbitrator, as well as increase the believability of the proceedings.

'Many of the people who show up in television's reality courtrooms come seeking a sympathetic hearing, maybe knowing that they will not have to pay a judgment or maybe just to be on television', suggests Leroux.[35] Even so, Sheindlin expresses little concern for the 'backstory' of litigants. From time to time, however, she demonstrates her goodwill by showing empathy and compassion for those who have been wronged by friends, family members, or strangers. In particular, she will take on a motherly persona[36] while offering support and advice to young victims of domestic violence. For instance:

> Life can be a beautiful thing. You have been granted several gifts. Reasonable health, right? You seem to be actually a reasonably intelligent young lady. You know, the few things that

---

[33] WA Haskins, 'Ethos and Pedagogical Communication: Suggestions for Enhancing Credibility in the Classroom' (2000) *Current Issues in Education* 3, no 4, (para 18) www.cie.asu.edu/volume3/number4/index. html.

[34] *Judge Judy* (Big Ticket Productions, CBS Distribution, 12 March 2010).

[35] C Leroux, 'The Gavels of TV: Your Guide to Those Who Have Traded Courtroom for Television Studio' *Chicago Tribune* (11 December 2008), available at www.articles.chicagotribune.com/2008-12-11/entertainment/0812100582_1_judge-judy-judith-sheindlin-judge-joe-brown.

[36] CR Foust, 'A Return to Feminine Public Virtue: *Judge Judy* and the Myth of the Tough Mother' (2004) *Women's Studies in Communication* 27, no 3, 269–93.

you have said to me suggest to me that you are a reasonably intelligent young lady. God has graced you with beauty and the gift of choice. If you make the wrong choices, when you are 18, they can stay with you forever. You can either be a winner or a victim. If for three years you have been a victim and you continue to let it happen to you, there has to be a reason. [There is] something [in the back of your mind that is telling you,] 'I am not worthy of somebody who treats me like I am supposed to be treated, and I have to accept somebody who abuses me physically and emotionally because I don't deserve any better' ... and that's not true. Somebody has to make you believe it. Somebody has to work with you so that you actually believe it. That's why [you require therapy,] because everybody has unique gifts and is special. You just haven't found yours yet.[37]

The degree of power exuded by Sheindlin pertains to whether she can provide some form of reward or punishment to the litigants.[38] Clearly, the plaintiff can benefit from a monetary award. However, considering that 60 per cent of cases are either dismissed or result in an exchange of property,[39] the 'presumed innocent' are nevertheless subject to Sheindlin's pointed humiliation, browbeating, and haranguing, as a juvenile delinquent found out:

I have power. You have nothing. You know why you have nothing? Because you have no brain. Because you are not doing anything with the brain. All you are doing is streaking your hair, putting nice eye makeup on, and putting on earrings. Right? And thinking you're a real smarty-pants. But you are not. You're nothing. And you are going to continue to be nothing unless you go to school, unless you get yourself an education, and unless you park your attitude someplace else![40]

To be perceived as having a high degree of idealism, the source must exude the values and qualities that the audience esteems and desires.[41] The parties that appear on the show 'seem to stem from dysfunctional families, romances gone sour, [and] roommates from hell. They tend to be on the lower rungs of the ladder of success, and many have had previous brushes with the law in criminal courts.'[42] Be that as it may, the parties seem to have warmed to Sheindlin's tough love approach. In fact, as Randy Douthit, one of the show's executive producers, points out, the parties perceive Sheindlin as a stern mother, one with whom they identify and aspire to emulate.[43] Hence, to appeal to a group of followers, the reality television arbitrator embodies the traits of a group or opinion leader. These include:

— Having greater exposure to external communication. This suggests more exposure to relevant mass media ... and a more cosmopolitan (worldly) orientation than [her] followers.
— Having greater social participation than [her] followers.

[37] *Judge Judy* (Big Ticket Productions, CBS Distribution, 9 November 2009).
[38] RP Hart and SM Daughton, *Modern Rhetorical Criticism*, 3rd edn (Boston, Allyn & Bacon, 2005).
[39] CNN, 'Larry King Live: Judge Judy Lays Down the Law' *CNN* (18 February 2000), available at transcripts.cnn.com/TRANSCRIPTS/0002/18/lkl.00.html.
[40] *Judge Judy* (Big Ticket Productions, CBS Distribution, 3 March 2010).
[41] Hart and Daughton, *Modern Rhetorical Criticism* (n 38).
[42] Leroux, 'The Gavels of TV' (n 35).
[43] P Albiniak, 'Judge Judy Sheindlin: Her Appeal is Undeniable' *Broadcasting and Cable* (25 January 2010), available at www.broadcastingcable.com/article/print/445708-Judge_Judy_Sheindlin_Her_Appeal_Is_Undeniable.php.

— Having a 'somewhat' higher social status than [her] followers.
— Being more innovative than [her] followers.
— Having more expertise than [her] followers.[44]

Finally, the more similar a source is to a message recipient, the more persuasive the communicator will become to the recipient. Similarities do not influence persuasive effectiveness directly; instead, they influence persuasive outcomes indirectly[45] by affecting the perceived competence, trustworthiness, and likeability of the communicator.[46] To draw viewers away from the entertainment aspect of the programme, Sheindlin occasionally provides explanations of legal terminology and court proceedings. Most devout viewers would probably agree that, more so than any other syndi-court show, *Judge Judy* provides them with the opportunity to learn about the law not only through Sheindlin's teachings, but also through the eyes of people like themselves. Hence, to reflect the average American's dressing habits, the litigants dress for comfort and conformity, not for extravagance and style. The deep shades and saturated hues of the litigants' apparel further enhance their perceived sociability, outgoingness, and sincerity.[47] Moreover, the show averages approximately 10 million viewers each day,[48] 75 per cent of whom are women.[49] Even though the show's primary demographic consists of 25- to 54-year-olds, the programme recently gained considerable popularity among younger adults aged 18 to 24. Consequently, the plaintiffs and members of the gallery are predominantly women of comparable ages. The litigants and actors are equally comprised of Caucasians and African- and Asian-Americans from diverse socioeconomic backgrounds. Racial and socioeconomic diversity among the litigants and actors helps demonstrate that all may access Sheindlin's playpen, regardless of race or class—especially after the programme was sued for alleged racial screening.[50]

V. More than Words: The Power of Nonverbal Communication

In *The Sage Handbook of Nonverbal Communication*, Keating puts forward the following argument:

> Nonverbal communication is tuned to motives and orchestrated to accomplish goals. Thus, displays of anger can be used to cloak signs of guilt, smiles can serve as a disguise

---

[44] TS Robertson et al, *Consumer Behavior* (Glenview, IL: Scott, Foresman and Company, 1984) 406.

[45] DJ O'Keefe, *Persuasion: Theory and Practice*, 2nd edn (Newbury Park, CA, Sage, 2002).

[46] RG Hass, 'Effects of Source Characteristics on Cognitive Responses and Persuasion' in RE Petty et al (eds), *Cognitive Responses in Persuasion* (Hillsdale, NJ, Lawrence Erlbaum Associates, 1981) 141–72.

[47] LB Rosenfeld and TG Plax, 'Clothing as Communication' (1977) *Journal of Communication* 27, 24–31.

[48] L Elber, '*Judge Judy* Marks a Decade of Tough Love' (Lexis Nexis, 14 February 2006), available at www.lexisnexis.com/hottopics/lnacademic/?sfi=AC00NBGenSrch&csi=147876&shr=t.

[49] J Benson, 'Judy Judy Judy: How a Tough-Talking Brooklyn Judge Led a Courtroom Revival' *Broadcasting and Cable* (3 September 2005), available at www.broadcastingcable.com/article/print/157970-Judy_Judy_Judy.php.

[50] TMZ, 'Lawsuit Says "Judge Judy" Sends Blacks Packin'' *TMZ* (2007), available at www.tmz.com/2007/12/31/lawsuit-says-judge-judy-sends-black-packin.

for psychological pain, and 'blank' looks may be enacted to convey irony or sarcasm. This brand of *nonverbal impression management* reflects how individuals 'spin' nonlanguage cues in ways intended to project images that produce desired social outcomes.[51]

Likewise, *Judge Judy* uses various nonverbal communication strategies to create and maintain favourable impressions of Sheindlin within the minds of viewers and thus promote her commonsense approach to law and justice.

Society generally considers physically attractive communicators as better per-suaders.[52] Over the years, Sheindlin's facial features have become more pronounced. However, as she points out, 'People don't watch my show for what I look like. They wouldn't be watching if they wanted to see a looker. They're watching for a message, action, or something else.'[53] So, to detract viewers from these unsightly lineaments, the camera operators do not shoot Sheindlin in focus. In addition, a diffuse light sits on the bench, away from the line of sight of the cameras and litigants, and sweeps across Sheindlin's face; the presence of the illuminant becomes evident as Sheindlin sways her hands across the source. To further soften her stern and sharp appearance, Sheindlin wears a lace collar[54] and has progressively lightened the colour of her hair.

Toward the end of each episode, the deep and authoritative voice of the announcer calls for aggrieved individuals who seek justice, are embroiled in a family dispute, or are victims of scams. This voice not only promotes the accessibility[55] of Sheindlin's court, but also stimulates the viewer to imagine him or herself on the show. For these reasons, socially attractive peer models typically comprise the plaintiffs. As the series features 'real cases' and 'real people', a viewer is more likely to respond favourably to litigants who reflect the viewer's perceptions of his or her own appearance and values. This favourable response, in turn, encourages the viewer to submit his or her case to the show. By the same token, the parties who appear on the programme are not overly attractive individuals with whom the average American cannot identify.

Direct gaze 'is the preliminary step of interpersonal interaction and during inter-action, it is frequently used for contextually evaluating oneself and others'.[56] Hence, when Sheindlin 'was commanded to look into one of the six cameras on the set,

---

[51] CF Keating, 'Why and How the Silent Self Speaks Volumes: Functional Approaches to Nonverbal Impression Management' in V Manusov and ML Patterson (eds), *The Sage Handbook of Nonverbal Communication* (Thousand Oaks, CA, Sage) 321–39.

[52] Richmond and McCroskey, *Nonverbal Behavior in Interpersonal Relations* (n 28).

[53] M Starr, 'Starr Report' *New York Post*, 22 February 2010, available at www.nypost.com/f/print/enter-tainment/tv/starr_report_iCkQeloUIvZkc2Zs5J00CN.

[54] When asked about the story behind her trademark lace collar, Sheindlin replied 'At just about the time that I was appointed to the bench, my husband and I were traveling in Greece and at the foot of the Acropolis there was a lady making lace collars. I said, "You know, male judges wear a white shirt and usu-ally a brightly colored tie, so they look terrific, but the women have this black robe right up against their faces. I'm going to try that lace collar." It's a little disarming, you walk in and see a nice lady sitting there with a lace collar, and you think, "She wouldn't hurt a fly"' (Judith Sheindlin, 2009).

[55] According to Erickson, in 'a typical two-week program cycle, the show's staff contacts 500 litigants by phone, 40 [of whom] are brought into the [Los Angeles based] studios to be interviewed. If their stories hold up and they are still confident they could win, they appear on the show—forfeiting the right to appeal, agreeing to a jurisdictional award limit of $5,000, and going along with the show's policy of using the money to establish a "fund", with either the winner or the loser getting the bigger half depending on Judge Judy's whim': H Erickson, *Encyclopedia of Television Law Shows: Factual and Fictional Series About Judges, Lawyers and the Courtroom, 1948–2009* (Jefferson, NC, McFarland & Company, 2009) 140.

[56] L Conty et al, 'The Mere Perception of Eye Contact Increases Arousal During a Word-Spelling Task' (2009) *Social Neuroscience*, 5 no 2, 172.

she replied, 'I'm not going to look at any camera. You follow me.'[57] In other words, Sheindlin is not the one on trial and definitely not the one to be scrutinised by the cameras or viewers at home. Nevertheless, the mutual gaze she maintains with the litigants demonstrates her involvement and interest[58] in the hearing and is central to her adept lie-detection abilities. Likewise, as she is continually shown in profile, her credibility,[59] honesty, and sincerity[60] are enhanced, and the camera position at eye level with Sheindlin further reinforces her perceived neutrality and objectivity.[61]

Eye contact is equally instrumental in establishing and defining relationships.[62] Thus, to better connect and identify with the television audience, the programme shows the litigants in direct address, allowing the viewer to assess the credibility, trustworthiness, and persuasiveness of the litigants' arguments.[63] The camera operators shoot both plaintiffs and defendants from above eye level, preventing either from looking directly into the lenses of their respective cameras. Although the angle is subtle, the director employs this technique for two distinct reasons: it reaffirms Sheindlin's superior status while emphasising the less-than-prominent stature of the litigants, and renders the members of the gallery more visible.

The gallery consists of background actors or—more specifically—paid distracters. When a litigant rambles, the gallery members begin to talk amongst themselves, or the members avert their gaze to signal the irrelevance of the evidence and gently guide the viewer's attention to the more pertinent verbal and visual information. The members also appear to laugh on cue, emphasising select disparaging moments that the viewer should retain. All in all, the gallery's actions are difficult to ignore as (a) the actors' gaze figures directly in the middle of the screen, and thus is captured by our detailed central vision; (b) the use of the narrow angle lens enlarges the background, giving the impression that all objects, distant and near, are of the same size; and (c) the extras are dimly lit and softly out of focus, which, in consequence, give rise to the desaturation of colour effect described earlier.

The diminutive Sheindlin uses her brashness and blunt nature to maintain control of the courtroom. Nevertheless, she does not quickly dismiss the role of the director in the taping of the proceedings:

> Do you hear me speaking? You're trying to talk over me? That's not going to happen. I have control over this set, and the people who are recording what's going on here are going to record me, not you![64]

The tempo of her delivery further conveys her energy and expressiveness. The quick pace and lack of disfluencies in the stream of her speech enable Sheindlin to assert

---

[57] Benson, 'Judy Judy Judy' (n 49).

[58] VP Richmond et al, *Nonverbal Behavior in Interpersonal Relations*, 2nd edn (Englewood Cliffs, NJ, Prentice–Hall, 1991).

[59] J Baggaley et al, *Psychology of the TV Image* (New York, Praeger, 1980).

[60] P Webbink, *The Power of Eyes* (New York, Springer, 1986).

[61] In the title sequence of the show, Sheindlin poses as Lady Justice and holds an evenly balanced scale to further suggest that all parties will benefit from fair and equal justice.

[62] Richmond and McCroskey, *Nonverbal Behavior in Interpersonal Relations* (n 28).

[63] M Argyle, *Bodily Communication*, 2nd edn (London, Methuen, 1975).

[64] *Judge Judy* (Big Ticket Productions, CBS Distribution, 18 May 2009).

her point of view, while increasing her persuasiveness, credibility, and competence.[65] Not surprisingly, she has little tolerance for those who express themselves in a crackly and muffled tone; thus, she encourages the litigants to speak in a strong and clear voice. As a result, the plaintiff and defendant will be perceived as being significantly more composed, qualified, and dynamic, and the viewer is likely to maintain a greater interest in the proceedings.[66]

As North Americans, we generally keep people with whom we are not familiar at arm's length. In that regard, the show consists primarily of medium- and long-shots to present a neutral, objective point of view. By contrast, the show selectively employs the more subjective point of view associated with close-ups to emphasise statements that could make or break a case, and to profile individuals perceived less favourably and often shunned by society or Sheindlin herself. As a matter of fact, she

> routinely grills litigants about their employment history, marital and parental status, income, drug habits, sexual practices, incarceration record, and past or present 'dependency' on public welfare. ... In addition to this biographical scrutiny, Sheindlin mocks the accents of non-English speakers, scorns the uneducated and low-paid, accuses litigants of lying and abusing the 'system,' and frequently orders them to spit out gum, stand up straight, and 'control' bodily functions to her liking.[67]

The show also uses this shot designation during the closing interview sequence, as the litigants praise Sheindlin for her expeditious and definitive judgments and reiterate key elements of the case or of the adversary's unseemly actions or behaviours. Interestingly, the show juxtaposes the successful plaintiffs—who win monetary judgments—against the unsuccessful defendants, showing the plaintiffs in front of the courtroom, while showing the defendants positioned against a taupe-coloured wall alongside a tropical plant. Due to this suggestive positioning, viewers are therefore more likely to perceive the expressed views of the plaintiff as those attitudes, values, and beliefs espoused by the court, while regarding the views of the defendant as frivolous and gratuitous.

Last, in order to maintain the interest and attention of prospective litigants, the producers succeeded in creating an environment in which they would feel comfortable presenting their case. First, shades of red and brown adorn the courtroom. Psychologically, reds 'encourage action and confidence [and yet] provide a sense of protection from fears and anxiety',[68] whereas browns convey a sense of stability, reliability, and orderliness.[69] Second, to be perceived as being approachable, the show's producers position Sheindlin's bench within close proximity of the litigants' tables. Third, to convey the impression that the cases presented before Sheindlin are subject

---

[65] JK Burgoon et al, 'Nonverbal Behaviors, Persuasion, and Credibility' (1990) *Human Communication Research* 17, no 1, 140–69.

[66] EP Kaminski and GR Miller, 'How Jurors Respond to Videotaped Witnesses' (1984) *Journal of Communication* 34, 88–102.

[67] L Ouelette, 'Take Responsibility for Yourself: *Judge Judy* and the Neoliberal Citizen' in S Murray and L Ouelette (eds), *Reality TV: Remaking Television Culture* (New York, University Press, 2009) 228.

[68] Kate Smith, 'All About the Color Red,' *Sensational Color*, available at www.sensationalcolor.com/color-messages-meanings/color-meaning-symbolism-psychology/all-about-the-color-red.html.

[69] Kate Smith, 'All About the Color Brown' *Sensational Color*, available at www.sensationalcolor.com/color-messages-meanings/color-meaning-symbolism-psychology/all-about-the-color-brown.html.

to the rigours of the law,[70] a collection of legal volumes is prominently displayed in the background when the litigants enter the courtroom; with the same setting appearing in the judge's chambers. Fourth, the careful interplay of positive and negative masses connotes the relative structural stability of the objects or events within the television screen.[71] Finally, the producers have based *Judge Judy* on reality television shows with which the audience is familiar, providing the viewer with well-known conventions of such programmes that not only contribute to a feeling of ease, but also heighten the viewer's arousal and interest values and increase the positivity, pleasantness, and preference with which the programme's environment is rated.[72]

VI. Understanding Influence: The Art of Persuasion

Communication scholars have defined persuasion in myriad ways: as 'a process in which the communicator seeks to elicit a desired response from his receiver';[73] as 'a conscious attempt by one individual to change the attitudes, beliefs, or behavior of another individual or group of individuals through the transmission of some message';[74] as 'a symbolic activity whose purpose is to effect the internalization of voluntary acceptance of new cognitive states or patterns of overt behavior through the exchange of messages';[75] and as 'a successful intentional effort at influencing another's mental state through communication in a circumstance in which the persuadee has some measure of freedom'.[76] Taken together, these definitions have identified key factors that are central to our understanding of the art of persuasion—it is a symbolic, noncoercive[77] form of influence. Nevertheless, for the viewer to regard Sheindlin as a convincing and authoritative judge, she must also convey a sense of believability.

---

[70] When asked to comment on the operations of the court, Sheindlin replied:

'The way you run a courtroom is, you have a complaint and an answer. The complaint is written by the litigants, stating their position, the answer by the defendant, and if there's a countersuit, the countersuit. That's what I get to read. And when a producer came in to discuss the case with me, I said, I have no interest meeting you. You're a nice person. You do your job. I do my job. If the public wanted your opinion on how this case should be decided, they would give you a black dress with a collar and I would be doing your job. You do your job. I am not going to interfere with the way you do your job, if you do it well. And you can't interfere with the way I do my job. So we all have what we do. We don't do [production notes.] We don't use somebody else's opinion. I don't take a break to go and research what the law is. You know, go in the back and call for people ... We do a case start to finish, that's it.' (Judith Sheindlin, 2009).

[71] Zettl, *Sight Sound Motion* (n 23).

[72] RF Bornstein, 'Exposure and Affect: Overview and Meta-Analysis Research 1968–1987' (1989) *Psychological Bulletin* 106, 265–89.

[73] K Andersen, *Persuasion: Theory and Practice* (Boston, Allyn & Bacon, 1971) 6.

[74] EP Bettinghaus and MJ Cody, *Persuasive Communication*, 4th edn (New York, Holt, Rinehart & Winston, 1987) 3.

[75] MJ Smith, *Persuasion and Human Action: A Review and Critique of Social Influence Theories* (Belmont, CA, Wadsworth, 1982) 7.

[76] O'Keefe, *Persuasion* (n 45) 5.

[77] To avoid any possible coercion, persuasion must involve 'a *perception of choice* regarding the acceptance or rejection of symbolic appeals'. See Smith *Persuasion and Human Action* (n 75) 10.

Judge Judy presents us with a vision of the judge as a great, charismatic lawgiver who appeals to extralegal and perhaps supernatural sources (e.g., intuition) as a foundation for judgment. We are led to believe that Judge Sheindlin herself, billed as 'the ultimate truth machine,' embodies the power of justice and is not merely a passive conduit for the general principles of the official doctrine of the law.[78]

However, in view of the limited evidence presented in a case, Sheindlin continually faces the challenge of convincing viewers of the appropriateness of her rulings. To therefore convey her arguments in an honest and believable manner, Sheindlin provides analogies that are well within a layperson's level of understanding, and presents her views with the attitude of 'it would be natural for you to have this idea if you don't know all the facts, but when you know all the facts, you will be convinced'.[79] In the case of *Powers v Powers*, the defendant maintained that she should not be held accountable for her son's medical expenses, for the minor had decided to leave home to live with his grandmother. Driven by a passion for family law, Sheindlin refuted the defendant's claim in a strident tone, as follows.

Sheindlin: Ms. Powers, it was your choice, as his mother, to let him stay there.

Defendant: No.

Sheindlin: No, listen to me very carefully. Yes, because he can go. But if you are his mother and you want him home, you go to the police, you go to the family court, and you say to the family court, 'They are interfering with my role as a parent, I want my son to come home.' But if you choose to let him stay with his grandparents or an aunt, an uncle, a neighbor, a friend, or whatever, that does not absolve you of the responsibility of supporting him. Now the fact that his grandparents have not come after you for support, I don't understand why, because you are absolutely responsible. Is his father alive?

Defendant: Yes.

Sheindlin: Does his father support him?

Defendant: No.

Sheindlin: Well, then his grandparents have the absolute right to sue you and his father for support while he is under their roof. Because under the law, you are responsible for his necessaries—all of his necessaries while he is a minor. And the fact that you choose to let him live with somebody else does not absolve you of the responsibility of supporting him. So, if he has a medical bill, and despite the fact that his grandparents have been footing the bill for his living for the last two years, that does not mean that they cannot come against you for his medical. Do you understand?

Defendant: Yes, your honor.

Sheindlin: That, madam, is the law![80]

---

[78] SA Kohm, 'The People's Law Versus *Judge Judy* Justice: Two Models of Law in American Reality-Based Courtroom TV' (2006) *Law & Society Review* 40, 693–728.

[79] M Karlins and HI Abelson, *Persuasion: How Opinions and Attitudes are Changed*, 2nd edn (New York, Springer, 1970) 26.

[80] *Judge Judy* (Big Ticket Productions, CBS Distribution, 12 February 2009).

Fear appeals have enormous potential in resolving disputes as well:

> Their effectiveness, [however,] depends in large part on the structure of the messages. At the least, [they] must include a severe threat, evidence suggesting the target is especially vulnerable to the threat, and solutions that are both easy to perform and effective.[81]

Even if Sheindlin dismisses the case or does not award monetary damages, the plaintiff may still feel that 'justice was served' as Sheindlin threatens to destroy the defendant's reputation and leave him or her financially ruined. In the matter of *Pacheco v Googins*, a used car dealer illegally repossessed and subsequently damaged the plaintiff's vehicle. In the supposed interest of showing good faith, the defendant offered to repair the sedan. Nevertheless, in view of his less than stellar composure and unlawful ways, Sheindlin questioned the veracity of the defendant's intentions:

Sheindlin: I'll have her bring you the car and you can fix it … But, I don't want to hear that you did any patch job on it. Do you understand that?

Defendant: [*Nods his head.*]

Sheindlin: Do you understand Mr. Googins, I know where you live.

Defendant: [*Gives a nervous smile.*]

Sheindlin: I do.

Defendant: Yes, your honor.

Sheindlin: I do. Are you still in business?

Defendant: Yes, your honor.

Sheindlin: I could put you out of business in a second. Nobody will buy another car from you, sir. So, if you say you're going to fix her car, you're going to fix her car. Otherwise, this case is going to have a postscript with what the car looked like after you fixed it. And I guarantee you, nobody in Jacksonville, Florida, will come and buy a car from you. Do you understand?

Defendant: Yes, your honor.

Sheindlin: Perfect.[82]

Be that as it may, Sheindlin contends that her

> viewers are smart. They know [she has] a contract with a television show and that [she] makes a lot of money. In a way, [Sheindlin maintains that she is] presiding over a real court. But the difference between [her] court and a real-world court is that [she is] making the right thing happen at the end of the trial.[83]

---

[81] JL Hale and JP Dillard, 'A Staged Social Cognitive Approach to Message Design Fear Appeals in Health Promotion Campaigns' in EW Maibach and RL Parrott (eds), *Designing Health Messages: Approaches From Communication Theory and Public Health Practice* (Thousand Oaks, CA, Sage, 1995) 78.

[82] *Judge Judy* (Big Ticket Productions, CBS Distribution, 12 February 2010).

[83] J Dempsey, '*Judge Judy* on a Roll: Syndication Star Sentenced to Two More Years' *Variety* (15 February 2008), available at www.variety.com/index.asp?layout=print_story&articleid=VR1117981008&categoryid=2522.

Thus, to convince viewers of the validity of her verdicts, she explicitly states the conclusions upon which they are based, as evidenced in the case of *Reynard v Rinker*:

> There is an actual dispute over rent and then there is vindictiveness and venality, and you crossed the line, Ms. Rinker. If she made a mistake and thought that she was supposed to give you notice, that's a mistake. But when you cross the line into the parameters of somebody else's safety because you are being vicious, that's something that courts won't tolerate. I certainly won't tolerate it.[84]

Finally, active participation results in greater attitude change than the passive reception of information. So, to encourage viewers to think about the ramifications of their actions, and those of the litigants, Sheindlin offers viewers lessons in life and in law on her website. To demonstrate, let us consider the following family adage:

> One of my grandmother's favorite expressions was ten times measure, one time cut. In plain parlance that means, before you make a decision that could be life altering like signing on to cosign a debt for somebody that you hardly know, giving somebody to use your car that you hardly know, giving some guy that you met last Tuesday a credit card or cell phone with the bill in your name, or worse, think about the consequences. Think about all of the consequences. Think about the fact if you take a piece of cloth, and you don't measure what you need and you cut it, it is very hard to put it back again. Ten times measure, one time cut.[85]

Thus, as the clip outlines the types of disputes *Judge Judy* customarily showcases, Sheindlin expects these words of wisdom to not only influence the viewer in his or her decision making, but also allow the viewer to evaluate the proceedings as well as Sheindlin's credibility for accuracy and honesty.

VII. Conclusion: The Medium is the Message

9 May 2012 marked the 815th consecutive week in which *Judge Judy* was ranked as television's top-rated, courtroom-themed, reality-based series. Its success is predicated on the paucity of

> moral conundrums or technical wrinkles. [Viewers] love Sheindlin's show because she offers them a fantasy of how they would like the justice system to operate—swiftly, and without procedural mishaps or uppity lawyers. They get to see wrongdoers publicly humiliated by a strong authority figure. There is no uncertainty after Sheindlin renders her verdict and bounds off the bench, and there are certainly no lengthy appeals.[86]

Still, as Erickson points out,

> in light of the enduring popularity of the series, it is difficult to remember that *Judge Judy* was not regarded as a sure-fire success when it first came out. Many of the major local stations took a pass on the property, writing off Sheindlin as an unknown and the court-show format as passé. So, Big Ticket Productions all but gave the show away, cutting prices to the

---

[84] *Judge Judy* (Big Ticket Productions, CBS Distribution, 2 May 2010).
[85] CBS Studios, '*Judge Judy*—Judy's Tips', available at www.judgejudy.com/judys_tips.php.
[86] BI Koerner, '*Judge Judy*: The Most-Watched Court Show for 452 Straight Weeks' (27 May 2005), available at www.slate.com/id/2118556.

bone while retaining only three 30-second ad slots in each episode, and shipping it to second-echelon stations in smaller markets.[87]

The problem, in Sheindlin's view, was that 'the seat was not [hers] yet'.[88] However, the fact is that both Sheindlin and her producers had yet to learn the conventions of the medium and to successfully implement the elements discussed herein. Thus, whereas the distributors of *Judge Judy* are selling Sheindlin's unique sense of sight and hearing as well as her unparalleled ability to reach instant verdicts, the viewers are buying into the notion that they too have the requisite qualities and legal prowess to someday appear on the show to seek monetary compensation and emotional vindication.

[87] H Erickson, *Encyclopedia of Television Law Shows* (n 55) 140–41.
[88] Judith Sheindlin, interview by Stephen J Abramson (n 1).

14

Reality TV and the Entrapment of Predators

MARK TUNICK

I. Introduction: *'To Catch a Predator'*

Dateline NBC's *To Catch a Predator*, which aired from 2004 to 2008, was a reality TV programme in which NBC staff worked with police and a watchdog group of private citizens called 'Perverted Justice' (PJ) in order to televise arrests of men who were lured by the prospect of having sex with a minor. A typical episode worked like this: a member of PJ, collaborating with NBC, poses as a 14-year-old girl in an online chat room and engages in a lurid exchange with a 40-year-old man, eventually inviting him to Dateline NBC's 'undercover house', which is wired with hidden cameras. The man shows up at the house and after he briefly talks with a 19-year-old actress posing as the 14-year-old girl, Dateline Correspondent Chris Hansen enters and asks his squirming target a series of questions: 'What are you doing here?' 'Who did you come to see?' 'How old is she?' 'How old are you?' 'Why did you bring condoms and lotion?' 'Do you think it's appropriate that you're here?' If the man reveals he has his own children, Hansen will ask, 'How would you feel if it was your 14 year old daughter home alone?' After this exchange, people with hand-held cameras enter, at which point Hansen reveals that he is a correspondent for Dateline. The sting target tries to exit. The police, waiting outside in ambuscade, rush at him shouting, guns pointed, and push him to the ground and cuff him. Viewers then see video clips of an ensuing police interrogation of the suspect, who is charged with attempting to engage in sex with a minor.

To Catch a Predator continually found ways to maintain audience interest.[1] At first there was no police presence. In series I, many of the men just walked out, their only punishment being Hansen's chastisement ('Clearly this man knows he's done

---

[1] NBC broadcast 12 sting operations, which I cite as: I (Long Island, NY, aired Nov 2004), II (Herndon, Virg, Nov 2005), III (Riverside, CA, Feb 2006), IV (Ohio, April/May 2006), V (Ft Myers, FL, May 2006), VI (Fortson, GA, Sept 2006), VII (Petaluma, CA, Sept–Oct, 2006), VIII (Long Beach, CA, Jan–Feb 2007), IX (Murphy, TX, Feb 2007), X (Flagler Beach, FL, Feb–March 2007), XI (Ocean County, NJ, July 2007), XII (Bowling Green, KY, Jan 2008).

something wrong'), although PJ did turn online chat dialog over to the police, which in some cases pursued misdemeanour charges for engaging in sexual dialogue online with someone thought to be underage. The third series began by Hansen observing that NBC received numerous inquiries from audience members who wondered why these men were able to walk away. Apparently in response to viewer demand, the sting targets were now arrested by the police on film as they attempted to leave the under-cover house. With police involved, prosecutors could pursue more serious charges because showing up at the house with the intent to have sex with someone believed to be a minor is a felony.

Series IV shifted to a small town in Ohio, to demonstrate that predators lurk even in rural America. For the first time we saw video of the courtroom arraignments, and arrestees in striped jail suits. For series five, in Ft Myers, Florida, police now tackled the suspects violently when they left the sting house; Hansen explained that in Florida the police needed to be proactive because it is legal to have a concealed weapon. Police violence escalated further in series VIII, in which a taser gun was used on one man who 'didn't respond fast enough'. The arrests on *To Catch a Predator* were more likely to be of high intensity, not because the suspect was potentially violent or likely to evade police, but because the cameras were rolling, and shouting and gun-wielding police add to the humiliation and make for good ratings. As the show progressed, the decoys got younger. In series VIII, one 'girl' said she was only 11, although a study of internet sex-crimes revealed that no reported victim was under the age of 12.[2] Another innovation, begun in series VII, was that the decoy spoke with the sting target in person before Hansen appeared. In the earlier shows, the decoy would typically shout from another room as the target entered the house, and before they could meet, Hansen would arrive on scene. NBC played on the increased tension the audience felt in observing the suspect and decoy together, especially in series XI, where the man and the decoy would be alone on a beach with Hansen nowhere in sight—although he assured us that he and police were nearby.

Crime-based reality TV series tend to promote a law and order ideology.[3] Their message is that bad people permeate society and the police are catching them. *To Catch a Predator* in particular portrays a society teeming with child predators, many of whom are people we would never suspect.[4] Like other crime-related reality TV pro-grammes, *To Catch a Predator* arguably overstates the crime threat.[5] Internet-initiated statutory rape offences are relatively infrequent, offenders are rarely violent, and one

---

[2] See Janis Wolak, et al, 'Online "Predators" and their Victims' (2008) *American Psychologist* 63(2) 115.

[3] Cf Aaron Doyle, 'Cops: Television Policing as Policing Reality' in Mark Fishman and Gray Cavender (eds) *Entertaining Crime: Television Reality Programs* (New York, Aldine de Gruyter, 1998).

[4] Hansen labels one section of his book 'An Epidemic?' (7); and emphasises how NBC was 'besieged' by predators showing up at its sting house (23). Chris Hansen, *To Catch a Predator* (New York, Penguin, 2008).

[5] Barry Blasser, *The Culture of Fear* (New York, Basic Books, 1999) 32, 35, 39–40; Vanessa Grigoriados, 'The New American Witch Hunt' (2007) *Rolling Stone* 1032, 64–71; Douglas McCollam, 'The Shame Game' (2007) *Columbia Journalism Review* 28–33; Steven Kohm, 'Naming, Shaming, and Criminal Justice: Mass-Mediated Humiliation as Entertainment and Punishment' (2009) *Crime, Media, Culture* 5(2), 188–205. Some studies suggest that those exposed to reality-based police programmes overestimate the prevalence of crime—Mary Beth Oliver and G Blake Armstrong, 'The Color of Crime' in Fishman and Cavender (eds) (n 3) 30.

study reported that more men were arrested for soliciting online sex in undercover sting operations than for soliciting actual youths.[6] Although his goal is to convince us that children face a grave threat from strangers prowling online, Hansen, in his book about the show, cannot conceal evidence to the contrary. One person he quotes concedes that 'Your child has an almost zero percent chance of being harmed by anyone on the Internet.' In fact, in most cases of child molestation, the abuse is committed by family members.[7]

Feeding on a fear that it helped stir, the show's strangely captivating character made it among Dateline NBC's highest rated programmes.[8] One reason the show was popular was its voyeuristic appeal: the audience can witness the hidden depravities of outwardly respectable people: teachers, doctors, a district attorney, a rabbi. Viewers get to see them caught red-handed, and then partake in their punishment by bearing witness to their shame. More perversely (and hypocritically for a show taking the moral high ground by shaming men for succumbing to their sexual fantasies), To Catch a Predator dwells on racy, titillating details of their sexual desires and deviancies, appealing to the prurient interests of the viewing audience. Hansen reveals to his national audience that a 28-year-old man chatted online with a decoy about sex acts with a dog (II), relates to us another's online boast about the size of his genitals (VII), and tells us that one man likes to suck on toes (VIII). In videotapes of police interrogations, viewers learn that one arrestee, a married man, has had sex with other men (III), that another uses Viagra (III), and, another, a penis pump (VII). We see police ask an arrestee, 'Do you wear condoms when you have sex with your wife?' (IV), and 'Do you masturbate while you (chat with 13 year olds)?'(IV).

The entertainment value of the show comes at a price. One sting target, Texas Assistant District Attorney Louis Conradt, shot himself as a SWAT team entered his home. He had declined his chat room decoy's invitation to go to an undercover house, so police came to him, at Hansen's urging, and he could not live with the humiliation of an on-air exposure of his depravities. Conradt's sister and his estate brought a lawsuit against NBC, seeking $100 million in damages. After a federal district court judge ruled that a reasonable jury could find that NBC acted outrageously, created a substantial risk of suicide, and that there was no legitimate law enforcement need for a heavily armed SWAT team to enter Conradt's home, the case was settled under undisclosed terms, and the show ended shortly thereafter.[9] But many of its episodes remain viewable online; and the premise of baiting criminals has been copied by other shows such as Tru-TV's Bait-Car, in which people are enticed to steal an unlocked car with keys in the ignition, while cameras hidden in the car allow the crime to be publicly aired.[10]

---

[6] Wolak et al., 'Online "Predators" and their Victims' (n 2) 114–15, 119.

[7] Hansen, To Catch a Predator (n 4) 119; cf 6, 193–4.

[8] Brian Stelter, '"To Catch a Predator" is Falling Prey to Advertisers' Sensibilities' New York Times, 27 Aug 2007.

[9] Conradt v NBC Universal 536 F. Supp. 2d 380 (2008); 'NBC Resolves Lawsuit Over "To Catch a Predator" Suicide', Los Angeles Times, 24 June 2008, available at http://latimesblogs.latimes.com/showtracker/2008/06/nbc-resolves-la.html [accessed 26 Mar 2010].

[10] See www.trutv.com/video/bait-car/index.html [accessed 2 June 2011].

To Catch a Predator differs from most other reality-TV programmes, where the programme's subjects want to be on the air. It differs even from most reality-TV crime shows. It is not a ride-along show in which cameras merely accompany the police, as in *COPS*; nor does it re-enact past crimes, as does *America's Most Wanted*. Nor, like *COPS*, does it digitise the faces of those appearing on camera who decline to sign a release form.[11] It is helpful to compare *To Catch a Predator* with A&E's *Investigative Report: Cybersex Cops* (1996). The A&E show used surveillance camera footage and cameras following law enforcement agents as they investigated a crime. The faces of suspects whose cases were still pending were blurred. Where a child predator's face was shown undistorted, the man had been convicted and his face had already appeared in the newspapers following his arrest. *To Catch a Predator*, in contrast, does not show past crimes, or crimes that the police happen upon by chance or are dispatched to. Rather, it entices people to commit a crime which it then captures on air, and it has no interest in blurring the faces of the predators it shows. Hansen makes this clear when, in his book, he relates a story about the episode that ensnared a rabbi. The rabbi was upset and berated the producer, writes Hansen, 'as if we were the cause of all his trouble'. NBC offered to let the rabbi tell his side of the story and he said he'd agree only if NBC promised to obscure his face, not mention he was a rabbi, and not use the video of him being confronted by Hansen. Hansen replied, 'These were obviously conditions we couldn't comply with.'[12] 'Could not' here means 'were unwilling to' because obscuring a predator's face would detract from what makes the show such compelling TV—the public shaming of an outwardly respectable but deviant person.

To Catch a Predator engenders conflicting responses: Did NBC act as a news provider and fulfill a public service by informing the public about a real danger and deterring potential predators? Or did it take advantage of human weakness by entrapping and then inappropriately shaming and humiliating men before they could be properly tried and convicted in a court of law, all to entertain and garner ratings? Because the show captures people widely regarded as among the most abhorrent and threatening, it might be seen as a force for justice.[13] I shall argue, rather, that the 'justice' it metes out is perverse. My argument has three parts: Dateline-NBC usurps the authority of the state as the exclusive instrument of punishment (section II); it inappropriately bears the First Amendment shield of the press to publicise private facts, disguising entertainment as news, and in doing so it hypocritically appeals to the very prurient interests it seeks to condemn by dwelling repeatedly on men's sexual fantasies and desires (section III); and it uses promiscuous decoys to evoke these fantasies and desires, luring and entrapping people rather than meting out justice (section IV).

---

[11] Doyle, 'Cops: Television Policing as Policing Reality' (n 3) 96.

[12] Hansen, *To Catch a Predator* (n 4) 27.

[13] See Bridget Boggess, 'Attempted Enticement of a Minor: No Place for Pedophiles to Hide Under 18 U.S.C. Sec. 2422(B)' (2007) 72 *Mo L Rev* 909 and Hansen, *To Catch a Predator* (n 4).

II. Public Shaming and Punishment

Perhaps the most striking feature of *To Catch a Predator* is how it shames and humiliates those it lures.[14] When Hansen finally reveals that he is a reporter who is interviewing the sting target for a national television broadcast, the revelation can be traumatic. One man was put into diabetic shock and carted off to a hospital (V); another had an asthma attack (V); and another man became ill and collapsed (XI). One man said he wanted to kill himself, and tried to use a pen as a shiv in a half-hearted attempt (IV). Conradt did kill himself (IX). Lest we feel remorse for sting targets whose unbearable pain is exposed, Hansen reminds us of what they were planning to do. For example, he tells us 'this is the same man who chatted online for more than 3 weeks' to a girl he thought was 14 (VI). Much of Hansen's dialogue with his sting targets is intended not to provide newsworthy information about the dangers of internet predators, but to shame them. Hansen asks, 'What made [having sex with a 13 year old girl] tempting for you? (VI)'; You ask [online] if she can do a "deep throat". Explain that to me' (VI). Hansen succeeded at shaming one of his sting targets when the target pleaded, 'Can I just go to jail, sir? You guys win'. But Hansen was not satisfied and continued reading lewd chat room dialog for his national audience (VII). Hansen humiliates his targets, sometimes by making fun of them for reasons other than their moral failings. Hansen noted how it took one sting target 'extra time to get on a stool because he's five feet tall' (IV). Another sting target said 'I don't want to be on the news, dawg'; Hansen replied, 'Well it's a little late for that, dawg!' (V) In another segment, a man told Hansen about how he had once met a woman who turned out to be a transvestite. Hansen interjected, '[so she] had a little Adam's apple thing going on? How'd that work out for ya?' (VIII).

This public shaming and humiliation is particularly troubling because it is inflicted by someone who falsely passes himself off as having the authority to judge and punish. Hansen notes that the sting targets 'think I'm a cop' (IV); 'he has no idea if I'm the father or the police. He has no idea he's on film' (V). Hansen takes advantage of this deception by acting as if he has authority. While Hansen sometimes tells the sting target he is free to leave at any time (although he says this with a smirk, knowing that police lie in wait outside), he often takes an authoritative tone, saying such things as 'I'm not finished asking questions yet' (V). He frequently barks orders we would expect to hear from the police but not a journalist: 'Keep your hands out of your pocket for me' (III, VII); 'I need you to sit down' (III); or 'I want to see what's in your pocket' (III). Hansen even revels in his position of pseudo-authority, boasting on one occasion that he made one sting target so nervous the man sweated and had to take his jacket off (V).

---

[14] *Cf* Steven Kohm, 'Naming, Shaming, and Criminal Justice: Mass-Mediated Humiliation as Entertainment and Punishment' (2009) *Crime, Media, Culture* 5(2), 188–205. Kohm characterises *To Catch a Predator* broadcasts as shaming punishment. See also Robert Lissit, 'Gotcha' (1995) *American Journalism Review* 17(2), 16–22, quoting Neville Johnson concerning an ABC Prime Time Live show: 'Imagine being scourged and whipped in front of 24 million people. You're tried, convicted, sentenced and buried at sea, with no right of appeal.'

At times Hansen acts like a prosecutor, confronting his suspect with evidence proving his guilt. Hansen's stock charge is that sting targets came to the home to have sex with someone they thought was underage, and he frequently produces transcripts of the online chat to prove they were told the decoy was a child. For example, one man said 'I was here to look at real estate. I thought she was 18'. Hansen replies: 'come clean', and then reads from the transcript: 'she tells you she was 12. So 18 was a lie' (II). Some of these men try to defend themselves by saying they didn't believe the decoy was really that age. Most of the men themselves lied about their own age, and several claimed that they used chat rooms in order to role-play. They might have assumed that no one was being entirely truthful. But Hansen ignores this and on at least one occasion browbeats his interrogee:

Sting target: 'She said she was 13, but…'

Hansen interrupts him: 'She said she was 13. And how old are you?' (VII)[15]

In addition to police officer and prosecutor, Hansen sometimes plays the judge who will mete out retribution. On one occasion Hansen says, 'He's not going to get off so easy. It's time to tell him who I am' (V). On another, Hansen, after reading a chat transcript, asks a man, incredulously, 'You were gonna make a 14 year old perform a sex act on a cat?' The man laughs, and Hansen responds like a disciplining authority, 'So it's funny?' (V).

Hansen's deception works: the sting targets believe he is in authority. Some targets invite Hansen to search them to prove they didn't bring condoms (I). It is striking how consistently they deferentially call him 'Sir'. Many apologise to him. One man says 'Thank you for kicking me in the pants and setting me straight, Chris …' (V).

The men snared on *To Catch a Predator*, while publicly shamed and humiliated, were not always punished legally. Fewer than half of 256 arrestees were convicted; most had no prior arrests, or even traffic citations, although they are now registered as sex offenders.[16] In its series in Murphy, Texas which included the Conradt incident, 23 men were arrested, but no indictments were pursued.[17] Many *To Catch a Predator* targets who were convicted for attempted lewd or lascivious behaviour with a child received as little as probation or a few months in jail, a far cry from the sentence of 12 years in prison that a man recently received for meeting an actual 14-year-old girl for sex.[18]

However, while *To Catch a Predator* does not (because it cannot) punish legally, it judges its targets and *in effect* punishes them by publicly shaming them and airing their sexual fantasies and behaviour. *To Catch a Predator* aims to fulfill the primary

---

[15] On another occasion, a sting target tries to explain that the online exchanges were fantasy and Hansen retreats from the moral high ground and just says, 'but it is illegal' (IV).

[16] Brian Stelter, '"To Catch a Predator" is Falling Prey to Advertisers' Sensibilities' *New York Times*, 27 Aug 2007.

[17] Luke Dittrich, 'Tonight on Dateline this Man Will Die' (2007) *Esquire* 148(3), 233–44.

[18] *Nguyen v State* 676 SE 2d 246 (2009). According to MSNBC's website, sentencing of 16 Ohio *To Catch a Predator* sting targets ranged from 30 days to 11 months; there were a few sentences of three years in Riverside, CA; the state's standard offer in Long Beach, CA was 18 months and many defendants received probation and no jail time, though they were required to register as sex offenders. Georgia was tougher, with sentences ranging from two to six years; and a rabbi received a federal sentence of six and a half years; see Chris Hansen, 'Reflections on "To Catch a Predator"', *Dateline NBC* (13 Mar 2007), available at www. msnbc.msn.com/id/17601568/ns/dateline_nbc/?page=4 [accessed 11 May 2010].

purposes of punishment by deterring potential predators—although it did not deter a few sting targets who said they had seen the show before; and by meting out retributive justice.[19] The punishment it metes out could mean loss of one's career, friends and family, and be far more devastating than a prison term.

Although the men *To Catch a Predator* exposes are deviant and deserve blame, and society needs to deter people from preying on children, there are good reasons to object to NBC's handling of its sting targets. Perhaps the most compelling is that only the state and no one else may legitimately punish lawbreakers. Punishment is hard treatment imposed by one with the authority to punish.[20] Only the state can administer legal punishment, just as only a child's parents can mete out parental punishment and only a teacher or school administrator can punish students. In all of these cases, the punisher is guided by formal and informal rules.[21] I can't punish someone else's children, even if I think they deserve it, because I lack authority over them.[22] Taking justice into your own hands is revenge, not punishment.[23]

One reason we reserve the power to punish to the state is that its agents must provide due process. They must ensure that the accused have the opportunity to explain and defend themselves at greater length than Chris Hansen affords in his brief interviews with his sting targets, the editing of which is under NBC's control.[24] NBC metaphorically prosecutes, judges and punishes its targets—accusing and making them defend themselves on air is punishment itself—before there is a trial with an impartial judge. Apart from instances of outrageous conduct intended to inflict emotional distress, it is normally not illegal for private parties to humiliate others, though in some circumstances doing so can be immoral. NBC exposes its sting targets to a peculiar form of hard treatment in the form of public humiliation, using media resources that far exceed what most private parties could muster. Even if NBC's actions did not rise to the level of tortious conduct, it acts irresponsibly by abusing the power accorded to it as a member of the free press. NBC uses its credentials as news provider, and collaborates with the police, in passing itself off as an instrument of public justice when in fact it is but a force of summary vengeance. Were the state to proceed in punishing the predators NBC exposes, it is not clear that it should humiliate and shame them even while exposing them as criminals.[25]

---

[19] See Mark Tunick, *Punishment: Theory and Practice* (Berkeley, CA, University of California Press, 1992).

[20] Joel Feinberg, 'Expressive Function of Punishment', (1965) *Monist* 49(3), 397–408.

[21] John Rawls, 'Two Concepts of Rules', (1955) *Philosophical Review* 64(1), 10; HLA Hart, *Punishment and Responsibility* (New York, Oxford University Press, 1968).

[22] Cf John Locke, *Second Treatise of Government*, edited by CB Macpherson (Indianapolis, Hackett, 1980) §74.

[23] Leo Zaibert disagrees and speaks of non-state or private punishment, see Leo Zaibert, *Punishment and Retribution* (Aldershot, UK, Ashgate, 2006) 17–18, 23–24, 29–42. According to his point of view, I can punish a friend who doesn't keep a secret, or an acquaintance who cheats at a game, and presumably a stranger's child who misbehaves. As long as I find someone blameworthy, I can punish them. Whereas others, including myself, regard the above examples as 'metaphorical' and distinct from legitimate punishment, Zaibert rejects that distinction. For Zaibert, retributive punishment is warranted because it is imposed upon those 'we find blameworthy'. The problem with his view is that not just anyone gets to decide who is blameworthy.

[24] Cf Grigoriadas, The New American Witch Hunt' (n 5).

[25] See Annabelle Lever, 'Mill and the Secret Ballot' (2007) *Utilitas* 19(3), 371 (arguing that 'public shame and humiliation threaten our ability to see and treat each other as equals').

The rush to judgement that we see in *To Catch a Predator* is endemic to reality TV crime shows that present only pieces of information about a person and the circumstances surrounding their arrest. One important reason why we protect a person's privacy is to avoid formation of judgements that are based on snippets of information taken out of context that lead people to falsely assess a person's character.[26] Anderson notes that shows like *COPS* relieve us 'of the burden of knowing what has come before, or what will come after'; 'there are no second-or third-person perspectives offered to provide a context for the action at hand'.[27] In the case of *To Catch a Predator*, we do not see unexpurgated transcripts of the online chat exchanges that lead up to the arrests.

This objection may ring hollow to some since the people captured by *To Catch a Predator* have demonstrated their guilt—they are caught red-handed; and the degree to which they deserve blame may seem magnified by the seriousness of their offence. One problem with this response is that private punishment is inappropriate regardless of the seriousness of the offence or guilt of the offender. The job of catching predators is not NBC's, but the state's. The state has a monopoly on the power to punish criminals and must adhere to rules in place to protect all citizens against potential abuses of this power. All of us are at risk if vigilantes, unconstrained by these rules, usurp this power. While NBC may claim it is no vigilante because it collaborates with the police, it metes out effective punishment (shaming) before the police enter the scene, by rolling the cameras as a predator approaches. The police are like mere actors in NBC's show.

III. Publication of Private Facts

Even if police were running the show, broadcasting to a national audience the events and dialog leading up to and following the sting targets' arrests is inappropriate. The magnitude of this publication is vast—the show reaches millions, and because it is archived on the web, it is likely to continue to be in the public view for generations. *To Catch a Predator* metes out such harsh metaphorical punishment because it so grossly violates privacy by widely publicising private facts.

NBC exposes a national audience to the inner struggles and demons within people that they most want to keep hidden. The sting targets do not want their behaviour to be broadcast. When the cameras finally appear, one pleads: 'Could you please turn the camera off?'[28] Catching them when they are in a state of shock and most vulnerable, Hansen gets many of these men to reveal their deepest inner thoughts, often unaware they are sharing these thoughts with a national viewing audience. Some men, for example, reveal how lonely they are (IV, XI). Hansen asks one apparently religious

---

[26] See Jeffrey Rosen, *The Unwanted Gaze* (New York, Random House, 2000).
[27] Robin Anderson, '"Reality" TV and Criminal Injustice' (1994) *The Humanist* 8; *cf* Gray Cavender, 'In Search of Community on Reality TV' in Su Holmes and Deborah Jermyn (eds), *Understanding Reality Television* (London, Routledge, 2004) 167.
[28] Hansen replied: 'I can't do that' (VII).

person to justify himself: 'I want you to square [your asking a young girl if she can do "deep throat"] with what's on your Myspace website where you talk about how "Jesus rocks!"' Hansen promises we'll learn more about this person's 'inner struggle' later on, a promise he keeps when we hear the man say he is still a virgin, confronting the conflict between his spirituality and his desire for sex with teenage girls (VI). In some cases NBC shines a spotlight on people with obvious psychological problems. The second series focuses on one man who showed up at the house naked and who attempted to meet another decoy the very next day. Hansen asks him on air: 'Why do you do it?'; he responds, 'I need help—that's why I'm seeing a psychologist'. As if to confirm the man's mental problems, NBC shows a close up of his untied shoe laces. We might wonder what business NBC has in exposing to the world the troubled mental state of people who are not public figures, just as we can wonder what business NBC has in punishing individuals.

NBC might defend itself by saying it is just bearing witness to behaviour that is of legitimate public interest and newsworthy. Hansen has defended *To Catch a Predator* by saying that because Dateline NBC is a 'news broadcast' and part of the news division, NBC may legally film people and use their names on TV without their consent.[29] These people have already committed a crime by talking about sex online to someone they believe is a minor, illegal in almost every state;[30] and their conduct is 'not only illegal, it is outrageous'.[31] Hansen and NBC might argue that the public has a legitimate interest in knowing about outrageous or criminal conduct, that the predators it captures on video cannot reasonably expect privacy in such activities, and that NBC, as part of the free press protected by the First Amendment, has a right, perhaps even a duty, to expose their dark secrets to the world. Does this defence succeed?

NBC could rightly broadcast the arrest of a public figure, or of someone accused of a notorious crime that has captured the public's attention and concern, such as gunning down a member of Congress. Showing such an arrest may put the public at ease. Public figures have reduced expectations of privacy, as do people who become newsworthy by thrusting themselves into the public eye.[32] But the people caught on *To Catch a Predator* are neither public figures nor accused of a notorious crime.

Today, however, the expectation of privacy even for non-public figures may be less than it once was, given the wide use of digital cameras to upload photos or video to websites such as Facebook and YouTube. By merely attending a public event one may forfeit an expectation of privacy against being broadcast, perhaps to the surprise of the overweight man who attends a major league baseball game and, in one of the close-ups of the crowd, is shown on TV eating a salad while the broadcasters comment with a chuckle that 'salad won't be enough for this guy'.[33] Courts have allowed such embarrassing broadcasts. CBS was permitted to broadcast a video clip of a man and woman holding hands in public, over their vehement protests, each being in relationships with

[29] Hansen, *To Catch a Predator* (n 4) 12.
[30] See, for example, Fla Stat Ann §847.0135 (2009): 'Any person who knowingly uses a computer online service ... to seduce, solicit, lure [a person] believed by the person to be a child ... to commit any illegal act' commits a felony of the third degree, punishable by up to 5 years in prison.
[31] Hansen, *To Catch a Predator* (n 4) 4–5.
[32] *Sipple v Chronicle Pub Co* 201 Cal. Rptr. 665 (1984); *Gertz v Robert Welch* 418 U.S. 323 (1974).
[33] Broadcast of Florida Marlins homegame on Fox Sports Florida in 2009 (date unknown).

other people; the court noted that the plaintiff could not refute the reality captured.[34] Even if you are indoors, courts have held, if you are in a public place where you cannot reasonably expect privacy and are engaged in a newsworthy activity, photos or video of you may be published or broadcast, with the proviso that you may have a cause of action for appropriation of your name or likeness if the publication is for commercial gain.[35] One might argue in NBC's defence that with the exception of Conradt, who was in his own home, its sting targets are not filmed in a place where they can reasonably expect privacy; and that their arrest is a public fact which one cannot keep private, any crime being newsworthy and of legitimate public interest.

We know from their shock at discovering they are on video that the men lured by *To Catch a Predator* did not expect or want to be on television. They expected privacy. They were not in a public place such as a stadium, gym, or bar. Conradt's suicide, like the suicide of Tyler Clementi, the college student whose roommate posted a video he secretly took of Tyler kissing another student in their dormitory room on the internet, illustrate just how devastating an unwanted intrusion upon privacy can be. In the coming years, the law will need to adapt to unprecedented technological advances that permit people's private affairs to be widely broadcast.[36] As it does develop, a strong case can be made that society should not regard it as legitimate to broadcast surreptitiously-recorded videos that deeply intrude upon one's privacy, whether or not the cameras 'catch a predator' in the act. The interest in fighting crime can be served by keeping such video evidence *in camera* and not broadcasting it to the world.

While it is true that crimes are newsworthy and arrests are often publicised,[37] suspects of non-notorious crimes who have yet to be convicted still retain some reasonable expectations of privacy. At least one court has hinted that broadcasting the arrest of such people may not be appropriate.[38] But *To Catch a Predator* does far more than merely publish a photo or broadcast a video of a person being brought to the stationhouse for booking. It details the moral failings of people who are not public figures, using deception to get them to give an account of themselves when they are most vulnerable. It then broadcasts this to the world without the individuals' consent. Even if their arrest were a public fact, their inner struggles are not.

Under the protection of the First Amendment, NBC may broadcast what is newsworthy, or of legitimate public concern. Some courts have defined what is newsworthy quite broadly to include any subject of public interest.[39] *Harper's Magazine* was permitted to publish a photo of a couple posing in Los Angeles' Farmer's Market for a story

---

[34] *DeGregorio v CBS* 473 N.Y.S. 2d 922, 926 (N.Y. Sup. Ct. 1984); *cf Sweenek v Pathe News* 16 F. Supp 746, 747–8 (E.D. N.Y. 1936) (permitting broadcast of women using a new gym apparatus to lose weight).

[35] Daniel Solove and Paul Schwartz, *Privacy and Media* (New York, Aspen, 2008) 206–07.

[36] Don Terry, 'Eavesdropping Laws Mean that Turning on an Audio Recorder Could Send You to Prison' *New York Times*, 22 Jan 2011 ('Our society is going through a technological transformation ... [T]ens of millions of Americans carry around a [d]evice in their pocket that has an audio-video capacity. Ten years ago, Americans weren't walking around with all these devices' (quoting lawyer Adam Schwartz)).

[37] Anyone arrested in Palm Beach County, Florida, for example, might see their mug shot appear online even though they have not yet been convicted, see *The Palm Beach Post News* (Florida), available at www.palmbeachpost.com/news/crime/ [accessed 11 May 2010]. *Cf Penwell v Taft Broadcasting* 469 N.E. 2d 1025 (1984) (permitting multiple broadcasts of a false arrest in a public bar).

[38] *Cf Lauro v Charles* 219 F. 3d 202, 213 (2002) (acknowledging while refusing to address the issue of whether a television broadcast of an arrest is appropriate).

[39] *Messenger v Gruner + Yahr Printing and Pub* 208 F. 3d 122 (2000).

about everyday people in love, as the publication served 'the function of entertainment as a matter of legitimate interest'.[40] But some courts have set limits to what counts as news. Publicising private facts about someone who is not a public figure can be a cause of legal action if they are published merely to satisfy the public's curiosity rather than to fulfill a legitimate public interest, or if the publication amounts to morbid and sensational prying into private lives for its own sake.[41] For example, privacy rights may be violated by the broadcast of a tape of a victim's sexual assault if the broadcast serves only sensational interests and is inessential to the news that a rape took place.[42] One court held that publishing the details of someone's private life, such as who they date or other gossip about their love life, even if true, violates privacy rights insofar as a person's romantic life 'is not a matter of public concern'.[43] Some courts have set limits to the publication even of public facts if they serve little purpose apart from satisfying the public's curiosity.[44]

Does *To Catch a Predator* serve a legitimate public interest as a provider of news, or does it merely satisfy the public's prurient curiosity and desire for entertainment?

Several reality TV crime programmes present themselves as news providers by using interviewers who describe themselves as correspondents. That status has been challenged by those who characterise these programmes as 'infotainment' rather than news, and point to the shows' use of subjective camera angles or tension-heightening music that a genuine news broadcast would not employ.[45] Notably, *To Catch a Predator* does not use such devices. It does use hidden cameras as part of its sting operation, a tactic Hansen defends by arguing that it is often 'the only way to capture a crime'.[46] While some journalists criticise the use of hidden cameras as unethical because they create mistrust,[47] most people seem to agree with Hansen that hidden cameras can be a legitimate tool for news providers. They have been fruitfully used to expose corruption or other illicit activities.[48]

---

[40] *Gill v Hearst Publishing Co* 253 P. 2d 441, 444 (Cal. 1953). *cf Meetze v Associated Press* 95 S.E. 2d 606 (S.C. 1956) (that a 12-year-old girl gave birth would 'naturally excite public interest' and so the identity of the woman and her 20-year-old husband could be published).

[41] See the cases discussed in Amy Gajda, 'Judging Journalism: The Turn toward Privacy and Judicial Regulation of the Press' (2009) 97 *Cal L Rev* 1066, 1081–86, 1104.

[42] *Doe v Luster*, Not Reported in Cal.Rptr.3d, 2007 WL 2120855 (Cal. App. 2 Dist. 2007). Compare with *Anderson v Blake*, Not Reported in F.Supp.2d, 2006 WL 314447 (W.D. Okla. 2006).

[43] *Benz v Washington Newspaper Publishing Co. and Bisney* 34 Media L. Rep. 2368 (D.C. 2006).

[44] In *Briscoe v Reader's Digest Association* 483 P. 2d 34, 39–40 (Cal. 1971), California's Supreme Court ruled that while facts about past crimes may always be published, names of past criminals who are rehabilitated should be kept private so that they can return to an anonymous life. *Gates v Discover Communications Inc,* 101 P. 3d 552, 560 (2005), largely undermined *Briscoe* by holding that in light of intervening opinions by the US Supreme Court, the media may air facts about a previous crime that were obtained from 'public official court records'.

[45] Fishman and Cavender (eds), *Entertaining Crime: Television Reality Programs* (n 3) 4, 10–12. *Cf* Gajda, 'Judging Journalism' (n 41) 1096.

[46] Hansen, *To Catch a Predator* (n 4) 3.

[47] See Cavender, 'In Search of Community on Reality TV' (n 27) 164–65; Ron Smith and H Eugene Goodwin, *Groping for Ethics in Journalism* (Iowa, Iowa State University Press, 1999) 221–23; Lissit, 'Gotcha' (n 14).

[48] *Desnick v ABC* 44 F. 3d 1345, 1355 (1995); Gajda, 'Judging Journalism' (n 41).

However, *To Catch a Predator* does not merely use hidden cameras to uncover criminal activity: it creates the specific crime.[49] The show may not create child predators, but it entices individuals to commit a felony. This distinguishes it from legitimate investigative journalism. When ABC's *Prime Time Live* secretly sent undercover producers into Food Lion stores to videotape unsafe food handling practices, they did not 'create a situation that would not have otherwise existed'.[50] In contrast, NBC does not merely report a story; it makes it. That casts doubt on Hansen's claim that *To Catch a Predator* is broadcasting news or simply portraying a reality that cannot be refuted. Arguably, it constitutes entrapment (see section IV).

To Catch a Predator purports to serve a legitimate news function by informing parents of the dangers awaiting their children on the internet.[51] On occasion the show offers advice to parents, such as noting the existence of software that monitors children's computers (I); and NBC might argue that only by broadcasting the predators entering a home and seducing someone they think is a minor, and showing the sorts of behaviour they may be capable of, can it convincingly and effectively demonstrate the real nature of the threat they pose and show that the problem is not remote or hypothetical.[52] Sometimes this account of the show's purpose may seem credible, as when we see a man bring a case of Smirnoff Vodka to a girl who presented herself as a young teen (III). Hansen asks: 'What would have happened if I wasn't here?' This is surely an important question but also a misleading one because if Hansen and NBC weren't there, the man would not be either. Not many children profess to be as sexually promiscuous as the decoys PJ uses to lure men like him to the undercover house.[53] These decoys are a far cry from the innocent children they are supposed to represent. One decoy, Samantha_gurl001, for example, tells her sting target that she got laid four months before (VIII). Another decoy tells her target, 'my mom is gone, and I'm 13 … and we can get naked' (VII). Hansen and NBC never once address the incoherence of their project: they invoke the fearful image of dangerous predators preying on innocent children, but employ decoys who act anything but innocent to reel in men.

To Catch a Predator's broadcasts of graphic sexual dialogue and staged arrests in which police brandish guns and tackle suspects for no legitimate law enforcement needs smacks more of entertainment rather than news meant to fulfill a legitimate public interest.[54] The show does not provide an objective assessment of an existing threat. In one case, Hansen tell us that some of the men *To Catch a Predator* exposed

---

[49] See Steven Kohm, 'Naming, Shaming, and Criminal Justice' (2009) *Crime, Media, Culture* 5(2), 195; Douglas McCollam, 'The Shame Game' (2007) *Columbia Journalism Review* 32, and s IV, below.

[50] *Food Lion v ABC* 964 F. Supp. 956, 964 (1997).

[51] Hansen says the '"real reason for the show" is "of course" to bring home the dangers …' (V); *cf* XII: the purpose of *To Catch a Predator* is to warn people about the dangers of predators.

[52] See Gajda, 'Judging Journalism' (n 41) 1090 and fn 310, citing Judge Posner in *Haynes v Alfred A. Knopf*, Inc, 8 F. 3d 1222 (7th Cir. 1993).

[53] See Janis Wolak, et.al, 'Online "Predators" and their Victims' (n 2) 116. Only 5% of youth report talking online to unknown people about sex.

[54] Luke Dittrich, 'Tonight on Dateline this Man will Die' (n 17); *cf* Deborah Jermyn, 'This is About Real People! Video Technologies, Actuality and Affect in the Television Crime Appeal' in Su Holmes and Deborah Jermyn (eds), *Understanding Reality Television* (London, Routledge, 2004) 71–90. Discussing *Crimewatch*, Jermyn argues that showing still images rather than film would suffice to reconstruct the crime for the audience, but notes one producer's view that 'it is fair to help people be entertained at the same time'. Ibid 83.

'have criminal histories that are frightening'—these potential predators, he says, had 'real victims'. One expects to hear that one of the men was convicted for a violent rape, perhaps even for murder. Instead, we hear that one man was convicted of stalking a woman, and another of manslaughter (III). Such men could be frightening, but we aren't told the circumstances of their crimes. Was the stalker a dangerous brute like Max Cody in *Cape Fear* or a husband in a contested divorce? Was the manslaughter conviction for a vicious assault or a hunting accident?

The show's purpose is not to objectively report about actual dangers;[55] it is to alarm, shock, shame, humiliate, and titillate. *To Catch a Predator* played clips in which it ensnared a rabbi and a member of the NYFD on multiple episodes (in I and II) not because parents need to be warned of the dangers of rabbis and firemen, but because it is shocking to see the moral depravities of people in such greatly respected roles. Revealing one man's foot fetish (IV), asking another man about his rape fantasies (VIII), and sharing that one target likes to be treated like a dog and a toilet (X) constitute egregious intrusions upon privacy. Dwelling on sexual acts that will make some audience members blush may titillate others. None of this is needed to warn parents about the dangers their children face on the internet.

Its ratings success demonstrates that *To Catch a Predator* broadcasts something people are interested in seeing. But '[i]nvading privacy because people are interested is the moral equivalent of stripping someone in public against their will'.[56] The public might be interested in seeing an adulterer get caught cheating, a wife learn that her husband is gay, or a job applicant's deceptive resume exposed. But just because this might be interesting does not mean it is newsworthy and would not justify reality shows such as *To Catch an Adulterer*, *To Catch a Homosexual*, or *To Catch a Liar*. That actual predators, unlike the cheat or liar or self-identifying homosexual, are likely to cause serious harm is an argument for pursuing them diligently with the full force of the law, but not for broadcasting a deviant person's private struggles with temptation.

Even if the fact that a crime took place is newsworthy, details about the crime may not be.[57] That a 7-year-old girl has been allegedly abused is newsworthy, but the identity of the particular child might not be.[58] A story about a coach who sexually abuses young athletes is newsworthy, but a photo of his Little League team may not be.[59] NBC could have satisfied the legitimate public interest of alerting the public to a general threat of child predators without identifying the men it ensnares.[60] If they were found guilty, their names will be publicly available in court records and broadly accessible, and they might serve a jail or prison term. They will register as sex offenders and police and residents of their neighbourhood will be notified. NBC had the ability

---

[55] Dangers surely exist, but some studies indicate that men using the internet to have sex with minors are rarely violent. Wolak et al, 'Online "Predators" and their Victims' (n 2) 119.

[56] Karen Sanders, *Ethics and Journalism* (London, Sage, 2003) 90.

[57] *Briscoe v Reader's Digest Association, Inc* 483 P.2d 34, 38, n.7 (Cal. 1971). *Cf* Elizabeth Pater-Simpson, 'Private Circles and Public Squares: Invasion of Privacy by the Publication of "Private Facts"' (1998) *Modern Law Review* 61(3), 318–40.

[58] *Foretich v Lifetime Cable* 777 F. Supp. 47 (1991).

[59] *MG v Time Warner* 107 Cal. Rptr. 2d 504 (2001), cited in Gajda, 'Judging Journalism' (n 41) 1075.

[60] One might think that criminal suspects deserve less privacy than victims do, but that would fly in the face of a cherished principle that people accused of crime still have rights.

to blur faces and protect individuals' identities.[61] The only reason it does not is to maximise the voyeuristic appeal and entertainment value of the show by humiliating someone. Showing the face of the rabbi who enters NBC's undercover house and identifying him might promote deterrence and retribution; but those functions are reserved to the state and not NBC. No legitimate news purpose is served by graphically describing the sting targets' sexual fantasies and idiosyncrasies and pointing out their use of Viagra or penis pumps.

IV. Entrapment

To Catch a Predator does not passively capture newsworthy images it finds in a public place. While much news reporting involves some ferreting out of facts that goes beyond mere passive discovery, *To Catch a Predator* does not merely report on crime with a healthy aggressiveness: it creates the conditions that result in the crime. That makes it problematic for NBC to shield itself from privacy tort claims by arguing that it is a news provider. It also casts doubt on whether the public shame, humiliation, and hard treatment NBC metes out, while punishment only metaphorically, is in any case just.

Some crimes are hard to detect, especially when there is no victim or witness to the crime, as may be the case with consensual sex offences. To catch the criminal in these cases police may need to use deception, by going undercover. In offering enticements to expose criminals, the police risk convincing a normally law-abiding person to commit a crime that they would not have otherwise committed. If that happens, enticement may become entrapment: rather than catch a true criminal, the police make someone a criminal.

If I commit a crime by taking advantage of an opportunity wholly created by the police but it is an opportunity I could readily have been presented with in my encounters with ordinary citizens without any involvement by the police, it is reasonable to conclude that I was predisposed to commit the crime and am therefore a true criminal who deserves to be punished. However, if the police do more, offering me inducements I would not otherwise receive, I may not be a true criminal deserving of punishment.[62] (If a man is enticed to commit a sex offence by an actual 14-year-old girl, no matter how persistent she is, he has no excuse as there is no private entrapment defence. However, although NBC and the members of PJ are not state actors, because they collaborate with the police the distinction between private and state entrapment dissolves.)[63] Many courts decide whether a defendant was entrapped simply by asking whether the defendant was predisposed, looking at, for example, their past criminal

---

[61] In one segment, a man comes to the sting house with his little boy, and NBC blurs the boy's face (but not the father's) (V).

[62] *Cf* Richard McAdams, 'Political Economy of Entrapment' (2005) *Journal of Criminal Law and Criminology* 96(1), 126–29.

[63] See *US v Morris* 549 F. 3d 548 (7th Cir. 2008); and Mark Tunick, 'Entrapment and Retributive Theory' in Mark White (ed), *Retributivism: Essays on Theory and Policy* (New York, Oxford University Press, 2011) 171–91, 176–77.

record.[64] But some courts also look at the means used to entice the defendant. If the police were so persistent as to risk luring an ordinarily law-abiding citizen, a defendant could still be entrapped even if he was predisposed.[65]

It may be appropriate for the police to target people who they have reasonable cause to suspect are true criminals, in order to secure sufficient evidence to convict them, but doing that is not the same as testing the susceptibility of ordinary people to the lure of ill-gotten gains. In an early entrapment case, Judge Marston of the Michigan Supreme Court offers a reason why doing the latter is troubling:

> Human nature is frail enough at best, and requires no encouragement in wrong-doing. If we cannot assist another and prevent him from violating the laws of the land, we at least should abstain from any active efforts in the way of leading him into temptation.[66]

To Catch a Predator tests the virtue of people who may not be predisposed to crime. The police and NBC do not passively observe someone who they reasonably suspect is a criminal based on prior record or witness accounts. Rather, they lure targets in chat rooms, using promiscuous decoys to create opportunities the sting target is unlikely to encounter otherwise.

Hansen defends *To Catch a Predator* against the charge that it entraps by claiming that the PJ decoys 'never make the first contact'—the potential predator does.[67] The predator sees a profile set up by a PJ decoy with a picture of an underage teen, and sends an instant message.[68] It is certainly true that NBC and PJ do not pick out people randomly: their targets come to them in the online chat room, and one might argue that this conduct itself constitutes reasonable suspicion that the person is up to no good.

'First contact', however, can be misleading. On at least one occasion we see that PJ used a Craigslist ad that said, 'Boy looking for friends', which seems like an invitation or offer (VII). Even though the sting targets may make first contact in the online chat room, unlike true predators they may be merely curious, and reluctant to turn their fantasy into reality. The decoys can be aggressive in getting them to make that transition.[69] We may not know how aggressive they were. There is reason to be skeptical of the transcripts of PJ's online conversations with sting targets that NBC makes public: one of NBC's producers accused PJ of providing incomplete transcripts and was subsequently fired.[70] But the show provides some evidence that the sting targets were lured with considerable persistence. One encounter escalates from chat room

---

[64] See *Sorrells v US,* 287 U.S. 435 (1932); *Hampton v US* 425 U.S. 484 (1976). This is called the 'subjective test'.

[65] This is called an 'objective test'; see *State v Kummer* 481 N.W. 2d 437 (N.D. 1992). See generally Paul Marcus, *The Entrapment Defense,* 3rd edn (Newark, NJ, Lexis-Nexis, 2002).

[66] *Saunders v People* 38 Mich. 218 (1878).

[67] Hansen, 'To Catch a Predator' (n 4) 5. In *To Catch a Predator* (I), Katie Couric asks Hansen, 'you didn't make the first move?' Hansen replies, 'No, they entered the chatroom'.

[68] Ibid 21.

[69] On the aggressiveness of PJ decoys, see Douglas McCollam, 'The Shame Game' (2007) *Columbia Journalism Review* 31; Brian Montopoli, 'Does "Dateline" Go Too Far "To Catch A Predator?"' *CBS News Online* (7 Feb 2006), available at www.cbsnews.com/8301-500486_162-1290135-500486. html?tag=mncol;lst;1; Vanessa Grigoriados, 'The New American Witch Hunt' (2007) *Rolling Stone* 1032.

[70] *Bartel v NBC Universal, Inc* 543 F. 3d 901, 903 (7th Cir. 2008). The producer sued for breach of contract. While not challenging her account of the facts as true, the US Court of Appeals affirmed the dismissal of her claim since her contract contained no restrictions on allowable reasons for firing.

exchange to phone conversation at the suggestion not of the target but of the decoy (II). Another decoy senses that her target is having a change of heart and so she tries to keep him interested in her by saying 'I'm so bored' (IV). A cancer doctor who was publicly shamed on air when he showed up to meet a young girl said: 'she asked to meet me on several occasions. I declined. And today she asked (again)' (VII). One target says, 'She was the one who started' the talking about sex (VII). And the oldest sting target, a 60-year-old man, tried to walk away from the decoy, but she said, 'Come on, it's okay' (XI). Conradt in particular was lured with unusual perseverance.[71]

The US Supreme Court supported an entrapment defence for a man who was targeted by undercover government agents in a sting operation to catch purchasers of pornography that showed nude boys engaged in sex. The defendant, Jacobson, became a person of interest after he ordered magazines with pictures of nude pre-teens which, at the time, were legal since the law only prohibited pictures showing boys actually having sex. Over a two-year period the government encouraged Jacobson to buy illegal pornography. Jacobson eventually succumbed, and was arrested. A majority of the Court held that while the defendant had certain 'generalized inclinations', that itself did not establish a predisposition to commit a crime. The idea of committing a crime was implanted in Jacobson by the government.[72] Many of To Catch a Predator's targets have generalised inclinations; but before they actually meet an underage teen for sex they may, like Jacobson, have to be coaxed. To know for sure if this is the case, we would need to see the complete online exchange.

By definition, predators do not need to be lured; they actively seek out their prey. They are 'true criminals' but difficult to catch. When police are aware that someone is attacking runners in a park, they may set up a decoy target with the hope of catching the attacker. If they succeed, they will have nabbed a true criminal. Their use of an inducement—a potential victim—does not constitute entrapment as they are not implanting the idea to commit a crime into a susceptible person's mind; rather, the police are using a strategy of surveillance to detect a crime they do not create.[73] To Catch a Predator's sting targets, in contrast, may not be true criminals. They may be susceptible, as Mr Jacobson was, but the idea of meeting a minor for sex may, nevertheless, have been implanted in them by PJ decoys. The operations of NBC and PJ are more analogous to an undercover agent's offering of drugs to a man undergoing treatment for drug addiction, knowing he has a weak trigger. Courts have held that to be entrapment.[74] That the entrapped target ensnared by To Catch a Predator is tempted to commit an act of a kind that can cause great harm, whereas the entrapped drug offender commits a self-regarding act that may cause no harm, does not necessarily matter in deciding if a defendant deserves punishment. A child predator may be worse than a drug user, but a false criminal induced to attempt to have sex with a minor is no more a criminal than a false criminal induced to commit a drug offence; both may be equally entitled to a defence of entrapment.[75]

---

[71] Dittrich, 'Tonight on Dateline this Man Will Die' (n 17).

[72] *Jacobson v US* 503 U.S. 540 (1992).

[73] See Tunick, 'Entrapment and Retributive Theory' (n 63).

[74] *Sherman v US* 356 U.S. 369 (1958); *cf State v Lively* 921 P.2d 1035 (Wash. 1996).

[75] In s II, I made a similar point: private punishment is inappropriate regardless of the seriousness of the offence.

Whether a legal defence of entrapment would succeed for a defendant caught in a *To Catch a Predator* sting may hinge on the extent to which the defendant was predisposed to having sex with a minor before contacting PJ's decoy. Even if an entrapment defence could not be made in particular cases, NBC's methods distinguish its show from a legitimate news broadcast and makes the justice it metes out suspect.

V. Conclusion

To Catch a Predator targets are not sympathetic. They attempt to have sex with a child whom they think is a minor. It is no defence that the defendants were mistaken about the decoy's age—only their intent matters.[76] And the fact that they fail to complete the crime is irrelevant because most laws punish individuals who make a substantial step towards commission of the crime.[77] Although children would most likely not be as sexually promiscuous as the decoys NBC employs, there are actual children who respond to online advances of adult strangers. They are often troubled, depressed, and may have suffered previous sexual abuse.[78] The men who manipulate them for their own sexual gratification deserve to be blamed. But it is the state and not NBC that is the proper institution to blame them and, in our society, shaming a person on national television should not be a permissible means of expressing blame.

To Catch a Predator seduces its viewers with the immediate gratification of seeing a perverted crime followed by an arrest, conviction, and punishment all in the span of minutes. The viewers themselves become the punishers by bearing witness to the sting target's shame and humiliation. The show itself is a perverted enterprise in disguising entertainment as justice. Hansen and his crew deceptively present themselves as agents of the law and instruments of justice but fail to afford any of the due process protections essential to a system that provides genuine justice. They use sexually promiscuous decoys to lure men with inducements they are unlikely to encounter otherwise. They take the moral high ground by shaming these men for succumbing to their sexual fantasies while parading the lascivious details of their sexual deviancies, and don the First Amendment armour of 'news media' to do so, even though broadcasting deeply private details about people who are not public figures serves no legitimate news purpose and merely entertains.[79]

---

[76] *US v Morris* 549 F. 3d 548 (7th Cir. 2008) 550, citing *US v Cote* 504 F. 3d 682 (7th Cir. 2007); *cf US v Helder* 452 F.3d 751 (8th Cir. 2006).

[77] *State v D Stephens-Tun* 2008 WL 2698639 (Ohio App. 2 Dist. 2008), but see Bridget Boggess, 'Attempted Enticement of a Minor: No Place for Pedophiles to Hide under 18 U.S.C. Sec. 2422(B)' (2007) 72 *Mo L Rev* 909.

[78] Wolak et al, 'Online "Predators" and their Victims' (n 2) 116–17 and studies cited therein.

[79] I thank Alan Gray and this volume's editors and anonymous reviewers for their helpful feedback.

References

Books and Journals

Anderson, R, '"Reality" TV and Criminal Injustice' (1994) *The Humanist* 8–13.

Blasser, B, *The Culture of Fear* (New York, Basic Books, 1999).

Boggess, B, 'Attempted Enticement of a Minor: No Place for Pedophiles to Hide Under 18 U.S.C. Sec. 2422(B)' (2007) 72 *Missouri Law Review* 909.

Cavender, G and Fishman, M, 'Television Reality Crime Programs: Context and History' in Fishman and Cavender (eds) *Entertaining Crime: Television Reality Programs* (New York, Aldine de Gruyter, 1998).

Cavender, G, 'In Search of Community on Reality TV' in Holmes and Jermyn (eds), *Understanding Reality Television* (London, Routledge, 2004).

Dittrich, L, 'Tonight on Dateline this Man Will Die' (2007) *Esquire* 148(3), 233–44.

Doyle, A, 'Cops: Television Policing as Policing Reality' in Fishman and Cavender, *Entertaining Crime*, 1998.

Feinberg, J, 'Expressive Function of Punishment' (1965) *Monist* 49(3), 397–408.

Fishman, M and Cavender, G, *Entertaining Crime: Television Reality Programs* (New York, Aldine de Gruyter, 1998).

Fishman, M, 'Ratings and Reality: The Persistence of the Reality Crime Genre' in Fishman and Cavender ibid.

Gajda, A, 'Judging Journalism: The Turn toward Privacy and Judicial Regulation of the Press' (2009) 97 *California Law Review* 1039.

Grigoriados, V, 'The New American Witch Hunt' (2007) *Rolling Stone* 1032, 64–71.

Hansen, C, *To Catch a Predator* (New York, Penguin, 2008).

Hart, HLA, *Punishment and Responsibility* (New York, Oxford University Press, 1968).

Holmes, S and Jermyn, D, (eds) *Understanding Reality Television* (London, Routledge, 2004).

Jermyn, D, 'This is About Real People! Video Technologies, Actuality and Affect in the Television Crime Appeal' in Holmes and Jermyn ibid.

Kohm, S, 'Naming, Shaming, and Criminal Justice: Mass-Mediated Humiliation as Entertainment and Punishment' (2009) *Crime, Media, Culture* 5(2), 188–205.

Lever, A, 'Mill and the Secret Ballot' (2007) *Utilitas* 19(3), 354–78.

Lissit, R, 'Gotcha' (1995) *American Journalism Review* 17(2), 16–22.

Locke, J, *Second Treatise of Government*, edited by CB Macpherson (Indianapolis, Hackett, 1980).

Marcus, P, *The Entrapment Defense*, 3rd edn (Newark, Lexis-Nexis, 2002).

McAdams, R, 'Political Economy of Entrapment' (2005) *Journal of Criminal Law and Criminology* 96(1), 107–85.

McCollam, D, 'The Shame Game' (2007) *Columbia Journalism Review* 28–33.

Oliver, MB and Blake Armstrong, G, 'The Color of Crime' in Fishman and Cavender, *Entertaining Crime*, 1998.

Pater-Simpson, E, 'Private Circles and Public Squares: Invasion of Privacy by the Publication of "Private Facts"' (1998) *Modern Law Review* 61(3) 318–40.

Rawls, J, 'Two Concepts of Rules' (1955) *Philosophical Review* 64(1) 3–32.

Rosen, J, *The Unwanted Gaze* (New York, Random House, 2000).

Sanders, K, *Ethics and Journalism* (London, Sage, 2003).

Smith, R and Eugene Goodwin, H, *Groping for Ethics in Journalism* (Iowa State University Press, 1999).

Solove, D and Schwartz, P, *Privacy and Media* (New York, Aspen, 2008).

Tunick, M, *Punishment: Theory and Practice* (Berkeley, CA, University of California Press, 1992).

—— 'Entrapment and Retributive Theory' in M White (ed), *Retributivism: Essays on Theory and Policy* (New York, Oxford University Press, 2011).

Wolak, J et al, 'Online "Predators" and their Victims' (2008) *American Psychologist* 63(2), 111–28.

Zaibert, L, *Punishment and Retribution* (Aldershot, England, Ashgate, 2006).

Newspapers and Websites

Montopoli, B, 'Does "Dateline" Go Too Far "To Catch A Predator?"' *CBS News Online* (7 Feb 2006), available at www.cbsnews.com/8301-500486_162-1290135-500486.html?tag=mncol;lst;1.

Stelter, B, '"To Catch a Predator" is Falling Prey to Advertisers' Sensibilities' *New York Times*, 27 Aug 2007.

Terry, D, 'Eavesdropping Laws Mean that Turning on an Audio Recorder Could Send You to Prison' *New York Times*, 22 Jan 2011.

Part III: Specific Shows

Bordering on Identity: How English Canadian Television Differentiates American and Canadian Styles of Justice

UMMNI KHAN

Canadians are forever taking the national pulse like doctors at a sickbed: the aim is not to see whether the patient will live well, but simply whether he will live at all.[1]

But surely the search for the fabled Canadian identity is like a dog chasing its own tail. Round about and round about it goes, with the tail whisking out of sight; whereupon it proclaims the tail elusive, fragile, threatened, or absent. And yet, as everyone can plainly see, there is the tail as firmly attached to the dog as ever...[2]

I. Introduction

While the boundary between Canada and the United States has rhetorically been dubbed 'the longest undefended border in the world', Canadian narratives have vigorously sought to defend the border in symbolic terms. In 1972, Margaret Atwood suggested this nationalist project to withstand American cultural hegemony reflected the recurring theme of *survival* in Canadian fiction.[3] Similarly, theorists of Canadian television have found that discerning Canadian identity, separate from that of its southern neighbour, is a frequent (and anxious) theme in its programming.[4]

This chapter examines this symbolic border-defending through a discursive analysis of two successful English Canadian television shows, *Due South* and *The Border*, with

---

[1] M Atwood, *Survival: A Thematic Guide to Canadian Literature* (Toronto, Anansi, 1972) 41–42.
[2] M Atwood, *Strange Things* (Oxford, Clarendon Press, 1995) 8.
[3] Atwood, *Survival* (n 1).
[4] B Beaty and R Sullivan, *Canadian Television Today: Op/Position: Issues and Ideas Series; no. 1.* (Calgary, University of Calgary Press, 2006) 13.

particular emphasis on the ways in which they differentiate Canadian and American styles of justice. Although the shows represent different genres, occupy different settings, and take place in different time periods, both articulate Canadian national pride in terms of law enforcement. Both plots devote a substantial amount of time dramatising the tension, and often the conflict, between Canadian and American approaches to justice. While the Canadian approach is usually vindicated in the storyline, both shows also offer the promise of productive collaboration between the nations.

In the 1990s show *Due South,* this fraught collaboration is comically portrayed when an upstanding Royal Canadian Mounted Police (RCMP) member teams up with a cynical American cop to solve crimes in Chicago. Debuting in 2008, *The Border* takes Toronto as its setting, and the outsider is Bianca LaGarda (Sofia Milos), a brash American agent sent by the United States Department of Homeland Security (Homeland Security) to represent its interests on Canadian soil. Both shows feature a *fish-out-of-water*, albeit two very different kinds of fish. The Canadian fish is hyperbolically polite in the midst of American obnoxiousness, while the American fish is hyperbolically pugnacious in the midst of Canadian diplomacy. Other important distinguishing features of Canadian law enforcement officers in these programmes include their intelligence, temperance, tolerance, heroism, connection to nature, Aboriginal ties, and commitment to the rule of law. While these values and characteristics often aggrandise Canadian law enforcement characters, the shows also suggest that *sometimes* Canadians must rely on American strong-arm tactics to secure justice. Indeed, the last season of *The Border* finds the two national security agencies in sync as they battle inside corruption and cross-border criminality.

An examination of national approaches to justice in *Due South* and *The Border* positions English Canadian popular television as an artefact of the Canadian imaginary.[5] In Canada, both cultural critics and government commissions have identified television as a principal stage upon which Canadians perform and solidify their national identity in opposition to American culture.[6] Yet, despite a regulated broadcasting infrastructure that subsidises Canadian products and imposes Canadian content quotas, most Canadian television viewers watch American shows most of the time.[7] As exceptions to this dominant trend, the relatively successful runs of *Due South* and *The Border* are significant because their narratives are both reflective of nationalist fantasies, and productive of the social order. As John Fiske points out, 'Television-as-culture is a crucial part of the social dynamics by which the social structure maintains itself in a constant process of production and reproduction: meanings, popular pleasures, and their circulation are therefore part and parcel of this social structure'.[8] This theoretical and methodological approach seeks to understand these televised cultural articulations as strategies that engage politics, generate identity, manage anxiety, and

---

[5] Throughout the rest of the chapter, when I refer to Canadian television or the Canadian imaginary, I am specifically addressing English Canadian culture.

[6] B Feldthusen, 'Awakening from the National Broadcast Dream: Rethinking Television Regulation for National Cultural Goals' in DH Flaherty and FE Manning (eds), *The Beaver Bites Back? American Popular Culture in Canada* (Montreal, McGill-Queens University Press, 1993) 42.

[7] Z Druick and A Kotsopoulos (eds), *Programming Reality: Perspectives on English Canadian Television* (Waterloo, Wilfred Laurier University Press, 2008) 1–2.

[8] J Fiske, *Television Culture* 2nd edn (New York, Routledge, 2010) 1.

harness pleasure. As this is a two-part study, my analysis elucidates the ways the social dynamics and ideological stakes have shifted from the 1990s to the 2000s in the production of difference between Canadian and American styles of justice.

This chapter will thus explore Canadian characterisations and how they differentiate from their American counterparts, beginning with *Due South* and then turning to *The Border*. As will become evident, the events of September 11th serve as a significant landmark that divides the imaginaries of the two shows. I argue that a comparison of the televised shift from 'self-othering' a Canadian against an American backdrop in *Due South*, to 'othering' an American against a Canadian backdrop in *The Border*, reflects both the political climate of the day, and a strengthening sense of self in the Canadian imaginary. Amidst America's 'war on terror', and in relation to international protest against American foreign policy, many episodes of *The Border* depict Canada as a mature and progressive nation that strikes a better balance between security and rights. No longer needing to just *survive*, Canadian policing identity appears robust and confident.

The Border shifts perspective in the last half of its run, however. A review of the latter episodes indicates that Canadian identity ceases to hinge on distinguishing Canadian and American law enforcement. Instead, the show shifts to emphasise binational compatibility between security officers on both sides of the border, allied against two other groups: terrorists and politicians. Terrorists, usually racialised and often Muslim, are portrayed as self-absorbed fanatics out to murder innocent Westerners. Interestingly, the security officers' other adversaries are much closer to home. Canadian and American politicians and their aides are often portrayed as elitist, morally questionable and concerned solely with staying in power. These grandstanders and bureaucrats do not prioritise security and human rights, particularly for non-citizens and/or racialised people. *The Border* thus capitalises on the entertainment value of vilifying racialised and ethnicised people, while still portraying its law enforcement protagonists in contradistinction to racist politicians.

This examination of the parameters of Canadian identity in crime shows demonstrates that *survival* does not depend on being the fittest, but rather the most flexible. The Canadian approach to justice in the popular imagination reflects the ways Canadian national identity must be flexible enough to sometimes stand in opposition to American styles of justice, and sometimes in alliance when going up against Other maligned subjectivities.

II. Due South

Benton Fraser, Constable for the Royal Canadian Mounted Police: 'If you treat people with respect more often than not they'll respond accordingly.'

Ray Vecchio, detective for the Chicago police department: 'You know at a certain point, you gotta stop calling yourself a cop.'

Due South originated as a made-for-TV movie in 1994, co-produced by CTV in Canada and CBS in the United States. Because of its high ratings, the networks developed the story into a weekly comedy-action series. Despite a number of cancellations and renewals, it became one of the most successful Canadian television shows ever aired.[9] It ran for four seasons from 1994 to 1998, was broadcast locally and internationally, and continues to be re-run to this day.[10] It has attracted a loyal following from all over the world, with a fan convention having been held as recently as 2010—a full 12 years after the final episode aired.[11] In the context of a struggling Canadian television culture where, despite government protectionist policies, English Canadian audiences usually prefer American shows over domestic programming, *Due South* stands out for its fan culture, longevity and success.[12] Some critics have hypothesised that it might be the greatest Canadian television show of all time.[13] In the following analysis, I aim to deconstruct *Due South* in order to explore how this exceptional televised success story signifies and produces the Canadian imaginary.

Perhaps one reason for *Due South's* popularity could be its lampooning of national stereotypes.[14] Set in Chicago, *Due South* features a Canadian and American buddy-cop team whose contrasting methods of law enforcement heighten both the action and the comedy of the show. Constable Benton Fraser (Paul Gross) is a courteous Mountie who works as liaison officer with the Canadian consulate in Chicago, but spends most of his time with his local friend, Detective Ray Vecchio (David Marciano), a tough-as-nails misanthropic cop. Together they solve mysteries, apprehend criminals and improve public safety. But make no mistake, most of the time it is Fraser who carries the day. As Reid Gilbert points out, in the Canadian imaginary, 'Mounties remain both a central icon of Canadian pride and a source of common Canadian humour'.[15] In *Due South,* the show portrays Fraser's saintly outlook and superhuman skills both smugly and facetiously.

A. The Canadian Superhero

The show likens Fraser to a superhero, both literally and symbolically. In the episode 'Witness', a cop refers to Fraser as 'Spiderman' after he scales the side of a building to examine evidence. In the later episode, 'Dead Men Don't Throw Rice', a detective from the police station exclaims, 'Fraser's like Superman; he can't die'. After witnessing Fraser's extraordinary policing skills for four years, the Mountie has attained mythic status in the eyes of his American colleagues. Fan culture also designates Fraser as larger than life, as attested by his listing in the 'International Catalogue of Superheroes'.[16]

---

[9] J McKay, 'Mountie Always Gets his Renewal: Dollars from Europe Rescue *Due South'* (1997) *Edmonton Journal* section B7, www.westlaw.com.proxy.library.carleton.ca, cited in MA Tate and V Allen 'Integrating Distinctively Canadian Elements into Television Drama: A Formula for Success or Failure?: The Due South Experience' (2003) Canadian Journal of Communication 28, 1, 72–73.

[10] A Strachan, 'Summer Silliness Scales New Heights in Downfall' *The Montreal Gazette*, 22 June 2010), www.montrealgazette.com/life/Summer+silliness+scales+heights+Downfall/3185036/story.html.

[11] The Original Convention for Fans of Due South (Toronto, Canada 2010), www.rcw139.org/.

[12] Tate and Allen 'Integrating Distinctively Canadian Elements into Television Drama' (n 9).

[13] 'VisionTV Adds Classic Canadian Series Due South to Lineup' (CHANNEL CANADA, Canada's Entertainment and Broadcasting Information, 9 June 2010), www.channelcanada.com/Article4652.html.

[14] Tate and Allen 'Integrating Distinctively Canadian Elements into Television Drama' (n 9) 77.

[15] R Gilbert, 'Mounties, Muggings, and Moose: Canadian Icons in a Landscape of American Violence' in DH Flaherty and FE Manning (eds), *The Beaver Bites Back?: American Popular Culture in Canada* (Montreal, McGill-Queen's University Press, 1993) 187.

[16] International Catalogue of Superheroes, www.internationalhero.co.uk/b/benny.htm.

Like many superheroes, Fraser signals his exceptional status through a flamboyant outfit. Most often, he wears the iconic RCMP uniform, composed of a red serge tunic and accented with riding breeches, boots and a Stetson hat. While the red of his outfit could be reminiscent of the red in Superman's cape, more significantly, the outfit seems to endow him with superhuman skill, strength and resilience. When Fraser is dressed in official RCMP gear, he can leap between tall buildings or float to the ground with a parachute fashioned out of a cape-like tarp, as seen in the episode 'Perfect Strangers'.

Fraser leaping between buildings in pursuit of a suspect.[17]	Fraser floating to the ground with a makeshift parachute.[18]

Fraser's uniform also signifies his communitarian outlook. By wearing a standard uniform, even when he is not working in his official capacity as an RCMP officer, Fraser performs his deference to authority and conveys a collective sense of self. Vecchio and Kowalski choose informal apparel, which suggests a more individualistic sense of self and a rebellious attitude towards authority. And while a number of Canadian critics have mocked the image of the RCMP as 'foppish' and 'sexless', in Fraser's case, his attention to RCMP dress code might better be associated with the gallantry of a gentleman.

Fraser's style of justice, however, goes beyond simple aesthetics. The Mountie's progressive approach to crime fighting reveals his compassion and his community-building skills. While he obviously assists victims of crime, as one would expect of any superhero figure, he reaches out to offenders as well. In 'Free Willie', Fraser befriends and rehabilitates a 13-year-old purse-snatcher who initially threatens him with a gun. In 'Pizza and Promises', Fraser insists to his partner that they must help a young offender to comply with his onerous probation orders. Vecchio responds in disgust: 'There are still a few people in this neighbourhood without a criminal record. Why don't you try helping one of them?' From Vecchio's moral perspective, time should

---

[17] *Due South*, 'Perfect Strangers' season three (1997–1998).
[18] Ibid.

not be wasted helping criminals, even if they become victimised themselves. Fraser, on the other hand, treats criminals with the utmost respect and offers them alternatives to their criminal lifestyles. This reinforces the stereotypes of the United States as 'tough on crime' and Canada as 'soft on crime'. However, virtually every criminal in whom Fraser invests his rehabilitative energy subsequently becomes an upstanding member of society. The normative message of the show is that Fraser's approach is actually *smarter* on crime.

Another way that Fraser occupies a superhero role is through his ability to fight. Like most superheroes, Fraser does not rely on a gun to capture the bad guy. Again, demonstrating his respect for the rules, the Constable refuses to carry or shoot a gun because he is not licensed to do so in the United States. Instead, he disarms suspects through skilful battle, and sometimes with the assistance of his companion, wolf.

In contrast, Ray and Stanley, like ordinary cops, use guns to fight crime. The show explicitly ties this approach to nationality when Ray states in the pilot episode: 'Being an American, I also know where my strength lies, and that's in being as heavily armed as possible.'[19] While this may be less impressive than Fraser's extraordinary combat skills, Fraser often relies on his American partner to back him up or detain a suspect with the threat of a gun. Thus, while the show may perpetuate the stereotype of gun-toting Americans and restrained Canadians, the synergy of both approaches is frequently shown to be the most effective way of ensuring public safety.

Fraser's unarmed state also has gendered significance. As many film critics have pointed out, the gun often operates as a phallic symbol that reinforces the bearer's masculinity.[20] A cop without a gun is not necessarily emasculated, but he occupies a softer masculinity. But while Fraser's masculinity might be softer, like most superheroes, he is also irresistible to women. His ability to subdue a criminal and save the damsel in distress with his bare hands registers as *more* attractive in the eyes of many heterosexual female characters. This conveys the idea that Canadian justice is not just less violent, but also *sexier* than American justice.

Besides brawn, Fraser also has brains. His keen sense of touch, taste, sight, smell and hearing is exaggerated to the point of magic realism. In addition, Fraser draws upon an encyclopaedic knowledge when interpreting what his senses are registering. In the episode 'Body Language', Vecchio looks on in revulsion as Fraser smells the breath of a rat to determine what it had eaten. Fraser not only identifies barbeque sauce, he ascertains the exact ingredients of the sauce ('tomatoes, vinegar, sugar—both brown and white, mustard, Worcestershire sauce, jalapeño peppers and raw comb honey in a 1 to 4 combination'). After sampling every type of barbecued ribs in the city, Fraser is able to locate the specific restaurant in which the rat had feasted.

---

[19] *Due South*, pilot episode/made-for-television movie.
[20] Fiske, (n 8) 214.

Vecchio looks on in disgust as Fraser smells the breath of a rat to track a suspect.[21]	Fraser tasting the bottom of a dead man's shoe to determine where the victim had been.[22]

B. Nature Lover and Aboriginal Insider

Fraser's hands-on, and often tongues-on, approach to detection (see figure above) connects him to nature. This naturalisation of Canadian identity draws on canonical and colonial literary themes in Canadian literature and parodies them in a pop cultural context. In *Due South*, Fraser's ties to nature are rooted in his upbringing in the Northwest Territories and the Yukon where much of his social community and mentorship came from Inuit friends and neighbours. As Katherine L Morrison explains, nature and Aboriginal peoples are imbricated in the Canadian literary imaginary,[23] and this thematic tradition continues in televised narratives. In contrast to his American colleagues who are urbanised and tech savvy, Fraser is indigenised in the narrative, as he draws on Inuit knowledge systems to scrutinise evidence.[24] In 'Hawk and a Handsaw', Fraser states, 'You know, the Inuit have 60 words to describe snow, Ray. One-third of them concern the colour.' Vecchio is often incensed with this cultural frame of reference. In 'An Eye for an Eye', he rants at Fraser:

> This is what's wrong with you, Fraser. You see a problem and you have to fix it. You can't even go to the men's room without stopping to tell some simple stupid charmingly witty Inuit story that inspires people to take on the world's social ills.

From this voice of American justice, we hear cynicism, sarcasm and contempt towards do-gooders. And significantly, Vecchio's comic diatribe against Fraser connects the Mountie's altruism to traditional Aboriginal culture.

However, the show does not completely romanticise or reify Aboriginal culture. In subsequent episodes, stereotypes are explicitly mocked. At an office party, when

[21] *Due South*, 'Body Language', season two (1995–1996).

[22] *Due South*, 'Mountie and Soul', season three (1997–1998).

[23] KL Morrison, *Canadians are Not Americans: Myths and Literary Traditions* (Toronto, Second Story Press, 2003) 85.

[24] Terry Goldies coined the term 'indigenization' to describe the portrayal of heroic White people internalising indigenous customs, moral frameworks and epistemologies in T Goldie, *Fear and Temptation: The Image of the Indigene in Canadian, Australian and New Zealand Literatures* (Kingston, McGill-Queen's University Press, 1989) 13.

Fraser suggests playing a 'traditional Yukon game: bobbing for trout' he is asked by a colleague, 'Is that a traditional Inuit game?' He replies, 'No, the locals favour something called Twister.'[25] Irony and self-reflexivity are displayed in a later episode when Fraser's childhood mentor, an Aboriginal man named Tom Quinn (Gordon Tootoosis), comes to Chicago to try to stop the construction of a hydroelectric dam that will flood his native community.[26] When a representative of the company assures Quinn that consultations have been carried out with the affected parties, Quinn replies, 'What about the caribou, the elk, the beaver, did you talk to them? Because they too can talk.' Later, Quinn shares the inside joke with Fraser, '... I thought the Tonto act might impress that little jackass.' In other words, Quinn was attempting to appropriate the exotic figure of the Noble Red Man to subvert American corporate violence.[27] The fact that Fraser is trusted to understand Quinn's strategy positions the Mountie as an insider to Aboriginal culture. This is further demonstrated in Fraser's attempts to sensitise Ray to the violence associated with colonial language, for example, when he instructs his partner not to use the term 'Eskimo' in reference to Inuit people.[28] He likens the derogatory practice to two icons associated with American baseball teams: the symbol of the tomahawk chop for the Atlanta Braves and the figure of Chief Wahoo for the Cleveland Indians. Thus, the narrative draws upon a long-standing Canadian nationalist myth that constructs Americans as perpetuating colonial oppression, while Canadians are portrayed as champions of Aboriginal causes.[29]

This rendering of the heroic White Canadian as ally to Aboriginal peoples does not extend, however, to Canadian bureaucrats. In the episode 'The Mask', a Tsimshian religious artefact has been appropriated by the Canadian and French governments. Fraser rescues the mask from a corrupt Canadian official and returns it to the Tsimshian people, allowing a forgery to be returned to the government who holds legal title. This is one of the rare moments when Fraser's principles contradict the law. He appears to be even more devoted to Aboriginal interpretations of title and property than to the Canadian government's legal system. The plot thus contributes to historical amnesia. As Christopher Gittings states,

> *Due South*, in its attempts to translate the Mountie from racial gatekeeper and reproducer of Anglo-Saxon Canadian culture to a Tsimshian speaker on intimate terms with First Nations people and their cultural practices, elides the racist origins of the police force.[30]

This elision in *Due South* also draws on a long-standing colonial fantasy of the White saviour working for the betterment of the down-trodden, the racialised and the neo-colonised.[31]

---

[25] *Due South*, 'Eclipse' season three (1997–1998).

[26] *Due South*, 'Easy Money' season four (1998–1999).

[27] For a discussion of Tonto as Noble Native American friend, see M Hilger, *From Savage to Nobleman: Images of Native Americans in Film* (Lanham, Scarecrow Press, 1995) 5.

[28] *Due South*, 'Dead Men Don't Throw Rice'.

[29] E Mackey, *House of Difference, The: Cultural Politics and National Identity in Canada* (Taylor & Francis, 1998) 1–2, www.lib.myilibrary.com.proxy.library.carleton.ca/Browse/open.asp?ID=14373&loc=xvi.

[30] C Gittings, 'Imaging Canada: The Singing Mountie and Other Commodifications of Nation' (1998) *Canadian Journal of Communication* 23, 4, 507–22, www.proquest.com.proxy.library.carleton.ca/.

[31] For an overview of the Hollywood tradition of the white saviour in the cinematic imagination, see H Vera and A Gordon, *Screen Saviors: Hollywood Fictions of Whiteness* (Lanham, Rowman & Littlefield Publishers, 2003), 'Chapter 3: The Beautiful White American: Sincere Fictions of the Savior'.

C. White Canadian Saviour

Fraser's whiteness is a key trope for his pure and heroic heart. This is contrasted to the compromised whiteness of his American partners. As Ross Chambers reminds us, there are shades of white in the colonial imaginary, whereby certain ethnicities and class characteristics will separate an ostensibly White subject from the White ideal.[32] Put simply, 'some white people are whiter than others'.[33] Ray Vecchio's adherence to all the clichés of the Italian-American figure undermines his whiteness. He is hot-headed, wears Armani suits, maintains some connections to the mob, has a sweet nagging mother, and still lives at home with his family. Fraser's second American partner, Stanley Kowalski, is less obviously ethnicised in his personal life, but still stands in contrast to the mountie's Anglo-Saxon identity. The surname indicates Polish roots and to emphasise this ethnic background, we later learn that he was named after Marlon Brando's rendition of 'Stanley Kowalski' in the cinematic version of *A Streetcar Named Desire*. Like Brando's character, he has a passionate, even violent, temper and is marked as working class. Vecchio and Kowalski's whiteness is tainted in relation to Canadian whiteness. And as Dyer reminds us, whiteness as colour, race and symbol are interconnected to convey the ideal in morality and beauty.[34] Fraser's racial status thus emblematises superior ethical and aesthetic qualities in relation to his American partners within the economy of whiteness. Furthermore, within the Canadian colonial imaginary, Fraser's indigenisation does not detract from his whiteness; rather, it adds to his nobility. As Russell Lawrence Barsh discusses, the construction of Canadian whiteness as tolerant and beneficent hinges on the fantasy that Canada treated and continues to treat Aboriginal peoples better than those 'trigger-happy cowboys' to the South.[35]

D. American Guns versus Canadian Battle Lances

However, the show is careful to construct Fraser's benign and unmarked whiteness in stark contrast to American white supremacist movements. *Due South* dedicates multiple episodes to the Bolt family, a group of American fanatics who have formed a racist militia called the 'Father's of Confederation'. The Bolts specifically make reference to the United States Constitution's Second Amendment to defend and justify their right to bear arms and challenge a government that has 'chosen to betray its people'.[36] Within the show's imaginary, the supreme law of the land is complicit in fostering the xenophobic vigilantism of American culture.

---

[32] R Chambers, 'The Unexamined' in M Hill (ed), *Whiteness: A Critical Reader* (New York, New York University Press, 1997) 187–25.

[33] R Dyer, *White* (London, Routledge, 1997) 51.

[34] Ibid 70.

[35] RL Barsh, 'Aboriginal Peoples and Canada's Conscience' in Daniel JK Beavon et al (eds), *Hidden in Plain Sight: Contributions of Aboriginal Peoples to Canadian identity and Culture* (Toronto, University of Toronto Press, 2005) 272.

[36] *Due South*, 'All the Queen's Horses'; 'Red White or Blue' and 'Call of the Wild'.

In contrast to Bolt's gun-worship and Ray's reliance on ammunition to enforce the law, Fraser's gunless approach to justice establishes Canadians as more temperate and rational. In 'Red White or Blue', Mr Bolt's nefarious plans are ultimately foiled by unarmed RCMP officers. First, Meg Thatcher (Camilla Scott), Fraser's boss, uses her bare hands to throw the villain off his vehicle, and then the RCMP musical riders use their red and white battle lances to detain him. The image is a powerful ideological statement of Canadian solidarity, collectivism, and discipline that vindicate over rampant American individualism. Significantly, the circular arrangement the RCMP characters form in *Due South* replicates the most famous ceremonial 'dome' pose of the actual RCMP musical riders, who stage elaborate sequences and cavalry drills throughout the world.[37] The nationalist significance is further established because this image is featured on the back of the Canadian $50 bill.[38]

Bolt, the gun-toting Amercian White-supremacist is foiled and surrounded by spear-carrying Canadian Mounties.[39]	The back of the former Canadian $50 bill.[40]	The RCMP musical riders in the dome formation.[41]

E. The Death Penalty

Nationalist pride is also tacitly conveyed in the one episode that addresses the death penalty. In his article 'Two Nations under Law', The Honourable Roger P Kerans hypothesizes: 'If I ask what Canadians consider special or unique about American justice ... Almost all would mention the death penalty.'[42] In the Canadian imaginary, the continued use of the death penalty signifies the authorisation of vengeance over human rights in the American justice system. The episode entitled 'The Ladies Man' performs this indictment in a subtle story of corruption and redemption. At the start of the episode, we find Kowalski wracked with guilt as he confesses to Fraser that he might be responsible for the execution of an innocent woman. Six years ago, Kowalski accidentally tampered with evidence when arresting Beth Botrelle for the murder of

---

[37] Royal Canadian Mounted Police, official website (www.rcmp-grc.gc.ca/mr-ce/index-eng.htm).
[38] Royal Canadian Mounted Police, official website (www.rcmp-grc.gc.ca/mr-ce/index-eng.htm).
[39] *Due South*, 'All the Queen's Horses' season two (1995–1996).
[40] See www.specialx.net/specialxdotnet/evileye-images/50rcmp.jpg.
[41] See www.rcmp-grc.gc.ca/mr-ce/images/formations-figures/dome.jpg.
[42] Hon RP Kerans, 'Two Nations Under Law' in DM Thomas (ed), *Canada and the United States: Differences That Count*, 2nd edn (Peterborough, Broadview Press, 2000) 359.

her husband, a police officer. Kowalski is now convinced that this error has enabled someone to frame Botrelle for a murder she did not commit. As Fraser and Kowalski fight against time to uncover the truth, Kowalski has to defy a direct order from the State Attorney to back off and face his colleagues who are gleefully counting down the days until Botrelle's lethal injection. In the nick of time, Kowalski and Fraser apprehend the culprit behind the frame job to demonstrate that the victim's death was actually a suicide. Police corruption caused both the death and the cover up. The denouement achieves its catharsis with Botrelle forgiving Kowalski with a comforting kiss.

Not once do any of the characters condemn capital punishment, nor does Fraser mention the fact that Canada has abolished the practice, and yet the episode still expresses censure of the death penalty. Firstly, if Kowalski and Fraser had been unable to present the evidence to the authorities in time, an innocent woman would have been killed by the state, *because* of state corruption. One fan of the show described the episode as affirming her stance against the death penalty, stating, 'what nearly happened to Beth, happens to a lot of people in real life too!!'[43] Many other fans identify 'The Ladies Man' as the best *Due South* episode of all time.[44]

One reason for this endorsement might rest on the episode's affective contrast between an innocent woman's forgiveness and compassion against the state actors' vengeance and cruelty. Early in the episode, Kowalski visits Botrelle on death row. Instead of being angry, she says, 'Let your conscience be clear, Officer Kowalski … I killed him.' Kowalski recognises the confession as a ruse telling his partner, 'She's lying, Fraser. She's gonna die, and she tried to make me feel better.' In the end, Botrelle forgives Kowalski and holds him in her arms even though she has spent six years on death row, and was taken to the execution room on five separate occasions before the conviction was overturned. The mercy she expresses is in stark contrast to the political climate and the police behaviour. There is a sense that the criminal justice system is more interested in satisfying blood-lust and maintaining a clean image than ensuring that the right person is being punished. It is this narrative privileging of mercy over vengeance that clinches the show as normatively against capital punishment.

F. Utilitarian versus Deontological Approaches to Crime Fighting

More generally, the most important normative contrast in the show features Fraser's deontological approach to law enforcement, and his partners' more utilitarian philosophy. While Fraser is committed to upholding the rule of law, Vecchio expresses total disregard for the rights of suspects. As he states to Fraser: 'All right, stand back and watch how we do things here in America. No neighborhood watch, no caring for your fellow man, just good old-fashioned intimidation.' Vecchio frequently breaks into suspects' homes without a warrant and uses the threat of violence to obtain information.

---

[43] William and Elyse's DS Web Page, Fan Episode Reviews, 'Ladies Man' Review #5 by 'Petra', www.home.hiwaay.net/~warydbom/duesouth/review/lm.htm.

[44] Ibid.

The episode 'Juliette is Bleeding' dramatises this clash of perspectives when Vecchio sees a chance to finally put his criminal nemesis, Frank Zuko, behind bars. Zuko, a ruthless mob boss who has terrorised Vecchio's neighbourhood for years, is wrongfully accused of murder. Fraser presents evidence that would exonerate Zuko to his partner, but Vecchio initially wants to ignore it. In Vecchio's view, even if Zuko didn't kill this particular victim, he is guilty of murder in other cases where there was insufficient evidence. The ends justify the means because they can finally put this mobster away. Fraser refuses this logic. As he states in a later episode, 'Nothing good can come from a bad act.'[45] The audience finds out that Fraser learned this maxim from his mentor Tom Quinn, again connecting Fraser's philosophy on life to his exposure to Aboriginal morality. While *Due South* gives voice to more utilitarian approaches to crime-fighting, at the end of most episodes, Fraser's commitment to duty, due process and the rule of law is presented as the morally correct choice.

G. Canadian as Other or Queering the Canadian Nation

All of these characterisations seem to glorify Canadian styles of justice, yet it should be noted that the show is based on the idea of peculiarising Canadians. As Aniko Bodroghkozy suggests, *Due South* was premised on 'playing at being Canadian' against an American backdrop.[46] *Due South* is set in Chicago, and although the Mountie stands out because of his ingenious abilities and unwavering politeness, Fraser is nonetheless rendered the exotic *Other*. This rendering conveys a self-deprecating conceit in relation to the United States, where Fraser's distinctively Canadian qualities become visible only through his identity as a patriotic expatriate (ex-pat). While some scholars have suggested this cultural practice conveys an inferiority complex and a failure to achieve a self-contained national identity, Jason Morgan suggests that it actually evidences a queering of nationhood.[47] Although Morgan's comments address cinematic representations, his interpretive framework sheds light on the articulations of nationhood in *Due South* as well. Morgan suggests that the use of 'queer' as a trope disrupts the binary of self/other, and recognises the 'fundamental contradictions (the innate 'queerness') in the formation of any community, including the nation'.[48] Morgan's queering of the nation parallels recent scholarship that has sought to queer heterosexuality; each queering initiative seeks to deconstruct stable hegemonic categories to expose their inherent instability, their slippages and their contradictions.

Due South exemplifies this instability in its portrayal of the protagonists' heterosexuality in conjunction with their national identities. In the show, both national and heterosexual relations are naturalised and presented as self-evident and contained

---

[45] *Due South*, 'Easy Money' season four (1998–1999).

[46] A Aodroghkozy, 'As Canadian as Possible ...: Anglo-Canadian Popular Culture and the American Other' in H Jenkins et al (eds), *Hop on Pop* (Durham, Duke University Press, 2002) 581.

[47] J Morgan, 'Queerly Canadian: 'Perversion Chic' Cinema (and Queer) Nationalism in English Canada' in S Petty et al (eds), *Canadian Cultural Poesis: Essays on Canadian Culture*, Cultural Studies Series (Waterloo, Wilfrid Laurier University Press, 2006) 211.

[48] Ibid 217.

organisations of community and intimacy. However, at the same time, *Due South* also subverts both sets of relations. From the national angle, *Due South's* explicit reliance on an American background to highlight Fraser's Canadianess demonstrates an intersubjective sense of self that transgresses hegemonic and insular constructions of the nation. In other words, to borrow Morgan's analytical frame, Fraser's dislocation and *Due South's* self-othering 'emphasize[ ] the subversion of dominant models of belonging by positioning intersection and difference as the foundations of community.'[49] From the interpersonal angle, the show not only privileges male bonding over heterosexual desire, but goes further by infusing homoerotic tension into the buddy-cop dynamic.

As the narrative unfolds, we see Fraser at the centre of two love triangles, one heterosexual, the other homosocial. Vecchio's sister has been in love with Fraser from the start, and Meg Thatcher, Fraser's uptight RCMP boss, has also fallen in love with him. However, Fraser shares deep affection for his two American male partners, first Ray Vecchio and then Vecchio's replacement, Stanley Kowalski. In another signal of queerness, the bond between Fraser and Kowalski proves, in the end, to be the most long-lasting.

Almost from the moment they meet, the sparks fly between Fraser and Kowalski in a fashion that is reminiscent of a typical Harlequin romance. While Fraser's cerebral ways grate on Kowalski's nerves, they also develop a deep intimacy. By the end of the third season, this 'bromance'[50] takes a surprisingly homoerotic turn in the two-part episode 'Mountie on the Bounty'. The story begins with Fraser and Kowalski both being offered transfers to other postings that would, on the surface, be more suitable for each. Both men are sorely tempted to seize the opportunity, as they have been bickering over their different approaches to crime-fighting. Kowalski is frustrated with Fraser's commitment to logic, while Fraser fails to see the benefit of following gut instinct. Later in the episode, Fraser leads Kowalski underwater in a daring escape, but notices that Kowalski is having difficulty holding his breath. He returns to offer Kowalski some air from his own lungs, but this survival technique registers visually as a three-second kiss. Afterwards, they have a humourous exchange that implies romantic tension:

Kowalski: What was that, Fraser?

Fraser: What was what?

Kowalski: That thing you were doing with your mouth.

Fraser: Oh, that. That's buddy breathing. You seemed to be in a bit of a, well, having a problem. I have excess lung capacity, so…

Kowalski: Buddy breathing.

[49] Ibid 212.

[50] Bromance is a portmanteau of the two words: brother and romance. The Urban Dictionary defines 'bromance' as '1. the complicated love and affection shared by two straight males'; 2. A non-sexual relationship between two men that are unusually close'; and '3. A close relationship between two bros to such a point where they start to seem like a couple.' (www.urbandictionary.com/define.php?term=Bromance).

Fraser:	Standard procedure.
Kowalski:	Good … Okay … All right … Nothing's, like, changed or anything, right?
Fraser:	No.
Kowalski:	Okay.
Fraser:	Yeah.
Kowalski:	Thanks.
Fraser:	You're thanking me?
Kowalski:	Look, don't get too excited, Fraser. The jury's still out on this … partnership thing, okay?
Fraser:	Oh, well, don't worry, Mr. Instinct, I'm not excited.[51]

Kowalski's desire to re-establish normalcy, and the discussion/denial of 'excitement', suggest an underlying attraction that is being vigorously disavowed. The episode further establishes the slippages between professional and romantic partnership through the voice of Fraser's ghost father, who states, 'Partnership is like a marriage, son. Give and take, up and down, who left the empty butter dish in the fridge... It isn't easy.' When Fraser finally allows Kowalski to make a strategic decision based on his instinct, he learns the give and take of this special partnership. At the end of the episode, both have decided to decline their offers of transfer and remain together.

But it is the final episode that really establishes Fraser and Kowalski's devotion to one another. The two-part 'Call of the Wild' repositions Kowalski as the fish-out-of-water, when the bi-national team stumbles upon a case that leads them into northern Canada. By the middle of the plot, times are desperate. Fraser and Kowalski are trudging through frozen tundra when suddenly they both tumble into a deep crevice. As in the episode 'Mountie on the Bounty', their dire predicament forces them into intimate contact, where their bodies are pressed up against one another.

Another plot device to get Kowalski and Fraser pressed up against each other.[52]

---

[51] *Due South*, 'Mountie on the Bounty—Part 2' season three (1997–1998).
[52] *Due South*, 'Call of the Wild—Part 2'. season four (1998–1999).

While they wait for help, Fraser recounts to Kowalski the Canadian folk story of Sir John Franklin's doomed expedition to find the Northwest Passage in the mid nineteenth century. Franklin's body was never recovered, though, as Fraser explains, 'Many went in search of his hand reaching for the Beauford Sea.' An inspired Kowalski vows, 'If I get out of this, I live through this, gotta find that hand, I gotta find that reaching out hand.' Fraser warns, 'It might be the hand of death.' Fraser then sings a famous Canadian folk song about Franklin's fate, again intertextually linking *Due South* to the Canadian literary tradition of re-telling the explorer's fate.[53] When the episode concludes, marking the end of the series, Fraser narrates that he and Kowalski remained together in the Great White North to begin another adventure. The last words of the show are: 'And off we went to find the hand of Franklin … And if we do find his hand, the reaching out one, we'll let you know.' Notice that Fraser repeats Kowalski's colloquial language 'the reaching out one', indicating a harmonious blending of their separate outlooks. The bromance has a happy ending!

Fraser's hand on Kowalski's shoulder as they set out on their adventure.[54]	Fraser leading Kowalski to find the hand of Franklin 'reaching for the Beauford Sea'.[55]

In setting out on this journey, Fraser chooses Kowalski over his female suitors, Francesca Vecchio (Ramona Milano) and Meg Thatcher, despite the fact that he has expressed romantic interest towards both women at various points in the series. Yet, it is significant that Fraser's continued relationship with Kowalski occurs in Northern Canada, and not in Chicago or Ottawa. Mother Nature provides a feminine presence through which their homosocial relationship can be triangulated. As Margaret Atwood stated in a lecture she wrote on the literary treatment of Sir John Franklin, 'the North c[a]me to be thought of as a frigid but sparkling fin de siècle *femme fatale,* who entices and hypnotizes male protagonists to their doom'.[56] As we saw, Fraser and Kowalski almost died in this *femme fatale's* icy embrace, and have now been lured by the *call of the wild,* even if it means touching 'the hand of death'. The show thus rejects the dominant happily-ever-after denouement, which would have seen each man return to his country of origin to begin or continue sexual

[53] Stan Rogers, 'Northwest Passage'. Go to www.youtube.com/watch?v=TVY8LoM47xI to hear the song.
[54] *Due South* 'Call of the Wild—Part 2' season 4 (1998–1999).
[55] Ibid.
[56] Atwood, (n 2) 3.

relations with an appropriately gendered object choice. Instead, homoerotic and bi-national tension will converge and continue as Fraser and Kowalski team up to explore the Canadian north (the wilderness, of course, also provides a clandestine space for same-sex desire to manifest, most recently and vividly exemplified in the film *Brokeback Mountain*).

But what does this have to do with styles of justice? While the homosocial relationships that were building throughout the show, first with Vecchio, then with Kowalski, signified the compatibility of the two national approaches to justice, it is now clear that Canadian subjectivity has been repositioned at the centre. Or, to use a sexual metaphor: Fraser is now 'on top'. The story concludes with Kowalski as the ex-pat and Fraser in his element. While much of *Due South's* four seasons are dedicated to displaying Fraser's naiveté when negotiating big city life, the last episode features Kowalski's big city inexperience in navigating the harsh Canadian climate. Kowalski is Other in this environment. In their next adventure, Kowalski will now have to trust Fraser completely to steer their course, both literally (see figure above) and symbolically. As we will see in our analysis of *The Border*, Canadian television has continued in this vein by perpetuating the narrative fantasy of Canadians guiding Americans towards a more just system of law enforcement.

III. The Border

Bianca LaGuarda, United States Department of Homeland Security: 'Mine is bigger than yours; get used to it Major...'

Major Mike Kessler, Canadian Immigration, Customs and Security: 'There you have it, the voice of American diplomacy.'

In the early episodes of *The Border*, this kind of exchange between American and Canadian high-ranking security officials is typical. The accusation that American security rests on a 'might-is-right' philosophy connects the series to *Due South* and its earlier construction of American over-reliance on force at the expense of due process or genuine diplomacy. Unlike the dyadic team in *Due South*, however, each episode of *The Border* features an ensemble cast of characters working for Immigration Customs and Security (ICS), a fictional agency that protects the Canadian people from threats that cross the border. As mentioned, Bianca LaGarda, a liason officer with the United States Department of Homeland Security, acts as a continual thorn in the squad's side after she is sent to Toronto to assist ICS and safeguard American interests. Of course, her interventions are frequently characterised as interference. While portrayed as both intelligent and gutsy, LaGarda continually amazes her Canadian colleagues with her monomaniacal fixation on potential terrorist threats and her disregard for the human rights, and even the lives, of non-Americans. Although LaGarda's attitude mellows as the show progresses, the real shift happens when Agent Liz Carver (Grace Park) replaces her in the middle of the second season. With the arrival of Carver, the show ceases to condemn American styles of justice, and instead starts to focus more squarely on shared enemies to both nations.

While *The Border* played for only three seasons and produced roughly half as many episodes as *Due South*, it too gained considerable acclaim and a solid fan base during its run between 2008 and 2010. By Canadian standards, the show was quite a success. And despite its cancellation, it lives on both locally and internationally.[57] All three seasons are available for purchase on iTunes or DVD, 22 countries have bought the rights, it is currently being played on the American station ION, and it has been translated into 10 different languages.[58] Since the announcement of its cancellation, fans have bombarded the Canadian Broadcasting Corporation with complaints, and created a Facebook group, 'Bring Back The Border', in an attempt to overturn the network's decision.[59]

A. Wikileaks and the Political Stakes of Televised Crime Drama

The exceptional popularity of *The Border*, as with *Due South*, indicates its significance as a text reflective and productive of the imagined Canadian community. However, its post 9/11 context actuated narrative shifts and drew political attention. I will address the narrative shifts below, but first I want to consider some recently publicised official documents that allude to the political stakes in this show. In December 2010, the whistle-blowing website Wikileaks disclosed US diplomatic cables to Washington that conveyed a frustration with Canadian television. In January 2008, when *The Border* debuted, an American diplomat stationed in Ottawa complained, 'Primetime images of U.S.-Canada border paint U.S. in increasingly negative light'.[60] The cable provides plot points from the first three episodes of *The Border*, as well as other Canadian shows, that purportedly portray 'nefarious American officials carrying out equally nefarious deeds in Canada'. The message laments:

> While this situation hardly constitutes a public diplomacy crisis per se, the degree of comfort with which Canadian broadcast entities, including those financed by Canadian tax dollars, twist current events to feed long-standing negative images of the U.S.—and the extent to which the Canadian public seems willing to indulge in the feast—is noteworthy as an indication of the kind of insidious negative popular stereotyping we are increasingly up against in Canada. (para 1)

The cable proceeds to outline more plot detail of *The Border* and other Canadian television shows deemed anti-American. The conclusion states that action must be taken to counter such pejorative characterisations:

> While there is no single answer to this trend, it does serve to demonstrate the importance of constant creative, and adequately-funded public-diplomacy engagement with Canadians, at all levels and in virtually all parts of the country. ...While there are those who may rate the need for USG public-diplomacy programs as less vital in Canada than in other nations because our societies are so much alike, we clearly have real challenges here that simply must be adequately addressed. (para 10)

---

[57] Amber Dowling, 'Boarded Up' (*T.V. Guide.ca*, 29 March 2010), tvguide.ca/Interviews/Insider/Articles/100329_the_border_AD.

[58] Ibid.

[59] Facebook group, 'Bring Back The Border', www.facebook.com/group.php?v=wall&gid=384890931958#!/group.php?gid=384890931958&v=info. See also www.facebook.com/pages/The-Border/246837539217?v=info#!/pages/The-Border/246837539217?v=wall.

[60] See www.wikileaks.ch/cable/2008/01/08OTTAWA136.html.

The cable suggests that political actors, like academics, engage in ideological analysis of pop cultural products and consider their impact on the zeitgeist of a nation. From my review of the disclosed cables on Wikileaks, the American Embassy did not have concerns about other plot-driven narrative products like Canadian films or books.[61] Thus, television is singled out. I want to suggest that the temporal rhythm of weekly shows may offer a partial explanation as to why this is. Unlike the vast majority of films and books, television shows are episodic; the plotlines and characters are works in progress. The recurring characters and the continual development of the storyline give television shows a particularly powerful performative effect. As Judith Butler has theorised, performativity should be cast 'not as the act by which a subject brings into being what she/he names, but, rather as the reiterative power of discourse to produce the phenomenon that it regulates and constrains'.[62] The reiterative nature of these stories may cause politicians to be concerned with the image of US-Canada relations conjured by the viewership. And as John Hartley suggests, government officials imagine television viewers as representative of a reified 'public' whose world views must be canvassed, and ideally managed, for political purposes.[63]

Weekly television shows are also unique in their ability to adapt or adjust. Characters can be killed off, bad guys can turn into romantic heroes and, as with the case of *The Border*, the political direction of the show can change, or even reverse course. The second season's ideological shift from caricaturing to celebrating American militancy attests to the plasticity of televised narratives. Of course, it would be pure (and perhaps paranoid) conjecture on my part to suggest that 'USG public diplomacy engagement' had any impact on the evolution of the show. Indeed, the election of Barack Obama in 2008, when presumably the writers were crafting the second season, is a more defensible hypothesis to explain the change. But whatever the reason, *The Border's* ability to reconceive its ideological premise reveals television's potential dialogic interaction with political forces.

B. The Border's Textual Politics

In her essay, 'Soft Power: Policing the Border through Canadian TV Crime Drama', Yasmin Jiwani analyses the first season of *The Border* as an expression of Canadian nationalist ideology centred on 'soft power'. She explains that the concept exemplifies a hegemonic strategy of social control that veils violence and produces docile bodies.[64] As I understand it, 'soft power' can refer to the ways the crime drama itself is an exercise of soft power, through its ideological structuring of reality that naturalises and disguises unequal power relations on a weekly basis. But soft power also draws upon Canadian mythology that in the land of 'peace order and good government', government exercises its powers benevolently and proportionately. Although Jiwani

---

[61] (213.251.145.96/origin/58_0.html).

[62] J Butler, *Bodies That Matter* (New York, Routledge, 1993) 2.

[63] J Hartley, 'The Constructed Viewer' in T Miller (ed), *Television Studies* (London, British Film Institute, 2002) 60.

[64] Y Jiwani, 'Soft Power: Policing the Border through Canadian TV Crime Drama' in J Klaehn (ed), *The Political Economy of Media and Power* (New York, Peter Lang Publishing, 2010) 273–91.

wrote her analysis before seasons two and three were aired, her conclusion can be generally applied to the entire series. She states:

> The Border asserts and reasserts the Canadian national imaginary; that of a nation that is subordinate to yet more humane and compassionate than its powerful neighbour to the south. However, despite these differences, the core message underscores the necessity of uniting to confront a common enemy and enjoining the forces of law and order.[65]

This section of my chapter expands Jiwani's analysis, with a focus on how the US–Canada relationship developed and shifted over the three seasons, and how racialised subjects, in particular Muslims, were eventually evicted completely from symbolic citizenship. I will bring in Due South to identify how The Border replicates the production and reconciliation of national difference, as well as point out the distinguishing features that speak to a post-9/11 shift in the Canadian imaginary.

C. The Americanisation of Canada's Public Safety Infrastructure

Unlike Due South, the popularity of The Border rests less on laughing at the differences between American and Canadian styles of justice and more on bemoaning them, at least in the initial episodes. And yet ironically, the premise of the show actually reflects an Americanisation of discourse and identity.

A comparison between the fictionalised culture of The Border and the political culture in Canada demonstrates this point. The existing infrastructures regarding security and safety in Canada and the United States in the real world evince different preoccupations and ideologies. In the United States, 'the Department of Homeland Security [has] identified the predominant threat to America as a terrorist threat coming from outside the country, and established priorities that relegated preparedness for domestic emergencies, and natural hazards to a lower level'.[66] In contrast, the Canadian equivalent umbrella agency, Public Safety Canada, emphasises a broader mandate which includes emergency management, national security, law enforcement, corrections, and crime prevention.[67] These distinct mandates reflect different political understandings of risk, security and notions of preparedness.

However, The Border did not capitalise on this organisational distinction in its production of national difference. Instead it created a fictional organisation, Immigration, Customs and Security (ICS), an elite squad empowered to detain suspects and use force to protect Canada from foreign intrusions and hazards. The fictionalised ICS mimics the ideology of the Department of Homeland Security in its fixation on external threats. In its mission statement, Public Safety Canada does not deal with immigration matters; such issues are managed by a separate agency, Citizenship and Immigration Canada. The conflation of these two mandates within the fictional culture of The Border reflects the organisational structure of the United States and situates the

---

[65] Ibid 288.
[66] VA Konrad and HN Nicol, Beyond Walls: Re-Inventing the Canada-United States Borderlands, Border Regions Series (Burlington, Ashgate Publishing, 2008) 11.
[67] Public Safety Canada webpage, www.publicsafety.gc.ca/index-eng.aspx.

non-citizen as always already suspect; a risk about which ICS must be hyper-vigilant. However, because *The Border* draws on current events to inspire plotlines and makes reference to real and well-known agencies in its narrative, such as the Royal Canadian Mounted Police (RCMP) and the Canadian Security Intelligence Services (CSIS), the genre can be described as 'hybrid realist', as it appropriates non-fictional discourses, events and organisations to authenticate its imaginative world.[68] This mediated reality conforms to the Department of Homeland Security's leery gaze upon 'foreign' subjects, which includes immigrants, refugees, racialised people (even if citizens) and residents without official status. However, through a semiotic sleight of hand, *The Border* still manages to construct Canada as more tolerant towards foreign subjects.

D. Canada's Balance between Security and Human Rights

The pilot episode exemplifies *The Border's* image of Canada as effectively dealing with terrorists while protecting innocent citizens. The scene begins in Toronto airport where ICS arrests Tariq Haddad, a Muslim terrorist responsible for the bombing of a Canadian embassy. They also detain Nizar Karim, a Canadian citizen who had been seated next to Haddad on the aeroplane, and who spoke with him briefly. ICS finds no evidence to link Karim to the infamous terrorist; however, CSIS intervenes, takes Karim into custody, and then promptly delivers him to Homeland Security. Karim is shipped off to Syria's Tadmoor prison to undergo a brutal interrogation. This gross violation of the rule of law is blamed on both American and Canadian political agents. However, the head of ICS and protagonist of the show, Major Mike Kessler (James McGowan), refuses to abandon the innocent Canadian to this American-backed torture chamber.

Kessler's efforts for this wrongfully detained Muslim can be seen as a spin-off of Fraser's efforts to help reform low-level offenders in *Due South*. In both cases, the Canadian series' protagonists are confronted with the attitude that effort should be reserved for more innocent citizens. But like Fraser, Kessler does not quit. Despite the fact that he has been ordered off the case by the Deputy Minister, Kessler manipulates the press to draw links between Karim's situation and that of another innocent Canadian whom CSIS had previously delivered to Homeland Security. The case of Aram-al-Kir was a media spectacle when it came out that he was tortured on a daily basis for 18 months before his innocence was established and he was returned to Canada. Kessler's behind-the-scenes manoeuvrings work; the media exposure forces the Canadian government to intervene on Karim's behalf to clear his name and bring him home. Enhancing the hybrid realism of the show, Canadian viewers will likely make the connection between the fictional innocent men and the real Maher Arar, a Canadian citizen who was detained by the United States and subsequently sent to Syria, where he was allegedly tortured for over a year before his innocence was established.[69] The guilty Muslim men also tap into hybrid-realism, not because

---

[68] Z Druick and A Kotsopoulos (eds), *Programming Reality: Perspectives on English-Canadian Television*, Film and Media Studies Series (Waterloo, Wilfrid Laurier University Press, 2008) 1.

[69] Note that the United States denies any wrongdoing and maintains that Arar is connected to terrorist organisations. For more information on Maher Arar, see www.cbc.ca/news/background/arar/index.html.

they signify a specific person, but because they conform to the generic caricature of Muslim monsters who are ubiquitous in news media,[70] as well as entertainment programming.[71]

Whether they end up being good or bad, the show clearly constructs Muslims as presumptively suspicious persons whose loyalty to Canada must be investigated by ICS. However, the moral battle in the pilot is really between the good Canadians at ICS and the nasty American agenda, enforced by CSIS lackeys and servile Canadian politicians. While there are no American characters in the first episode, it is clear that it is American disrespect for due process that results in Karim's wrongful detention and presumable torture. This rendition of American abuse of power takes Vecchio's minor violations of due process to the nth degree. As a human rights lawyer, Yvonne Castle (Debra McCabe), states on *The Border*, 'torture by proxy, a Syrian growth industry. Why do I sense the Americans are involved?' When Kessler manages to finesse the return of Karim, CSIS representative Andrew Mannering (Nigel Bennett) and the Deputy Minister are furious. Kessler learns that because of this interference, 'the Americans are not happy'. In response, Homeland security sends an American agent, Bianca LaGarda, to oversee ICS activities and intervene when necessary.

With the introduction of an American Homeland Security agent into the narrative, the production of national difference gets personal. While *The Border* is clearly premised on an ensemble cast, the only two recognisable characters featured in the opening credits are LaGarda and Kessler. They are the main protagonists. Agent LaGarda personifies the United States as hot-headed, unscrupulous and self-centred, while Major Kessler represents Canada as restrained, principled and progressive. Although the show portrays both as sexy and seductive, their respective charms reflect their national character. LaGarda's sexiness is associated with her forceful, take-charge attitude, which is specifically nationalised when the computer geek character, Hieronymus Slade (Jonas Chernick), refers to her as an 'American dominatrix'. Kessler's sexiness stems from his reserved manner and quiet authority that women seem to find irresistible. Like Fraser, Kessler gets a lot of female attention, but unlike the Mountie, he gets a lot more action. Thus, *The Border* updates heroic Canadian masculinity by replacing the gentleman's image with that of the ladies' man.

As stated, Kessler and LaGarda are not quite the buddy-cop team that we saw in *Due South*. Instead, the *Border* translates Vecchio's aggressiveness into LaGarda's militarism, and Fraser's niceness into Kessler's diplomacy. As was the case with *Due South*, the earlier episodes hinge on the dramatic tension between American and Canadian styles of justice as enacted by these two figures. I will address how this contrast is racially coded later, but for now I want to focus on the ways in which the representation of American militancy creates a backdrop to emphasise Canada's ability to balance security and rights more effectively.

This is acutely dramatised in the third episode, 'Bodies on the Ground'. Again, the episode features Muslim terrorists, but as in the pilot, the moral battle is between

---

[70] P Gottschalk and G Greenberg, *Islamophobia: Making Muslims the Enemy* (Lanham, Rowman & Littlefield Publishers, 2008).

[71] See JG Shaheen, *Guilty: Hollywood's Verdict on Arabs After 9/11* (Northhampton, Olive Branch Press, 2008).

American and Canadian security forces. The story begins dramatically with an American rendition flight crashing in Quebec and letting three Muslim detainees loose on Canadian soil. Agent LaGarda explains that the fugitives are, 'Enemy combatants with high intelligence value.' When LaGarda refuses to divulge where the prisoners were headed, Kessler asks, 'Albania, Serbia, somewhere where the gloves can come off?' LaGarda explains that these terrorists are so evil and so resistant to American interrogation techniques that she has '...no problem handing [them] over to people who are not so squeamish'. In other words, it is suggested that Americans outsource torture, something that not only marks the United States as a human rights-violating state, but also as a threat to Canadians.

Thanks to American policies and screw-ups, the terrorists initially escape and end up killing two Canadian officers and wounding more. The situation escalates when, prior to the terrorists being apprehended, LaGarda decides that the situation is too dangerous and orders American F16 jet fighter planes to bomb the region of rural Quebec where they believe the fugitives are hiding. This order is given despite the fact that there are two ICS agents (and perhaps unknown civilians) who are also in the region. Thankfully, ICS apprehends the terrorists in the nick of time and the American bombing is called off. This almost comical exaggeration of American aggression suggests a total disregard for international law, Canadian sovereignty and Canadian lives.[72] This portrayal is an intensified version of Vecchio and Kowalski taking the law into their own hands when they intimidate suspects or break into homes without a warrant. And as in *Due South*, we find that the Canadians, with less firepower and fewer technological resources than the Americans, still manage to catch the bad guys by virtue of their superior crime-fighting skills.

E. American White Supremacy versus Canadian Racial Harmony

Canada's more effective law enforcement also applies to combating racist crimes. As with *Due South*, American white supremacists rear their ugly heads a few times during the series. In 'Gross Deception', Kessler and LaGarda investigate an arms smuggling deal, with Canadian military weaponry being trafficked across the border. At the end of the episode they discover that the culprits were American 'home-grown terrorists': white supremacists who had formed a group called the 'Sons of Paul Revere'. LaGarda explains that the group had planned to bomb an INS (Immigration and Naturalization Service) office. Kessler connects the crime to the work of Timothy McVeigh and the Unabomber and knowingly recites the Second Amendment as an explanation for such aggression. As in *Due South*, blame for American vigilante terrorism is partially attributed to the constitutional right to bear arms. In addition, the name of the white supremacist organisation makes reference to the American war hero Paul Revere, rooting the current day violence in the discourse of America's bloody revolutionary past. The Canadian gaze implicitly elevates Canada's piecemeal

---

[72] Not surprisingly, the American diplomatic cable disclosed on Wikileaks was particularly offended by this portrayal. See www.wikileaks.ch/cable/2008/01/08OTTAWA136.html.

process of nation-building and loyalty to government over America's violent process of revolution and hostility to government.[73]

While *The Border* does recognise the existence of Canadian white supremacists, the show subtly places responsibility for these miscreants on Americans. In the episode 'Hate Metal', a racist militia group in British Columbia is revealed to be a small chapter of a larger organisation spawned by a notorious American white supremacist. Even though the Canadian operation is planning an attack on the Sikh community in Vancouver, there is a sense that Canadian racism is an infection from the United States. The most vicious and seasoned white supremacist is still an American who has inspired the crew and mobilised the attack.

In other episodes, historical white supremacy is explicitly invoked to construct Canada as a haven from American racism. In 'Enemy Contact', Darnell Williams (Jim Codrington), an ICS agent, is interrogating Sorraya, an American Muslim convert and, as it turns out, a terrorist. She refers to Williams as an African man and he rebuts, 'Actually, I'm a Canadian man.' When Sorraya challenges his patriotism considering his ancestors were 'dragged here in chains', he says proudly, 'To America. They came to Canada to be free.' The construction of Canada as safe house is again invoked in the episode 'Stop Loss', where three American soldiers seek refugee status in Canada. Kessler's daughter, Zoe, tries to convince her father that the soldiers should be allowed to stay by citing the Underground Railway as precedent for Canada assisting oppressed Americans. These two references produce national difference by drawing upon 'the image of Canada as 'freedom's land' [which] has lodged itself in the national psyche and become part of our national identity'.[74] Thus the show not only imagines the Great White North as the real refuge for the 'huddled [African-American] masses longing to be free', it also contributes to the collective amnesia of Canada's historical participation in slavery, systemic racism and violent assimilation practices.

As in *Due South*, these forgotten atrocities are also linked to a disavowal of current day oppression of racialised people, in particular Aboriginal peoples. *The Border* reinscribes the oft-repeated nationalist notion that Canada respects Aboriginal peoples' autonomy, while America still views them as unrestrained savages. In the episode 'Grey Zone', Homeland Security and ICS investigate an Albanian money-laundering scheme at an Aboriginal-run casino. Kessler is sensitive to the fact that their investigation trespasses on Mohawk territory, while LaGarda is eager to send US agents onto the reserve without Mohawk authorisation. Her view—which is not the view of the show—constructs Aboriginal people as criminals who endanger the real Americans: 'Today the Mohawks are sending us drugs, tomorrow terrorists and plutonium'. She further resents their special jurisdiction complaining that, 'It's bad enough the Natives run contraband with impunity.' When she is confronted with an admonishing stare from Kessler, she sarcastically corrects herself: 'Okay, exercise their cross-border treaty rights.' Kessler, on the other hand, insists on respecting the conditions of Frank Arthurs, the Mohawk Sheriff, when they begin their investigation at the casino.

---

[73] KL Morrison, *Canadians Are Not Americans: Myths and Literary Traditions* (Toronto, Second Story Press, 2003).

[74] A Cooper, *The Hanging of Angélique: The Untold story of Canadian Slavery and the Burning of Montréal* (Toronto, HarperCollins, 2006) 69; cited in A Bakan, 'Reconsidering the Underground Railroad: Slavery and Racialization in the Making of the Canadian State' (2008) 4 *Socialist Studies / Études Socialistes* 1, www.socialiststudies.com/index.php/sss/article/view/3.

There is a sense of cooperation and mutual respect between ICS and Aboriginal law enforcement, again drawing upon the myth—which was also perpetuated in *Due South*—that Canadian law enforcement officers have a collaborative relationship with Aboriginal peoples, both in the past and the present.

Canadian and Mohawk law enforcement officers working together to bring down the bad guys.[75]

Yet it is important to note that while ICS works with the Aboriginal officers, it is Kessler, the white man, who heads the investigation and leads the final takedown. The Aboriginal officers look for Kessler's signal for authorisation before they proceed. Colonial domination and images of paternalism are thus regenerated, even as the show attempts to perpetuate a rosy picture of multiculturalism.

Like Fraser, Kessler performs the figure of the White saviour as he works to sort the bad racialised Others from the victimised racialised Others. As we saw in the pilot episode, Kessler rescues a Canadian-Syrian, Nizar Karim, from an unlawful detention by American and Syrian authorities. The closing scene features Kessler looking on with satisfaction as Karim is reunited with his family at Toronto airport after his ordeal in the Syrian prison. As the show spends much time showcasing surveillance technology, this image suggests that by constantly looking at racialised people, ICS is actually *looking after* their best interests. Kessler, who goes unnoticed by the Karim family, is situated behind as a white protective figure. His constant gaze reassures the viewer that ICS surveillance and racial profiling is all to identify and protect the innocents from the thugs.

Kessler looking at the racialised Other that he saved.[76]

---

[75] *The Border*, 'Gray Zone', season one (2008).
[76] *The Border*, 'Pockets of Vulnerability' season one (2008).

Aboriginal victims are also recipients of Kessler's protection. In the episode 'Double Dealing', Kessler rescues an Aboriginal woman, Tamara Hardistry (Leanne Poirier Greenfield), who has been kidnapped by mobsters. Kessler enters the crime scene accompanied by Homeland Security Agent Liz Carver, who by this point had replaced LaGarda in the series. When the two agents discover Hardistry chained in a basement, she gratefully launches herself into Kessler's arms, sobbing, 'Thank you' while Kessler says soothingly, 'You're safe.'

The Aboriginal victim encircled in Kessler's protective embrace as DHS agent looks on.[77]

It is significant that Hardistry does not go to Carver first, but to Kessler. Again we get the image of Canada as defender of the maltreated and the victimised. Aboriginal feminine subjectivity is brought in as a prop to enact this self-congratulatory image. As Eva Mackey notes, 'Aboriginal people are necessary players in nationalist myths: they are the colourful recipients of benevolence, the necessary 'others' who reflect back white Canada's self-image of tolerance.'[78]

F. Canadian Whiteness and American Racialisation

As with the racial subjectivity of Fraser in relation to his American partners, Kessler's whiteness stands in contrast to the racialisation of LaGarda and Carver. In the second episode, we learn that LaGarda was born to an Italian mother and a Cuban father. Like Vecchio and Kowalski, she too has a violent streak, not so much in her personal interactions but through the security orders she sometimes gives to effect torture and collateral damage on innocent people. Her character is bossy, aggressive and tactless. As Jiwani points out, 'LaGarda herself suffers from the quintessential stereotypical Latina flaw—her temper and inability to be diplomatic.'[79] The show connects this personality defect to her American citizenship and patriotism. For example, when Kessler refers to her as a 'cowboy',[80] he likens the agent to the iconic figure of American gun-toting individualism. And as in *Due South*, each episode concludes with the inevitable vindication of the Canadian way over that of the cowboy.

---

[77] *The Border*, 'Double Dealing' season two (2008).
[78] Mackey, *House of Difference* (n 31) 2.
[79] Jiwani, 'Soft Power' (n 64) 281.
[80] *The Border*, 'Gray Zone'. season one (2008).

When LaGarda is replaced by Carver, an Asian-American, the show takes a significant turn towards reconciling national differences. However racial difference, along with sex difference, is still invoked to contrast Carver and Kessler's personalities. In the final episode of the series, 'No Refuge', we see Carver and Kessler having an argument with Mannering, the nefarious CSIS representative. Afterwards Carver asks Kessler, 'How do you keep yourself from punching that asshole's lights out?' Kessler responds, 'Emotional repression; it helps to be a white male.' While Kessler's answer calls attention to race and sex instead of allowing patriarchal whiteness to remain invisible and thus more powerful, it nonetheless reveals the way that Carver's racialised and gendered identity is tied to a particular personality: one that is hot-tempered and impatient. Again, it is not a coincidence that both American agents share this volatile temperament, just as Vecchio and Kowalski did in *Due South*. Canadian superior styles of justice thus hinge on reinforcing the image of in-control whiteness versus out-of-control racialised subjectivity.

G. Post-9/11 and the Otherisation of Americans

I want to return now to the fish-out-of-water premise of both shows. In *Due South*, the show identifies Fraser as the misfit: his sympathetic attitude towards criminals, non-violent law enforcement techniques, and quaint Canadian quirks all conflict with the ethos of the Chicago police station in which he unofficially works. In *The Border*, we see LaGarda as the freak: her ruthless attitude towards suspects, excessively violent strategies, and abrasive manner all clash with the ethos of the ICS headquarters she frequents. While both scenarios elevate Canadian styles of justice over American, as I stated in the previous section, *Due South* does so by engaging in a self-othering process. The American way, even if subtly denigrated in the narrative, becomes the benchmark against which to measure Canadian superiority. Yet *The Border* shifts this dynamic to such an extent that the Canadian way becomes the benchmark by which to measure American shortcomings. I want to suggest that American foreign policy post-9/11 has generated, and in some cases furthered, global Anti-American frustration, in a way that reinvigorated the Canadian imagined community. In *America Alone*, Stefan A Halper and Jonathan Clarke canvass the many studies that document how American foreign policy post-9/11 has engendered diminished, and often downright negative, opinions of the 'Stars and Stripes' across the world. In this best-selling book, these self-identified 'center-right' thinkers sharply criticise American policy of the past decade that has dismissed diplomacy as a 'tiresome constraint on American 'unipolarity''.[81] In the Canadian imaginary, Canadians look pretty good compared to them!

The *Border* capitalises on this feeling, which is reflected not just in the ways in which Canadian styles of justice are elevated over American—after all, we saw this

---

[81] SA Halper and J Clarke, *America Alone: The Neo-Conservatives and the Global Order* (Cambridge, Cambridge University Press, 2004) 4, lib.myilibrary.com.proxy.library.carleton.ca/Browse/open.asp?ID=54096&loc=Cover.

in *Due South* as well—but in the ways LaGarda is 'otherised' within the narrative. Her position in Toronto, surrounded by Canadians, means her excessive unilateral militancy is constantly being challenged. At one point, Kessler specifically makes reference to her myopic worldview when he asks her in frustration: 'Have you ever been posted out of the US? Things have been broken for a while. You have to stop swatting flies with bunker busters.'[82] While American superior military power and technological resources are undisputed, Canadian morality and proportionality in response to terrorist threats are affirmed. *The Border* suggests that the Canadian strategic and ethical compass must attempt to steer its misguided neighbour to a more prudent and rights-respecting path.

H. Reconciling American and Canadian Styles of Justice through Eros

In *The Border*, as in *Due South*, the nations' clashing styles of justice slowly work themselves out into a harmonious partnership as the show progresses. Interestingly, as was the case in *Due South*, this is also expressed in part through eros, although in a much more explicit and heterosexual fashion. Over time, Kessler and LaGarda develop a mutual respect, bridge many of their differences, and even come to flirt brazenly with one another. One concession that Kessler makes to his American colleague right from the start is in direct opposition to the normative subtext of *Due South*. When LaGarda presents extradition papers for a murder suspect in Canadian custody, Kessler informs her that he technically can't extradite someone to a death penalty state. LaGarda is furious, but Kessler simply instructs her to lower the charge to kidnapping, and then upgrade to murder once they have the suspect in American custody. Thus, while the death penalty was represented as immoral and subject to gross error or corruption in *Due South*, *The Border* shows a Canadian facilitating capital punishment by sidestepping Canadian law. LaGarda too bends the rules for the benefit of ICS as she learns to trust Kessler's tactics and principles. In the episode 'Nothing to Declare', she gives Kessler access to a top secret FBI file because she knows it will assist his investigation. And in the last episode where LaGarda operates as the official Homeland Security liaison officer, she unites with Kessler to defy direct orders from both CSIS and the CIA in order to stop a deadly pharmaceutical scam. The crucial differentiation is thus no longer between American and Canadian law enforcement, but between law enforcement officers and spy agencies taking orders from politicians. In the last scene, we learn that LaGarda has been recalled back to Washington DC because her superiors believe she has 'lost perspective'. She and Mike share a bottle of wine at his home, and both admit they will miss each other. The show suggests that had she stayed, their relationship might have become more intimate. Tensions between styles of justice are translated into erotic tension that ultimately

---

[82] *The Border*, 'Bodies on the Ground' season one (2008).

mutes the differences between the two nations. During this exchange, the camera angle does a close-up shot that emphasises the intimacy of their relationship.

Kessler and LaGarda have reconciled their differences through eros.[83]

However, the Canada–US relationship is finally consummated with the introduction of Liz Carver (Grace Park).

Grey Jackson (Graham Abbey), the prototypical rough-and-tumble white man on the ICS team, first meets Carver on an assignment that takes place on the US-Canada border. It doesn't take long for the two to give into their mutual desire. In the next bedroom scene, their sexual relationship is explicitly linked to collaborative crime fighting when we see them post-coitus and naked, surveying information of their suspects.

Jackson and Carver post-coitus examining evidence together.[84]

When Carver is assigned to replace LaGarda, she is at first adamant that all romantic contact between her and Jackson must end. She explains to him: 'The DHS has a policy against close and continuing bonds of affection with foreign nationals.' This directive is another indication of the extreme xenophobia of the United States. But after again succumbing to Jackson's rugged Canadian charm, she grumbles the next morning: 'If my superiors find out I'm screwing a foreigner...' Grey responds indignantly, 'It's not like I'm an Iraqi!!' In other words, racial profiling is fine, but Canadians should not be considered a suspect group. His protest indicates the direction in which the series will soon turn, by suggesting that American and Canadian alliance comes at the price of displacing abjection onto Other communities.

83 *The Border*, 'Prescriptive Measures' season two (2008).
84 *The Border*, 'Articles of Faith' season two (2008).

I. Demonising Muslims

While the *The Border* capitalises on a number of stock racial figures, including Tamil extremists, Albanian mobsters, Russian mobsters, Chinese spies, Hindu fundamentalists, Congolese warlords, Croatian warlords, Kenyan drug dealers, and Latino gangs, the most recurrent bad guy is the Muslim terrorist. In an interview with Peter Raymont, co-creator of *The Border*, he boasts that the show cast 217 actors from visible minority groups over its three-year run.[85] However, Raymont's claim that these actors were given 'interesting and positive roles—not negative roles', is belied by even a cursory examination of the weekly plots, particularly of those involving Muslims. While there were, of course, a few Muslim victims of abuse or torture, as we saw in the episode entitled 'Pockets of Vulnerability', the majority were bad guys: intolerant fundamentalists at best, terrorists at worst.

Perhaps Raymont was focusing instead on the recurring South Asian Muslim character, Layla Hourani, an ICS agent for the first two seasons before being killed in the line of duty. From the first episode, Hourani establishes an ambivalent relationship to Islam. At a multicultural school, Hourani defends the right to wear the hijab to her white partner, Jackson. But when Jackson asks whether she ever wore one, she replies, 'Please, I was deep into grunge.' In this statement, the audience is reassured that although a Muslim, Hourani has always been a proper assimilated Other who can be trusted. As Jiwani points out, wearing the hijab casts someone in the 'bad Muslim' category as a fundamentalist or a victim of fundamentalist oppression.[86] Throughout the show, Hourani establishes her 'good Muslim' status first by wearing Western-identified clothing, then by flirting with white men and eventually by having an affair. Again, eros plays a role, this time in containing and familiarising the Other. Her rejection by conservative Muslims, who dismiss her as a 'traitor' and 'obsessed with her looks', demonstrates she is on the right side. She clinches her commitment to the Western point of view when she chases down Muslim terrorists and shoots them down if necessary. But despite all these traits that code her as an acceptable citizen, Hourani is still killed off at the end of the second season. Even reassuring assimilationists like Hourani are not allowed to stay in the show. This decision was not because the actress chose to leave, but because the producers chose to have her character eliminated.[87] Significantly, she is replaced by Agent Khalida Massi—racialised but not identified as Muslim—whose mother died in a Muslim terrorist attack. Thus, the one 'good Muslim' character in the cast who, at the very least, buffers the ubiquitous image of Muslim maniacs, is discarded for someone who symbolises victimisation at the hands of 'jihadists'. By the time the third season begins, it is clear that in the show's imaginary, the only good Muslim is literally a dead Muslim.

---

[85] A Dowling, 'Boarded Up' *TV Guide*, 2010-03-29 tvguide.ca/Interviews/Insider/Articles/100329_the_border_AD.

[86] Jiwani, 'Soft Power' (n 64) 287, drawing on insights from M Mamdani, *Good Muslim, Bad Muslim: America, the Cold War, and the Roots of Terror* (New York, Pantheon Books, 2004).

[87] B Brioux, 'Goodbye, Mr. Bauer' *The Toronto Star*, 22 May 2010), www.thestar.com/entertainment/television/article/813094.

J. Justifying Torture

This Islamaphobic subtext actuates American and Canadian solidarity in the third season of *The Border*. In the episode entitled 'The Broken', the plot is centred on the 'ticking bomb scenario' to convey the necessity for Canadians to ally with Americans, and the acceptability of torture for the greater good. In this episode, LaGarda returns for a special assignment to escort Ali Jabir, a 17-year-old prisoner from Guantanamo Bay back to Canada. Jabir, a resident but not a citizen of Canada, had been in 'Gitmo' since he was 13, and the show acknowledges that he was continually tortured, requiring over 30 medical treatments during his incarceration. However, Jabir's release is not for the sake of his health or his innocence, even though LaGarda concedes that he was unfairly given the rap while the real terrorist, Nasim Mujab, got away. Homeland Security believes that by releasing Jabir, they will catch Mujab. The trap works, but of course, it cannot be that easy. ICS discovers that a terrorist attack is being planned in the next 24 hours in Toronto and their only leads are Mujab and Jabir. They interrogate Jabir who they discover has no 'good intel', but after four years of torture, he will say anything to make them stop the harsh questioning. During a musical montage with an Arabic soundtrack, we witness ICS alternately interrogating Mujab and trying to decipher a terrorist code, with a clock literally ticking down to 'D-Day'. The suspense that is built and the imminence of the attack are meant to justify their subsequent course of action. Kessler strikes on a brilliant idea: build upon the foundation of torture inflicted on Jabir and use his post-traumatic stress against Mujab. ICS arranges for Mujab to observe Williams fiercely interrogating Jabir, who has completely broken down and is begging for mercy. In the figure below, you can see Mujab in the reflection of the glass as he witnesses the abuse.

Darnell psychologically torturing Jabir in order to extract information from Mujab.[88]

Kessler and LaGarda keep repeating that they will stop the interrogation if Mujab reveals the terrorists' target. When Mujab does not crack initially, Kessler screams, 'He was tortured because of you.' This is the third time in the episode that Mujab is blamed for the torture Jabir received at the hands of American authorities. Mujab breaks down and reveals the target.

---

[88] *The Border*, 'The Broken', season three (2009).

Torture is justified and rationalised on a number of levels in this episode, but much of it will not be recognised as such because, as Jinee Lokaneeta argues, the popular understanding of torture focuses exclusively on physical brutality and grievous bodily harm.[89] While this latter type of torture is briefly alluded to by Slade (the ICS character taken the least seriously) when he expresses disapproval of Jabir's initial torture from the ages of 13 to 17, La Garda transfers moral approbation onto the previous US government. In addition, blame is also displaced onto Mujab for allowing Jabir to 'serve the sentence' that was meant for him. The logic of this accusation is that bad Muslims are blamed for the torture of good Muslims, and not that the United States has contravened international law by systematically inflicting torture on detainees. The right to be free from torture is a non-derogable right and applies to all people, not just 'innocent' ones. But *The Border* suggests that Muslims are excluded from this protection.

As it turns out, thanks to Guantanamo torture of an innocent Muslim boy, the agents have a weapon to use against Mujab, the evil Muslim man. In addition, their final tactic against Mujab would, I submit, violate the United Nations Convention against Torture and Other Cruel, Inhuman or Degrading Treatment or Punishment. The Convention defines torture as 'any act by which severe pain or suffering, whether physical *or mental*, is intentionally inflicted on a person for such purposes as obtaining from him *or a third person* information or a confession...' [*emphasis added*].[90] In this incident, Williams purposefully inflicts psychological torture on Jabir in order to extract information from Mujab, who is tormented by the sight of his victimised friend. It should be noted that Kessler is saved from getting his hands dirty by having the one racialised man on his team carry out Jabir's psychological torture.[91] And, as with most ticking bomb hypotheticals, the narrative framework establishes that the means of torture justify the ends of saving innocent lives.[92]

This moral universe is shared by both Canada and the United States. After they manage to prevent the terrorist attack, Bianca praises her Canadian colleague: 'You did good work in there, Mike...I always thought we'd make an outstanding team.' Here, the viewers get the voice of American authority patting Canada on the back. Canadians are now in line with the Americans; they not only tolerate American torture, they also engage in the practice themselves *when necessary*. The show seems no longer interested in defending the border between the two law enforcement worlds; instead Canadian national pride comes from receiving American approval of their

---

[89] J Lokaneeta, 'A Rose by another Name: Legal Definitions, Sanitized Terms, and Imagery of Torture in *24*' (2010) *Law Culture and the Humanities* 6, 246, 263.

[90] Convention against Torture and Other Cruel, Inhuman or Degrading Treatment or Punishment, Adopted and Opened for Signature, Ratification and Accession by General Assembly Resolution 39/46 of 10 December 1984, entry into force 26 June 1987, in accordance with art 27 (1), www2.ohchr.org/english/law/cat.htm.

[91] This is not the first time that Williams is associated with the seamier side of law enforcement. In the episode 'Blowback', Kessler was planning to kill a Croatian war criminal against direct orders from his superiors, but Williams does the killing before his boss has a chance to do it, in order to protect him. In addition, in the episode 'Double Dealing', unbeknown to Kessler, Williams delivers a suspect to a remote location where it is implied that he will be tortured in order to extract information. It works and no one at ICS is any the wiser.

[92] Lokaneeta, 'A Rose by another Name' (n 89) 257.

counter-terrorism tactics. Unlike Fraser, who established his heroism in part by his kindness to offenders, Kessler's willingness to make suspects suffer for the greater good signals his heroic status. In addition, in the world of *The Border*, Canadians would never have known about the impending terrorist attack if Homeland Security had not shared information on Mujab. There is a sense, reinforced in other episodes in the second and third season, that the American 'war on terror' is also protecting Canadian soil. This cozy picture of compatibility between Canadian and US styles of justice is in distinct contrast to the first season and a half, which showed the 'war on terror' endangering Canadian lives. In these earlier episodes, the clash between Homeland Security and ICS created the moral tension upon which the narrative was built. Kessler specifically condemned 'ends justify the means' approaches. But by the end, we see him embracing a consequentialist philosophy that wins favour from Homeland Security. For ICS, the enemies and the moral opponents now mostly consist of racially marked Others, who either hail from outside of Canada, or are citizens who have resumed the atavistic practices of their ethnic/religious origins.

K. The Never-Ending Struggle against Bad Racialised People

The final episode of *The Border*, 'No Refuge', celebrates this US–Canada collaborative teamwork by making Latino youth occupy the role of shared enemy. ICS is working with Carver and Homeland Security to protect Toronto's residents from a Mexican drug cartel looking to distribute north with the assistance of the street gang, MS-13. The show ends on a dramatic cliffhanger with the ICS team trapped in a refugee centre surrounded by MS-13 members. The gang has cut all power and telephone communication and, like zombies, are slowly penetrating the ad hoc barriers put up by Kessler and his cohorts. Much to the fans' dismay, there was no resolution to this dire predicament, as the series was then abruptly cancelled.

While the producers may not have known that this was their last hurrah, the story does provide some closure. The final image we get of the team shows them heroically protecting good racialised people (refugees) against their bad counterparts (the Latino gangs). There is a sense that this is a never-ending struggle. In the last few seconds of the show, an MS-13 gang member has hacked through a door and peers in like a predator locating his prey. His tattooed face, with the number 13 branded on his forehead, emphasises his construction as primitive and animalistic within the clean-cut imaginary of the show.

These racialised men are not just animalised by the camera shots, but by what goes unmentioned on screen. Missing from the show is any reference to the socio-economic and political context that contributed to the creation of such gangs. As Juan Fogelbach argues, the existence of MS-13 can be attributed, in part, to the systemic and persistent marginalisation, victimisation and imposed poverty that El Salvadorian refugees experience in the United States.[93] The American practice of deporting members has

---

[93] JJ Fogelbach, 'Mara Salvatrucha (MS-13) and Ley Anti Mara: El Salvador's Struggle to Reclaim Social Order' (2005–06) 7 *San Diego Int'l LJ* 224.

exacerbated the problem and increased the gang's membership. Without any of this context, the young Latino men simply appear as hateful and bloodthirsty animals.

While the violent closing of *The Border* in an urban jungle is in stark contrast to the peaceful conclusion of *Due South* in the icy wilderness, the harmony between American and Canadian law enforcement is still verified, in both shows, through eros. Recall that in *Due South*, Fraser and Kowalski remain partners, not because of their jobs, but because they choose to seek adventure together in Northern Canada, and as Keohane states, 'Nature is constructed as the locale for eroticism in the Canadian imaginary.'[94] In *The Border*'s final episode, violent criminality forms the erotic backdrop for the Canadian-American duo. In the midst of fighting off the MS-13 hooligans, Jackson and Grey—who have had their ups and downs—take a moment to express their commitment to one another. Love, apparently, conquers national differences.

IV. Conclusion

To close, I would like to return to the trope of queer to further nuance the differences between the imaginations of Canadian nationhood in *Due South* and *The Border*. Recall that in my analysis of the fish-out-of-water subjectivity in *Due South*, I drew upon Jason Morgan's suggestion that Canadian texts refusing the insularity of a discrete nation are queering the imagined community. For most of the series, the audience recognises Fraser's Canadianness by looking at him through the American gaze. His adoption of Inuit epistemological and moral frameworks further marks him as extraordinary. Notwithstanding the symbolic violence of claiming kinship with Aboriginal peoples whilst maintaining colonial power structures, Fraser's Inuit-Canadian hybridity and US–Canada oppositionality does not simply invoke the cherished notion of Canada as mosaic, but rather advances Canada as '... contradiction and paradox at the expense of an imagined homogeneity'.[95] This fragmentation of national identity disrupts the borders of the collective nationalist subject. When Kowalski remains in Canada to continue his homosocial relationship with Fraser, national difference is queered not merely because of the suggestion of same-sex, cross-national desire, but also because of the narrative picture of binational interdependence. While the two men will literally need each other to survive the harsh landscape, they also need each other in order to identify themselves as recognisable national subjects. The *survival* of Canadian identity depends on the Other. However, hegemonic conceptions of Canada as the site of benign whiteness continue to be perpetuated in the narrative. What remains entrenched and undisrupted is Fraser's whiteness as a blank screen to project the indefinite negotiation of difference.

---

[94] Kieran Keohane, *Symptoms of Canada: An Essay on the Canadian Identity* (University of Toronto Press, 1997) 111.

[95] Morgan (n 49) 218.

While *The Border* presents a more multicultural picture of Canadian identity, whiteness still operates as the hegemonic norm where difference is not just negotiated, but disciplined and managed. Canadian identity pivots on two axes of difference in the series. First, there are the racialised bad guys; whether foreign intruders or unassimilated immigrants, they represent a threat to national survival within the zeitgeist of post-9/11 Canada. But danger also comes from Canadian allies. The first half of the series' run suggests that the American 'war on terror' infringes Canadian sovereignty and sometimes endangers Canadian lives, particularly racialised innocents caught in the over-inclusive net of counter-terrorism tactics. This second axis of difference between Canada and the US is ultimately resolved through an accentuation of the first. Although eros plays its part, the solidarity that is built between Canadian and American law enforcement officers does not register as queer. If anything, the trope of queerness would be better deployed to elucidate how camaraderie is built through a kind of 'queer bashing', expressed in the violent measures of ICS and Homeland Security against suspected terrorists and other fiends. To be clear, the descriptor 'queer bashing' is not mere metaphor where I substitute race for sex to convey the fear of racialised and ethnicised subjects in the US–Canada psyche. As Jasbir Puar and Amit Raj argue, the figure of the modern terrorist registers not only as racial, but also as a sexual monster that has elicited belligerent heteronormative patriotism.[96] As we watch LaGarda and Kessler take turns interrogating racialised bad guys, we see their heterosocial bond strengthen and their national differences soften. In the final episode, the confrontation with Latino gang members compels Carver to no longer view Jackson as a 'foreigner', but as a committed romantic partner.

As stated, *The Border* was cancelled after this episode. While most of the on-line commentary suggests this was because of its time-slot, which placed the Canadian drama in stiff competition with popular American shows, it is possible that other reasons may have contributed to its falling ratings. As a Muslim who grew up in the United States but now calls Canada home, allow me to indulge in some far-fetched conjecture. I would like to think that the elimination of Layla Hourani was a contributing factor. I would like to think that on some level, it was appreciated that there was representation of a recurring Muslim character who was *good*, and that when she was killed off, there was a feeling of betrayal. Make no mistake, I agree with all of Jiwani's critiques of Hourani's character, and I understand that the image of the assimilated Muslim reassures the Islamaphobic imaginary that it only targets *bad* Muslims for contempt. But it was still a deep blow to my sense of belonging to find out that Hourani was replaced by a character portrayed as a victim of Islamic terrorists. I would like to think that the ideological shift in the second half of the series, which integrated Canadian and American security tactics against racialised Others, was alienating to some viewers. Again, make no mistake: I know that the notion of multicultural Canada as mosaic and acculturated America as melting pot is a distortion (usually

---

[96] JK Puar and AS Raj, 'Monster, Terrorist, Fag: The War on Terrorism and the Production of Docile Patriots' (2002) 20 *Social Text* 72, 118.

perpetuated by Canadians) of the complexity of both countries, and a reification of national difference.[97] But perhaps the show's failure to *survive* points to something in the Canadian imaginary that still wants to witness this difference as a moral battle-field. And maybe, just maybe, its initial popularity and subsequent decline in ratings points to a political interest in having a pop cultural critique of the gross human rights abuses that have accompanied America's 'war on terror'. While I acknowledge this may be wishful thinking on my part, it at least demonstrates the contested meanings that can be extracted from the commodity culture of Canadian television.

[97] Recent data suggests that Americans may actually support the ideals of multiculturalism more than Canadians: D Tandt, 'Cross-border Amity Eroding: Poll' *The Globe and Mail* (Toronto, Ontario, 9 May 2005) A.1, cited in B Beaty and R Sullivan, *Canadian Television Today* (Calgary, University of Calgary Press, 2006) 12.

16

Television Divorce in Post-Franco Spain: *Anillos de oro* (*Wedding Rings*)

ANJA LOUIS

I. Introduction

The transition from dictatorship to democracy in Spain was a time of unprecedented social change. Given the reluctance of the old guard to cede power, the interim period between General Franco's death in 1975 and the Socialist Party's (PSOE) election victory in 1982 was a time of extreme social tension. The process of democratisation rested very much on the shoulders of a new generation, where young and innocent lawyers (or not so young, but politically above suspicion) were called upon to participate in—and construct—democracy. What better way to celebrate 'hero lawyers'[1] than with a series set in one of the most challenging times of recent Spanish history, in which democracy was in the making and law was instrumental, both real and imagined, in major social changes of the time. The Constitution of 1978 proclaimed democratic principles after almost 40 years of dictatorship; in 1981 the Divorce Law allowed full dissolution of marriage rather than judicial separation. This groundbreaking new law exacerbated tensions between the Catholic Church and the state, becoming the focus of a wide-ranging public and parliamentary debate. The television show *Wedding Rings*[2] (1983) convincingly captures these social tensions. The series tells the story of two 'hero lawyers', Lola Martínez Luque (Ana Diosdado) and Ramón San Juan (Imanol Arias), describing them as personifications of progress who create a law firm together to specialise in divorce cases. Each episode deals with a particular divorce case, and each narrative guides the viewer through the social reality and change that

---

[1] The term 'hero lawyer' is used to refer to an archetypal hero and honourable lawyer as a representative of justice and social change.

[2] The series was called *Anillos de oro* in its original form, which literally means golden rings. In this chapter it will be referred to as *Wedding Rings* to capture the clear reference to weddings and wedding rings in the opening credits of the series.

the Divorce Law created within the country. It might seem odd that the 13 episodes of this highly acclaimed and award-winning television show[3] set during the time of the Spanish transition should concentrate solely on the issue of divorce, and odder still is the fact that most episodes do not actually end in divorce. The mostly conservative endings, however, attest to the anxiety about the supposed breakdown of marriage and its consequences for the family as the basis of society.

Wedding Rings can be read as a careful mediation between the opposing factions of the old and new Spain. Not only was the series an emblematic representation of Spain's transition to democracy, but the series also captured the public imagination.[4] The series made both main actors famous nearly overnight, especially Imanol Arias, who became the heartthrob of his generation (and the imaginary son-in-law the older generation of Spain would love to have). One element of the series' success could have been the long list of prestigious actors who guest-starred, such as Hector Alterio, José Bódalo, Alberto Closas, Juan Luis Galiardo, and María Luisa Ponte. These actors and actresses' stunning performances have become part of popular memory, and it is no coincidence that the best-scripted episodes star at least one of these actors or actresses. The Spanish film director and film critic José Luis Garci hailed *Wedding Rings* as a masterpiece of television, declaring that both Ana Diosdado's script and Pedro Masó's direction had a certain 'street smell', or rather authentically repre-sented the lived experiences during Spain's transition. The obvious social relevance of *Wedding Rings* testifies to its closeness to contemporary Spanish audiences. In his introduction to Ana Diosdado's script, Garci assured her that the series had been 'democratically declared of public interest by the audience'.[5] Pedro Masó, the series' director, confessed that everyone involved with the series was quite surprised at the great success of *Wedding Rings*, and gave credit for the success to Arias's versatile talent. Arias noted '[i]n those days it was considered a very progressive series'. Arias also acknowledged that 'having the scriptwriter [Ana Diosdado] on set meant we couldn't easily get away with changing the script when we had problems filming something'.[6] The series' incredible success quickly expanded to Latin American countries such as Cuba and Argentina, while at home women's magazines celebrated 'Arias fever'.[7] Arias himself acknowledged that he did not appear as much in the series as people remember, instead appearing no more than three times per episode on average. Alvares attributed the series' success partly to the social impact of the general phenomenon of TV series at the time; this is an interesting observation to make, especially if compared

[3] See L Díaz, *La television en España [Television in Spain], 1949–1995* (Madrid, Alianza, 1994).

[4] See also comments on YouTube.com, for eg at www.youtube.com/watch?v=aFwChmQq5Zk&feature= PlayList&p=704086904D83F8B1&playnext=1&index=8, for more anecdotal evidence of viewers' nostalgia.

[5] JL Garci, 'Introduction' in A Diosdado (ed), *Anillos de oro [Wedding Rings]* (Madrid, Espasa-Calpe, 1985) 19–20. Garci himself directed one of the emblematic films of the Transition, *Asignatura pendiente* [Unfinished Business], a love story about a generation who lived through socially and politically ambiguous times.

[6] R Alvares, *Imanol Arias* (Barcelona, Belacqva, 2003) 198–99. See also Díaz, *La televisión en España* (n 3) 249, where he gives details about Diosdado's prior work as a scriptwriter for Spanish national televi-sion. Her breakthrough is undoubtedly due to *Wedding Rings*.

[7] Alvares, *Imanol Arias* (n 6) 198–99.

to today's public attitude to television, most aptly summarised in the common label of *telebasura* (or tele-rubbish).[8]

Implicit in the huge success of *Wedding Rings* was a broader socio-political context that was evoked. The opening credits of the DVD explain that the television series is an essential point of reference for those interested in viewing an 'historic document' of the Spanish transition. Apart from the obvious social anxiety regarding the restructuring of Spanish society and the construction of democracy, *Wedding Rings* also convincingly captured two generations that lived through politically challenging times, and examined how their convictions on everyday issues (such as marriage and divorce) clashed with startling regularity.

II. Historical Background

The transition also included one of the most infamous attacks on lawyers' lives in Spanish legal history: the assassination of the so-called 'Attorneys of Atocha'. On 24 January 1977, two right-wing extremists entered the Atocha Street office of a group of labour law attorneys in Madrid and opened fire, killing five and wounding four. The massacre earned public indignation as a direct attack on the figure of the lawyer as someone who was instrumental in the application of democratic values—and also the process of democratisation itself—and, as a result, it is commemorated to this very day.[9] The original viewers of *Wedding Rings* would have watched the show against this historical backdrop and it is no coincidence that Ramón's hero status is re-enforced by the fact that he is both a labour and divorce attorney, the epitome of hero lawyers in post-Franco Spain.

It might be appropriate here to give a historical overview of the Spanish divorce laws. As early as 1932, Spain boasted one of the most modern divorce laws in Europe, as a result of the proclamation of the Second Republic in 1931 and its political commitment to equality. These laws provided for the dissolution of marriage by mutual consent without any further precondition. Predictably, this law was also the first one to be repealed in 1938, even prior to the end of the Spanish Civil War. More than 40 years later, divorce was again a yardstick for the new democracy that tried to bring Spanish divorce legislation in line with other European countries (France 1975,

---

[8] See Ibid 199, where she adds that once the Arias fever had started, Masó cashed in on it with another very successful series called *Brigada Central* [Central Brigade] in which Arias plays a Spanish version of Dirty Harry. See also PJ Smith, *Contemporary Spanish Culture* (Cambridge, Polity Press, 2003) 14, where he explains that television is generally scorned by Spaniards themselves despite the fact that Spain is one of the biggest producers of series drama in Europe, overtaking France and Germany, while also selling original formats abroad.

[9] In 2003 a monument was erected on Madrid's Plaza Antón Martín, near the Atocha Street office. Its plaque reads as follows: 'On January 24, 1977, in a labour law firm that was located at number 55 on Atocha Street, four lawyers and a trade unionist were killed and four more lawyers were injured. All were members of the *PCE* [Spanish Communist Party] and *CCOO* [Workers' Union]. This monument reproduces the sculpture of Juan Genovés known as "El Abrazo" [The Hug], a symbol of the restoration of freedom. It was opened by the City Council of Madrid on June 10, 2003, as a tribute to those who died in that office. It is a tribute to those who died for freedom in Spain.' For Juan Genovés's sculptures, see also www.juangenoves.com/en/work/sculptures/sculptures.html.

Germany 1976, Italy 1975).[10] The debate—at least in its parliamentary form—was not so much about divorce per se, but rather about the scope and extent of the new legislation. While the political left pressed for legislation similar to that of 1932, the political centre and right-wing parties were unsurprisingly conservative in their approach to family law. Unlike the 1932 Divorce Law that permitted immediate divorce, the 1981 Divorce Law imposed waiting periods of varying length. This law nearly always required the proceedings for judicial separation to precede those for the dissolution of marriage. According to Glos, the law thus imposed on the parties an 'unnecessary hurdle of duplicated proceedings. The duplication involves time, effort and expense on the part of the parties, and unnecessary clogging of court calendars and expense on the part of the courts.'[11] The Spanish legislature clearly hoped that compliance with these formalities would prevent hasty divorces in a final attempt to keep families together and prevent speedy marriages to third parties.

The Union of the Democratic Centre (UCD), the ruling political party in Spain at the time, struggled against the considerable anti-divorce sentiment of a large segment of its membership. Before the constitutional referendum of 6 December 1977, the Prime Minister at the time, Adolfo Suárez, categorically declared that 'the constitution is not pro-divorce',[12] in an attempt to assuage the conservative quarters' fears of 'a liberal revolution'. After lengthy debates in both parliament and the Judiciary Committee, two issues remained unresolved: first, the mutual consent clause (and following from that the question of fault or no-fault divorce); and second, the so-called *cláusula de dureza* (severity clause) in which the judge would be allowed to use his discretion to decide particularly difficult cases and deny a divorce altogether. Predictably, the Socialist Workers' Party (PSOE) and the Communist Party (PCE) favoured a no-fault divorce system, while the Democratic Coalition (CD) and the Union of the Democratic Centre (UCD) opposed this. The proposed no-fault divorce system produced heated debates between parties, but also considerable disagreement amongst the governing UCD parliamentary members, which culminated in some members breaking party discipline and voting against their own party in the final vote on 22 June 1981.

Regardless of this protracted political debate, the Divorce Law of 1981 came into force as a law that failed to include a mutual consent clause; it would take until 2005 before Spain reformed the Divorce Law to include a no-fault divorce provision.[13]

---

[10] See also GE Glos, 'The Spanish Divorce Law of 1981' (1983) 3 *International and Comparative Law Quarterly*, 688, where he adds that: 'The new concept of *civil* marriage in Spain might have been as important a change as the reintroduction of divorce. Civil marriage legislation was first enacted during the Second Republic in 1932, but it lasted only until its repeal in 1938. [...] It has abolished the virtual monopoly of the Catholic Church over marriages in that it gives the parties, including Catholics, the choice of entering into a civil marriage before an officer of state or into a religious marriage before a minister of any recognised religion. The law thus expresses the democratic approach to the issue by stressing the element of choice the parties have in entering into a marriage.'

[11] Ibid 680–81.

[12] Adolfo Suárez declared it on television. For printed evidence, see the letter to the editor by Manuela Gil Alonso entitled 'El ataque a la familia' [Attacking the family], in the Madrid daily *ABC*, 11 July 1980.

[13] For an interesting article on divorce rates in Europe, see L González and TK Viitanen, 'The Effect of Divorce Laws on Divorce Rates in Europe' (2006) *European Economic Review* 53.2, 127–38, in which they analyse the increase in divorce rates between 1950 and 2003. See also AB Jones, *Women in Contemporary Spain* (Manchester, Manchester University Press, 1997) 91, where she states that: 'Owing to pent-up

The public debate during the time of the law's initial passage was equally intense as the political debate, and a cursory look at the headlines at that time, describes the emotive content. For instance, on 19 October 1980, the ultra-conservative newspaper *ABC* gave an overview of the divorce laws of other countries; the headlines read as follows: 'One in Two [Divorces] in the States, One in Three in the USSR'; 'Belgium, by Mutual Consent after Six Months'; 'Sweden, Denmark and Norway, Quick Access to Divorce'; 'In Italy there's a Distinction between Religious and Civil Marriage'; 'Portugal Allows Mutual Consent after Two Years of Marriage'.[14]

It should also be noted that, at the time of this public debate, the spectre of Francoism still loomed quite large over the country, and artists used television to erode Francoist values. The pedagogical value of television shows should not be underestimated at a time like that, when democracy needed to be imagined and democratic values taught through narratives of private lives. Although the Divorce Law had come into force, social mores and attitudes did not change overnight, and the political and public debates in the series attest to that. If we consider television as a primary mediator in the public sphere and one of the most influential agents of value construction, then *Wedding Rings* can be considered a powerful mechanism in guiding its viewers through the moral climate of the time.

Television's blurring of the boundaries between public and private supplement transitional moments in history, as television is the ideal medium for the message of change and the creation of a 'mediated democratic polity'.[15] Manuel Palacio, in his excellent book *Historia de la television en España*, analyses the impact television might have had on the transition process. Palacio is careful not to overestimate television's impact, while also sharing important details with the reader. For example, on 15 June 1977, the night of Spain's first democratic elections since 1936, TVE (Spanish national television) celebrated election night by coining the phrase 'fiesta de la democracia' [party for democracy], in an attempt to establish a clear link between the celebration of democracy and the programming for that night. Similarly, on the night of the referendum on the Constitution (6 December 1978), TVE offered a whole array of entertainment programmes celebrating the momentous occasion. TVE's coverage of the assassination of the Atocha lawyers demonstrated another clear example of TVE's commitment to the democratic process. Palacio described the news coverage during the 'seven days in January'[16] as a particularly strong example of how the newspresenters communicated the political message of non-violence through visibly remorseful

---

demand over 21,000 [divorce suits] took place in the first full year after reintroduction, and in 1995 (after some fluctuation) the figure stood at 33,000. Separations consistently and increasingly exceed divorces—in 1991, for example, there were 29,000 divorces and 39,000 separations—reflecting a preference for judicial separation among the middle and upper classes, partly for financial reasons.'

[14] Compare *El País*'s less emotive headlines, 23 October 1980: 'Divorce Possible after 2 Years of Separation'; 'Reduced Power of Courts to Deny Divorce'. See also *El País*, 23 June 1981: 'Separation and Divorce Suits Start from August'; 'Congress Rejects 'Tough Clause' of Divorce Bill in Secret Ballot'.

[15] J Corner, *Critical Ideas in Television Studies* (Oxford, Clarendon Press, 1999) 114.

[16] The assassination of the Atocha lawyers is often referred to as 'seven days in January' due to the film with the same title, directed by Juan Antonio Bardem.

faces. The public display and coverage of communist mourning on television was a crucial 'distancing act from Francoism'.[17]

III. Overview of *Wedding Rings*

Citizens used the topic of divorce as a litmus test for democracy, and the fictional discussions in *Wedding Rings* reflect the range of opinions expressed in the national press. At the start of the pilot episode, Ramón has a very telling conversation with a taxi driver, who—fitting for his profession—is the *vox populi*:

Taxi Driver: There just aren't any civilised people any more. [...] It's scary to walk on the street these days.

Ramón: Particularly when you have to work at night.

Taxi Driver: No, I don't mean robberies, I mean people! People are so impolite, everybody barks at each other. You ask them something politely and they bark at you, particularly in the city centre. [...] It's like this divorce thing that they've just come up with. Do you think that's a good idea?

Ramón: Good idea? In what sense?

Taxi Driver: In the good old days nobody would get divorced. Everybody put up with their fate. But today...

Ramón: Every now and then there is progress. We've also abolished the Inquisition.

Taxi Driver: Progress? What progress? Today people get divorced for any old thing: 'you are a pig'... 'you're betraying me with the secretary'... 'you're a drunkard and you hit me'... 'you're a whore'. And they get divorced for silly little things ... I find that ridiculous.

Ramón: I know, it's really bad. It would have to be compulsory.

Taxi Driver: Exactly! Like it used to be.

Ramón: No, I'm talking about divorce. Divorce would have to be compulsory. If not, nobody will make use of the new legislation. Or do you think that happily married couples will get divorced?

Taxi Driver (*in an angry voice*): Happy? Do you honestly think there is such a thing as a happily married couple?

In a smooth cut, the episode links to a scene that introduces the viewer to Lola, the heroine lawyer and colleague of Ramón. Lola speaks to a flower shop assistant, saying, 'Well, for example mine. My marriage is a happy one. I've been happily married for 20 years.' Lola organises the flower arrangements for her daughter's wedding, and thus sets the narrative frame nicely for the entire series: the juxtaposition of scenes cross-cutting from one extreme to the other, from Ramón celebrating divorce to Lola

---

[17] M Palacio, *Historia de la television en España* [History of Television in Spain] (Barcelona, Gedisa, 2001) 92–97.

celebrating happy marriages—her own and that of her daughter—as a representative of the next generation.

Wedding Rings is an interesting hybrid between a domestic sitcom, a workplace drama and a lawyer show. Staple scenes take place in the lawyer's office, at the local bar, at Lola's family home or at Ramón's hip bachelor pad overlooking the *Plaza Mayor*.[18] The series does not separate the personal and the professional easily: most of the lawyers' clients are friends or distant relatives and, not unlike many American legal dramas, the series also focuses heavily on Lola and Ramón's private lives. Lola's bourgeois family life and Ramón's bohemian lifestyle feature heavily in each episode, making their own private lives a case study and an integral part of the ongoing debate about divorce. The series mixes narrative strands of deep-level plot lines about the lawyers' private lives that remain unresolved with surface stories about divorce cases that conclude by the end of the episode. These patterns of repetitiveness and unresolved storylines inscribe themselves in the viewer's memory after only a few viewings, and give the audience a sense of connection and continuity. Every episode leaves the viewer eager to know what Ramón's flavour of the month looks like, how Lola copes with her rebellious adult children and how *doña* Trini (Aurora Redondo), the Francoist voice of the past, insults anyone willing to set foot in the lawyers' office in search of a better life.

Because the series centres around divorce, the entire series is implicitly or explicitly gendered. Many of the scenes revolve around the family setting of the divorce cases. Of 13 episodes, only four narratives end in divorce, and viewers witness only one divorce before a judge. Narrative closure in each episode results more from reconciliations or de facto separations than from divorce. The series never actually explains the new Divorce Law to the viewer: does the law require a serious matrimonial offence (typically adultery or physical abuse) to occur, or does one spouse have the right to file for a divorce by mutual consent? Is it a fault or a no-fault divorce? The series fails to explain any of these legal details to the viewer, and in a sense the series provides little specific popular-legal education. The strength of the show is perhaps this self-conscious dramatisation of social issues such as divorce, and the sacrifice of legal proceedings or the details of the juridical process.

The creators of *Wedding Rings* aimed the series at a generalist interpretative community, re-enacting the fictionalised divorce debates at different levels and offering more indirect than direct educational value for the viewer in the sense that the series looks at 'real' cases of marital melodramas rather than the legal technicalities of a divorce. The emotional engagement generated by fiction, in particular by television dramas, informs the social understanding of private issues. The prime questions each episode asks seem to be: why is this particular marriage at risk? Is it anybody's fault? And to what extent can the legal profession help, if at all?

The audience itself then plays the role of both judge and jury. The series displays both a cross-section of society as well as divorce cases, including: aristocratic marriages as a cover-up of homosexuality; a medical doctor whose wife betrays him; the emotionally abused lower-middle-class woman who has finally had enough and falls in love with an actor; a butcher who has an emotionally abusive wife; a mother of

---

[18] Main square in Madrid.

two who finally wants to leave her marriage of convenience to lead a self-determined life; the young wife of a much older husband who falls in love with a man of her own age; a man who's been living in sin for decades and had children with his de facto partner rather than his de jure wife can now finally divorce the latter. The series uses this assortment of cases as a careful mix of injustices in which neither gender is blamed for their supposedly egotistical desires of filing for divorce. In each case, the viewer empathises with the spouse who wishes to leave, and this empathy—through storytelling—gives the viewer indirect educational value. Personalised emotive accounts of claimants lend themselves to melodramatic narratives of family life and law. At its simplest, then, divorce is where law meets melodrama, and maybe therein lies the success of *Wedding Rings*.

The stigma of divorce looms understandably large within the logic of *Wedding Rings*. The first hurdle for the series' attorneys is obtaining office space, complicated by their admission that they specialise in divorce cases. The landladies, two elderly ladies representing the voice of a Francoist past, are disgusted at their tenants' professional convictions. In a comical misunderstanding at the beginning of the pilot episode, the landladies assume Lola is a prostitute and Ramón her pimp. While not delighted by the prospect of prostitution in their private home, the landladies would have considered it for their own financial gain. At the end of the first episode Ramón comments while sitting in the local bar with his friends: 'If we started a human trafficking, money laundering or an arms trade business, they would have been delighted. But that divorce stuff, good God, none of that! That goes against their principles.' One of the landladies in question, *doña* Trini, becomes a recurring commentator in the series, reminding Lola and Ramón of their 'dirty business', and of the good old days under Franco when everything was better and people were less egotistical. *Doña* Trini also continually mentions that she believes Lola and Ramón are single-handedly responsible for the downfall of Spanish society. The voice of the Francoist past here is taken to such comical extreme that no one takes *doña* Trini seriously, but she nevertheless represents an important reminder of the conservative, and sometimes fascist, factions that were still very much part of the new and now democratic Spain. Many people preferred the stability that arose from law and order to the perceived insecurity of the new democratic system.

IV. The Heroine Lawyer Lola

The series characterises the hero lawyers as struggling partners in a downtrodden law firm. The lawyers' economic struggles are further complicated by the fact that Lola receives anonymous phone calls threatening her because of her chosen legal career. While sewing a button on one of her husband's shirts, Lola explains to him:

> I think I'm going to give it up. I'm very vulnerable, these phone calls really frighten me. I'm not a natural rebel and I don't need to be given medals. I'm happily married, what do I care [...] It's not gonna make a big difference anyway if I'm around or not...

These anonymous threatening phone calls were not a fictional exaggeration, but rather a significant part of social reality at the time and reminiscent of the threats to which attorneys were subjected to in Spain at the time. The Lola character is continuously justifying her anxious existence as a divorce lawyer.

Contrary to the default feminist representation in the 1980s (the more career-oriented the character, the more feminist she is), Lola is not a heroine lawyer who wanted to become an icon of feminist progress; rather, Lola is simply a woman struggling with her career. The extent to which Lola struggles to maintain both her career and family is never more obvious than the summarising sections of the series' divorce narratives. In these scenes set in Lola's kitchen—the female private space *par excellence*—she comments and reflects on her current cases while cooking a meal and talking to her husband, implicitly reminding viewers that it seems natural to ask women to juggle professional and private duties. Simply examining Lola's screen presence could prompt viewers into thinking that she is mainly a housewife who also happens to turn up at the office in the afternoons. When some of Ramón's clients assume Lola is his secretary, she sets them straight with a tone of voice mixing both anger and satisfaction: 'No, I'm one of the partners.' Nevertheless, Lola is not motivated in choosing her profession by overt feminism, other than the 'liberal' conviction that divorce can benefit society and women have a right to self-determination. Calista Flockhart once commented on her role as Ally McBeal: 'Men are just characters. The moment a woman is on television as a lead character, she is expected to be a role model.'[19] If that holds true for Ally McBeal, it must be doubly true for Lola who, as a token personification of progress, comes as little surprise in a television show depicting a new and democratic Spain.

In this sense, Lola can be considered a representative character through which the series communicates larger sociological questions about gendered symbolism. During Spain's transition, women fought for both democracy *and* women's rights, the latter not necessarily being automatically subsumed by the former, even if the 1978 Constitution proclaimed de jure equality. Arguably, the series writers imposed—and resisted—cultural narratives on the Lola character; Lola can be read as vacillating between the two poles of a self-confident mother-of-three/divorce-lawyer-superwoman, or a middle-aged back-to-work-type mom, constantly on the verge of a nervous breakdown, and who desperately needs the support of her male colleague and husband. The viewer can find evidence for both constructions in the television show.

We should also distinguish between feminist issues at the character/private level and feminist issues at case level. Lola's female clients appreciate her views regarding feminist issues, and in one particular episode, when a client wants to leave her husband and children to live a self-determined life, Lola's words of wisdom about the ultimate form of female selfishness (abandoning one's children), are significant:

> The part of the self-sacrificing mother who would never leave her children I know all too well. And there are two types: those who decide to leave with their children and need to make ends meet from one day to another. To those, chapeau! But I also know the other type, the sinister mother who uses her children as a bargaining point in the divorce settlement. And on top of it they feel like saints. I don't have the slightest prejudice against a woman who, for whatever reason, decides to divorce her husband and give up her children because they are

---

[19] A Lotz, 'In Ms McBeal's Defense: Assessing Ally McBeal as a Feminist Text' in E Watson (ed), *Searching the Soul of Ally McBeal* (Jefferson, McFarland, 2006) 156.

better off with their father. I have much more respect for that kind of mother, I consider her less egotistical and much braver.

Lola's observations, because the viewer has come to love her as the motherly career woman, have more power than most other characters' would have in a similar situation. It is, perhaps, in comparison to other characters in the show that her views, and their significance, become obvious.

Despite constant family quarrels, Lola is happily married, and part of the series' narrative function of Lola's character is juxtaposing her good marriage and happy family life with the bad marriages of the divorce cases. Clearly, the strength of the show lies partly in depicting lawyers as human beings who have as many relationship problems as the next person. *Wedding Rings* does not depict a perfect world of powerful lawyers who carelessly decide upon the destiny of other people. Both Lola and Ramón constantly struggle with their own private lives. Due to her family situation, Lola can easily relate to complex narratives of family life (and law), and she understands that people are entangled in webs of complicated relationships. For Lola nothing is ever clear-cut; in contrast, Ramón is a self-professed lawyer for the socially disadvantaged that seeks divorce for his clients at almost any price. Lola is also the voice of reason and harmony whenever couples decide not to pursue divorce, while Ramón sees justice in divorce and gets frustrated at the limited usefulness of legal change. Lola is a seemingly conservative family woman in her private life, and hence maybe more suspicious of divorce, while Ramón is the anti-establishment hero lawyer supportive of people who attempt to get out of oppressive marriages.

V. The Hero Lawyer Ramón

Ramón stands as the series' most forceful voice of progress for women's equality and often disagrees violently with Lola, thereby leaving Ramón as the one who strengthens the feminist message of the show. Ramón's choice of profession has clear political motivation based upon his background as the illegitimate child of a working class mother; this gives him ample left-wing credentials, as well as a hunger for social justice. He frequently castigates Lola for not having the courage of her convictions and calls her 'Milady' (using the English term) to denigrate her bourgeois background, her age and marital status. Ramón teases Lola by calling her a 'bastion of traditional values' and reminding her that her seemingly conservative life is inapposite of her profession as a divorce lawyer. Lola, in turn, calls Ramón *el progre* (the lefty), alluding to his anarchist views that denounce legal marriage sanctioned by church or state. Ramón advocates the complete revolution of intimate relationships, and rejects not only marriage's legal framework but its traditional link to monogamy and nuclear family primacy. Ramón has this conviction tested a few times: twice at a private level and once at case level. In two episodes, he falls seriously in love with two women and immediately establishes conservative rules of monogamous relationships in order not to lose them, only to find the women just wanted affairs and would never leave their husbands for him.

As early as episode two, Ramón's human need for connection becomes apparent when he, almost against his will, falls in love with a client who pretends she would like to divorce her husband in order to start a relationship with him. Although Ramón adamantly proclaims that he does not believe in the fairytale of happy marriages, he cannot help but feel happy about the love given by Rosa (Ana Obregón). When Ramón finds out that Rosa will never leave her husband, he finds it surprisingly difficult to accept that their relationship will never be more than an affair. As hard as this realisation may be for Ramón, this particular episode has a fairytale ending of sorts. At the end of the episode, the real reason for Rosa's behaviour is revealed—her husband had become disabled and wheelchair-bound after a sports accident—and, despite Rosa's frivolous behaviour of serial adultery, she cares deeply for her husband and still loves him. When Ramón learns of this, he is full of admiration for Rosa's commitment to her husband. The episode ends with a dialogue between Ramón and his friend Pepe, a bar owner, where Pepe asks him to explain his 'theory that marriage is a utopia' to a group of people in the bar. Ramón, lovingly looking at Rosa, answers succinctly: 'I can't Pepe. I got it wrong. It exists [love and marriage]. I've just learnt what it means.' This admission of error so early on in the series foreshadows later developments in his own life when—at the end of the series—he decides he would like to get married himself. Throughout the series, however, the tension between Ramón's convictions and his own desires become a recurring motif.

Similarly, at case level, Ramón's ambivalence regarding marriage becomes apparent when he takes on a case for an elderly gentleman looking to divorce his de jure wife in order to marry his long-standing de facto partner. The final scene of that episode shows the happy newly-weds in the foreground while the camera zooms in on Ramón's face in the background. Ramón finds himself shedding near tears of joy, proud to have been involved in somebody else's marital bliss. As in all quality drama shows, writers use continuing narrative threads to lend regular characters unexpected traits and thus render them 'round'. At the end of the day Lola is not quite as bourgeois as Ramón would assume, nor is Ramón quite as anarchist as he would like to be.

VI. When Life Deals a Bad Hand

In one of the series' best episodes, entitled 'When Life Deals a Bad Hand', an embittered wife emotionally abuses her husband, a butcher. Husband Alfredo Astigarraga, the butcher, and his wife Asun are played by guest stars José Bódalo and María Luisa Ponte, and give brilliant performances as two people who cannot stand each other's company anymore. This episode is representative of the series' general format. The episode features constant cross-cutting—technically and metaphorically—between the private and public lives of the lawyers and their clients, and thus between legal issues and everyday life. The episode gives fictional answers to a few vital questions of the parliamentary and public divorce debates: is love a *sine qua non* of marriage? Is mutual consent necessary for a divorce? The episode also poses the implicit question of whether divorce is socially necessary and desirable, assuming there is an element of luck in both life and a person's choice of partner. Although divorce had become a legal reality, society had not yet considered it socially acceptable. This episode then asks whether there should be legal mechanisms to counteract a marriage contract when life deals a bad hand.

The opening scene has Lola worrying about a supposedly missed period, which later turns out to be the beginning of her menopause. The episode treats this as much a stroke of fate as her husband Enrique's denial of promotion. While Lola is menopausal and cannot have any more children, Enrique is frustrated because his company did not make him a director, his last chance of promotion. Both Lola and Enrique have reached a middle age plateau, and their frustrations are foretold in the storyline. Lola's family ignores her recurrent cry for 'help' (she literally shouts 'help' as if there was an emergency when she is at home and feels nobody helps her), with her son sarcastically telling her not to end up like the 'boy who cried wolf'.

Meanwhile, in the legal part of the storyline, Alfredo, the butcher, actually cries for help and turns to Ramón:

> *Alfredo*: I don't have any legal reasons to separate from my wife. She's a decent woman and attends to everything at home. But I can't stand her anymore. Always in a bad mood, nothing is good enough, nothing cheers her up. She drove our son away and now that he's married she is turning against his wife. Our grandchild is two years old and she hasn't even met him yet. In short, it's a nightmare.

The episode's title, 'When Life Deals a Bad Hand', refers then to both couples, and the episode juxtaposes their crises throughout. When Alfredo tries to explain to his wife that he cannot stand her bitterness anymore, Asun rejects the accusation and claims that love and marriage do not necessarily go hand-in-hand. This retort falls under a 'dialogue of the deaf' and renews the viewer's conviction that this marriage is beyond repair. In one particular cross-cutting, the episode contrasts two marital fights; while both fights are symbolic in nature, Lola's marital fight ends quickly in resolution, while the bitterness of the other couple's argument shows why a divorce would be liberating for both parties. For the considerate viewer, the beauty of the message lies in the subtle juxtaposition: a robust exchange of opposing views ending in affectionate truce, as compared to an emotional and bitter argument of melodramatic proportions. That is the sum total of difference between good and bad marriages.

Alfredo convinces Asun to go and see Ramón to get advice on the divorce proceedings. In her conversation with the lawyer, she admits that:

> Asun: I'm not going to miss him. But I don't want to feel incomplete. What benefits do I get out of a separation?
>
> Ramón: Isn't it sad to view it in those terms?
>
> Asun: I don't understand.
>
> Ramón: Doesn't matter. Anyway, financially you don't have to worry about anything.
>
> Asun: Listen, I'm not a very educated person, but I asked around. [...] And I was told that if I didn't agree, there wouldn't be a divorce. You can't allege anything against me.
>
> Ramón: I could have explained that to you as well.
>
> Asun: Well, if it's true, don't count on me. I don't and won't agree to a divorce. And if you want to go to court, do it. Let's see who gets the bigger slice.

Ramón (*with an angry voice*): That's an issue you need to sort out between the two of you. But now that you've taken the trouble to come to my office, let me explain something to you: the only thing that your husband tried to do is legalise a situation that is going to happen anyway. The slice in question—which he doesn't deny you – would have been given to you through legal channels and with proper procedures. The decision you've just taken means he's going to do whatever he damn well pleases. [...] With or without divorce Alfredo won't be living with you anymore.

The dialogue represents the difference between legal possibilities and real-life complications caused by a lack of understanding of the nature of divorce. Asun fears loneliness and social stigma and tries to avoid the unavoidable. Love is not part of the equation for her, and she really cannot understand what she might have done wrong. According to her, marriage is a social institution that is dissolved only by death.

VII. Conclusion

At the end of the series Lola's happy marriage comes to an abrupt end precisely due to her husband's accidental death. Nevertheless, there is an almost fairytale conclusion to the show: Lola and Ramón become a couple; all's well that ends well, although I am sure that this ending would have really annoyed educated viewers for being cheesy, happy and unrealistic. And at a surface level it is, but it also shows how conservatism and anti-establishment attitudes go hand in hand in *Wedding Rings*. Ramón relinquishes his stern bachelorhood to a woman 10 years his senior, which in 1980s Spain was certainly going against social conventions. They declare each other's love in a fake, and deliberately unromantic, ceremony in a car. Ramón, ridiculing the wedding vows, asks:

Do you take this complete wreck as your partner…for better or worse, etc.etc? [Puts wedding ring on her finger] Do you take this stupid cow who is going to spoil your life from this day forward? Yes, I do. Inside your ring it says 'Ramón'. As you can see, I'm very vulgar.

The conservative ending of the entire show and the mostly conservative endings of each episode remind us that *Wedding Rings* represented a careful mediation between the opposing factions of the old and the new Spain. It cautiously locates its ambiguous liberal politics in an unstable combination of modernisation and tradition and thus includes something for everybody. However, despite its highly emotive content, or maybe because of it, attention is more focussed on the sociological and psychological explanations rather than an obvious 'right or wrong' conceptualisation of moral and legal concepts. *Wedding Rings* is also a good example of how some cultural texts reveal an interpretative space that can work against the seemingly conservative textual surface. The point that needs stressing here is that it may precisely be this apparent conservatism, and hence wider acceptance, which could conceivably convert it into a tool of social critique and change. The careful mediation of values might also, at a macro-level, explain why the Spanish transition is one of the more successful in recent history.

17

'McNutty' on the Small Screen: Improvised Legality and the Irish-American Cop in HBO's *The Wire*

SARA RAMSHAW*

This article interrogates the boundaries of justice through the fictional television series, *The Wire*. This programme, sold to HBO[1] as a subversion of the network cop show, depicts police bureaucracy as 'amoral' and 'dysfunctional' and criminality as bureaucratic.[2] The article's purpose here is twofold: (1) to explore the relationship between improvisation and realism in the televisual mass media (thereby saying something about television); and (2) to assess the acceptability of improvisation as more or less just and/or justified in light of the laws from which they depart (thereby saying something about law). Unlike other studies in improvisation, which often focus around the African-American jazz musician, this one looks to portrayals of the Irish-American cop[3] in *The Wire* to unpack the justice of improvisation and the

---

* I would like to thank the editors of this volume, along with the anonymous reviewers, for their insightful comments and guidance. Thanks also to Eugene McNamee for introducing me to *The Wire*, and spending hours watching it with me; but, even more so, for his suggestions for change on earlier drafts.

[1] Without sponsors to please, the subscriber-based HBO network is 'more willing to experiment with subversive reinterpretations of old formats': A McMillan, 'Heroism, Institutions, and the Police Procedural' in T Potter and CW Marshall (eds), *The Wire: Urban Decay and American Television* (New York and London, Continuum, 2009) 52. According to *The Wire*'s creator, David Simon, the show 'could not exist but for HBO, or, more precisely, a pay-subscription model such as HBO': David Simon, 'Introduction' in R Alvarez (ed), *The Wire: Truth be Told* (Edinburgh, London, New York and Melbourne, Canongate, 2009) 10–11. The distinction between network and subscription cable channels in the United States will be discussed in further detail below.

[2] David Simon, 'Letter to HBO' in Alvarez (ed), *The Wire: Truth be Told* (n 1) 33.

[3] It may seem strange to focus on the Irish when so much of *The Wire* is about African American culture in the United States. As James Poniewozik writes:

'The Wire* is also TV's best—and nearly its only—drama about race and class. Because Baltimore is largely a city of black people, *The Wire* is a show largely about black people, all kinds. Black people are the criminals, and they are the cops and the politicians. What's more, they are the good cops and the lousy cops, the decent pols and the ones on the take, the vicious criminals and the sympathetic ones, and none

improvisation of justice. Ultimately, I hope to demonstrate that, while improvised legality is necessary for justice,[4] sometimes improvisations in or on law are not always critically conceived 'improvisations', but instead are scripted illegalities and therefore corrupt or unjust. Spotting the difference is not always easy, but, when read through *The Wire*, is made far more enjoyable.

I. Why The Wire?

As a medium for serious storytelling, television has precious little to recommend it—or at least that has been the case for most of its history. What else can we expect from a framework in which the most pregnant moment in the story has for decades been the commercial break, that five-times-an-hour pause when writers, actors, and directors are required to juke the tale enough so that a trip to the refrigerator or bathroom does not mean a walk away from the television set, or, worse yet, a click on the remote to another channel.

In such a construct, where does a storyteller put any serious ambition? Where are the tales to reside safely and securely, but in the simplest paradigms of good and evil, or heroes, villains, and simplified characterization? Where but in plotlines that remain accessible to the most ignorant and indifferent viewers. Where but in the half-assed, don't rattle-their-cages-uselessness of self-affirming, self-assuring narratives that comfort the American comfortable, and ignore the American inflicted; the better to sell Ford trucks and fast food, beer and athletic shoes, iPods and feminine hygiene products.[5]

The above encapsulates the view held by David Simon, creator of and writer for *The Wire*, of contemporary American television; television designed to sell not just stories, but 'intermissions' to stories. As Simon said, 'For half a century, network television wrapped its programs around the advertising—not the other way around, as it may have seemed to some.'[6] Simon contrasts the network television approach to storytelling to that of cable channels, such as HBO, where 'the only product being sold is the programming itself', even though the media conglomerates' (in the case of HBO, Time Warner Corp), who own these stations, 'absolute interest' remains 'selling to consumers'.[7] 'In the distinction', argues Simon, 'there is all the difference'.[8]

---

of them (nor the whites) are wholly, simply good or evil'; J Poniewozik, 'Connecting the Dots' *Time* (3 Jan 2008), available at www.time.com/time/printout/0,8816,1699870,00.html. The decision to focus on the Irish-American cop is explained and defended in s III of the chapter.

[4] The complex interaction between law, justice and improvisation must be assumed for the purposes of this chapter. For a more detailed discussion of the relationship between the two, see S Ramshaw, 'Deconstructin(g) Jazz Improvisation: Derrida and the Law of the Singular Event' (2006) 2 *Critical Studies in Improvisation* 1, 19; and S Ramshaw, 'Jamming the Law: Improvised Theatre and the "Spontaneity" of Judgment' (2010) *Law Text Culture* 14, 133.

[5] Simon, 'Introduction' (n 1) 1–2.

[6] Ibid 2.

[7] Ibid.

[8] Ibid.

With nothing being sold on HBO but the stories themselves,[9] Simon sold the story of *The Wire* to HBO as 'the greatest ever cop show that isn't actually a cop show'.[10] In a letter to HBO dated 27 June 2001, Simon reasoned that although in the past HBO had 'seize[d] a share of the drama market by going to places where no network could compete',[11] it was time to 'find a different—perhaps even more fundamental—way to differentiate [their] programs'.[12] Simon writes:

If you continue to seek worlds inaccessible to other networks, it will, creatively, become a formula for diminishing returns. ... Having achieved with prisons, drug corners, criminality, and the young and sexually active, HBO has, I would argue, gone about as far as it can in bringing fresh worlds to television.

At the same time, this formula has, by default, ceded the basic dramatic universe of politics, law, crime, medicine, to the networks. In the past, this was wise. These things were the networks' bread and butter, and they are at their most competitive in the hour-long ensemble drama.

But *The Wire* is, I would argue, the next challenge to the network logic and the next challenge for HBO. It is grounded in the most basic network universe—the cop show—and yet, very shortly, it becomes clear to any viewer that something subversive is being done with that universe. Suddenly, the police bureaucracy is amoral, dysfunctional, and criminality, in the form of the drug culture, is just as suddenly a bureaucracy. Scene by scene, viewers find their carefully formed prescriptions about cops and robbers undercut by alternative realities. Real police work endangers people who attempt it. Things that work in network cop shows fall flat in this alternative world. Police work is at times marginal or incompetent. Criminals are neither stupid nor cartoonish, and neither are they all sociopathic. And the idea, as yet unspoken on American TV, that no one in authority has any reason to care what happens in an American ghetto as long as it stays within the ghetto, is brought into the open. Moreover, within a few hours of viewing, the national drug policy—and by extension our basic law enforcement model—is revealed as calcified, cynical, and unworkable.13

Simon therefore suggests that HBO

take the essence of network fare and smartly turn it on its head, so that no one who sees HBO's take on the culture of crime and crime fighting can watch anything like *CSI*, or *NYPD Blue*, or *Law & Order* again without knowing that every punch was pulled on those shows.[14]

HBO executives must have found Simon's reasoning to be sufficiently persuasive, because HBO first aired *The Wire* in the United States the summer after the 9/11 attacks on New York City,[15] when the line between 'good' and 'evil' seemed relatively clear-cut (democracy and rule of law = good, terrorism = evil). The show however challenged this simplistic dichotomy. According to Simon, 'instead of the usual good

---

[9] Ibid.

[10] J Wilde, 'Why *The Wire* is the Greatest TV Show Ever Made' in S Busfield and P Owen (eds), *The Wire Re-Up* (London: Guardian Books, 2009) 5.

[11] Simon, 'Letter to HBO' (n 1) 33.

[12] Ibid.

[13] Ibid.

[14] Ibid 34.

[15] M Wood, 'This is America, Man' (2010) 32 *London Review of Books* 10, 20.

guys chasing bad guys framework, questions would be raised about the very labels of good and bad, and, indeed, whether such distinctly moral notions were really the point'.[16] Rothkerch also explains:

> Shunning the black-and-white simplicity of most TV police dramas, Simon examines the parallel lives of both the drug dealers and the cops, finding a morally skewed universe where the dealers are pragmatic entrepreneurs and the cops are apathetic political animals driven more by ambition than altruism.[17]

Most other television cop shows follow the format of the 'police procedural'.[18] McMillan, quoting Stephen Stark, summarises the basic appeal and moral character of this genre:

> Legal stories… feature clear winners and losers, stock scenarios, compelling characters, and recognizable villains and heroes. Moreover, the moral imperatives that television usually has injected into these melodramas—respect the law, good conquers evil, the system works— strike a responsive chord with corporate advertisers who sponsor network programming.[19]

Police dramas have thus been overpopulated with characters heroic in nature:

> Driven by their own virtuous nature, such characters stopped at nothing to root out crime and villainy. The validity of the laws they pledged to uphold was beyond question. Sustained by individual heroism, triumphing over evil time after time, the legal system was portrayed as a well-oiled machine in the service of justice.[20]

In contrast to the police procedural of other TV cop shows, *The Wire* 'had ambitions elsewhere'.[21] Simon explains:

> Specifically, we were bored with good and evil. To the greatest possible extent, we were quick to renounce the theme. After all, with the exception of saints and sociopaths, few in this world are anything but a confused and corrupted combination of personal motivations, most of them selfish, some of them hilarious.[22]

The Wire challenged 'the conventions of television by altering the good-bad moralism that inhibits much of popular entertainment'.[23] It did so through 'realism, good writing, and a more honest and more brutal assessment of police, police work, and the drug culture'.[24]

The Wire's realism greatly impacted how Simon chose to challenge the conventions of television. As a former journalist for the *Baltimore Sun* newspaper and a resident of the city, David Simon is, according to Jeremy Kahn, 'dedicated to authenticity'.[25] Actual police officers and reporters who double as *The Wire*'s viewers have rewarded Simon's dedication. As some cops have stated, 'the HBO drama is the only cop show

---

[16] McMillan, 'Heroism' (n 1) 50.
[17] I Rothkerch, 'What Drugs Have not Destroyed, the War on them Has' *Salon* (29 June 2002), available at dir.salon.com/story/ent/tv/int/2002/06/29/simon/print.html.
[18] McMillan, 'Heroism' (n 1) 51.
[19] Ibid 52.
[20] Ibid.
[21] Simon, 'Introduction' (n 1) 3.
[22] Ibid 3.
[23] MA Fletcher, 'Barack Obama: Wire Fan' in Alvarez (ed), *The Wire: Truth be Told* (n 1) 39.
[24] Simon, 'Letter to HBO' (n 1) 34.
[25] J Kahn, '*The Wire* is Not Escapism' in Busfield and Owen (eds), *The Wire Re-Up* (n 10) 250.

they've seen that is "remotely accurate"';[26] it is impressive how 'every side of an issue [is layered], how *The Wire* is not—like an old cop car—merely black and white'.[27] Patrick O'Connell, a newspaper reporter, stated similarly, 'I liked it because it was *real*—more than any show I'd watched'.[28] The next section of this article will theorise the show's realism or 'spot-on portrayal of cops and drug dealers and their respective bureaucracies'[29] through both its content and its form, explain the relationship between this realism and improvisation, and explain the effect this relationship has on the television police drama genre.[30]

II. Why Improvisation?

The Wire's content is extremely important to the show's realism, especially the written dialogue and subject material. Compared to other TV cop shows, *The Wire* has an 'utterly different rhythm';[31] 'It's loose and rambling; its dramatic climaxes don't coincide neatly with the conclusion of any given episode. Its dialogue, overseen by creator David Simon ..., is so good it often sounds improvised'.[32] This improvised quality depends not only on the performers' ability to make scripted material sound spontaneous, but also on the material itself, which pushes past 'preconceived ideas of how certain stock figures in sitcoms or dramas are supposed to behave'.[33] Simon described his writing as 'kinda like blues music': 'The trick is to take what can become a calcified universe and try to find some new way to do it. It's kinda like blues music, you know. There's 12 bars. It's all the same. But if you're listening it's not'.[34]

The Wire's scripted yet improvisational-sounding dialogue, and its material, which challenges the pre-conceived and stereotypical, provide the show with a sense of realism and spawns viewers to ask, 'How much improvisation do you allow your actors to do?'[35] Highlighting the talent of his writers 'to capture the real', Simon quickly dismisses any actual spontaneity in content and stresses that 'improvisation is kept to a minimum' on the show:

> ... the dialogue is on the page. *The Wire* is not big on ad libs, as the plotting is too ornate and detailed to allow for such. In the case of a few of those portraying our characters, for whom professional acting is a relatively new endeavor, we allow a certain leeway. But even in those cases, there is a writer on set making sure that the specific intent of every line is being

---

[26] VP Alvarez and G Garland, 'Cop Reporters and *The Wire*' in Alvarez (ed), *The Wire: Truth be Told*, 411 (n 1).

[27] Ibid 413.

[28] Ibid 414, emphasis added.

[29] Ibid 414–15.

[30] J Fiske, *Television Culture* (London and New York, Routledge, 1987) 33.

[31] K Tucker, '*The Wire*' *Entertainment Weekly* (28 June 2002), available at www.ew.com/ew/article/0,,264531~3~~wire,00.html.

[32] Ibid.

[33] Ibid.

[34] Rothkerch, 'What drugs' (n 17).

[35] J King, 'Exclusive David Simon Q&A' *Borderline Productions* (16 August 2006) available at www.borderline-productions.com/TheWireHBO/exclusive-1.html.

achieved. And with the majority of the cast, comprised as it is of experienced actors, we want them to stay on book. If an actor has an idea for an ad lib, he runs it by the writer on set for that episode and a decision is made on a line-by-line basis. Sometimes an actor's idea for a phrase or sentence can enhance a script; just as often, such a change can prove problematic, and it is the writer, who is aware of the context of the dialogue and who is responsible for protecting the story, that makes the decision. At least on this show that is how it works.[36]

Regardless of whether the dialogue is actually improvised, it does have an improvisational quality, which the show's audience thereby views as more authentic and real.[37]

A second way realism can be theorised in relation to *The Wire* is through its *form*. According to John Fiske:

This relates it to what it does rather than what it is or what it shows (its content). Realism does not just reproduce reality, it makes sense of it—the essence of realism is that it reproduces reality in such a form as to make it easily understandable. It does this primarily by ensuring that all links and relationships between its elements are clear and logical, that the narrative follows the basic laws of cause and effect, and that every element is there for the purpose of helping to make sense: nothing is extraneous or accidental.[38]

This would seem to suggest that realism in television cannot exist if any part of the show's formatting is improvised. As with its content, however, *The Wire*'s realistic format also relies upon improvisation, actual or perceived. Simon aimed, at least in season one of *The Wire*, to 'teach folks to watch television in a different way, to slow themselves down and pay attention, to immerse themselves in a way that the medium had long ago ceased to demand'.[39] While Simon spent much time 'thinking about the exacting structure and the inherent message',[40] the audience watching *The Wire* embarked on an improvisational journey into an unknown world of television where they were no longer left wondering—'in cop-show expectation'—whether 'the bad guys will get caught'. Instead, the audience began to ask 'who the bad guys are and whether catching them means anything at all'.[41] Re-training viewers in the 'art of watching television'[42] required improvising on known techniques of observation and analysis in order to learn how to watch *The Wire* 'properly': 'the promise is that, as they go along, they'll understand more and more, and maybe by the end they'll understand most if not all of it'.[43] Thus, the realism of this form meant not telling the viewer everything, or not explicitly detailing the relationship between the elements with logic and clarity, but instead letting the viewer do the grunt work, improvising on taken-for-granted assumptions to develop a new—and more sophisticated—way of detecting and responding to the televisual narrative form.

Form and content alone do not define realism, but the interaction of the two elements, as demonstrated by the viewer's understanding of legal reality via storylines

---

[36] Ibid.

[37] John Fiske points out that unfinished sentences and redirections in argument give dialogue 'an immediacy, a thinking with [the] tongue that, in its rawness, gives a sense of authenticity'. J Fiske, *Media Matters: Race and Gender in U.S. Politics* (Minneapolis and London, University of Minnesota Press, 1996) 30.

[38] Fiske, Television Culture (n 30) 24.

[39] Simon, 'Introduction' (n 1) 3.

[40] Simon, 'Letter to HBO' (n 1) 35.

[41] Ibid.

[42] O Burkeman, 'Interview: David Simon,' in Busfield & Owen, *The Wire Re-Up* (n 10) 246.

[43] Ibid.

involving Detective Jimmy McNulty, one of the only characters given top billing in season one[44] and absolution in season five.[45] McNulty is 'the most typical of tough street cops from other shows'.[46] As one viewer notes, it appears 'as if [McNulty] is written to be a bit of a stereotype to juxtapose with the quality of the characterisation of the gangsters when contrasted'.[47]

English actor Dominic West[48] heads *The Wire*'s cast list as McNulty, 'the hard-drinking, bed-hopping, working-class Irish-American'.[49] He is a 'rakish hero', 'simultaneously attractive and dangerous, trading on the currency of temptation, the thrill of adventure, and the promise—almost never, ever fulfilled—that he'll reform for the "right" woman'.[50] McNulty[51] is a 'stock character type', as Rundacille explains:

> This kind of hero—the one who straddles the line between the criminal and the police, and who charms and betrays women left and right, but still seems to embody a true code of honor—lingers in all manner of crime and detective fiction today.[52]

Many critics argue that McNulty 'was obviously designed as an easily recognisable way in for the viewer in a show with more than its fair share of unfamiliar elements'.[53] As one audience member wrote, 'It's such a cliché, after all; the hard-drinking, authority-bucking, maverick cop with the disastrous personal life … it's something that is easily recognised from countless other TV shows'.[54] Paul Owen concurs with this description, stating,

> McNulty—at his most basic, a roguish, talented Irish-American cop—was an easy 'in' for the viewer, a recognisable character you could latch on to in the first series as you got used to the unfamiliar settings and dialect and the relatively demanding style of writing.[55]

In an interview with Oliver Burkeman, David Simon explains that '[t]he first season of *The Wire* was a training exercise. We were training you [the viewer] to watch television differently.'[56] According to Steve Busfield, '…series one is, by necessity, a much simpler story than in later series. While nuanced and layered unlike most cops

---

[44] 'Billed first in the credits, Dominic West began the programme as its star': P Owen, 'Episode 6—Where's Jimmy' in Busfield & Owen (eds), *The Wire Re-Up* (n 10) 172. See also A Anthony, 'Interview: Dominic West' in ibid.

[45] D Rudacille (with contribution from S Alvarez), 'The Drunkard's Opera: Jimmy McNulty in Life and Letters' in Alvarez (ed), *The Wire: Truth be Told* (n 1) 489.

[46] bistryker, 'Episode 2—Getting away with murder' in Busfield & Owen (eds) *The Wire Re-Up* (n 10) 199.

[47] Ibid.

[48] Nothing in the plot of *The Wire* could rival the fact that Irish-American cop McNulty was actually played by an Englishman, 'and not just any Englishman, but that most curious and mythologised of creatures: an Old Etonian': Anthony, 'Interview: Dominic West' (n 44) 65.

[49] Ibid.

[50] Rudacille, 'The Drunkard's Opera' (n 45) 486.

[51] The character was originally going to be called 'Jimmy McArdle' but Bob Colesberry convinced Simon to change the name to his grandmother's family name as 'no one likes the name Jimmy Ardle': Simon, 'Introduction' (n 1) 17.

[52] Rudacille, 'The Drunkard's Opera' (n 45) 486.

[53] P Owen, 'Episode 11—The True McNulty' in Busfield & Owen (eds), *The Wire Re-Up* (n 10) 54.

[54] Lingli, 'Episode 22—The True McNulty' in ibid 55.

[55] Owen, 'Episode 6' (n 44) 172.

[56] Burkeman, 'Interview: David Simon' (n 42) 246.

and crooks shows, it is also essentially about the police[57] and their attempts to catch criminals.'[58] As the seasons progressed, the show needed the stock McNulty character less and less to help orient the viewer to the (legal) reality of *The Wire* and, by season four, throughout which McNulty appears infrequently, Simon (and Ed Burns, his co-creator and writer) 'credit the viewer with no longer needing McNulty to hold their hand'.[59]

In light of the argument offered above that the show exploited the McNulty character in season one as a stereotypical hard-drinking, maverick Irish-American cop to orient viewers to the (legal) reality of *The Wire*, what does the programme actually say about justice and the necessity of improvised legality in relation to a steadfastly bureaucratic legal system? The subsequent section will unpick the importance of McNulty's characterisation and the relevance of his Irish heritage to the realism of *The Wire*, both in terms of content and form and the relationship of both to conceptions of law and order in the television programme.

III. Why Irish?

The world of 'law and order' in *The Wire* is one in which the line between legal and illegal, just and unjust, moral and immoral is always in a state of flux. That the show claims an Irish-American represents this world should not surprise viewers, for fundamental to stereotypical notions of Irish-American-ness is 'the presumption that the border between legal and illegal was a question of convenience rather than morality'.[60] This presumption has a long history and, unfortunately, this chapter does not have enough room to sufficiently canvas the issue. It should suffice to say that the story of Irish Catholic immigration to America, especially after the Potato Famine of 1845, is one steeped in hardship and discrimination. The 'initial sympathy [in America] for the starving peasants [soon] gave way to anti-Catholic hostility as they began to arrive in droves, forming enclaves in Northern cities'.[61] Signs appeared throughout the nation stating, 'No Irish need apply now'[62] and '[h]ostility often turned violent'.[63] These

---

[57] This spelling of police signifies, for the viewers of the show, '"good" or "real" or "natural police"', or 'POE-leese', as it is pronounced in a Baltimorean accent. As Brooks points out, 'In the Baltimore accent, noticeable in several of the show's characters, "police" is pronounced 'POE-leese'—making the compliment "real POE-leese" seem all the more authentic and distinctive': R Brooks, 'The Narrative Production of "Real Police"' in Potter & Marshall (eds), *The Wire: Urban Decay and American Television* (n 1) 65, 76, fn 1.

[58] S Busfield, 'Episode 10—From Script to Screen' in Busfield & Owen, *The Wire Re-Up* (n 10) 51.

[59] Owen, 'Episode 6' (n 44) 172.

[60] P Quinn, 'Looking for Jimmy' in J Lee & MR Casey (eds), *Making the Irish American: History and Heritage of the Irish in the United States* (New York, NYU Press, 2006) 672.

[61] 'Irish American' *Answers.com*, available at www.answers.com/topic/irish-american (accessed 27 March 2011).

[62] DP Moynihan, 'The Irish' in Lee & Casey (eds), *Making the Irish American* (n 60) 493.

[63] Ibid.

episodes of violence, 'etched in Irish American memory',[64] contributed to 'a separatist mentality long after they achieved success'.[65]

In the mid-1800s, many Irish immigrants 'accepted the low pay and the long hours of police work as the price for job security—though the low pay might be supplemented by coins buried in the apples proffered by protection-seeking street vendors.'[66] Sonja Massie writes; 'Many Irish men took to walking a policeman's beat, armed with a billy club, that gift of gab that served them so well in all other areas of life, and a "way with people" that could turn a quarrel into a truce.'[67] In 1855, 27 per cent of those policemen conducting arrests in New York City (NYC) were Irish (slightly greater than the Irish proportion of the city's population).[68] According to Massie,

> The stereotype of the big, swaggering cop with the Irish brogue twirling his nightstick and dispensing a bit of street justice here and there became a common sight, because many of the peace officers in the large cities of the Eastern Seaboard were Irish.[69]

Somewhat ironically, the majority of those arrested in cities such as NYC in the 1850s were also Irish-born.[70] In fact, the term 'paddy wagon', as the vehicle used to transport prisoners, was coined in NYC during the mid-1800s because many of its passengers were Irish, with names such as 'Padraic or Patrick'.[71]

Not only did the propensity of the Irish to be on both sides of the law reinforce 'a prevailing racialist sentiment that the Irish were by nature an inherently violent people',[72] it also led to the image of the 'conflicted police officer', one 'who is torn between enforcing the law and watching the backs of his relatives or buddies'.[73] This conflict may have stemmed in part from the 'settled tradition' the Irish 'brought to America... regarding the formal government as illegitimate and the informal one bearing the true impress of popular sovereignty'.[74] The Penal Laws of eighteenth-century Ireland, imposed under British rule, 'totally proscribed the Catholic religion and reduced the Catholic Irish to a condition of de facto slavery'.[75] Moynihan cites Cecil Woodham-Smith, who explains, 'that the lawlessness, dissimulation, and revenge which followed left the Irish character, above all the character of the peasantry, "degraded and debased"':[76]

---

[64] Ibid.

[65] Ubid.

[66] D Barry, 'Begorrah! Irish Cops, Yet Again' *The New York Times*, 26 October 2008, available at www.nytimes.com/2008/10/26/movies/26barr.html?_r=1&pagewanted=print.

[67] S Massie, *Complete Idiot's Guide to Irish History and Culture* (Indianapolis, Alpha Books, 1999) 178. It is argued that 'the Irish have an advantage over many other groups of immigrants because they already spoke English when they arrived in America': ibid.

[68] K Kenny, 'Labor and Labor Organizations' in Lee & Casey (eds), *Making the Irish American* (n 60) 376.

[69] Ibid.

[70] Massie, *Complete Idiot's* (n 67) 184.

[71] Ibid.

[72] K Kenny, 'Race, Violence, and Anti-Irish Sentiment in the Nineteenth Century' in Lee & Casey (eds), *Making the Irish American* (n 60) 370.

[73] Barry, 'Begorrah!' (n 66).

[74] Moynihan, 'The Irish' (n 62) 480.

[75] Ibid.

[76] Ibid.

His religion made him an outlaw; in the Irish House of Commons he was described as 'the common enemy,' and whatever was inflicted on him he must bear, for where can he look for redress? To his landlord? Almost invariably an alien conqueror. To the law? Not when every person connected with the law, from the jailer to the judge, was a Protestant ...[77]

Quite understandably, such conditions bred the 'suspicion of the law' and 'of the ministers of the law and all of the established authority'.[78] Since the law did not give the Irish peasant justice, he set up his own law: 'The secret societies which have been the curse of Ireland became widespread during the Penal period ... dissimulation became a moral necessity and evasion of the law the duty of every God-fearing Catholic.'[79]

While there is some historical basis for the conflicted relationship of the Irish-American cop to the law he or she pledged to uphold, the tale of the Irish and 'loyalty-protected corruption'[80] has become a familiar storyline in Western popular culture, and *The Wire* does little to challenge this stereotypically Irish approach to law and justice. The viewers, however, appeared to appreciate—and even welcome— this stereotypical characterisation (and McNulty's hand-holding) as they settled into the unsettling world of *The Wire*. In the first few seasons, McNulty's irreverence to authority and failure to follow legal protocols or the chain of command was met with playful audience tallies of 'McNulty giving a fuck when it's not his turn'.[81] This playful dismissal of McNulty's actions all changed in season five when long-time viewers of *The Wire* labelled McNulty's actions, in relation to law and justice issues (specifically his creation of a fictional serial-killer in order to obtain more funding for police investigations), as 'villainous',[82] 'wacko',[83] 'absurd or crazy',[84] hence the 'McNutty' nickname.[85] In light of the audience response to McNulty's exploits, the next section of this article will unpick the limits of justice and explore the distinction between improvisations in or on law, which improvisations are just or justified, and which improvisations are seen simply as corrupt or wrong.

IV. The Limits of Justice as Improvised Legality

Scholars have theorised that improvisation operates as a possible response to hardship and discrimination, much like that experienced by the Irish Catholic immigrants to New York City. According to two of the leading theorists in the new and emerging

---

[77] Ibid.
[78] Ibid.
[79] Ibid.
[80] Barry, 'Begorrah!' (n 66).
[81] See, eg the 'Running Totals' section throughout *The Guardian*'s guide to *The Wire*: Busfield & Owen (eds), *The Wire Re-Up* (n 10). The guide also tracks the number of times McNulty gets drunk on the show, signifying the perpetuation of another stereotype: the tie between Irish Americans and alcohol and the 'unstable and unreasonable temperament' that results from this tie: Quinn, 'Looking for Jimmy' (n 60) 675.
[82] R Alvarez, 'Season Five Overview,' in Alvarez (ed), *The Wire: Truth be Told* (n 1) 405.
[83] Joedoone, 'Episode 7—A shot at redemption,' in Busfield & Owen (eds), *The Wire Re-Up* (n 10) 219.
[84] ShelfsideAndy, 'Episode 7—A Shot at Redemption' in Busfield & Owen (eds), *The Wire Re-Up* (n 10) 221.
[85] See, for example, Busfield & Owen (eds), *The Wire Re-Up* (n 10) 196.

field of 'critical studies in improvisation' (CSI),[86] Ajay Heble[87] and Daniel Fischlin,[88] improvisation is a complex and dynamic social phenomenon, that interrupts traditional orthodoxies of judgement and assumes a shared responsibility for participation in the community, all the while accepting the challenges of risk and contingency.[89] Improvisation, these critics argue, is a 'social practice'[90] that 'emerged out of those cultures who most suffered the effects of colonialism (in particular indigenous and African slave populations)'.[91] It requires a 'dissonant relation to hegemony', to colonialism, which, for them, is 'predictably manipulative and adaptive, dictated by the self-interested goals of the imperial ideology [it seeks] to enforce.'[92] To be 'truly improvisatory in relation to otherness', argues Fischlin and Heble, requires

> turning away from the predictable acts of imperial greed and destruction to initiate something quite different—like a peaceful and productive alliance with indigenous cultures in the name of forming a transcultural community based on dialogue and 'true' improvisation rather than on the monological deployment of European power.[93]

[86] For more on this field of study, see the journal of *Critical Studies in Improvisation/Études critiques en improvisation*, available at www.criticalimprov.com/public/csi/index.html. Also, many of the theorists working in this field are involved in the Improvisation, Community and Social Practice (ICASP) project, which is a $4 million international community/university research project headed by Ajay Heble, a professor at the University of Guelph, Canada. This project involves researchers from 18 universities across Canada, the United States, England and Australia and is supported by a very rare and prestigious $2.5 million Major Collaborative Research Initiatives (MCRI) grant from the Social Sciences and Humanities Research Council of Canada (Canada). For more information, see 'Musical Improvisation, Social Change Focus of Major Research Grant' *University of Guelph News Release* (4 Sept 2007), available at www.uoguelph.ca/news/2007/09/musical_improvi.html (accessed 27 March 2011). According to the ICASP website: 'This project investigates the ways in which improvised music plays a role in shaping notions of community and "new forms" of social organization, with the goal of developing a new field of interdisciplinary scholarly endeavour, one that promises to place the civic function of improvised artistic practices firmly at the centre of both broad public debate and informed policy decisions about the role of arts in society': 'About ICASP: Research', available at www.improvcommunity.ca/about/research (accessed 27 March 2011).

[87] Dr Ajay Heble is a Professor at the School of English and Theatre Studies at the University of Guelph, Canada. He is the author of several books on improvisation, including Landing on the Wrong Note: Jazz, Dissonance, and Critical Practice (New York and London, Routledge, 2000); The Other Side of Nowhere: Jazz, Improvisation, and Communities in Dialogue (with Daniel Fischlin) (Middletown, Connecticut, Wesleyan University Press, 2004); and Rebel Musics: Human Rights, Resistant Sounds, and the Politics of Music Making (with Daniel Fischlin) (Montréal, New York and London, Black Rose Books, 2003). He is the founding editor of the journal of *Critical Studies in Improvisation/Études critiques en improvisation* and the founder and artistic director of the Guelph Jazz Festival in Guelph, Ontario, Canada. He is also the Project Leader of the ICASP project.

[88] Dr Daniel Fischlin is a Shakespearean and jazz/music scholar at the University of Guelph, Canada. He has co-edited two books on the socio-political implications of improvisation with Ajay Heble (ibid). He is also a researcher and Management Team member of the ICASP project.

[89] This description of improvisation is taken from my notes from the one-day workshop on 'Improvisation, the Arts, and Social Policy' held on Thursday 18 June 2009 at McGill University, Montréal, Québec, Canada. The workshop was organised and sponsored by the Improvisation, Community and Social Practice (ICASP) project out of Canada. It was ICASP Project Leader, Ajay Heble, who made these comments.

[90] D Fischlin and A Heble, 'The Other Side of Nowhere: Jazz, Improvisation, and Communities in Dialogue' in D Fischlin and A Heble (eds), *The Other Side of Nowhere: Jazz, Improvisation, and Communities in Dialogue* (Middletown, Connecticut, Wesleyan University Press, 2004) 14.

[91] Ibid.

[92] Ibid.

[93] Ibid.

By reading Fischlin and Heble's critical vision of improvisation through a postcolonial perspective,[94] the distinction between law and corruption becomes somewhat less straightforward. Much dominant law is viewed to be 'the product of imperialism and thus inherently questionable. More particularly, hibernocentric[95] postcolonial jurisprudence perceives many dominant legal rules as historically anglocentric and for that reason suspect'.[96] For the Irish-Catholic diaspora in America, a sense of exile and even nostalgia were common themes. By theorising improvisation as a response to such oppression, scholars better understand how aggrieved communities, such as Irish-Catholic immigrants in the United States, excelled at 'adapting to new (and changing) circumstances',[97] and troubled 'the very assumptions of fixity'[98] by using 'the materials at hand to create powerful and enduring resources for hope'.[99] Indeed, diasporic communities often 'cultivate[d] resources for hope out of seemingly hopeless situations, ... find[ing] "a way out of no way"'.[100]

In light of the above, the question becomes whether McNulty's improvised legality, along with his 'distain for authority and tendency to circumvent the chain of command to set up investigations',[101] entail a 'dissonant relation to hegemony'[102] and are therefore improvised reactions to perhaps his or his ancestors' experience of colonial domination as an Irish Catholic in both America and back in Ireland. If so, his actions may be considered, if not just, then at least justifiable. In contrast, are McNulty's actions instead 'predictably manipulative and adaptive, dictated by ... self-interested goals'[103] and thus not improvised legality at all, but instead scripted illegality and therefore corrupt or unjust? To answer these questions, we need to examine in more detail his actions in season five, and the audience reaction to these actions.

To provide some background, season five of *The Wire* had Baltimore's mayor severely cutting the city's police department's budget in order to redress the city's education deficit, which was the focus of season four. These budget cuts forcibly shut down a year-long investigation of the drug lord Marlo Stanfield, and in response, a very frustrated McNulty concocts a way to divert resources back to the police department by manipulating evidence at death scenes to make it appear that a serial killer is murdering homeless men in Baltimore. McNulty hopes that the mayor, in an attempt to avoid or lessen the bad publicity that comes with having a serial killer in any city,

---

[94] According to Walter Walsh, 'a postcolonial perspective is one that identifies and rejects those political, aesthetic, and intellectual structures and canons that are imperialist in origin and form....By definition, colonizers exert power far beyond their numbers': WJ Walsh, 'The Priest-Penitent Privilege: An Hibernocentric Essay in Postcolonial Jurisprudence' (2005) *Indiana Law Review* 80, 1038.

[95] Hibernocentric, according to Walter Walsh, 'means seen from an Irish standpoint. ... Hibernia, the land of winter, was the Roman name for that far-flung Celtic island in the Atlantic Ocean, where the Roman writ never ran, on the seeming edge of the world': ibid. Walsh adds: 'Of alternative voices the postcolonial Irish perspective is among the most interesting, coming from both the earliest of England's overseas prizes and from the first indigenous population to regain independence from British colonial rule and establish a democratic republican regime.' Ibid.

[96] Ibid.

[97] Fischlin and Heble, 'The Other Side' (n 90) 12.

[98] Ibid.

[99] Ibid.

[100] Ibid.

[101] 'Jimmy McNulty,' Wikipedia, en.wikipedia.org/wiki/Jimmy_McNulty (accessed 27 March 2011).

[102] Fischlin and Heble, 'The Other Side' (n 90) 15.

[103] Ibid.

will reapportion some much-needed funds to the Police Department. McNulty would then use the money to reignite the investigation of Marlo Stanfield, which he feels is very close to closing.

McNulty's inspiration for the creation of the 'fictional serial killer' came from a trip to the morgue during an investigation into an accidental death. At the morgue, McNulty encountered two Baltimore County homicide detectives arguing with the new medical examiner. One detective who McNulty knows explains that, although the recent victim was an accidental death, the paramedics actually had to grab the deceased's neck in order to remove him from behind a toilet. Because the paramedic's actions create the appearance of a strangulation, the medical examiner intends to rule the death as a homicide. The discovery that post-mortem strangulation is indistinguishable from strangulation causing death amazes McNulty.

This scene is followed by another in which a frustrated and angry McNulty, infuriated by the cuts to the police department's budget and the lack of overtime pay, drinks heavily while on the job. He is assigned a probable overdose with his partner, Bunk Moreland. After surveying the scene, McNulty dismisses the other officers (except Bunk), grabs a bottle of Jameson whiskey from the trunk of his car, and begins to manipulate the crime scene so that it looks like a struggle occurred. McNulty then strangles the already-deceased victim, much to the amazement and outrage of Bunk, who wants no part in McNulty's plan. The relevant dialogue is as follows:

Jimmy: 'There's a serial killer in Baltimore. He prays on the weakest among us. He needs to be caught' [takes a drink].

Bunk: 'I'm gone. I don't want a part of this'.[104]

Back in his office, McNulty searches for unsolved cases to link to his fake strangulation, in the hope of creating the appearance that a serial killer is killing homeless men in Baltimore. After much effort on McNulty's part, including leaking the story to the local newspaper, *The Baltimore Sun* (which ends up, much to McNulty's dismay, relegating the story to the middle of the paper and not the front page), news finally breaks about the serial killer. While at first the mayor pays lip service to addressing the problem, he refuses to actually move any money around in order to enable the police department to increase its investigatory efforts. McNulty then decides to enlist the assistance of Lester Freamon, another police officer with whom he has worked before in the Major Crimes Unit. With the help of Lester's former patrol partner, McNulty and Freamon are able to get to dead homeless victims before other officers. McNulty becomes more perverted in his evidence-tampering by creating the impression that the serial killer is sexually motivated in his killings of homeless men. When a reporter for *The Baltimore Sun* similarly fabricates an interview with the serial killer in order to gain promotion, the story garners national attention, and the mayor decides to give the police department all the resources it needs to catch the killer.

In doing so, the mayor actually gives McNulty more money and resources than he needs to rekindle his investigation—including a wiretap—of Marlo Stanfield. Because

---

[104] *The Wire*, 'Unconfirmed Reports', Episode 52, Season Five. Directed by Ernest Dickerson. Story by David Simon and William F Zorzi; teleplay by William F Zorzi. See also R Alvarez (ed), *The Wire: Truth be Told* (n 1) 426–27.

of this new allocation of resources, Jimmy 'Boss' McNulty begins 'running the police department's finances',[105] apportioning resources to others in the department working on different cases, which he then expenses to the serial killer case. McNulty becomes a department hero, for at least a brief period. In the end, it all goes pear-shaped when a guilt-ridden McNulty confesses his antics to another officer, Kima Griggs, who has been taken off a real case in order to work the fictional serial killer one with him. Regardless of her close friendship with McNulty, Griggs decides to tell her and McNulty's former superior, who then tells the department's Commissioner, who in turn breaks the news to the mayor. But as the mayor is running on the issue of homelessness in his bid to become Governor of Maryland, McNulty and Freeman are not arrested for their deception, but instead forced to retire quietly from the police force.

As mentioned previously, long-term fans of the show severely criticised the 'fictional serial killer' storyline as 'crass, ludicrous or just plain silly'.[106] For a series that prided itself on telling the 'real' story of the Baltimore streets, fans viewed McNulty's faking of evidence, messing with crime scenes and lying to fellow police officers and medical examiners as too far-fetched, thus violating the signature realism of the show.[107] The audience reaction to this storyline should not surprise scholars when viewed in relation to the dominant conception of Western legality. This conception accepts that the law may have its flaws, but such blatant and scripted illegality—especially by police officers hired to uphold the law—definitely crossed the line between justice and corruption. A fan of the show wrote: 'How would we feel if we found out that a police here forged evidence in order to pursue a prosecution against someone he 'knew' was guilty.'[108]

Viewers cannot claim that police officers—fictional or otherwise—cannot be corrupt. However, *The Wire* packaged or 'sold' McNulty to viewers as the (perhaps too clichéd) hero 'who straddles the line between the criminal and the police, ... but still seems to embody a true code of honor'.[109] As one viewer explains:

> McNulty has always been an insubordinate ass, but he has always been honest. He's never cut corners in his police work, and while he has always fought with his bosses, rarely toeing the company line, he has always taken a moral high ground. This move struck me as being

---

[105] Busfield, 'Episode 7—A Shot at Redemption' in Busfield & Owen (eds), *The Wire Re-Up* (n 10) 217.

[106] Alex Boothroyd, '*The Wire* re-up: McNulty, Templeton and Dexter' *The Organgrinder Blog* (27 Oct 2008), available at www.guardian.co.uk/media/organgrinder/2008/oct/27/wire-television-mcnulty-templeton-dexter.

[107] Christopher Monfette, in his review of *The Wire*, writes that season five '[c]entred around a storyline [i.e., McNulty's fictional serial killer] that arguably departed from the series' persistent level of realism...'. Later in the review he adds that 'McNulty's storyline this season [is] perhaps the most *fictional* narrative device ever utilized by *The Wire*'. C Monfette, '*The Wire*: The Complete Fifth Season DVD Review' *IGN* (15 Aug 2008), available at uk.dvd.ign.com/articles/899/899184p1.html (emphasis in the original). Another viewer wrote: 'As for the reality of the show, ... Everything except McNulty's crazy serial killer plot rang true to me': bmoregirl, '*The Wire*: 'Every Villain Has Their Reasons' *Irish Left Review*, (6 July 2009), available at www.irishleftreview.org/2009/03/12/wire-every-villain-reasons/.

[108] Marwood 1974, 'Episode 8—Obituary: Omar Little' in Busfield & Owen (eds), *The Wire Re-Up* (n 10) 227.

[109] Rudacille, 'The Drunkard's Opera' (n 45) 486.

dishonest to the character, and a cheap plot device. I think Executive Producer David Simon, like McNulty, is cutting corners.[110]

Viewers and critics made many references throughout the series about those on the Baltimore City Police Force who were 'pOlice,' that is, "good" or "real" or "natural police".'[111] 'Good police work' 'connotes pursuing order in reality' as opposed to 'bad' police who pursue 'order in appearance only', that is, those 'obsessed with improving the clearance rate'.[112] And yet '[g]ood police don't always play by the rules, especially when the rules are set up for the good police to fail to do their jobs... .'[113] For such police:

> ... order is maintained only when criminals are actually *convicted*, not just arrested, and only when the person who orders the crime is also brought to justice ... A degree of lawlessness on the part of both the uncorrected criminal and the cop who exempts himself form strict application of the law is the condition of possibility for the detail's pursuit of justice.[114]

Moreover, this particular characterisation of a police officer—one who 'defies bureaucrats for a good cause'—is, according to McMillan, 'a common heroic figure in police dramas'.[115]

What is it, then, about McNulty's season five antics that so irked viewers? According to McMillan:

> We may respect his courageous defiance of the bosses, but eventually his motives and principles become altogether suspect. Insofar as he never really puts his ideal scenario of pursuit and triumph to the question, his principles are deeply problematic. His motive, on the other hand, becomes self-evident in Season Five, when he fabricates a serial killer to cover for an illegal and ultimately futile wiretap of Marlo Stanfield's organization. Unmistakably, this becomes more of a vendetta than a quest for justice. The conclusion of McNulty's story thereby knocks the biggest hole of all in the heroic image suggested by the early episodes in Season One, revealing his readiness to discard ethics and law in pursuit of a fantasy of domination.[116]

To be 'truly improvisatory in the relation to otherness',[117] and thus just, McNulty would have had to turn away from the predictable acts of pride, conceit or greed to initiate something quite different.[118] Much like McMillian, I too am not so certain that this was the case here, finding support for this assertion in an interview with David Simon, who 'described his goal of presenting McNulty as ambiguous in his motivations'.[119] Based on his experiences with real detectives, Simon feels that

---

[110] C Pearson, '*The Wire*: Season 5 Episode 2 Self-Righteous Indignation' *Wordpress.com Blog* (8 Jan 2008), available at urbanfervor.wordpress.com/2008/01/08/the-wire-season-5-episode-2/ (accessed 27 March 2011).

[111] Brooks, 'The Narrative Production' (n 57) 65. See also McMillan, 'Heroism' (n 1) 55.

[112] Brooks, ibid 70–71.

[113] foxtrotdelta, 'McNutty: Season 5 Episode 2—Getting Away with Murder' in Busfield & Owen (eds), *The Wire Re-Up* (n 10) 199.

[114] Brooks, 'The Narrative Production' (n 57), emphasis added.

[115] McMillan, 'Heroism' (n 1) 55.

[116] Ibid 57.

[117] Ibid.

[118] Ibid.

[119] 'Jimmy McNulty', Wikipedia (n 101).

... most crime dramas present their police characters with the inherent falsehood that they care deeply about the victims in the cases they are investigating. Simon states that in his experience a good detective is usually motivated by the game of solving the crime—he sees the crime as an 'insult to his intellectual vanity' and this gives him motivation to solve it.[120]

At the same time, however, some of the best musical improvisation, for example, has resulted from the jam session 'cutting contest', a form of 'musical duelling',[121] which emphasised *individual* self-interest and talent and provided the musicians with the necessary tools to improve as improvisers. These contests were fiercely competitive, testing the 'skill and creativity'[122] of the individual musicians. Yet, 'the ultimate purpose was to raise the quality of performance all around'.[123]

The relationship between the individual and the collective is extremely important when discussing the merits of improvisation. According to Marcel Cobussen, '[i]mprovisation is about interaction. Musicians [and people in general] do not improvise in isolation'.[124] An integral part of improvisation is the emotional bonds that are forged with others through a shared experience of 'risk, vulnerability and trust'.[125] Improvisation is not simply a spontaneous action, but is an 'empathetic, hermeneutic interaction that is constituted upon a recognition of the powerful synergy and responsibility that arises when humans with multiple perspectives come together'.[126] Fischlin and Heble even go so far as to assert that 'improvisation is less about original acts of self-creation than about an ongoing process of community building'.[127]

Applied to McNulty's situation, we find that while his improvised legality forged a temporary communal bond between himself and Lester Freeman, the improvised legality cost both their jobs in the end, shattering the bond between the two. Although McNulty's apportioning of financial resources to others in the police department did lead to some sense of interdepartmental community, the community was driven apart when an officer began blackmailing McNulty for unearned resources. Finally, any community and emotional bonding displayed in earlier seasons of *The Wire* were almost non-existent in season five, as shown by McNulty's own partner Bunk, and those officers closest to him deeply questioning his choices.

At the end of *The Wire*, the question of McNulty's improvised legality remains. McNulty's story is not just his story, but also the story of bringing the series back around on itself. In the final section, I return to the beginning in order to end with some concluding remarks on law and television and the limits of justice as improvised legality in *The Wire* and beyond.

[120] Ibid.
[121] D Belgrad, *The Culture of Spontaneity: Improvisation and the Arts in Postwar America* (Chicago and London, University of Chicago Press, 1989) 180.
[122] Ibid.
[123] S DeVeaux, *The Birth of Bebop: A Social and Musical History* (London, Picador, 1997) 211.
[124] M Cobussen, 'Improvisation. An Annotated Inventory' (2008) *New Sound* 32, 6.
[125] Ibid.
[126] Stanyek, cited in ibid 7.
[127] Fischlin and Heble, 'The Other Side' (n 90) 17.

V. The Other Side of The Wire

Critics often judge the skill or talent of an improviser by his or her ability to return, after a period of 'wild' improvisation, to the original melody, to 'somehow [return] to *sense* when he seemed to have unleashed mere *chaos*'.[128] This ability to return is perhaps the most difficult part of improvisation, bringing it all to a 'successful' end where there is a resonance beyond the end, where the end does not just come as a collapse back into the order of things, but orients us towards the possibility of otherness,[129] and towards 'the other side of nowhere'.[130] McNulty returns to hand-holding in season five, but this time with the aim of orienting the viewers away from the reality of *The Wire*, or towards a reality in which *The Wire* no longer exists.

In the final season, McNulty becomes a degraded reflection of the thing that he fights and in doing so loses all connection to Irish justice. McNulty stops being Irish, and he knows it. In the words of one viewer; 'McNulty's incredulous catch phrase, "What the f**k did I do?" no longer applies. He knows exactly what the f**k he did.'[131] The season closes with McNulty's career in tatters and his closest friendships—and last-chance relationship—all but destroyed.[132] And yet, at the very end, the writers of *The Wire* pardon McNulty from a life of misery and pain.[133] With McNulty's release, *The Wire* also releases itself from realist television programming, which had been both a prison and a playground throughout the duration of the show's running. Absolution for McNulty, specifically the Irish 'wake' held for him by his work colleagues to mourn his departure from the police department, signalled the end of a five-year improvisation and the return to the familiar, redemptive storylines, which dominate network television police dramas. The 'wake' also signalled the 'death' of *The Wire* and McNulty's return to Irishness (during his 'eulogy' he gets to say one final, 'What the f**k did I do?').

The wire is in essence the wiretap, but also a metaphor of how things are held together not by solidity, but by wire, a fragile flexible connection of communication and binding.[134] These connecting wires are also those of television and their fragility stems from the laws of realism, a concept that asks televisual storytelling to be more real than reality itself in order to perpetuate its realism. In its devotion to authenticity, *The Wire* became—in a sense—too real and, along the way, lost confidence in its own metaphor of wire. The show instead became about the institutional resilience of power as the irresistible propensity of institutions to corrupt; there is only the possibility of deeper cycles of degradation. *The Wire* becomes the wall—and the programme's televisual portrayal of law and order, although lauded as 'revolutionary',[135] finds its limit.

---

[128] J Jones, 'Wild Ones' *The Guardian Weekend* 11 December 2004 64 (emphasis added).

[129] Fischlin and Heble, 'Other Side' (n 90) 11.

[130] Ibid 1.

[131] Joedoone, 'Episode 8—Obituary: Omar Little' in Busfield & Owen (eds), *The Wire Re-Up* (n 10) 227.

[132] Rudacille, 'The Drunkard's Opera' (n 45) 489.

[133] Only one other character in *The Wire*, Bubbles, the recovering heroin addict, is offered the same. Ibid.

[134] Poniewozik writes: 'A wire is something that connects': Poniewozik, 'Connecting the Dots' (n 3).

[135] Burkeman, 'Interview: David Simon' (n 42) 245.

References

Books and Journals

Alvarez, R, (ed) *The Wire: Truth be Told* (Edinburgh, London, New York and Melbourne, Canongate, 2009).
—— 'Season Five Overview' in Alvarez ibid 401–08.
Alvarez, VP and Garland, G, 'Cop Reporters and *The Wire*' in Alvarez ibid.
Anthony, A, 'Interview: Dominic West' in S Busfield and P Owen (eds), *The Wire Re-Up* (London, Guardian Books, 2009) 65–68.
Belgrad, D, *The Culture of Spontaneity: Improvisation and the Arts in Postwar America* (Chicago and London, University of Chicago Press, 1989).
Brooks, R, 'The Narrative Production of 'Real Police' in T Potter and CW Marshall (eds), *The Wire: Urban Decay and American Television* (New York and London, Continuum, 2009) 64–77.
Burkeman, O, 'Interview: David Simon' in Busfield and Owen, *The Wire Re-Up*, 2009, 244–49.
Busfield, S and Owen P, (eds) *The Wire Re-Up* (London, Guardian Books, 2009).
Busfield, S, 'Episode 7—A Shot at Redemption' in Busfield and Owen ibid 217.
—— 'Episode 10—From Script to Screen' in Busfield and Owen ibid 51.
Cobussen, M, 'Improvisation. An Annotated Inventory' (2008) *New Sound* 32 4–15.
DeVeaux, S, *The Birth of Bebop: A Social and Musical History* (London, Picador, 1997).
Fischlin, D and Heble, A (eds), *Rebel Musics: Human Rights, Resistant Sounds, and the Politics of Music Making* (Montréal, New York and London, Black Rose Books, 2003).
—— (eds), *The Other Side of Nowhere: Jazz, Improvisation, and Communities in Dialogue* (Middletown, Connecticut, Wesleyan University Press, 2004).
—— 'The Other Side of Nowhere: Jazz, Improvisation, and Communities in Dialogue' in Fischlin and Heble ibid 1–42.
Fiske, J, *Media Matters: Race and Gender in U.S. Politics,* revised edn (Minneapolis and London, University of Minnesota Press, 1996).
—— *Television Culture* (London and New York, Routledge, 1987).
Fletcher, MA, 'Barack Obama: Wire Fan' in Alvarez, *The Wire: Truth be Told*, 2009, 37–41.
Heble, A, *Landing on the Wrong Note: Jazz, Dissonance, and Critical Practice* (New York and London, Routledge, 2000).
Kahn, J, '*The Wire* is Not Escapism' in Busfield and Owen, *The Wire Re-Up*, 2009, 250–52.
Kenny, K, 'Labor and Labor Organizations' in J Lee and MR Casey (eds), *Making the Irish American: History and Heritage of the Irish in the United States* (New York, NYU Press, 2006) 354–63.
—— 'Race, Violence, and Anti-Irish Sentiment in the Nineteenth Century' in Lee and Casey ibid 364–77.
Massie, S, *Complete Idiot's Guide to Irish History and Culture* (Indianapolis, Alpha Books, 1999).
McMillan, A, 'Heroism, Institutions, and the Police Procedural' in T Potter and CW Marshall (eds), *The Wire: Urban Decay and American Television* (New York and London, Continuum, 2009) 50–63.
Moynihan, DP, 'The Irish' in Lee and Casey, *Making the Irish American*, 2006, 475–25.
Owen, P, 'Episode 6—Where's Jimmy' in Busfield and Owen, *The Wire Re-Up*, 2009, 172–74.
—— 'Episode 11—The True McNulty' in Busfield and Owen ibid 53–54.
Quinn, P, 'Looking for Jimmy' in Lee and Casey, *Making the Irish American*, 2006, 663–79.
Ramshaw, S, 'Deconstructin(g) Jazz Improvisation: Derrida and the Law of the Singular Event' (2006) 2 *Critical Studies in Improvisation* 1, 19.

—— 'Jamming the Law: Improvised Theatre and the "Spontaneity" of Judgment' (2010) 14 *Law Text Culture* 133–59.

Rudacille, D (with contribution from Sofia Alvarez), 'The Drunkard's Opera: Jimmy McNulty in Life and Letters' in Alvarez, *The Wire: Truth be Told*, 2009, 485–91.

Sidhu, DS, 'Wartime America and *The Wire*: A Response to Posner's Post-9/11 Constitutional Framework' (2009) *George Mason University Civil Rights Law Journal* 20, 37–82.

Simon, D, 'Introduction' in Alvarez, *The Wire: Truth be Told*, 2009, 1–31.

—— 'Letter to HBO' in Alvarez ibid 32–36.

Walsh, WJ, 'The Priest-Penitent Privilege: An Hibernocentric Essay in Postcolonial Jurisprudence' (2005) *Indiana Law Review* 80, 1037–89.

Wilde, J, 'Why *The Wire* is the Greatest TV Show Ever Made' in Busfield and Owen, *The Wire Re-Up*, 2009, 4–5.

Wood, M, 'This is America, Man' (2010) 32 *London Review of Books* 10, 20–21.

Newspapers and Websites

'About ICASP: Research' Improvisation, Community and Social Practice' www.improvcommunity.ca/about/research.

Barry, D, 'Begorrah! Irish Cops, Yet Again' *The New York Times,* 26 October 2008.

Heble, A and Siemerling, W, 'Voicing the Unforeseeable: Improvisation, Social Practice, Collaborative Research' http://myuminfo.umanitoba.ca/Documents/2206/HebleSiemerlingVV_revised.pdf.

'Irish American' *Answers.com* www.answers.com/topic/irish-american.

'Jimmy McNulty' *Wikipedia* http://en.wikipedia.org/wiki/Jimmy_McNulty.

Jones, J, 'Wild Ones' *The Guardian Weekend*, 11 Dec 2004, 61–65.

King, J, 'Exclusive David Simon Q&A' *Borderline Productions* (2006) www.borderline-productions.com/TheWireHBO/exclusive-1.html.

Monfette, C, '*The Wire*: The Complete Fifth Season DVD Review' *IGN* http://uk.dvd.ign.com/articles/899/899184p1.html.

'Musical Improvisation, Social Change Focus of Major Research Grant' (University of Guelph News Release, 4 September 2007) www.uoguelph.ca/news/2007/09/musical_improvi.html.

Pearson, C, '*The Wire*: Season 5 Episode 2 Self-Righteous Indignation' *Wordpress.com Blog* (8 January 2008) http://urbanfervor.wordpress.com/2008/01/08/the-wire-season-5-episode-2.

Poniewozik, J, 'Connecting the Dots' *Time.com* www.time.com/time/printout/0,8816,1699870,00.html.

Rothkerch, I, 'What Drugs Have Not Destroyed, the War On Them Has' *Salon.com* http://dir.salon.com/story/ent/tv/int/2002/06/29/simon/print.html.

'*The Wire*: 'Every Villain Has Their Reasons' *Irish Left Review* www.irishleftreview.org/2009/03/12/wire-every-villain-reasons.

'*The Wire* re-up: McNulty, Templeton and Dexter' *Organgrinder Blog* www.guardian.co.uk/media/organgrinder/2008/oct/27/wire-television-mcnulty-templeton-dexter.

Tucker, K, '*The Wire*' *EW.com* www.ew.com/ew/article/0,,264531~3~~wire,00.html.

Wordpress.com Blog http://urbanfervor.wordpress.com/2008/01/08/the-wire-season-5-episode-2/.

18

Torture and Contempt of the Law in '24': Selling America New 'Patriotic' Values

RYAN J THOMAS AND SUSAN DENTE ROSS

The social fabric of the United States was, according to many commentators, irrevocably altered on 11 September 2001. For one commentator, the terrorist attacks of 9/11 constructed a 'bleak landscape of personal loss, paranoia, and political cynicism... American culture has been forever changed'.[1] Another proclaimed that 'everything has changed since the terrorist attacks... and nothing will be quite the same again'.[2] Of particular concern to media scholars is the way that various forms of mass communication have articulated the fears and tensions of the post-9/11 era. In her review of television culture following 9/11, Lynn Spigel argued that, 'after the attacks of September 11, traditional forms of entertainment had to reinvent their place in US life and culture'.[3] However, while studies on news discourses have been plentiful, little attention has been given to how entertainment media has shaped the post-9/11 epoch. For Spigel, 'the scholarly focus on news underestimates (indeed, it barely considers) the way the "reality" of 9/11 was communicated across the flow of television's genres, including its so-called entertainment genres'.[4] Such research routinely underestimates the extent to which the atmosphere of fiction tends to render invisible the pervasive struggles over meaning and power, the tensions among ideologies, and the divides between producers and consumers that undergird television texts. Any assumed line between reality and fiction, knowledge and imagining is infinitely thin and porous, and any distinction that may exist is immaterial in affecting how we perceive events and how we choose to respond to them.

---

[1] W Dixon, 'Introduction: Something Lost—Film After 9/11' in W Dixon (ed), *Film and Television After 9/11* (Carbondale, Southern Illinois University Press, 2004) 36.

[2] D Sterritt, 'Representing Atrocity: From the Holocaust to September 11' in ibid 64.

[3] L Spigel, 'Entertainment Wars: Television Culture after 9/11' (2004) 56 *American Quarterly* 56, 235.

[4] Ibid 238.

One of the most prominent issues of the post-9/11 age is torture. In this chapter, we argue that the discursive construction of torture in the television show *24* has real and important implications for how people in the United States and around the world understand torture as a legal and ethical issue. After we define the concept of torture, we survey some of the prominent issues central to its practice. We then discuss the show itself within the context of research that examines the 'normalising' function of mass media. The second half of the chapter applies a discursive analysis of one full season of *24*, focusing on its representation of torture. Using a critical discourse analytic framework, which allows for a nuanced understanding of the relationships between discourse and ideology, text and context, we argue that *24* normalises torture as a necessary part of 'the way things are', an unquestionably justifiable course of action in the 'War on Terror'. This construction, we contend, positions the law as an *impediment to* rather than an *instrument of* justice.

I. Torture after 9/11

On 15 May 2007, during a televised debate among the prospective Republican candidates for president, moderator Brit Hume illustrated 'a fictional but we think plausible scenario involving terrorism and the response to it', describing a situation in which the United States has come under terrorist attack and a further attack 'has been averted when the attackers were captured... and taken to Guantanamo [Bay]', while 'US intelligence believes that another, larger attack is planned'. Hume then posed the question: 'How aggressively would you interrogate the captured suspects?' The question, which seemed to be snatched from the script of a Hollywood thriller, elicited fascinating responses from the candidates, from former New York Mayor Rudy Giuliani calling for the use of 'every method [interrogators] can think of', to Massachusetts Senator Mitt Romney's demand to 'double Guantanamo [Bay]' and use 'enhanced interrogation techniques'. One of the most startling responses came from Colorado Representative Tom Tancredo, who replied: 'I'm looking for Jack Bauer at that time, let me tell you... [the US should take actions that] make the bad guy fearful'. Tancredo's response drew laughter and applause from a studio audience amused at the mention of Bauer, the main character in the television series *24*. However, Tancredo's comment is one made by a candidate for the highest office of the globe's most prominent superpower. In response to a serious question about intelligence gathering and interrogation, he calls up a fictional television character to signify his position. This instance is illustrative of a blurring of lines between reality and fiction in contemporary society. It highlights how televised and dramatised portrayals of law and justice and the 'appropriate' use of force and torture transfer rapidly and glibly from the small screen to the world stage, while simultaneously indicating the prominence of torture as a political issue in the twenty-first century.

Since the revelations of prisoner abuse and extreme interrogation methods at Abu Ghraib and Guantanamo Bay detention facilities, torture has been a prominent topic of US social and political discourse. In April 2004, when the news media distributed leaked photographs of prisoner mistreatment, the public learned that US guards at the Abu Ghraib detention facility in Baghdad had been torturing detainees. The photographs demonstrated the 'normalcy of exceptional brutality'[5] in the facility and revived international debate over the 'rules' of war and the use of torture, returning nearly forgotten arguments to the centre of political and social deliberations.

Studies show a significant increase in the presentation of torture on television since 9/11, with a dramatic peak in 2003.[6] Madelaine Hron noted that torture became a prominent plot feature on television for the first time following 9/11. In this era, she said, 'the representation of torture has become even more realistic and graphic... takes place in politicised real-life contexts... and is increasingly associated with terrorism, military operations, and law enforcement'.[7] In shows like *The Agency* and *Spooks*, torture comes to be represented as an instrument of justice committed by the '*good* guys' against the '*bad* guys'. Human Rights First found that television portrayed 'heroic American characters [using] torture—and... depicted [it] as necessary, effective, and even patriotic'.[8]

Such portrayals have consequences. Interviews with former military interrogators suggest that such fictional representations of torture are 'having an undeniable impact on how interrogations are conducted in the field. US soldiers are imitating the techniques they have seen on television—because they think such tactics work'.[9] However, torture is illegal and,

in the real world, torture does not work like that at all. ... Overwhelming evidence shows that the use of violence and coercion in interrogation actually hinders the ability to get good information. Unfortunately, you rarely see what does work. Very few shows take the time to truly explore the issue.[10]

And although the information gained from illegal, time-consuming, and inhumane torture is, at best, of highly questionable value, the belief in torture's productivity persists; 'The larger problem here', an active CIA officer told *The Washington Post*, 'is that this kind of stuff just makes people feel better, even if it doesn't work'.[11]

II. Torture's Shifting Opprobrium

The origins of the word 'torture' lie in ancient Greece, devolving from the concept of a 'touchstone that tests gold', which broadly equates to a method or device by which

---

[5] A Gordon, 'Abu Ghraib: Imprisonment and the War on Terror' (2006) 48 *Race and Class* 1, 45.

[6] Human Rights First, 'Scenes of Torture on Primetime Network TV 1995–2005' www.humanrightsfirst. org; Parents Television Council, 'PTC Calls for More Network Responsibility Over Violent Content' www. parentstv.org; D Bauder, 'Group: TV Torture Influencing Real Life' (11 February 2007) www.usatoday.com.

[7] M Hron, 'Torture Goes Pop!' (2008) 20 *Peace Review: A Journal of Social Justice* 27.

[8] Ibid.

[9] Ibid.

[10] J Rosenblum, '"Criminal Minds" Wins Human Rights Award for Portrayal of Interrogation' (15 October 2007) www.humanrightsfirst.org).

[11] Darius Rejali, 'Five Myths about Torture and Truth' *The Washington Post* 16 Dec 2007 (www. washingtonpost.com).

to obtain that which is genuine or true. Torture, as defined by the UN Convention of 10 December 1984, is:

> Any act by which severe pain or suffering, whether physical or mental, is intentionally inflicted on a person for such purposes as obtaining from him or a third person information or a confession, punishing him for an act he or a third person has committed or is suspected of having committed, or intimidating or coercing him or a third person, or for any reason based on discrimination of any kind, when such pain or suffering is inflicted by or at the instigation of another person acting in an official capacity.

The US Code, title 18, chapter 113C, section 2340, similarly defines torture as an action by someone 'acting under the color of law *specifically intended to* inflict severe physical or mental pain or suffering... upon another person *within his custody or physical control*' (our emphasis). The federal statute establishes US jurisdiction over this crime when committed by a US national anywhere in the world, and it sets penalties that include death or life imprisonment.

The illegality of torture is well established in foundational documents of both national (US) and international law. Indeed, 'one of the most fundamental aspects of human rights law is the universal proscription of torture'.[12] The Eighth Amendment to the US Constitution prohibits the use of cruel or unusual punishments. Similarly, article five of the UN Universal Declaration of Human Rights declares that torture is a violation of human rights. This principle is strengthened and elaborated in both the 1975 UN Declaration on Protection of All Persons from Being Subjected to Torture and other Cruel, Inhumane or Degrading Punishment and its 1984 Convention Against Torture and Other Cruel Inhumane or Degrading Treatment or Punishment. The Third and Fourth Geneva Conventions (which the US signed) bind signatories to prohibit torture of prisoners in times of conflict. Article five of the Universal Declaration of Human Rights, which holds that '[n]o one shall be subjected to torture or to cruel, inhuman or degrading treatment or punishment', is echoed in article seven of the International Covenant on Political and Civil Rights, article three of the European Convention for the Protection of Human Rights and Fundamental Freedoms, article five of the African Charter on Human and Peoples' Rights, and article five of the American Convention on Human Rights.

Despite the plethora of national and international codes and covenants recognising torture as a profound violation of human rights and a serious criminal offence, its use continues. Too often the black letter of the law appears to take the proverbial back seat to the more abstract, discursive concept of justice or, in colloquial terms, 'getting the job done'. Thus, for example, the US relies on the broadly worded congressional resolution of Authorization for the Use of Military Force passed during the post-9/11 frenzy as its legal foundation for its use of extraordinary interrogation techniques and indefinite detention without judicial review for those it labels 'enemy combatants'. The War on Terror has 'revived debates that one thought were definitively buried in Western democracies',[13] initiating a paradigm shift in both the use and justification

---

[12] W Nagan and L Atkins, 'The International Law of Torture: From Universal Proscription to Effective Application and Enforcement' (2001) 14 *Harvard Human Rights Journal* 95.

[13] I Avelar, *The Letter of Violence: Essays on Narrative, Ethics, and Politics* (New York, Palgrave Macmillan, 2004) 25.

of torture. The perception of torture as cruel and unusual punishment may no longer dominate. Rather, torture may be sufficiently salient and acceptable as vital to the prevention of major disasters, the protection of civilian security, and, not incidentally, suitable as an almost frivolous topic for political jokes and posturing. In this context, television news and entertainment have amplified and reinforced the mistreatment of prisoners at Abu Ghraib and Guantanamo Bay in ways that make the brutal routine and normalise torture as a standard procedure of operations in the public conscious-ness. As one scholar argued, it is conceivable that 'the [US Supreme] Court might now rule that it is neither cruel nor unusual to torture a convict ... or even a mere suspect, if the information that *might* be wrung from that person *could* save thousands of innocent lives' (our emphasis).[14]

These controversies have created a moral grey area and revived age-old debates over the ethics of the use of torture as an interrogation tool and whether torture has a place in civilised society. Many scholars adopt the absolutist position, such that Michael Ignatieff asserts, that torture 'expresses the state's ultimate (and unacceptable) view that human beings are expendable'.[15] In contrast, others, perhaps most notably the promi-nent civil rights attorney Alan Dershowitz, argue that torture *is* ethical under limited conditions or within a specific scenario. In what some might view as moral relativism, Dershowitz says the wrongdoing of torture is 'cancelled out' by the lives saved as a result of its use. He asks: 'Would torturing one guilty terrorist to prevent the deaths of thousands of innocent civilians shock the conscience of all decent people?'[16] Dershowitz uses the example of the 'ticking time bomb' scenario—'the situation in which a captured terrorist who knows of an imminent large-scale threat refuses to disclose it'[17]—to rhetorically question whether saving hundreds or thousands of lives ethically justifies the torture of a single captive. He says that it *would be justified*; the *ethical* answer is to permit the torture to allow the interrogator to obtain information needed to save innocent lives.

The ticking time bomb scenario, which is also embedded in the structure of *24,* is a complex rhetorical construct that highlights the tension between ends and means. If one applies the teleological principle of utilitarianism, the choice to torture can be rationalised by a calculation of the greater good and which group comprises the greater number. In weighing the right of the suspect to an interrogation free of 'cruel, inhuman or degrading treatment or punishment' against the right to life of manifold innocent civilians, protagonists in such a scenario may (and, according to Dershowitz, *should*) feel morally compelled to make a calculation in favour of the majority. However, such a calculation requires the fulfillment of specific criteria for it to be internally consis-tent; the ethics of torture presumes absolute and infallible knowledge on the part of the authorities regarding the nature and likelihood of the impending catastrophe, the certainty the captive has vital knowledge, and the necessity for officials to rely on the

[14] H Silverglate, 'The Government Should Not Authorize the Use of Torture to Combat Terrorism' in J Torr (ed), *Civil Liberties: Current Controversies* (San Diego, Greenhaven Press, 2003) 186.

[15] M Ignatieff, *The Lesser Evil: Political Ethics in an Age of Terror* (Princeton, Princeton University Press, 2004) 143.

[16] A Dershowitz, 'The Use of Torture May be Justified in Certain Circumstances' in J Torr (ed), *Civil Liberties: Current Controversies* (n 14) 173.

[17] Ibid.

captive as the sole source of essential information. Furthermore, this scenario fails to acknowledge the possibility that a suspect or informant may provide *false* information to halt the torture *and* protect the planned act of terror. Finally, this resolution breezily ignores the fact that torture is illegal under both US and international law.

What the above debate makes clear is that torture is no longer a taboo subject. Instead, torture is an increasingly prominent topic of presidential debates and the entertainment world alike. As the stuff of policy, democracy, and fiction in the twenty-first century, torture has gained a new popular cachet to parallel, or perhaps overshadow, its centuries-old notoriety and proscription.

III. TV Torture before 9/11

In her review of the history of the representation of torture on film and in television, Madelaine Hron noted that, until the 1990s, most depictions of torture arose in adaptations of literary works such as the James Bond series or Anthony Burgess' *A Clockwork Orange*, reinforcing the fictive otherworldliness of torture as a phenomenon outside the boundaries of normalcy. Hron argued that torture scenes began to multiply in the 1990s in films such as *Natural Born Killers* and *Reservoir Dogs*, which 'banalised torture'[18] and in the 2000s' treatment of torture as 'pure fear and spectacle'[19] in horror movies such as *Hostel* and the *Saw* series. After 9/11, however, an increasing number of television shows 'reflexively comment[ed] on current torture practices—sometimes critically, at other times ambiguously, and in certain instances, even approvingly'.[20] One of the most prominent shows within this emerging genre was *24*.

A. 24 Hours of Torture

Following its premiere on 29 October 2001, *24* became one of the most popular and critically acclaimed, yet controversial, US television dramas of recent years. The show, which concluded in 2010 after eight seasons, pivoted around Jack Bauer and his colleagues at the Los Angeles Counter Terrorist Unit (CTU), their frontline fight against terrorism, and the rapid and difficult decisions they made to protect national security. Debuting seven weeks after the 11 September attacks, the show both chronologically and thematically paralleled the 'War on Terror', dealing with the same issues of terrorism and counter-terrorism that were simultaneously taking centre stage in national and international US policy discourse and actions.

The show was heralded for its dramatic innovations. One of the most innovative premises of the show was its setting in 'real-time', wherein the events of the show

---

[18] Hron, 'Torture Goes Pop!' (n 7) 26.
[19] Ibid.
[20] Ibid.

unfolded on a 24-hour timeline, spanning a day in the lives of the protagonists.[21] *24*'s hallmark premise of occurring throughout one 24-hour day positioned the show as a fictive embodiment of 'the ticking time bomb' scenario, as the urgency prompted by the ticking time bomb functions not only as an apt metaphor but also as the central narratological framework, building tension, velocity, and immediacy through the constant, ominous movement of the clock toward impending disaster. The time compression and perceived urgency of decisions created by the literal and figurative countdown of the clock 'takes an unusual situation and turns it into the meat and potatoes of the show',[22] ramping up the intensity for an audience of millions.

Observers suggested the show adopted an implicitly, if not explicitly, pro-torture stance in its portrayal of counter-terrorism. Bauer was portrayed as 'the sympathetic vigilante', uninterested in legalities and '[speeding] rapidly ahead in his battle to save humanity… with humanity here reduced to the United States only'.[23] With 'astonishing regularity',[24] the show's overriding 'context of suffering and violence… instill[s] in viewers a strong presumption that *24* is grounded in the starkest exigencies of the real world',[25] constructing a world in which the realities are extreme and dangerous.

In *24,* routine acceptance of torture was one facet of a world view in which the rule of law was secondary to practical and pragmatic concerns about the speedy resolution of an imminent threat. The show did 'not moralise about the use of abuse and torture by Americans interrogating terrorists'.[26] Rather, torture was presented as an acceptable, even honourable, course of action. Concerns about legality and consequences were trivialised, and profound questions about the costs of torture were brushed off as the nit-picking of pencil-pushing nay-sayers. Viewers who 'participated' voyeuristically were invited to adopt the same perspective: the law be damned!

Beyond the television screen, questions about the show's presentation of torture gained weight because the show's co-creator, Joel Surnow, was a well-known supporter of then President George W Bush and a financial contributor to the Republican Party.[27] Public figures with influence on popular opinion, such as conservative commentator Rush Limbaugh, former Homeland Security Secretary Michael Chertoff, former Secretary of Defense Donald Rumsfeld,[28] and, evidently, Tom Tancredo, made it known that they watched and enjoyed the show. As Surnow once said, 'People in the [Bush] administration love the series … It's a patriotic show'.[29]

Such comments suggest either flippancy or an easy acceptance of torture within the administration then leading the global 'War on Terror'. However, in 2007, US military

---

[21] That said, some creative license must be used to allow for commercial breaks. Thus, *24* cannot be said to truly occur in real-time, rather the viewer must accept that for those three to five minutes while the commercials are airing, there is nothing consequential happening that will move the plot forward.

[22] Quoted in J Mayer, 'Whatever it Takes: The Politics of the Man Behind "24"' *The New Yorker*, 19 February 2007 (www.newyorker.com).

[23] Dennis Broe, 'Fox and its Friends: Global Commodification and the New Cold War' (2004) 43 *Cinema Journal* 101.

[24] Matt Feeney, 'Torture Chamber: Fox's *24* Terrifies Viewers into Believing its Bizarre and Convoluted Plot Twists' *Slate* (6 Jan 2004) (www.slate.com).

[25] Ibid.

[26] Frank Rich, 'We'll Win this War—On "24"' *The New York Times*, 9 Jan 2005.

[27] Mayer, 'Whatever it Takes' (n 22).

[28] Ibid.

[29] Ibid.

spokesmen seemed to take the show more seriously. Citing the frequency and explicitness of depictions of torture, as well as the show's routine reliance on torture as an information-gathering technique, the military requested that *24* tone down the torture scenes over concerns about 'the impact the [scenes] are having both on troops in the field and America's reputation abroad... Jack Bauer is giving us a bad name'.[30] Even '[m]ilitary educators claimed that the popular depiction of torture... present[ed] an enormous training challenge', because Bauer routinely circumvented the legal process and presented torture as the cure-all.

IV. Television: Normalising and Naturalising

The true impact and significance of fictional depictions of torture, like those on *24*, is difficult to assess. Horace Newcomb argued that television dramas and popular entertainment are a 'crucially important' area of study because they bring 'massive audience[s] into a direct relationship with particular sets of values and attitudes'.[31] Newcomb alluded to well-established findings that fictional narratives bypass certain cognitive gatekeepers in ways that enable their messages to be more readily and uncritically internalised by viewers.

Thus, because television characters 'tend to become familiar figures, loved, or excused with a tolerance that is quite remarkable',[32] the actions of a character like Jack Bauer tend to touch viewers deeply. The 'values and attitudes' contained within fictional shows, therefore, are not 'just entertainment'. When Bauer adopts torture as routine and normal, it makes it easier for viewers to shift torture from the category of unacceptable and immoral (or even a last resort when everything else fails) to simply 'the way things are', an ethical means of combating terrorism. And while audiences are not passive, public understandings of the law and the complex calculations necessary to protect human rights in an era seemingly overtaken by terror are shaped by mediated discourses such as those on *24*. The ways in which shows like *24* present the law and its violation, torture and its appropriate response come to represent the world, and 'by representing the world, [they help to] constitute it'.[33]

Television, among other cultural texts, constitutes a particular world as it cultivates particular attitudes and opinions of it. Through naturalising cultural texts that incorporate dominant ideologies, such as television shows, consumers assimilate a worldview consistent with dominant social norms. Television inculcates in viewers 'standards for deciding what is, standards for deciding what can be, standards for deciding how one feels about it, standards for deciding what to do about it, and standards for deciding how to go about doing it'.[34] According to Douglas Kellner,

---

[30] A Buncombe, 'US Military tells Jack Bauer: Cut out the Torture Scenes ... or Else!' *The Independent*, 13 Feb 2007 (www.independent.co.uk).

[31] H Newcomb, 'Toward a Television Aesthetic' in H Newcomb (ed), *Television: The Critical View* (New York, Oxford University Press, 1976) 274.

[32] J Ellis, *Visible Fictions* (London, Routledge & Kegan Paul, 1982) 139.

[33] J Silbey, 'What We Do When We Do Law and Popular Culture' (2002) 27 *Law and Social Inquiry* 155.

[34] W Goodenough, *Culture, Language, and Society* (Massachusetts, Addison-Wesley, 1971) 22.

certain... cultural texts advance *specific ideological positions* which can be ascertained by relating the texts to the political discourses and debates of their era, to other artifacts concerned with similar themes, and to ideological motifs in the culture that are active in a given text (our emphasis).[35]

Much research has examined the workings of ideology in television texts. John Fiske argued that texts perform ideological work by creating 'common sense out of dominant sense'[36] through a process of coercion by consent that naturalises particular worldviews and perspectives. Naturalisation, by which a subject 'present[s] itself as an objective, innocent reflection of the real',[37] invites the audience toward an uncritical acceptance of the phenomenon as simply part of the natural order.

Such effects take on added significance when viewed within the wider political context in which *24* was situated. The show did not occur in a political or historical vacuum. Its central focus on national security and terrorism arose in the wake of 9/11, at a time when national security (and the measures taken to protect it) was among the most prominent social and political issues. Its treatment of torture coincided with the exposure of prisoner mistreatment by the US military at Abu Ghraib and Guantanamo Bay. The show's tendency to denigrate or ignore the constraints of law came during increasing public and political debate over abuses of power by the Bush administration and the willing diminishment of civil liberties by the US Congress. The specific ideological positions advanced by *24* related directly to the contentious and volatile issue of torture and the conditions, if any, under which the intrinsic value of human beings might be dismissed in the pursuit of the 'greater good'.

V. Analysis

We now turn to an analysis of a full season of *24*. A season of *24* contains 24 episodes and each episode is an hour in length, with each episode representing one hour within a single day. As Birk and Birk argued, this real-time setup 'constituted a single narrative' spanning all the shows of one season.[38] We therefore elected to analyse the entire fourth season of the show, which aired from 9 January 2005 to 23 May 2005. We selected this season because it aired most proximately to the revelation of Abu Ghraib prisoner abuse in April and May of 2004, which pushed the issue of torture to public prominence in US social and political discourse. We focused our analysis on how the show represented the law and ethics of torture. However, before moving into that discussion, a short summary of the plot will be helpful.

---

[35] D Kellner, *Media Culture: Cultural Studies, Identity, and Politics Between the Modern and the Postmodern* (London, Routledge, 1995) 93.

[36] J Fiske, 'The Discourses of TV Quiz Shows, or School + Luck = Success + Sex' in L Vande Berg and L Wenner (ed), *Television Criticism: Approaches and Applications* (New York, Longman, 1991) 447.

[37] J Fiske, *Television Culture* (New York, Methuen, 1987) 42.

[38] E Birk and H Birk, '"Today is Going to be the Longest Day of My Life": A Narratological Analysis of *24*' in G Allrath and M Gymnich (ed), *Narrative Strategies in Television Series* (New York, Palgrave Macmillan, 2005) 48.

The fourth season of *24* deals with a 'day in the life' of those who work to protect, and to threaten, US national security. The central protagonist is Jack Bauer (Kiefer Sutherland), who was recently fired from his job at the Los Angeles Counter Terrorist Unit (CTU) by its director, Erin Driscoll (Alberta Watson), due to a heroin addiction picked up while working undercover for the unit.[39] Bauer now has a desk job working for Secretary of Defence James Heller (William Devane), alongside his lover Audrey Raines (Kim Raver), who is also Heller's daughter. As the day progresses, Jack returns to action with CTU as he and his colleagues uncover and move to counter an increasingly elaborate terrorist plot that causes the US Government to lurch from crisis to crisis.

The season begins with the bombing of a commuter train, which enables the theft of a device capable of commandeering all 104 nuclear power plants in the US. However, before CTU can address that, they must rescue the kidnapped Secretary of Defence and his daughter, whose threatened execution is streamed live on the internet. Bauer succeeds in a solo rescue as the device stolen after the train bombing causes a meltdown of the San Gabriel Island nuclear reactor. Other reactors are hijacked but CTU's herculean efforts avert further meltdowns. As that crisis resolves, a terrorist who has stolen a stealth fighter launches a direct attack on Air Force One, causing it to crash. The injuries sustained by the President in the attack necessitate the elevation of the Vice President to the presidency, under the terms of the twenty-fifth Amendment,[40] and the crash also enables the theft of the controls to the US' nuclear arsenal. In the climax of the season, a stolen nuclear warhead is fired at Los Angeles but is deactivated in the final hour/episode of the season/day.

24's fourth season features the torture of five characters: Tomas Sherek (in episode one), Richard Heller (episodes three, four, six, seven, and 22), Sarah Gavin (episodes eight and 13), Paul Raines (episodes 11 and 20), and Joe Prado (episode 18). Viewers are 'entertained' with scenes of torture in 11 episodes, or nearly half of the episodes comprising the fourth season.

Tomas Sherek (Faran Tahir) is introduced as a terrorist who participated in the train bombing that opened the season. He is tracked down by CTU and brought in for questioning in the first episode. Bauer happens to be at CTU and attempts to explain to Driscoll that something is amiss; a terrorist of Sherek's prominence would not risk his cover for a relatively minor operation such as the train bombing. Driscoll dismisses Bauer's advice, asserting that CTU has the situation under control. When Driscoll and a CTU agent fail to obtain information from Sherek, Bauer knocks out a CTU security guard, gains access to the interrogation room, and demands information from the suspect. When Sherek refuses to comply, Bauer, without hesitation, shoots him in the leg. Sherek cries out in agony and immediately divulges the information to Bauer that a kidnapping of the Secretary of Defence is planned.

Here, CTU's by-the-book methods, which are within the law, are portrayed as weak and ineffective, while Bauer's renegade violence gets results. Bauer's shooting of Sherek is presented as essential in gaining timely access to vital information.

---

[39] His firing takes place off-screen, between the end of season three and the beginning of season four.

[40] The twenty-fifth Amendment clarifies the issues of succession to the presidency, establishing procedure in the event of the death, resignation, or incapacity or the President, where the Vice President assumes the office of the President in the event of such an instance occurring.

Nonetheless, the information comes too late. The kidnapping has occurred and the secretary's guard detail has been killed. The implicit suggestion is that had Bauer tortured Sherek sooner, or had Driscoll and CTU employed more ruthless measures, the kidnapping and murders would have been averted. This is a teachable moment for Driscoll that is revisited later in the season.

At the end of the first episode, terrorists kidnap the Secretary of Defence Richard Heller and his daughter, Audrey, while they are visiting the Secretary's son, Richard (Logan Marshall-Green). CTU agents suspect some insider double-crossing as the only people aware of the Secretary's whereabouts were his children and his guards, who were killed in the attack. When the son is brought in for questioning and fails a polygraph test, Driscoll authorises the use of extreme measures:

> Driscoll: It'll take days to go through his phone records. I want you to see if you can get the name out of him another way.
>
> Agent: What do you mean?
>
> Driscoll: You know what I mean.
>
> Agent: Erin, we're not even sure he's guilty of anything.
>
> Driscoll: This is how we'll find out. Get started.

This exchange follows Bauer's success in obtaining information from Sherek with violence and suggests that Driscoll has learned the benefits of extreme (illegal) measures. Unsure whether Richard Heller has any knowledge of the kidnapping, Driscoll says that torture is the way to ascertain his innocence or guilt. Torture is presented not as the way to obtain vital information but as the way to determine *whether* the suspect has any information at all. Circumventing other strategies that would benefit from the colour of law, Driscoll authorises torture, prompting the following scene:

> Richard: What the hell are you doing? Get your hands off me!
>
> Agent: Who else knew your father would be at your house this morning?
>
> Richard: I told you, no one.
>
> [A second CTU agent pulls a syringe out of his briefcase.]
>
> Richard: What are you, crazy?
>
> Agent: It works on a neurotransmitter level. It makes every nerve ending within your body feel like it's on fire.
>
> Richard: You're bluffing. I know you can't get away with this.
>
> Agent: By the time you're released, the mark on your arm will be gone. It'll be just your word against mine.

The agent abruptly ends the interrogation, believing torture without just cause is inappropriate, but Driscoll, the authority figure who previously opposed Bauer's ready reliance on violence, orders the torture to continue. The agent then adopts a different interrogation technique: sensory deprivation, where the son is deprived of sight and intense, uncomfortable noises are played through headphones into his ears. After 30 minutes, Richard protests, exclaiming, 'This isn't legal. You can't keep me here'. The agent replies calmly, 'You'll be here until you tell me what I need to know'. He then resumes the sensory deprivation. The agent is willing to prolong Richard's suffering for as long as necessary in order to obtain any information the son may hold. The agent is presented as aware that his actions are illegal, but as accepting orders because he believes the end is sufficient in justifying the means.

One might expect the Secretary of Defence to be outraged at CTU's torture of his son. That is not the case. When the Secretary is rescued, Driscoll informs him his son, as a suspect, had been subjected to extreme interrogation methods. After his initial mild annoyance, the Secretary meets with his son, learns of Richard's refusal to cooperate, and takes a different view:

Secretary: They said they were using some interrogation techniques.

Son: Totally out of line. I'm gonna sue them blind.

Secretary: I think it'll be a little more effective if you let me deal with it. I promise you, if they were out of line, heads will roll.

Son: What do you mean, 'if?'

Secretary: Why did they think you were holding something back from them?

Son: I don't know!

Secretary: Richard, if you know something that would shed some light on what happened to me...

Son: Wait, you don't think I would tell them if I thought it was relevant?

Secretary: So there is something?

Son: Now *you're* giving me the third degree?

Secretary: Son, do you have any idea what your sister just went through? If you know anything that would help us find the people behind this, tell me now!

Richard: Dad, I'm glad you're alive, I really am, but I am not going to tell these people things about my private life that they don't need to know.

Secretary: That you don't *think* they need to know. Richard, these people were trying to save our lives!

Richard: These people can't be trusted! What they did to me is proof.

Secretary: [Turning away from Richard.] Agent Manning, could you come in here please?

[The agent enters the interrogation room.]

Secretary: Agent Manning, I am authorising you to do whatever you feel is necessary to get this information out of my son.

Richard: Dad...

Secretary: I love you, son. But I have a duty to my country.

Here, the Secretary, like Driscoll before him, is converted to, or perhaps naturally embraces, torture as *the* method to obtain information even though his release makes its possession less urgent. Here, the Secretary of Defence, who serves as the principal adviser to the President on matters of national defence, is presented as condoning the torture of his own son based on a suspicion that the son *may* have information related to national security. Throughout the show, the Secretary of Defence is portrayed as an upright man with a strong sense of integrity who is saluted as a patriot. Viewers are invited to identify with him and to accept that the torture is justified because he *says* it is justified. The use of torture is naturalised as an intrinsic part of the national security regimen when the Secretary explains, 'These people were trying to save our lives'. Rather than being horrified or frightened by CTU's criminal behaviour, the Secretary seems dumbfounded by his son's failure to recognise that 'they' are only doing what's best for 'us'. For the father, and one of the leaders of the US military, the question is not about the tactics of the CTU agents but about his son's refusal to cooperate.

Sarah Gavin (Lana Parrilla), a CTU analyst, appears to be the trusted confidante of her supervisor, Driscoll. Driscoll asks Gavin to spy on her CTU co-workers, whom Driscoll suspects of disloyalty. However, Gavin soon after makes an enemy of a CTU colleague, Marianne Taylor (Aisha Tyler), who is secretly a 'mole' in the employ of terrorists. Taylor directs her colleagues' suspicions away from herself by framing Gavin as the source of a leak to terrorists. Gavin is hauled off for questioning, where her continuous pleas of innocence only frustrate Driscoll and 'force' the use of torture to obtain information from Gavin which she does not have. Gavin repeatedly pleads that 'there's been some kind of mistake... [that she] would never betray... [her] country or endanger people's lives'. Driscoll's response encapsulates the season's perspective: 'I learned my lesson today with Sherek, and I am no longer going to err on the side of caution in these interrogations. Do you get my meaning?' Gavin is then repeatedly tasered to the point where she sobs for mercy. Driscoll's apparent epiphany suggests that she has not only come to appreciate Bauer's methods, but understands that they work. Further, she has come to understand them as a necessary first, rather than last, resort given the time constraints placed upon her and her unit. She makes the sweeping statement that she will *no longer* err on the side of caution; caution is the wrong way, and ruthlessness gets results. Friendship, like family, must join the rule of law in falling before the exigencies of fighting terror.

The torture of Gavin is one of the most uncomfortable scenes of the season, as viewers are aware that Gavin is innocent. Yet, her guilt is presumed by the other members of the CTU. She is treated like a criminal whose claims of innocence are mere subterfuge, and the truth she speaks has no power to alter her condition. The paradox is painful: her truths are dismissed, and only a false statement of knowledge can stop her torture. Gavin's supervisor refuses to believe her innocence or to follow the law, refuses to provide legal protection to suspects, or even delay the adoption of extreme methods of interrogation. Gavin is the victim of Driscoll's epiphany, and she is one of the primary vehicles for delivering the ideological message of the season.

Paul Raines (James Frain) is the estranged husband of the daughter of the Secretary of Defence, Audrey. He reappears at the time of the kidnapping, expressing concern for Audrey's safety. When Audrey is rescued, Paul reveals his desire to reconcile, but she says she loves Bauer. In the eleventh episode, Paul is thrust back into the narrative as the holder of the lease on the building where the terrorists planned their attacks. Bauer suspects Paul is involved and, with Audrey looking on, interrogates Paul in his hotel room. The following excerpt sets the scene:

Audrey: What are you going to do to him?

Bauer: Whatever I have to.

When Paul refuses to cooperate, Bauer tortures him by cutting a lamp's electrical cord to shock him:

Audrey: Jack, I don't think that Paul would be a traitor to this country!

Bauer: Right now Paul is a prime suspect, and he's not cooperating with me and I don't have time to do this any other way. I need to know for sure.

After Audrey protests, Bauer says, 'There are five nuclear power plants ready to melt down. All I care about right now is making sure that that doesn't happen.' His sole motivation, according to the narrative, is to safeguard the national security of the United States and save the lives of the innocent. So, Bauer shocks Paul multiple times until he reveals the necessary information.

Here again, torture is effective, and the time bomb of a (potential) crisis makes it *essential*; there is no time 'to do this any other way'. The narrative projects Bauer's personal responsibility for the torture to absolve viewers of their voyeuristic complicity. This projection of his sole responsibility also functions to protect audience notions (ones the show also implicitly asserts represent the audience's delusive belief) that national security can be protected when the law is followed. However, according to the social and fictional narrative, a national security crisis eliminates the space for certain legal niceties. Bauer, and those like him, sacrificially and benevolently assume the heavy responsibility for actions citizens and viewers alike wish to be shielded from, the painful reality that effective terror prevention is ugly and messy.

The electrical torture of Paul is uncomfortable viewing. This time viewers are not omniscient and must wait for the results of Bauer's interrogation to ascertain Paul's innocence (or guilt), making them somewhat complicit in his actions through their desire for the revelatory outcome. When Bauer learns that Paul is an innocent dupe, it is not Bauer but Paul who apologises for his gullibility. Paul's savage handling at Bauer's hands is virtually erased as the narrative drives forward. Here, despite Paul's innocence, viewers see that torture works. The information procured through Paul's torture permits Bauer to prevent successive nuclear reactor meltdowns. Millions of innocents are saved, and torture is reaffirmed as the essential tool to prevent terrorism. Law and its cumbersome procedures are secondary concerns at most.

Joe Prado (John Thaddeus) is introduced as a mercenary assisting one of the terrorists to flee the country. Prado kills the terrorist he claimed to be helping, in what he calls self-defence, and is arrested by CTU for his involvement in the terrorist plot. When the season's central villain hears of Prado's arrest, he contacts Amnesty Global (a fictional group overtly modelled on Amnesty International and/or the American Civil Liberties Union), asking them to prevent an innocent man from being tortured by CTU Los Angeles. Indeed, Prado is about to be tortured when an Amnesty Global attorney presents a signed court order to halt the interrogation:

CTU Agent: We have a problem. This is David Weiss from Amnesty Global.

Attorney: And I have a signed court order here protecting the rights of one Joseph Prado whom you have in custody. This US Marshall is here to assure that I am taken to the prisoner immediately.

CTU Agent: That's ridiculous.

The initial comment in this exchange signals the legal process as 'a problem', while the final statement makes it clear how legal or ethical interruptions of torture are represented as frivolous and absurd in *24*. Here an invocation of the law and the US Constitution are ridiculed as almost alien concepts, out of place and worse than useless. The scene continues:

Attorney: That's your opinion, but Mr. Prado's rights will not be violated. Take me to him now.

CTU Agent #1: We have no choice, Curtis. Do what he says.

CTU Agent #2: There's a nuclear warhead missing. This is our only lead, Bill.

CTU Agent #1: I'll get into this with the Justice Department. In the meantime, do what he says.

The CTU official later claims that 'this [situation] does *not* fall outside the boundary of the Patriot Act'. Another CTU analyst states: 'I don't like what's happening here. We have some prissy lawyer holding us up from doing our job'.

Throughout this scene involving three separate CTU employees, the attorney and his reliance on the law are portrayed as an impediment to national safety, and lawyers and the law are the 'prissy' stuff for sissies too emasculated to step up in a manly way to 'do the right thing' in order to protect the country. The law is not the domain of these investigators. Rather the law prevents them from 'doing their job', and the job is naturalised to incorporate torture as the only way to avert nuclear annihilation. As these scenes demonstrate, the stakes involved that 'require' torture escalate progressively throughout the season.

Bauer arrives at CTU and is confused by the lack of interrogation of Prado. 'What the hell's going on here?' he demands. 'You've got a key witness on a missing warhead. We should be pressing this guy *with everything we've got!*' When the CTU official informs him, with regret and anger in his voice, that 'If we want to appeal, we'll have to wait until 7:00 a.m. to take it to an appellant judge', Bauer seems baffled and asks, somewhat plaintively, 'Does he know what the stakes are?' The notion of 'knowing what the stakes are' is important; the stakes are high, lives are at stake, and Bauer, the ultimate national security insider, is profoundly aware of this. Lawyers and the courts that are removed from 'doing the job' presumably do not understand the stakes.

Bauer then questions how Prado managed to get a lawyer so soon after being arrested, and the following exchange takes place between Bauer and the attorney:

Bauer: You and I both know that your client isn't clean, and that he conspired to steal a US nuclear warhead.

Attorney: All my client wants is due process.

Bauer: Mr. Weiss, these people are not gonna stop attacking us today until millions, and millions of Americans are dead. Now, I don't wanna bypass the Constitution, but these are extraordinary circumstances.

Attorney: The Constitution was born out of extraordinary circumstances, Mr. Bauer. This plays out by the book, not in a back room with a rubber hose.

Bauer: I hope you can live with that.

This exchange is remarkable; Bauer's notion of 'extraordinary circumstances' is reminiscent of the scenario painted by Brit Hume before the presidential nominee debaters. But here the attorney, unlike any of those aspirants, responds that the Constitution 'was born out of extraordinary circumstances', meaning that its protections are expressly intended to stand strong in times of crisis. The attorney presents his request as modest and basic, but the context casts 'due process', that most fundamental process which civilised societies are due to give their citizens, as an extreme and illegitimate demand. For Bauer, the Constitution seems to be little more than bureaucratic red tape that muddies the waters of national security.

Further, the reference to Amnesty Global, with its awkward yet knowing wink toward Amnesty International and other 'liberal' organisations, plays toward popular conservative ire over legal procedures that assure the rights of alleged terrorists and criminals and undermine the safety of the people of the United States. Bauer's parting shot—that he hopes the attorney can live with himself—suggests that Bauer has little problem living with himself and his routine use of torture. In contrast, it is the man of law whose conscience and actions are questioned, casting them as dubious or worse. The clear message is that the United States would be a much scarier place if national security were left to people like the attorney.

When Bauer later contacts the President to obtain executive permission to torture Prado, the following exchange takes place:

> Bauer: If we want to procure any information from this suspect, we're gonna have to do it behind closed doors.
>
> President: You're talking about torturing this man?
>
> Bauer: I'm talking about doing what is necessary to stop this warhead from being used against us.

For Bauer, torture is 'necessary', but the President says they need to wait while he seeks the advice of the Justice Department. Bauer unsuccessfully pleads, 'With all due respect, sir, please let us *do our jobs*'. Here, again, torture is the definition of 'our job'. Protecting the nation 'naturally' and routinely requires the 'extraordinary' power to employ the option of torture.

Ignoring the President, Bauer plans to 'resign' his official post, to free Prado, and (now fully outside of the law or any 'official' role) to interrogate Prado as a private citizen. Prado questions his release and expresses concerns about his own safety but is told not to worry. Then Bauer arrives, knocks out the Federal Marshall guarding Prado, and handcuffs Prado to the dashboard of his car. Prado refuses to talk, so Bauer holds a knife to his throat and then cuts his fingers one by one until Prado reveals the information Bauer wants. Then, in a twist of violence as humour, Bauer gives Prado something to 'help... with the pain' by knocking him out.

VI. Wither the Lawman?

In *24*, torture consistently trumps the bonds of family, friendship, collegiality, and institution. Those who wield its power are presumed to exercise it with absolute knowledge and clear motive. In this context, the law is not only an irrelevance but an impediment to obtaining information and protecting national security. Bauer, the central character employing the tool of torture again and again, is the 'good guy' of the plot, the sole individual with sufficient foresight and fortitude to fight those who would conspire to destroy the United States. Bauer is presented as a benevolent vigilante, operating outside the law as he deems necessary and often resorting to torture as the *first* option to achieve his objectives.

Bauer is also unafraid to act outside the law in other ways to get results. At the end of episode three, in order to buy time to enable CTU to establish satellite surveillance, he stages a robbery of a gas station where a suspect has stopped. During the robbery, he threatens a police officer and a group of innocent customers. Then, in the latter part of the season, he stages a raid on the Chinese Consulate, the legal territory of a foreign nation, to obtain information from a terrorist conspirator there.

Through these episodes it is not the law, but its violation, that is a tool of national security. This message is particularly pronounced in the handling of the 'Amnesty Global' lawyer and given the fact that it is the villain of the season who contacts Amnesty Global on behalf of Prado. In this instance, the law is presented as the tool of the villain, as the puppet of terrorists, as a means of literally slowing, inhibiting, and distracting the law enforcement officials attempting to avert catastrophe. US law is a weapon in the terrorist arsenal, used against CTU and, by extension, the people CTU seeks to protect and defend.

Despite his disregard for protocol, procedure, and the law, Bauer is very much cast as the hero of the show. That role and Bauer's moral position are reinforced by the consistent portrayal of those that oppose him, both individuals and the processes of the law, as either incompetent or naïve. One of the major obstacles to Bauer in the early episodes of the season is Driscoll, his former boss at CTU who fired him for drug addiction. Driscoll repeatedly thwarts Bauer's methods, determined to go 'by the book' and follow protocol. This female supervisor is presented as rather weak and ineffective at dealing with crises. She lacks the tough, ruthless edge that makes Bauer such an effective agent and protector of national security. Her later about-face, in which she embraces Bauer's tactics, only strengthens Bauer's projected superiority. As viewers come to trust Bauer, they distrust the law-abiding Driscoll, her disrespect for Bauer and his methods, and her failure to notice what Bauer finds glaringly obvious.

Bauer is continually painted as the man making the right decisions, the decisions that 'pay off'. Bauer is fearless and indomitable, willing to go to any lengths to do what he believes is necessary to protect national security interests. This image is reinforced by colleagues who continually vouch for him and, alternately, by the bumbling and foolhardy colleagues who resist him. Getting his hands dirty, in the form of engaging in torture and other crimes, is the mark of Bauer's true honour, his real heroism. The implicit logic is that because terrorists play dirty, the good guys can win only by playing dirty too. *24* repeatedly presents a stark contrast between those willing to 'do the job' and those too weak-willed, shortsighted, or spineless, who also work within the law.

Although Bauer is clearly the hero of *24*, with viewers asked to identify with him and his struggle against sinister terrorist threats, he is far from infallible. In the opening season of the show, Bauer's wife was murdered by a colleague-cum-terrorist, and subsequent seasons provide insight into Bauer's lonely, dysfunctional personal life. Being on the frontline in the war against terror has scarred him. The start of the fourth season finds Bauer working a desk job after having left 'field work'. He explains his choice:

> Bauer: I wanted to get my life back. I wouldn't have been able to do that if I was still doing field work... I wanted something different from my life. It might not seem like a lot to you, but for me, to be able to have this kind of a connection with somebody... I couldn't do that before.

However, Jack's comfortable life is disrupted when he is thrust back into the job he has been desperate to escape from. Throughout the season, we see that 'doing what needs to be done' causes problems in Jack and Audrey's relationship. Following Jack's torture of Paul Heller, Audrey has this exchange with her father:

> Audrey: A couple of hours ago, when we thought that Paul was somehow involved with the attacks, Jack questioned him, and Paul has his pride, so he resisted, but...
>
> Heller: Jack was pretty rough.
>
> Audrey: Very.
>
> Heller: That's his job. He had to make sure. You have to believe that Jack had no choice.
>
> Audrey: I know. I guess it was just a shock to see it. Somehow he seemed like a different person.
>
> [Audrey starts crying.]
>
> Heller: We need people like that, Audrey.

This interaction normalises torture as the alternative available to agents in the field. If the United States is to remain secure, 'we need people like' Jack Bauer. The implicit message is that these are tough, uncertain times where people like Bauer, who can make tough decisions, are highly valued. Nevertheless, Bauer's actions damage his personal life. Later, Tony Almeida and Audrey discuss Bauer's job shift:

> Tony: I couldn't believe it when I heard that Jack had taken a desk job at D.C.
>
> Audrey: He said he was happier this way.
>
> Tony: Well, you've gotten the chance to see him in both worlds today. You think he'll go back to wearing a suit?
>
> Audrey: After the hell Jack's been through today, you think he'll want to come back to this?
>
> Tony: Some people are more comfortable in hell.

Tony's analysis is astute. Bauer and Audrey's relationship breaks down, with the torture and then death of Paul Raines a major contributing factor. Ultimately, it is Bauer's frontline work in the fight against terror that destroys the relationship:

> Jack: Audrey, I never believed you could ever really love me if you'd known about everything I've done.
>
> Audrey: Jack, I can't...
>
> Jack: Audrey, please, let me finish. These were the things that I was running away from. That's why I moved to D.C. That's why I stopped doing fieldwork. That's why I don't work at CTU.

Audrey: All I know is that you're back in it, and it's too much for me, Jack.

Jack: I know. I know. The last thing I ever wanted to do was push you away from me. God, Audrey, I love you. But this is how the job has to be done. I just want you to know how sorry I am that it had to involve you and the people you care about. Look, you don't have to say anything now. Please, just promise me, as soon as this is over we can talk about everything that's happened. Audrey, please.

Even as a flawed human being, however, Bauer is shown as honourable. Amid emotional pain and in danger of losing the woman he loves, he refuses to disavow his commitment to the nation and his conviction that his way is the right way: 'This is how the job has to be done'.

At the end of the season, Bauer fakes his own death and goes into hiding to escape a contract put out on him by the Chinese government, aided and abetted by the cowardly Logan administration. He is forced to adopt a new identity and start over. His life has to begin anew, without Audrey, without a job, without his colleagues. He has lost everything. Bauer is also conflicted: he is filled with remorse at his actions but convinced he did what he had to.

One could argue that through this loss of everything he values, Bauer pays the price for his torturous acts. Certainly, his remorse and loss inject nuance into a character that, at other times, has embodied the reductive portrait of security agents as unthinking automatons committed to torture. Yet, this nuance renders 24's handling of torture all the more problematic. It invites viewers to watch Bauer rationalise his own suffering, and the suffering of those around him, as the necessary sacrifice for a greater cause. This utilitarian calculation indicates that Bauer firmly believes in the cause he is fighting for and in the means he is deploying. It is this belief—illogical, fallible, and ultimately illegal though it may be—that is valourised throughout 24. In the end, and despite the woe they cause, the actions that Bauer (and others like him) take in the name of national security are painted as necessary, a vital cog in the War on Terror. In short, the fallibility of Bauer adds to, rather than detracts from, the normalisation of torture as an instrument of justice.

VII. Coda

This chapter has illustrated the discursive construction of torture in the television show 24 and offered ruminations regarding its implications for popular understandings of the law, ethics, and civil liberties. We argue that 24 normalised torture as a routine practice by counter-terrorism agents in the ongoing 'War on Terror'. Furthermore, the show positioned the law as an impediment to, rather than an instrument of, justice. Where the law is explicitly discussed, it is an irritation, an unnecessary complication that only slows the course of justice. We argue that such representations are highly problematic because they position the phenomenon of torture, which is unequivocally illegal in both national (US) and international law, as part of 'the way things are', a natural element of international struggles against terror.

24 came to an end, with its eighth season concluding in May 2010. While we have discussed only one season in this chapter, a focus on any of the remaining seven seasons

of the show would similarly uncover torture as one of the defining characteristics of the show, the ominous 24-hour clock embodying the necessity to torture now, torture fast, and torture hard. Revealingly, in the seventh season of the show, when Bauer is hauled before the US Senate and asked to explain his actions, he argued that torture saved innocent lives and he had 'no regrets' about anything he had done in the name of national security. It makes perfect sense that a fictional character can explain away his actions within the confines of a narrative that can bend reality to create maximum drama and suspense. That, after all, is one of the primary functions of drama. What is less sensible and more alarming, however, is the proverbial bleed from the fiction of *24*, and its depiction of torture, to the perceived reality it has helped to etch into the national consciousness, where the rule of law, civil liberties, and due process become subservient to the imagined needs of national security agents. The problem, then, is not so much, or solely, that Jack Bauer tortures terrorists; it is, to return to Tancredo's quote, that, through the power of narrative, we may all 'be looking for Jack Bauer' when we want fast solutions to real, complex, global problems.

References

Books and Journals

Avelar, I, *The Letter of Violence: Essays on Narrative, Ethics, and Politics* (New York, Palgrave Macmillan, 2004).

Birk, E and Birk, H, '"Today is Going to be the Longest Day of My Life": A Narratological Analysis of 24' in G Allrath and M Gymnich (eds), *Narrative Strategies in Television Series* (New York, Palgrave Macmillan, 2005) 47–61.

Broe, D, 'Fox and its Friends: Global Commodification and the New Cold War' (2004) *Cinema Journal 43*, 97–102.

Dershowitz, AM, 'The Use of Torture May be Justified in Certain Circumstances' in JD Torr (ed), *Civil Liberties: Current Controversies* (San Diego, CA, Greenhaven Press, 2003) 172–74.

Dixon, WW, 'Introduction: Something Lost—Film after 9/11' in WW Dixon (ed), *Film and Television After 9/11* (Carbondale, IL, Southern Illinois University Press, 2004) 1–28.

Ellis, J, *Visible Fictions* (London, Routledge & Kegan Paul, 1982).

Fiske, J, *Television Culture* (New York, Methuen, 1987).

—— 'The Discourses of TV Quiz Shows, or School + Luck = Success + Sex' in LR Vande Berg and LA Wenner (eds), *Television Criticism: Approaches and Applications* (White Plains, NY, Longman, 1991) 445–62.

Goodenough, WH, *Culture, Language, and Society* (Reading, MA, Addison-Wesley, 1971).

Gordon, AF, 'Abu Ghraib: Imprisonment and the War on Terror' (2006) 1 *Race and Class* 48, 42–59.

Hron, M, 'Torture Goes Pop!' (2008) *Peace Review: A Journal of Social Justice* 20.

Ignatieff, M, *The Lesser Evil: Political Ethics in an Age of Terror* (Princeton, NJ, Princeton University Press, 2004).

Kellner, D, *Media Culture: Cultural Studies, Identity, and Politics between the Modern and the Postmodern* (London, Routledge, 1995).

Nagan, WP and Atkins, L, 'The International Law of Torture: From Universal Proscription to Effective Application and Enforcement' (2001) *Harvard Human Rights Journal* 14, 88–121.

Newcomb, H, 'Toward a Television Aesthetic' in H Newcomb (ed), *Television: The Critical View* (New York, Oxford University Press, 1976) 273–89.

Silbey, J, 'What We Do When We Do Law and Popular Culture' (2002) *Law and Social Inquiry* 27, 139–68.

Silverglate, HA, 'The Government Should Not Authorize the Use of Torture to Combat Terrorism' in Torr, *Civil Liberties*, 2003, 184–89.

Spigel, L, 'Entertainment Wars: Television Culture After 9/11' (2004) *American Quarterly* 56, 235–70.

Sterritt, D, 'Representing Atrocity: From the Holocaust to September 11' in Dixon, *Film and Television After 9/11*, 2004, 63–78.

Newspapers and Websites

Bauder, D, 'Group: TV Torture Influencing Real Life; *USAToday.com* (11 February 2007), www.usatoday.com/life/television/2007-02-11-tv-torture_x.htm.

Buncombe, A, 'US Military tells Jack Bauer: Cut out the Torture Scenes ... or else!' *The Independent*, 13 February 2007, www.independent.co.uk/news/world/americas/us military-tells-jack-bauer-cut-out-the-torture-scenes--or-else-436143.html.

Feeney, M, 'Torture Chamber: Fox's *24 Terrifies* Viewers into Believing its Bizarre and Convoluted Plot Twists' *Slate* (6 January 2004), www.slate.com/id/2093269/.

Human Rights First, 'Scenes of Torture on Primetime Network TV 1995-2005' (28 June 2010), www.humanrightsfirst.org/us_law/etn/primetime/index.asp.

Mayer, J, 'Whatever it Takes: The Politics of the Man Behind "24"' *The New Yorker*, 19 February 2007, www.newyorker.com/reporting/2007/02/19/070219fa_fact_mayer.

Parents Television Council, 'PTC Calls for More Network Responsibility over Violent Content' (2007), www.parentstv.org/ptc/publications/emailalerts/2007/wrapup_021607.htm.

Rejali, D, 'Five Myths about Torture and Truth' *The Washington Post*, 16 Dec 2007, www. washingtonpost.com/wp-dyn/content/article/2007/12/13/AR2007121301303.html.

Rich, F, 'We'll Win this War—On "24"' *The New York Times*, 9 January 2005.

Rosenblum, J, '"Criminal Minds" Wins Human Rights Award for Portrayal of Interrogation' *Human Rights First* (15 October 2007), www.humanrightsfirst.org/media/etn/2007/alert/160/ index.htm.

19

Decoding the Dark Passenger: The Serial Killer as a Force for Justice. Adapting Jeff Lindsay's *Dexter* for the Small Screen

ANGUS NURSE

Jeff Lindsay's *Dexter*[1] depicts a serial killer who happens to be a police forensics expert, *or perhaps* a police forensics expert who happens to be a serial killer. Adapting *Dexter* for the small screen has arguably altered the status and authority of pre-existing versions of the text and conceptions of this serial killer as a vigilante. Berger acknowledges that theories of remediation and heteroglossia hold that there is fluidity and exchange between literature, theatre, cinema, radio, television and videogames so that, rather than literary texts remaining authoritative, the adaptation can become 'canonical' and act as the source text.[2] Film and television reach audiences beyond that of the original source novels, both in size and scope, and adaptations also allow for an alternate realisation of *Dexter's* characters and their wider world. Violence hidden beneath the surface is the central metaphor of the television adaptation, depicted not only in the violence hidden beneath Dexter Morgan's law enforcement officer persona, but also inherent in the violence hidden beneath the surface of tourist-friendly cities like Miami and the violence integral to the justice system. If 'adaptation reveals the connection between texts',[3] the adaptation of *Dexter* reveals novels and television as consistent in their view of a vigilante anti-hero created by a failed justice system and the harnessing of his unnatural urges to operate within a specific code of justice.

---

[1] At time of writing Lindsay has published six books; *Darkly Dreaming Dexter* (London, Orion Books, 2004), *Dearly Devoted Dexter* (London, Orion Books, 2005), *Dexter in the Dark* (London, Orion Books, 2007), *Dexter by Design* (London, Orion Books, 2009), *Dexter is Delicious* (London, Orion Books, 2010), and *Double Dexter* (London, Orion Books, 2011).
[2] R Berger, 'Are There Any More at Home Like You?: Rewiring Superman' (2008) *Journal of Adaptation in Film & Performance* 2, 87–101.
[3] Ibid.

Dexter Morgan (played by Michael C Hall) is the central character in Showtime's television series *Dexter*.[4] The six seasons broadcast thus far have earned a number of awards,[5] conferring icon status on its central character. *Dexter* primarily revolves around Morgan's work as police forensics blood spatter expert, his nocturnal activities as a serial killer and his interactions with his adopted sister, police officer Debra Morgan, colleagues in the Miami Police Department and his relationships with girlfriend (and later wife) Rita and her children, son Cody and daughter Astor. Each season of *Dexter* follows the search for a specific serial killer while examining the conflicts between Dexter's serial killing, day job and personal relationships.

Cinematic and television depictions of serial killers combine genre conventions and social anxiety about violent crime. The cinematic serial killer is typically shown as being hunted by federal authorities and representing a seemingly random threat of violence, thus acting 'as a substitute and a shield for a situation so incomprehensible and threatening it must be disavowed'.[6] Serial killers are a powerful symbol of deviance and abnormality, reinforcing notions of 'otherness' in criminality. *Dexter* provides a complex portrayal of both a serial killer and an unconventional vigilante/detective, who operates according to a strict code (which dictates killing only 'bad' guys). It provides for a study of the adaptation of literary crime fiction to the small screen and contemporary discourse on the serial killer and the failings of the justice system. Lindsay's novels show life, death and police work in Miami solely from Dexter Morgan's viewpoint as he serves the 'Dark Passenger'.[7] Yet while the novels, written from Dexter's viewpoint, provide only his perspective and justification, the television adaptation, while retaining Dexter as narrator, reveals how his interior monologue contrasts with reality. Adapting the novels to a visual medium allows for the use and development of alternate viewpoints. The show expands the roles of other characters and reveals the effect of Dexter's interactions with, and reactions to, them. The resulting complex picture of moral culpability, the workings of the justice system and vigilante justice is explored within the serial television format.

This chapter examines the literary and television texts and the tensions inherent in a lead character occupying conventional law enforcement, vigilante and signature-based serial killer roles within the small screen depiction. First, it defines *Dexter* within its genre conventions and outlines the basic elements of its television adaptation. Second, it argues that the series reflects social anxieties about crime, particularly the impact of escalating violence on the socially disadvantaged, ethnic communities and the law enforcement officers involved. Third, it considers how the television adaptation reflects a fascination with, and anxieties about, justice and the failings of the justice system on the part of the viewer, and how through its manipulation of crime imagery it enhances viewer engagement with the subject material. Finally, this chapter analyses the development of the series' central

---

[4] At the time of writing, six seasons of *Dexter* have aired on US television, while five seasons have been broadcast in the UK. Season seven premieres on Showtime in the US in September, 2012.

[5] Including the 2010 Screen Actors Guild 'best' male actor in a drama series (Michael C Hall), Outstanding performance, 2010 Golden Globes for best supporting television actor (John Lithgow) and best actor in a television series (Michael C Hall), 2009 Saturn Award for best television guest star (Jimmy Smits) and the 2008 Saturn Award for best syndicated/Cable television series.

[6] A Taubin, 'The Allure of Decay' (1996) 6 *Sight and Sound* 1, 22–24.

[7] The 'Dark Passenger', as Dexter comes to refer to his impulse to kill, is accepted by him and his police officer step-father Harry as an impulse to be channelled rather than corrected.

character, Dexter, from crime-victim to a vigilante anti-hero operating within a specific code of justice. In doing so, this chapter considers the cultural importance of the adaptation and the reasons for its success.

I. Defining Dexter: Genre and Adaptation

Dexter opens with a shot of the moon reflected in a pool of water. Filtered red, the image foreshadows the blood that is to follow. The shot then shifts to images reflected in a moving car's side-mirror, and then the shot widens to give the view of a silhouetted man driving through a city at night. In voiceover a man tells us 'tonight's the night and it's going to happen again and again. It *has* to happen'. The driver in silhouette then gives way to a chorus of uniformed children, their angelic voices singing in unison, suggesting the promise of the future. One boy steps forward and the camera pulls back to reveal a smiling middle-aged man who turns away from the boy and nods towards an unseen crowd, applauding the end of the song. The scene is a park bandstand where a choral recital has taken place for wealthy white patrons. The middle-aged man is seen hugging some children before the voiceover reveals, 'there he is. Mike Donovan. He's the one'. The brightly lit park gives way to a dim car park. Donovan gets into his car and settles into his seat only for a cord to be whipped around his neck by our driver/narrator, waiting in the back seat. 'You're mine now', says the assailant, 'do exactly as I say'.

These opening scenes establish *Dexter's* credentials both as crime drama and within the serial killer subgenre, which is firmly established as a distinctive genre of cinematic narrative, but is less prevalent on the small screen. Conventional cinematic serial killer narratives concern the efforts of law enforcement professionals seeking to apprehend a lone killer, usually identified by his signature (unique way of killing). Cinematic narratives usually present a lone or flawed detective, whereas television narratives rely on an ensemble cast, usually characterised by an older senior detective and a range of supporting team members. From the outset *Dexter* depicts a world in which violence is integral to the narrative and in which characteristics from other genres, most notably the 'slasher', 'monster' or 'vigilante' film are easily incorporated.[8] Dexter's credentials as a killer are established within the series' opening and subsequent execution scenes, where there is also early confirmation that Donovan is a child molester and killer. This provides justification for Dexter's execution of Donovan, but the ritualised manner in which this is carried out still carries multiple meanings. Dexter could, at this stage, be a vigilante forcing Donovan to confront his victims before he is killed, but his acknowledgement of his own helplessness while committing Donovan's murder hints at something more. From the outset, the viewer is invited to consider that moral ambiguity and conflicting notions of justice are at the heart of *Dexter*.

Film and television studies frequently ask the question, what do writer and film-maker intend when they transfer the reading experience of a novel to the visual and

---

[8] A Young, *The Scene of Violence: Cinema Crime Affect* (Abingdon, Routledge, 2010).

aural experience of film or television? The adaptation of a literary text can involve illustration, translation or interpretation (or a mixture of all three), but requires the filmmaker to make some changes to the literary text in order to meet the demands of a visual format. Sinyard argues that, 'no television adaptation can simply offer a pictorialisation of the story and the characters'.[9] Other changes are required to meet the demands of a different medium. *Dexter*, as a television series, considerably expands the relatively insular world of Lindsay's novels to provide for new visual settings, characters and situations.

While many television crime series generally consist of self-contained episodes with no final resolution and limited consideration of characters' personal lives, *Dexter's* serial format continues the storyline 'over from one instalment to another' and contains detailed analysis of the personal life, conflicts and motivations of its central character.[10] It thus departs from the episodic 'monster of the week' format of shows like *Criminal Minds*, which primarily detail weekly self-contained searches for different serial killers. *Dexter* also subverts genre conventions by using a serial killer as its quasi-protagonist series lead within the wider format of an ensemble cast. Central to the adaptation is a manipulation of the crime-image and the audience's expectations, achieved by developing a seductively sympathetic, yet murderous central character. This interpretation of the novels' texts involves the further development of Dexter's character, from a serial killer merely playing at socially acceptable parts to an individual actually engaging with other characters. The television medium enables viewers to connect with its central character such that Dexter's awkwardness, failure to understand social conventions and identification with other serial killers, described in the novels by his narration, becomes visual depiction eliciting sympathy in the viewer. As audiences require characters they care about, the television adaptation presents Dexter Morgan as victim as much as it does killer. It does so through combining conventional catch-the-bad-guy narratives with horror and thriller motifs, alongside the human drama involved in revealing Dexter's serial killer origins, the problems law enforcement officers experience in dealing with serial killers and the wider social problems caused by violence. Each of Dexter's seasons has a continuing narrative primarily consisting of the search for one serial killer, with subplots concerning the lives and fortunes of its ensemble cast. Examined are Dexter's domestic relationships, his growing self-awareness concerning his serial killer origins (achieved primarily through flashbacks to his childhood and adolescent training with his stepfather Harry) and the lives of Dexter's police 'family', specifically Debra Morgan (his step-sister), detective Angel Batista, Lieutenant LaGuerta and Dexter's nemesis, Sergeant Doakes. Despite their rarity, law enforcement and academic studies of serial killers[11] have established that many operate according to a specific code and have a distinct 'kill signature' (eg type of victim, method of execution) through which they can be distinguished and identified. Dexter conforms to these real life and genre conventions, portraying

---

[9] N Sinyard, 'The Classic Serial on British Television' in Chapman (ed), *Film and Television History: Television Genres* (Milton Keynes, The Open University, 2003).

[10] G Creeber, '"Taking Our Personal Lives Seriously": Intimacy, Continuity and Memory in the Television Drama Serial' (2001) 23 *Media, Culture and Society* 439–55.

[11] J Douglas and M Olshaker, *Obsession* (London, Simon and Schuster, 1999). A Vachss, *Sex Crimes* (New York, Random House, 1993).

signature serial killers whom the justice system is unable to apprehend, but whose guilt Dexter (in keeping with his 'peace' officer role) is able to determine with sufficient certainty, such that (while adhering to 'Harry's Code') he can take steps to rectify the mistakes or omissions of the justice system.

Central to the thriller element of the series is the escalation of the particular season's serial killer from controlled signature killer, who has managed to evade capture, into a wilder and less controlled offender who commits subsequently sloppier and/or more brazen killings. The forces of law and order thus face an increased threat to the citizens they seek to protect while Dexter faces a race against time, one in which he seeks to aid in the apprehension of the given serial killer as he learns as much as he can from this other sociopath before he is caught or killed. While season one closely follows the plot of its corresponding novel, *Darkly Dreaming Dexter*, the following seasons retain only thematic elements from their respective novels while introducing new stories, characters and narrative devices.[12] In part, this is a necessity of adapting novels to a visual medium[13] discussed further below.

II. Engaging the Audience: Aspects of Illustration

Illustration vis-a-vis film or television requires more than mere pictorialisation of the story and characters, even where Lindsay provides such strong visual characterisation of both lead and supporting characters. Lindsay's narrative provides specific sets of signals to which an adaptive illustrator might heed, such as Debra Morgan's intensely driven persona, her liberal use of foul language and physical characteristics. Within Dexter's narration, forensics colleague Vince Masuka is described as Asian with a fake smile, as if 'he had learned to smile from a picture book'.[14] Such specific description indicates Dexter's relationship with his working world colleagues and its basis in a shared forced conformity to ritual niceties. The television adaptation, however, in that each adaptation is a reworking of the foundation text, has the task of creating its own particular expression of the crime-image, separate from that described or alluded to in Lindsay's novels.

Monaca explains that 'the reader of a page invents the image, the reader of a film does not'.[15] Yet both 'readers' have to work to interpret the signs they receive from their texts in order to complete their understanding. Adaptation can trade 'upon the memory of the novel'[16] but television reaches a different audience than the novel. In the case of crime fiction on cable television, it will potentially reach an audience largely unfamiliar with the source material. The casting of recognisable TV actor

---

[12] The title sequences in seasons two through to five, however, retain the notice 'based on the novel *Darkly Dreaming Dexter* by Jeff Lindsay'.

[13] S McDougal, *Made into Movies: From Literature to Film* (Fort Worth, Harcourt College Publishers, 1985).

[14] Lindsay, *Dearly Devoted Dexter* (n 1).

[15] J Monaco, *How to Read a Film: The Art, Technology, Language, History and Theory of Film and Media* (New York, Oxford University Press, 1977).

[16] J Ellis, 'The Literary Adaptation' (1982) 23 *Screen* 1, 3–5.

Michael C Hall (*Six Feet Under*) as Dexter was undoubtedly intended to draw some viewers who might otherwise have been initially unattracted to the material. For the television series to succeed, however, it needs to provide its own compelling point of view and aesthetic in order to simultaneously re-engage those familiar with the novels, while reaching out to a new audience. In this respect, the adaptation of *Dexter* translates Lindsay's novels into a new televisual language that, while respecting the original premise, displaces the novel's primary focus on Dexter Morgan the serial killer with a refocusing on Morgan as part of an ensemble 'police family' fighting crime together in Miami. Such ensembles are generally familiar to television audiences, with their genre conventions of plot and sub-plot, and their portrayals of often highly idiosyncratic central and supporting characters. *Dexter* thus incorporates serial killer genre/ subgenre crime fiction elements but also retains familiar thriller and police procedural drama components, in particular by showing detectives at work and immersing the audience in its puzzle-solving elements.

The television adaptation, particularly serialisation, allows its creators more time to expand the novel's narrative. Although each television episode requires sufficient self-containment to avoid excluding the casual viewer, serialised television can take time with such elements as character and plot development, introduce new subplots and characters not contained within the novel and, while deploying an appropriate *mise-en-scene* to approximate the novel's descriptiveness, provide for visual shocks appropriate to its genre and audience expectations. Audience expectation of slasher/ horror films and the serial killer genre includes graphic depictions of killing and its accompanying rationale. While the scope of television is such that its exploitation of visual spectacle is less than cinema's, there is still an expectation that the genre's visual depiction of serial killer activities[17] will be present, especially on cable television with its often explicit portrayals of nudity and violence, and its freedom to employ what is generally considered obscene language.[18] Serial killer narratives in film typically commence with establishing shots, which show the communal order that will later be threatened. Examples often include montages showing the world of culture and sophistication,[19] detectives undergoing training,[20] or the business of investigating 'ordinary' murders.[21] Such scenes frequently presage the showing of a more deviant and brutal crime that confirms the extraordinary nature of the killer, raising the question of whether ordinary detectives and standard police methods are sufficient. Serial killer narratives on television frequently start either by showing the killer at work or by showing the brutality of the killer's crimes while hiding their identity, thus establishing the procedural requirements of identification and apprehension. *Dexter* simultaneously conforms to and subverts these conventions by establishing its lead as a killer from the outset. This choice also allows the audience to witness the ritualistic

---

[17] J Demme (Director), *The Silence of the Lambs* [Motion Picture] (United States, Orion Pictures Corporation, 1991). D Fincher (Director), *Seven* [Motion Picture] (United States, New Line Cinema, 1995). R Scott (Director), *Hannibal* [Motion Picture] (United States, Metro-Goldwyn-Mayer/ Universal Picures, 2001). B Evans (Director), *Mr Brooks* [Motion Picture] (United States, Twentieth Century Fox, 2007).

[18] J Potter and S Smith, 'The Context of Graphic Portrayals of Television Violence' (2000) 44 *Journal of Broadcasting and Electronic Media* 3, 301–23.

[19] Evans, *Mr Brooks*; Scott, *Hannibal* (n 17).

[20] Demme, *The Silence of the Lambs* (n 17).

[21] Fincher, *Seven* (n 17).

aspect of Dexter's killing, his meticulous preparation and his confrontations with his victims, thereby continuing to meet while inverting the audience's genre expectations.

III. The Killer Confesses: Narrative Viewpoints and Translation

The adaptation of a novel can involve translating the original text into a new televisual language that displaces, more than it merely translates or illustrates, the original. In this respect the adaptation's appropriation of the novel can sometimes rely more on cultural memory than actual reading.[22] Thus, *Dexter's* television adaptation, in what almost seems a structural meta-commentary on the process of adapting the material, adopts the use of shifting viewpoints as a primary audience engagement tool. This device extends the story dynamic well beyond Dexter's narration, which at best represents his biased or incomplete perspective on his own behaviour and the behaviour of others. At its worst it might be the mere narcissistic expression of an unreliable, manipulative narrator seeking self-justification.

The television adaptation preserves Dexter's viewpoint and lead character status but requires that the questionable reliability and focus of his narration be offset by the inclusion of genre appropriate scenes that supplement the novels' first person viewpoint. Thus, while characters frequently conform to detective/criminal and victim/witness archetypes, providing images viewers can easily identify and recognise, both Dexter Morgan and the season's 'other' serial killer primarily occupy the narrative foreground. Seen through the prism of Dexter's understanding in contrast to the expressed understandings of the other characters, and as a result of this mosaic quality the viewer is often privy to a greater number of facts and insights than any one character at any given time. From a narrative viewpoint, this incremental revelation of the offender's actions, as explored during each series instalment, contrasts Dexter's own serial killings against those of the 'guest' serial killer, and serves to highlight the counterpoise provided him by 'Harry's Code'.

Television audiences need characters that they can care about. Otherwise, they will not be invested in the outcome of the story and the fate of the central and secondary characters. This requires *Dexter's* supporting cast to be sufficiently 'real', that they contribute to the demands of story and character development while maintaining the necessary dramatic tension and a context for the various conflicts facing its central character. The television adaptation thus relies partly on the novelist providing sufficient visual cues to inform an engaging visual representation, and partly on sufficient development of supporting characters so that they do not become mere ciphers or plot exposition devices. *Dexter* as television thus requires transforming the novel's confessions-of-a-serial-killer approach into a sympathetic character journey in which audiences can emotionally invest.

---

[22] Ellis, 'The Literary Adaptation' (n 16).

IV. Dexter as Anti-Hero

The fascination with serial killers is such that *Dexter* is not the first attempt to turn a serial killer into the central protagonist of a fictional drama. The charismatic and high-IQ serial killer is firmly established within literary crime fiction, as well as in film. Thomas Harris's Dr Hannibal 'the Cannibal' Lecter has appeared in four novels[23] and five films,[24] and has sold millions of books; there have also been other television series depicting the hunt for serial killers[25] or which have followed vigilante killers.[26] While *Dexter* is representative of the hunt-for-offender crime fiction, its adaptation of the serial killer genre contains analysis of the killer's moral universe, the good/evil dichotomy inherent in its central protagonist, and the law enforcement and cultural imperatives that determine societal reaction to serial killer activity.

While serial killers are relatively rare among criminals, they exert powerful cultural fascination via fictional narratives through which their motivations and the law enforcement response to their killing are examined. Charismatic killers such as Hannibal Lecter thus resonate with the public imagination and lure audiences back to the novels and films.[27] Oleson argues that the high-IQ criminal 'who deliberately and coolly commits his crime, not because he must, but because he *can*—because he *likes it*—is both mysterious and terrifying'.[28] The serial killer's 'indifference to the legal order'[29] is a key factor in the public's fascination, as his intellect places him outside the parameters of ordinary understanding and he is aware that traditional law enforcement techniques are unlikely to result in his apprehension. *Dexter's* television adaptation exploits this aspect of viewer engagement by manipulating Dexter Morgan's composite identities of killer, victim and agent of justice. This is accomplished within a narrative where, as a law enforcement agent, he has special knowledge of serial killers and their techniques, and exploits his own high-IQ-killer status to identify the signature of other killers, while evaluating the success of their techniques and attempts at integration into the social world.

While Lindsay's novels depict Morgan as remote and detached, merely pretending to be human, the series' visual adaptation (and Hall's interpretation) makes Dexter likeable and aloof through lack of understanding rather than purely through genetic

---

[23] T Harris, *Red Dragon* (New York, GP Putnam's Sons, 1981); T Harris, *The Silence of the Lambs* (New Yrok, St Martin's Press, 1988); T Harris, *Hannibal* (New York, Delacourte, 1999); T Harris, *Hannibal Rising* (New York, GP Putnam's Sons, 2006).

[24] Demme, *The Silence of the Lambs* (n 17); M Mann (Director), *Manhunter* [Motion Picture] (United States, De Laurentis Entertainment Group, 1986); B Ratner (Director), *Red Dragon* [Motion Picture] (United States, De Laurentis Entertainment Group, 2002); R Scott, *Hannibal* (n 17); P Webber (Director), *Hannibal Rising* [Motion Picture] (United States, The Weinstein Company/ Metro-Goldwyn-Mayer, 2007).

[25] See, for example, *Criminal Minds* (2005 to present).

[26] See, for example, the supernatural crime thriller series *Brimstone* (1998) or its contemporary *Supernatural* (2005 to present).

[27] J Oleson, 'King of Killers: The Criminological Theories of Hannibal Lecter, Part One' (2005) 12 *Journal of Criminal Justice and Popular Culture* 186–210.

[28] J Oleson, 'King of Killers: The Criminological Theories of Hannibal Lecter, Part Two' (2006) 13 *Journal of Criminal Justice and Popular Culture* 29–49.

[29] R Salecl, 'Crime as a Mode of Subjectivization: Lacan and the Law' (1994) IV *Law and Critique* 1, 3–20.

disposition. Television adaptation dictates that the reactions of other characters are displayed through the process of shot and reaction to convey meaning, understanding and impact. Through this mechanism Dexter's confusion at his surroundings and the role required of him in social situations is frequently portrayed as genuine innocence and misunderstanding rather than malevolent dismissal. However, his high-IQ status is explicit in Dexter's forensic science expertise, reinforced through his solving of crimes that frustrate the wider Miami Police department. Thus, as a serial killer who understands other killers and makes moral judgements concerning their actions as he seeks to understand them, he not only kills because he can and likes it, but also because he *must*. Dexter is thus a high-IQ killer who is charismatic, charming and at ease within the justice system, both exploiting and remedying its flaws within a series narrative that analyses the motives of serial killers, while providing commentary on certain aspects of the justice system and broader social concerns about crime, law and order.

V. Visions of Violence

Depicting the world of a serial killer within the serialised television format requires presentation of crime images that both compel and repel. The violence and moral culpability of *Dexter's* universe is explicit in the duality of his own desire to kill, while preventing violence towards the innocent. The conflict at the heart of the justice system is explicit from the opening sequence (discussed earlier). Justice for all is often promised but rarely delivered; in one story arc children who have put their trust in adults are betrayed and the justice system has failed to identify and convict their killer, possibly because his respectable social status is anathema to the expected profile of a deviant serial killer.[30] *Dexter* thus portrays Miami as a city with persistent violent crime problems[31] and an overstretched police department inadequate to the task of combating everyday crime and deviance. Lindsay's literary descriptions of Miami emphasise its violent nature and relationship with despair linked to crime, while the adaptation shows crime as a problem primarily affecting the vulnerable, eg prostitutes (season one), ethnic minorities (seasons two and three) and women (season five). Notions of ethnicity as both backdrop and a target of deviancy are further reinforced with the liberal use of non-subtitled Spanish and the prominence of Cuban music in the television score.

---

[30] The opening scenes broadly replicate those of *Darkly Dreaming Dexter*, yet in the novel Dexter's narration explicitly states that Father Donovan is a priest who teaches music at an orphanage (Lindsay's text states that, 'Everything he did, it was all for the kids.'). Father Donovan's victims are identified as children from the orphanage. The implication is that the justice system would not look too hard into the disappearance of orphaned children and the system would be unwilling to question or even countenance a priest as both paedophile and murderer.

[31] Actual figures from the Miami-Dade County Police show an 11% drop in overall violent crimes from 2008 to 2009 (source: MDPD Crime Data Warehouse).

Dexter presents a specific picture of deviance showing the serial killer's actions in the context of its labelling by society.[32] Deviance is defined not by the quality of the act the person commits, but is a consequence of the application of the rules and sanctions to an offender.[33] In both novels and television, Dexter portrays himself as an artificial or pretend human, embracing his identity as killer and 'monster' according to the dictates of society, while not entirely accepting himself as a criminal. 'The Code of Harry' (discussed later), contextualises Dexter's actions within both moral justification (fatherly and implied police sanction) and genre convention. Matza[34] developed drift theory to explain how delinquents often accept a moral obligation to be bound by the law but can drift in and out of delinquency. Dexter typifies this, fluctuating between total freedom and total restraint, drifting from one extreme of behaviour to another, accepting the norms of society (attendance at work, a generally law abiding lifestyle) while also developing a special set of justifications for his behaviour which allows him to rationalise the violence that violates social norms. These techniques of neutralisation[35] allow Dexter to express guilt over certain illegal acts, but also to reason between those whom he can victimise and those he cannot. Dexter is thus visualised as not being immune to the demands of conformity, but is, rather, able to rationalise when and where he should conform and when it may be acceptable to break the law. In addition, the adaptation's portrayal of Dexter as part of an extended police family dictates that some aspects of conformity are necessary aspects of his culture, environment and status within the community. While within this community he employs both primary and secondary deviance characteristics, rationalising and defending his behaviour in response to perceived societal reaction.[36] This offers both a striking translation and interpretation of the source novels, visually situating Dexter's actions within the lives of other characters while providing access to both his inner thoughts and exterior reactions.

Dexter portrays the serial killer as rational, operating according to a distinct set of motivations and *modus operandi*, which shows the serial killer as organised, thoughtful and premeditated as long as he operates according to a specific rationalisation. It also portrays Dexter as 'conditioned' towards being criminal.[37] The novels show Dexter as victim to an interior controlling force, but the television adaptation dispenses with this supernatural explanation, instead dictating that Dexter can control his homicidal urge when exercising it according to a specific code (discussed below). The audience thus engages with Dexter's growing understanding of his own nature and recognition of a societal reaction that views his killing as deviant. The television

---

[32] J Muncie and M Fitzgerald 'Humanising the Deviant: Affinity and Affiliation Theories' in Fitzgerald, McLennan and Pawson (eds), *Crime and Society: Readings in History and Theory* (London, Routledge, 1994).

[33] H Becker, *Outsiders: Studies in Sociology of Deviance* (New York, Free Press of Glencoe, 1963).

[34] D Matza, *Delinquency and Drift* (New Jersey, Transaction, 1964).

[35] G Sykes and D Matza, 'Techniques of Neutralization: A Theory of Delinquency' (1957) 22 *American Sociological Review* 664–73; S Eliason, 'Illegal Hunting and Angling: The Neutralization of Wildlife Law Violations' (2003) 13 *Society & Animals* 3.

[36] E Lemert, *Social Pathology: Systematic Approaches to the Study of Sociopathic Behaviour* (New York, McGraw-Hill, 1951).

[37] R Clarke and D Cornish, 'Rational Choice' in R Paternoster and R Bachman (eds), *Explaining Crime and Criminals: Essays in Contemporary Criminological Theory* (Los Angeles, Roxbury, 2001) 23–42; S Eliason, 'Illegal Hunting and Angling' (n 35).

adaptation also deals explicitly with Dexter's fear of discovery, and in this aspect of the televisual narrative is the acknowledgement of the wider threat any serial killer represents. Likewise, in each of its five seasons Morgan is challenged professionally and personally by another serial killer, which offers yet another angle through which the audience can perceive the ramifications of his moral ambiguity. Thus, the conflict inherent in the duality of his role as high-IQ killer and law enforcement agent is one shared by the audience, able to see the 'benefits' of his execution of killers who have escaped the justice system, while also viewing the harm and anxiety he causes to his police colleagues, immediate family and the wider society.

VI. The Code of Harry

From the outset, the show establishes 'The Code of Harry' as Dexter's moral compass. His first victim in both the television series and novel is a paedophile, and the code dictates that the most heinous criminals deserve death. The effect of his indoctrination into 'Harry's Code', its internalisation by Dexter, is early evidenced when he comments on the paedophile, 'Children. I should have killed him twice.'[38] His second victim is a drunk driver responsible for several deaths across the country.[39] This person too is a deserving criminal, aware that his actions have resulted in the deaths of others yet continuing to drive drunk. The code has the effect of humanising Dexter, integrating his actions as part of the wider law and order narrative with his own internal struggle.

The series uses flashbacks to reveal the origins of the young Dexter and Harry's indoctrination of him into the code, which (among other things) teaches him that being organised is the key to his continued freedom and successful killing. Dexter's nature necessitates an in-depth training in police procedure to enable him to eliminate any evidence through which the 'typical' serial killer could be apprehended. So too, encapsulated within the same practical rules that ensure his safety, the code simultaneously sets forth its moral and ethical dimensions as summarised by the following key rules:[40]

1. Killing must serve a purpose; otherwise it's just plain murder.
2. Be sure.
3. Blend in—maintain appearances.
4. Control urges; channel them.

Harry instils in Dexter an understanding that killing innocents is never allowed, and that Dexter should blend in with others and choose his victims carefully. This is a clear replication of the value system and culture adopted by police officers,[41] a

---

[38] Lindsay, *Dearly Devoted Dexter* (n 1).
[39] Portrayed in the episode entitled 'Crocodile'.
[40] ShowTime (2010).
[41] See, eg R Graef, *Talking Blues* (London, Collins, 1989) and R Reiner, *The Politics of the Police* (Hemel Hempstead, Harvester Wheatsheaf, 1992).

culture where some aspects of criminal behaviour are considered part of legitimate police work, and where successful emulation of criminals (at the very least in terms of undercover work) is considered worthwhile, challenging and rewarding.[42]

Both the series and novels show Dexter conducting his own investigations into those whom the justice system is unable to reach, taking time and gathering evidence to establish certainty of guilt. Harry's rules also dictate that Dexter should be careful with both his killing and preparation, such that the method of killing satisfies the need to kill.[43] This facet of his character dynamic is also an important factor in eliciting viewer sympathy for a central character operating outside the law. The television Dexter thus goes beyond Lindsay's narrative viewpoint to methodically establish his victims' guilt and the failure of the justice system to apprehend them before he gives himself permission to take any action. In his novels, Lindsay describes Dexter's victim selection as 'very complicated, but very necessary'.[44] By showing the (usually) careful victim selection process and evidence of their crimes, the viewer is invited to condone Dexter's judgement and acknowledge this necessity in the prevention of further crime. Dexter's ritualised killing in accordance with the code thus serves multiple purposes; it satisfies his own need to kill, allows him to confront his victims with their guilt, and ensures that the police will never be able to solve his murders. All this goes to eliciting viewer sympathy for his actions. As a result, the audience thus acknowledges the failure of the justice system to deal with serious criminals and the anxiety generated by offenders who escape justice. All of this is explicitly displayed, analysed and resolved within the narrative scope of the series.

VII. Dexter Morgan: Vigilante Family Man

While the *Dexter* novels adopt a narrative viewpoint that reinforces Dexter's identity as a disturbed individual compelled to kill, the paradox of the television version of Dexter Morgan is that he is an ordinary and soft-spoken forensics 'nerd' who shows little outward sign of his capacity for violence. He is fully integrated into his law enforcement role and respected for his scientific expertise. Dexter's 'ordinary man' persona is, however, consistent with the reality of many serial killers who 'don't look or act like monsters, and that is why they become successful. We see them, but we look right through them'.[45] The pilot episode (discussed earlier in this chapter), directly comments on the irony of a police department trained to notice aberrant behaviour, yet seemingly unable to spot Dexter's true nature.[46] Notwithstanding audience fascination with intelligent killers and gruesome death scenes,[47] Dexter's apparent normality is itself a significant factor in the show's success. It suggests to the viewer

---

[42] Reiner, ibid.
[43] Lindsay, *Dearly Devoted Dexter* (n 1).
[44] Ibid.
[45] Douglas and Olshaker, *Obsession* (n 11).
[46] With the exception, initially, of Sergeant Doakes.
[47] See, eg the success of the *Saw* and *Final Destination* film franchises, primarily built upon the innovative death scenes.

that the notion of evil is less important than the impact of circumstances. The killers portrayed all have a distinctly logical (if extreme) justification for their actions and kill signature. In essence, the viewer considers Dexter as one who could have been a somewhat highly intelligent, if otherwise average, American, and one turned into a persistent killer as a direct consequence of events. The question of how long he will get away with it, and how many lives he will eventually destroy, makes for compelling viewing.

Lindsay's novels explicate Dexter's urge to kill as the result of a controlling force or separate personality, reflecting claims made by real life serial killers. Take for example William Heirens, who attributed his kills to a man named George Murman who he claimed lived inside him.[48] Lindsay's novels provide strong descriptions of the dark impulse to kill, 'the Need inside, the *entity*, the silent watcher, the cold quiet thing',[49] characterising the Dark Passenger as an interior voice whispering advice and guidance. Yet the Dark Passenger as a controlling force is downplayed during *Dexter's* first season, which provides childhood trauma (discussed later) as the catalyst for Dexter's propensity towards serial murder. As with other real life serial killers, whose signatures frequently involve specific murder rituals and the collection of trophies that allow them to repeatedly relive their crimes, Dexter's rituals and trophies prove no less enigmatic and complex.

Television adaptation provides for an evocative visual depiction of the serial killer rituals employed by Dexter Morgan, which according to a specific code (discussed earlier) involve a direct confrontation with his victims. Dexter takes his victims openly, injecting them with an animal tranquiliser, primarily in scenes that show him emerging from the shadows, unmasked and calm in appearance. He then transports his prey to a prepared room where they are stripped naked, bound using tape and clear plastic to an 'operating' table, and made to look at prominently displayed evidence and/or pictures of their own victims. Central to the ritual is the victim's conscious knowledge of the reasons for their death and their ultimate acceptance that they have not escaped the justice system. Prior to killing his victims, Dexter makes a small incision on their cheek in order that he may capture a single drop of blood, which he preserves on a glass slide so as to make it part of the collection he keeps hidden within his air conditioning unit.

The majority of his 'kills' include dialogue heavy scenes where Dexter discusses with his victims the nature of their offending, aspects of serial killer practice and domestic life. The ritual not only provides Dexter with a means of satisfying his urges, but it is also an opportunity for him to reinforce his status as a servant of the justice system. Having fulfilled the dualistic dictates of his impulses (having his kill, but elevating it into something more than mere murder through the code), he is further able to enter into discussions with some of his victims about the 'serial killer nature' and the mechanisms through which it can be disguised or subsumed within an otherwise normal-seeming life. Such scenes also serve to emphasise the extent to which Dexter sees himself as an 'artist', as his discussions with his victims often involve aesthetic

[48] Douglas and Olshaker, *Obsession* (n 11).
[49] Lindsay, *Darkly Dreaming Dexter* (n 1).

considerations through which he shows his appreciation for the other killer's artistry or their ability to integrate into society.

Crime fiction and serial killer stories largely operate through a duality that emphasises the good/evil dichotomy as essential parts of a whole story. The serial killer is the embodiment of evil, driven by dark forces and/or childhood traumas (abusive fathers, neglectful mothers, neighbourhood brutalisation), while the forces of law and order are generally good, protecting the public and relentlessly pursuing the aim of bringing the serial killer to justice. *Dexter* conforms to these archetypes, yet its five television seasons and novels explore the tensions between Dexter Morgan's different roles, portraying the evolution of Dexter the killer as both vigilante and mass murderer, in a way that does not conform to criminological stereotypes. While the origins of Dexter's crimes may be found in the coupling of the trauma of his childhood and contemporary conceptions of evil, viewing his actions within the wider context allowed by television adaptation more solidly roots them within concepts of vigilante justice, thus lending them a more sympathetic appearance than the novels allow.

A. Season One: The Nature of Evil

Acknowledging the character of Dexter Morgan as a serial killer invites audiences to view him as evil. Yet, any portrayal of the good/evil dichotomy inherent in an adaptation of the novels dictates that audiences are provided with ambiguous answers regarding Dexter's nature. Lindsay's novels portray events solely from Dexter's point of view. As a result, the moral descriptions that readers must consider are problematic. Dexter himself acknowledges that he 'belonged to the Dark Passenger',[50] an interior controlling force which he cannot overcome. However, there are tensions between the scientific and theological explanations for Dexter's crimes. He is not inherently evil. He is, rather, the victim of a specific childhood trauma that provides not just the psychological explanation for his nature but which also determined his criminal methodology. Season one *Dexter* graphically shows the infant Dexter left sitting in his mother's blood for several days prior to rescue, having witnessed her brutal dismemberment. While these become repressed memories, the parallels between his mother's death and his killings are self-evident, whereby the question of whether Dexter is evil resists simple interpretation.

Sociologists frequently view evil as a result of social forces that determine the behaviour of individuals and social institutions, whereas theologians view evil as sin, while psychologists consider the mental states of individuals and the deep-seated motivations for their deeds. In its adaptation of *Darkly Dreaming Dexter*, the initial season widens the consideration of the nature of evil to encompass its social context. The narrative arc that deals with the search for the 'Ice Truck Killer' shows the nature of evil in several different guises. Dexter is revealed as a serial killer who has been 'made' not born; he dismembers his victims because his earliest (repressed) memories are of his mother's dismemberment. Similarly, he works as an expert in forensic serology because he was birthed in blood. Like the murders committed by Hannibal Lecter,

---

[50] Lindsay, *Dearly Devoted Dexter* (n 1).

Dexter's killings are arguably a form of repetitive compulsion by which he seeks to relive and understand the brutal murder of his mother.[51] Yet through his analysis and understanding of blood, and its importance, he seeks to save the victims of other killers (and subconsciously his mother) and to understand the etiology of killing. This is how he honours his rescuer and adoptive father, by working for the police and by following 'Harry's Code' which, among other things, dictates that those who commit murder for pleasure and escape the justice system are deserving of death.

Evil is also present in Dexter's brother, Biney (Brian). Brian suffered the same childhood fate as Dexter, but grew up without the guiding hand of the justice system and the nurturing support of a family structure, and so became the 'Ice Truck Killer'. Brian murders for pleasure and solely to serve his own needs, including killing others to facilitate a reunion with his younger brother. Dexter's rejection and murder of his brother[52] demonstrates that from a psychological perspective Dexter, while committing acts generally considered to be evil, is not mentally ill. The season finale invites contemplation that Dexter's killings serve the needs of justice, reflecting the non-criminal killing of serial murderers sometimes practiced by the justice system, and reinforces viewer perceptions of Dexter's killings as morally justified. All this is depicted in direct contrast with his brother's killings, and ultimately through Dexter's ritualised killing of him.

The season's closing scene, which takes place shortly after his brother's death, is a fantasy sequence in which Dexter is given a ticker tape hero's welcome, complete with banners showing enthusiastic support by members of the general public and police officers. Here, in the season's final moment, Dexter's self-perception and the perception of the audience, both the fantasised on-screen crowd and those sitting in front of the screen, merge. One soccer mom shouts out, 'you keep our children safe'. A police officer smilingly affirms, 'way to take out the trash'. The perspective of the killer, who has been established as an instrument of justice by overcoming and accepting his traumatic past through the nurturing support of his justice 'family', is thus firmly established.

B. Season Two: Learning to Fly

Serial killer films (and television depictions) bring audiences to 'a sensual awareness of evil in the forms of dread, defilement, transgression, vengeance, sacrilege and sacrifice'.[53] In the second season the show explores the evolution of Dexter's role as vigilante and protector, alongside his increasing integration into his own domestic family, the further realisation of his true nature, and his growing awareness of his own moral culpability. This set of episodes also examine the nature of Dexter's compulsion and societal responses to it, reflected in the various reactions of the other characters to aspects of Dexter's behaviour—from his step-sister's annoyance

---

[51] P Messent, 'American Gothic: Liminality in Thomas Harris's Hannibal Lecter Novels' (2000) 23 *Journal of American Comparative Cultures* 23–26.

[52] The conclusion to the first season.

[53] J Katz, *Seductions of Crime: Moral and Sensual Attractions in Doing Evil* (New York, Basic Books, 1990).

at his distant nature, and Rita's growing concern over his late-night disappearances, to Doakes' inkling suspicion that there is something deeply wrong with Dexter.

The controlling metaphor of season two is that of secrets coming to the surface. Textual issues also surround notions of the hidden self, the acceptable behaviour of law enforcement officers given the demands of dealing with the underbelly of society, confidence in (and public support for) the justice system, and its perceived versus its actual effectiveness. The good/evil dichotomy is again present when the dumping ground for Dexter's victims is revealed and the bodies are brought to the surface to undergo forensic examination. Season two explicitly delves into the revulsion Dexter's police colleagues display at the number of victims dispatched by one killer, reinforcing his outsider status and the inherent paradox in his working for the justice system while also acting outside of its mores. Yet, when it becomes known that the victims of the 'Bay Harbor Butcher' were themselves all killers who had escaped the justice system, the 'Butcher' begins to attract some public support. Again, the good/evil dichotomy is shown to be more complex than a simple duality. While the activities of the 'Butcher' are undoubtedly unlawful, this sympathetic expression by the public reflects an awareness of and identification with the killer's moral imperative, which dictates that the killer only kills those who have escaped the justice system and thus are seen as being 'deserving' of extreme treatment; the show reveals that this outlook is privately endorsed by some within the police force, and more forthrightly so by members of the public and the media. The season thus grapples with the challenges facing law enforcement and the justice system in relation to maintaining public support for their crusade to catch 'The Butcher' in light of the obvious pressure generated by an unsympathetic public perspective towards tracking him down. The impact of this sort of pressure on the justice officers themselves, and the solidarity of 'cop culture', subsequently plays an integral part in the dynamic explored in the arc of season two.

In this season, Dexter's status as a high-IQ killer is reinforced by revelations about his martial arts training and excellence in medical school and it is also revealed that he swapped a medical career to pursue police forensics work. Yet, the good/evil dichotomy is also glaringly re-encountered when Dexter's culpability in the death of Rita's abusive husband, Paul, is admitted. Within the season's early episodes Rita also becomes suspicious about his late-night activities, and in order to shift her focus away from his oddly timed forays he encourages a misunderstanding on her part and thus confesses to an addiction assumed by her to be an addiction to narcotics. In the context of his stressful law enforcement occupation, exceptions are made for Dexter's presumed drug addiction. In the culture of the show's police family his behaviour is 'accepted' and 'understood' as something resolvable through attendance at Narcotics Anonymous (NA) meetings. The assumption of an acceptable level of drug abuse indicates the closeness of the police family, but it also indicates a tacitly agreed to acceptance of such behaviours as the normalised societal response to the pressures that they face.

This sidestepping the reality that drug dependency results in impaired job performance and often leads to the commission of crimes, such as Dexter's theft of evidence and fabrication of Paul's drugs crimes (which resulted in an 'innocent' man being sent to prison to face an untimely death), is yet another expression of the good/evil dichotomy inherent in the storyline. The viewer thus witnesses another manifestation of acceptable rule 'bending' as inherent in the justice system. As a result of the narrative threads surrounding the presumed narcotics issue, there is the introduction of a female sponsor for Dexter. This provides even further temptation for, and examination of, his addictive nature, as he freely confesses to his NA meeting that his Dark Passenger controls him and he is powerless to resist its urges. Initially, his relationship with his sponsor (Lila) provides the acceptance of his 'darkness' that he craves from another, as well as a means through which Dexter strengthens his relationship with Rita. However, even this stage in Dexter's development provides only a temporary stay against his desire for that understanding and acceptance of his darker impulses. As with all of Dexter's previous relationships based on an understanding of his 'true self', aside from that which he had with Harry, the relationship between Lila and the show's quasi-protagonist takes a violent turn, and his evolution into a family protector is visually confirmed when he kills his sponsor in order to protect Rita's children, whom she threatens.

C. Season Three: Kindred Spirits

Interest in serial killers and depictions of real life 'monsters' is indicative of the uncertainty of the society in which we live and our fear about the frailties of the justice system. Picart suggests that when crime control policies are perceived as weak or the justice system is seen as being ineffectual, 'magical solutions for controlling the monstrous are sought, often imaginatively worked out through narratives in film and popular culture'.[54] Season three of *Dexter* explicitly deals with these concerns. Here, the narrative leads the audience towards considerations not just of the failings of the justice system and the nature of vigilante justice, but also towards different perspectives on justifying action outside of the law, which ultimately serve the needs of justice.

Dexter's proposal to the pregnant Rita squarely confronts the question of how law enforcement officers view the type of society their children will be born into and how this impacts on their dealing with crime. This consideration of vigilante justice is facilitated by introducing Assistant District Attorney Miguel Prado, a vigilante who aids Dexter in killing criminals, who becomes his friend and best man at his wedding. Season three departs significantly from its corresponding novel, yet that also deals with the protection of children and the nature of vigilante justice. Manuel Prado sees himself as an honourable man fighting a corrupt and ineffectual justice system. On his discovery that Dexter has killed drug dealer 'Freebo' (in self defence), Prado congratulates him acknowledging that the fractured elements of the justice system sometimes require the rules to be broken in order to achieve its aim of justice. Yet while Prado is willing to live with this paradox and embraces it wholeheartedly, Dexter, despite his growing doubts about Harry Morgan's honesty with him, remains uncomfortable with any killing that takes place outside of the

[54] C Picart, 'Crime and the Gothic: Sexualizing Serial Killers' (2006) 14 *Journal of Criminal Justice and Popular Culture* 3, 1–18.

code. The viewer is thus invited to consider how far the rules should be bent for the greater good of protecting society and when Prado kills a defence attorney by himself because, in his view, she is responsible for frustrating the justice system, his failure to adhere to 'Harry's Code' creates a conflict between them that ultimately leads to Dexter killing Prado.

Shots near the season's conclusion reveal Dexter again embracing 'Harry's Code', now fully able to reconcile his roles as serial killer and agent of justice. The final wedding scene indicates the addition of family protector to his role as protector of the larger public. At the same time this gives him an opportunity to integrate his serial killer persona into an idealised vision of normality.

D. Season Four: Vigilante

Season four's primary story arc follows the search for a serial killer known as Trinity (because he always kills in threes), who has been the subject of an FBI manhunt tracing his killings back 15 years. Working together, Dexter, his sister and an FBI serial killer specialist (Agent Lundy) identify the fact that Trinity has more likely been killing for 30 years. Yet, as season four opens, the viewer is presented with a subversion of the initial scenes from the pilot episode, showing Dexter driving at night as his voiceover again asserts 'tonight's the night'. This scene alternates with shots of a seemingly ordinary middle-aged man drawing a bath. However, Dexter's nocturnal drive is not a victim hunt. Rather, it is a desperate attempt to encourage his son Harrison to sleep, while the middle-aged stranger is running a bath for his intended victim, a woman unaware of the killer within her home. Here, yet again, is an underscoring of one of the show's dominant themes, the manner in which the banalities of suburban family life sometimes hide something much darker.

Crime fiction and thriller narratives frequently deal with 'the disruption (usually violent) of normality with the forces of chaos'.[55] While in traditional crime stories the protagonist as servant of law and order descends into a world immersed in chaos to restore the status quo and enforce its rules, *Dexter* shows how the forces of chaos exist naturally within and exploit the status quo through the family unit, using its norms as 'cover' for deviance. This notion, that the suburban ideal provides a perfect cover for deviancy, is reinforced by both Trinity and Dexter, as both are family men with children. The season also depicts vandalism and anti-social behaviour as coming from within the idyllic community that Dexter and family have moved to, which functions as a visual representation of the multifaceted nature of the American Dream. Explicit within the television texts is the message that secrets hidden within families can have extreme consequences, but also that the nature of criminality defies conventional boundaries. Trinity, a respected man within his own community, has successfully concealed his true nature (as a murderer) from that community, his family and the justice system.

---

[55] J Chapman, *Saints & Avengers: British Adventure Series of the 1960s* (London, IB Tauris, 2002).

In the character of Trinity, the adaptation charts out what Dexter might have become without 'Harry's Code' and the support of his police family. Further assumptions by the law enforcement officers involved in the case, that Trinity would have shunned all but the most rudimentary connections to community are shown as inherently flawed, reflecting social misunderstandings of the nature of serial killers. As the character of Trinity, a family man, so amply reflects, many serial killers are outwardly normal, even likeable in many respects, rather than being the monsters that the public expects and perhaps *needs* them to be. Always the counterpoint to the serial killer 'other' operating in the storyline, season four gives Dexter full acceptance of his status as family man, at peace with the past that has created his urge to kill, and fully operative as a vigilant killer serving the ends of justice according to the dictates of his specific code of ethics while protecting his family.

E. Season Five: The Limits of Control

The narrative of season five primarily examines Dexter's actions as serial killer rather than as agent of justice, while exploring the nature of humanity and violence towards, and the protection of, women. At the conclusion of season four Rita, Dexter's primary connection to humanity, is murdered as a consequence of Dexter's identification with the Trinity killer and his failure to consider the wider implications of Trinity's actions. As a result, his step-children go to live with their grandparents and he is forced to confront the nature of his feelings for his dead wife, his links with humanity and his identification with other killers. Dexter retains parental control over Harrison, his infant son, who like him has witnessed a brutal murder as a child. The violence hidden below the surface is now explicitly a part of Dexter's life, as he confronts not only the possibility that his son could become a killer but also the reality that his pursuit of his own interests has wider consequences.

Season five also deals with the roles of fathers and protectors, and depicts an evolution of Dexter's character that goes beyond the narrative of the novels. Dexter not only now has a son who relies on him for protection and support, but the season introduces the character of Lumen, a rape victim who seeks revenge on the men who captured and abused her. Dexter kills one of the gang responsible for the attack on Lumen and joins her hunt for the other men, adopting the role of teacher, protector and surrogate father figure (and later, lover). Thus, the series, given the story arc as presented to this point, has come to deal openly and explicitly with Dexter's evolution as a killer and his identification with other killers.

Yet, this explicit depiction of Dexter's evolution is not the main driving force behind the success of the series. The success of *Dexter* as a television adaptation relies on its ability to transcend the literary texts. Primarily, through a dynamic interpretation and translation of the source texts, it achieves a new reading of the serial killer as vigilante by deploying an appropriate *mise-en-scène* to approximate the novels' descriptiveness. Clearly, it also goes beyond the novels in terms of character realisation, its manipulation of televisual crime images and the incorporation and subversion of genre conventions. In the end, audiences are aware that Dexter is a violent serial killer. However, the moral universe in which he operates is expansively portrayed in order to elicit viewer sympathy for his status as victim and the influence of that fact on his actions. As mediation on the confessions of a serial killer the television adaptation has become 'canonical', eclipsing the novels in popularity and achieving the status of *the* definitive view of Dexter the serial killer.

References

Books and Journals

Becker, H, *Outsiders: Studies in Sociology of Deviance* (New York, Free Press of Glencoe, 1963).

Berger, R, 'Are There Any More at Home Like You?: Rewiring Superman' (2008) 1 *Journal of Adaptation in Film & Performance* 2, 87–101.

Chapman, J, *Saints & Avengers: British Adventure Series of the 1960s* (London, I.B. Tauris, 2002).

Creeber, G, '"Taking our Personal Lives Seriously": Intimacy, Continuity and Memory in the Television Drama Serial' (2001) 23 *Media, Culture and Society* 439–55.

Douglas, J, and Olshaker, M, *Obsession* (London, Simon and Schuster, 1999).

Eliason, SL, 'Illegal Hunting and Angling: The Neutralization of Wildlife Law Violations' (2003) 11 *Society & Animals* 3.

Ellis, J, *The Classic Serial on Television and Radio* (Basingstoke, Palgrave, 1982).

—— 'The Literary Adaptation' (1982) 23 *Screen*1, 3–5.

Felthous, A and Kellert, S, 'Childhood Cruelty to Animals and Later Aggression against People: A Review' (1987) *American Journal of Psychiatry* 144, 710–17.

Graef, R, *Talking Blues* (London, Collins, 1989).

Harris, T, *Hannibal* (New York, Delacourte Press, 1999).

—— *Hannibal Rising* (New York, G.P. Putnam's Sons, 2006).

—— *Red Dragon* (New York, G.P. Putnam's Sons, 1981).

—— *The Silence of the Lambs* (New York, St. Martin's Press, 1988).

Katz, J, *Seductions of Crime: Moral and Sensual Attractions in Doing Evil* (New York, Basic Books, 1990).

Lemert, EM, *Social Pathology: Systematic Approaches to the Study of Sociopathic Behaviour* (New York, McGraw-Hill, 1951).

Lindsay, J, *Darkly Dreaming Dexter* (London, Orion Books, 2004).

—— *Dearly Devoted Dexter* (London, Orion Books, 2005).

—— *Dexter in the Dark* (London, Orion Books, 2007).

—— *Dexter by Design* (London, Orion Books, 2008).

—— *Dexter is Delicious* (London, Orion Books, 2010).

Matza, D, *Delinquency and Drift* (New Jersey, Transaction, 1964).

McDougal, SY, *Made into Movies: From Literature to Film* (Fort Worth, Harcourt College Publishers, 1985).

Messent, P, 'American Gothic: Liminality in Thomas Harris's Hannibal Lecter Novels (2000) *Journal of American and Comparative Cultures* 23, 23–26.

Monaco, J, *How to Read a Film: The Art, Technology, Language, History and Theory of Film and Media* (New York, Oxford University Press, 1977).

Nurse, A, 'Perspectives on Criminality and Criminal Justice Policy in Wildlife Crime in the UK' [Unpublished dissertation] (Birmingham, Birmingham City University, 2008).

Oleson, JC, 'King of Killers: The Criminological Theories of Hannibal Lecter, Part One' (2005) *Journal of Criminal Justice and Popular Culture* 12, 186–210.

Picart, CJ, 'Crime and the Gothic: Sexualizing Serial Killers' (2006) *Journal of Criminal Justice and Popular Culture* 14(3), 1–18.

Potter, JW and Smith, S, 'The Context of Graphic Portrayals of Television Violence' (2000) *Journal of Broadcasting and Electronic Media* 44(3), 301–23.

Reiner, R, *The Politics of the Police* (Hemel Hempstead, Harvester Wheatsheaf, 1992).

Salecl, R, 'Crime as a Mode of Subjectivization: Lacan and the Law' (1994) *Law and Critique* IV(1), 3–20.

Sinyard, N, 'The Classic Serial on British Television' in Chapman (ed), *Film and Television History: Television Genres* (Milton Keynes, The Open University, 2003).

Skolnick, J, *Justice without Trial: Law Enforcement in Democratic Society* (New York, Wiley, 1966).

Sykes, GM and Matza, D, 'Techniques of Neutralization: A Theory of Delinquency' (1957) *American Sociological Review* 22, 664–73.

Taubin, A, 'The Allure of Decay' (1996) *Sight and Sound* 6(1), 22–24.

Vachss, A, *Sex Crimes* (New York, Random House, 1993).

Young, A, *The Scene of Violence: Cinema Crime Affect* (Abingdon, Routledge, 2010).

Films

Demme, J, (Director), *The Silence of the Lambs* [Motion picture] (United States, Orion Pictures Corporation, 1991).

Evans, BA (Director), *Mr Brooks* [Motion picture] (United States, Twentieth Century Fox, 2007).

Fincher, D (Director), *Seven* [Motion picture] (United States, New Line Cinema, 1995).

Mann, M (Director), *Manhunter* [Motion picture] (United States, De Laurentis Entertainment Group, 1986).

Ratner, B (Director), *Red Dragon* [Motion picture] (United States, De Laurentis Entertainment Group, 2002).

Scott, R (Director), *Hannibal* [Motion picture] (United States, Metro-Goldwyn-Mayer/ Universal Pictures, 2001).

Webber, P (Director), *Hannibal Rising* [Motion picture] (United States, The Weinstein Company/ Metro-Goldwyn-Mayer, 2007).

Websites and Data

MDPD, 'MDPD Five Year Crime Comparison 2005–2009' (MDPD Crime Data Warehouse, 2010).

ShowTime Television, 'Dexter: The Code of Harry', available at http://dexterwiki.sho.com/ page/The+Code+of+Harry [accessed 23 June 2010].

20

Canada: ADR and *The Associates*

JENNIFER L SCHULZ[*]

I. Introduction and Context

This book examines lawyers and justice on television. There are detailed descriptions of British and American television lawyers and legal processes. However, what about Canadian lawyers and legal processes? What about Canadian justice? Is there such a thing? Is it unique? This chapter will examine law and justice on Canadian television. I will analyse a Canadian legal TV programme called *The Associates*[1] with a view to discovering what, if anything, might be different or distinct about Canadian television law.

The Associates is now off the air. This hour-long prime time dramatic series ran for two seasons on CTV, in 2001 and 2002. It featured five new associates in a large Toronto law firm. Importantly, the show never tried to hide its Canadian-ness. Canadian landmarks such as the CN Tower, Canadian place and street names, and Canadian license plates all featured prominently in *The Associates*. As a result, it was always clear to viewers that they were watching a Canadian programme set in Toronto, featuring a Bay Street law firm,[2] called Young, Barnsworth & King, or YBK. The series chronicled the legal and personal ups and downs of the new associates, paying particular attention to one associate, a young woman named Robyn Parsons, who has been described as the 'heart of the show'.[3] Peter Robson would define *The Associates* as a legal drama because it maintained the general trope that, 'whatever the personal situation may be, the job and the client come first'.[4] *The Associates* is thus part of the television lawyer show genre. The only other Canadian legal drama

[*] I am grateful to the participants at the Canadian Initiative in Law, Culture & the Humanities who provided helpful commentary in November 2009 in Ottawa, and for the opportunity to present a portion of this research to the Association for the Study of Law, Culture & the Humanities at Brown University, Rhode Island in March 2010.
    [1] *The Associates* (Alliance Atlantis Communications and CTV, 2001) Created by Greg Ball, Steve Blackman and Alyson Feltes. Produced by Brian Dennis and Anne Marie La Traverse.
    [2] Bay Street in Toronto, Ontario is Canada's equivalent to Wall Street in New York City, New York.
    [3] Anne Marie La Traverse, the executive producer of *The Associates*, in a telephone interview on 10 November 2009.
    [4] Peter Robson, 'Lawyers and the Legal System on TV: The British Experience' (2007) 2, 4 *International Journal of Law in Context* 333, 342.

that falls into the genre is another off-the-air series called *Street Legal.*[5] With only two legal dramas in the entire Canadian repertoire, I cannot say anything definitive about who the lawyer in Canadian TV is. My indigenous television is not fulsome enough to provide an answer to the question of what a Canadian television approach to law looks like. And, unlike other countries, Canada does not have a television history to mine in order to trace the historical popular culture construction of Canadian lawyers. While other law and popular culture scholars can take a thematic approach, make a typology, or trace the development and cultural representation of the TV lawyer over time,[6] I cannot. With only two shows, there is simply not enough material. Marsha Ann Tate describes some of the reasons why there is little programming, legal or otherwise, in Canada as compared to the United States:

> Canada's two official languages and a television market size of approximately ten percent of the United States (where most production costs can be recovered domestically) combined with easy transborder reception of US stations by much of the populace have traditionally been impediments to the growth of indigenous programming in Canada.[7]

So, the first problem is our lack of programming and therefore data. The second is our lack of viewers. Although by Canadian production design standards *The Associates* was an excellent show, most Canadians have never watched it.[8] This is likely because other than news and sports viewing, most Canadians overwhelmingly prefer to watch American TV.[9] Furthermore, it has been that way from the very beginning. Our first public television broadcasts, by the CBC in 1952, came *four years after* US networks began regular broadcasting in Canada.[10] Thus, there has never been a time when Canadians did not watch American TV. Given that Americans produce far more legally-themed programmes than Canadians do, most Canadian TV-watchers are much more familiar with American programmes than Canadian. If we accept that much of what people think they know about law is derived from television's depictions,[11] we may conclude that the law most Canadians think they know about is actually American (TV) law, not Canadian (TV) law. As a Canadian scholar writing about law and TV in Canada, I am very aware of the fact that American TV is a 'cultural juggernaut that spans the globe'.[12] American 'television is consumed in massive amounts by nearly all members of the general public. It transmits a consistent set of images and messages about social reality into nearly

---

[5] *Street Legal* (Canadian Broadcasting Corporation (CBC), 1987). Created by William Deverell and Guy Mullally. Produced by Douglas Wilkinson and Brenda Greenberg.

[6] Robson, 'Lawyers and the Legal System on TV' (n 4) 354.

[7] Marsha Ann Tate, 'Canada, Culture & Broadcasting: An Examination of the Cultural Components of Canada's Broadcasting Policies' (Pennsylvania State University, College of Communications, 2000), available at http://mtateresearch.com/cancult.pdf 9.

[8] The executive producer of the show said *The Associates* was cancelled after only two seasons because of low viewership and low ratings. (Anne Marie La Traverse, telephone interview on 10 Nov 2009). In response to my question, 'Why were the ratings low?' she answered: 'The audience was not connecting with the characters. *The Associates'* characters were not "larger-than-life" like the characters on *Ally McBeal*, and the legal stories were not as sophisticated or quirky as those on American law shows airing at the same time.'

[9] Tate, 'Canada, Culture & Broadcasting' (n 7) 7, referencing the work of many others.

[10] Ibid 6 (emphasis added).

[11] Michael Asimow and Shannon Mader, *Law and Popular Culture: A Course Book* (New York, Peter Lang, 2004) 7; and Steven Penney, 'Mass Torts, Mass Culture: Canadian Mass Tort Law and Hollywood Narrative Film' (2004) 30 *Queen's Law Journal* 205, 211 fn 43.

[12] Tate, 'Canada, Culture & Broadcasting' (n 7) 1.

every home.'[13] As a result, Canadian TV has always, and must still, operate very much in the shadow of American TV, and my work must highlight this additional consideration. Canadian work in television and the law is complicated by issues of cultural domination and national identity.[14]

Due to Canada's fears of American cultural domination, Canadian television exists in a context of protective legislation. Given Canadian TV's secondary status at home, our federal government has historically tried to statutorily protect some sense of national identity and Canadian culture, even though most Canadians would be hard-pressed to define what those might be. As Andrew Wernick notes, 'the seductive embrace of American entertainment, sport, and advertising raises some serious issues of national autonomy, for what that is worth, vis-à-vis the United States'.[15] Despite the fact that 'Canadian' national identity is most often only understood in opposition to or as something different than 'American', it is accepted that local cultural production enriches our cultural life. Therefore, government policies protect the production and distribution of Canadian content.[16] We have Canadian content regulations, subsidisation of indigenous film and TV production, foreign ownership restrictions, tax incentives, and governmental agencies that have been established solely to fund productions, such as the Canada Council, and promote our films, such as Telefilm Canada.[17] Indeed, our Broadcasting Act states that 'the Canadian broadcasting system provides, through its programming, a public service *essential* to the maintenance and enhancement of national identity and cultural sovereignty'.[18] It also states that 'the Canadian broadcasting system should serve to safeguard, enrich and strengthen the cultural, political, social and economic fabric of Canada'.[19]

Both our public (CBC) and private (CTV) broadcasters are regulated by the Canadian Radio-Television and Telecommunications Commission, or CRTC. The CRTC allows Canadian broadcasters to import US shows, but then requires them to use a portion of the income so derived to produce domestic shows.[20] This process is called 'simulcasting', or 'simultaneous program substitution'. Canadian networks buy the broadcasting rights for American shows and then air them at the same time, except with Canadian advertisements. Simulcasting therefore allows Canadian viewers to

---

[13] Michael Asimow, 'Popular Culture Matters' in Michael Asimow (ed), *Lawyers in Your Living Room! Law on Television* (Chicago, American Bar Association, 2009) xxi.

[14] Andrew Wernick, 'American Popular Culture in Canada: Trends and Reflections' in David H Flaherty and Frank E Manning (ed), *The Beaver Bites Back? American Popular Culture in Canada* (Montreal, McGill-Queen's University Press, 1993) 300.

[15] Ibid 294.

[16] Catherine Murray, 'Silent on the Set: Cultural Diversity and Race in English Canadian TV Drama' (prepared for the Strategic Research and Analysis (SRA), Strategic Policy and Research, Department of Canadian Heritage, August 2002) 4–5. For a discussion of British protective policies, see Sarah Street, *British National Cinema* (London, Routledge, 1997) 22–27.

[17] Murray, 'Silent on the Set' (n 16) 4–5.

[18] Broadcasting Act, SC 1991, c 11, s 3(1)(b), emphasis added.

[19] Ibid c 11, s 3(1)(d). However, in Lawson A Hunter, Edward M Iacobucci, and Michael J Trebilcock, 'Scrambled Signals: Canadian Content Policies in a World of Technological Abundance' (28 January 2010) C.D. Howe Institute Commentary, No 301, 1–34, the authors note that this will change. Now that we are in an era where television content is available on demand, many current regulatory tools will eventually be rendered obsolete. In the opinion of Hunter, Iacobucci, and Trebilcock, regulations regarding ownership and content quotas will be unenforceable online and should therefore be abolished.

[20] Tate, 'Canada, Culture & Broadcasting' (n 7) 10.

watch the American shows they enjoy, but also provides advertising revenues that are used to produce Canadian shows.[21] *The Associates* was one of these shows.

II. Literature Review and Methodology

Only one article has been written about *The Associates*.[22] Otherwise, a review of the television lawyer scholarship reveals that nothing has been written about Canadian law shows. Therefore, in order to situate this chapter, I read the international literature, which demonstrates different methodological approaches to engaging with television's lawyers. Peter Robson has focused on different trends in lawyer depictions over time in Britain.[23] Barbara Villez has researched historical development phases and women lawyers in France.[24] Michael Asimow has described different legal subject areas as found on TV in the United States,[25] and Elayne Rapping has examined American politics and TV law shows.[26] Andrew Wernick notes that popular culture theory

> derives from countries—mainly England, France, and the United States—whose intelligentsia have been able to read their local urban cultures [and TV shows] as straightforwardly exem- plifying global developments, without needing to think about the specific relation of those developments to their national context.[27]

I, on the other hand, must think about my national context and do something different. Firstly, out of necessity. Without a Canadian legal TV genre to mine, I must closely focus on one series. Then, rather than speculate what that one off-the-air series may have to say about global developments, I will focus on what it says about the Canadian context. Secondly, because I want to do something original. I want to examine Robyn Parsons, a young, female lawyer on a Canadian show, something that has never been done before.[28]

As I trace the character of Robyn Parsons on *The Associates*, I will employ the work of WJT Mitchell.[29] In his book, *What Do Pictures Want? The Lives and Loves of Images,* Mitchell offers a thought experiment—an invitation to try—to put our

---

[21] Paul Rutherford, 'Made in America: The Problem of Mass Culture in Canada' in David H Flaherty and Frank E Manning, *The Beaver Bites Back? American Popular Culture in Canada* (Montreal, McGill-Queen's University Press, 1993) 275; and Tate, 'Canada, Culture & Broadcasting' (n 7) 10.

[22] Jennifer L Schulz, 'Settlement and Mediation in Canadian Legal Television' (2011) 1 *Journal of Arbitration and Mediation* 77.

[23] Robson, 'Lawyers and the Legal System on TV' (n 4) 354.

[24] Barbara Villez, *Series Tele: Visions de la Justice* (Paris, Presses Universitaires de France, 2005).

[25] Michael Asimow and Shannon Mader, *Law and Popular Culture: A Course Book* (New York, Peter Lang, 2004).

[26] Elayne Rapping, 'The History of Law on Television' in Michael Asimow (ed), *Lawyers in Your Living Room! Law on Television* (Chicago, American Bar Association, 2009).

[27] Wernick, 'American Popular Culture in Canada' (n 14) 300.

[28] In previous work, I examined young, female lawyers on an American legal TV drama, but this is the first time a young Canadian woman TV lawyer has been closely studied. See Jennifer L Schulz, '*girls club* Does Not Exist' in M Asimow (ed), *Lawyers in Your Living Room! Law on Television* (Chicago, ABA Press, 2009) 243.

[29] WJT Mitchell, *What Do Pictures Want? The Lives and Loves of Images* (Chicago, The University of Chicago Press, 2005).

relations to images in question. Following Mitchell, I will shift the question from what the TV show *does*, to what it *wants*. Mitchell wrote that this involves shifting 'from power to desire, from the model of the dominant power to be opposed, to the model of the subaltern to be interrogated, or (better) to be invited to speak'.[30] So, rather than worrying about opposing the dominant power of American television, I want to invite the subaltern, or Canadian TV show, to speak, and have us listen, for the first time.

According to Mitchell, images' desire to speak is strong because their power is weak: 'The power they want is manifested as *lack*, not as possession.'[31] Therefore, Mitchell asks pictures what they desire. He asks what the picture wants in terms of lack.[32] Then, I argue, we have to listen to the answer. This is an interesting twist, given our usual preoccupation with meaning. As Mitchell describes it, we must be 'less concerned with the meaning of images than with their lives and loves'.[33] Therefore, in this chapter I am attempting to determine what *The Associates* wants or desires, remembering that the question is about the picture's desire, not the producer's intent. Listening to the answer is to some extent made easier because unlike traditional two dimensional pictures, televised images give *The Associates'* pictures both voice and motion. To turn analysis of TV shows toward questions of voice and affect, and to question the viewer: what is the target of desire expressed by the picture?[34], is unique. When we approach a television programme this way, we can ask, what does *The Associates* want? And, how do Canadian TV shows inform the construction of Canadian socio-legal life?

In order to attempt to discern what *The Associates* might want, I needed to watch the show. Unfortunately, the show is extremely difficult to access. The series cannot be rented on DVD nor downloaded from the internet. After weeks of searching, I eventually obtained all 31 episodes after convincing the distributor's legal counsel that I would pay someone in their technology department to copy the show onto DVDs. I then purchased those DVDs directly from the distributor, for $400 CDN. I view this lack of availability as somewhat problematic from a methodology perspective. It means that the comments I make and the conclusions I draw about what the show wants are to a certain extent unverifiable. You simply cannot go home and watch an episode in order to check my conclusions.[35] While both Canadian and international scholars whom I asked at conferences did not seem to care too much about this—responding that it is often the case that readers cannot verify conclusions based upon

---

[30] Ibid 33.
[31] Ibid 36, emphasis in original.
[32] Ibid 37.
[33] Ibid 343.
[34] Ibid 49.
[35] I have twice chosen off-the-air television programmes as the focus of my scholarly interest—first, *girls club*, (Schulz, '*girls club* Does Not Exist' (n 28) 243) an American programme, and now, *The Associates*. This made my task easier, because these shows each represent a finite body of work. All episodes can be watched before embarking upon the writing process, which is akin to choosing to write about a film instead of a TV show. By choosing these shows, I am able to trace developments over time. As Robson, 'Lawyers and the Legal System on TV' (n 4) notes at 353: 'This affords the opportunity for a more nuanced approach to both the issues and how the world in which the professional operates responds to changing pressures.' Robson's further point, that 'tracing this is a challenge for scholarship in this area', was alleviated for me by the fact that only two episodes of *girls club* and 31 of *The Associates* ever aired. However, the challenge still remains for readers who may wish to verify my conclusions about off-the-air programmes, and cannot do so.

obscure texts or archival research[36]—I am not entirely persuaded. I often watch the films and TV shows that popular culture scholars write about—either because their articles intrigued me, or because I wanted to see if I agreed. However, if my chapter piques your interest in *The Associates* or you want to check if you concur, you cannot do so, and in my view, that is less than ideal.

Once I obtained all 31 episodes, I watched them at home, during quiet evenings, in comfortable clothes, on my living room couch, without a single commercial. I purchased a new DVD player and first used it to watch episode one on 4 August 2009 and episode 31 on 10 September 2009, which means I watched two seasons or two years of a television show in one month. Watching all of the episodes so close together, with no interruptions, and with ample opportunities to pause and rewind in order to facilitate note-taking and dialogue-transcription, was wonderful. It then came time to record my observations in this chapter, which, as with all written work in the law and popular culture field, puts my audience at a disadvantage. Instead of watching the shows, you are reading about them. As Mitchell notes, 'Vision is as important as language in mediating social relations, and it is not reducible to language, to the "sign", or to discourse. Pictures want equal rights with language, not to be turned into language.'[37] Be that as it may, the nature of the scholarly book mandates that, despite *The Associates'* pictorial desires, and despite the nuances, sounds, and feelings that are lost in so doing, I had to turn my observations about *The Associates* and its desires into words.

III. Observations: ADR and *The Associates*

My very first observation was that *The Associates* was classy television that felt expensive and well produced. As such, it was better-than-usual Canadian prime time drama. In fact, it felt 'American' in its production values.[38] Viewers were treated to Canadian lawyers and clients addressing Canadian common law issues, in English Canadian court rooms. As a result, episodes of *The Associates* were rarely about guns, because Canada does not have a real gun culture. The cases on the show were seldom about huge sums of money, because Canadian courts have capped allowable damage awards. Lawyers were shown advising clients against launching frivolous lawsuits, because Canadian rules of civil procedure require the losing party to pay the legal costs of the winner. Lawyers on *The Associates* also wore robes in court the way that Canadian and British lawyers do, did not put on 'shows' for the jury because Canadian courts rarely use juries, and finally, simply did not move around that much, pace, or lean on the witness box, because Canadian rules of court do not permit them

---

[36] Thanks to the participants at both the Canadian Initiative in Law, Culture & the Humanities (CILCH) 2009 conference in Ottawa, and the Association for the Study of Law, Culture & the Humanities (ASLCH) 2010 conference in Providence.

[37] Mitchell, *What Do Pictures Want?* (n 29) 47.

[38] Mary Jane Miller, 'Inflecting the Formula: The First Seasons of *Street Legal* and *L.A. Law*' in David H Flaherty and Frank E Manning, *The Beaver Bites Back? American Popular Culture in Canada* (Montreal, McGill-Queen's University Press, 1993) 114.

to do so. These things, together with an overtly Canadian setting, made the show different. It looked and felt different than the American legal programmes we are used to watching, because the writers and producers made an effort to depict distinct characteristics of the Canadian common law system. However, like all shows in the legal television genre, *The Associates* liked 'to "juice" up the conflicts'[39] because 'exact reality does not always make for scintillating television'.[40] As a result, viewers were treated to some unlikely legal scenarios, and more sex and nudity in the Canadian law firm than is realistic.

Importantly however, *The Associates* also treated viewers to something crucially different than what is seen in other (American) law shows. *The Associates* highlighted the alternative dispute resolution or ADR work of lawyers. What I observed when I watched the show, and what I read in my notes later, was scene after scene of dispute resolution interventions. *The Associates* was full of instances where lawyers, and especially Robyn Parsons, chose to use alternative dispute resolution processes such as negotiation, mediation, and arbitration, instead of litigation. And, they did so often, paralleling the growing use of these processes in legal practice. In Canada and the United States, mediation and negotiation are the most popular forms of ADR. The vast majority of cases no longer go to trial because more than 90 per cent of all civil and criminal cases end in negotiated settlement. The use of dispute resolution processes is growing, and mediation is increasing in popularity daily. Yet, virtually all American legal programming is focussed on the trial. This inaccuracy was, in a sense, corrected on *The Associates*. Instead of being exclusively bombarded with images of dramatic, adversarial trials, viewers also saw the collaborative tasks of lawyering. Problem solving, negotiation, and mediation formed the core of many of the storylines in the show. *The Associates* therefore more accurately depicted the reality of North American legal practice than most American legal television programmes do.[41] For example, in the first season, while the first episode introduced the show's characters and had no legal or ADR storylines, five of the 12 remaining episodes (episodes 105, 106, 109, 112, 113) featured dispute resolution storylines.[42] This means that 42 per cent of the first season's storylines were focussed on mediation and other ADR processes. In the second season, five episodes focused on dispute resolution, though this time that was five episodes out of 18, or 28 per cent of the storylines (episodes 201, 203, 206, 207, 209). This is simply unprecedented. Unlike the vast majority of American legal television dramas that solve all client problems in the court room, *The Associates* depicted lawyers using dispute resolution processes such as negotiation,

---

[39] Carrie Menkel-Meadow, 'Is There an Honest Lawyer in the Box? Legal Ethics on TV' in Michael Asimow (ed), *Lawyers in Your Living Room! Law on Television* (Chicago, American Bar Association, 2009) 44.

[40] Jill Goldsmith, 'Writing for Television: From Courtroom to Writer's Room' in Asimow (ed) ibid 14. In the same collection, Charles Rosenberg, '27 Years as a Television Legal Advisor and Counting...' correctly points out at 19: 'The problem is that audiences would find watching what lawyers mostly do in real life—read, write, talk on the phone, answer email and, sometimes, meet with people—visually boring (even snoring) to watch.'

[41] Jennifer L Schulz, 'Law and Film: Where are the Mediators?' (2008) 58 *University of Toronto Law Journal* 233, 239.

[42] The episodes from the first season begin with the number 101 and end with episode 113 (i.e. 13 episodes). Season two had 18 episodes—numbers 201 to 218—for a total of 31 episodes.

mediation, and arbitration to resolve client disputes. This is very unique, and it is the key observation of my study.

When I closely examined the many mediation and ADR-themed episodes I discovered that *The Associates* often commented on the benefits of ADR approaches: its speed as compared to litigation, its cost effectiveness, and its ability to, if not restore relationships, at least not damage them further. For example, in the second season, an episode entitled 'Ground Zero' highlights the benefits of ADR and the difference in Canadian and American approaches to settlement.[43] In this episode there has been a major plane crash with no survivors and YBK's New York office has been retained by the American defendant who manufactured the plane's faulty tyres. However, since the crash happened in Ontario, the American CEO of the defendant tyre company attends at YBK's Toronto offices to discuss strategy. The CEO, a black woman, is concerned about legal fees and whether litigation or settlement would be a better strategy. This scene is unprecedented for several reasons. First, because it is so rare to see CEOs on TV depicted as women, and even rarer as women of colour, and second, because of the discussion of the pros and cons of settlement. I will address each of these points in turn.

The Canadian Association of Broadcasters has set out guidelines for voluntary cultural diversity. The guidelines state that 'private broadcasters shall make an effort: to reflect, ...the ....multicultural and multiracial nature of ....Canadians, and the special place of aboriginal peoples within Canadian society.'[44] Catherine Murray's analysis of racial diversity in English Canadian television drama examined our television shows to see whether these diversity guidelines are being adhered to.[45] Her study relied on subjective audience review of plots with racial themes and content. Over 50 variables were used in a qualitative content analysis protocol to examine the contribution of visible minority people to the narratives of the top 10 television shows produced for the English market in 1999 or later.[46] *The Associates* was one of these shows. Murray found that visible minority characters appeared in 43 per cent of the storylines, and 'in this respect, Canada may be at least equal or marginally ahead of representation of visible minorities compared to Australian, American, or UK precedents'.[47] So, this episode of *The Associates* is important because it demonstrates gender and racial diversity and also that the producers of *The Associates* adhered to the Canadian Association of Broadcasters' guidelines.

The episode is also exceptional because the CEO wants to discuss the costs of litigation and whether or not settlement would be a good strategy. She meets with two YBK partners, Gary, the white American from the New York office, and Terrance, the white Canadian, former Brit (with accent to match), from the Toronto office. As the two white male lawyers face off to debate the pros and cons of litigation versus settlement, and to advise their client, ominous music begins to play in the background. The music sounds like music from an old Western, and the two lawyers have an almost classic standoff. We are used to seeing this kind of posturing and competitive,

---

[43] Episode 209.
[44] Murray, 'Silent on the Set' (n 16) 14.
[45] Ibid.
[46] Ibid 21.
[47] Ibid 28.

positional behaviour on legal shows. What we are not used to seeing is a discussion of fees and cost consequences. Even rarer is the depiction of a real debate on the merits of different legal strategies—settling as compared to litigating. In the course of Gary and Terrance's debate, Gary, the American lawyer, describes settlement as 'a gutless, Canadian solution', and proceeds to very strongly encourage the CEO to go to court. As a consequence, Terrance, the Canadian lawyer, threatens to report Gary to the law society for pressuring the client to litigate. This is an overt television depiction of an American versus a Canadian approach to justice. What does it tell us? What does this scene want?

This scene wants viewers to really think about settlement. Is it true that settlement is a gutless, Canadian solution? Is this what viewers think? What does it say about others' perspectives on Canadian approaches to justice? Is prioritising settlement good? Is it in keeping with our international reputation as peacekeepers? Or, is it weak, and not as good as an adversarial American approach? *The Associates* is asking us to consider these questions, and it wants us to come up with the answers for ourselves. Dispute resolution, feminist, and race perspectives all contribute to the analysis of this scene and all inform the answer to Mitchell's question: what does *The Associates* want?

The Associates seems to want more time—both on the air and in legal practice—for dispute resolution. It also appears to want to legitimise dispute resolution. It does so by deliberately articulating the benefits of settlement. Later in the scene, the five associates are invited to provide their opinions on settlement versus litigation to the client, the CEO. The associates have researched the question, so together they outline the benefits of settlement (faster, cheaper, able to craft solution) and its potential downside (may not obtain as much as you could in court). In so doing they emphasise the fact that working together brings results, and that research proves that settlement makes sense for most clients. As Carrie Menkel-Meadow notes, the TV series is:

> an appropriate forum for demonstrating the camaraderie and colleagueship of group practice. While movies typically explore the developmental and moral challenges faced by individuals, a television series shows us the interplay of many people sharing decisions, caring for, and mentoring each other in the workplace.[48]

In *The Associates,* when lawyers share work and jointly communicate well-reasoned, well-researched opinions to clients, clients are in a better position to make decisions. This episode, as well as many other episodes of *The Associates*, demonstrates the value of collaborative conflict resolution approaches. In the Canadian context, justice can be obtained both adversarially *and* through dispute resolution strategies. Both approaches can provide justice if done in clients' best interests, with competent, ethical counsel. *The Associates* did not make it an either or choice—both the courtroom and the mediation chamber were locations of justice in the show. Significantly, and differently than most American TV programmes, *The Associates* often showed the dispute resolution strategy as the more optimal; at the end of this particular scene, the CEO chooses settlement. Her choice to settle rather than litigate was the more collaborative and less painful choice for her company and her employees. It was, arguably, a more Canadian choice.

---

[48] Menkel-Meadow, 'Is There an Honest Lawyer in the Box?' (n 39) 45.

What else does *The Associates* want to tell us? It wants to say something about Robyn Parsons too. When the majority of the five associates espouse the benefits of settlement, only one associate, Robyn Parsons, mentions or seems to care about the hundreds of people who have died in the plane crash. Robyn is a white, blonde, heterosexual, woman lawyer, and she is *The Associates'* fairness compass. Robyn is portrayed as caring very much about her clients and cases, achieving fair results, and using mediation to get there. She could be described as emotional and ethical, and she, of all the associates, is the one who most often suggests a dispute resolution approach. Robyn falls into Barbara Villez's description of the third generation of television lawyer.[49]

The third generation of television lawyer, according to Villez, is a woman.[50] Shows about her, like *Ally McBeal* and *The Associates*, focus on the woman lawyer and her professional and personal life. Through the two-year arc of *The Associates*, viewers see Robyn develop professionally and personally, and we like her. (In my notes for episode 216 of 218 I noted that I was a bit sad because I had almost finished watching the series and I knew I would miss watching her.) Professionally, Robyn changes from an insecure new lawyer to competent legal counsel, using mediation instead of litigation whenever possible. Personally, she learns to navigate a difficult relationship with her mother and two romantic relationships with male associates at her firm. In *the practice* and *Ally McBeal*, Joan Gershen Marek argues that the female lawyers are bright, successful professionals who are developing their careers and are not being made to suffer for so doing.[51] They are competing well with the male lawyers on their shows, and, by the second season of *The Associates*, so is Robyn. (This is noteworthy because in filmic portrayals, women lawyers are rarely depicted competently.)[52] Robyn is also not being made to suffer for her success; by the end of the series, Robyn is happy in all aspects of her life.

So, what does *The Associates* want to say about Robyn Parsons? The depiction of her character does not really provide an answer, since her character could be described as sexist, or conversely, as favourable to women. And, of course, she is also entertaining. There were sexist scenes in *The Associates*, but there were also scenes that depicted Robyn making well-reasoned choices for herself. So, while parts of the show ratified traditional sexist conventions, others tried to portray the empowerment that comes from being able to make choices in a third wave feminist world. Jonathan Cohen argues that third wave women lawyers (or Villez's third generation women lawyers) represent a new type of woman.[53] According to Cohen, women lawyers like those on *Ally McBeal* represent 'a new type of woman for whom second wave feminism has

---

[49] Barbara Villez, *Television and the Legal System* (New York, Routledge, 2010).

[50] Villez, *Series Tele* (n 24) 37 and Villez, *Television and the Legal System* (n 49) 37–40.

[51] Joan Gershen Marek, 'The Practice and Ally McBeal: A New Image for Women Lawyers on Television?' (1999) *Journal of American Culture* 77, 83.

[52] Jennifer L Schulz, 'The Cook, the Mediator, the Feminist, and the Hero' (2009) 21 *Canadian Journal of Women and the Law* 177, 183, 191. Virtually all legally themed films starring women lawyers portray them as in some way incompetent. See, e.g. Carole Shapiro, 'Women Lawyers in Celluloid: Why Hollywood Skirts the Truth' (1995) 25 *University of Toledo Law Review* 955.

[53] Jonathan Cohen, 'Deconstructing Ally: Explaining Viewers' Interpretations of Popular Television' (2002) 4 *Mediapsychology* 253.

provided choices, and who when faced with these choices, is trying to figure out her own life.'[54] Robyn on *The Associates* is this type of woman.

Like *Ally McBeal*, *The Associates* had its funny, unrealistic, and entertaining moments. Following Jonathan Cohen's approach in his study of 251 Israeli students and their responses to *Ally McBeal*,[55] one might ask which of the three responses—favourable, sexist, or funny—is the dominant, resistant, or negotiated reading of *The Associates*. Cohen would describe the dominant reading as comporting with the favourable view, seeing positive images of women in the show. The resistant reading would view the show as sexist, and those who found the show funny would likely be conducting a negotiated reading where 'viewers focus on the dilemmas humorously portrayed in the program, rather than on the characters and the ideological "bottom line" they deliver'.[56]

Ultimately, however, it does not matter whether *The Associates* was favourable to women, sexist, or funny. That is because labelling *The Associates* 'favourable to women', 'sexist', or 'funny' is the viewer's response. None of these labels answer the question, what does *The Associates* want? If we are really asking pictures, images, and TV shows what they desire, then we must move from *our* impressions to *their* wants. Mitchell argues that the gender of pictures is feminine. Since Robyn is the centre of the series or the picture, in Mitchell's view, '[t]he question of what pictures want, then, is inseparable from the question of what women want'.[57] So, what does Robyn Parsons want? In the first season, Robyn wants to be a good lawyer, to be taken seriously as a legal professional, and to find a boyfriend. By the second season, Robyn is a good lawyer and she has found love. Whether her desires suggest a sexist meaning for *The Associates* is not the issue. As Mitchell states, we must be 'less concerned with the meaning of images than with their lives and loves'.[58] Robyn cares about how fulfilling her life is, on both professional and personal levels. Because she feels fulfilled by the end of season two, if we ask what does she want (in terms of lack), the answer is she wants for nothing.

'What pictures want in the last instance, then, is simply to be asked what they want, with the understanding that the answer may well be, nothing at all'.[59] What is important is that for the first time, a Canadian legal television drama is being asked what it wants, and people are listening to the answer. Pictures may not know what they want, or they may want nothing. But whatever they might want can only be determined through dialogue with others.[60] This dialogue is what I am hoping to start with this chapter. Mitchell suggests that we move away from our preoccupation with 'meaning' and think of pictures as complex individuals with multiple identities.[61] If we do so, we can readily see how Robyn may have varied aspects to her personality

---

[54] Ibid 256.

[55] Ibid 253.

[56] Ibid 259.

[57] Mitchell, *What Do Pictures Want?* (n 29) 35. According to Mitchell, the power that both pictures and women want 'is manifested as *lack*, not as possession' (at 36, emphasis in original).

[58] Ibid 343.

[59] Ibid 48.

[60] Ibid 46. Mitchell does note that some images can transcend specific, local, cultural forms of social construction and can be universal (at 344).

[61] Ibid 47.

and how she may sometimes be funny, other times be 'unfeminist', and at other times be a favourable model for women. More importantly, Mitchell proposes we treat visual cultural images such as Robyn Parsons as 'go-betweens' in social transactions, as screen images that structure our encounters with other human beings.[62] Robyn is thus a screen image who is a go-between for viewers and *The Associates'* storylines. In this way, Robyn, the proponent of mediation in *The Associates*, is a go-between, or a mediator of sorts. She structures our encounter with TV ADR and she is central to our relationship with *The Associates*. When we watch *The Associates*, Robyn, our go-between, mediates our understanding of how Canadian law can truly be about dispute resolution. She is actively involved in constituting law and justice through her dispute resolution initiatives. Robyn Parsons is crucially implicated in how *The Associates* informs the construction of Canadian socio-legal life.

Through the character of Robyn Parsons, viewers come to see the central role of ADR in Canadian law and justice. The final episode of the first season is illustrative. In episode 113, the partners of the law firm are discussing Robyn in the context of her performance review.[63] Although Robyn has felt unsure of her legal abilities for most of the first season, and indeed, is a low biller, she has proven herself very competent in the area of ADR. At the performance review, Robyn is described by one of the law firm's partners, Cindy, who says that Robyn 'displays mediation skills beyond her years'. A true compliment. However, another partner, Walter, counters Cindy's comment with, 'mediation is half-assed lawyering for those who are scared of a fight'. Cindy disagrees with him and says, 'mediation is the future of law—good to have someone who is interested'. Here again, Robyn is a go-between; she is between the two ends of the spectrum. Robyn mediates between the positions of 'ADR is vital' and 'ADR is useless', thereby not only bringing the question of the utility of ADR to television (unique in and of itself), but also allowing viewers to reach their own conclusions on the matter. When viewers ask themselves, what does *The Associates* want? They start to think about dispute resolution in a sustained way, perhaps for the first time in the context of a legal drama. Does *The Associates* want to profile dispute resolution? Debate its utility? How, if at all, do our answers change when we know that the reason Robyn pursues ADR alternatives is because she is scared of litigating? Robyn admits this to her friends, the other associates. Does this suggest that Walter was right? Is mediation soft and weak, perhaps like Robyn? Is mediation the choice for lawyers who cannot really handle 'real' legal work? Or, does *The Associates* want us to side with Cindy and appreciate ADR as the future of law?

Given the sheer number of mediation-themed storylines in *The Associates* (almost half of the first season's episodes), and the fact that mediation is made to look as interesting and exciting as courtroom work, I think the show wants us to agree with Cindy that mediation is the future of law.[64] More lawyers should participate in non-adversarial dispute resolution processes so that their clients can take advantage of

---

[62]   Ibid 351.

[63]   Episode 113, 'Should I stay or should I go?'

[64]   *The Associates* featured many more mediation storylines than I could outline in this chapter, although not all of them could be described as 'true' mediation. For eg, in Episode 109, 'Family Values', the lawyers were said to be attending mediation, though there was actually no mediator present. See Schulz, 'Settlement and Mediation in Canadian Legal Television' (n 22) 94.

the creative, collaborative benefits of interest-based, facilitated negotiations. This conclusion, articulated on Canadian TV in 2001, is quite incredible; it is something we never hear on television legal dramas. It is simply unprecedented for a show from 10 years ago to showcase so much ADR, especially given how non-existent ADR processes were, and still are, on US television programmes.[65]

IV. Conclusions

I began this chapter with a question: what is different or distinct about Canadian television law? The answer is its focus on ADR. Highlighting the importance of ADR and especially mediation, focusing on a young woman lawyer, and depicting Canadian law firm life made *The Associates* unique. And, choosing this Canadian show, asking what it wants, and then listening to the answer, makes my approach unique. This chapter was the first attempt to see Canadian legal television and ask what it wants. Based on my observations, I conclude that *The Associates* wants time and legitimacy for dispute resolution. *The Associates* wants lawyers to use mediation and to respect it. Watching the show convinces viewers that they should think about settlement and the value of collaborative conflict resolution approaches, because justice can be obtained both adversarially and through dispute resolution strategies.

Although *The Associates* had something to say about how essential dispute resolution processes are to a just legal system, it is not clear that many people heard the message. The reality is that very few Canadians actually watched the show, and it was cancelled after only two seasons. Is this because, as Asimow argues, 'people like to consume media that echoes and reinforces their preferences and preconceptions'[66] and *The Associates* did not reinforce Canadian preferences? Perhaps Canadians do not actually prefer less adversarial approaches? Do we just like American shows, with their focus on adversarial justice, too much? The answer may be 'yes'. Despite its high production values, great cast, and good acting, the show was cancelled after only 31 episodes. Canadians were simply not watching *The Associates*, which brings us back to the thorny problem I began this chapter with—namely the American versus Canadian dilemma. It appears that Canadians prefer American television and consume American popular culture as if it was our own. Andrew Wernick writes:

Canadian consciousness is depicted as an ironic duality that borrows the clothes but not the spirit of American razzle-dazzle, and self-deprecatingly knows itself to be rooted in the dull daily experience of living in a peripheralized region in which nothing really happens... this ambivalence is reflected in the preference of Canadian TV viewers for American entertainment and Canadian news—that is the key to the Canadian difference.[67]

---

[65] There is one exception. In January 2011 the USA Network premiered a new TV show, entitled *Fairly Legal*. This primetime, hour-long drama features a female mediator as its protagonist. Mediator Kate Reed performs at least two ADR interventions per episode, so this American show depicts more ADR than all other US television programmes before it. For more on *Fairly Legal*, see ibid 103–04.

[66] Asimow, Popular Culture Matters' (n 13) xxi.

[67] Wernick, 'American Popular Culture in Canada' (n 14) 297.

Thus, Canadians happily watch American TV over their own domestic television for entertainment purposes, but for the news, we recognise our difference from Americans and therefore prefer Canadian news. Quite simply, Canadians are loyal to their national news programmes, but not to their indigenous drama programmes.[68] Therefore, and very unusually, Canadian national television broadcasters must actually compete for their own domestic market, and other than for news and sports, find themselves losing. Paul Rutherford is correct when he comments that our seldom watched and often derivative TV 'has been a bitter pill for any devout nationalist to swallow'.[69]

However, does the fact that we like American programmes so much pose a threat to our Canadian identity? Paul Rutherford argues:

> But mass culture in itself does not pose, and never has posed, a direct threat to the Canadian identity, because consumers have 'read' its messages through a special lens made in Canada. Canada is living proof that the doctrine of nationalism does not really explain how things work.[70]

So, perhaps, even if Canadians prefer American legal dramas, it does not matter, because a steady diet of American shows is not a direct threat to our identity. This is either because we are able to read American TV through our Canadian lenses, or perhaps more likely, because 'a Canadian nationality in any typical sense of the word is an impossibility'.[71] In our subordinated context, our national identity is comprised of what we want, or rather, lack; we define ourselves as 'not American', and any sense of a Canadian identity is 'founded in the determined absence of any such thing'.[72]

If this is true, statements about the historical domination of Canadian popular culture by American popular culture have to be newly understood. The historical situation has been complicated by economic elements and cultural interpenetration, and this must be recognised. 'There is a process of global assimilation associated with international capitalist development'[73] and Canada's is not the only national culture to be submerged. Other cultures and countries too have been flooded. 'The global character of contemporary capitalism and the ubiquity of its cultural forms'[74] means that we are not alone. We are not the only non-Americans watching 'too much' American TV. 'The cultural space that Canadians inhabit is continuous not just with the rest of the continent but with the whole "advanced" world.'[75] Therefore, we must (perhaps grudgingly) accept that the United States' popular television is part of our

---

[68] This means that Elayne Rapping's statement in 'The History of Law on Television' (n 26) is probably not true for Canadians. Rapping argues at xxx that: 'fictional programming actually has a much greater influence than the news on how people view the legal system. That's because people watch more entertainment series than news, and they take these series much more seriously than one might realize.' Since Canadians are very loyal Canadian news watchers, they get some accurate information about their own legal system from the news, and the news may have a greater influence on how Canadians view their legal system than it does on how Americans view their legal system.

[69] Rutherford, 'Made in America' (n 21) 260.

[70] Ibid 280.

[71] Ibid 278.

[72] Wernick, 'American Popular Culture in Canada' (n 14) 298.

[73] Ibid 295.

[74] Ibid 295.

[75] Ibid 295.

popular culture, and it is probably part of Australia's, Britain's, and many other countries' as well.

However, American TV law is not all there is to know about law or justice, and it is certainly not all there is to know about dispute resolution. *The Associates* stresses the benefits of ADR and the differences between Canadian and American approaches to incorporating ADR into legal practice. No matter whether we take Mitchell's approach and ask what *The Associates* wants, or if we agree with Asimow that 'popular culture reflects what people actually believe (or at least what the makers of pop culture believe that people believe)',[76] we come to the same conclusion. *The Associates* wants lawyers to employ mediation, and *The Associates* reflects that Canadians believe in mediation. Mediation is the future of law, and therefore, ADR may be the just, civil, Canadian approach.

The Associates stresses the importance of non-adversarial dispute resolution processes and depicts them as a great Canadian choice. Quite simply, *The Associates* desires a Canadian approach to achieving justice through mediation instead of litigation. If we want to communicate this Canadian approach, we must accept that popular culture has gone global, and broadcast our unique approach to the global market. Rather than worrying about opposing the dominant power of American television, or being overly concerned about the failure of Canadian TV at home, we need to be more concerned with the failure of Canadian TV in other markets, because that failure means we are not able to trumpet our wants and our desires globally. *The Associates* knew that settlement was not a gutless solution, but rather, often the optimal solution. Since *The Associates* is now off the air, we must come up with new ways to broadcast that Canadian truth.

References

Asimow, M, 'Popular Culture Matters' in M Asimow (ed), *Lawyers in Your Living Room! Law on Television* (Chicago, American Bar Association, 2009).

Asimow, M and Mader, S, *Law and Popular Culture: A Course Book* (New York, Peter Lang, 2004).

Cohen, J, 'Deconstructing Ally: Explaining Viewers' Interpretations of Popular Television' (2002) 4 *Mediapsychology* 253.

Flaherty, DH and Manning, FE (eds), *The Beaver Bites Back? American Popular Culture in Canada* (Montreal, McGill-Queen's University Press, 1993).

Goldsmith, J, 'Writing for Television: From Courtroom to Writer's Room' in Asimow, *Lawyers in Your Living Room!*, 2009.

Marek, JG, 'The Practice and Ally McBeal: A New Image for Women Lawyers on Television?' (1999) *Journal of American Culture* 77.

Menkel-Meadow, C, 'Is There an Honest Lawyer in the Box? Legal Ethics on TV' in Asimow, *Lawyers in Your Living Room!*, 2009.

Miller, MJ, 'Inflecting the Formula: The First Seasons of *Street Legal* and *L.A. Law*' in Flaherty and Manning, *The Beaver Bites Back?*, 1993.

---

[76] Asimow, 'Popular Culture Matters' (n 13) xx.

Mitchell, WJT, *What Do Pictures Want? The Lives and Loves of Images*, (Chicago, The University of Chicago Press, 2005).

Murray, C, 'Silent on the Set: Cultural Diversity and Race in English Canadian TV Drama' (prepared for the Strategic Research and Analysis (SRA), Strategic Policy and Research, Department of Canadian Heritage, August 2002).

Penney, S, 'Mass Torts, Mass Culture: Canadian Mass Tort Law and Hollywood Narrative Film' (2004) 30 *Queen's Law Journal* 205.

Rapping, E, 'The History of Law on Television' in Asimow, *Lawyers in Your Living Room!*, 2009.

Robson, P, 'Lawyers and the Legal System on TV: The British Experience' (2007) 2, 4 *International Journal of Law in Context* 333.

Rosenberg, C, '27 Years as a Television Legal Advisor and Counting...' in Asimow, *Lawyers in Your Living Room!*, 2009.

Rutherford, P, 'Made in America: The Problem of Mass Culture in Canada' in Flaherty and Manning, *The Beaver Bites Back?*, 1993.

Schulz, JL, 'Settlement and Mediation in Canadian Legal Television' (2011) 1 *Journal of Arbitration and Mediation* 77.

—— 'The Cook, the Mediator, the Feminist, and the Hero' (2009) 21 *Canadian Journal of Women and the Law* 177.

—— '*girls club* Does Not Exist' in Asimow, *Lawyers in Your Living Room!*, 2009.

—— 'Law and Film: Where are the Mediators?' (2008) 58 *University of Toronto Law Journal* 233.

Shapiro, C, 'Women Lawyers in Celluloid: Why Hollywood Skirts the Truth' (1995) 25 *University of Toledo Law Review* 955.

Tate, MA, 'Canada, Culture & Broadcasting: An Examination of the Cultural Components of Canada's Broadcasting Policies' (Pennsylvania State University, College of Communications, 2000).

Villez, B, *Series Tele: Visions de la Justice* (Paris, Presses Universitaires de France, 2005).

—— *Television and the Legal System* (New York, Routledge, 2010).

Wernick, A, 'American Popular Culture in Canada: Trends and Reflections' in Flaherty and Manning, *The Beaver Bites Back?*, 1993.

21

Stranger Danger?: Sadistic Serial Killers on the Small Screen

ANNETTE HOULIHAN

I. Act One, Scene One: Culturally Violent Strangers

This chapter examines the most gruesome of crime fantasies which is now commonly portrayed on American television; the sadistic serial killer. It will analyse episodes of American crime dramas, *Criminal Minds, Dexter* and *Law and Order: SVU*, which feature sadistic serial killers in the plots. By examining these representative crime dramas, the manner in which television narratives of violence are disconnected from the corporeality of gendered, heterosexual violence through imaginations of sadism as a form of criminal violence, will come clear. However, popular cultural constructions of fictional sadistic serial killers do not recognise the differences between sadomasochism and criminal violence. Rather, the criminally violent offences depicted are often fused with elements of sadism, especially sexual sadism, to produce a neatly defined culpable body.

The label 'sadism', especially sexual sadism, is attached to popular cultural profiles of serial killers as part of a social construction which insists that expressions of violence are foreign and strange. This identity is based on visual imagery and evidence of torture, rather than on recognition of sadomasochism (s/m) as a mutually consensual form of desire (as defined by those who practice it). Sadism becomes a metaphor for torture, a simplistic formula of extreme cruelty displayed by inflicting corporeal suffering on unconsenting and random victims. At other times a character's sadism is loosely signified by certain traits, which have little or no relation at all to the practices involved in actual sadomasochism, but rather embody extreme anti-social or egotistical behaviour. This distorts the image of sadomasochism as not only pathological, but as an excessively inhumane form of criminality/violence. This hyper-pathology of criminality creates, for the viewers of these crime dramas, a terrifying monster, one that is sexually, socially and psychologically terrifying.

In this newly emerging genre, women appear especially vulnerable to excessive violence from random offenders with whom they have little or no relationship. However, most women are at a much greater risk of violence from someone they know, particularly an intimate partner or family member.[1] Sadomasochism, depicted in crime dramas, bears little resemblance to s/m as a form of consensual desire, as discussed in the recent and relevant literature.[2] Instead, s/m as a trope deployed in these types of shows functions as a hyperbolic spectacle of violence intended to titillate.

II. Sadomasochism and Moral Panics

As Moser and Kleinplatz write in 'Themes of SM Expression', 'SM is *consensual* by definition. Just as the difference between consensual coitus and rape is consent, the difference between SM and violence is consent. Non-consensual acts are criminal'.[3] Sadism refers to personal desires involving various practices, including the giving of pain for pleasure.[4] Sadism is not only about pain, but the infliction of pain is perhaps the most troubling aspect of sadism for its dissidents. These dissidents rely on exclusive categorisations of pleasure and pain as entirely separate concepts, but also the extension of neat classifications of pain as bodily injury/harm in criminal law.[5]

Pleasure and pain are not exclusive categories. They share many intersections and overlaps. S/m represents the seeming paradox of pleasurable pain, which can be socio-legally confusing. Popular culture is littered with references to the interconnections between pleasure and pain. Examples range from explicit references, such as John Cougar's 1982 song entitled 'Hurts so Good'. Burr outlines how the pain/pleasure nexus was also celebrated in the television show *Buffy the Vampire Slayer*, which contained sub-textual elements of s/m.[6] The pain/pleasure nexus has also featured in movies including *Secretary* and *9 1/2 Weeks*, which contain explicit s/m references. More recently, Rihanna's pop single *S&M* directly references s/m themes and the

---

[1] R Hunter, 'Law's (Masculine) Violence' (2006) *Law and Critique* 17, 27–46.

[2] T Edwards, 'Spectacular Pain: Masculinity, Masochism and Men in the Movies' in V Burr and J Hearn (eds) *Sex, Violence and the Body: The Erotics of Wounding* (Palgrave Macmillan, 2008) 157–176; D Langdridge and M Barker, 'Situating sadomasochism' in D Langdridge and M Barker (eds), *Safe, Sane and Consensual: Contemporary Perspectives on Sadomasochism* (Houndmills, Palgrave, 2008) 3–9; C Moser and PJ Kleinplatz, 'Themes of SM Expression' in Langdridge and Barker (eds) ibid 25–54; D Langdridge (2008). 'Speaking the Unspeakable: S/M and the Eroticisation of Pain' in Langdridge and Barker ibid 85–97.

[3] Moser and Kleinplatz, 'Themes of SM Expression' (n 2) 38.

[4] Langdridge, 'Speaking the Unspeakable' (n 2) 85–97.

[5] This extension of sadism to harm is at the heart of legal punishment for s/m. The most recognised example of criminalising s/m is the English case of *R v Brown* [1992] 2 All ER 552, [1992] QB 491, (1992) 94 Cr App R 302 (CA) and *Laskey, Jaggard and Brown v The United Kingdom* [1997] 2 EHRR 39. *Brown* involved the prosecution and subsequent appeals of 16 same-sex desiring men who engaged in various sadomasochistic activities. Prosecutions were initiated solely from police intervention following the 1987 'Operation Spanner' investigation in Manchester, England. The men video-recorded some of their activities, these recordings comprised a significant component of the evidence. Much of the initial hysteria stemmed from incorrect police assumptions that the activities were non-consensual and involved torture and murder. For more information about the case, see A Houlihan, 'When "No" means "Yes" and "Yes" means Harm': Gender, Sexuality and Sadomasochism Criminality' (2011) *Tulane Journal of Law & Sexuality: A Review of Lesbian, Gay, Bisexual, and Transgender Legal Issues* 20, 31–60 and M Weait, 'Sadomasochism and the Law' in Langdridge and Barker (eds), *Safe, Sane and Consensual* (n 2) 63, 65–79.

[6] V Burr, 'Ambiguity and Sexuality in *Buffy the Vampire Slayer*: A Sartrean Analysis (2003) *Sexualities* 6, 343–60.

video features s/m costumes and paraphernalia. The music video for 30 Seconds to Mars' *Hurricane* also features s/m apparatus and clothing. Both of these videos have received special censorship classification and been banned in many countries because of the depiction of s/m, highlighting the social prevalence of discomfort with s/m.[7]

The categories of pleasure and pain have been debated and explored within philosophy, perhaps most famously by Jean-Paul Sartre's theory of 'Phenomenology'. In this work, he suggests that sadism is an expression of a failed desire, which occurs when mutual incarnate love is unsuccessfully reciprocated.[8] While he recognises that love and desire are imbued with tension and conflict, offering that sexuality is fundamentally sadomasochistic,[9] there are problems with his treatise. What is troubling about these types of theories about sadism is that s/m is rendered strange, a failure or something lacking. Another issue with this outlook is that sadism is treated as a metaphor for absolute pain. There is an assumption that sadism is about one being wholly selfish and cruel, as expressed through the television dramas discussed in this chapter, rather than recognising the mutual, consensual and desirable aspects of sadomasochism between selves. Sadomasochism is the giving and receiving of pleasure, at times through pain, but it is also a complex set of desires infused with, and expressed through, intricate modes of consent.

Sadomasochism makes the interconnectedness between pain and pleasure explicit, and highlights the complex nature of desire. Essentially, s/m celebrates pleasure as multiple and diverse. This is troubling for socio-legal histories of sexuality, which have demonised sexual difference.[10] These works often express perspectives on sadism that represent socio-legal panics about the stranger who does not fit the mould of procreative heteronormativity. There are still numerous legal prescriptions about desires and procreative heteronormativity.[11] This is where narratives about sadistic killers gather their meaning, from these histories which have criminalised and pathologised desire. But, the demonising of s/m extends to other realms, including psychology, psychiatry and medicine.

The historical pathologisation of sadism is grounded in psychiatric discourse. There is an entry for sadism in the *Diagnostic and Statistical Manual of the American Psychiatric Association* (DSM-IV) and the *International Classification of Diseases* (ICD-10), despite a lack of evidence to support s/m as psychopathology.[12] This pathologisation informs legal discourses and judgments, which criminalise s/m.[13] Sadomasochism is celebrated globally with annual events (eg Leather Pride Week in the US city of San Francisco, Leather Pride Week in the Netherlands city of

---

[7] See the following media articles that discuss these bans and censorship: www.mtv.com/news/articles/1657144/rihanna-s-m-video-banned.jhtml;www.billboard.com/column/viralvideos/video-ban-30-seconds-to-mars-too-sexual-1004132701.story.

[8] JP Sartre, *Being and Nothingness: An Essay on Phenomenological Ontology* (Hazel E Barnes translated 1993, first published 1943) [trans of *L'Être et le néant: Essai d'ontologie phénoménologique*].

[9] Burr, 'Ambiguity and Sexuality' (n 6) 343–60.

[10] D Dalton, 'Genealogy of the Australian Homocriminal Subject: A Study of Two Explanatory Models of Deviance' (2007) *Griffith Law Review* 16, 83–106.

[11] M Thompson, 'Viagra Nation' (2006) *Law, Culture and the Humanities* 2, 259–83.

[12] Langdridge and Barker, 'Situating Sadomasochism' (n 2) 3–9.

[13] See Houlihan, 'When "No" means "Yes" and "Yes" means Harm' (n 5) 31–60 for a further discussion of the criminalisation of s/m within the UK, especially the now infamous *Brown* decision that described s/m as a non-consensual form of assault.

Amsterdam and Leather Pride Week in Sydney, Australia). Yet, many people still view sadism as deviant, dangerous or illegal, and it is these constructions and understandings of s/m that underpin popular cultural constructions of the sadistic serial killer.

These imagined boundaries between pain and pleasure and sadism from normative sociality underpin popular cultural narratives of violence, discussed in this chapter. The argument made here is that popular culture relegates violence to the foreign, imagined realm of television drama. Violence, like s/m, is socio-legally positioned as something deviant and unusual, something that is both strange and unfamiliar. While s/m may be unfamiliar (strange) to many people's lived experience, especially those who do not practice s/m, violence may have a more familiar place. Violence has a presence in popular cultural imaginations (eg television, film, gaming), the dissemination of current affairs (eg newspaper, television, the internet) and the actuality of violence in our familial, social and professional lives. The examples of violence shown through the fantasy of sadistic serial killers overshadow the more usual occurrences of violence, diverting our attention away from probable corporeal instances of violence to fantastical imaginations of crime. The concept of domestic/family violence is silenced within popular cultural narratives of criminality by associating violence with the extreme, the bizarre and the imaginary—that being, sadistic serial killers.

III. Criminal Casting Call: Sadistic Serial Killer and Ideal Victims

Popular cultural crime narratives (ie film and television) are cluttered with serial killers. However, an even more terrifying killer has recently emerged within popular culture; the sadistic serial killer. These criminals pose a threat of even more harm than the serial killer because they commit several crimes: abduction, serious assault, grievous bodily harm, torture, sexual assault and murder. This couples a slow and painful death with particularly heinous assaults. Yet, the sadistic serial killer identity is based more upon notions of torture, which bear little or no resemblance to sadism as a consensual identity-choice.

Criminal Minds, Dexter and the *Law & Order* franchises include murders with sadistic serial killers as offenders. These cultural constructions of victimology reflect a fictionalised landscape, more than the actuality of violent offenders and their victims. This chapter outlines numerous examples of female victims who have been murdered by allegedly sadistic male serial killers in episodes of *Criminal Minds, Dexter* and *Law & Order: SVU*. It will argue that this construction of violent crime attempts to bifurcate bodies into unusually exaggerated deviant offenders and their idealised victims.

The offender in these shows is often an exaggerated stranger, an archetypal figure who reflects various cultural biases about that which is considered alien. In short, the killer is unknown to the victim and is sadistic. Popular cultural constructions of sadism are not based on consensual sexual practices involving domination and submission, control and/or pain for pleasure, but on torture and death. This gives rise to depictions of a sensationalised violent offender based upon moral panics concerning the unknowable stranger, rather than the embodied risks of gendered and sexualised violence. The collocation of sadism with the murder usually occurs through a post-mortem examination of a female victim and crime scene. Devoid of clues and without knowledge of the offender, criminal justice professionals scrutinise the victim and her location. This analysis leads to a hunt for a sadistic serial killer based upon images of torture or offender profiles.

Describing offenders as sadistic has many thematic functions, such as construct-ing a complex 'otherness' based on much more than mere criminality. The sadist serial killer has a perverse sexual deviance, as well as layers of sociopathy and psychopathy. These popular cultural constructs of deviance and victimology reflect social and legal discomfort with sadomasochism. The naming of torture is almost absent in television crime dramas. Instead, it has been replaced with these lingering notions of sadism. Also, domestic/family violence rarely occurs in television scripts. Depictions of these types of violence have been washed away, and replaced by extreme conceptualisation of serial killers and xenophobic notions of the dangers posed by strangers.

Popular culture fictionalises violence through the presentation of the paradox of a killer who may seem slightly familiar, yet is ultimately someone who is strange. These criminals have an essence of familiarity for audiences as well, because they often appear to be strangers lurking in the shadows, cutting the figure of an oddly recognisable unrecognisable. Offenders are cast as 20- to 40-year-old Caucasian males, who work or live near their victims. Examples of the 'familiar stranger' lurking in the metaphorical shadows include reclusive neighbours, shy co-workers, professional acquaintances (eg mail worker, service staff, barista, bank teller) or other persons with whom the victim has had some fleeting contact. Simultaneously, the killer wears the mask of the social outsider (eg criminal, loner, single/unmarried, childless with few relatives and friends—the non-familiar). These narratives also rely on the construct of ideal victimology, as the sadistic serial killer seeks out idealised targets as his victims, and they are almost invariably unsuspecting, Caucasian and female.

Christie[14] describes ideal victims as 'a person or category of individuals—who—when hit by a crime—most readily are given the complete and legitimate status of being a victim'. He also suggests that exaggerated criminal caricatures of offenders inform ideal victim status. Extremely violent (and viscerally frightening) offenders make the victim seem more innocent and less deserving of victimisation. Employing these caricature-like tropes of sadism within depictions of the imaginations of violent criminals exaggerates the offender's criminality and the victim's undeserving status.

Dowler, Fleming and Muzzatti (2006)[15] highlight idealised gender stereotyping of victims within popular culture, whereby female victims are categorised either as innocent and undeserving or corrupted and blameworthy. Female victims who symbolise innocence and moral goodness are more likely to be seen as victims. Dowler, Fleming and Muzzatti also suggest that race influences social imaginations of victims, asserting that Caucasian victims are assumed to illicit more public sympathy.

---

[14] N Christie, 'The Ideal Victim' in E Fattah (ed), *From Crime Policy to Victim Policy: Reorienting the Justice System* (London, Macmillan, 1986) 18.
[15] K Dowler, T Fleming and SL Muzzatti, 'Constructing Crime: Media, Crime, and Popular Culture' (2006) Canadian Journal of Criminology and Criminal Justice 48, 837–50.

Therefore, women of colour are cast less frequently in the fictional role of victim. In film and television narratives, serial killers mostly target Caucasian females who are young and attractive. While the serial killer may have preyed on sex workers in previous crime-drama depictions, the focus of each story that currently airs is usually framed around a victim who is law-abiding and innocent (or, rather, an idealised version of 'normality').

This research analyses television crime shows to demonstrate how popular culture relies on a misinformed construction of victimology, beyond that of the ideal victim described by Christie. Victimology developed out of the emergence of criminology in the late nineteenth century. Victims were previously silenced, as their injuries were absorbed by the 'law and order' regime, which acknowledged only the state as the injured party, as each individual was but an extension of the state. Initially, citizens and workers began to claim rights during the French and American revolutions.[16] Then, individuals started asserting socio-legal recognition of their rights when employment shifted from agricultural to dense industrial workplaces. Further, the victim's movement also reflects developments in international human rights, such as civil rights, women's liberation and gay, lesbian, bisexual, transgender and queer rights.[17]

While academic victimology refers to the study of victims and to victim services, support and advocacy, popular cultural victimology has rather different meanings. Television programmes have implicit and explicit definitions of victimology. In *Criminal Minds* the term 'victimology' refers to victim characteristics and methods of harm. *Dexter* and *Law & Order: SVU* create more implicit meanings of victimology and do not use the term 'victimology' in the same way. In these two shows, victimology implicitly refers to specialised forensic investigation. Violent victimisations evidenced by dead, and often mutilated, bodies are integral to their plots and the immediate and overarching quests for justice. The figure of the victim is seemingly omnipresent in narratives of violence, and in most cases the plot revolves around one or several dead bodies.

IV. Press Play—The Episodes and Analysis

The following episodes under consideration were randomly selected episodes from three high-rating crime series broadcast on free-to-air and cable television. They include an episode of *Criminal Minds*, *Dexter* and *Law & Order: SVU*. The *Criminal Minds* episode analysed is titled 'Penelope' (series three, episode nine). 'Dexter' is the title of the first episode of season one of the series by the same name (season one, episode one). Finally, the *Law & Order: SVU* episode was titled 'Uncle' (season

---

[16] T Beauchamp, *Philosophical Ethics: An Introduction to Moral Philosophy*, 3rd edn (New York, McGraw-Hill, 2001).

[17] M O'Connell, 'Victims and Criminal Justice' in H Hayes and T Prenzler (eds), *An Introduction to Crime* (Sydney, Pearson, 2007) 249–63.

eight, episode four). That said, while sadistic serial killers frequently feature in crime dramas, this chapter does not attempt to quantify the existence of sadistic serial killers in popular culture depictions. Instead, it seeks to explore these fictional narratives and how they are dislocated from gendered, heterosexual victimologies of violence and s/m identities.

A. Criminal Minds

In the *Criminal Minds* episode entitled 'Penelope', the Federal Bureau of Investigations' (FBI) Behavioral Analysis Unit (BAU) investigates the shooting of Penelope Garcia, a computer expert with their unit. In this episode the BAU is hyper-vigilant, as they are investigating a crime committed against a fellow employee who is also their friend. At the conclusion of the previous episode, a man Garcia met at a café shot her. Their initial meeting appears to be by chance, when Garcia fixes the man's laptop computer. He is in his 30s, well dressed and handsome. During their initial dinner date, he tells Garcia his name is James 'Colby' Baylor, and that he is an Ivy League educated lawyer, all of which turns out to be lies.

After heavy prompting from the behavioural analysts, Garcia tells her colleagues that Baylor took charge during the date by ordering for her and that he insisted on sitting with his back to the wall. Based on this rather general information about his behaviour, the FBI agents announce that he may be a sadist who gains women's trust and attempts to murder them. They construe him as arrogant and cocky because of the way he describes his education and employment. Later, Baylor is revealed to be John Clark Battle, a police officer who mistakenly thought that Garcia knew he was killing people in his professional capacities. He is described as an 'Angel of Death', someone who places lives at risk in order to be seen as a hero and saver of lives. The episode concludes with a standoff between Battle and FBI officers at the BAU headquarters, during which a female agent fatally shoots Battle.

B. Dexter

Dexter is a serial drama about a blood spatter analyst who works for the Miami Metro Police Department (PD). Through flashbacks to his adolescence, the audience learns that Harry Morgan, a Miami Metro PD officer, is Dexter's foster father. Dexter and Harry share a deep bond. In the initial seasons, Harry is the only person who knows about Dexter's secret homicidal desires. The flashbacks portray an emotionally detached adolescent with an intense desire to kill. Harry detects this, encouraging Dexter to enact his desires on criminals who escape punishment. Through further episodes, the audience learns that Dexter has killed many people, but only in accordance with the 'Code of Harry', which stipulates that the killing must serve a purpose and that Dexter must be sure that his victim deserves to die because of their violent actions. Usually, Dexter's targets prey on 'innocent' people.

The first episode shows Dexter stalking Jamie Jaworski, a hotel valet in his 30s. Dexter suspects Jaworski violently murdered a young mother named Jane

Saunders. He was arrested for the crime, but escaped conviction because a search warrant was deemed invalid in court. After Jaworski's release from custody, Dexter breaks into his apartment to find evidence that he murdered Saunders. If Dexter can prove to himself that Jaworski murdered an innocent person, this will allow him to enact his own form of justice defined through 'Harry's Code'. Jaworski's apartment is a miniature bondage den, furnished with whips, restraints and specialised pornographic magazines. On a fetish website called 'Scream Bitch Scream', a site dedicated to violent hard-core pornography saved in Jaworski's browser, Dexter discovers a posted video recording of the murder. The victim is seen in the video alongside a man with the same tattoo as Jaworski. Later in the episode Jaworski confesses to Dexter that he is the man in the video and that it is a snuff movie, after which Dexter kills him.

C. Law & Order (SVU)

The *Law & Order: SVU* (*SVU*) episode entitled 'Uncle' ('Sadist' in Germany) opens with the brutal rape and murder of a mother and her young daughter. Their naked bodies are wrapped in clear plastic, both have been strangled, their breasts and genitals bear incision marks and the young girl is positioned holding a crucifix. Detectives Elliot Stabler and Dani Beck from the New York Police Department's (NYPD) Special Victims Unit investigate the crime. Each episode opens with a voice-over stating this NYPD unit investigates 'sexually based offences' which are considered to be 'especially heinous'. The NYPD: SVU includes various specially-trained professionals, including detectives and other forensic specialists. In most episodes, the unit works closely with a medical examiner, an assistant district attorney and a forensic psychiatrist.

In 'Uncle' the unit's forensic psychiatrist, Dr George Huang, profiles the offender as someone who is aroused by inflicting pain, a sadist. The detectives become interested in a man whose fingerprints were found on an advertisement the murdered woman posted for her daughter's bicycle at a convenience store. This man was jailed as a teenager for rape and kidnapping and his name is Brent Allen Banks. He is in his 30s, well groomed, handsome and fit. Acting on this evidence, Stabler and Beck bring Banks into the police station for questioning. Then, behind the two-way mirror looking into the interrogation room where Banks awaits, Dr Huang prepares the detectives for the interview, proposing a formula of how the suspect will act during questioning. When interviewed, Banks exhibits extreme egotism and smugness, even going so far as to flirt with Detective Beck. The detectives inquire about his sexual preferences, suggesting he engages in s/m with reference to his rape conviction and by producing photographs of bite marks on the complainant's body. Banks responds that the sex was consensual and denies he engages in s/m. He also claims he was wrongly convicted.

During the interview, the detectives psychologically bait Banks into taking a piece of chewing gum left in front of him in the interviewing room. This is a ploy to obtain evidence connecting him with the murders. Once he chews the gum and discards it, they will have the imprint of his bite pattern as evidence, and the idea that he will take the gum is based on his psychological profile as charted out by Dr Huang. This is somehow supposed to reinforce the idea that he is a sadist, that he is a taker who presumes his own superiority. Without Banks' confession, the prosecution relies on two pieces of forensic evidence (ie the fingerprints and the gum). The gum is used during the trial as the primary evidence, presented by the prosecution as matching Banks' teeth, and directly linking him to the injuries on the victims' bodies. Not surprisingly, given such scant evidence, the case is dismissed and Banks escapes conviction. However, at the end of the episode a civilian kills him by pushing him in front of a moving subway train.

V. Dangerous Liaisons: Sadistic Serial Killer Themes

In all three of these violent narratives the offenders are male, and their victims are female. The offenders are all portrayed as serial criminals. There are explicit statements that *Criminal Minds*' Baylor/Battle has murdered multiple people and that he harbours an irrepressible desire to kill. Dexter's targets are mostly serial killers who have preyed on multiple victims. The audience can easily imagine that Jaworski may already be a serial killer, or that he is well on the path to becoming one. Banks has a previous conviction for a violent rape, and the detectives describe him as someone whose criminality is escalating. Several parts of the story indicate that he will go on to kill other women, if he has not already done so.

All three offenders are young (ie in their 30s), Caucasian, single, childless males. They have no familial or intimate relationship with their victims. Although their desires are heterosexual, their sexuality is relocated through the strangeness of sadism. However, sadism is very narrowly defined through these depictions as extremely violent, non-consensual and undesired. The violence is unforeseen by the victim, who is chosen somewhat randomly to satisfy the sadistic and insatiable desires of the offenders. This is an expression of one of the baseline dichotomies that the sadist as serial killer format relies upon. Violence is seen as being foreign from our commonly held idea of sociality, and it is dislocated from the realm of families and intimacy. Moreover, the offenders seem to inflict violence on their victims instead of engaging in intimate relationships. This implies two things; that sadism is a form of violence unrelated to human sexuality and that violence occurs outside of relationships. This reinforces the myth that sadists are grotesquely cruel predators and that violent offenders are strangers who bear no resemblance to men we know (eg husbands, partners, boyfriends, fathers, brothers, uncles, cousins, etc). Yet it is known to those, even only somewhat familiar with studies of violence committed against women, that most female victims of sexual violence are accosted by male members of their own families or men they may otherwise already know prior to the time of the attack.

Although the various justice professionals in these dramas define the offenders as sadists, that sadism they speak of is actually better categorised as extreme violence or torture. None of the offenders name themselves as s/m practitioners. Dexter labels Jaworski as sadistic when he discovers his stash of s/m paraphernalia. However, Jaworski does not see himself as an s/m practitioner. In *SVU*, Detective Stabler says to the offender that many people legitimately engage in s/m, however the offender says he does not. The offenders are all portrayed as egotistical and see themselves as being 'above the law', which in some way explains why they engaged in violence. All three plots imply that the offenders see themselves enacting a masculine right to inflict any degree of violence they so choose upon the female body.[18] Violence is constructed as an extension of gender and sexual desire, albeit pathological desires in their case. Although the violence is criminal and pathological, this is very much a uni-directionally gendered violence. In these episodes, sadistic violence is almost exclusively centred in the masculine domain, and is perpetrated against women and children. While these stories acknowledge women's subjective experiences of violence, they redirect it through the largely hyperbolic mythical figure of the stranger who poses a threat.

The victims are young (ie three of the women are in their 20s or 30s, and the other victim is the young daughter of one of these women). They are unmarried women who have little or no relationship with their attackers. Although the victims are unmarried, they are layered with symbols of heteronormativity. Two of the victims are mothers (the victims in *SVU* and *Dexter*). The other, Penelope Garcia, is looking for a boyfriend (the audience can imagine that she may become a mother later in her life). All of the female victims are Caucasian. Even Penelope Garcia is a Caucasian American who merely acquired a Spanish surname from her stepfather. The victims are law-abiding citizens who contribute to society through employment and/or motherhood. They are portrayed as virtuous females who are harmed by 'bad' men, reflective of Christie's notion of ideal victims.

The female victims are defined around culturally common notions of femininity (ie heteronormative gender tropes like wearing dresses and make-up, having long styled hair and through occupying gendered roles like mother, potential girlfriend/date and sexual object). They display a particular heterosexual and gendered vulnerability by which their attacks are somehow linked to their heterosexuality. That is, all the plots imply that these bodies were victimised/vulnerable because of their gender and that these crimes would not be perpetrated on heterosexual male bodies, or homosexual male or female bodies. Further to this, these narratives imply that women are vulnerable in a particular way, which is directly linked to notions of the dangerous stranger. Female vulnerability is embodied through depictions of violence visited upon the female characters by male strangers (seeking out single, heterosexual women). This reinforces the myth that violence occurs in public and silences the corporeality of most violence which occurs in private spaces.[19]

Sadism is measured through its proximity to death in all three cases. The victims in *Dexter* and *SVU* died as the result of violent acts committed by willful perpetrators. In *Criminal Minds*, the victim was shot intentionally, but pretended to be dead. The plot clearly outlines that the offender intended to kill her. This suggests that death is either

---

[18] Heterosexual s/m case law reflects this masculinist entitlement to the female body, especially amongst married couples and the case of *R v Slingsby* [1995] Crim LR 570. See Houlihan, 'When "No" means "Yes" and "Yes" means Harm' (n 5) for further discussion.

[19] Domestic/family violence rarely appears in crime dramas. There is a domestic/family violence storyline in *Dexter*, involving Dexter's girlfriend and her ex-husband, who is a career criminal and drug user. However, it follows the dichotomisation of victim and offender where the victim is layered with symbols of feminine vulnerability and the offender is positioned as strange. This reinforces the myth that violence comes from the strange and that violent offenders are recognisable by a delinquent, criminal facade.

the intended result or the ultimately aimed at form and outcome of sadism. Sadistic desire is shown as either an uncontrollable desire to kill or an uncontrollable desire for extreme forms of sexual gratification, the pursuit of which results in death. McCosker makes some interesting assertions about s/m in his analysis of the film *Crash*, which includes s/m themes within its plot.[20] He tacitly argues that s/m participants may actually be exploring the limits of living, rather than toying with death. That is, s/m may be about a consensual, mutual exploration of the body's experiences of painful pleasure. At any rate, his thesis highlights the multiple meanings s/m participants may express these inclinations in relationship to, meanings that are in conflict with notions of criminal violence and the violations of the 'other' endemic of these types of crime dramas.

In these television plots, s/m is also often portrayed as a series of acts through which men seek to kill females with whom they have little or no relationship. This aspect of anonymity opens up the group of potential victims to encompass literally almost anybody, and thus creates a limitless supply of victims and opportunities for violence. This simultaneously reinforces the idea that sadism is the expression of an uncontrollably violent desire. Thus, sadists appear as horrifyingly, violent killers who have little self-control. This is in stark contrast to the literature on s/m that emphasises its consensual elements.[21] There is considerable academic literature that describes s/m, gender and sexuality from a more fluid position. These theories are based upon Pat Califia's work that highlighted how the s/m scene and her intimate, sensual experiences were not defined by sex/gender.[22] Further, as mentioned earlier, s/m is often misunderstood as violence and conflated with criminality, and notions of consensuality and mutual pleasure are denied and silenced.

In crime dramas, the sadistic killers engage in acts of violence with 'innocent' bodies in place of the (female) self, who is most often heterosexual and Caucasian. Masochistic partners are displaced in favour of the unsuspecting, unknown victim. This is because masochists may also be construed as strangers. Mainstream audiences may have trouble with masochistic bodies, potentially seeing them as deviant and culpable for their own victimisation because they engaged in deviant desires. These narratives of violence, whether purposely or instinctively, utilise the familiar/strange dichotomy, whereby the heterosexual male body functions as the protector, the heterosexual female body is cast as the victim, and the stranger is the one who performs violent acts. However, the gender roles are exaggerated within these plots, representing extreme notions of femininity and masculinity—feminine bodies are vulnerable and in need of protection, while male bodies are either cruelly violent or protectors. Even given that it could be argued that the character of the sadistic serial killer functions to signal the extreme limits of men's entitlement to women's bodies, these fictions of violence incorrectly locate gendered, heterosexual violence (against women) within

---

[20] A McCosker, 'A Vision of Masochism in the Affective Pain of Crash' (2005) *Sexualities 8, 30–48*.

[21] Houlihan, 'When "No" means "Yes" and "Yes" means Harm' (n 5) and Moser and Kleinplatz, 'Themes of SM Expression' (n 2),

[22] P Califia, 'A Personal View of the History of the Lesbian S/M Community and Movement in San Francisco' in P Califia, *Coming to Power: Writings and Graphics on Lesbian S/M* (Boston, Alyson Publications, 1982). Califia transitioned from female to male in the 1990s, but has written about lesbian sexuality and lesbian s/m sexuality since 1979 (See also P Califia, *What Color is Your Handkerchief: A Lesbian S/M Sexuality Reader* (SAMOIS, 1979) and P Califia, *Lesbian Sadomasochism Safety Manual* (Alyson Books, 1988)).

the boundaries of extreme and unusual assaults. Popular culture imagines violence through the dead bodies of victims and the unknown body of the random, sadistic, homicidal stranger. This situates violence as something that happens elsewhere, while also subsuming these violent expressions in the realm of fantasy. It reconfigures violence as an illusion and improbability.

These exaggerated gender roles clash with the more fluid and playful roles frequently found within actual queer and s/m spaces. For example, bondage, discipline, sadomasochism (BDSM) practices can provide spaces in which to disrupt more traditional gender categories by creating playgrounds that challenge gender norms and recognise gender diversities.[23] These more elaborate gender identities may provide alternate narratives to negotiate intimate relationships. Further, heterosexual, gendered and violent imagery within these television crime dramas are disempowering for men and women alike because they replicate and reinforce notions about abusive gender relationships. The domains of s/m play encompass gender polemics, but also create new ways for individuals to explore their gender and sensuality. For example, Bauer's work puts forth the idea that those who engage in s/m tend to experience increases in 'consciousness around gender identity and social and power relations (especially in regard to gender)'.[24] Normative social and power relations enable violence against women, while s/m creates spaces within which individuals can challenge society's gender norms. Given all this, it becomes clear that television crime dramas largely falsify their narratives of gendered violence and s/m as torture.

S/m represents an erotic transgression.[25] It has also been described as 'the erotics of wounding'.[26] On a superficial level s/m symbolises the confluence of sex and violence. Yet, its complexities extend far beyond the mere mixture of sex and violence, and those who practice it may argue (and often do) that they are exploring psycho-social and cultural discomforts with sensual violence. Upon this point actual s/m practice is made distinct from the s/m killer represented in these crime dramas. S/m is a type of consensual sensuality embodying the expression of complex and intricate, yet highly controlled, desires. This is why s/m should not be classified as criminally violent, for violent crime, by contrast, is non-consensual and uncontrolled.

VI. Closing Credits: Sadistic Serial Killers and the Familiar Criminal Stranger

Sadistic serial killers have recurring roles within crime dramas, especially given that sadism is therein loosely defined around notions of cruelty and torture. This typology of criminality is evidenced repeatedly in television shows like *Criminal Minds*

---

[23] R Bauer, 'Playgrounds and New Territories—The Potential of BDSM Practices to Queer Genders' in Langdridge and Barker (eds), *Safe, Sane and Consensual* (n 2) 175–94.

[24] Ibid 198.

[25] Houlihan, 'When "No" means "Yes" and "Yes" means Harm' (n 5).

[26] J Hearn and V Burr, 'Introducing the Erotics of Wounding: Sex, Violence and the Body' in V Burr and J Hearn (eds), Sex, Violence and the Body: The Erotics of Wounding (Palgrave Macmillan, 2008) 2–3.

and the *CSI* franchises, which often utilise gruesome victim-imagery. The characters referenced in this chapter are highly representative of how villains are contemporarily portrayed in film and television in several ways. Yet, aside from these portrayals of sadistic serial killers embodying the fear of that which is unknown, these characters function, among other things, to blur the boundaries between evilness and desire by making the strange more familiar.

The sadistic serial killer is based on two premises. First, those who inflict violence and torture on their victims are presented through evidence of sadism as a genuine and archived offender typology. Second, these definitions rely on textbook definitions of psychopathology, which results in a one-dimensional construction of criminals as strangers. The sadistic serial killer theme in television crime dramas explores a conglomeration of difference and sameness, with these themes in conflict until the conclusion, where culpability is assigned and the killer becomes emphatically synonymous with the strange. The gaze of the camera continually switches between the normalcy of the suspect body and social, psychological and/or sexual pathology. This is achieved by various techniques, including intertwining the usual with the extraordinary. For example, a suspect may be depicted at work, at home, on a date or doing some other ordinary task which fills the average person's everyday life, but this may be spliced with imagery of the suspect viewing pornography, experiencing social isolation or engaging in criminal activity. But perhaps more importantly, the sadistic serial killer often fulfills the narrative of his culpability by evidencing his absolute and compound evilness through a relationship which signifies an s/m lifestyle. Thus, this labeling of offenders as sadists reinforces their extreme culpability. The innocent victim of the sadist serial killer is a polarised contrast of the offender in many ways—they are a locus for pathos in the narrative, a de-contextualised presentation of hyperbolically pure suffering asserted through the lack of connection between themselves and the perpetrator.

The offenders depicted within the crime dramas analysed here offer a neat characterisation of violent offenders and their culpability. And these depictions have a tendency to deflect our gaze from the more usual cases of violence, which are prosecuted within global legal systems in continuing abundance. These sorts of cases have been widely discussed in the referenced literature on the topic, including domestic/family/intimate partner violence in the United States,[27] the United Kingdom and Canada,[28] as well as in Australia.[29] Popular culture realises its vision of violence through distorted and extreme stories of victimology, through narratives that dislodge the plausibility of gendered, heterosexualised violence enacted by familiar people (a lived experience for many women). Finally, s/m imagery within crime dramas displays little recognition of those consensual practices identified by s/m practitioners. Instead, serials killers are given as extremely violent and cruel predators who inflict torture on random, unknown victims in a manner indicative of involvement in the practice of s/m.

[27] J Belknap and H Potter, 'The Trials of Measuring the "Success" of Domestic Violence Policies' (2005) *Criminology and Public Policy* 4, 559–66.

[28] A Sev'er, M Dawson and H Johnson, 'Lethal and Nonlethal Violence against Women by Intimate Partners: Trends and Prospects in the United States, the United Kingdom and Canada (2004) *Violence Against Women* 10, 563–76.

[29] H Douglas, 'The Criminal Law's Response to Domestic Violence: What's Going On? (2008) *Sydney Law Review* 30, 426–69 and Hunter, 'Law's (Masculine) Violence' (n 1).

LIBRARY, UNIVERSITY OF CHESTER

Index

Note: numbers are filed as if spelt out (eg *24* is under '*24*' as if spelt out as 'twenty-four')

Abbey, Graham 338
abortion 23
Abu Ghraib, prisoner abuse at 382–3, 385, 389
abuse of power 331
access to production, gaining 69–73
acquaintance rape 154–5, 161–3, 171
active audience paradigm 124–5
actor-network theory (ANT) 64–9, 71, 76–7, 84–5
adaptations 403, 405–13, 415
ADR (alternative dispute resolution) 431–7, 439
adversarial process 3, 17, 19, 21–4, 261, 431, 433, 437
advertising 235–6, 362
'affect', concept of 37–9, 50–4
African Charter on Human and Peoples' Rights 384
age 137
Agency and the Spooks, the 383
agenda setting 93–4, 101
aggression 202–4, 255, 257–8, 260–4, 266
al Qaeda 199–200, 203, 206
Alchemy of Race and Rights, the. Williams, Patricia 30–1
Ally McBeal 6, 113, 144, 148, 355, 434–5
alternative dispute resolution (ADR) 9, 431–7, 439
Alterio, Hector 348
altruism 124
Alvares, R 348–9
Amazing Race, the 216
America Alone 336
American Convention on Human Rights 384
American Idol 216
America's Most Wanted 119, 292
America's Psychic Challenge 188
Andenæs, Kristian 265
androids 16–17, 21–32
Anillos de oro see Wedding Rings (Anillos de oro) and divorce in post-Franco Spain
anti-essentialism 24–8
anti-heroes 137–45, 403, 405, 410–11
  see also heroes
Arar, Maher 330
archetypes 82, 444
Arias, Imanol 347–8
Arquette, Patricia 178–9, 183
Asimow, Michael 4, 116–17, 207, 428, 437, 439
Associates, the 425–40
  alternative dispute resolution 9, 431–7, 439
  availability of series, lack of 429–30
  Canada 425–40

costs of litigation 432–3
cultural diversity, guidelines on 432
fairness 434
feminism 434–6
gender 432–7
'Ground Zero' episode 432
images 428–9, 435–6
literature review and methodology 428–30
personal relationships 434
popular culture 428, 430, 439
race 432–3
settlement as a strategy 432–4
United States 429–33, 439
Attorneys of Atocha, assassination of the 349, 351
Atwood, Margaret 311, 325
Ausubel, DP 274
availability of material 3–4, 231, 327, 429–30
Avatar 31–2

'bad apple' explanation for police corruption 64–5, 73–84
'bad barrel' explanation for police corruption 64, 78, 81, 85
bad character evidence in rape trials 154–6, 160–3, 168–72
bailiffs in reality court shows, race and gender of 233–4
Bait-Car 291
Baltimore Sun 364, 373
Banks, Lovell 96
Barker, C 121, 125, 129
Baron, Carla 182
Barrett, Jackie *182*
Barsh, Russell Lawrence 319
Bauer, R 452
behaviourist approach 119–20, 124–5
beliefs
  cultivation theory 88, 89–90, 102, 119–20, 153
  rape evidence rules, TV portrayals of 152–4, 161
  violence and crime, beliefs about increase in 89–90, 119
Bennett, Nigel 331
Berger, R 403
Bergman, Paul 4
Bertinelli, Valerie 179
Bharachua, Rustom 60, 227
Big Brother 216
Biggest Loser, the 216
Birk, E 389
Birk, H 389

'bitch', use of word 140–1, 144
Block-Lieb, Susan 221–2
Boal, Augusto 37
Bódalo, José 348, 357
Bodroghkozy, Aniko 322
Bond, James 386
bondage, discipline, sadomasochism (BDSM) 452
books, noteworthy television and law 5–7
Border, the 311–14, 326–44
  aboriginal insiders 334–5
  American racialisation and white
    supremacy 332–6
  Canada
    identity 313, 328–9
    racial harmony 332–6
    United States justice, comparison with
      311–13, 326–43
    whiteness 335–6, 344
  colonial domination 334
  death penalty 337
  gender 336
  Guantanamo Bay 340–1
  human rights 326, 330–2
  ideology 328, 344–5
  Immigration, Customs and Security 311–13,
    326–43, 344
  individualism of Americans 335
  Latino gangs 342–3, 344
  multiculturalism 334, 339, 344–5
  Muslims 313, 329–32, 339–42, 344–5
  nationalist ideology 328
  'otherness' 313, 336–9
  personal relationships 337–8, 344
  political stakes of televised crime dramas 327–8
  popularity 327
  Public Safety Infrastructure, Americanisation
    of 329–30
  race 313, 329, 332–6, 338–45
  security and human rights, balance
    between 330–2
  September 11, 2001 terrorist attacks 313, 327,
    329, 336–7, 344
  soft power 328–9
  stereotyping 335
  terrorist threats 313, 326–7, 329–33, 336–42, 344
  textual politics 328–9
  ticking time bomb scenario 340
  torture of terrorist suspects 330, 335, 340–2
  United States and Canadian justice, comparison
    between 311–13, 326–43
  xenophobia of Americans 338
  war on terror 313, 342, 344
  white supremacy 332–6
  Wikileaks 327–8
Boston Legal 193
Brando, Marlon *319*
Breaker Morant 21
Bridge, the 73–85
  actor-network theory (ANT) 76–7, 84–5
  aesthetic appeal 82
  'bad apple' explanation for police corruption
    64–5, 73–84

'bad barrel' explanation for police corruption
  64, 78, 81, 85
Canadian/US co-production 64, 73–6,
  79–80, 82–3
CBS Network Executives 74–5, 82–3
CBS Standards & Practices of broadcast
  networks 80, 83
commercial appeal 82
Emergency Task Force, Toronto 79–84
Errors & Omissions insurance 65, 80–2
fictionalising and translations 80, 81–2, 84–5
Flashpoint 77–80
generalisations 81–2
high production values 75
ideology 83
knowledge sources 76–8
local knowledge of policing and police
  corruption 76–7
local newspapers 76–7
locally-made police dramas, watching 76–7
modular narratives 74–5
narratives 74–5
production 64–5
prosocial content 83–4
serial narratives 74–5
showrunners 82
Standards & Practices of broadcast networks
  65, 80, 83–4
technical consultants 76–80
Toronto, Canada 76–82
translations 80, 81–2, 84–5
'Unguarded Moment' episode 76, 84
untried shows 83
Wire, the 74
writers' rooms 75–6, 77–9
Brokeback Mountain 326
Browne, Sylvia 181–2
Buchanan, Ruth 5
Buffy the Vampire Slayer 442
Bull Kovera, Margaret 105
Burgess, Anthony 386
Burkeman, Oliver 367
Burns, Ed 368
Burns, Robert 24
Burr, V 442
Busfield, Steve 367–8
Bush, George W 31, 387, 389
Butler, Judith 328

cable shows *see also* **particular shows**
  (eg *Deadwood*)
  age 137
  'bitch', use of word 140–1, 144
  Closer, the 135–43, 146–8
  Damages 135–48
  DVD sales 143
  economic and market considerations 136,
    143, 147
  feminism 136, 138–47
    post-feminism 145
    second-wave 142, 144–6
    third-wave 140–2, 144–6

format, transformation of 7
gender 135–51, 163
heroes and anti-heroes 138–47
heterosexual femininity 138, 145, 147
identity 7
mainstream TV, impact on 137–8
man-of-action heroes 139–41, 143
masculinity, model of heterosexual 137–8, 145
men, acting like 135–6, 146
network broadcasts to cable, from 7
new images 146–7
norms, reflection of cultural 137
post-feminism 145
public perceptions of lawyers 148
race 163
rape evidence rules, TV portrayals of 163
reconfigured stereotypes 146–7
religion 142
Saving Grace 135–43, 146–8
sexual promiscuity 141–2, 146
stereotyping gender 139–47
Wire, the 83, 362
women legal actors 135–51
Cagney and Lacey 142
Califia, P 451
Callon, Michel 67
Canada *see also Bridge, the; Due South*
actor-network theory (ANT) 69
alternative dispute resolution 431–7, 439
Associates, the 425–40
behind-the-scenes perspective 67
Border, the 311–14, 326–44
colonial domination 334
cultural diversity 432
cultural domination 427, 438–9
death penalty 337
DVD marketing strategies 67
gender 336
human rights 326, 330–2
identity 313, 317, 322, 328–9, 427, 438
ideology 328, 344–5
indigenous people 317–18, 319, 322,
 334–5, 343
justice, difference between US and Canadian
 311–13, 326–43
multiculturalism 334, 339, 344–5
Muslims 313, 329–32, 339–42, 344–5
national identity 313, 317, 322, 328–9, 427, 438
news programmes 438
'otherness' 313, 336–9
private broadcasters 427–8, 432
productions, access to 70–2
public broadcasters 427–8
race 313, 317–20, 329, 332–6, 338–45
September 11, 2001 terrorist attacks 313, 327,
 329, 336–7, 344
simulcasting 427–8
stereotyping 335
superhero 314–17
terrorist threats 313, 326–7, 329–33, 336–42, 344
Til Debt Do Us Part 211–27
torture of terrorist suspects 330, 335, 340–2

United States
 Border, the 331–6
 difference from Canadian TV 426–8, 437–9
 justice, difference from Canadian 311–43
 September 11, 2001 terrorist attacks 313, 327,
  329, 336–7, 344
 terrorist threats 313, 326–7, 329–33,
  336–42, 344
 viewers, lack of 426–7, 437–8
 whiteness 318, 319, 332–6, 343–4
Cape Fear 301
capital, concentration and circulation of 65
capital punishment 320–1, 337
Chambers, Ross 319
Changing Images of Law in Film and Television.
 Lenz, T 115–16
character of defendant rules in rape trials 154–6,
 160–3, 168–72
Chertoff, Michael 387
child abuse *see To Catch a Predator*
Chomsky, Noam 63–4
Christie, N 445–6
cinema *see* film
Citizens United v Federal Election Commission 32
civil liberties *see* **rights of suspects/defendants**
civil rights era 30
Claire 179
Clarke, Jonathan 336
class 235–6
Clementi, Tyler 298
Clinton, Bill 206
Clockwork Orange, A 386
Close, Glenn 137, 144
Closer, the 135–43, 146–8
Cobussen, Marcel 376
Codrington, Jim 333
Cohen, Jonathan 434–5
cold cases 175, 178, 180, 181
Cole, Simon 100
colonialism and imperialism
 Border, the 334
 Canada 318, 319, 334, 343
 culture 36
 Deadwood 34–5, 38–43, 45, 49, 54, 60–1
 discursive formations 35–6
 Due South 318, 319, 343
 'empire of force' 34, 36
 free trade (informal and interactive)
  imperialism 35–6
 indirect colonial rule 35
 inequality, persistence of 35
 literature 36
 postcolonial scholarship 35
 replication imperialism 35, 43
 strategies 35
 United States
  Canada 318, 319, 334, 343
  Deadwood 34–5, 38–43, 45, 49, 54, 60–1
  Due South 318, 319, 343
  Wire, the 371–2
 Wire, the 371–2
commercials 235–6, 362

community spirit 315–16
comparative law 2
compassion 278–9, 315–16, 33
concentration, levels of 272
confidence in legal system
    Dexter and the serial killer 404–5, 411, 418–19
    gender 141, 148
    judges in reality TV in Germany 252, 259, 262–6
    psychic detective effect 175, 180–1, 185–6
    rape evidence rules 163, 165, 167–8, 172
    technicalities, defendants' getting off on 175,
        177, 181, 187
conformity 412
Conradt, Louis 291, 294, 298, 304
consciousness, recognition of legal 128
conservatives
    United States, growth of right in 6
    Wedding Rings and divorce in post-Franco Spain
        348, 350–1, 354, 356, 359
constitutional rights *see* rights of
    suspects/defendants
consumerism 212, 217–18, 221, 227
consumption 212, 224–5
content analysis 8, 63, 84, 89, 97, 103–6, 114, 117–21
COPS 119, 292, 296
Corcos, Christine 138–9, 144, 146
corporations, rights of 15–16, 32
corruption and illegality *see also* **torture of terrorist
    suspects in United States; 24 (TV series)**
    and torture
    'bad apple' explanation 64–5, 73–84
    'bad barrel' explanation 64, 78, 81, 85
    Bridge, the 64–5, 73–85
    illegally-founded communities 40–1, 43
    Wire, the 372–7
costs of litigation 432–3
Cougar, John 442
court reality TV *see* **reality TV judges; reality TV
    judges in Germany**
Court TV 148
Cover, Carol 19
Crash 451
Cra$h and Burn 73
credibility of reality TV judges 277–80, 282–3, 287
'crime scripts' 104–5
Crime Stories 115
Criminal Court, the (Strafgericht, Das) 257–8
criminal justice system *see* **confidence in legal system**
Criminal Minds 406, 441, 444, 446, 447, 449–53
critical discourse analysis 126
cross-examination of rape victims 154–72
Crucible, the. Miller, Arthur 16
CSI 74, 93, 95, 98–101, 104–5, 118, 174, 453
'CSI effect' 98–101
    acquittal rates 100
    anti-prosecution effect 99–100
    empirical research on law and justice 98–101
    fact, as being turned into 101
    forensic evidence 98–101
    jurors 98–101
    media coverage 101
    myth, as 98–101, 118

'Perry Mason syndrome' 98–9
    pro-prosecution effect 100–1
    quantitative analysis 118
cultivation theory 88, 89–90, 102, 119–20, 153
culture *see also* **popular culture**
    Canada 427, 432, 438–9
    colonialism and imperialism 36
    cultural capital, mobilising 71–3
    Deadwood 40, 60–1
    Dexter and the serial killer 405, 410, 414
    diversity 432
    empirical study of audiences 120, 124
    ethnography 67–9, 84–5, 112–13, 120–9
    femininity 450
    film 4–5
    gender 137
    identity 124
    Judge Judy 213
    judges on reality TV in Germany 252
    neoliberalism 213, 226–7
    norms, reflection of cultural 137
    productions, gaining access to 71–3
    serial killers 405, 410, 414, 441–4, 446–7,
        450, 452
    Til Debt Do Us Part 212, 226–7
    torture of terrorist suspects 388–9
    United States 40, 60–1, 427, 438–9
    victimology 446
Culture and Imperialism. Said, Edward 36

Damages 6, 103, 135–48
Darkly Dreaming Dexter 407, 416
Daskal, Jennifer 200
de Waal, Frans 28
Deadwood 33–61
    'affect', concept of 39, 50–4
    cinematic technique 50–4, 60
    colonialism 34–5, 38–43, 45, 49, 54, 60–1
    counting coup 55–7
    cultural imaginings 40, 60–1
    economy 39–43, 59
    feeling, structure of 54–60
    forgetting, politics of 60
    frontier myth 39
    genocide 38–9, 44–54, 60
    illegally founded community, as 40–1, 43
    implantation of settlers 40
    indigenous people 38–60
    justice 42, 59
    law, absence of 41–3, 54–60
    market, law of the 42–3
    national identity 60
    natural law 42–3
    replication imperialism 43
    re-visualising law 54–60
    self-defence, use of force in 53–4, 57–8
    seriality, place of 39, 44–50
    sexual violence 47
    structure of feeling 41
    violence 34–5, 39–60
    Western genre, place in 39–44
death penalty 320–1, 337

defendants, rights of *see* **rights of suspects/defendants**
Defender, the 5
Defenders 3
deontology 201, 321–2
Dershowitz, Alan 385
Devane, William 390
deviance 412–13, 444–5
Dewey, John 26
Dexter **and the serial killer** 403–23, 441, 444, 447–51
  adaptations 403, 405–13, 415
  anti-hero, Dexter as an 403, 405, 410–11
  'Bay Harbor Butcher' 418
  childhood trauma as explanation 415–16, 447
  confidence in criminal justice system 404–5, 411, 418–19
  conformity 412
  control, limits of 420–1
  conventions 408–9
  culture 405, 410, 414
  'Dark Passenger' 404, 415, 416, 419
  '*Darkly Dreaming Dexter*' novel 407, 416
  deviance, labelling of 412–13
  'Dexter' episode 446, 447–51
  discovery, fear of 413
  disruptions of normality 420–1
  drug abuse 418–19
  engaging the audience 407–9
  ethnic communities, effects of crime on 404, 411
  family man, Dexter as a 417, 419–21
  forensics expert, Dexter as 403–4, 411, 414, 416–18
  genre 405–9, 412, 421
  good/evil dichotomy 416, 418–19
  'Harry's Code' 409, 412, 413–14, 417, 419–21, 447–8
  high-IQ killers 410–11, 413, 414, 418
  'Ice Truck Killer' 416–17
  identification with other killers 421
  justification 404, 409, 412, 415, 417
  kindred spirits 419–20
  mental illness 417
  moral judgments 404, 411–13, 416–17, 421–2
  narrator, Dexter as 404–8
  neutralisation, techniques of 412
  'ordinary man' persona 414–15
  'otherness' 404
  personal relationships 404, 406–7, 417–19
  rationality of serial killers 412–13
  rituals of killings 405, 414, 415–16
  sadistic serial killers 441, 444, 446, 447–51
  serial format 404, 406, 408, 411
  signatures of killers 404, 406–7, 410
  social anxiety 404
  social disadvantaged, effects of crime on 404, 411
  theology 416
  'Trinity' 420–1
  victim selection process 413–14
  victimology 446

  vigilante, serial killer as a 403–5, 410, 414–22
  visions of violence 411–13
  women, effects of crime on 411
Dickens, Charles 44, 46
Diosdado, Ana 347–9
Dioso-Villa, Rachel 100
discrimination and inequality *see also* **gender; race**
  colonialism and imperialism 35
  Irish, against the 368–71
  Wire, the 368–71
Dispute at 3pm (Streit um Drei) 253–4, 256, 257
divorce *see* *Divorce Court; Wedding Rings (Anillos de oro)* **and divorce in post-Franco Spain**
Divorce Court 231, 233–7, 241
documentary viewers, reality TV viewers compared with 272–4
doing law and television scholarship, methods of 7
domestic abuse 240, 441–2, 444–5, 449–50, 453
Douthit, Randy 279
Dowd, Nancy 147
Dowler, K 445–6
Drop Dead Diva 188
drug abuse 418–19
drug dealers 365, 372–4
DSM-IV 443–4
DuBois, Allison 182–6
due process *see* **rights of suspects/defendants**
Due South 69, 311–26
  aboriginal insiders 317–18, 319, 322, 334, 343
  arms smuggling 319–21
  Canada
    Canadian Superhero 314–17
    identity 317, 322
    United States justice, comparison with 311–26, 329, 331, 343
    whiteness 318, 319, 343
  colonial oppression 318, 319, 343
  community spirit 315–16
  compassion 315–16, 330
  death penalty 320–1
  deontological versus utilitarian approach to crime fighting 321–2
  gender 316
  guns, carrying 316, 319–21, 332
  heterosexuality 322–6
  homoeroticism 323–6, 343
  individualism of Americans 315, 320
  music riders of RCMP 320
  nature lovers 317–18, 325
  'otherness' 313, 322, 326, 336–7, 343
  personal relationships 322–6, 343
  popularity 314, 327
  queering the Canadian nation 322–6, 343
  race 317–18, 319–20, 332–3
  Royal Canadian Mounted Police 311–15, 320, 323
  September 11, 2001 terrorist attacks 313–26
  sex appeal 316, 331
  stereotypes 314, 316, 317–18
  Superhero 314–17
  United States and Canadian justice, comparison between 311–26, 329, 331, 343

utilitarian versus deontological approach to
   crime fighting 321–2
war on terror 313
whiteness of Canadians 318, 319, 343
white supremacists 319–20, 332–3
Dunwoody, Philip T 103, 118
Dupont, Benoit 100
Durkheim, Emile 254, 259
DVD marketing strategies 66–7
Dyer, R 319

economic and market considerations 136, 143, 147
education *see* **legal education**
Elkins, James 4
empathy 28, 29, 242, 278–9
'empire of force' 34, 36
empirical research 106 *see also* **law and justice,
   empirical research on TV depictions of;
television audiences, role of empirical methodology
   in exploring**
engaging the audience 274–6, 407–9
entrapment 292, 300, 302–5
epistemology 64, 201
Erickson, H 287–8
Errors & Omissions insurance 65, 80–2
essentialism 24–30
Estrich, Susan 154
ethics/morality
   content analysis 97
   deontology 201, 321–2
   Dexter and the serial killer 404, 411–13,
      416–17, 421–2
   empirical research 96–8, 117–18
   judges on reality TV in Germany 259, 263–6
   law students 96–7
   moral panics 442–4
   moral relativism 385
   sadomasochism 442–4
   terrorism thrillers 193–202
   torture of terrorist suspects 385
ethnographic research 67–9, 84–5, 112–13, 120–9
European Convention on Human Rights 384
evidence *see* **rape evidence rules, TV portrayals of
evil/good dichotomy** 363–4, 416, 418–19
Ewick, Patrick 18

facial expressions 28
Fairly Legal 6
familiar people as perpetrators 441–2, 444–5,
   449–50, 453
fear, appeals to 286–7
feeling, structure of 54–60
feminism
   Associates, the 434–6
   cable shows 136, 138–47
   post-feminism 145
   second-wave 142, 144–6, 434–5
   third-wave 140–2, 144–6
   Wedding Rings and divorce in post-Franco
      Spain 355–6
femininity 138, 145, 147, 450
fictionalising and translations 80, 81–2, 84–5

film
   access to productions 70–1
   'affect', notion of 37–8
   cinematic medium, focus on 37
   decline in cinema-going 2
   'film-as-law' approach 4–5
   law and film scholarship 1–2, 35, 36–8
   'law-in-film' approach 4
   legal culture beyond film 4–5
   narrative structure 36–8
   reader/response spectatorship 36–8
   rhetorical power of film 4–5
financial literacy 211–13, 218–27
firearms, carrying 316, 319–21, 332
Fischlin, Daniel 371–2, 376
Fiske, John 212, 225, 312, 366, 389
Flashpoint 77–80, 83
Fleming, T 445–6
Flockhart, Calista 355
focus groups 122–5
Fogelbach, Juan 342–3
forensic evidence, 'CSI effect' on 98–101, 118
forgetting, politics of 60
Frain, James 393
framing 91–2, 101, 104
Franco, Franscisco 351–2, 354
Frankenstein. **Shelley, Mary** 16
Franklin, John 325
**free trade (informal and interactive)
   imperialism** 35–6
freedom of speech and corporations 32
freedom of the press 292, 297–8, 305
Friedman, Lawrence 1, 18
Friedman, Thomas 31
Friends 137
frontier myth 39

Galiardo, Juan Luis 348
game shows 212, 216, 276
Garci, José Luis 348
gay and lesbian people 32, 219, 322–6, 343
gender
   age 137
   Associates, the 432–7
   bailiffs in judge reality TV shows 233
   'bitch', use of word 140–1, 144
   Border, the 336
   cable shows 7, 135–51
   Closer, the 135–43, 146–8
   commercials 235–6
   confidence in legal system 141, 148
   cultural tropes of femininity 450
   Damages 135–48
   Dexter and the serial killer 411
   Due South 316
   economic and market considerations 136,
      143, 147
   empirical study of audiences 114–15
   feminism 136, 138–47, 355–6, 434–6
   femininity 138, 145, 147, 450
   guns, carrying 316
   heroes and anti-heroes 138–47

heterosexuality 137–8, 145, 147
    ideal victims 445–6
    judges on reality TV 96, 230, 232–8
    mainstream TV, impact on 137–8
    man-of-action heroes 139–41, 143
    masculinity, model of heterosexual 137–8, 145
    men, acting like 135–6, 146
    new images 146–7
    norms, reflection of cultural 137
    personal relationships 6, 135
    post-feminism 145
    psychic detective effect 179
    public perceptions of lawyers 148
    race 445–6
    reconfigured stereotypes 146–7
    religion 142
    role models 355
    Saving Grace 135–43, 146–8
    self-determination 355–6
    serial killers 411, 441–52
    sexual promiscuity 141–2, 146
    social context 4
    stereotyping gender 139–47
    United States 336
    Wedding Rings and divorce in post-Franco
        Spain 353–6
generalisations 81–2
Geneva Conventions 384
genocide 38–9, 44–54, 60
Germany see reality TV judges in Germany
Gerritsen, Tess 143
Ghost Whisperer 173–4, 176, 179, 188, 192
Gideon v Wainwright 175
Gies, L 116, 128
Gilbert, Reid 314
Gilliam, Franklin D 104
Giroux, Henry 60
Gittings, Christopher 318
Giuliani, Rudy 382
Gladwell, Malcolm 241–2
Glaser, Barney 128
Glos, GE 350
Goldberg, Whoppi 29
good/evil dichotomy 363–4, 416, 418–19
Good Wife, the 261
Goodman, Douglas 19
Greenfield, S 114
Grid, the 193, 197, 200, 207
Gross, Karen 221–3
Gross, Paul 314
Guantanamo Bay 199–200, 340–1, 382, 385, 389
guns, carrying 316, 319–21, 332

Hall, Michael C 404, 408
Hall, Stuart 18, 124–5
Hallstein, D 146
Halper, Stefan A 336
Haltom, William 18
Hamdan v Rumsfeld 200
Hansen, Chris 289–300, 303, 305
Harper's Magazine 298–9
Harris, Thomas 410

Hartley, John 328
heavy viewing of reality TV, effects of 272–4
Heble, Ajay 371–2, 376
hegemony 371–2
Heirens, William 415
hemispheric lateralisation 272
Herman, Edward S 65–6
hermeneutics 125–6
heroes 137–45, 314–17, 347, 349, 352–7 see also
    anti-heroes
Herz, Ruth 256–8, 261, 267
heteronormavity 450
heterosexuality
    Due South 322–6
    femininity 138, 145, 147
    gender in cable shows 138, 145, 147
    homoeroticism 323–6, 343
    nuclear families 219–21
    sadistic serial killers 441, 447, 449–52
heuristics 90–1, 119
Hewitt, Jennifer Love 178–9
high involvement tactics 274–6
high-IQ killers 410–11, 413, 414, 418
Hill Street Blues 5
Historia de la television en España. Palacio,
    Manuel 351–2
historical approach to production study 65, 66–7
Hobbes, Thomas 42
Holder, Eric 200
Holmes, Su 215–16
homosexuals 32, 219, 322–6, 343
Hornbeck, Shawn 181
Hostel series 386
Hron, Madelaine 383, 386
human rights see also rights of suspects/defendants
    Border, the 326, 330–2
    Canada 326, 330–2
    contested legal rights 17
    corporations, rights of 15–16, 32
    freedom of speech and corporations 32
    human, what qualifies as 17, 20, 22–4
    security and human rights, balance
        between 330–2
    Star Trek: the Next Generation episode
        'The Measure of a Man' 17, 20
    torture 341, 384
    treaties and conventions 341, 384
    United States 326, 330–2
human, what qualifies as 15–17, 20–32
    androids 16–17, 21–32
    anti-essentialist model 24–8
    empathy 28, 29
    facial expressions 28
    human rights 17, 20, 22–4
    racial subordination 29–31
    rights-bearing status 17, 20, 22–4
    sentience, principle of 16, 22, 24–5, 29
    slavery analogy 20, 23, 27, 29–31
    Star Trek: the Next Generation episode
        'The Measure of a Man' 15–17, 20–32
    visualisation 28
Hume, Brit 382, 396

Hunter, Holly 137
Hurricane 443
Hurricane Katrina 31
Hurts So Good 442

ideal victims 444–6
idealism 279
identity
    Canada 313, 317, 322, 328–9, 427, 438
    cultural identity 124
    Deadwood 60
    Due South 317, 322
    national identity 9, 60, 313, 317, 322, 328–9,
        427, 438
ideology
    actor-network theory (ANT) 64, 67–8
    Border, the 328, 344–5
    Bridge, the 83
    Canada 83, 328, 334–5
    content analysis 63
    definition 63
    empirical study of audiences 114–15,
        118, 128
    epistemological question, as 64
    justice 63
    knowledge, as 67–8
    nationalism 328
    neoliberalism 213, 224–7
    production 63–4
    reception 63–4
    sources 64
    Standards & Practices of broadcast
        networks 83
    Til Debt Do Us Part 212–13, 224–7
    torture of terrorist suspects 382, 389
    Wire, the 83
Ignatieff, Michael 385
illegality *see* corruption and illegality; torture of
    terrorist suspects in United States; *24* (TV series)
    and torture
images 428–9, 435–6
immigration, customs and security 311–13,
    326–43, 344
impartiality of reality TV judges 243
imperialism *see* colonialism and imperialism
Imperialism and Civic Freedom. Tully, Jim 35–6
implantation of settlers 40
improvisation 361–2, 365–8, 370–7
indigenous people
    Border, the 334–5
    Canada 317–18, 319, 322, 334–5, 343
    Deadwood 38–60
    Due South 317–18, 319, 322, 334, 343
    genocide 39, 47–8, 60
    law, absence of 54–6
individualism 315, 320, 335
insurance 65, 80–2
International Covenant on Civil and Political
    Rights 384
interrogations *see* torture of terrorist suspects in
    United States
Investigative Report: Cybersex Cops 292

Irish people
    discrimination 368–71
    improvisation 372
    Irish-American cops 361–2, 368–72, 377
    Potato Famine 368–9
    stereotypes 368–70
    Wire, the 361–2, 368–72, 377
Islam *see* Muslims
Iyengar, Shanto 104

Jacobson, Keith 304
Jama Scheerer 259
Jarvis, Robert M 5
Jermyn, Deborah 215–16
Jiwani, Yasmin 328–9, 335
Johnson, Rebecca 5
Jordan v Johnson 278
Joseph, Paul R 5
Judge Alex 230, 231–4, 236, 239, 241, 246
Judge Christina 95
Judge Hatchett 95, 231–8, 245
Judge Joe Brown 95, 231, 233, 236, 240–1
Judge Judy 229–38, 271–88
    bailiff, race and gender of 233
    clarity 19
    commercials 235–6
    competence 277–8, 283
    complaints 245
    credibility 277–80, 282–3, 287
    cultural support for neoliberal regulatory
        project, as 213
    demographics of watchers 280
    direct gaze 281–2
    empathy and compassion 278–9
    eye contact 282
    fairness 243
    fear, appeals to 286–7
    gallery members 282
    game shows, comparison with 276
    German equivalents 253, 256
    idealism 279
    impartiality 243
    jurors, effect on 118, 245
    justice 272
    knowledge rehearsal 276
    legal education 279–80
    mathemagenic strategies 275
    message design approach 8, 272
    nonverbal communication 280–4
    number of cases heard 231
    organisation structure 274
    overview of cases at beginning of episodes 274
    passive learning 276
    perception of judge's behaviour 95, 148, 245,
        277–87
    personality of judge 229, 243, 245–6, 277–87
    persuasion 277–87
    popularity 19, 229, 280, 287–8
    psycholinguistic pauses 276
    race 232, 235
    simplification 19
    teasers 274–5

trustworthiness 278
visual practices 276–7
Judge Mathis 231–4, 236, 239, 244–5
Judge Nancy 245–6
Judge Pirro 231–40, 242–3
judges *see Judge Judy;* reality TV judges;
    reality TV judges in Germany
Judging Amy 6
Jugendgericht, Das (the Juvenile Court) 256–8, 267
Jungians 82
juror decision-making and verdicts 98–105
    African-Americans and Latinos as criminals 104
    'crime scripts' 104–5
    'CSI effect' 98–101
    empirical research 98–105, 118
    Judge Judy 118, 245
    judges on reality TV 118, 244–5
    Oprahisation 99
    'Perry Mason syndrome' 98–9
    pre-trial publicity 105
    psychic detective effect 177, 190–2
    rape 105
justice and law 87–110
    African-Americans and Latinos as criminals 104
    agenda setting 93–4, 101
    approaches to research 88–92
    audiences, empirical study of 122–3
    'crime-scripts' 104–5
    'CSI effect' 98–101
    cultivation theory 88, 89–90, 102, 119–20
    Deadwood 42, 59
    empirical study 87–110
    ethical or moral, perceptions as to whether
        judges are 96–8
    factual legal knowledge 101–2
    formats 88
    framing 91–2, 101, 104
    genre-specific viewing 90
    heuristic processing 90–1
    ideology 63
    impact of TV's depictions of law 92–106
    importance of TV to law 88
    improvisation 361–2, 370–6
    judges on reality TV 95–6, 119, 272
    Judge Judy 272
    juror decision-making and verdicts 98–105
    Kantian/Rawlsian model 24
    law students, impact on 96
    limitations of empirical study 105–6
    Miranda warnings, popular knowledge of 102
    modelling behaviour 102–3
    norms 92–3, 102–3
    psychic detective effect 176–7, 180–1, 185–6,
        188, 192
    public ideas of justice 122–3
    social justice 6, 18, 32, 356
    socialisation 88, 92–3, 103
    Star Trek: the Next Generation episode
        'The Measure of a Man' 24–8
    violent crime, disproportionate coverage of
        94, 119
    Wire, the 361–2, 370–6

Juvenile Court, the (Jugendgericht, Das)
    256–8, 267
juvenile crime, perceptions of 119

Kahn, Jeremy 364–5
Kant, Immanuel 24–6
Katyal, Neal 200
Keating, CF 280–1
Keep America Safe 199–200
Kellner, Douglas 388–9
King, Martin Luther 30
King, Tom 61
Kitchener, Herbert 21
Kleinplatz, PJ 442
knowledge *see also* legal education
    actor-network theory (ANT) 67–8
    Bridge, the 76–8
    corruption, local knowledge of 76–8
    empirical research on law and justice 101–2
    factual legal knowledge 101–2
    ideology, as 67–8
    Miranda warnings 102
    rehearsal 276
    sources 76–8
Kohl, Helmut 256
Kohts, Nadia 28
Königlich-Bayerisches Amtsgericht (The Royal
    Bavarian Magistrates' Court) 252–3, 266
Kunen, James 199

LA Law 1, 3, 5, 6, 97, 144, 161–5, 193
Larry King Live 178, 181
Latinos
    Border, the 342–3, 344
    lawbreakers and criminals, as 104
Latour, Bruno 67–8, 76
law, absence of 41–3, 54–60
law and film scholarship 35, 36–8
law and justice *see* justice and law
Law and Justice As Seen on TV. Rapping,
    Elayne 6, 115
Law and Order 5, 6, 19, 95, 97–8, 103–5, 113,
    118–20, 141, 148, 160–1, 193, 444
Law and Order: SVU 167–8, 441, 444, 446–51
law in culture studies 2–3
'law-in-film' approach 4
Law, John 67
Lawyers in Your Living Room! Television Lawyers.
    Asimow, Michael 207
legal education
    altruism 124
    Judge Judy 279–80
    empirical research 96, 122–4, 126
    ethical or moral, perceptions as to whether
        judges are 96–7
    ethnography 122–4
    Germany, judges on reality TV in 253,
        256, 258–63
    identity of law students 122–4, 126
    judges on reality TV 238–42, 253, 256,
        258–63, 279–80
    passive learning 272, 276

perpetrators, on 260
Star Trek: the Next Generation episode
  'The Measure of a Man' 21–4
victimisation, on 260
legal system *see* **confidence in legal system**
legitimacy of law, undermining the 120
Lenz, T 115–16
Leroux, C 278
lifestyle programming 212, 216
Limbaugh, Rush 387
Lindh, John Walker 205, 206
Lindsay, Jeff 403–4, 407–8, 410–11, 414–16
litigation crisis, perception of 18
'litigation lottery' 94
Locke, John 42
Loeffler, Charles 100
Lokaneeta, Jinee 341
loyalty 24–8, 31–2

Macaulay, Stewart 1, 18, 121
Machura, Stefan 265
Mackey, Eva 335
man-of-action heroes 139–41, 143
Marciano, David 314
Marek, Joan Gershen 434
marriage 219–21
Marshall-Green, Logan 391
Marston, Isaac 303
Marx, Gisela 256
masculinity
  cable shows, gender in 135–41, 143, 146
  heroes 137–45
  man-of-action heroes 139–41, 143
  men, acting like 135–6, 145
Marxism 65
Masó, Pedro 348
Massie, Sonja 369
Matlock 5
Matza, D 412
Mazzariello, Michael 232–6, 244–5
McCabe, Debra 331
McCann, Michael 18
McCarthyism 19
McCosker, A 451
McDermott, Dylan 197
McGowan, James 320
McMillan, A 364, 375
McVeigh, Timothy 332
meanings, making of 112, 124–6
Measure of a Man, the see Measure of a Man, the.
  King, Martin Luther; *Star Trek: the Next*
  Generation episode 'The Measure of a Man'
Measure of a Man, the. **King, Martin Luther** 30
Medium 173–4, 176, 179, 182–92
memory systems 272–4
men *see* **gender; masculinity**
Menkel-Meadow, Carrie 97, 433
mental illness 417
Merleau-Ponty, Maurice 28
message design approach 8, 272
Meyer, P 117
Miami Vice 38

Michael Clayton 144
Milano, Ramona 325
Milch, David 39–41
Milian, Marilyn 233–4, 236, 238–40
Miller, Arthur 16
Miller, Nancy 147
Miranda **warnings** 102, 175, 202, 203–4, 205
Mitchell, WJT 428–30, 435–6, 439
mob rule 21
Mohammed, Khalid Sheikh (KSM) 202–3
modelling behaviour 102–3
Monaca, J 407
Montel Williams Show 181–2
Montemurro, Beth 216, 221
Moore, Michael 198
morality *see* **ethics/morality**
Morgan, Jason 322, 343
Morley, D 121
Morrison, Katherine L 317
Moser, C 442
Moussaoui, Zacarias 205–7
Moynihan, DP 369
multiculturalism 334, 339, 344–5
Murder One 5
Murray, Catherine 432
Murray, Susan 215
Muslims
  Border, the 313, 329–32, 339–42, 344–5
  Canada 313, 329–32, 339–42, 344–5
  United States 313, 329–32, 339–42, 344–5
Muzzatti, SL 445–6

national identity 9, 60, 313, 317, 322, 328–9, 427, 438
national security *see* **terrorism thrillers; torture of**
  terrorist suspects in United States; *24* **(TV series)**
  and torture
nationalist ideology 328
Natural Born Killers 386
natural law 42–3
naturalisation of torture 388–9, 393
NCIS 83
negative characterisation of defence lawyers 7,
  193–204, 207, 394–7
neoliberalism 213, 224–7
Newcomb, Horace 388
Neumann, Guido 253–5
neutralisation 412
New York v Quarles 204
New York Times 31
9 ½ Weeks 442
nonverbal communication 28, 280–4
normalisation of torture 382, 386, 388–9, 398
norms 92–3, 102–3, 137
noteworthy television and law books 5–7
nuclear families 219–21
NYPD Blues 5

Obama, Barack 31, 200, 328
Obregón, Ana 357
O'Connell, Patrick 365
O'Connor, Sandra Day 234–5
Oleson, J 410

Oprah 99, 271, 299
'ordinary man' persona 414–15
Osborn, G 114
O'Sullivan, Sean 46
'otherness'
   Border, the 313, 336–9
   Dexter and the serial killer 404
   Due South 313, 322, 326, 336–7, 343
   serial killers 404, 445
Ouellette, Laurie 215
Owen Marshall Counselor at Law 157–60
Owen, Paul 367

Pacheco v Googins 286
Palacio, Manuel 351–2
Papendorf, Knut 265
Paper Chase 5
paranormal *see* psychic detective effect
Paranormal Cops 174, 191
Parrilla, Lana 393
Park, Grace 338
passive learning 272, 276
past sexual history of victims, cross-examination
   on 154–72
Peckham, Morse 24
Penn & Teller 182
People's Court 231, 233–4, 236, 238–40, 253
perceptions of lawyers *see* public perceptions
   of lawyers
Perks, Lisa Glabatis 217
Perloff, RM 277–8
Perry Mason 5, 98–9, 198, 261
'Perry Mason syndrome' 98–9
personal relationships *see also Wedding Rings
   (Anillos de oro)* and divorce in post-Franco
Spain
   Associates, the 434
   Border, the 337–8, 344
   Dexter and the serial killer 404, 406–7, 417–19
   Divorce Court 231, 233–7, 241
   Due South 322–6, 343
   gender 6, 135
   judges in reality TV 231, 233–7, 240–1, 275, 282
   LA Law 6
   serial killers 404, 406–7, 417–19, 449–52
   Star Trek: the Next Generation episode
     'The Measure of a Man' 20, 28
   Til Debt Do Us Part 213–16, 219, 221
   24 (TV series) 398
   Wire, the 377
personality of reality TV judges 8, 95, 229,
   243–6, 277–87
Petrocelli 3
Phil Donahue 99
Picart, C 419
Picket Fences 5
Plato 26
pleasure/pain nexus 442–3
Podlas, Kimberlianne 99, 101, 118–21
Poirier Greenfield, Leanne 335
police procedurals 74, 77, 79, 88, 203, 364–5, 408
Police Woman 142

political economy approach to production study
   65–6, 68–9
political stakes of crime dramas 327–8
Ponte, Maria Luisa 348, 357
popular culture
   Associates, the 428, 430, 439
   cult TV 17
   empirical study of audiences 111–29
   interest, growth in 6–7
   law in culture studies 2–3
   object of study, TV as own 2
   perceptions of law 1
   representations of legal practice 17–21
   sadistic serial killers 441
Porsdam, Helle 253–4
Potato Famine 368–9
Powers v Powers 285
Practice, the 113, 115, 148, 165–9, 193, 434
pre-trial publicity 105
primates, facial expressions of 28
Prime Time 300
Prime Time Law. Jarvis, Robert M and Joseph,
   Paul R 5
prisoner abuse at Abu Ghraib and Guantanamo
   Bay 382–3, 385, 389
private facts, publication of 292, 296–302, 305
production study
   access, gaining 69–73
   actor-network theory (ANT) 65, 67–9, 71
   behind-the-scenes perspective 66–7
   being in the right place at the right time 70–1
   'big picture', focusing on the 66
   Canada 70–2
   capital, concentration and circulation of 65
   cultural capital, mobilising 71–3
   day-to-day practices of journalism and media
     production 66
   DVD marketing strategies 66–7
   established versus untried dramas 70–1
   ethnographic research 67–9
   historical approach 65, 66–7
   Marxism 65
   movies-of-the-week versus television dramas 70
   political economy approach 65–6, 68–9
   propaganda model of mass media 65–6
   service productions versus original
     productions 70
   untried dramas, access to 70–1, 72
propaganda model of mass media 65–6
psychic detective effect 173–92
   accused, fears on protection of rights of 175,
     180–1, 185–6
   best evidence rule 177
   camera, investigative function of the 176
   certainty, attraction of 176, 180
   cold cases 175, 178, 180, 181
   common claims 177–83
   confidence in legal system 175, 180–1, 185–6
   constitutional protections/rights of suspects 175,
     180–1, 186–7
   gender 179
   genetic, psychic skills as 184

Ghost Whisperer 173–4, 176, 179, 188, 192
jurors 177, 190–2
justice 176–7, 180–1, 185–6, 188, 192
law enforcement agencies use of psychics
    177–8, 182–92
loners/outsiders 176, 180
Medium 173–4, 176, 179, 182–92
    'Allison Rolen Got Married' episode 187
    'In Sickness and Adultery' episode 185–6
Paranormal Cops 174, 191
popularity, reasons for 7, 192
presentation of psychic claims 183–91
Psychic Detectives 174, 182, 188, 192
Psychic Witness 174
reality shows 174, 182–3, 191–2
sceptical third parties 179–80, 184, 187
scientific evidence 7, 174
standard of proof 174
technicalities 175, 177, 181, 187
tricks of defence attorneys 175
truth 7, 177, 180–1, 191
victims, proof from 174, 176, 180–1, 192
Psychic Detectives 174, 182, 188, 192
Psychic Witness 174
psycholinguistic pauses 276
psychopathology 443–4, 453
Puar, Jasbir 344
**public opinion and legal policy, relationship
    between** 116
public perceptions of lawyers
cultivation theory 119–20, 153
Damages 148
empirical study of audiences 113–26
gender in cable shows 148
Germany, judges on reality TV in 252, 258–66
Judge Judy 95, 148, 245, 277–87
juvenile crime, perceptions of 119
litigation crisis, perception of 18
quantitative content 120
reality TV show judges 95–6, 119, 148, 229–30,
    245, 252, 258–66, 277–87
violence and crime, beliefs about increase
    in 89–90, 119
**Public Safety Infrastructure, Americanisation
    of** 329–30
public shaming and punishment 293–6, 301
public interest 297–301

qualitative analysis 8, 112, 121–2, 127
quantitative analysis 8, 94, 118, 120

R v Young 190–1
race
Associates, the 432–3
bailiffs in judge reality TV shows 233
Border, the 313, 329, 332–6, 338–45
cable shows 7
Canada 313, 317–20, 329, 332–6, 338–45
commercials 235–6
Dexter and the serial killer 404, 411
Due South 317–18, 319–20, 332–3, 343
human, what qualifies as 29–31

Judge Judy 232, 235
judges on reality TV 96, 230, 232–8
Latinos 104, 342–3, 344
lawbreakers and criminals, Afro-Americans
    as 104
serial killers 404, 411, 445–6, 451
Til Debt Do Us Part 220–1
United States
    Border, the 313, 329, 332–6, 338–45
    white supremacy 332–6
victims 445–6, 451
white supremacy 319–20, 332–6
whiteness 31–20, 332–6, 343–4
Raddack, Jessalyn 205
Raj, Amit 344
Randi, James 182
rape evidence rules, TV portrayals of 153–72
acquaintance rape 154–5, 161–3, 171
sbeliefs 152–4, 161
cable services 163
changes in rules 161–4, 169–72
character of defendant rules 154–6,
    160–3, 168–72
confidence in legal system 163, 165, 167–8, 172
consent defence 153, 155, 162–5, 168
cross-examination of victims 154–72
false accusations 166–7
'Get Tough on Rapists Era' 7, 154–72
    evidence rules after 161–3
    evidence rules before 155–6
    TV shows after 163–70
    TV shows before 156–61
juror decision-making and verdicts 105
LA Law 'Noah's Bark' episode 163–4
Law and Order
    'Discord' 161
    'Helpless' episode 160
Law and Order: SVU 'Doubt' episode 167–8
Owen Marshall Counselor at Law
    'A Girl Named Tham' episode 159–60
    'Victim in Shadow' episode 157–9
past sexual history of victims, cross-examination
    on 154–72
Practice, the 165–9
rape shield laws 154–6, 161–72
reflection, reinforcement and revision of beliefs
    153–4, 161
reporting 154–5, 157, 161, 170–2
satellite services 163
second rapist, criminal justice system as 154,
    157, 161
Shark 'In the Grasp' episode 170
third rapist, TV shows as 155, 170–2
Rapping, Elayne 6, 115, 428
rationality and reason 24–7
Raver, Kim 390
Rawls, John 24–5
Raymont, Peter 339
reader/response spectatorship 36–8
realism 364–8, 374–5, 377
reality TV *see* **reality TV judges; reality TV judges
    in Germany; reality TV shows**

reality TV judges 6, 8, 229–49 *see also Judge Judy;* **reality TV judges in Germany**
  actual judges, effect on 246
  bailiffs, race and gender of 233–4
  broad role of judges 241–3
  children, support of 240–1
  class 235–6
  commercials 235–6
  concern, causes for 243–6
  Court TV 148
  demographics 230, 232–8
  diversity 230, 232–8
  Divorce Court 231, 233–7, 241
  domestic abuse 240
  empathy 242
  empirical study of audiences 118
  entertainment and judging, blurring lines between what is 244–5
  evidence 239–40
  fathers, role of 240–1
  gender 96, 230, 232–8
  Judge Alex 230, 231–4, 236, 239, 241, 246
  Judge Christina 95
  Judge Hatchett 95, 231–8, 245
  Judge Joe Brown 95, 231, 233, 236, 240–1
  Judge Mathis 231–4, 236, 239, 244–5
  Judge Nancy 245–6
  Judge Pirro 231–40, 242–3
  jurors, effect on potential 118, 244–5
  legal education, providing 238–42
  negative lessons 229
  number of cases heard 231
  People's Court 231, 233–4, 236, 238–40, 253
  perceptions of behaviour 95–6, 119, 148, 229–30, 245, 252, 258–66, 277–87
  personal relationships 231, 233–7, 240–1, 275, 282
  personality of judges 8, 95, 229–30, 243–6
  positive lessons 229, 237–41
  qualitative analysis 8
  quantitative analysis 8
  race 96, 230, 232–8
  Street Court 231–6, 244–5
  translators, judges as 242–3
  types of cases 237
  winners and losers, gender and race of 236–7
reality TV judges in Germany 8, 251–69
  aggressive behaviour in court 255, 257–8, 260–4, 266
  Bochum area study 258, 261–5
  Criminal Court, the 257–8
  cultural significance 252
  Dispute at 3pm 253–4, 256, 257
  entrepreneurial competition 255–8
  fairness 259, 264, 266
  Judge Judy 253, 256
  Juvenile Court, the 256–8, 267
  legal education 253, 256, 258–63
  legal significance 252–3
  morality 259, 263–6
  orientation seekers 258
  perpetrators, education on 260

  procedural fairness 259
  public broadcasters 255–6
  public perceptions 252, 258–66
  race to the bottom 255
  Richter Alexander Hold 257–8
  Richter Neumann 253–5
  Richterin Barbara Salesch 253–8
  Royal Bavarian Magistrates' Court 252–3, 266
  social change, fears of 253–4
  stereotypes of trials 261, 264–5
  traditional values 253–4
  trust in courts, effect on public 252, 259, 262–6
  truth, search for 260–1
  victimisation, education on 260
reality TV shows *see also* **reality TV judges; reality TV judges in Germany;** *To Catch a Predator*
  concentration, levels of 272
  content analysis 8
  definition 215–16
  documentary viewers, reality TV viewers compared with 272–4
  engaging viewers 274–6
  heavy viewing, effects of 272–4
  high involvement tactics 274–6
  memory systems 272–4
  obsession, as an 8
  passive learning 272
  psychic detective effect 174, 182–3, 191–2
  Til Debt Do Us Part 212–13, 215–18, 221, 227
  visual components 273
  voyeurism 216–17
relationships *see* **personal relationships**
religion 142 *see also* **Muslims**
replication colonialism 35, 43
Rescue Me 145
Reservoir Dogs 386
responsibilisation 224–7
Revere, Paul 332
Reynard v Rinker 287
Richter (Judge) Alexander Hold 257–8
Richter (Judge) Neumann 253–5
Richterin (Judge) Barbara Salesch 253–8
rights-bearing status 17, 20, 22–8
rights of suspects/defendants
  Miranda warnings 102, 175, 202, 203–4, 205
  psychic detective effect 175, 180–1, 186–7
  torture of terrorist suspects 193–207, 394–6, 399
  24 (TV series) 193–9, 200, 394–8, 399
Rihanna 442–3
Rizzoli & Isles 143
Roberts, John 243
Robson, Peter 114, 425–6, 428
Roddenberry, Gene 16, 19
Romney, Mitt 382
Rookie Blue 77–8
Rothkerch, I 364
Rorty, Richard 24–5
Rose, Nikolas 212, 225
Royal Bavarian Magistrates' Court (Königlich-Bayerisches Amtsgericht) 252–3, 266

Royal Canadian Mounted Police (RCMP) 311–15, 320, 323
Rumpole of the Bailey 5
Rumsfeld, Donald 387
Rundacille, D 367
Rutherford, Paul 438

sadistic serial killers 441–53
  archetypes 444
  bondage, discipline, sadomasochism (BDSM) 452
  consensual desire 441–4, 451
  Criminal Minds 441, 444, 446–7, 449–53
    'Penelope' episode 446–7, 449–51
    victimology 446
  cultural victimology 446
  culture 441–4, 446–7, 450, 452
  deviance 444–5
  Dexter 441, 444, 446, 447–51
    'Dexter' episode 446, 447–51
    victimology 446
  domestic/family violence 441–2, 444–5, 449–50, 453
  DSM-IV 443–4
  familiar people as perpetrators 441–2, 444–5, 449–50, 453
  femininity, cultural tropes of 450
  gender 441–52
  heteronormativity 450
  heterosexuality 441, 447, 449–52
  ideal victims 444–6
  Law and Order: SVU 441, 444, 446–51
    'Uncle' episode 446–51
    victimology 446
  moral panics and sadomasochism 442–4
  'otherness' 445
  pleasure/pain nexus 442–4
  popular culture 441
  private violence 450, 453
  psychopathology 443–4, 453
  race of victims 445–6, 451
  sadomasochism 441–5, 449–53
  sexual sadism 441–5, 450–1
  strangers, killers as 443–5, 449–53
  themes 449–52
  torture and cruelty 444–5, 449–50, 452–3
  victim imagery, employment of gruesome 453
  victimology 444–6
  xenophobia 445
sadomasochism
  consent 441–2, 444, 451
  DSM-IV 443–4
  moral panics 442–4
  psychopathology, as a 443–4
  serial killers 441–5, 449–53
Sage Handbook of Nonverbal Communications. Keating, CF 280–1
Said, Edward 36, 41
Salcido, DeAnn 246
Salzmann, Victoria S 103, 118
S&M 442–3
Sartre, Jean-Paul 16, 443

Saving Grace 135–43, 146–8
Saw series 386
Schimanski, Horst 256
Schudson, Michael 66
Scott, Camilla 320
search warrants 205–7
Secretary 442
Sedgwick, Kyra 137
self-defence 53–4, 57–8
self-determination of women 355–6
self-incrimination, privilege against 199
Sellers, Wilfred 26
Sensing Murder 182, 188
sentience, principle of 16, 22, 24–5, 29
September 11, 2001 terrorist attacks
  Border, the 313, 327, 329, 336–7, 344
  Due South 313–26
  terrorism thrillers 7, 193–4, 199, 202–3, 381–5, 389
  torture of terrorist suspects 193, 381–5, 389
  24 (TV series) 193, 381–5, 389
  Wire, the 363–4
serial killers *see Dexter* and the serial killer; sadistic serial killers
serial narratives 39, 44–50, 74–5
settlements 432–4
sex *see also* rape evidence rules, TV portrayals of
  Border, the 337–8, 344
  Deadwood 47
  Due South 316, 323–6, 331, 343
  gender in cable shows 141–2, 146
  promiscuity 141–2, 146
  sadistic serial killers 441–5, 450–1
Shahzad, Faisal 204, 206
Shakespeare, William 16, 49
shaming and punishment in public 293–6, 301
Shark 170
Sheindlin, Judith *see Judge Judy*
Shelley, Mary 16
Shelton, Donald E 99–100
Shermer, Michael 182–3
Sherwin, Richard 18, 117, 120
Shield, the 74, 83, 145
Showden, Carisa 146–7
Shugart, H 146
Silbey, Susan S 18
Simon, David 362–8, 375–6
simulcasting 427–8
Sinyard, N 406
slavery 20, 23, 27, 29–31
Slotkin, Richard 39
social change 253–4, 347–9
social construction 23–5
social context 4, 404
social justice 6, 18, 32, 356
socialisation 88, 92–3, 103
soft power 328–9
solidarity 24–8, 32, 254, 320, 340, 344, 418
Sotomayor, Sonia 28, 29, 242–3
Spain *see Wedding Rings (Anillos de oro)* and divorce in post-Franco Spain
Spigel, Lynn 381

St John, Gale 182
Standards & Practices of broadcast networks 65, 80, 83–4
Star Trek 137 *see also Star Trek: the Next Generation* episode 'The Measure of a Man'
Star Trek: the Next Generation episode 'The Measure of a Man' 15–32
  adversarial legalism 19, 21
  anti-essentialist model 24–8
  binary quality of legal decisions 23
  courtroom drama 17, 20–6
  essentialism 24–30
  human rights 17, 20
  human, what qualifies as 15–17, 20–32
  justice 24–8
  legal form and narrative form, homology between 19
  loyalty 24–8, 31–2
  personal relationships 20, 28
  rights-bearing status 17, 20, 22–8
  social constructions of essences 24–5
  solidarity 24–8, 32
  teaching material, episode as 21–4
  thinness of law 23–4
Stark, Steven 1, 364
state, punishment by the 292, 295–6, 302, 305
Stedman, RW 44–5
stereotyping
  Border, the 335
  Canada 314, 316, 317–18, 335
  Due South 314, 316, 317–18
  gender in cable shows 139–47
  Irish-American cops 368–70
  reconfigured stereotypes 146–7
  trials 261, 264–5
  United States 335
  Wire, the 367–70
Stevens, John-Paul 32
Stierhammer, August 252–3, 266
Stimson, Charles 199
Strafgericht, Das (The Criminal Court) 257–8
strangers, killers as 443–5, 449–53
Strauss, Anselm 128
Street Court 231–6, 244–5
Street Legal 426
Streetcar Named Desire, A 319
Streit um Drei (Dispute at 3pm) 253–4, 256, 257
students *see* legal education
Suárez, Adolfo 350
suicide 291, 293, 298
Supernanny 216
Surnow, Joel 387
surveillance 8, 9, 194, 201, 205–7, 334, 397 *see also To Catch a Predator*
Survivor 216
suspects, rights of *see* rights of suspects/defendants
Sutherland, Kiefer 390
Swan, the 216

Tahir, Faran 390
Tancredo, Tom 382, 387, 400
Tate, Marsha Ann 426

Tatort 256
technical consultants 76–80
technicalities, defendants' getting off on 175, 177, 181, 187
Television and the Legal System. Villez, Barbara 6
television audiences, role of empirical methodology in exploring 111–32
  active audience paradigm 124–5
  behaviourist approach 119–20, 124–5
  content analysis 114, 117–18, 120–1
  critical discourse analysis 126
  cultivation theory 119–20
  cultural identity 124
  cultural studies 120
  day-to-day activities of lawyers 118
  ethical standards 117–18
  ethnographic research 112–13, 120–9
  gender 114–15
  hermeneutics 125–6
  ideology 114–15, 118, 128
  jurors, effect of syndicated courtrooms on 118
  justice, public ideas of 122–3
  lawyers, perceptions of 113–14, 117–18, 123–6
  legal consciousness, recognition of a 128
  legitimacy of law, undermining of 120
  meanings, making 112, 124–6
  panoramic perspectives of law 114
  persistent legal themes 114
  popular culture 111–29
  public opinion and legal policy, relationship between 116
  public perceptions 113–26
  qualitative empirical research 112, 117–18, 121–2, 127
  quantitative empirical research 118, 120
  representation 114
  social issues 114–15
  status quo of research 113–21
  student identity 122–4, 126
  textual critique/analysis 66, 68, 114, 120
  transnational study 117–18, 122
  viewer talk 125–7
terrorism *see* September 11, 2001 terrorist attacks; terrorism thrillers; torture of terrorist suspects in United States; *24* (TV series) and torture
terrorism thrillers 193–208
  24 193–9, 200–2, 204, 207
  aggressive legal positions 202–4
  antagonists, lawyers as 193–8
  Border, the 313, 326–7, 329–33, 336–42, 344
  Canada 313, 326–7, 329–33, 336–42, 344
  cognitive bias 201
  constitutional protections/rights of suspects 193–207, 394–6, 399
  exclusionary rule 198–9
  FISA search warrants 206–7
  government lawyers
    aggressive legal positions 202–4
    over-cautiousness 204–7
  Grid, the 193, 197, 200, 207
  Guantanamo Bay 199–200
  illegal and immoral actions 193–202, 396–9

interrogation methods 193, 198, 201–2
killings 193
lawyers, representation of 193–208
Miranda warnings 202, 203–4, 205
negative characterisation of defence lawyers 7,
    193–204, 207, 394–7
obstacles, lawyers as 193–8
real life defence lawyers versus TV defence
    lawyers 198–201
search warrants 205–7
self-incrimination, privilege against 199
September 11, 2001 terrorist attacks 7, 193–4,
    199, 202–3
surveillance 201, 205–7
ticking time bomb scenario 193, 201, 203–4,
    385–7
torture 193–204, 385–400
truth 198–9, 202
24 (TV series) 193–9, 200–2, 204, 207, 394–7
utilitarian arguments 194, 202, 389
war on terror 313, 342, 344, 382, 384–8, 399
ways of depicting lawyers, alternative 201–7
textual critique/analysis 66, 68, 114, 120
Thaddeus, John 394
Thin Blue Line, the 19
30 Seconds to Mars 443
Thym, Barbara 258, 261
ticking time bomb scenario 193, 201, 203–4,
    340, 385–7
Til Debt Do Us Part 212–27
    attachment 215
    audience participation 215, 217
    Canada 211–27
    children 219–21
    cohabitees 219
    consumerism 212, 217–18, 221, 227
    consumption 212, 224–5
    cultural support for neoliberal regulatory
        project, as 213, 226–7
    diversity 219–21
    disabilities, persons with 220
    employment 220
    empowerment 212–13
    fault 226
    financial literacy 211–13, 218–27
        regulatory projects, programs as 212, 218–27
        Task Force on Financial Literacy
            212, 222–3
    game shows 212, 216
    heterosexual nuclear families 219–21
    ideology 212–13, 224–7
    individual responsibility 213
    lifestyle programming 212, 216
    marriage 219–21
    neoliberalism 213, 224–7
    personal relationships 213–16, 219, 221
    race 220–1
    reality TV 212–13, 215–18, 221, 227
    regulation 212–13, 218–27
    responsibilisation 224–7
    same-sex couples 219
    self-regulation 213

socio-economic location of participants 212,
    218, 219–21, 227
Task Force on Financial Literacy 212, 222–3
transformation 212, 216–17
United States 212, 213, 215
voyeurism 216–17
To Catch a Predator 289–307
    communication techniques 8
    content analysis 8
    entrapment 292, 300, 302–5
    freedom of the press 292, 297–9, 305
    Investigative Report: Cybersex Cops 292
    overstating the threat 290–1
    police 289–90, 293, 296, 300–2
    private facts, publication of 292, 296–302, 305
    pseudo-authority 293–4
    public interest 297–301
    public shaming and punishment 293–6, 301
    social ills, exacerbating 8
    state, punishment by the 292, 295–6, 302, 305
    suicide 291, 293, 298
    surveillance techniques 8
    voyeurism 291, 302
To Kill a Mockingbird 261
Toler, Lynn 234–7, 241
tort reform 94
torture of terrorist suspects in United States
    381–401 *see also 24* (TV series) and torture
    Abu Ghraib, prisoner abuse at 382–3, 385, 389
    banalisation 386
    Border, the 330, 335, 340–2
    Canada 330, 335, 340–2
    cognitive bias 201
    constitutional protections/rights of suspects
        193–207, 394–6, 399
    cultural text, TV as a 388–9
    definition 202, 341, 383–4
    deontological objections 201
    efficacy objections 201
    enemy combatants 384
    epistemological objections 201
    false information, provision of 386
    Guantanamo Bay 382, 385, 389
    human rights treaties and conventions 384
    ideology 382, 389
    illegality 384–8, 396–9
    justification 340–1, 385–6
    memo 202–3
    moral relativism 385
    naturalisation 388–9, 393
    negative views of defence lawyers 7, 193–204,
        207, 394–7
    normalisation 382, 386, 388–9, 398
    origins of word 383–4
    September 11, 2001 terrorist attacks 193,
        381–5, 389
        after 9/11 382–6
        before 9/11 386–8
    terrorism thrillers 193–204, 385–400
    ticking time bomb scenario 193, 201, 203–4,
        340, 385–7
    Torture Convention (UN) 341, 384

utilitarianism 202, 385–6, 399
war on terror 382, 384–8, 399
Touched by an Angel 142
transformation 212, 216–17
translations 80, 81–2, 84–5, 242–3
Tully, Jim 35–6, 43
12 Angry Men 21–2
24 **(TV series) and torture**
  Abu Ghraib, prisoner abuse at 389
  constitutional protections/rights of suspects
    193–9, 200, 394–6, 399
  contempt of the law 396–9
  justification 200–1, 207, 382, 387–400
  negative views of criminal defence lawyers
    193–204, 394–7
  naturalisation 393
  normalisation of torture 388–9, 398
  September 11, 2001 terrorist attacks 193,
    381–5, 389
  ticking time bomb scenario 201, 204, 385–7
  utilitarianism 202, 399
  war on terror 386–8, 399
truth
  judges in reality TV in Germany 260–1
  psychic detective effect 7, 177, 180–1, 191
  scientific evidence 7
  terrorism thrillers 198–9, 202
Tyler, Aisha 393

Unabomber 332
United States *see also* **Deadwood;** *Dexter* **and the
serial killer;** *To Catch a Predator;* **torture of
terrorist suspects in United States;** *24* **(TV series)
and torture;** *Wire, the*
  abuse of power 331
  agenda setting 94
  alternative dispute resolution 431–2
  Associates, the 429–33, 439
  Border, the 311–13, 326–43
  Bridge, the 64, 73–6, 82–3
  Canada
    Border, the 311–13, 326–43
    Bridge, the 64, 73–6, 82–3
    colonialism 318, 319, 334, 343
    Due South 311–26, 329, 331, 343
    Flashpoint 79
    justice, comparison with US 311–43
    programming, comparison of US with
      426–8, 427–9
    simulcasting 427–8
  case-focused dramas 6
  colonialism 34–5, 38–43, 45, 49, 54, 60–1, 318,
    319, 334, 343
  conservative right, growth of 6
  culture 40, 60–1, 427, 438–9
  Deadwood 34–5, 38–43, 45, 49, 54, 60–1
  death penalty 337
  Due South 311–26, 329, 331, 343
  Flashpoint 79
  gender 6, 135–51
  Guantanamo Bay 199–200, 340–1, 382,
    385, 389

human rights 326, 330–2
immigration, customs and security 311–13,
  326–43, 344
individualism 315, 320, 335
litigation crisis, perception of 18
office life and relationships, focus on 6
personal relationships 6
Public Safety Infrastructure, Americanisation
  of 329–30
race 332–6
simulcasting 427–8
stereotyping 335
Til Debt Do Us Part 212, 213, 215
tort reform as a result of agenda setting 94
xenophobia 338
white supremacy 332–6
women lawyers 6, 135–51
Universal Declaration of Human Rights 384
untried dramas, gaining access to 70–1, 72
utilitarianism 23, 194, 202, 321–2, 385–6, 399

Vaz-Oxlade, Gail 213–26
victims
  Criminal Minds 446
  cultural victimology 446
  education on victimisation 260
  gender 441–52
  gruesome imagery 453
  ideal victims 444–6
  judges in reality TV in Germany 260
  Law and Order 446
  race 445–6, 451
  rape victims, cross-examination with 154–72
  sadistic serial killers 441–53
  victimology 444–6
vigilante justice 9, 403–5, 410, 414–22
Villez, Barbara 6, 103, 428, 434
violence *see also* *Dexter* **and the serial killer;
sadistic serial killers**
  'affect', concept of 50–4
  agenda setting 94
  beliefs about increase in violence and crime
    89–90, 119
  cinematic technique 50–4
  Deadwood 34–5, 39–60
  empirical research on law and justice 94, 119
  sexual violence 47
visualisation 28
voyeurism 216–17, 291, 302

Waggoner, C 146
Walzer, Michael 24–5
Wapner, Joseph A 253
war on terror 313, 342, 344, 382, 384–8, 399
Washington Post 383
Watson, Alberta 390
Wedding Rings (Anillos de oro) **and divorce in
post-Franco Spain** 347–59
  assassination of the Attorneys of Atocha
    349, 351
  conservatism 348, 350–1, 354, 356, 359
  democracy, transition to 347–52

feminism 355–6
Francoism 351–2, 354
gender 353–6
hero lawyers 347, 349, 352–7
historical background 349–52
mutual consent 350–1, 357
overview 352–4
popularity 348–9
role models, women as 355
self-determination of women 355–6
social change 347–9
stigma of divorce 354, 359
'When Life Deals a Bad Hand' episode 357–9
Weil, Simone 34, 36
Wernick, Andrew 427–8, 437
West, Dominic 367
Western genre 39–44
Wetzel, Ulrich 257
When Law Goes Pop 120
What Do Pictures Want? The Lives and Loves of Images. Mitchell, WJT 428–30, 435–6, 439
whiteness
    Border, the 332–6
    Canada 318, 319, 332–6, 343–4
    Due South 318, 319, 343
    United States 332–6
    white supremacy 319–20, 332–6
Wiener, Richard 221–2
Wikileaks 327–8
Williams, Bernard 25
Williams, Patricia 30
Williams, T 225

Winfrey, Oprah 99, 271, 299
Wire, the 361–79
    advertising 362
    Bridge, the 74
    bureaucracy 83
    cable TV 83, 362
    colonialism 371–2
    discrimination against Irish 368–71
    drug dealers 365, 372–4
    good and evil dichotomy 363–4
    hegemony 371–2
    ideology 83
    illegality/corruption of police 372–7
    improvisation 361–2, 365–8, 370–7
    Irish-American cops 361–2, 368–72, 377
    justice 361–2, 370–6
    personal relationships 377
    police procedurals 364–5
    realism 364–8, 374–5, 377
    September 11, 2001 terrorist attacks 363–4
    stereotypes 367–70
women see feminism; gender
Woodham-Smith, Cecil 369
Woolgar, Steve 68–9
writers' rooms 75–6, 77–9

xenophobia 338

Young, Alison 38, 51

Zettl, H 275
Zubaydah, Aby 202